# CLINICAL ASSESSMENT FOR SOCIAL WORKERS

# Also available from Lyceum Books, Inc.

Advisory Editor: Thomas M. Meenaghan, *New York University*

*Understanding and Managing the Therapeutic Relationship*
by Fred R. McKenzie

*Using Statistical Methods in Social Work Practice: A Complete SPSS Guide*
by Soleman H. Abu-Bader

*Advanced and Multivariate Statistical Methods for Social Science Research:
With a Complete SPSS Guide*
by Soleman H. Abu-Bader

*Research Methods for Social Workers: A Practice-Based Approach*
by Cynthia A. Faulker and Samuel S. Faulkner

*Social Work Evaluation: Enhancing What We Do*
by James R. Dudley

*Complex Systems and Human Behavior*
by Christopher G. Hudson

*Essential Skills of Social Work Practice*
by Thomas O'Hare

*Psychoeducation in Mental Health*
by Joseph Walsh

*Straight Talk about Professionals Ethics*
by Kim Strom-Gottfried

# CLINICAL ASSESSMENT FOR SOCIAL WORKERS

## Quantitative and Qualitative Methods
### Third Edition

**Edited by**

**CATHELEEN JORDAN**
University of Texas, Arlington

and

**CYNTHIA FRANKLIN**
University of Texas, Austin

LYCEUM
BOOKS, INC.

Chicago, Illinois

# DEDICATION

To David Cory, who did a brief assessment and concluded that my work-play balance needed adjustment. The best is yet to come. —Catheleen Jordan

To my brother Charlie K. Southern, for all the happy past memories on the farm and now on the ranch. The best is yet to come. —Cynthia Franklin

© Lyceum Books, Inc., 2011

Published by

LYCEUM BOOKS, INC.
5758 S. Blackstone Ave.
Chicago, Illinois 60637
773+643-1903 (Fax)
773+643-1902 (Phone)
lyceum@lyceumbooks.com
http://www.lyceumbooks.com

7 6                14 15

ISBN 978-1-933478-80-7

Printed in the United States of America.

## Library of Congress Cataloging-in-Publication Data

Clinical assessment for social workers : quantitative and qualitative methods / edited by Catheleen Jordan, Cynthia Franklin.—3rd ed.
    p. cm.
Includes bibliographical references and index.
ISBN 978-1-933478-80-7 (pbk.: alk. paper)
 1. Psychodiagnostics. 2. Psychiatric social work. 3. Needs assessment.
4. Behavioral assessment. 5. Family assessment. I. Jordan, Catheleen, 1947–
II. Franklin, Cynthia.
 RC469.J67   2010
 616.89′075—dc22

                                                        2009039871

# CONTENTS

# TABLES

# FIGURES

## APPENDICES

# Preface

*Clinical Assessment: Quantitative and Qualitative Methods* increases the expertise of social workers and other professionals in choosing the best scientifically based assessment methods and in using them with children, families, and adults. This book reviews several assessment methods from different theoretical models as well as some of the new advances in measurement and interviewing, including evidence-based frameworks; it also integrates measurement and clinical assessment into a practice text. Even though we cover assessment methods from various theoretical perspectives, we do not assume that the reader adheres to a particular theoretical orientation or epistemology. We believe assessment information can be collected using a variety of different formats. Having a repertoire of tools for performing assessment, derived from different perspectives, allows professionals more flexibility in data gathering and intervention planning. For example, some clients might readily provide information by filling out a standardized questionnaire, whereas other clients might be happier sharing information through a genogram or an ecological map. Professionals can also combine different types of information to help create the most effective treatment plans.

*Clinical Assessment* is designed for graduate and undergraduate social work students, as well as for social work practitioners and other related helping professionals—licensed professional counselors, marriage and family counselors, and psychologists. The book shows how to incorporate testing and measurement into practice and how to conduct empirically focused assessments on clients. Every chapter in this third edition includes new information and updated information. This book has always advocated the use of measurement and an empirical orientation to practice, so in keeping with the goals of the text, this new third addition emphasizes evidence-based assessment and tries to distinguish further assessment methods that are not based on research evidence from those that have a basis in evidence. A new chapter 5 has been added, which reviews frequently used assessment methods in social work that are based on pseudoscience. The critiquing of assessment methods based on pseudoscience has been neglected in the literature and is long overdue for attention. Some popular methods for social work assessment appear to be good ways to gather information from clients but, when examined more closely, are not able to provide valid and reliable assessments. Methods such as anatomically correct dolls and personality typing and testing are examples of the assessment methods reviewed in chapter 5. In addition to the new chapter, the population chapters (chapters 6–10) have the following updates: references and reference materials; integration of information on evidence-based assessment, including criteria for evidence-based assessment tools; reviews and illustrations of measures that relate specifically to *Diagnostic and Statistical Manual of Mental Disorders* (DSM) diagnoses and criteria; the addition of three to five Internet and quick reference resources on how to obtain evidence-based reviews of assessment and measurement instruments and how to stay abreast of measurement updates in the field; and updated case applications, including examples of how to use evidence-based assessment measures and approaches. Chapters 1 and 2 are combined into a new Chapter 1 and updated corresponding to the previous evidence-based standards as well. Chapter 11 is also updated with new information.

We thank the reviewers for their insightful and helpful reviews of the manuscript, the chapter contributors, and the social workers who have used this book into its third edition. We also thank our publisher, David Follmer, for his continued support of our work. Finally, we thank our families and friends for their tolerance, support, and sense of humor. We love you!

# Introduction to Clinical Assessment

Part I introduces the evolving field of assessment methods. The clinical practitioner will find in these pages a plethora of quantitative and qualitative assessment techniques. This approach is particularly suited for busy practitioners who work in today's high-accountability practice settings, because each chapter focuses on brief but thorough assessment and tools for determining the outcomes of interventions, as well as examples for how to translate assessment information into viable intervention plans. This edition emphasizes the important evidence-based approach, which these early chapters introduce. Chapter 1, "An Integrative Skills Assessment Approach," introduces the reader to the complex practice skills involved in assessment and provides an integrative assessment framework using several models, such as psychosocial and solution-focused assessment. It further shows the reader how assessment is important to treatment planning and to measuring the outcomes of social work interventions.

# CHAPTER 1

# An Integrative Skills Assessment Approach

## Cynthia Franklin and Catheleen Jordan

This book reviews and illustrates different methods and tools for clinical assessment in social work practice. In this chapter, we provide a definition of social work assessment and a framework for understanding how to conduct a comprehensive social work assessment. Social work assessment requires a complex set of practice skills that range from making accurate judgments based on practice theory to using the best methods available to obtain information to creatively and competently using various sources of information to make valid and reliable decisions concerning client care. We briefly describe many facets of social work assessment in this chapter. We also discuss ways that students and practitioners use theory to guide practice and common practice skills that are needed for being able to do assessment, particularly, clinical decision making, problem specification, problem monitoring, and treatment planning. This chapter and other ones following it guide practitioners to use evidence-based knowledge to guide their assessments with clients. In particular, this chapter highlights the importance of using evidence in assessment and describes criteria for evaluating assessments.

Finally, this chapter highlights an integrative, technical-eclectic approach for choosing which elements go into a comprehensive assessment, which is supported through the review of several social work practice models. We use technical eclecticism to integrate assessment information across the models reviewed into the Integrative Skills Assessment Protocol, which practitioners can use to guide assessment, and we introduce issues related to moving from assessment to intervention.

## DEFINITION OF SOCIAL WORK ASSESSMENT

Barker (2003) defines social work assessment as "the process of determining the nature, cause, progression, and prognosis of a problem and the personalities and situations involved therein; the social work function of acquiring an understanding of a problem, what causes it, and what can be changed to minimize or resolve it" (p. 30).

This definition suggests that assessment involves looking into people and their social environments and ascertaining problems, causes of problems, and plans for changing those problems. Austiran (2009) describes assessment as an ongoing process involving five steps:

1. Exploration through multiple methods, such as listening, observation, and other means of data collection.
2. Inferential thinking, which leads to clinical judgments that are grounded in empirical knowledge and guide the decision making about a case.
3. Evaluation of the capacity of a client's functioning and skills, as well as of the stressors of social environments that may impede a client's optimal functioning.
4. Problem definitions that are well defined and agreed on by client and social worker.
5. Intervention planning with the client, which leads to more effective outcomes.

Chapters in this book flesh out this definition with clinical examples and cover these five steps in some detail, demonstrating many methods and techniques that social workers can use in conducting clinical assessments. A person-in-environment, systems approach to examining clients and their concerns guides assessment in social work. Diverse methods are used in an assessment to identify and measure specific problem behaviors and protective and resilience factors, and to determine when treatment is necessary and which treatments might work best in a given situation. When conducting an assessment, social workers usually gather information from a variety of sources (e.g., the client, family members, case records, observation, rapid assessment tools, genograms). Types of assessment include biopsychosocial history taking, multiple-dimension crisis assessment, symptom checklists, functional analysis, and mental status exams (Levine, 2008). This text defines and illustrates multiple methods of assessment first in chapters about the assessment methods themselves and later in chapters that apply specific methods to population groups.

The methods of assessment illustrated herein are diverse and include face-to-face interviews with people (for essential questions to ask, see Box 1.1), behavioral observations, reviews of written documents, and the use of measurement instruments. As suggested, in the five steps mentioned earlier, *assessment* also refers to ongoing analysis and synthesis of information about the client and his or her social environment for the purpose of formulating a diagnosis or coherent intervention plan to help the client. Particular elements of an assessment are usually guided by practice theories and a case construction process, which involves the cognitive

**Box 1.1**
**Twelve Essential Questions to Be Asked in a**
**Brief Assessment Interview**

1. Why is the client entering therapy now?
2. Are there any signs of psychosis, delusions, or thought disorders that would indicate that the client needs immediate medical/psychiatric treatment?
3. Are there signs of illness indicating the need for neurological or other medical treatment?
4. Is there evidence of depression or suicidal or homicidal ideations?
5. What are the presenting complaints?
6. What are the important antecedent factors of the client's problem?
7. Who or what is maintaining the problem?
8. What does the client wish to derive from therapy?
9. What is the client's preference for therapy style? How can you match that style?
10. Are there clear indications for a specific modality of treatment based on a person-environment assessment?
11. Can a therapeutic alliance be maintained or should the client be referred?
12. What are the client's positive attributes and strengths?

SOURCE: Adapted from Franklin, C., & Jordan, C. (1999a). The clinical utility of models and methods of assessment in managed care. In B. S. Compton & B. Galaway (Eds.), *Social work processes* (p. 289). Pacific Grove, CA: Brooks/Cole.

appraisal of information, use of diverse theories and clinical judgment, and the incorporation of that information into a written psychosocial study or report. We now examine the importance of using evidence-based knowledge in assessment.

## Using Evidence-Based Practice in Assessment

Evidence-based practice is a scientific paradigm that encompasses clinician expertise, client characteristics, and contextual variables (chapter 2 and subsequent chapters further define evidence-based practice). Evidence-based approaches to assessment assume that social workers use the best-available scientific evidence, along with critical-thinking skills, their knowledge of best practices, and client input. Assessment is an ongoing process that begins with problem (and strength) identification using both quantitative and qualitative techniques. This book covers a range of both quantitative and qualitative techniques that social workers can use in practice and further offers critiques of those techniques.

Basing our assessments on evidence means that we act in the best interest of our clients, that we use the best-available scientific knowledge, our best-available skills, and the client's own perspective to do our best helping. The field of clinical assessment has been working to improve on assessment methods that are based on scientific evidence and that lead to the best intervention planning and outcomes. Evidence-based assessment has been defined as "the use of research and theory to inform the selection of targets, the methods and measures used in the assessment, and the assessment process itself" (Hunsley & Mash, 2007, p. 29). The primary focus of evidence-based assessment is on locating the best evidence regarding the most effective assessment instruments and protocols that fit best with a client's situation, culture, values, and preferences. Four major factors to consider when engaging in assessment underlie this broad definition:

1. Psychometric adequacy of standardized instruments or assessment protocols (reliability and validity)
2. Diversity issues and individual client characteristics, and the fit of various assessment instruments or protocols with these characteristics
3. Issues of comorbidity
4. Clinical utility of standardized instruments or assessment protocols

Chapter 3 defines and covers these specific issues in much more detail. Other chapters include illustrations of assessment methods and suggestions for how to use methods grounded in the best evidence-based practice.

Evidence-based practice has made it possible for us to evaluate empirically supported practices to develop treatment protocols that are grounded in empirical knowledge about what works with clients. As we progress in our knowledge about evidence-based assessments, certain protocols have emerged about the best assessment methods for certain populations and problem areas. What this means is that a protocol may specify which assessment techniques and standardized measures are best for assessing particular problem areas or may provide lists or choices for the best tools to use. This text does not create evidence-based protocols for assessing different populations or problem areas but serves as a foundation text for learning about different assessment methods that social work practitioners can use. Further, it teaches the steps of evidence-based practice that social workers can follow in identifying and formulating the best assessment protocols for clients. Although we agree that evidence-based assessment protocols can useful and guide practitioners toward the best assessment practices, here we offer an approach to empower practitioners to develop their own best evidence-based assessments based on client needs.

## Searching for the Best Evidence-Based Assessment Methods

Chapter 3 provides a list of sources for finding assessments based on the best scientific evidence. It is also important to know how to search for the best assessment methods. Leff and Conley (2006) provide a review of how to best search for evidence-based mental health information, and this also applies to instruments and protocols to follow in an evidence-based assessment. There are three basic sources of information that lead to rapid reviews of the information:

1. Narrative reviews, which review the literature but do not include any quantitative analysis
2. Systematic reviews, such as meta-analysis, which include a secondary statistical analysis of studies
3. Registries developed by federal agencies and independent groups that provide reviews and ratings of different programs and interventions, including assessment instruments (e.g., the What Works Clearing-house, kept by the Institute of Educational Sciences at the Department of Education; the Cochrane Collaboration; for a description of how registries work and how practitioners can use them, see Kim, Trepper, Smock, McCollum, & Franklin, 2010)

Each of these sources has strengths and weaknesses. Leff and Conley (2006) recommend that practitioners combine the sources to make use of the best information. Franklin and Kelly (2009) further discuss the need for training once the practitioner discovers evidence-based information and the importance of working as a team with other professionals in making the decisions on which evidence-based practices to use.

## Further Assessing the Evidence

Once they have reviewed assessment methods, practitioners need criteria for deciding on one or more methods. Holmbeck et al. (2008) delineate requirements for evidence-based assessment in relationship to reviewing standardized measures, and these criteria can be applied more broadly to other assessment techniques: "The three possible evidence-based categories [are] as follows . . . (a) Well-established assessment, (b) Approaching well-established assessment, and (c) Promising assessment (see Cohen 2007 for a more thorough discussion of the criteria for each of these three categories)" (p. 960). These authors further suggest that practitioners use the best-researched measures by adopting those that meet well-established criteria, which the literature on psychological treatments also recommends. That means that assessment techniques and methods should have a foundation in research and should have been found to be valid, reliable, and clinically useful in at least two studies, preferably completed by independent investigators. Later chapters in this book discuss further the definitions of *reliability* and *validity* and discuss how to select the best assessment measures.

## PRACTICE MODELS GUIDING ASSESSMENT

The practitioner's practice model dictates the type of information the practitioner gathers and how the practitioner thinks about that information and synthesizes it into a conclusion. In this way, all practice models offer, to a greater or lesser degree, their own case construction processes. The next section describes several models of social work intervention from the perspective of their unique contribution to social work assessment and their utility for performing current-day assessments. Although the models are distinct, it is common for practitioners to combine or integrate features from different models into their own unique way of thinking about client problems.

### Psychosocial Assessment Model

Some of the major contributors to the psychosocial approach were Hollis and Wood (1981) and Woods and Robinson (1996). The goal of the psychosocial approach, sometimes called the diagnostic approach, is to determine a psychosocial diagnosis for the client. Factors such as history and developmental processes, are taken into account in making this diagnosis and in implementing the change efforts. The term *person-in-environment* originated with the thinking of this model. Ego psychology is the major theoretical basis of the psychosocial assessment framework, but appreciation for the interplay of biopsychosocial processes is an inherent part of the model, as well as an orientation toward environmental modification (for an overview of the areas of assessment to cover when following a comprehensive biopsychosocial framework, see Figure 1.1). The reader may also interested in reviewing other ego approaches that use ego psychology in social work, such as Parad and Miller (1963), Blanck and Blanck (1974), Maluccio (1981), Gitterman, Goldstein, and Rose (1988), Goldstein (1986, 2002), and Brandell (2008).

Over the years, the psychosocial model has adapted to variations of other models, such as aspects of the shorter-term functional casework model, which deemphasizes history and focuses on solving problems in the here and now through the use of agency resources. Some of the outcomes of these adaptations include shortening the amount of history taken in a diagnostic interview and working more collaboratively with the client to solve problems. In one of the most recent explications of the psychosocial approach, Goldstein (2002) explains that, compared to the

**Figure 1.1**    Areas for Assessment Using Biopsychosocial Framework

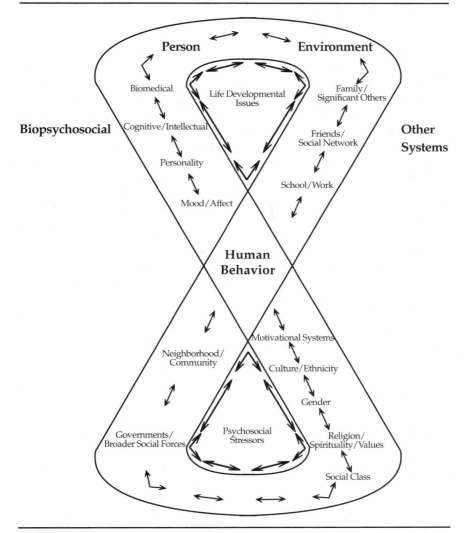

classical psychoanalytical thought that dominated early social work practice, ego psychology presents a more optimistic and sociocultural view of human behavior. Ego psychology concepts were used to refocus the study and assessment process on (a) the client's person-environment transactions in the here and now, particularly the degree to which he or she copes effectively with major life roles and tasks; (b) the client's adaptive, autonomous, and conflict-free areas of ego functioning, as well as ego deficits and maladaptive defenses and patterns; (c) the key developmental issues affecting the client's current reactions; and (d) the degree to which the external environment creates obstacles to successful coping.

**Unique Methods in Psychosocial Assessment.**    Turner (2005) suggests that psychosocial assessment and treatment is an ongoing process of identifying and labeling problems, as well as recognizing client strengths. Detailed psychosocial interviewing has become a key component of assessment in the psychosocial model. Specific assessment techniques include classical psychiatric interviewing for the purpose of making a diagnosis, use of standardized and projective testing to aid accurate diagnosis, psychosocial and developmental study to identify problem patterns, observations and interpretations of the client-social worker relationship to help clients understand their problem patterns and to provide a corrective emotional experience, use of standardized interviews to obtain an accurate mental health diagnosis, and further monitoring of symptoms to make sure they are changed in treatment plans.

The person-in-environment perspective offered by the psychosocial model is perhaps one of the most popular ways to understand clients in social work practice. It has also influenced many other important social work models, such as the problem-solving and task-centered models. Despite its popularity, the model actually has little research support other than some links to the medically based, biopsychosocial perspectives. More research on the contributions of the person-in-environment perspective is definitely needed.

## Problem-Solving Assessment Model

In the 1950s at the University of Chicago, Helen Harris Perlman attempted to integrate the two prominent models of the day, the diagnostic and the functional perspectives, into a framework known as the problem-solving social casework model. The diagnostic model integrated psychoanalytic theory into social casework, whereas the functional model, based on the work of the psychologist Otto Rank, focused on growth and realization of potential and the agency function. Perlman (1957) stated that the problem-solving model was an eclectic construct. Johnson (1981) later suggested that the problem-solving approach was theoretically eclectic, drawing on ego psychology, symbolic interactionism, role theory, and John Dewey's rational problem solving.

**Unique Methods in Problem-Solving Assessment.**    The goal of problem-solving assessment is to help the client cope by identifying the problem in the context of relevant intrapersonal issues (Johnson, 1981). Perlman (1957) suggested using the four Ps—person, problem, place, and process—as a way to collect and organize assessment data from clients.

Others have added further assessment criteria. Doremus (1976) added the four Rs: roles, reactions, relationships, and resources. Sheafor, Horejsi, and Horejsi (1988) added the four Ms: motivation, meanings, management, and monitoring. The authors suggest the following questions that practitioners can ask clients when collecting data on the four Ps, four Rs, and four Ms:

## Four Ps

- *Person or personality*: What personality characteristics are important to understanding the problem? What is the interaction between the client's personality and other people or the environment?
- *Problem*: What is the definition of the problem? Is the client's perception of the problem the same or different from others' perception of it? What are the specifics of the problem (e.g., frequency, magnitude)? Is the situation a crisis? What other solutions have been attempted and with what outcomes?
- *Place or agency*: What concerns and fears does the client have about being in contact with this particular agency? Is this agency setting the most helpful setting for this client with this particular problem? What barriers to helping the client can be attributed to the agency?
- *Process*: What type of helping process is best for this particular client? What are the consequences of the helping process for the client and his or her significant others?

## Four Rs

- *Roles*: What roles must the client perform, and how well does he or she perform them? What do significant others report about the client's role performance?
- *Reactions*: What are the client's psychological, emotional, behavioral, and physical reactions to the problem?
- *Relationships*: Who are the client's significant others, and what is their relationship to the problem? What are the consequences of the problem for them?
- *Resources*: What resources does the client already have that may be used in this situation, and what resources need to be developed?

## Four Ms

- *Motivation*: How motivated is the client to change, and does discomfort or optimism motivate that change?
- Meanings: What is the client's perception of the problem, or what meaning does he or she attribute to the problem? What client beliefs and values are important in order for the practitioner to understand the problem?

- *Management*: How will the practitioner structure casework activity to work with the client?
- *Monitoring*: How will the practitioner monitor the problem and evaluate the outcome? Who is available to help collect data?

## Cognitive Behavioral Assessment Models

Cognitive behavioral therapy focuses on clients' present functioning and attributes clients' problem behavior to learning processes, the formation of maladaptive cognitive schemas, errors in information processing, and proactive cognitive structures or meaning systems (Beck, 1995). Social workers who have integrated cognitive and behavioral techniques into social work practice include Gambrill, Thomas, and Carter (1971), Gitterman, Goldstein, and Rose (1988), Rose (1977), Stuart (2003), Gambrill (1983), Thyer (1983, 1987, 1988), Mattaini (1990), Shorkey and Sutton-Simon (1983), Brower and Nurius (1993), Berlin (1996), and Granvold, (1996). Cormier, Nurius, and Osborne (2008) integrate the cognitive behavioral perspective into their practice text.

The cognitive behavioral model is complex and includes numerous schools of therapy and practice models. For this reason, cognitive behavioral therapy has become more of a school of thought than a unitary theory or set of practices. It has been influenced by diverse theoretical and philosophical positions, ranging from psychoanalytic and behavioral to constructivist and experiential therapies. The approach has been associated most with behavior therapies, which has resulted in the term *cognitive behavior therapy*.

**Unique Methods in Cognitive Behavioral Assessment.**    The goal of cognitive behavioral assessment is to specify the behavior (thoughts, feelings, or overt behavior) to be changed, along with its antecedents, consequences, and underlying cognitive mechanisms. From Gambrill et al.'s (1971) nine-step behavioral assessment, behavioral assessment has evolved into a multidimensional contextual model (Barth, 1986; Gambrill, 1983; Mattaini, 1990; Whittaker & Tracy, 1989). Gambrill (1983) identified sources of influence on clients' behavior, including the actions of others, thoughts, emotions, physiological factors, setting, events, physical characteristics of the environment, ethnic and cultural factors, material and community resources, past history, societal factors, and developmental factors. Other influences include obstacles and opportunities, consequences of attempted solutions, environmental deficiencies, and motivations and/or inhibitions, as well as behavioral deficits inherent to the individual. Specific assessment approaches used in the cognitive behavioral model include behavioral analysis theory, interviewing, identification of underlying cognitive schemas, logs, self-anchored scales, and standardized measures (Bellack & Hersen, 1988; Hudson, 1982; Kanfer &

Schefft, 1988; Shorkey & Sutton-Simon, 1983). Chapter 2 summarizes and illustrates these methods.

In assessment systems, cognitive behaviorists have focused on theoretically and experimentally based approaches to identifying and tracking specific behaviors and cognitions that need to be changed. Now there is an increasing focus on putting people in their social contexts and on understanding how clients' developmental history and attachment relationships have influenced their current schemas and automatic thoughts. Also, in this type of assessment, it is important to collect data on the frequency and duration of cognitions and behaviors to observe the difficulties that clients experience and to monitor their changes. Among the popular earlier models was the ABC model, which focused on tracking antecedents (A), self-talk or automatic thoughts or beliefs (B), and behaviors and consequences of particular problems (C). The identification of automatic thoughts and their underlying schemas and the assessment of behavioral deficits and excesses are at the center of current models.

In general, cognitive behavior therapists have been forerunners in advocating valid and reliable methods for client assessment. Beck and Beck (2002), for example, developed measures for depression and suicide (see http://www.beckinstitute.org).

It is impossible to describe a full spectrum of cognitive behavioral approaches to assessment because of the increasing numbers of specific models and their unique features. One comprehensive assessment framework developed from the cognitive behavioral approach is multimodal assessment (Lazarus, 1989), and we describe that model here.

## Multimodal Assessment

Using the multimodal assessment framework, practitioners evaluate client problems in great depth and detail across different modalities, including behavior, affect, sensation, imagery, cognitions, interpersonal relationships, and physiological factors of client functioning—and the interactive effects of all of these (Lazarus, 2006). Lazarus (1991) developed a multimodal life-history inventory to help practitioners gain information about different modalities. Lazarus uses the acronym BASIC ID to describe the components that go into a comprehensive behavioral assessment: behavior, affect, sensation, imagery, cognition, interpersonal, and drugs.

The multimodal model helps practitioners formulate a brief but comprehensive assessment by developing a modality profile. A modality profile organizes information according to the BASIC ID assessment. Using BASIC ID, the practitioner is able to make differential decisions about effective treatments. It is also possible to scale the modality preferences to see in which areas a client may show a more favorable response to treatment (Lazarus, 1981). For example, some clients may experience difficulties in behavior, whereas others have more difficulties with affects or interpersonal relationships. Even a client with a presenting problem such as anxiety (an affect) may experience the problem in a way that responds to treatments that focus on another modality. For example, one of us had a client who experienced anxiety attacks mainly as physiological sensations (rapid pulse and tight muscles). The modality profile indicated that a treatment that focused on the sensation modality should be used as the first approach. As it turned out, teaching the client progressive muscle-relaxation exercises helped him. Using BASIC ID, it is possible for a practitioner to systematically plan interventions based on the client's assessment profile.

## Life-Model Assessment

Germain and Gitterman (2008), of the Columbia University of Social Work, developed the life model of social work practice. The authors suggest that an ecology metaphor best describes their approach. The underlying theory is ecological, concerned with interactions between people and their environments. Important concepts include stress, coping, and adaptation, as well as competence, autonomy, social networks, and organizations. Germain and Gitterman explain assessment as being concerned with "the interplay of dynamic forces within the life space, including the influence of the agency as a presence in the client's ecological context" (p. 633). The primary goal of assessment is to determine problems by examining three areas of the life space—life transitions, environmental pressures, and maladaptive interpersonal processes (Germain & Gitterman, 2008).

Gitterman identified five major aims of the life model (Gitterman, Goldstein, & Rose, 1988). The first aim is to develop a perspective to give equal attention to people and to the environment. The second aim is to develop a model of practice to build bridges among the traditional specializations of casework, administration and planning, and family therapy. Third, the model aims to mirror life processes closely so that social workers fit in with clients; clients should not be required to fit in with social workers' theoretical orientations. The fourth aim is to build on people's strengths rather than on their pathologies; labeling is viewed as blaming clients for their problems. The fifth and final aim is to build bridges between treatment and social reform.

**Unique Methods in Life-Model Assessment.**    Life-model assessment techniques include interviewing and ecomaps or social network mapping and standardized social support assessment instruments. The ecomap is one of the most important assessment tools to have evolved from this model (see Figure 1.2).

**Figure 1.2**    Ecomap

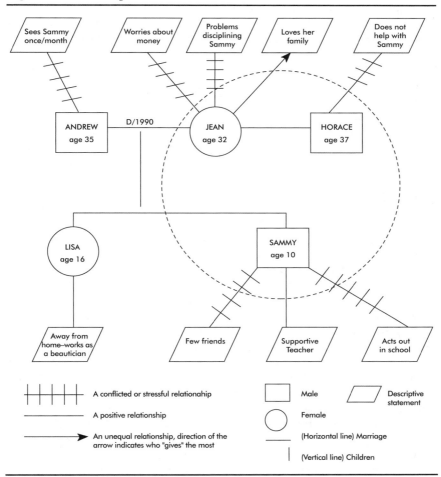

### Ecobehavioral Assessment Model

The work of Mattaini (1990, 1992, 1999, 2007) focuses on combining the ecological assessment model with specific, targeted interventions from the more empirical behavioral practice. Using an ecological systems framework is an important step in assessment, and the model provides practitioners with useful computerized assessment tools for generating ecomaps and other graphics-based assessments. This model's main contribution is that in combines ecological systems theories with contemporary behavioral practice from behavioral analysis traditions. There has been ongoing criticism from behavioral researchers and theorists that clinicians practicing behavioral therapies have not updated their knowledge about newer learning theories and thus have not keep abreast of the empirical and theoretical work going on in experimental psychology. The ecobehavioral model, however, does make use of knowledge from newer learning theories. Contemporary behavioral practice addresses overt behaviors and private experiences such as cognition and emotion, and it focuses on the social environment and major systems that shape humans (Mattaini, Lowery, & Meyer, 2002). The model also considers the structure and function of language (verbal behavior).

Three major developments guide the new behaviorism. First is the questioning of a mechanistic view of clients: mechanistic stimulus and response, simple contingency analysis (i.e., antecedents and consequences), and mediation models have been determined to be limited in explaining human behavior. Second is the development of contextual behavioral models that argue in favor of holism and a full contextual analysis for understanding of behavior: contextual behaviorists believe that no type of human response (e.g., overt behavior, cognition, emotion) can be separated from its contexts. This includes all forms of interaction, such as thinking, feeling, doing, and verbal behavior (rule governed), and the environmental contexts in which the behaviors take place. Contextual behaviorism rejects simple cause-and-effect relations because one area of observation, such as behavior or cognition, cannot explain psychological events; they must be analyzed in their full context, which includes all domains of responding. This is a systemic view, and contextual behaviorists are interested in the functions of behavior across contexts and in why a behavior is occurring. This means that they see both the history of the client and his or her current situation as important. Third is research on human verbal behavior (rule governed) and how humans derive bidirectional relations in learning. This research has led to an understanding of the importance of indirect contingencies for behavior. Experiments have shown, for example, that once humans learn one set of assumptions or a distinct pattern, they can transfer that pattern to another similar pattern without any further direct learning.

Humans may also learn through observation and verbal associations instead of direct experience. This means that they can learn by watching others and can talk themselves into responding a certain way in the present on the basis of a past association. Indirect contingencies often mediate more direct contingencies. This means that the internal meanings and expectations dictate responses to current experiences. So, what is aversive to one person may not be to another person who responds differently. Psychological problems such as phobias are usually learned indirectly through rule-governed behavior and not through direct experiences. Research on rule-governed, verbal behavior has led contemporary behaviorists to use more covert psychological events, such as valued elements (the potency of private reinforcers), different expectations (rules), and different meanings (equivalence relations), to understand the functional analysis of a behavior (Mattaini, 1999).

As with most contemporary behavioral models, the ecobehavioral model has broadened behaviorism as it was originally conceived. It shares features with other models. For example, it shares many features with the cognitive-ecological model of Brower and Nurius (1993), the life model, and the psychosocial model. The ecobehavioral model also incorporates knowledge and research from culture-analytic theory to help practitioners better assess and plan interventions with groups of people such as families. Using culture-analytic theory, the practitioner becomes acquainted with how culture shapes reinforcers, or rules for behavior, and sets the stage for individuals to form different meanings from their experiences (Mattaini, 1999).

**Unique Methods in Ecobehavioral Assessment.** The ecobehavioral model assumes that human behavior is complex and highly interconnected and that the best way to understand human behavior is to assess it using an ecological framework. Assessment is understood as the process of defining the difference between a client's current state and his or her goal state. This method is similar to that used in solution-focused therapy (to be reviewed later in this chapter) in that the focus is on change, goals, and new behavior and not on past pathology. The assessment process involves engaging, determining the difference in the goal state and the current state, envisioning how the client wants a situation to change, and planning the intervention. Assessment is completed in a framework of collaboration or shared power between the client and the practitioner (Mattaini, 1999). The ecobehavioral model is useful with individuals, families, groups, communities, and organizations, but it is better developed for micro practice than for macro practice.

In ecobehavioral assessment, the ecomap is an essential tool, along with other graphic methods that allow practitioners to map the context and relations of behavior. Mattaini (1993) provides detailed instructions and computer-based tools for graphing (available at http://www.nasw press.org/publications/bestbuys/thousand-words.html), as well as a framework and outline for conducting assessment following the ecobehavioral model (see Box 1.2).

Behavioral principles are used as analytical tools to map the exchanges between individuals, families, and their environment. For example, in the ecobehavioral model, practitioners use graphic tools or maps to help them understand the ecoscan (i.e., a mini-psychosocial history). This involves identifying focal issues and using contingency analysis to understand the consequences of overt and covert behavior that may reinforce a behavior. The practitioner also seeks to determine who is

**Box 1.2**
**Ecobehavioral Assessment**

I. Ecobehavioral Scan

I'd like to ask you a few questions so that we can develop a clear picture of your situation together and so that I can be sure I understand your life as it is now. (The social worker may wish to draw a transactional ecomap with the family during this stage.)

a. Let's start with what's going right. What areas of your family life are currently going the best?

b. What about connections you have outside the immediate family? How much contact do you have with relatives or extended family? On a scale of 0 (not at all) to 5 (a lot), how much satisfaction do you get from those contacts? Are there any struggles with those folks? On a scale of 0 to 5, how much pain do those struggles cause? (Use a similar scale with each of the following areas that appears particularly relevant.)

c. Do you have many friends? How often do you see friends? How are those relationships going? Anyone else?

d. What about work and school? What's going well there? So on our 0 to 5 scale, are there things that aren't going so well? About a __ on our scale?

e. Tell me a little about where you live. How satisfied are you with your home and neighborhood?

f. Any religious or church affiliation? Are you active?

g. Is anyone in the family active in other groups or organizations?

h. Any legal involvement?

i. How is everyone's health? Any problems there?

j. How much alcohol do people in the family use? Anyone take medication or drugs?

k. Now let's turn to your family itself. What's going right in the family? Who gets along best with whom? Who have more struggles getting along? (Elaborate and quantify as necessary to explore the relationships within the family.)

l. Does anyone else live in your home? How do you all get along? (Explore both positive and negative exchanges, and quantify if possible.)

m. What would you like to do more of in your family? What would you like to do less of? (Suggest self-monitoring or observational measures to expand data.)

II. Identification of Focal Issues

(Remember that focal issues may involve the behavior of only one person; however, to the extent possible, try to shift toward transactional definitions. Also, remember that focal issues need not involve only family members, but may involve transactions with other people or systems.)

a. So, out of all of this, where would you like to begin? What's most important to you?

b. I notice that you seemed to struggle a bit with ___. Is that one thing we should pay attention to?

**Box 1.2**  *Continued*

---

c. What do you think would be a realistic goal here? (Expanding with specifics, but build on the envisioning that occurred earlier.)
d. Do you think that there is anything else we should work on at this point?
e. So, specifically, one of our goals right now is (Explicate in behavioral terms.)

III. Contextual Analysis of Focal Issues

Now, let's see if we can get a really clear picture of our first goal (or focal issue), which is. (The general flow is from current undesirable situation to goal state; this kind of analysis should occur for each identified focal issue, although all may not be done at the same time. Focal issues left aside for later should be clearly stated and written down, however, so that the family knows they will be addressed later.)

a. As near as you can tell, how did this problem start?
b. When was that?
c. Does this problem behavior ever pay off in any way for anyone? Does it ever produce any advantages for anybody?
d. Who else acts a little like this sometimes?
e. Who or what supports the current pattern?
f. What are the costs? What other problems does it cause?
g. What seems to trigger the problem? Are there times when it does not happen? (Identify occasions.)
h. Are there some times when this is not a problem? Tell me about those times. When is the problem most likely to come up? (Search for motivating antecedents.)
i. What do you think it would take to get from where you are to where you want to be? (Explore resources, including tangible, personal, and social.)
j. Who would be willing to help you achieve this goal or resolve this problem?
k. Who or what might stand in the way?
l. How important is this to you? Why? How will reaching this goal enrich your lives? How quickly do you think that will happen? (Build motivation.)

IV. Identification of Interventive Tasks

(This part of the assessment process needs to flow from the information provided in earlier stages, and it should emphasize tasks that will address the areas identified in the contextual analysis. It should explore interventive options for mobilizing the resources and addressing the obstacles discussed in that analysis. Identify approaches with the best empirical support in the context of the family situation. Careful specification of the multiple steps required to work toward the goal may be required. Explore possible reinforcers to be used along the way as well.)

---

SOURCE: Mattaini, M. (1999).

involved in the issues and the motivating antecedents that may trigger a behavior. The final goal is to carry out the desired intervention tasks.

## Family Systems Assessment Model

Over the past forty years, the family therapy field has developed many methods for assessing families as a system. Family systems assessment focuses on the systemic or relational network characteristics of family functioning and associated presenting problems. Systemic functioning specifically refers to the circular, patterned way in which family groups are believed to behave. To effectively assess family systems, clinicians must use assessment methods that focus on the interactive sequences and relational network characteristics of the entire family. In this view, assessment serves a dual function: it is a way to discover how a family system is functioning and a method for intervening in the patterns of a family system. The processes of assessment and change interventions are not distinct but interactive and circular, which allows for assessment methods to contribute to information-gathering strategies and interventive methods. Viewing assessment as intervention blurs the boundaries between methods that are for the purposes of assessment and those that are for change. Family systems models have no distinct assessment phase; instead, they combine assessment with treatment.

**Unique Methods in Family Systems Assessment.**    In a family assessment, practitioners use special questioning techniques to gather information and to introduce information into a family system. Techniques include circular questions; conversational or therapeutic questions; hypothesizing, circularity, and neutrality; tracking problems, solutions, or exceptions to problems; and pretherapy change assessment. Graphic tools such as genograms are also used to assess longitudinal emotional and behavioral patterns in families (see Figure 1.3). Finally, family assessment uses empirically derived assessment models and standardized measures, which derive from research on the classification and assessment of family systems functioning (chapter 8 reviews and illustrates several family systems assessment methods).

## Task-Centered Assessment Model

The task-centered model was developed in the 1960s from a psychoanalytically oriented short-term model (Reid, 1988, 1992, 2000). Today, it is more akin to cognitive behavioral practice than to the psychosocial model. The model's focus is on specific problems that clients want to resolve. This approach has been used worldwide with many different types of social work clients (Fortune, Reid, & Reyome, 2009). The theoretical base of task-centered casework was designed to be open to integrating

**Figure 1.3**    Family Genogram

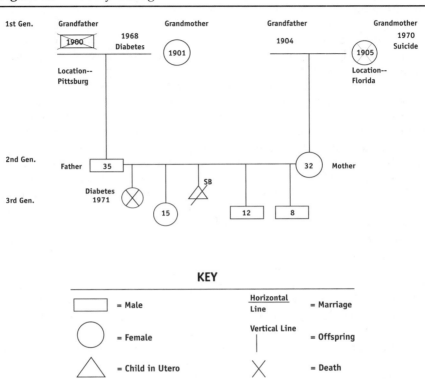

SOURCE: Foley, V. (1989). Family therapy. In R. Corsini & D. Wedding (Eds.), *Current Psychotherapies* (4th ed.). Itasca, IL: Peacock.

various theoretical and technical orientations (Reid, 1988). Ideas important to the original model were that casework is a problem-solving process (Perlman, 1957) and that the client's task is the focus (Studt, 1968). Theory and techniques were borrowed from crisis-intervention literature. More recently, theory and techniques from behavioral theory, cognitive and learning theory, and structural family therapy have been integrated into the task-centered model.

**Unique Methods in Task-Centered Assessment.**    The goal of assessment is to specify target problems and their desired outcomes. Reid and Epstein (1972) and Reid (1988, 2000) explain the assessment and task-planning process. The first activity is initial problem formulation. The clients' perception of the problem is important, though it has been recognized that clients may need help expressing or even acknowledging the full range of a problem. Practitioners may help in this process by exploring, clarifying, and specifying a problem. In the case of clients who are required to seek services (e.g., in the case of child abuse), practitioners begin with the problem that brought them to the service provider. After formulating the problem, the practitioner then places it in the context in which it occurs, including conditions that perpetuate the problem, resources, and interpersonal and intrapersonal systems. Standardized instruments may be used. Assessment continues into intervention and monitoring of case progress. In summary, the task-centered process includes task planning, implementation, and review (Reid, 1988).

The task-centered approach is useful for ensuring that assessment moves into specific intervention planning. The model has been shown to be helpful for both voluntary and nonvoluntary clients. It has been used in case management and clinical services with much success (Reid & Fortune, 2008). Task-centered assessment is prescriptive, in that specification of tasks and problems leads to specific intervention plans. The client and clinician usually define tasks through a collaborative process in a face-to-face interview. Specific forms and contractual agreements signed by both parties may be used to write down the problems, tasks, and goals. Task-centered assessment offers a tremendous amount of specificity on the desired outcomes of assessment, as the resulting service contract illustrates. It is, however, unclear which specific tasks work best with which clients and client problems. The link between assessment and intervention appears to be left up to the collaborative process of the interview and to the practitioner's own clinical judgment.

### The Strengths Perspective in Assessment

Dennis Saleeby (1997) pioneered the strengths perspective in social work practice. The essence of this model is the heart of social work's unique philosophical viewpoints on helping. Practicing from a strengths perspective incorporates a value system that encompasses belief in the dignity and worth of individuals, their self-determination, and the transformative power of humans and human relationships. Regardless of the model used, practicing with clients from a strengths perspective means viewing them through a humanistic lens that assumes that all clients can grow and change (Early & GlenMaye, 2000).

The strengths-oriented practitioner empowers clients, treating them as equals in a collaborative relationship. He or she looks beyond the individual and the oppressive systems that marginalize and define realities toward the larger community and cultural contexts that help the practitioner understand clients and their life circumstances. The practitioner also moves away from pathologizing language and diagnostic schemes, such as mental health classifications systems like the *DSM*-IV-TR in favor of broader, person-in-environment assessment for understanding client functioning. Saleeby (1997) argues that social work practice gives only lip service to strengths and that our continued practice within pathologizing, medical models has obliterated any strengths orientation. The importance of client strengths, however, can be traced to earlier models in social work, such as the functional, psychosocial, cognitive behavioral, and systems perspectives.

**Unique Methods in Strengths Assessment.**    As a practice model, the strengths perspective is more of a philosophical stance than a set of assessment and intervention skills. However, some important skills do emerge in the literature. These assessment and intervention skills mostly relate to the values and the therapeutic and helping stance of the practitioner. It is important in assessment, for example, for the practitioner to give preeminence to clients' viewpoints of the problem and their subjective interpretations and experiences. It is equally important for the practitioner to establish a collaborative helping relationship with clients as a part of a dialogic, ongoing assessment. As a part of assessment, clients participate in defining their problems, goals, and ways of being helped. The practitioner uses the words and language of the client to establish rapport and mutual understanding. The practitioner avoids simplistic, black-and-white thinking and/or simple cause-effect relationships in favor of longer narratives and complex explanations that are laden with situational and contextual meanings.

Finally, the practitioner focuses on assessing and defining competencies and uniqueness while avoiding blaming, pejorative labels, and debilitating diagnoses, which serve to disable clients (Cowger & Snively, 2008). In this manner, many social work practitioners practicing from the strengths perspective steer away from prescriptive and normative approaches to assessment, such as diagnostic and measurement approaches. These approaches are believed to be contrived and to produce limited options in their outcomes. Other practitioners, however, seek ways to integrate measurement approaches with the strengths perspective. The type of context-driven and open-ended assessment that strengths practitioners most value is consistent with qualitative and naturalistic approaches, which chapter 4 describes in some detail.

## Solution-Focused Brief Therapy Assessment Models

Several models of brief therapy exist, but this text covers only one here, solution-focused brief therapy, which has gained a considerable amount of popularity in social work practice in recent years. Solution-focused brief therapy is a strengths-based therapy model developed by two social work practitioners, Steve de Shazer and Insoo Kim Berg, and their associates at the Brief Family Therapy Center in Milwaukee, Wisconsin (Franklin et al., in press). De Shazer and Berg are deceased and the center has shut down, but the Solution-Focused Brief Therapy Association (http://www.sfbta.org) has continued the training and is a repository for information and resources. Solution-focused therapy has been compared to motivational interviewing. The two are conceptually similar and have some overlapping techniques, but solution-focused therapy is a unique approach to social work practice. The treatment manual for solution-focused therapy (available at http://www.sfbta.org) and has also been published in book form (Franklin, Trepper, McCollum, & Gingerich, in press). The book highlights research on solution-focused therapy and several studies that have found it to be an effective approach (Franklin et al., in press). Prominent social workers who currently conduct research, practice, and training on solution-focused therapy include Gingerich and Eisengart (2000); De Jong and Berg (2008); Kim (2008); Kim and Franklin (2009); and Kelly, Kim, and Franklin (2008). Peter Lehman (Lehman & Patton, in press) has developed a fidelity measure for solution-focused therapy and offers a certificate training program for solution-focused brief therapy at the University of Texas at Arlington.

**Unique Methods in Solution-Focused Brief Therapy Assessment.** Much like the family systems models described earlier, the solution-focused model does not separate assessment and intervention; assessment is part of the intervention process. A unique feature of this model is that practitioners assess in each particular case who is motivated to change. This assessment is guided by a case construction process that helps practitioners think about who in the case is the customer, complainant, or visitor. The customer is the person who is willing to make a commitment to the change process. The complainant is the person who is complaining about a problem and must be satisfied that a change has occurred—the complainant usually does not view him- or herself as part of the problem. The visitor is not very invested in the change process but is willing to be peripherally involved and may provide needed information. Solution-focused therapists use this assessment to develop goals and intervention strategies for a particular case. The solution-focused model also suggests that not all clients are customers and should not be treated in that manner by practitioners. The solution-focused model offers a wealth of information for assessing and working with mandated, or involuntary, clients who are required to seek services by other agencies, such as the child protection system, schools, and legal authorities (De Jong & Berg, 2001).

In working with a mandated client, practitioners are advised to change their relationship stance toward the client. For example, to begin the change process or to form a contract for the purposes of working with the client, it is not always necessary for practitioners to engage in a completely mutual, trusting relationship. Instead, practitioners may follow these principles for assessment and practice with mandated clients, summarized here by Franklin (2002):

1. Use nonjudgmental acceptance to investigate the client's problem. Use reflective listening skills and hear the client's version of the story. Let the client tell you how others view him or her. Listen to the explanation for how the client was referred. Empathize with the client's perceptions.

2. Increase motivational congruence by making the fit between what the client genuinely wants and the services you, the practitioner, provides as congruent as possible. Thus, find out what the client wants and to define roles in accordance with that purpose. For example, if the client wishes to have his or her children returned from child protective services, then discuss with the client ways that treatment can help that happen. Use reframing to help the client view his or her motivations and the system's or referral sources motivation as similar. For example, say, "You and child protective services both want to get your child back home as soon as possible."

3. Emphasize the client's choices when possible. Mandated clients often feel forced and helpless, like they have no choice but to come to see you. Emphasize that clients do have choices and point out areas in which such choices exist. For example, clients do not have to come to sessions; they can choose to take the consequences.

4. Educate clients about what to expect during intervention. Clients who are mandated may not know what to expect and may be very fearful of the situation. Their angry responses may be exacerbated by their fears. Practitioners should take care to inform clients about what to expect and to teach novice clients about the social services and legal systems.

5. Develop specific contracts and goals with the client. A contract can and should be different from the one developed with other systems. You can define what others expect differently than you define what you expect. The contract should involve your role and what the client agrees on with you.

6. Define for the client what is nonnegotiable from the standpoint of referring agencies. Offer or point out incentives for the client to comply with behavioral demands with which he or she does not agree. For example: "When Charles insults you, hitting Charles is not acceptable to the school. They want you to go to this dumb conflict resolution person instead. You do not agree with that idea and neither does your dad. You think it is a dumb practice that does not fit into being a man or staying alive in your neighborhood. However, if you go to the conflict

person, you can keep from being sent to the alternative school. Right? You said that you do not want to go to that place because you do not get to play basketball or leave school early. So, perhaps it is worth doing something dumb to avoid being sent to the alternative school. Anyway, I guess you have a choice on which way to go."

7. Use the client's goal of getting the system off his or her back as a way to gain compliance. For example: "As you see it, your teachers have it in for you, and it is difficult to get them to see you any differently. However, you have got to find a way to get them off your back so that they do not continue to call your mom every other day. So, are you willing to work on a few things they want just so you can get them off your back?"

Solution-focused brief therapy also offers a wealth of questioning techniques that can help facilitate client assessment and change. Solution-focused therapists are interested in clients' perspectives of their lives and in facilitating and co-constructing solution-building conversations with clients (De Jong & Berg, 2001). Practitioners therefore focus on exceptions to problems, strengths, and competencies of clients instead of on their weaknesses and pathologies. In particular, practitioners work with clients to co-construct specific goals that can move them in small steps toward their solutions. Box 1.3 briefly describes some of the questioning techniques used in solution-focused assessment.

---

**Box 1.3**
**Questions Used in a Solution-Focused Assessment**

---

**Tracking solution behaviors or exceptions to the problem.** The therapist identifies times when the problem does not occur, effective coping responses, and the contexts for the absence of the problem. The therapist says something such as, "Even though this is a very bad problem, in my experience, people's lives do not always stay the same. I bet that there are times when the problem of being sent to the principal's office is not happening or at least it is better. Describe those times. What is different? How did you get that to happen?" The therapist gathers as many exceptions to the problem pattern as possible by repeatedly asking the client, "What else . . .? What other times . . .?" Once an exception has been identified by the client, the therapist uses prompts, such as "tell me more about that," to help the client describe in detail the exceptions. The therapist also uses his or her own affects, tone, and intense attention to the client's story to communicate to the client that he or she is very interested in those exceptions. Such nonverbal gestures as nodding, smiling, leaning forward, and looking surprised are

**Box 1.3**  *Continued*

used. The therapist also may say something such as "how about that," "I am amazed," or "Wow!" as social reinforcement to the client. This encourages the client to talk on and to develop in more detail the exceptions story.

**Scaling the problem.** This approach uses scaling questions to assess the problem and to track progress toward problem resolutions. The therapist says, "On a scale of 1 to 10, with 1 being that you are getting in trouble everyday in class, picking on Johnny and Susi, getting out of your seat and being scolded by your teacher, and 10 being that instead of fighting with Johnny and Susi you are doing your work, and that you ask permission to get out of your seat, and your teacher says something nice to you, where would you be on that scale now?" With children, often smiley and sad faces are also used to anchor the two ends of the scale.

Other uses of the scaling technique in the therapy process include the following: 1) asking questions about where the client is on the scale in relationship to solving the problem; 2) using the scaling experience to find exceptions to problems, such as saying "How did you get to the 3?" or "What are you doing so you are not a 1?"; 3) employing scales to construct "miracles" or to identify solution behaviors. For example, the therapist inquires as to where the client is on the scale (with 1 representing low and 10 representing high). The therapist then proceeds to ask the client how he or she will get from a 1 to a 3. Or, the therapist inquires how the client managed to move from a 4 rating to a 5 rating, for example, by asking, "How did you get that to happen? What new behaviors did you implement or what was different in your life that made the changes?" Solution-focused therapists may also express surprise that the problem is not worse on the scale as a way of complimenting the client's coping behavior or as a way to use language to change the client's perception of the intractable nature of the problem.

**Using coping and motivation questions.** This is a variation on the scaling question that helps the therapist assess the client's motivation for solving the problem as well as how well the client perceives that he or she is coping with the problem. The therapist says something like, "On a scale of 1 to 10, with 10 being that you would do anything to solve this problem, and 1 being that you do not care so much for solving it, where would you say you are right now?" Or the therapist may say, "On a scale of 1 to 10 with 1 being that you are ready to throw in the towel and give up ever doing well in school, and 10 being that you are ready to keep on trying, where would you rate yourself right now?" After asking coping and motivation questions, the therapist should be able to determine the following:

---

**Box 1.3**  *Continued*

---

a) If the problem that has been defined is too overwhelming to the client. If the problem is too overwhelming, then the problem needs to be broken down into smaller steps and redefined for the client.

b) How much self-efficacy and hope the client possesses toward the problem resolution. If the client does not believe the problem can be solved, steps must be taken to change this belief. Here, the exception questions can be empowering.

c) What is the degree of commitment to work on the problem. If the client is not interested in committing to working on the problem, then the problem must be redefined to muster some degree of commitment.

d) If the problem that has been defined is the one that really interests the client and if it is a priority for him or her.

   **Asking the miracle question.** This type of question seeks to assess the client's priorities and to develop solutions. The therapist says, for example, "Let's suppose that an overnight miracle happened, and your problem disappeared; but you were sleeping and did not know it. When you woke up the next day, what would be the first thing that you would notice?" The therapist proceeds to help the client envision how things could be different. An extreme amount of detail is elicited to help develop a set of solution behaviors that are concrete and behaviorally specific. The miracle question helps the therapist to assess a detailed description of the client's perception of what life would be like without the problem. It also helps the therapist coconstruct with the client's input a specific set of behaviors, thoughts, and feelings that can be substituted for problem patterns. Ultimately, the therapist can assess what is most important to the client and others concerning which changes the client perceives will solve the problem.

---

SOURCE: Franklin, C., & Moore, K. (1999). Solution-focused therapy. In C. Franklin & C. Jordan, *Family practice: Brief systems methods for social work.* Pacific Grove, CA: Brooks/Cole.

## COMMON FEATURES OF SOCIAL WORK ASSESSMENT MODELS

Assessment information and social work practice models reviewed in this chapter share the following features concerning how assessment works:

- Social work assessment emphasizes both individuals and their social environments: viewing clients in their contexts of families, groups, and communities is the preferred approach to assessment.

- Social work assessments are evidence based and combine different approaches to develop best practices in assessment.

- Social work assessment includes the strengths and resilience of clients: it is equally important to assess competencies and strengths as it is to address problem areas and pathologies. The goals of most approaches include increasing the self-efficacy of clients, restoring or supporting their inherent problem-solving capacities, and returning clients to their best adaptive functioning.

- Most social work assessment models are integrative and rely on more than one underlying theory: the theory base of social work practice is eclectic. Social work models combine multiple theories in their assessment and practice focuses. Social work is interprofessional by nature, and social workers usually are employed in host settings. Social work assessment also integrates knowledge from several fields.

- Assessments deemphasize long history taking, even in models that traditionally focused on this information (e.g., psychosocial). Instead, only relevant history is used strategically to understand presenting problems and needed interventions.

- Assessments are organized around task-centered planning or goal orientations: the purpose of assessment across models is to resolve presenting problems or to move clients toward desired goals. Assessments across social work models focus mostly on the present context and future behaviors that clients' desire.

- Social work assessments share common types of information: even though different tools and methods are used across models to gather information from clients, social work models value information similarly, including definitions, identified strengths, specific goals, intervention planning or solution building, and outcome monitoring.

- Social work assessments use a collaborative process between client and practitioner: All models prefer collaborative work with clients in gathering information and goal construction. Shared power and client-centered perspectives are important to the clinical assessment process, in contrast to more authoritative approaches in which the practitioner is considered the only expert on the client and his or her problems.

- Assessments in social work emphasize brief, time-limited perspectives. All models reviewed here prefer brevity and short-term assessments, perhaps because of the realities of practice environments and the applied problem-solving nature of social work practice.

## INTEGRATING THE COMPONENTS OF PRACTICE MODELS FOR SOCIAL WORK ASSESSMENT

Similar to social work assessment models, this text takes an integrative approach to assessment. The integration of theory is a common approach to assessment and intervention in social work practice, as can be seen from the diverse practice models reviewed. We agree with Lazarus's (1981) technical eclecticism, which assumes that practice methods from different underlying theoretical models can be used together. Lazarus believes that it is not necessary to embrace the theory in borrowing techniques compatible with one's own theoretical and practice approach. Rather than choosing techniques based on one's theoretical philosophy, choice is based on research support for the technique or the best available practice wisdom. Although there are some limitations to a pragmatic approach like technical eclecticism, such as the lack of overarching or defining theory to guide practice, technical eclecticism allows for a more experimental and problem-solving approach that tests different assessment methods without being limited to one school of thought or set of practice methods. It is also important for the practitioner to evaluate assessment techniques with practice evaluation methods. Box 1.4 integrates the major assessment issues covered in each model reviewed and shows the elements that can be used in a comprehensive social work assessment.

---

**Box 1.4**
**Integrative Skills Assessment Protocol**

---

　I. Identifying Information
　　1. Name
　　2. Address
　　3. Home phone number
　　4. Work phone number
　　5. Date of birth
　　6. Family members living at home
　　　a. Name
　　　b. Age
　　　c. Relationship
　　7. Occupation
　　8. Income
　　9. Gender
　　10. Race
　　11. Religious affiliation
　　12. Briefly describe the presenting problem or symptom(s)
　II. Nature of Presenting Problem(s)
　　1. List all of the problems identified by the client and/or practitioner
　　　a. What is the specific problem(s)?
　　2. Specification of problem(s)
　　　a. History
　　　　i. When did the problem first occur?
　　　　ii. Is this a long-standing, unresolved problem? A recently established one?

**Box 1.4** *Continued*

      b. Duration
         i. How long has the problem been going on?
      c. Frequency
         i. How often does the problem occur?
      d. Magnitude
         i. What is the intensity of the problem?
      e. Antecedents
         i. What happens immediately before the problem occurs?
      f. Consequences
         i. What happens immediately after the problem occurs?
      g. Exceptions to the problem
         i. What exceptions to the problem exist?
         ii. How often have exceptions occurred?
         iii. When was the last time an exception happened?
         iv. What was different in the situation in which the exception occurred than in situations in which the problem happens?
         v. Who was involved in making the exception happen?
      h. Reason for seeking help
         i. What makes the client seek help now and not before?
      i. Prior efforts to solve problem(s)
         i. How has the client sought to solve the problem previously, including other therapy?
         ii. With what results?
      j. Client motivation
         i. What is the level of motivation for solving the problem?
         ii. Use scaling question to identify client motivation: "On a scale of 1 to 10 with 10 being you would do anything to solve this problem and 1 being that you do not care so much for solving it, where would you say you are right now?"
      k. Client resources/strengths
         i. What are the client resources available for solving the problem?
         ii. Use scaling question to assess coping: "On a scale of 1 to 10, with 1 being that you are ready to throw in the towel and give up and 10 being that you are ready to keep on trying, where would you rate yourself right now?"
      l. Other
         i. Are there other difficulties associated with or in addition to the problem?
  3. Prioritize problems and goals
      a. Through negotiations with the client, prioritize problems in terms of severity.
      b What are the client's goals? Goals should be something he or she is motivated to accomplish.
      c. What is a small, obtainable goal? What can the client do toward the goal immediately and before the next session?
      d. What, when, how, and with whom is the behavior to happen?
      e. What will the client do instead of the problem behavior?

---

**Box 1.4**  *Continued*

---

      f. Does the client understand that the goal is the first step and not the end to solving the problem?

      g. Is the goal something the client can do in the context of his or her life?

      h. Does the client understand that the goal is hard work and that effort must be put forth? Is the client committed to do so?

         i. Use the miracle question to prompt the client to set a goal or to envision a solution to the problem: "Let's suppose that an overnight miracle happened and the problem you are having disappeared, but you were sleeping and did not know it. When you woke up the next morning, what would be the first thing you would notice?" Guide the client in discussing what life would be like without the problem.

III. Client

  1. Intrapersonal issues

    a. Cognitive functioning

      i. What is the client's perception of the problem and its solution?

      ii. What are the client's most common upsetting thoughts?

      iii. What underlying beliefs and schemas support the client's upsetting thoughts and subsequent emotions and behaviors? Identify maladaptive cognitive schemas as the central focus of intervention.

  2. Maladaptive schemas around autonomy

    a. Dependence (on others for support, fear one can't take care of self)

    b. Subjugation (sacrifice of one's own needs to satisfy others' needs)

    c. Vulnerability to harm or illness (fear of disasters)

    d. Fear of losing self-control (over own mind, behavior, impulses, body, etc.)

  3. Maladaptive schemas around connectedness

    a. Emotional deprivation (expectation own needs won't be met)

    b. Abandonment/loss (fear of losing significant others and of being isolated forever)

    c. Mistrust (expectation of others to willfully hurt, abuse, cheat, lie, manipulate, or take advantage)

    d. Social isolation/alienation (feels different from others, not part of)

  4. Maladaptive schemas around worthiness

    a. Defectiveness/unlovability (feels inwardly defective, flawed, unlovable)

    b. Social undesirability (feels outwardly undesirable, ugly, of low status, dull)

    c. Incompetence/failure (believes self cannot perform)

    d. Guilt/punishment (believes self morally or ethically bad and deserving of punishment or harsh criticism)

    e. Shame/embarrassment (believes one's inadequacies are totally unacceptable to others)

  5. Maladaptive schemas around limits and standards

    a. Unrelenting standards (relentless striving to meet extremely high expectations of oneself at the expense of happiness, pleasure, health, satisfying relationships)

      i. Trace antecedents, beliefs, and consequences of upsetting thoughts and behaviors.

      ii. What are the "hot cognitions," or those cogntions that are related to underlying emotions and schemas?

      iii. What is the client's view of self, others, and the world?

      iv. What evidence is there for problem-solving capacity?

**Box 1.4**   *Continued*

      v. In what ways has client solved problems in the past?

     vi. Is there clear evidence of rational vs. irrational thoughts?

6. Emotional functioning
   a. Describe the client's affect and mood
   b. Can the client express a range of emotions?
   c. Is there evidence of appropriate vs. inappropriate emotions such as extreme anger, elation, or depression?
   d. Is there evidence that the client's cultural group or primary reference group views the client's affect or mood as being outside the norm?

7. Behavioral functioning
   a. Physical appearance
   b. Mannerisms
   c. Speech
   d. Abilities and disabilities
   e. Antisocial or acting-out behavior
   f. Behavioral deficits or excesses such as lack of social skills or addictions

8. Physiological functioning
   a. Has the client been seen medically during the past year?
   b. If so, with what results?
   c. Is there any evidence of drug and alcohol usage?
   d. Are any medications taken?
   e. Describe diet, caffeine, alcohol, and drug usage.

9. Client mental status
   a. Disturbances in appearance, dress, posture, etc.
   b. Disturbances in thoughts (hallucinations, delusions, etc.)
   c. Disturbances in level of awareness (memory, attention, etc.)
   d. Disturbances in thought processes (logic, intelligibility, coherence)
   e. Disturbances in emotional tone (deviations in affect or discrepancies in verbal reports of mood and client affect)
   f. Degree to which the client seems aware of the nature of the problem and the need for treatment

10. Ethnic/cultural/gender considerations
    a. What is the client's ethnic group?
    b. What is the degree of acculturation?
    c. What is the client's perception of how ethnic/cultural/gender group identification has helped or not helped?
    d. Are the sources of conflict related to ethnic/cultural/gender issues?

11. Motivation
    a. What stage of change is the client in?
    b. Is the client unaware of a need for changes?
    c. Is the client currently contemplating a need to change but has not made a full commitment to the change process?
    d. Has the client fully embraced the idea of change and is ready to move forward?
    e. Has the client already made some recent changes and needs help maintaining those changes?
    f. Has the client changed the problem behavior in the past but has since relapsed?
    g. What are factors that may contribute to client motivation, either causing client discomfort or causing client to have hope for the future?

**Box 1.4**    *Continued*

12. Client roles and role performance
    a. What roles does the client perform (wife, mother, etc.)
    b. What are the client's issues related to role performance?
    c. What are the client's issues related to satisfaction or dissatisfaction?
    d. What are the client's gender issues?
    e. Are there of social and economic injustices?
13. Developmental considerations?
    a. Trace the birth, developmental history of the client (the mother's pregnancy, developmental milestones, illness, trauma, etc.)
    b. Is there an "identified patient"? If so, whom?
    c. What is each family member's perspective of the problem(s)?
14. Marital status
    a. What is the client's sexual dating and/or marital history?
    b. What is the quality of the client's intimate relationships?
    c. How long has the client been married?
    d. How many times has the client been married?
15. Interpersonal: Family structure
    a. Quality of the client's family interactions
    b. Family boundaries
    c. Family alliances
    d. Family power structure
    e. Family communication patterns
    f. Family stories and narratives
    g. Family strengths
16. Interpersonal: Work or school
    a. Occupation or grade in school
    b. Satisfaction with work/school
        i. Are there indicators of successful achievement in this setting?
        ii. What are issues related to grades, pay, promotions, etc?
        iii. Describe relationships with colleagues/peers
    c. Effect of problem(s) on work/school
        i. Does the problem(s) occur in this setting? If so, how does the client get along with peers, teachers/bosses, other authority figures?
        ii. What is the academic/work history?
        iii. Any evidence of antisocial behavior?
17. Interpersonal: Peers
    a. Satisfaction with number of peers/friends?
        i. Who are the client's friends and what is the quality of these relationships?
IV. Context and Social Support Networks
    1. Agency considerations
        a. Does the agency setting have an effect on the problem/client (i.e., does the client have negative feelings about seeking services at this agency? Is the agency located too far away to be accessible to the client? Does the agency have the resources to deal with the client's problem in terms of worker time, interest, etc.?)
        b. Would referral be best for the client, and if so, what is the best referral source?

**Box 1.4** *Continued*

    2. Client's environmental context
       a. What environmental resources does client have? (adequate housing, transportation, food/clothing, recreation, social supports, educational opportunities, etc.)
       b. What environmental resources exist that the client is not currently utilizing (access to family or peer support, support from agencies in the neighborhood, etc.)
       c. What environmental resources do not exist and need to be developed? What gaps in resources exist for this client?
 V. Measurement (use global and/or rapid assessment instruments)
    1. Family functioning
    2. Marital (or significant other) functioning
    3. Individual functioning
    4. Social supports
    5. Strengths, resources, and protective factors
 VI. Summary
    1. Practitioner impressions
       a. Summarize areas for presentation to the client. List concerns of highest priority to the client. What is the goal? Generate a list of exceptions to the problem and a list of client strengths. Obtain client feedback.
       b. *DSM* diagnosis
       c. Problem(s) or solutions to be targeted for immediate intervention
    2. To be negotiated with client and prioritized
       a. What are some progress indicators?
       b. What are desired outcomes?
       c. What is the baseline?
       d. What are the results of either pretest or repeated measurement of targeted problems and strengths?
 VII. Treatment Plan
    1. Problem(s):
       a.
       b.
    2. Definition(s):
       a.
       b.
    3. Goal(s):
       a.
       b.
    4. Objective(s) (measurement):
       a.
       b.
       c.
       d.
    5. Intervention(s):
       a.
       b.
       c.
       d.

## Moving from Assessment to Intervention Planning

This final section describes how assessment is an integral part of forming treatment plans. Clinical decision making, problem monitoring, and treatment planning are a part of the social worker's assessment skills and are discussed here.

### Clinical Decision Making

What happens in the assessment phase of treatment affects interventions selected at later stages of treatment. The information collected during assessment helps the practitioner focus on specific problems to be targeted for intervention and to specify the type of intervention that will be of most help for those problems. Various treatment-planning manuals guide practitioners in selecting appropriate interventions (see, e.g., Jordan and Franklin, 2009; Reid, 2000). To meet this end, the social worker must make three important decisions during assessment: how much and which data to collect, which assessment tools to use, and the specific problem to target. Each chapter in this book offers information to help practitioners make these decisions.

The following seven steps that are associated with evidence-based practice give further guidance on selecting and evaluating assessment practices (adapted from Sackett, Sackett, Richardson, Rosenberg, & Haynes, 1997; see also Figure 1.4). The steps assume a collaborative approach with clients:

**Figure 1.4**    Evidence Informed Behavioral Practice

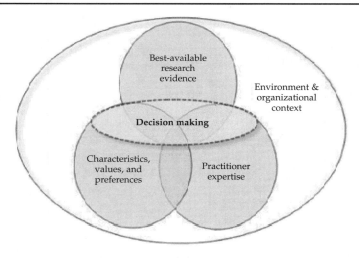

SOURCE: Spring, B., & Hitchcock, K. (2009). Evidence-based practice in psychology. In I. B. Weiner & W. E. Craighead (Eds.), *Corsini's Encyclopedia of Psychology*, 4th edition (pp. 603–607). New York: Wiley. Used with permission.

Step 1: Convert information needs into a relevant question for practice in a community and/or organizational context. Determine what data needs to be collected.

Step 2: Track down with maximum efficiency the best evidence to answer the question. When applying this step to the assessment process, determine what types of assessment tools are best to use.

Step 3: Critically appraise the evidence for its validity and usefulness. In this step, it is important to determine how effective and efficient the assessment tools are and to determine how much confidence we have in the information we have gotten from them.

Step 4: Provide clients with appropriate information about the efficacy of different interventions and collaborate with them in making the final decision on the best practice. This means sharing the results of our assessments with clients, including their limitations, and verifying information we have obtained with clients.

Step 5: Apply the results of this appraisal in making policy and practice decisions that affect organizational, community, or client change. Use the results of the assessment and client feedback to choose an intervention.

Step 6: Assess the fidelity of implementing the micro or macro practice intervention. Use ongoing assessments of the client to monitor the intervention and make sure it is delivered as planned.

Step 7: Evaluate service outcomes from implementing the best practice. Measure the outcomes of the intervention to determine whether it is working and then make any adaptations to ensure the best results.

**Collecting Data.**  We recommend performing assessment from a multidimensional perspective and across systems to gain the big picture of a client's issues; however, it also is important to know how to propose limits to data collection in assessment. Gambrill (1983) suggests that a thorough assessment should consider inter- and intrapersonal issues related to client functioning and that the assessment data collected should be *relevant*. In limiting the information to collect, consider who requested the assessment and for what purpose. For instance, if Child Protective Services is requested to perform an assessment and provide a report to a court, the judge may require a thorough assessment that includes a report of every detail of the child's life and environmental situation. However, if the assessment is performed in a managed care setting and the client requests time-limited help with a child management problem, only information pertinent to the parent-child relationship might be relevant.

The Integrative Skills Assessment Protocol covers the big systems picture about what might be relevant for a multidimensional perspective and covers details across the client's life to ask about (see Box 1.4). In a comprehensive psychosocial assessment, it might be important to learn as much as possible about each area, but not all the information on the protocol is necessary for every case. Box 1.5 provides a checklist to guide practitioners in selecting relevant information. Use of the checklist equires clinical judgment and decision making based on what is most relevant to each individual case. Note that the checklist asks the practitioner to consider the various areas that might be included in the assessment, such as client intrapersonal issues, family issues, or work issues. The practitioner should check off only the areas pertinent to the client; then only the checked-off areas are addressed in the Integrative Skills Assessment Protocol.

---

**Box 1.5**
**Checklist for Brief Assessment with the**
**Integrative Skills Assessment Protocol**

---

**Instructions:**  1. Check off the sections below as they apply to the client and/or the client's problem(s). (*Note*: Sections required for all clients are checked.)
2. Next, go to the Integrative Skills Assessment Protocol and complete only the sections checked.

### I. Identifying Information

_____ 1.–12.

### II. Nature of Presenting Problem

_____ 13.a. List all problems
_____ 14.a.–k. Specification of specific, discrete problem(s) behavior(s)
_____ 15.a. Prioritize problem(s)

### III. Client

_____ 16.a.–i. Intrapersonal issue
_____ 17.a.–d. Interpersonal: family
_____ 18.a.–b. Interpersonal: work or school
_____ 19.a. Interpersonal: peers

### IV. Context and Social Support Networks

_____ 20.a.–b. Agency consideration
_____ 21.a.–c. Client's environmental context

### V. Assessment Measures

_____ 22. Family functioning
_____ 23. Marital (or significant other) functioning
_____ 24. Individual functioning
_____ 25. Social supports

**Box 1.5**  *Continued*

**VI. Strengths and Resources**

_____ 26. Client strengths
_____ 27. Environmental strengths

**VII. Assessment Summary and Treatment Recommendations**

_____ 28.a. Baseline
_____ 29.a. Practitioner impressions
_____ 30. *DSM* IV-R
_____ 31.a. Problem(s) targeted for intervention
_____ 32.a.–b. Recommended treatment alternatives

**VIII. Methods Used in Assessment**

_____ 33. Standardized interview
_____ 34. Ethnographic interview
_____ 35. Nonstandardized interview
_____ 36. Background information sheets and questionnaires
_____ 37. Standardized assessment measures
_____ 38. Behavioral observations
_____ 39. Projective measures
_____ 40. Self-anchored or self-rating scales
_____ 41. Client logs or diaries
_____ 42. Graphs or maps
_____ 43. Experiential and task assignments
_____ 44. Information from collateral sources
_____ 45. Previous treatment or other social service records
_____ 46. Other (*please specify*: _____

## Specifying Problems

Problem definition follows from this assessment process and requires operationalizing the problems that are to be the focus of intervention. Problems might be overt or covert behaviors, including thoughts and feelings; problems also might be conceptualized at the environmental level, such as lack of needed resources. Measurement of the problems targeted for intervention requires the use of quantitative measures to ascertain the existence, extent, severity, duration, and so forth of the problems. These quantitative measures can be standardized measures, behavioral observations, self-anchored scales, and so on. Other qualitative measures may also be used to gather other information about the problems or to provide a more in-depth perspective. Chapters 2 and 4 provide more information on both quantitative and qualitative methods for problem specification.

## Problem Monitoring

After the assessment reveals problems targeted for change, the issue is monitoring the problems over the course of the therapeutic process. Quantitative data collection provides the clinician not only with information to determine the extent and severity of the problem during assessment but also with information to use in evaluations over the course of the assessment and treatment. The recommended monitoring system for evaluating practice activities is single-subject design. This evaluation design is different from the traditional group research design, which compares pre- and postintervention information. Rather than measuring the client's problems at only two points in time (pre- and postintervention), single-subject methodology requires repeated measurement of the problem over the course of assessment and treatment. This gives the practitioner a more in-depth look at the client's progress throughout the case activity. Single-subject data allows for changes to be made at any point during treatment if necessary. For example, if the data reveal that behavioral therapy is not making the anticipated difference in a client's level of depression, the practitioner might decide to change to an intervention such as cognitive therapy.

Bloom, Fischer, and Orme (2009) described the stages involved in single-subject design:

1. The measures are administered repeatedly, usually weekly or daily. The client, significant others, the practitioner, or a combination of interested parties can collect the data.

2. The data is collected systematically over the course of the treatment, using the same exact measurement instruments at all phases of the case.

3. The baseline phase of the case refers to the time before the formal intervention is begun when measurements are made.

4. The design of single-subject evaluation involves various phases, typically baseline, intervention, and follow-up. Comparisons are made between the phases to judge the success or failure of the treatment being implemented.

5. This approach requires a clear definition of intervention. Because the single-subject methodology relies on a comparison of phases—most important, the baseline and intervention phases—it is important for the practitioner to operationalize the selected intervention. To judge the effectiveness of a treatment, it is important to know when the intervention is being applied and when it is not.

6. Finally, the data is analyzed. Single-subject data is often analyzed simply by eyeballing or observing the level, trend, and stability of the data in the different phases. However, there are some simple tools to use

when the data are confusing to the eye. The Shewhart chart and celeration line are two examples of such tools.

The single-subject design is advantageous to clients, practitioners, and agency administrators. Clients may become more self-aware, and practitioners and administrators may benefit from increased practitioner accountability and improved agency performance (for more detail on the single-subject design, see chapter 11).

## TREATMENT PLANNING: CASE EXAMPLE OF TOM AND JULIE

Treatments should follow logically from and be related to the problems targeted for change, as the following case illustrates. Jordan and Cobb (1993) first discussed the case of Tom and Julie in *101 Interventions in Family Therapy*. Tom and Julie are a dual-career couple, both committed to their jobs and to their family life. In treatment, they presented difficulties about how to balance those two very demanding worlds. As a way to show the link between assessment and intervention, a summary of the assessment on Tom and Julie is presented here. Following the assessment summary is a list of problems targeted for intervention, measurements to be used for case monitoring, and a brief discussion of the interventions selected.

### Assessment Summary

Tom and Julie are dual-career spouses who each have promising careers, in banking and merchandising, respectively. In addition to a commitment to their jobs and to each other, they also have an eighteen-month-old daughter, CeCe. They came to therapy to resolve issues related to their busy lifestyle. Julie reported that Tom disagrees with her about who should be responsible for household chores, which results in yelling and screaming matches between them. Arguments also occur about who should be the primary caretaker for CeCe. CeCe is enrolled in a day school, but Tom and Julie disagree about who should drop her off and pick her up from school and about who should take her to the doctor and other appointments that occur during the day. Both Tom and Julie reported feeling "stressed out" most of the time. They feel like their relationship is suffering from their lack of time to complete their many jobs.

### Problem Selection

The practitioner identified the following problems as areas of concern: poor communication and stress.

## Problem Definition

The practitioner defined Tom and Julie's problems as follows:

> Poor communication: communication style described by angry arguments with yelling and screaming; disagreements remain unresolved.

> Stress: feelings of tension from inability to get jobs done; no time for important activities.

The practitioner presented the results of the assessment and the targeted problems to Tom and Julie and asked the couple for feedback. Both Tom and Julie agreed that communication and stress were the two major problems for them; they expressed a desire to continue in treatment to work on both problems.

## Goals

Goals for the treatment were to improve the couple's communication and to reduce the couple's stress.

## Objectives

During the assessment phase, the practitioner used three measures to assess the extent and severity of Tom and Julie's problems and to describe the objectives (note that the practitioner continued to collect data from Tom and Julie using these same measures over the course of treatment as a way to monitor outcomes):

1. The Primary Communication Inventory (Navran, 1967)—improvement on the inventory shows improved communication.
2. The Stress Arousal Checklist (Mackay, Cox, Burrows, & Lazzerini, 1978)—to measure reduced stress.

## Interventions Selected

The practitioner offered two types of intervention approaches to Tom and Julie: family therapy using a human validation process model and skills training. After hearing a brief description of each intervention, the couple chose the skills-training approach, which involved two components: communication training and stress management training.

For communication training, the therapist focused on teaching the couple both verbal and nonverbal skills of effective communicating, including use of "I" statements to communicate needs, active listening, correct timing of message delivery, expression of feelings, and editing of unproductive communications. Nonverbal techniques included appropriate facial expressions to match verbal content, posture, voice, physical proximity to partner, and other voice qualities. In addition, anger control techniques included recognition of escalating anger, taking a time-out, admitting one's own part in the argument, and problem-solving were also taught to the couple.

In stress management training, the practitioner helped both partners identify and analyze the stressors in their lives. In analyzing stress, Tom and Julie considered whether it came from lack of organization or from overwhelming responsibilities. The practitioner then designated four components of stress management as appropriate interventions for Tom and Julie: self-monitoring, daily relaxation exercises, cognitive restructuring of unproductive irrational beliefs contributing to stress, and environmental alteration.

## SUMMARY

This chapter provided a definition of social work assessment and a framework for understanding how to conduct a comprehensive social work assessment. We reviewed many facets of social work assessment in this chapter, including the ways that students and practitioners can construct information in a case and use theory to guide practice. This chapter and other ones following it guide practitioners to use empirical-based and evidence-based knowledge to guide their assessments with clients. The chapter highlighted the importance of using evidence in assessment and described criteria for evaluating assessments. The chapter further emphasized an integrative, technical-eclectic approach for the elements that go into a comprehensive assessment, supported through the review of several social work practice models. We also described common features for current-day assessment and the convergent elements found in the diverse practice models. We used technical eclecticism to integrate assessment information across the models into an Integrative Skills Assessment Protocol that practitioners can use to guide assessment. The final section of this chapter moved readers from assessment to treatment, introducing clinical decision making, problem monitoring, and treatment planning.

A final word: in writing this book and in our practice activities, we assume a broad approach to assessment and treatment planning. We believe that theoretical narrowness—limiting ourselves to only one method of collecting information about clients—does a disservice to our clients and to ourselves. We believe that broadening our approach by learning a variety of creative ways to obtain client information, both of a quantitative and a qualitative nature, helps us know and be sensitive to our clients. We encourage practitioners to use the techniques presented in this book while always thinking about the client's needs, style, and willingness to participate. It is when we put the client first and foremost in our practice that we can be of the most help.

## STUDY QUESTIONS

1. What are the major issues covered in social work assessment?
2. Describe the features of practice context, clients served, and practice model, and explain how those features impact social work assessment.
3. Describe the common assessment features that are found across social work practice models. What impacts do these features have on our work with clients?
4. What is the underlying eclectic theory behind the Integrative Skills Assessment Protocol?
5. Practice using the protocol by interviewing a friend.
6. What are the steps that can be used to select and evaluate an intervention using an evidence-based approach? Apply these to a specific problem.
7. How does single-subject design inform assessment and treatment? Describe the steps of single-subject design.
8. How has the prevalence of managed care affected assessment and treatment?
9. How would you time the movement from assessment to intervention? And chose the appropriate intervention?
10. Use a case example from the text and design a treatment plan.

## REFERENCES

Austiran, S. G. (2009). *Mental disorders, medications, and clinical social work* (3rd ed.). New York: Columbia Press.

Barker, R. (2003). *Social workers dictionary*. Washington, DC: National Association of Social Workers Press.

Barth, R. (1986). *Social and cognitive treatment of children and adolescents*. San Francisco: Jossey-Bass.

Beck, J. S. (1995). *Cognitive therapy: Basics and beyond*. New York: Guilford Press.

Beck, J. S., & Beck, A. T. (2002). *Beck youth inventories of emotional and social impairment*. San Antonio, TX: Psychological Corporation.

Bellack, A. S., & Hersen, M. (1988). *Behavioral assessment: A practical handbook* (3rd ed.). Elmsford, NY: Pergamon Press.

Berlin, S. B. (1996). Constructivism and the environment: A cognitive-integrative perspective for social work practice. *Families in Society, 77*, 326–335.

Blanck, G., & Blanck, R. (1974). *Ego psychology in theory and practice*. New York: Columbia University Press.

Bloom, M., Fischer, J., & Orme, J. (2009). *Evaluating practice: Guidelines for the accountable professional* (6th ed.). Englewood Cliffs, NJ: Prentice Hall.

Brandell, J. (2008). Using self psychology in clinical social work. In A. R. Roberts (Ed.), *Social workers' desk reference* (2nd ed., pp. 311–317). New York: Oxford University Press.

Brower, A. M., & Nurius, P. S. (1993). *Social cognition and individual change: Current theory and counseling guidelines.* Newbury Park, CA: Sage.

Cohen, D. K. (2007). Problems in education policy and research. In S. H. Fuhrman, D. K. Cohen, & F. Mosher (Eds.), *The state of education policy research* (pp. 349–371). Mahwah, NJ: Erlbaum.

Cormier, S., Nurius, P. S., & Osborn, C. J. (2008) *Interviewing and change strategies for helpers: Fundamental skills and cognitive behavioral interventions* (6th ed.). Pacific Grove, CA: Brooks/Cole-Thompson Learning.

Cowger, C. D., & Snively, C. A. (2008). Assessing client strengths. In A. R. Roberts & G. J. Greene (Eds.), *Social workers' desk reference* (pp. 221–225). New York: Oxford University Press.

De Jong, P., & Berg, I. K. (2001). Co-constructing cooperation with mandated clients. *Social Work, 46,* 361–374.

De Jong, P., & Berg, I. K. (2008). *Interviewing for solutions* (3rd ed.). Pacific Grove, CA: Cengage Learning.

Doremus, B. (1976). The four Rs: Social diagnosis in health care. *Health and Social Work, 1,* 121–139.

Early, T., & GlenMaye, L. F. (2000). Valuing families: Social work practice with families from a strengths perspective. *Social Work, 45,* 118–130.

Fortune, A. E., Reid, W. J., & Reyome, D. P. (2008). Task-centered practice. In A. R. Roberts (Ed.), *Social workers' desk reference* (2nd ed., pp. 226–230). New York: Oxford University Press.

Franklin, C. (1995). Expanding the vision of the social constructionist debates: Creating relevance for practitioners. *Families in Society, 76,* 395–407.

Franklin, C. (2002, October). Becoming a strengths fact finder. *American Association for Marriage and Family Therapy Magazine,* 39–46.

Franklin, C., & Kelly, M. (2009). Implementation of evidence-based practice in the real world of Schools. *Children and Schools, 31,* 46–56.

Franklin, C., Trepper, T., McCollum, E., & Gingerich, W. (in press) *Solution focused brief therapy.* New York: Oxford University Press.

Gambrill, E. (1983). *Casework: A competency based approach.* Englewood Cliffs, NJ: Prentice Hall.

Gambrill, E., Thomas, E., & Carter, R. (1971). Procedure for sociobehavioral practice in open settings. *Social Work, 16,* 51–62.

Germain, C., & Gitterman, A. (2008). *The life model approach to social work practice: Advances in theory and practice* (3rd ed.). New York: Columbia University Press.

Gingerich, W. J., & Eisengart, S. (2000). Solution-focused brief therapy: A review of outcome research. *Family Process, 39,* 477–498.

Gitterman, A., Goldstein, E. G., & Rose, S. (1988, March). *Alternative practice explanatory frameworks: A debate*. Presentation at the annual program meeting, Council on Social Work Education, Atlanta.

Goldstein, E. G. (1986). Ego psychology. In F. J. Turner (Ed.), *Social work treatment* (3rd ed., pp. 375–405). New York: Free Press.

Goldstein, E. G. (2002). *Object relations theory and self-psychology in social work*. New York: Free Press.

Granvold, D. K. (1996). Constructivist psychotherapy. *Families in Society, 77*(6), 345–357.

Hollis, F., & Wood, M. E. (1981). *Social casework: A psychosocial therapy* (3rd ed.). New York: Random House.

Holmbeck, G. N., Thill, A. W., Bachanas, P., Garber, J., Miller, K. B., Abad, M., et al. (2008). Evidence-based assessement in pediatric psychology. *Journal of Pediatric Psycholology, 33*, 958–980.

Hudson, W. W. (1982). *The clinical measurement package*. Homewood, IL: Dorsey Press.

Hunsley, J., & Mash, E. J. (2007). Evidence-based assessment. *Annual Review of Clinical Psychology, 3*, 29–51.

Johnson, L. (1981). *Social work practice: A generalist approach*. Boston: Allyn and Bacon.

Jordan, C., & Cobb, N. (1993). Treating dual career couples. In T. Nelson & T. Trepper (Eds.), *101 interventions in family therapy* (pp. 108–112). New York: Haworth Press.

Jordan, C., & Franklin, C. (2008). Treatment planning with families. In A. R. Roberts (Ed.), *The Social Workers' Desk Reference* (2nd ed., pp. 429–432). New York: Oxford University Press.

Kanfer, F. H., & Schefft, B. K. (1988). *Guiding the process of therapeutic change*. Champaign, IL: Research Press.

Kelly, M., Kim, J. S., & Franklin, C. (2008). *Solution-focused brief therapy in schools*. New York: Oxford University Press.

Kim, J. S. (2008). Examining the effectiveness of solution-focused brief therapy: A meta-analysis. *Research on Social Work Practice, 18*, 107–116.

Kim, J., & Franklin, C. (2009). Solution-focused, brief therapy in schools: A review of the outcome literature. *Children and Youth Services Review, 31*, 461–470.

Kim, J. S., Trepper, T., Smock, S., McCollum, E., & Franklin, C. (2010) Is solution-focused brief therapy evidence-based? *Families in Society, 91*, 300–306.

Lazarus, A. (1981). *Multi-modal therapy*. New York: McGraw-Hill.

Lazarus, A. (1989). *Multimodal therapy*. In R. Corsini & D. Wedding (Eds.), *Current psychotherapies* (4th ed., pp. 503–544). Itasca, IL: Peacock.

Lazarus, A. (1991). *The multi-modal life history inventory*. Champaign, IL: Research Press.

Lazarus, A. (2006). Multimodal therapy: A seven-point integration. In G. Stricker & J. Gold (Eds.), *A casebook of psychotherapy integration* (pp. 17–28). Washington, DC: American Psychological Association.

Leff, H. S., & Conley, J. A. (2006). Desired attributes of evidence assessments for evidence-based practices. *Administration and Policy in Mental Health, 33*, 648–658.

Lehman, P., & Patton, J. (in press). The development of a solution-focused fidelity instrument. In C. Franklin, T. Trepper, E. McCollum, & W. Gingerich (Eds.), *Solution-focused brief therapy.* New York: Oxford University Press.

Levine, E. R. (2008). Glossary. In A. R. Roberts (Ed.), *Social workers' desk reference* (2nd ed., pp. 829–849). New York: Oxford University Press.

Mackay, C., Cox, T., Burrows, G., & Lazzerini, T. (1978). An inventory for the measurement of self-reported stress and arousal. *British Journal of Social and Clinical Psychology, 17*, 283–284.

Maluccio, A. N. (Ed.). (1981). *Promoting competence in clients: A new/old approach to social work practice.* New York: Free Press.

Mattaini, M. A. (1990). Contextual behavioral analysis in the assessment process. *Families in Society, 7*, 236–245.

Mattaini, M. A. (1992). *More than a thousand words: Graphics in clinical practice.* Washington, DC: National Association of Social Workers Press.

Mattaini, M. A. (1993). Misdiagnosing assessment. *Social Work, 38*, 231–233.

Mattaini, M. A. (1999). *Intervention with families.* Washington, DC: National Association of Social Workers Press.

Mattaini, M. A., & Lowery, C. T. (2007). *Foundations of social work practice* (4th ed.) Washington, DC: National Association of Social Workers Press.

Mattaini, M. A., Lowery, C. T., & Meyer, C. H. (2002). *Foundations of social work practice* (3rd ed.). Washington, DC: National Association of Social Workers Press.

Navran, L. (1967). Communication and adjustment in marriage. *Family Process, 6*, 173–184.

Parad, H. J., & Miller, R. (Eds.). (1963). *Ego oriented casework.* New York: Family Service Association of America.

Perlman, H. (1957). *Social casework: A problem solving process.* Chicago: University of Chicago Press.

Reid, W. J. (1988). Brief task-centered treatment. In R. A. Dorfman (Ed.), *Paradigms of clinical social work* (pp. 196–219). New York: Brunner/Mazel.

Reid, W. J. (1992). *Task strategies: An empirical approach to clinical social work.* New York: Columbia University Press.

Reid, W. J. (2000). *The task planner.* New York: Columbia University Press.

Reid, W. J., & Epstein, L. (1972). *Task-centered casework.* New York: Columbia University Press.

Reid, W. J., & Fortune, A. E. (2008). The task-centered model. In A. R. Roberts & G. J. Greene (Eds.) *Social workers' desk reference* (pp. 101–104). New York: Oxford University Press.

Rose, S. (1977). *Group therapy: A behavioral approach*. Englewood Cliffs, NJ: Prentice Hall.

Sackett, D., Sackett, D., Richardson, W., Rosenberg, W., & Haynes, R. (1997). *Evidence-based medicine: How to practice and teach EBM*. New York: Churchill Livingstone.

Saleeby, D. (1997). *The strengths perspective in social work practice* (2nd ed.). New York: Longman.

Sheafor, B., Horejsi, C., & Horejsi, G. (1988). *Techniques and guidelines for social work practice*. Boston: Allyn and Bacon.

Shorkey, C. T., & Sutton-Simon, K. (1983). Reliability and validity of the Rational Behavior Inventory with a clinical population. *Journal of Clinical Psychology, 39,* 34–38.

Stuart, R. (2003). *Helping couples change: A social learning approach to marital therapy*. New York: Guilford Press.

Studt, E. (1968). *C-unit, search for community in prison*. New York: Russell Sage Foundation.

Thyer, B. A. (1983). Review of *Behavior modification in social work practice. Behavior Therapist, 8,* 161–162.

Thyer, B. A. (1987). Contingency analysis: Toward a unified theory for social work practice. *Social Work, 32,* 150–157.

Thyer, B. A. (1988). Radical behaviorism and clinical social work. In R. Dorfman (Ed.), *Paradigms of clinical social work* (pp. 123–148). New York: Brunner/Mazel.

Turner, F. (2005). *Social work diagnosis in contemporary practice*. New York: Oxford University Press.

Whittaker, J., & Tracy, E. (1989). *Social treatment: An introduction to interpersonal helping in social work practice* (2nd ed.). New York: Aldine de Gruyter.

Woods, M. E., & Robinson, H. (1996). Psychosocial theory and social work treatment. In F. J. Turner (Ed.), *Social work treatment* (4th ed., pp. 555–580). New York: Free Press.

# PART II

# Clinical Assessment Methods

Part II introduces quantitative and qualitative methods of assessment and shows how both ways of assessing are equally important and contribute different information. Part II also shows how to select sound approaches to assessment in order to teach practitioners how to pay close attention to the research basis of an assessment method and its clinical applicability. Chapter 2, "Quantitative Clinical Assessment Methods," provides a rationale for the inclusion of quantitative assessment methods in social work and summarizes the most frequently used measurements for assessing client behavior. Chapter 3, "Standardized Assessment Measures and Computer-Assisted Assessment," helps practitioners become informed consumers in the selection, use, and interpretation of standardized measurement instruments. Chapter 4, "Qualitative Assessment Methods," explains the unique contributions of qualitative assessment methods. Finally, Chapter 5, "Pseudoscience in Clinical Assessment," reviews several assessment methods that lack a sound research base and encourages students and practitioners both to evaluate clinical assessment methods according to their scientific merits before adopting them into practice and to discontinue assessment practices that may be questionable.

# CHAPTER 2

# Quantitative Clinical Assessment Methods

## Cynthia Franklin and Katherine Sanchez

## INTRODUCTION

Quantitative clinical assessment involves measurement that includes categorizing client characteristics, assigning diagnostic labels, developing behavior profiles and ratings, and systematically tracking problem behaviors, to observe change over the course of treatment and afterward. Measurements contribute to the practitioner's subjective and intuitive information (practice wisdom) and add specificity and concreteness. In keeping with an evidence-based approach to practice, this chapter on quantitative assessments helps the practitioner learn how to provide an objective and numerical assessment of a client. In this chapter, students and practitioners will learn how to conduct assessment so that measurement of client behaviors is part of the assessment process. Measurement assists practitioners in defining client problems and attributes, and in observing them over the course of treatment, as chapters 3 and 11 discuss further. In accordance with the person-in-environment approach of social work assessment, clinical quantitative measurement may also help practitioners define the client's environmental context by ascertaining situation-specific behaviors across settings. Examples include the rate of disruptive behavior in the school, home, and community; the functioning of social systems (e.g., families, friends); the quality of interpersonal interactions (e.g., peer relationships, classroom behaviors); available resources (e.g., finances, special assistance programs), and support networks (e.g., clubs, kin groups, close friends).

The main focus of this chapter is on providing a rationale for the inclusion of quantitative assessment methods in social work and on illustrating several different methods for assessing client behavior, including the following:

- Client self-reporting and monitoring
- Self-anchored and rating scales
- Questionnaires
- Direct behavioral observation

- Role play and analog situations
- Behavioral by-products
- Psychophysiological measures
- Goal attainment scaling
- Standardized measures
- Projective measures

Assessment methods discussed and illustrated here are also relevant to evaluating client change and effective intervention planning. Finally, because there will be times when practitioners simply cannot find a quantitative assessment tool that is right for their client's circumstances, this chapter provides guidelines for developing a more "homemade" instrument.

## RATIONALE FOR INCLUDING QUANTITATIVE MEASURES IN ASSESSMENT

Clinical assessment is designed to provide a portrayal of client functioning that is as complete as possible. The complexity of causes, the client's actual condition, and the social environment in which the condition arises are gathered into a clinical understanding that facilitates the social work intervention. As part of an assessment, social work practitioners usually develop a psychosocial assessment. This report is a narrative summary of the client's history and current life functioning. The report defines the presenting problem, tells the client's story, summarizes the major strengths and weaknesses of the client, and provides a formulation for treatment. Quantitative assessment can facilitate much of this because the client's concern and the accuracy of assessing the client's problem, behavior, and attribute are foremost in the social worker's mind.

Traditionally, the social assessment report has been based on social work practitioners' conceptual formulation of client problems and characteristics, which they observe during an interview with the client and significant others. The interview process is important, and the judgment of trained clinical practitioners as well as the viewpoints and values of clients are invaluable to the assessment process. The judgments and opinions of both practitioners and clients, however, may be subject to bias and to misformulations of client problems. Including quantitative measures as part of the social assessment helps practitioners and clients clarify and verify their opinions and provides multiple sources of data to consider in the assessment process.

The use of multiple sources of information is particularly important in obtaining accurate assessments (Hepworth, Rooney, Rooney, Strom-Gottfried, & Larsen, 2005). For example, in the case of a child with school problems, practitioners can interview the client (i.e., the child), the parents, and the child's teachers, and they can collect quantitative information from the parents and school using a questionnaire. It might be useful in some circumstances to observe the child in the classroom using a child behavior rating scale.

There are four reasons to collect quantitative measures on client behaviors as part of the assessment process, and the following sections discuss these reasons.

## Quantitative Measures Help Practitioners Improve Treatment

The objective assessment of client problems with measures improves treatment by increasing the accuracy of the practitioner's understanding of client problems and by providing feedback for the practitioner during treatment. Monitoring client progress with measures allows the practitioner to change treatment if progress is not being made, and several studies have shown this to improve treatment outcomes, as when the feedback from clinical measures are given to therapists (Hayes, Barlow, & Nelson-Gray, 1999; Slade, Lambert, Harman, Smart, & Bailey, 2008; Whipple et al., 2003).

## Quantitative Measures Enable Practitioners to Contribute to Clinical Research

The clinical practice field needs new methods to help bring about client change. By collecting measurements of individual client problems and changes across time, practitioners can demonstrate the effectiveness of treatments and contribute to the clinical research literature. Single-subject design methodology makes this possible, see also chapter 11 (Barlow, Nock, & Hersen, 2008).

## Quantitative Measures Provide a Basis for Practice Evaluation and Accountability

Practice evaluation is essential to good service provision in today's practice environment. Funding sources, such as federal agencies and insurance companies, demand that practitioners provide evidence of their accountability and effectiveness with clients. The federal government and other companies and agencies, for example, hire their own professional experts who require social workers to monitor the progress of intervention; consequently, they "certify" a certain number of sessions for payment. Measurement provides us with tools that we can incorporate into the assessment process and use as objective indicators of client problems and progress during the course of treatment (Barlow et al., 2008). In fact, clients may actually prefer the use of systematic data collection. Faul,

McMurtry, and Hudson (2001) found that the use of standardized scales and single-subject designs was associated with improved outcomes for clients. Social workers who used empirical clinical practice techniques showed significantly greater reductions in the severity of client problems. The use of such techniques may affect client outcomes beyond the effect of the intervention alone (Faul et al., 2001).

### Quantitative Measures Increase Practitioners' Skills Repertoire

If social workers are to function as independent practitioners, without consultation with other professions, it is important to conduct comprehensive assessments of clients. In doing so, measurement is a helpful tool. Competence in measurement will improve the status of social work and the ability of the profession to function autonomously. Measurement also provides an integral link between research and practice, which adds to the overall competence and effectiveness of the profession.

## QUANTITATIVE ASSESSMENT METHODS

We have been discussing reasons for including quantitative measures as part of social work assessment practice evaluation. The remainder of this chapter summarizes several assessment methods for measuring client problems, behaviors, and goals. It also suggests guidelines for developing a measurement tool.

### Client Self-Recording and Self-Monitoring

Client self-recording and self-monitoring are the most common methods of observing clients. The practitioner asks the client to record his or her thoughts, feelings, and behaviors. With self-recording, the practitioner asks the client to collect the observations and report the information in a retrospective fashion (e.g., record the number of times the client thought about leaving her husband in the previous week). In contrast, with self-monitoring, the practitioner asks the client to collect the observations every time the behavior occurs (e.g., record each time the client thinks of leaving her husband over the coming week). Methods of self-recording and self-monitoring vary and include such techniques as client logs, diaries, journals, and structured activities and behaviors.

Client self-recording and monitoring are useful clinical assessment tools that enable practitioners to obtain baseline measures of client problems. When baseline data show that the client is similar to a clinical sample or noticeably different from the general population, the measures tend to evidence the necessity of treatment (Corcoran & Boyer-Quick, 2002). Such information is particularly useful in settings that demand accountability (Corcoran & Vandiver, 1996). For example, the practitioner may ask the client to record the number of suicidal ideations he or she experiences and to report the specific nature of the ideations in a log (see table 2.1). Social work practitioners may use such a log to explore the seriousness or magnitude of clients' suicidal intent and to monitor any increase or decrease in the frequency or magnitude of suicidal ideations over the course of treatment. Figure 2.1 shows an anger diary of incidences of arguments between a client and spouse. Deschner (1984) has used this method to collect clinical data on clients in treatment for anger control. Figure 2.2 shows a journal kept by a client seeking treatment because of recurring and obsessive thoughts that led to compulsive behaviors. Table 2.2 is a structured form for observations in this type of

**Table 2.1**   Client Self-Recording, Self-Monitoring

|  | *Time* | *Duration* | *Situation* | *Nature of Thoughts* |
|---|---|---|---|---|
| Sunday | 11:00 A.M. | 2 hours | alone reading paper | Just wished I was dead, kept thinking about it, would like to be dead and not have to go through with my divorce. |
|  | 6:00 P.M. | 2.5 hours | husband came by to get his files | Thinking I would be better off dead than living alone. Didn't want to go on living without him. |
| Monday | 4:30 A.M. | 1.5 hours | alone, in bed at home | Don't want to face another day. Don't want to go to work, I'd be better off dead. I just want to go away. |
| Tuesday | 4:15 A.M. | 1.5 hours | same | same |
| Wednesday | 4:15 A.M. | 2 hours | same | Can't go on, it's getting worse, I am sure I want to die rather than live. Surely it must be easier to be dead. |
| Thursday | 5:00 A.M. | 1 hour | same | same |
| Friday | 6:00 P.M. | 2 hours | husband called said he wanted to move the rest of his things on weekend | I don't want to live. Maybe I will kill myself. I could take some pills or have a car accident. |
| Saturday | 7:00 A.M. | 3 hours | alone at home | same |
|  | 1:00 P.M. |  | at home with friend | same and might do it . . . |

## Figure 2.1    Anger Diary

Name: _____    Date: _____

How many arguments did you have this week? _____

How do you rate (0–10) your:

      Verbal: _____        Anger _____
                            Partner's Anger _____
                            Fear _____
      Physical _____    Anger _____
                            Partner's Anger _____
                            Fear _____

What were your internal signals when trouble began?

What signals came from your partner?

How many times did you call for time-out? _____

How many times did your partner call time? _____

Which steps did you use? (Answer Yes or No)

T sign _____    Exercise _____

Return of T _____    Error admitted _____

Leave quietly _____    Partner error  _____

How long did you stay apart in time-out? _____

What happened afterward?

What other anger-control methods did you use?

|  | Practiced | Used in Real Life |
|---|---|---|
| Relaxation | _____ | _____ |
| Cognitive realignment | _____ | _____ |
| 3-part assertion | _____ | _____ |
| Reflective listening | _____ | _____ |
| Diplomatic correction | _____ | _____ |

Rate your happiness with this relationship if things go on just as they are (0–10):

| Household responsibilities ____ | General happiness ____ | Spouse's independence ____ |
| Rearing of children ____ | Communication ____ | Occupational progress ____ |
| Money ____ | Social life ____ | Sex ____ |

## Figure 2.2    Journal of Obsessive Thoughts of Harm and Compulsive Behaviors

| Day and Date | Time of Day | Thought and Behavior |
|---|---|---|
| Monday, March 24th | 9:15 P.M. | I probably didn't lock the door, a killer may come in, I better check. Got up and checked the door and returned to bed. Same thought recurred, got up and checked door again. This happened *seven* times. |

**Table 2.2**  Structured Form for Observations

| A (Activator) | B (Belief) | | | |
|---|---|---|---|---|
| Description of the activating event | Self-statement you made at the time | Emotional consequences | Cognitive restructuring activity | New emotional consequences |
| *Negative event:* | *Irrational belief about event:* | *How I felt:* | *1) Dispute your irrational belief:* | *Now I feel:* |
| Supervisor does not accept recommendation for a new project I want very much. States my recommendations are unrealistic. | #1 #2 #3 I do have worthwhile ideas to share. | I feel inadequate, naive, embarrassed because this is a project I have boasted about. I feel depressed due to my project not being accepted. I must not be very intelligent. I am not a good employee. | My projects have been accepted in the past and complimented by my supervisor, therefore I am not inadequate, I should be proud of what I have done and not devastated because of this one nonacceptance. My supervisor still likes me even though he does not agree with this project. This project has its merits as well as its discredits | I am appreciated for my work. I feel I am a good employee. I feel disappointed that this project was not accepted, but I can improve on it to make it acceptable. |
| | | | 2) Now construct a positive statement | |
| *Positive event:* | *Positive self-statement about event:* | *How I felt:* | *1) Improve on your positive self-statement or add another one to it:* | *Now I feel:* |
| After the staff meeting today, Susan came up and complimented me on my ideas for the new promotional project. | I do have worthwhile ideas to share. | I felt encouraged and more confident. | No one is right all the time but when I do have good ideas there are people that appreciate me. I do my best and even if I fail people will still like me. | I feel I am a valuable part of our staff team. I am happy about giving my input at the meeting. |

situation. Practitioners ask clients to monitor their irrational beliefs according to Ellis's (1985) theory of rational-emotive therapy, which uses cognitive restructuring as a primary vehicle for facilitating client change.

Client self-recording and self-monitoring are relevant to clinical assessment and clinical intervention. Although they are not terribly rigorous scientific forms of quantitative measurement, they are appropriate tools for clinical observations of a client's thoughts, feelings, and behaviors. Clinicians can improve the accuracy of client reports from self-monitoring by encouraging clients to collect the information in real time instead of retrospectively, as when one keeps a log and writes things down as they occur or better yet makes immediate telephone calls to the practitioner to report when a behaviors happens. Quittner et al. (2008) found, for example, that self-reporting improved substantially for adherence to medical treatments if clients used telephone monitoring. Self-recording and self-monitoring are a supplement to, never a substitute for, clinical judgment; quantitative measures are used in addition to observe client change over the course of treatment. Self-recording and self-monitoring are compatible with other, more rigorous measurement tools, such as standardized scales, and they provide useful validation information. Chapter 3 covers standardized measures in detail.

## Self-Anchored and Rating Scales

Self-anchored scales are measures of client problems that the social worker and client construct together. Use of such scales is often necessary when a standardized instrument is not available or when a particular subtlety of the client's problem or goal needs to be part of the assessment. These do-it-yourself scales, as they are sometimes called (Bloom, Fischer, & Orme, 2005), allow for the development of an assessment tool that represents the client's specific problem or concern. For example, a self-anchored rating scale may be constructed that measures a client's particular experience of depression that lasted for six weeks from Thanksgiving and is recurrent since her marriage. The dimensions of the scale range from the maximum severity of depression (e.g., feeling tired, experiencing loss of appetite, feeling down in the dumps) to maximum improvement in depression (e.g., feeling energetic, feeling alive and vibrant). These two extremes are anchors, and they are used to describe the ends of a self-anchored rating scale. Practitioners ask clients to complete the self-anchored scale regularly—say, weekly or every other day or so (see figure 2.3). Scores on the self-anchored rating scale can be used to assess the client's depression and monitor its change over the course of treatment. Scale scores are practical and relevant because they are additional referents of the client's experience. By constructing a self-anchored rating scale, practitioners help clients define the problems by identifying the extremes. They construct the scale by identifying the extreme of the least magnitude as "1" and the

**Figure 2.3**   Self-Anchored Scale

Instructions: Circle the number that applies every day before 8:00 A.M.

1   2   3   4   5   6   7

| Energetic, | Tired, no energy |
|---|---|
| feel alive | feel like lying |
| and ready | down and never |
| to go to work. | getting up. |

extreme of the greatest magnitude a "7," which is an ideal scale range. It is important to capture sufficient deviations to reflect the client's experience, but not so many that the different intervals are not meaningful (Jordan, Franklin, & Corcoran, 2001). For example, say you construct a scale with 100 points, few clients would be able to meaningfully distinguish between 85 and 90 or 50 and 55. It is best to restrict the range of a self-anchored rating scale to five or seven intervals.

Self-anchored scales can be constructed for virtually any practice problem. They provide a systematic way for clients to observe their thoughts, feelings, and behaviors. Rating scales are similar to self-anchored scales in that the client and social worker co-construct them to reflect the client's presenting problem. However, someone other than the client completes a rating scale (see figures 2.4 and 2.5).

Figure 2.4 is an example of a rating scale used to track communication skills being taught in couples' counseling. During a clinical case, one of the authors created this rating scale to use with a couple to facilitate communication skills training. It is possible to substitute the generalized

**Figure 2.4**   Rating Scale for Communication

| | *Inadequate* | | | | | | | | | *Adequate* |
|---|---|---|---|---|---|---|---|---|---|---|
| Speak for self | 1 | 2 | 3 | 4 | 5 | 6 | 7 | 8 | 9 | 10 |
| Send I messages | 1 | 2 | 3 | 4 | 5 | 6 | 7 | 8 | 9 | 10 |
| Use a stop action | 1 | 2 | 3 | 4 | 5 | 6 | 7 | 8 | 9 | 10 |
| Ask for feedback | 1 | 2 | 3 | 4 | 5 | 6 | 7 | 8 | 9 | 10 |
| Give feedback | 1 | 2 | 3 | 4 | 5 | 6 | 7 | 8 | 9 | 10 |
| Listen | 1 | 2 | 3 | 4 | 5 | 6 | 7 | 8 | 9 | 10 |
| Summarize | 1 | 2 | 3 | 4 | 5 | 6 | 7 | 8 | 9 | 10 |
| Validate | 1 | 2 | 3 | 4 | 5 | 6 | 7 | 8 | 9 | 10 |
| Ask open questions | 1 | 2 | 3 | 4 | 5 | 6 | 7 | 8 | 9 | 10 |
| Build agenda | 1 | 2 | 3 | 4 | 5 | 6 | 7 | 8 | 9 | 10 |
| Check out | 1 | 2 | 3 | 4 | 5 | 6 | 7 | 8 | 9 | 10 |

SOURCE: Franklin (1982).

**Figure 2.5**    Rating Scale for Conflict Avoidance

|  | 1 | 2 | 3 | 4 | 5 | 6 | 7 |  |
|---|---|---|---|---|---|---|---|---|

Changes the subject, leaves the room, and refuses to talk about conflictual issues.

Stays on the topic and engages in conversation regarding conflictual issues.

anchors ("adequate" and "inadequate") with examples from the client's experience. For instance, on "use a stop action" the "inadequate" anchor could be substituted with "continues to insist and talk about difficulties after voices begin to rise," and the "adequate" anchor could be substituted with "calls a time-out when notices voice rising."

Figure 2.5 provides an example of a rating scale developed to assess the level of conflict avoidance of a couple in therapy. Rating scales allow the practitioner to obtain observations of client behavior from an outside observer, such as a spouse, a social worker, a teacher, or a member of a therapy group. These observations are helpful in that clients do not always observe themselves accurately; rating scales broaden the perspective on client functioning and substantiate progress in treatment.

Practitioners can use rating scales and self-anchored scales together as measures of client problems and behavior for even a broader scope and more accurate input.

Self-anchored and rating scales also provide opportunities for the practitioner and client to quantify the presenting problem in ways that are clinically meaningful to both. Similar to the client self-recording method described earlier, these scales are not rigorous, scientifically valid, or reliable. They are useful only as a self-referenced comparison of the client's performance relative to the same client's previous performance. Despite their limitations, these measures often represent the best or only instrument available for a client's particular problem.

## Questionnaires

Questionnaires are another useful way to collect assessment information about clients. They provide clients with opportunities to report a large repertoire of behaviors and background information. Questionnaires are flexible; many are designed to solicit both specific, detailed information from the client and more global, comprehensive material. Although many questionnaires are available through commercial publishers and in the professional literature, the social work practitioner can also design them to meet the demands of a particular practice situation. For example, the Multimodal Life History Inventory assesses clients on several dimensions: behavior, affect, sensation, imagery, cognition, interpersonal relations, drugs, and biology (Lazarus, 1991). This instrument provides comprehensive assessment data to use in conjunction with multimodal treatment. Questionnaires can also be developed for gathering information on clients. Appendix 2A provides an example, part of the Cassata History Questionnaire, which was designed for use with youths who are considering dropping out of high school (Franklin, McNeil, & Wright, 1990; Franklin & Streeter, 1992).

The chief advantage of questionnaires is that they are useful clinical tools for providing assessment information on clients in a simplified manner that does not require long interviews. Questionnaires are not particularly useful for monitoring clinical change, but they are helpful in gathering background information and formulating treatment plans, and they may guide our diagnosis and placement decisions. They may also point out to the social worker the need for a more specific measurement tool for a client problem.

## Direct Behavioral Observation

Behavioral observation is one of the most direct and effective measures of client behavior. Behavior is observed in terms of its frequency, duration, or both (i.e., interval) (Bloom et al., 2005). To gauge frequency of behavior, it is first necessary to operationalize the behavior to be observed and to decide whether it is to be observed constantly (continuous recording) or on different occasions (time-sampling recording). Observers must be trained in the behavior to look for and in how to recognize it when it occurs.

Use of more than one observer at a time makes it possible to establish interobserver agreement; that is, the occurrences of observed behaviors between the observers can be compared to know whether both are recording the same behavior. Interobserver agreement allows for calculation of a reliability statistic for observations to determine whether the ratings are consistent. Agreement of 80 percent or greater is believed to be acceptable for most clinical situations.

Direct behavioral observation that uses more than one rater is a very effective measurement strategy and has been used frequently in research on clinical practice (Nock & Kurtz, 2005). Although direct behavioral observation can be time consuming, expensive, and impractical in everyday practice, it is considered the most accurate assessment of client change. It is also an essential tool in the diagnosis of childhood behavior disorders. In practice, direct behavioral observation is easiest to use in residential settings and in schools, where numerous professionals can comprehensively observe behavior in a natural context. For example, in a hospital setting, a mental health aide and a nursing staff member can be trained to observe a client behavior such as withdrawal into the patient's room. Both staff may independently record the time the patient stays in his or her room for a work shift (duration measure). The two observers' recordings can then be compared to establish with greater confidence the actual occurrence of the behavior. Once we have established the frequency of behavior, we can continue to count the number of times the patient withdraws during a hospital stay to determine whether the patient's hospital stay is improving his or her social interaction.

Sometimes it is possible to use only one observer, either the social worker or a significant other of the client who is trained to observe the behavior. For example, the practitioner may ask a parent to record the amount of time a student studies during the week (duration measure). Behavioral observation with one rater lacks the scientific reliability of observation with two or more raters, but it remains an important measurement indicator in clinical assessments because it provides observations of the client's behavior in natural settings.

It is not always necessary to count every occurrence of a certain behavior to gain a sense of its frequency. Interval recording simplifies behavioral observations, which makes this measurement strategy more adaptable to clinical practice. In interval recording, the practitioner chooses a period of observation (e.g., twenty minutes) and divides it into equal (ten- to twenty-second) blocks (intervals). The social worker simply observes whether the client is performing the behavior (e.g., being off task in the classroom) during the interval. The practitioner records the behavior only once for that time interval no matter how many times it actually occurs (Bloom et al., 2005).

Interval recording is flexible in that almost any type of behavior can be recorded. It is also adaptable to clinical situations because it allows for observation of more than one behavior at a time. Interval recording is particularly useful for behaviors that are difficult to record using other methods (e.g., high-frequency behavior, behaviors of extended duration) (Bloom et al., 2005). Practitioners can also easily convert interval recording into percentages, by dividing the number of intervals during which the behavior occurs by the total number of intervals observed and then multiplying by one hundred. Figure 2.6 provides an example of an interval recording form used to monitor a child's behavior.

Direct behavioral observation of clients is one of the most effective tools for measuring client behavior, and when used with two or more observers, it is considered scientifically rigorous. When following specific observational procedures, clinicians can effectively identify, define, and assess target behaviors that can serve as a guide to intervention (Nock & Kurtz, 2005). This makes direct behavioral observation a useful tool for both practice and research.

**Figure 2.6** Interval Recording Form

| | |
|---|---|
| Observer: _____School Social Worker_____ | Date: _____28/10/78_____ |
| Reliability observer: _____paraprofessional_____ | day month year |
| Teacher: _____Mrs. Graves_____ | |
| School: _____Pine Elementary_____ | Time stop: _____11:16_____ |
| Subject area: _____reading-seatwork_____ | Time start: _____11:09_____ |
| Referred pupil (R): ___Chelsea___ Age: _8–6_ | Total time: _____7_____ |
| Comparison pupil (C): _____ Age: _8–5_ | |
| Class size: _____31_____ Class type: _regular_ | |

| Grouping Situation | Teacher Reaction Code: (T) | Observation Recording Method |
|---|---|---|
| R = student | T = teacher | (circle one) |
| C = student | AA = attention to all | (a) interval: size ___30"___ |
| X = behavior occurs | A+ = positive attention to | (b) time sample: _____ |
| O = behavior does | pupil | (c) event count |
| not occur | A– = negative attention | (d) duration for "out of |
| (circle one) | to pupil | seat" |
| L = large group | Ao = no attention to pupil | (e) latency |
| S = small group | An = neutral attention to | |
| O = one-to-one | pupil | |
| I = independent | = _____ | |
| F = free time | = _____ | |
| = _____ | | |

Explicit classroom rules in effect during observation: _1. work quietly 2. sit at desks 3. raise hand to ask question_

## Role Play and Analog Situations

Practitioners frequently use role playing and other analog situations to assess clients' performance of various behaviors. These allow clients to demonstrate certain behaviors in the social worker's office. Social workers create role plays or behavioral rehearsals in which clients demonstrate a behavior and the social worker observes. For example, a social worker might ask a client to play the role of a job applicant in a personnel interview. The observation serves as an assessment of potential skill and therapeutic feedback to facilitate goal attainment. In this example, the role play allows the social worker to assess the client's interviewing skills and provides data the social worker can use to coach the client to improve. Observing this role play on several occasions over a period of time makes it possible for the social worker to monitor improvement. The social worker can devise a plan for documenting this improvement, such as providing a rating scale of client performance or recording the client's improvements in a log, thus combining measurement strategies. The social worker can also document improvements through analog methods such as videotaping or audiotaping the role plays, which helps clients understand their own behavior. Videotapes and audiotapes also are used in therapy and clinical supervision, and they serve as an analog measure of behavior for direct observation by the social worker and others. Reasonably priced recording equipment can greatly enhance routine clinical practice.

Another analog measure is the use of vignettes and other contrived behavioral situations. Vignettes are more structured than role plays in that they usually provide the client with a set of questions to which he or she is to respond. The social worker asks clients to respond to a series of vignettes that approximate various behavioral situations. For example, a social worker can assess, at least hypothetically, an adolescent's problem-solving behavior by presenting the adolescent with a series of problem-solving vignettes or situations and asking him or her to respond. As with role plays, the practitioner can use this information to help the adolescent improve his or her problem-solving skills.

Role plays and other analog methods are useful assessment measures of client behavior. They are both indicators of client performance and mechanisms for helping clients improve their behavior. For example, a clinician may record a client's behavior and play it back to the client as a means of providing feedback for change.

### Behavioral By-Products

Behavioral by-products are specific items or evidences that can be collected or accumulated as indicators of client behaviors. For example, cigarette butts can be collected to assess clients in a smoking cessation program. Similarly, weight gained or lost may serve as an indicator of client health functioning. A scale can verify the client's weight, and the scale readings are a measurement of the behavioral by-product. As another example, clients who are agoraphobic (afraid to go into public places) may be asked to keep theater ticket stubs and other paraphernalia indicating their attendance at social or recreational events.

Behavioral by-products are objective indicators of client behaviors. They are naturally associated with and represent the behavior the client wants to change. Collecting behavioral by-products is also easier for some clients than keeping a log or other written assignment.

### Psychophysiological Measures

Psychophysiological measures are represented by mechanical and technological indexes of client behaviors. These measures assess the client's physiological performance as it relates to behavior. Several devices of clinical significance are currently used in clinical practice. Psychophysiological measures are frequently used in three categories of disorders: psychophysiological disorders (e.g., high blood pressure), anxiety disorders (e.g., stress symptoms, panic attacks), and sexual disorders (e.g., pedophilia, other deviant arousal syndromes) (Barlow et al., 2008). Examples of psychophysiological measures for each category follows.

**Psychophysiological Disorder.**  The sphygmomanometer, an instrument that measures blood pressure, is frequently used to measure psychophysiological disorders. Various clinical biofeedback measures such as the electromyographic activity (EMG), a measure of tension or muscular contraction, and galvanic skin response (GSR), a measure of skin conductance), are also used.

**Anxiety Disorder.**  Neurofeedback (NFB), also neurobiofeedback or electroencephalography (EEG) biofeedback, is used to assess clients' anxiety and stress. Technology has increased the sophistication of EEG biofeedback measures for clinical practice. For example, Davacon produces a computerized biofeedback system that can complete a full physiological assessment of clients, including measures such as heart rate, EMG, and GSR. This biofeedback program administers a stress test to the client in conjunction with the other measures. The EEG biofeedback technology holds promise as a methodology for retraining abnormal brainwave patterns. It has been associated with minimal side effects and is less invasive than other methods used to address biological brain disorders. The use of neurofeedback with anxiety disorders, including posttraumatic stress disorder and obsessive-compulsive disorder, and with depression has shown initial success with minimal intrusion (Hammond, 2005; Moore, 2000).

**Sexual Disorders.**  The most common psychophysiological measure used to assess and treat sexual disorders is the penile plethysmograph, a direct measure of of blood flow that increases penile circumference. In the clinical setting, males with sexual deviations (e.g., pedophilia) are exposed to both appropriate and inappropriate sexual stimuli, and measures of penile arousal are obtained in conjunction with self-reports of sexual arousal. The plethysmograph makes it possible to measure deviant sexual arousal and aids the assessment and treatment of clients with sexual disorders (Barlow et al., 2008; Ward, Laws, & Hudson, 2003).

Psychophysiological measures are important indexes of client behaviors. Technological and mechanical devices greatly increase our ability to make scientifically valid and reliable assessments of client functioning in this domain. These measures, therefore, have significance for both clinical practice and research.

## Goal Attainment Scaling Measures

Goal attainment scaling (GAS) is a method used to measure change in client problems according to clients' treatment goals (Corcoran, Gingerich,

& Briggs, 2001) and thus to evaluate practice. Social workers have used GAS primarily to evaluate specific client or program outcomes. Goal attainment scaling is useful to ongoing assessment and monitoring because it allows practitioners and clients to operationalize and determine different levels of progress toward treatment goals. Outcomes or progress indicators range from most unfavorable to best anticipated. Table 2.3 shows an example of a GAS used in a crisis intervention center to evaluate two problem areas: education and suicide.

**Table 2.3**   Goal Attainment Scaling

| Check whether or not the Scale has been mutually negotiated between patient & CIC interviewer. | Scale Headings and Scale Weights |
| --- | --- |
| | Yes ____   No ____   Yes ____ <br> No ____ |

| Scale Attainment Level (WI = 20) | Scale 1: Education (W2 = 30) | Scale 2: Suicide |
| --- | --- | --- |
| a. Most unfavorable treatment outcome thought likely. (−2) | Patient has made no attempt to enroll in high school. X | Patient has committed suicide. |
| b. Less expected success w/treatment. (−1) | Patient has enrolled in high school, but at time of follow-up has dropped out. | Patient had acted on at least one suicidal impulse since her first contact w/ the CIC, but has not succeeded.* |
| c. Expected level of treatment success. (0) | Patient has enrolled and is in school at follow-up, but is attending class sporadically (misses an average of more than a third of her class during a week). | Patient reports she has had at least 4 suicidal impulses since her first contact with the CIC but has not acted on any of them. |
| d. More than expected success with treatment. | Patient has enrolled, is in school at follow-up, and is attending classes consistently, but has no vocational goal.* | |
| e. Best anticipated success with treatment. (=2) | Patient has enrolled, is in school at follow-up, is attending classes consistently, and has some vocational goal. | Patient reports she has had no suicidal impulses since her first contact with the CIC. |

X = Level at Intake
* = Level at Follow-up

SOURCE: Reid, W. and Smith, A. (1981). *Research in social work*. New York: Columbia University Press.

Goal attainment scaling is an effective method for assessing clinical change in clients, and it is a relevant and adaptable form of measurement that has proved successful in measuring client change across diverse clinical settings.

## Standardized Measures

Standardized measures are ready-made instruments with proven records, in that their statistical and psychometric properties have been researched. Standardization refers to uniformity of procedures in scoring and administering the measure. In general, social work practitioners can have confidence in these measures and in their ability to assess the client behaviors for which they were developed. Even with excellent psychometric development, however, practitioners have to be aware of underlying flaws that may exist in scale properties and their clinical utility, which might lessen their usefulness for clinical practice. Chapter 3 describes these issues in detail in relationship to the use of standardized measures in clinical assessment.

Standardized assessment measures assess a broad spectrum of client behaviors, such as personality, intelligence, marital satisfaction, self-esteem, and just about all aspects of human behavior (Fischer & Corcoran, 2007a, 2007b). Some standardized measures assess global behaviors such as personality (e.g., the Personality Inventory for Children; Lachar, 1982), and others assess specific behaviors such as level of dysphoric mood (e.g., the Beck Depression Inventory II; Beck, 1978). Self-report standardized measures exist, as do measures that others can complete, such as parents, teachers, or some other informed individual. Both rapid assessment instruments and lengthy, comprehensive measures are available (for an example of a rapid assessment instrument—the Index of Self Esteem [Hudson, 1989]—see figure 2.7.

Standardized measures generally make use of two points of reference that aid in their interpretation: criterion referenced and norm referenced. These methods may be combined, however. Criterion-referenced measures interpret specific content to be mastered. Clients' scores are interpreted on the basis of clients' ability to master a certain number of items on the measure (Anastasi & Urbina, 1997). For example, criterion-referenced standardized measures are used frequently in education to measure educational achievement. Norm-referenced measures are used to interpret outcomes on a particular measure for a specific population. Client scores on the measure are compared with the scores from a normative group of persons who have completed the measure. Norm-referenced standardized measures are generally used in clinical situations to assess the normative characteristics of clients. However, both types of measures can be used in clinical situations.

**Figure 2.7**  Index of Self-Esteem (ISE)

---

**INDEX OF SELF-ESTEEM (ISE)**

Name: _____  Today's Date: _____

Context: _____

This questionnaire is designed to measure how you see yourself. It is not a test, so there are no right or wrong answers. Please answer each item as carefully and as accurately as you can by placing a number beside each one as follows.

1 = None of the time
2 = Very rarely
3 = A little of the time
4 = Some of the time
5 = A good part of the time
6 = Most of the time
7 = All of the time

---

1. ____ I feel that people would not like me if they really knew me well.
2. ____ I feel that others get along much better than I do.
3. ____ I feel that I am a beautiful person.
4. ____ When I am with others I feel they are glad I am with them.
5. ____ I feel that people really like to talk with me.
6. ____ I feel that I am a very competent person.
7. ____ I think I make a good impression on others.
8. ____ I feel that I need more self-confidence.
9. ____ When I am with strangers I am very nervous.
10. ____ I think that I am a dull person.
11. ____ I feel ugly.
12. ____ I feel that others have more fun than I do.
13. ____ I feel that I bore people.
14. ____ I think my friends find me interesting.
15. ____ I think I have a good sense of humor.
16. ____ I feel very self-conscious when I am with strangers.
17. ____ I feel that if I could be more like other people I would have it made.
18. ____ I feel that people have a good time when they are with me.
19. ____ I feel like a wallflower when I go out.
20. ____ I feel I get pushed around more than others.
21. ____ I think I am a rather nice person.
22. ____ I feel that people really like me very much.
23. ____ I feel that I am a likeable person.
24. ____ I am afraid I will appear foolish to others.
25. ____ My friends think very highly of me.

---

3, 4, 5, 6, 7, 14, 15, 18, 21, 22, 23, 25.

---

Standardized measures are some of the most useful quantitative clinical measurement tools available to practitioners because of the amount of research that often goes into their development so that they are evidence-based assessment tools. Box 2.1 provides a list of reference sources that practitioners can use to explore and review standardized measures.

---

**Box 2.1**
**Resources for the Review of Standardized Measures**

---

### Books

Corcoran, K., & Fischer, J. (2000a). *Measures for Clinical Practice: A sourcebook Vol. 1, Couples and Families and Children*. New York: Free Press.

Corcoran, K., & Fischer, J. (2000b). *Measures for Clinical Practice: A sourcebook Vol. 2, Adults*. New York: Free Press.

Hudson, W. W. (1997). *Walmyr Assessment Scales*. Tallahassee, FL: Walmyr Publishing.

Keyser, D. J., & Sweetland, R. C. (Eds.). *Test Critiques, Vol. 8*. Austin, TX: Pro Ed.

McCubbin, H. I., Thompson, A. I., & McCubbin, M. A. (1996). *Family Assessment: Resilience, Coping, and Adaptation. Inventories for Research and Practice*. Madison, WI: University of Wisconsin Press.

Murphy, L. L., Plake, B. S., Impara, J. C., & Spies, R. A. (2002). *Tests in Print VI*. Lincoln, NE: Buros Institute of Mental Measurement.

Olin, J. T., & Keatinge, C. (1998). *Rapid Psychological Assessments*. New York: Wiley.

Plake, B. S., Impara, J. C., & Spies, R. A. (2003). *The fifteenth mental measurements yearbook*. Lincoln, NE: Buros Institute of Mental Measurement.

### On-line Location Services and Reviews of Tests and Measures

See the comprehensive list and critical reviews of most commercially available tests and measures available on-line at Buros Institute http://www.unl.edu/buros.

Review tests through the ERIC TEST LOCATOR http://ericae.net/test-col.htm.

Find all kinds of test and measures located and reviewed at All the Tests.Com http://www.allthetests.com.

Review psychological tests at The American Psychological Association website http://www.apa.org/science/faq-findtests.html.

Discover measures and reviews of fun measures at Barbarians On-line Test page. Take the fun Learning Styles Inventory measure and have it scored on-line http://www.wizardrealm.com/tests/index.html.

---

Because of their importance to clinical assessment, chapter 3 is devoted to norm-referenced standardized measurement instruments.

## Assessing Outcomes Using Standardized Measures

Outcome measurement involves assesssing the clinical effectiveness of treatment with standardized measures of clinical severity. At least two data collection points are necessary to demonstrate change, one at the start of treatment and at least at one other follow-up point (Brown, Burlingame, Lambert, Jones, & Vaccaro, 2001). With the burgeoning interest in evidence-based interventions, it has become imperative to measure the results of interventions in social work practice. Indeed, tracking psychotherapy outcomes has become a requirement for most practitioners. Treatment outcome measurement should be an integral part of empirical clinical practice.

Chapter 1 identified an evidence-based practice (EBP) process in which clinicians engage in five steps that increase the likelihood of clients receiving the most effective assessment and intervention (for a more thorough discussion of this process, see Rubin & Parrish, 2007):

1. Converting one's need for information into an answerable question

2. Tracking down the best-available information to answer the question

3. Critically appraising the evidence for its validity, reliability, impact, and applicability

4. Integrating this critical appraisal to improve practice skills and match the client's values.

5. Evaluating the effectiveness and efficiency in executing steps 1–4 and seeking ways to improve both the next time.

Rubin and Parrish (2007) particularly elaborate on step 5, which has to do with evaluating outcomes (chapter 11 in this text also discusses this step in more detail). Following an EBP process as suggested throughout this book will improve assessment and intervention, but it does not guarantee that a client will improve. Many interventions lack evidence with particular types of clients or problems. Of course, by following the recommendations of systematic reviews and EBPs, a clinician is more likely to have success with a client than if the clinician relies only on his or her own judgments (Mullen, Bledsoe, & Bellamy, 2008) Standardized outcome measures can also assist practitioners in evaluating the effectiveness of any intervention for the client and in building the evidence base for the intervention itself, thereby engaging the social worker in the EBP process. So, following good measurement can help even when practitioners are not certain about the best way to help a client, because they can use the data collected on client outcomes to guide and fine-tune practices.

One such outcome measure developed for guiding practice with children and adolescents is the Youth Outcome Questionnaire (YOQ), which was designed to bridge the gap between traditional diagnostic measures and measures specifically designed to track outcomes (Burlingame et al., 2001; Wells, Burlingame, Lambert, Hoag, & Hope, 1996). A reliable and valid measure that can document and track treatment outcomes, clinicians, researchers, and managed-care administrators cooperatively designed the YOQ to meet the needs of all three. Its sensitivity to change in the client over time makes the YOQ an ideal instrument for evaluating client outcomes for EBP. Appendix 2B provides a case sample clinician report from the YOQ generated by Carepaths, and it provides several scores, which document client change over time.

## Projective Measures

Projective measures, used widely in clinical practice, are less structured than the other quantitative assessment tools we have discussed in this chapter. Projective measures typically assign a task that allows for an unlimited variety of responses. For example, a practitioner gives a client a partially completed sentence to finish or asks the client to describe what is happening in a picture. The most famous projective measure is the Rorschach test (Exner, 2001). Most projective measures are designed to assess global personality functioning and to uncover hidden or unconscious personality processes. Moreover, most of the measures are based on psychoanalytic concepts, and researchers have widely criticized them for their clinical inadequacies and lack of psychometric properties, such as reliability and validity (Fredman & Sherman, 1987; Leiter, 1989). From this perspective, they may not be quantitative measures at all in the psychometric sense (on psychometric properties, see chapter 3). Furthermore, with the exception of certain psychoanalytic constructs such as defense mechanisms, projective measures are not useful in tracking client progress in treatment.

Despite these criticisms, however, projective measures continue to be a favorite clinical assessment and measurement tool of clinicians (Shemmings, 2004; Viglione & Hilsenroth, 2001). Their continued popularity may be because of their viability as a clinical technique for unraveling the intricacies and subtleties of client functioning. Clinicians prefer projective measures because they reach for latent or broad aspects of client functioning; this allows clinicians to make more global interpretations than do narrow approaches to assessment, such as rapid assessment instruments. In this sense, projective measures are similar to the clinical interview, for they rely on the interpretations and judgments of the interviewer. Although projective measures have several quantitative weaknesses, they can be useful in a comprehensive assessment to generate global hypotheses about client characteristics such as personality or intelligence. Because they are vastly popular as a clinical technique and as a measure of client attributes, we describe a few commonly used projective measures here.

Incomplete sentence forms are a common group of projective measures. In this measure, the practitioner presents incomplete sentences to the client. This measure allows for almost-unlimited completions (e.g., "My mother never . . . ," "What worries me is . . . ," "My father . . ."). The practitioner uses incomplete sentences to solicit clinical themes and relevant personality and affective characteristics of the client.

The Draw-a-Person (DAP) test and the Good-Enough Harris Drawing test (Harris, 1963) are some other frequently used projective measures. The latter first gained respect as a nonverbal measure of intelligence. A set of norms has been developed for its use as a measure of intellectual maturity in children (Harris, 1963), though the norms are rather dated. In this measure, the practitioner instructs the child to draw the best picture he or she can of him- or herself and a woman. Credit is given for the inclusion of individual body parts, clothing details, proportion, perspective, and similar features. A level of intellectual maturity score can be determined on the basis of a standard score, with a mean of one hundred and a standard deviation of fifteen, which demonstrates the quantitative aspect of the measure (Harris, 1963; for a discussion of standard scores, see chapter 3). The DAP test has also been used to infer personality characteristics. There is some support for the use of the measure in assessing intellectual maturity (Dunn, 1967; Harris, 1963). However, it has been widely criticized as a personality measure (Fredman & Sherman, 1987).

The inkblot test known as the Rorschach test (Rorschach, 1921/1942) and the picture-story technique known as the thematic apperception test (TAT; Murray, 1938) are popular projective measures used in clinical practice. The Rorschach test requires clients to respond to a series of ten cards on which an inkblot is printed. Five cards are black and have shades of gray, two cards have some red, and the remaining three cards are of assorted pastel colors. The practitioner infers personality functioning from what the client reports seeing in the inkblots. Over the years, clinical psychologists have worked to standardize the answers a client may give to an inkblot shape and to develop norms for the cards. The Exner (2001) interpretive system for the Rorschach test provides such a standardization and has been both praised and criticized for its success in making the Rorschach test conform to the rigor of validity and reliability needed for a psychiatric diagnosis (for a review of the criticism of the Exner system, see Wood, Garb, Lilienfeld, & Nezworski, 2002). Two of the most glaring criticisms have to do with the fact that, with the Exner norms, many "normal" adults and children appear to have severe psychopathologies and the Exner scoring system does not conform to *DSM* diagnostic categories. The Rorschach measure has also failed in areas of construct validity by showing little or no correlation with more objective, self-report measures. Most notable for social work practice, the Rorschach may have little validity or reliability when used with ethnic minorities. Recent studies have shown that the Exner system did not perform well with American minorities (Ephraim, 2000; for further discussion of the limitations of measurement instruments with American minorities, see chapter 10).

The Exner (2001) system scores responses on a variety of dimensions, such as color, shading, movement, and location on the inkblot, but the Rorschach actually assesses a person's characteristic style of dealing with stimuli. Through Rorschach assessment, it is possible to ascertain a client's response style toward affective, ideational, perceptual, and interpersonal content. The practitioner can also infer a client's strengths and weaknesses, as well as a diagnostic profile (Viglione & Hilsenroth, 2001). The Rorschach measure requires a great deal of sophistication and training to administer and score. Recent research has documented a comprehensive, empirically based scoring system for the Rorschach (Viglione & Hilsenroth, 2001; Viglione & Taylor, 2003). Typically, clinical psychologists, not social workers or other counselors, administer the Rorschach (for a sample write-up from a psychological evaluation, see Pharis, 1990; appendix 2C).

The TAT, widely used by a variety of counseling professionals, consists of nineteen cards with simple black-and-white drawings of people interacting and one blank card (Anastasi & Urbina, 1997). Clinicians frequently use ten or twelve cards in their assessment. In the test, the client is asked to make up a story to represent each picture. The clinician further instructs the client to describe what is happening at that moment in the story, the events leading up to the story, how the characters are feeling, what they are thinking, and the outcome of the story. A good amount of information has been published on the typical responses for each card. Clinical practitioners, however, usually rely on their own interpretations of the themes, roles, and affective characteristics that clients express in the stories to develop an understanding of client personality and psychological functioning (Anastasi & Urbina, 1997). The TAT measure has lagged behind in its cultural relevance and should be used with caution for ethnic minority groups (Velasquez, 1995; for a write-up of a TAT from a psychological report, see Pharis, 1990; appendix 2C).

Projective measures are widely used in clinical practice and have become an entrenched part of clinical assessment. Regardless of their validity or reliability, they will continue to be used. Research indicates that projective measures as a quantitative measurement instrument have several weaknesses, but as a clinical technique they may be extremely valuable in generating global hypotheses about a client. Social workers should be skeptical, however, about what they can determine with these instruments, and they should make interpretations with extreme caution. Among all measures, projective assessment tools are the weakest of all psychological measures.

## GUIDELINES FOR USING MEASURES IN CLIENT ASSESSMENT

Thus far, we have discussed the need for using quantitative measurement as a part of assessment. We have also summarized ten methods of measuring client behaviors that practitioners can use. Table 2.4 presents

**Table 2.4**    Measurement Method Summary

| Ask & Interpret | Watch | Ask |
|---|---|---|
| Interpretive Report | Observe and/or obtain objective indicators from other sources | Self-Report and/or obtain objective indicators from the client |
| Projective Measures | Direct Behavioral Observation (frequency, duration, and interval), Rating Scales, Goal Attainment Scaling, Standardized Measures, Psychophysiological Measures, Role Plays/ Analogue Situations, Behavioral By-Products | Logs, Journals, Diaries, Structured Behavioral Report Forms, Goal Attainment Scaling, Standardized Measures, Role Plays/Analogue Situations, Behavioral By-Products |

a conceptual representation of these methods. With so many different methods available for measuring client behaviors, it can be difficult for social work practitioners to decide which methods to use in their assessment. This section offers guidelines to help practitioners develop a measurement system for client assessments. Specific suggestions for developing an assessment plan follow general guidelines.

When possible, practitioners should determine the best evidence-based approaches (i.e., determined through research studies) for their particular populations or problem areas to make their assessments more effective and efficient. Evidence-based assessment helps clinical assessment tools to be more precise and may lessen the number to tools a practitioner needs to develop a good assessment.

Chapter 3 further discusses the process of evidence-based assessment and the advantages of developing evidence-based assessments. In using evidence-based assessment, researchers and practitioners seek to learn the best ways to assess different problems and populations. As mentioned in chapter 1, as the field learns more about the best assessment tools for different populations, assessment protocols or guides to assessment for various populations or mental health disorders are becoming available. Guidelines based on evidence will make clearer which standardized measures or ways of collecting information are best for particular problem areas. For this reason, it is increasingly important for practitioners to be familiar with their populations and problem areas, as well as other client factors (e.g., ethnicity) in order to judge the best assessment practices. Following the steps of the evidence-based practice process described in this book will help guide practitioners to the best assessment tools. The second half of this book also discusses assessment issues in relationship to specific populations in more detail and offers directions for working with those populations. In the absence of good research and evidence-based assessment tools, it is always a good idea to use multiple methods to measure client behaviors and to always seek out the best measures available that can most efficiently provide an assessment—having to use other sources of information can become cumbersome in practice situations. We provide three guidelines for developing an assessment based on evidence in the following paragraphs.

First, develop baseline indicators of client functioning. Baseline data that are considerably different from data on a general population can evidence treatment necessity. Alternatively, scores at the baseline that are similar to those of a clinical sample suggest the need for treatment. All measures should be given at least on a pretest and a posttest basis. Follow-ups are also desirable.

Second, use at least one repeated measure. This ensures that practitioners measure client behavior on several occasions to monitor progress over the course of treatment. This approach is consistent with the single-subject design approach (see chapter 12), it provides feedback on the practitioner's interaction with the client, and it may improve treatment through that feedback.

Third, include specific and global measures of client problems. Doing so increases the likelihood of capturing changes in client behaviors.

Following these general guidelines, an ideal measurement system for client assessment might include the following:

- A standardized measure or a client log or self-anchored scale (self-report)
- A behavioral observation (self-report)
- A standardized or do-it-yourself rating scale (significant other report)

Ideally, in any assessment situation, the practitioner should use at a minimum both a client self-report and a report from another rater to help decrease bias of any one perspective. For example, a client reporting depression can be administered the Beck Depression Inventory, a self-report, standardized measure; the practitioner might also ask for a report from a relative on the client's specific behavioral symptoms of depression (e.g., crying, isolation, not going to work). In developing a measurement approach to aid assessment, it is important to consider whether the measure really captures client change in the real world and is sensitive to what the practitioner is asking of the client (e.g., in filling out forms and measures). It is important, for example, not overwhelm the client with too many assessment tools and measures—more is not necessarily better. On some occasions, only one measure may be enough. For example, even though there are many good ways to assess attention deficit/hyperactivity disorder in children, Evans and Baird (2006) suggest that the behavioral rating system called the daily report card, which teachers fill out, is one of the best evidence-based assessments and captures the behaviors of the child that need to be monitored and changed. Good measurement, like good practice, requires knowledge, creativity, and flexibility of the practitioner. As are other practice skills, clinical measurement is as much art as science. A clinical assessment and measurement approach should therefore be as unique as clients and their situations dictate.

## SUMMARY

Quantitative measurement requires practitioners to devise or use methods to assign numerical indicators to behaviors, emotions, or other attributes. Including measures as part of assessment provides quantitative sources of data and helps practitioners and clients verify and clarify their opinions and judgments concerning client functioning. The chapter discussed ten methods of measurement that practitioners can use: client self-reporting and self-monitoring, self-anchored and rating scales, questionnaires, direct behavioral observation, role play and analog situations, behavioral by-products, psychophysiological measures, goal attainment scaling, standardized measures, and projective measures. The chapter also provided examples of these measurements and guidelines for their use. Four important guidelines are use of multiple methods (at a minimum a self-report and another report), development of baseline indicators of client functioning, use of repeated measures, and use of both global and specific measures. Thus, this chapter has provided a broad overview of quantitative assessment methods that social workers can use in assessment, client evaluation, and intervention plans.

## REFERENCES

Anastasi, A., & Urbina, S. (1997). *Psychological testing* (7th ed.). Upper Saddle River, NJ: Prentice Hall.

Barlow, D. H., Nock, M. K., & Hersen, M. (2008). *Single case experimental designs: Strategies for studying behavior change* (3rd ed.). Boston: Allyn and Bacon.

Beck, A. (1978). *Beck Depression Inventory*. San Antonio, TX: Psychological Corporation.

Bloom, M. J., Fischer, J., & Orme, J. G. (2005). *Evaluating practice: Guidelines for the accountable professional* (5th ed.). Boston: Allyn and Bacon.

Brown, G. S., Burlingame, G. M., Lambert, M. J., Jones, E., & Vaccaro, J. (2001). Pushing the quality envelope: A new outcomes management system. *Psychiatric Services, 52,* 925–934.

Burlingame, G. M., Mosier, J. I., Wells, M. G., Atkin, Q. G., Lambert, M. J., Whoolery, M., & Latkowski, M. (2001). Tracking the influence of mental health treatment: The development of the Youth Outcome Questionnaire. *Clinical Psychology and Psychotherapy, 8,* 361–379.

Corcoran, K., & Boyer-Quick, J. (2008). How clinicians can effectively use assessment tools to establish treatment necessity and throughout the treatment process. In A. R. Roberts & G. Greene (Eds.), *Social workers' desk reference* (pp. 317–322). New York: Oxford University Press.

Corcoran, K., Gingerich, W. J., & Briggs, H. E. (2001). Practice evaluation: Setting goals and monitoring change. In H. E. Briggs & K. Corcoran (Eds.), *Social work practice: Treating common client practice* (pp. 66–84). Chicago: Lyceum Books.

Corcoran, K., & Vandiver, V. L. (1996). *Maneuvering the maze of managed care: Skills for mental health practitioners.* New York: Free Press.

Deschner, J. P. (1984). *The hitting habit: Anger control for battering couples.* New York: Free Press.

Dunn, J. A. (1967). Inter- and intra-rater reliability of the new Harris-Goodenough Draw-a-Man test. *Perceptual and Motor Skills, 24,* 269–270.

Ellis, A. (1985). Expanding the ABC's of rational-emotive therapy. In M. Mahoney & A. Freeman (Eds.), *Cognition and psychotherapy* (pp. 313–323). New York: Plenum Press.

Ephraim, D. (2000). Culturally relevant research and practice with the Rorschach comprehensive system. In R. H. Dana (Ed.), *Handbook of cross cultural/multicultural personality assessment* (pp. 303–327). Mahwah, NJ: Erlbaum.

Evans, S. W., & Baird, A. V. (2006). Evidence-based assessment of ADHD: Measuring outcomes. *Journal of the American Academy of Child and Adolescent Psychiatry, 9,* 1132–1137.

Exner, J. E. (2001). *A Rorschach workbook for the comprehensive system* (5th ed.). Asheville, NC: Rorschach Workshops.

Faul, A. C., McMurtry, S. L., & Hudson, W. W. (2001). Can empirical clinical practice techniques improve social work outcomes? *Research on Social Work Practice, 11,* 277–299.

Fischer, J., & Corcoran, K. (2007a). *Measures for clinical practice and research: A sourcebook: Vol. 1. Couples, families and children* (4th ed.). New York: Oxford University Press.

Fischer, J., & Corcoran, K. (2007b). *Measures for clinical practice and research: A sourcebook: Vol. 2. Adults* (4th ed.). New York: Oxford University Press.

Franklin, C., McNeil, J., & Wright, R. (1990). School social work works: Findings from an alternative school for dropouts. *Social Work in Education, 12,* 177–194.

Franklin, C., & Streeter, C. L. (1992). Social support and psychoeducational interventions with middle class dropout youth. *Child and Adolescent Social Work, 9,* 131–153.

Fredman, N., & Sherman, R. (1987). *Handbook of measurements for marriage and family therapy.* New York: Brunner/Mazel.

Hammond, D. C. (2005). Neurofeedback with anxiety and affective disorders. *Child and Adolescent Psychiatric Clinics of North America, 14*, 105–123.

Harris, D. B. (1963). *Children's drawings as measures of intellectual maturity: A revision and extension of the Goodenough Draw-a-Man test.* New York: Harcourt Brace Jovanovich.

Hayes, S. C., Barlow, D. H., & Nelson-Gray, R. O. (1999). *The scientist practitioner: Research and accountablility in the age of managed care* (2nd ed.). Boston: Allyn and Bacon.

Hepworth, D. H., Rooney, R. H., Rooney, G. D., Strom-Gottfried, K., & Larsen, J. A. (2005). *Direct social work practice: Theory and skills* (7th ed.). Pacific Grove, CA: Brooks Cole.

Hudson, W. W. (1989). *Computer assisted social services.* Tempe, AZ: Walmyr.

Jordan, C., Franklin, C., & Corcoran, K. (2001). Standardized measures. In R. M. Grinnell Jr. (Ed.), *Social work research and evaluation* (6th ed., pp. 198–209). Itasca, IL: Peacock.

Lachar, D. (1982). *Personality inventory for children (PIC) revised format manual supplement.* Los Angeles: Western Psychological Services.

Lazarus, A. (1991). *Multi-modal life history inventory.* Champaign, IL: Research Press.

Leiter, E. (1989). The role of projective testing. In S. Wetzler & M. M. Katz (Eds.), *Contemporary approaches to psychological testing* (pp. 118–126). New York: Brunner/Mazel.

Moore, N. C. (2000). A review of EEG biofeedback treatment of anxiety disorders. *Clinical Electroencephalography, 31*, 1–6.

Mullen, E. J., Bledsoe, S. E., & Bellamy, J. L. (2008). Implementing evidence-based social work practice. *Research on Social Work Practice, 18*, 325–338.

Murray, H. A. (1938). *Exploration in personality.* New York: Oxford University Press.

Nock, M. K., & Kurtz, S. M. S. (2005). Direct behavioral observation in school settings: Bringing science to practice. *Cognitive and Behavioral Practice, 12*, 359–370.

Pharis, M. (1990). *Sample write-up on the Rorschach and TAT.* Unpublished psychological report.

Quittner, A. L., Modi, A. C., Lemanek, K. L., Ievers-Landis, C. E., & Rapoff, M. A. (2008). Evidence-based assessment of adherence to medical treatments in pediatric psychology. *Journal of Pediatric Psychology, 33*, 916–936.

Rorschach, H. (1942). *Psychodiagnostics: A diagnostic test based on perception* (P. Lemkau & B. Kronenburg, Trans.). Berne, Switzerland: Huber. (Original work published 1921)

Rubin, A., & Parrish, D. (2007). Challenges to the future of evidence-based practice in social work education. *Journal of Social Work Education, 43*, 405–428.

Shemmings, D. (2004). Researching relationships from an attachment perspective: The use of behavioural, interview, self-report and projective measures. *Journal of Social Work Practice, 18*, 299–314.

Slade, K., Lambert, M. J., Harmon, S. C., Smart, D. W., & Bailey, R. (2008). Improving psychotherapy outcomes: The use of immediate electronic feedback and revised clinical support tools. *Clinical Psychology and Psychotherapy, 15,* 287–303.

Velasquez, R. J. (1995). Personality assessment of Hispanic clients. In J. N. Butcher (Ed.), *Clinical personality assessment: Practical approaches* (pp. 120–139). New York: Oxford University Press.

Viglione, D. J., & Hilsenroth, M. J. (2001). The Rorschach: Facts, fictions, and future. *Psychological Assessment, 13,* 452–471.

Viglione, D. J., & Taylor, N. (2003). Empirical support for interrater reliability of Rorschach Comprehensive System Coding. *Journal of Clinical Psychology, 59,* 111–121.

Ward, T., Laws, D. R., & Hudson, S. M. (2003). *Sexual deviance: Issues and controversies.* Thousand Oaks, CA: Sage.

Wells, M. G., Burlingame, G. M., Lambert, M. J., Hoag, M. J., & Hope, C. A. (1996). Conceptualization and measurement of patient change during psychotherapy: Development of the Outcome Questionnaire and Youth Outcome Questionnaire. *Psychotherapy, 33,* 275–283.

Whipple, J. L., Lambert, M. J., Vermeersch, D. A., Smart, D. W., Nielsen, S. L., & Hawkins, E. J. (2003). Improving the effects of psychotherapy: The use of early identification of treatment failure and problem solving strategies in routine practice. *Journal of Counseling Psychology, 58,* 59–68.

Wood, J. M., Garb, H. N., Lilienfeld, S. O., & Nezworski, T. (2002). Clinical assessment. *Annual Review of Psychology, 53,* 519–543.

# CHAPTER 3

# Standardized Assessment Measures and Computer-Assisted Assessment

**David W. Springer, Cynthia Franklin, and Danielle E. Parrish**

## INTRODUCTION

The goal of this chapter is to help social work practitioners become informed consumers in the selection, use, and interpretation of standardized measurement instruments. The chapter explores major issues in the development, evaluation, and interpretation of standardized measures, as well as applications of standardized assessment systems that use computer technologies. Previous chapters introduced the importance of conducting an evidence-based assessment. This chapter further defines what is meant by the term *evidence-based assessment* and shows how standardized measures can be an important part of conducting an evidence-based social work assessment.

## EVIDENCE-BASED PRACTICE PROCESS AND ASSESSMENT

Previous chapters have discussed the seminal definition of *evidence-based practice* (EBP), which originated in medicine and focuses on EBP as a process. As a matter of review, Sackett, Straus, Richardson, Rosenberg, and Haynes (2000) originally coined the term *evidence-based practice* as the "integration of the best available research evidence with clinical expertise and [client] values" (p. 1). This process involves the following steps:

1. Convert the need for information into an EBP question (e.g., about prevention, diagnosis, assessment, intervention, risk factors, cultural sensitivity).
2. Search for the best research evidence with which to answer that question (most often using Web-based resources).
3. Critically appraise that evidence for its validity and applicability,

4. Integrate the critical appraisal with clinical expertise and the client's unique characteristics, values, and circumstances.

5. Evaluate our effectiveness and efficiency in implementing the practice decision and the EBP process (adapted from Straus, Richardson, Glasziou, & Haynes, 2005).

To date, the primary focus and application of the EBP process has been on the selection of the most effective interventions, with little attention paid to the import of this process to guide evidence-based assessment (EBA) (Hunsley & Mash, 2005, 2007; Mash & Hunsley, 2005). To address this concern, a handful of journal special issues on the topic of EBA have emerged recently in the psychology literature, and the collective sentiment is perhaps best reflected in a comment by Achenbach (2005), who likens the use of EBP without evidence-based assessment to "a magnificent house with no foundation" (p. 547).

## Definition of Evidence-Based Assessment

As Chapter 1 mentioned, evidence-based assessment (EBA) has been defined as "the use of research and theory to inform the selection of targets, the methods and measures used in the assessment, and the assessment process itself" (Hunsley & Mash, 2007, p. 29). The primary focus of EBA is to locate the best evidence regarding the most effective assessment instruments and protocols that fit best with a client's situation, culture, values, and preferences. This chapter further defines and describes what is beneath this broad definition. Four major factors to consider when engaging in EBA include the following:

1. Psychometric adequacy of standardized instruments or assessment protocols (reliability and validity)

2. Diversity issues and individual client characteristics and the fit of various assessment instruments or protocols with those characteristics

3. Issues of comorbidity

4. Clinical utility of standardized instruments or assessment protocols

Although the consideration of these factors is not new, the explicit, thoughtful, and concurrent integration of such factors has come out of recent writings on EBA and is thought to increase the probability that assessment procedures selected will be the most effective and relevant to each individual client. The bulk of this chapter focuses on those four factors and their relation to EBA, but the factors constitute only the third, fourth, and fifth steps of the EBP process for answering EBP questions related to clinical assessment (critically appraising the research related to

EBA; integrating this information with client values, preferences, and circumstances; and using standardized measures to monitor treatment outcome).

## PSYCHOMETRIC ADEQUACY

Once thought to be the domain of psychologists, standardized measures and computer-assisted assessment technologies continue to gain popularity with social work practitioners and other counselors (Baird & Wagner, 2000; Bloom, Fischer, & Orme, 2005; Fischer & Corcoran, 2007; Grove, Zald, Lebow, Snitz, & Nelson, 2000). Practitioners from cognitive-behavioral and empirical practice orientations have long used standardized assessment measures. Recall from Chapters 1 and 2 that practitioners trained in the empirical practice models value scientific practice and single-case designs as important parts of the assessment process, which is why more empirically trained practitioners often use standardized measures more often. Unfortunately, many social workers have not been thoroughly trained in standardized assessment methodologies. So we have devoted this chapter to their uses in clinical assessment.

Standardized measures encompass a wide range of assessment tools, including but not limited to personality assessment instruments, behavior-rating scales, social attitude scales, measures of marriage and family functioning, achievement tests, measures of cognitive functioning, and aptitude measures (Fischer & Corcoran, 2007; Jordan, Franklin, & Corcoran, 2005; Kaplan & Succuzzo, 2009). Computerized assessment technologies have been developed for many standardized measures, and computers are increasingly being used to aid practitioners in making clinical judgments (Garb, 2000).

Standardization is essential to the development of useful measures for clinical practice; several authors define it differently, but most definitions are related (Jordan et al., 2005). All definitions share two characteristics that distinguish a standardized measure from a nonstandardized measure.

First, standardized measures have uniform administration and scoring procedures. Measurement conditions and outcomes are clearly and completely specified to ensure comparability of the results. The development of the measure provides detailed directions about how the measure is to be given, to whom it is to be given, and the exact meanings of the results. Detailed directions include such information as materials to be used, oral instructions to be given while administering the measure, preliminary demonstrations, exact ways to score the measure, and meanings of the scores. These directions are often reported in a measurement manual that accompanies the measure at its purchase. All directions in the manual must be followed precisely to reduce or eliminate the influence of factors extraneous to the characteristic(s) of the client being assessed (Kaplan & Succuzzo, 2009).

Second, standardization entails a process of establishing norms for a measure. A measure is thought to be standardized if it has gone through technical development involving a standardization sample (a large representative sample of people) used to establish its normalization (statistical properties). The establishment of norms is essential to the scoring and interpretation of the measure. Norms make the measure comparable across client groups and empirically define the limits and practicalities of the measure. For example, norms establish such relevant information as the average score on the measure, the deviations necessary to fall outside the average, and the client groups for which the measure is appropriate (Kaplan & Succuzzo, 2009).

For a measure to be standardized, it must go through a rigorous process of research and development aimed to empirically verify the measure's characteristics and usefulness. The level of research and development for different standardized measures varies greatly from minimal, crude standardization (e.g., testing on a small group of college freshmen) to state-of-the-art development (e.g., testing on a large, representative national sample). As a rule, practitioners should incorporate only the best and most technically developed standardized measures into practice situations (Jordan et al., 2005).

The remaining sections summarize important considerations for evaluating the psychometric properties of standardized measures. First, we discuss the assessment of reliability of measures. Second, we examine methods for determining measurement validity. Third, we summarize norms, scoring, and interpretation of standardized measures, as well as explain frequently used standard scoring systems explained. Fourth, we discuss the use of standardized instruments for assessing treatment outcome. Fifth, we summarize and illustrate the availability of computer-assisted assessment technologies. Sixth, we present the limitations of standardized instruments. Finally, we explain measurement error.

## DETERMINING RELIABILITY

Reliability refers to the consistency of a measure and to its dependability and stability (Bloom et al., 2005; Fischer & Corcoran, 2007). A tool is reliable to the extent that it performs consistently over repeated uses. Reliability is understood by examining the reliability coefficient or by using the standard error of measurement. A measure cannot be trusted if its reliability coefficient is low (Sattler, 2001). Reliability coefficients indicate the degree of consistency in the measurement of test scores, and they range from 1.00 (perfect reliability) to 0.00 (no reliability). High reliability is especially important for measures incorporated into practice situations that will be used to guide clinical decision making. As the reliability of a measure decreases, so should our faith in it.

From available measures, social workers should try to choose the assessment tools with the highest reliability. Four prominent methods for establishing reliability of measures are described in the following sections: test-retest, alternate form, split-half, and internal consistency.

## Test-Retest Reliability

Test-retest reliability is an index of a measure's stability. The same test is given to the same client groups (subjects) on two different occasions, usually within a relatively short time (one week to a month or two). The Pearson product-moment correlation (Pearson's $r$), which indicates the relationship between two interval or ratio variables, is applied to the scores (Rubin & Babbie, 2010). The obtained correlation coefficient indicates how consistent the measure performs over time (Kaplan & Succuzzo, 2009; Rubin & Babbie, 2010). To the extent that both sets of responses correlate with each other, test-retest reliability is established.

A challenge of establishing this type of reliability is that too much time between administrations of the measure allows for real change to take place in the group of clients, whereas too little time raises the possibility that the second set of responses are based on memory of the first administration. In either case, the obtained correlation coefficients will be misleading. This type of reliability may be difficult to establish and accurately interpret for scales that measure highly variable emotional and interpersonal traits (e.g., depression, anxiety). For this reason, test-retest reliability is not as useful as sometimes implied (Springer, Abell, & Hudson, 2002).

## Alternate-Form Reliability

Also called equivalent or parallel-form reliability, alternate-form reliability is obtained by giving two different but equivalent forms of the same measure to the same group of clients (Rubin & Babbie, 2010). The two sets of scores are then compared by computing a correlation coefficient (e.g., Pearson's $r$). If there is no measurement error, clients should score the same on both measures, which thus yields a high correlation coefficient. This type of reliability is most commonly encountered when a scale developer wishes to establish a shorter version of a scale, say, from twenty-five items to ten items, so that it is less time-consuming for clients to complete. A correlation coefficient of roughly 0.90 is needed to comfortably argue for the presence of alternate-form reliability (Springer, Abell, & Hudson, 2002).

## Split-Half Reliability

Split-half reliability is obtained by dividing a measure into two equivalent halves (Kaplan & Succuzzo, 2009; Rubin & Babbie, 2010). Basically, the split-half method consists of administering one form of a scale to a group of subjects. The developer then uses half the items to compute one total score and the other half to compute a second total score. The developer then computes a correlation between the two sets of scores. To the extent that the two halves correlate, split-half reliability is established. To use this method, all items must measure the same construct.

There is a limitation to this method of establishing reliability. The developer must decide how to divide the items. For example, on a thirty-item scale, one could create one set by taking the first fifteen items to create one score and the second set of fifteen items to create a second score. A more common practice is to create two sets of scores by using all of the odd-numbered items and even-numbered items to create two scores. The possibilities are infinite. In fact, for a thirty-item instrument, there are 77 million estimates for split-half reliability (Hudson, 1999). Rather than choosing one of these estimates to determine the internal consistency of a new measure, the next approach allows us to effectively compute the average of all 77 million estimates.

## Internal-Consistency Reliability

The coefficient alpha (Cronbach, 1951; Guttman, 1945) computes the mean of all possible split-half reliabilities. It is a measure of the internal consistency of a measure and is based on the positive intercorrelations of the scale's items (Kuder & Richardson, 1937). Computing the internal consistency of a measure allows one to estimate how consistently respondents performed across items of a measure. The internal consistency of a measure also lends support for evidence of its content validity.

Cronbach's alpha is appropriate for use with equal-appearing interval-level data (e.g., Likert-type responses). For measures with a dichotomous (e.g., yes-no) item response format, the Kuder-Richardson Formula 20 (an equivalent procedure) should be computed.

## Reliability Standards

A satisfactory degree of reliability depends on how a measure is intended to be used. Group research is typically concerned with mean differences among groups of subjects (e.g., experimental versus comparison groups). For scales that are used in large group research efforts or scientific studies, it used to be that a reliability coefficient of 0.60 or greater was needed (Hudson, 1982). Given the field's advancement in its ability to establish psychometrically sound scales in recent years, today we should not accept anything as credible for use in nomothetic research with a reliability coefficient below .70 (Abell, Springer, & Kamata, 2009). However, in clinical work, a higher reliability coefficient is needed for scales that will be used to help guide clinical decision making with individual clients. The reason for this standard is that, when working with an individual, there is no opportunity to average out the inevitable measurement error contained in the scale, as there is in group research.

Abell et al. (2009) assert that measurement tools that will be used to make decisions about a single individual should produce test scores with a minimum reliability coefficient of .80. Nunnally and Bernstein (1994) suggest that a reliability of .90 is even more appropriate.

These reliability standards can help social workers make decisions about a scale's degree of reliability. The greater the seriousness of the problem being measured (e.g., suicidal risk), and the graver the consequences of being wrong, the higher the standard should be held.

Reliability is a necessary but not sufficient condition for ensuring that a scale has solid psychometric properties. If an instrument measures something consistently (indicating reliability) but not accurately (indicating validity), then the measure lacks clinical utility.

## DETERMINING VALIDITY

Validity is concerned with the target and method of measurement of a particular measurement tool; that is, a tool is valid to the extent that it measures what it purports to measure. Any information gathered as part of the process of developing or using a measure becomes relevant to its validity. No one type of validity is appropriate for every measurement situation. Validity must be verified with reference to the specific intended use of a measure (Kaplan & Succuzzo, 2009). So, regarding a measurement tool, social workers must continually ask what and for whom is it valid? The answers to these questions can be determined only by examining the validity studies of a particular measure. All procedures for establishing measurement validity are concerned with the relationship between performance on the measure and other independent empirical criteria (Kaplan & Succuzzo, 2009). Four methods for establishing measurement validity are described here: content validity, criterion validity (concurrent and predictive), construct validity (convergent and discriminant), and factorial analysis.

### Content Validity

Content validity refers to the evaluation of items on a measure to determine whether the content contained in the items relates to and is representative of the domain that the measure seeks to examine (Kaplan &

Succuzzo, 2009; Rubin & Babbie, 2010). For example, to select a measure that assesses behavioral disorders in children, it is necessary to examine the item universe (total number of items) of the measure to determine whether the items on the measure include representative samples of the behavior of children. If the items relate only to depression, (e.g., "I feel sad"), the measure does not reflect the representative behavior domain of children. Although depression may be one dimension of that behavior domain, such a measure could not be said to have content validity (Jordan et al., 2005).

A measure reflecting representative samples of behavior for assessing behavior disorders in children is necessarily multidimensional (measuring several different traits or behaviors) rather than unidimensional (measuring one trait or behavior). For instance, the measure would include items covering hyperactive behavior, antisocial behavior, and anxious behavior, as well as depression. Several measures of this caliber have been developed (e.g., the Revised Behavior Problem Checklist [Quay, 1987], the Achenbach Child Behavior Checklist (CBCL) [Achenbach & Edelbrock, 1983], the Child and Adolescent Functional Assessment Scale (CAFAS) [Hodges, 2000]). Such measures are said to have good content validity because they reflect the domain of interest (behavior disorders of children) and include questions that reflect representative samples of the types of behavior to be measured (e.g., hyperactivity: fidgets in seat; antisocial: fights with other children; Jordan et al., 2005).

To ensure the representativeness of a measure and its subsequent content validity, items to be included in the measure must be chosen carefully. According to Hudson (1982), developing the content of an item is the single most important step in developing a measure or selecting one for use. Items should represent the specific characteristics one wishes to measure.

Hudson (1982) has proposed two rules for determining content validity of a measure: "A clear and unambiguous definition of the variable or construct to be measured should be available," and "each item should represent some aspect of the variable or construct being measured"(p. 142). Hudson suggests that social workers examine the items of the measure and use the best possible wisdom, training, experience, insight, and intuition in determining whether a measure has content validity.

## Criterion Validity

Criterion validity relates to the scores on the measure in relationship to some type of criterion (Kaplan & Succuzzo, 2009; Rubin & Babbie, 2010). Procedures for criterion validity help establish a measure's accuracy in identifying client characteristics or predicting client performance on specific activities (Kaplan & Succuzzo, 2009). The results are checked against an empirical criterion and must be measurable, free from bias, and relevant to the purposes of the measure (Kaplan & Succuzzo, 2009). Research is done to establish the correlations (relationships) between scores on the measure and the outcomes of these independent, empirical criteria. If appropriate relationships are found, then social work practitioners can be confident that the measure is a useful tool for categorizing or predicting behavior.

Confidence is based on the measure's ability to produce the same results as the independent, objective criterion. For example, if a team of mental health professionals evaluates the clients, and a psychiatric assessment measure constantly assigns the same diagnosis for clients, the measure is said to have good criterion validity.

The criterion that is used to validate the measure may be obtained at approximately the same time as the measure is given or at some future point. Authors often differentiate between concurrent and predictive criterion validity by these time relations (Kaplan & Succuzzo, 2009; Rubin & Babbie, 2010).

Concurrent validity is based on a current criterion or a criterion existing at the same time the measure is given and is useful for measures involved in diagnosis or assigning existing status (Kaplan & Succuzzo, 2009; Rubin & Babbie, 2010). The example given previously concerning a measure's ability to formulate a consistent psychiatric diagnosis in relationship to an independent criterion (diagnosis by mental health team) illustrates concurrent validity of a measure. There are two primary types of concurrent criterion validity: known-instruments validity and known-groups validity.

Known-instruments validity is established to the extent that one's new measure correlates highly with a preexisting instrument that measures the same construct of interest. For example, a newly developed scale to measure clinical depression could be compared with an already-existing scale that measured depression. If the scores from the two scales correlated, then there exists known-instruments validity.

To the extent that this new depression measure can distinguish between groups of people that one would expect to be clinically depressed from those that one would not expect to be depressed, known-groups validity is established; that is, a scale's ability to distinguish between groups of people who possess the construct being measured from those who do not demonstrates known-groups validity for that scale.

Predictive validity is based on a future, after-the-fact criterion and is necessary if a measure will be involved in specialized selection or classification (Kaplan & Succuzzo, 2009). For instance, college entrance exams are assumed to have a certain degree of predictive validity. To establish predictive validity, the scores on the measures are compared with a person's later college grade point average or other performance criteria.

High correlations between scores on the measure and subsequent behavior indicate that the measures have good predictive validity.

## Construct Validity

Construct validity ensures that we are measuring the client behaviors under assessment. This type of validity is concerned with the degree of measurement of a theoretical construct or trait (Kaplan & Succuzzo, 2009; Rubin & Babbie, 2010). A construct is a concept that has been invented for the purpose of inquiry. It is a variable that can be studied or measured and is believed to be important to the development of theories. Constructs derive from theories and are developed to explain and organize observed responses. Many measures are developed to assess various constructs. A measure that demonstrates construct validity is well developed and may be confidently used in practice situations as an indicator of the client characteristics under consideration.

## Factorial Analysis

The purposes of factorial analysis are to examine the interrelationships of behavioral data such as scale items, to group items, and to make it possible to identify the underlying dimension or trait for a set of items (Kaplan & Succuzzo, 2009). Simply stated, data can be simplified by reducing the number of items from many to the most relevant ones that best capture the construct of interest.

To illustrate, the Adolescent Concerns Evaluation (ACE; Springer, 1998) will be used. The ACE is a forty-item instrument that measures the degree to which a youth is at risk of running away from home. It consists of four separate but interdependent domains: family, school, peer, and individual. The family domain includes twelve items, each of which clusters (correlates) more strongly with the family domain than with the other domains; that is, together they create a domain of items that captures how an adolescent perceives his or her family life. In contrast, suppose items that were intended to measure school functioning loaded more strongly on the peer domain; this would call into question the factorial structure of both the school and the peer domains. However, for the ACE, the family domain (twelve items), school domain (nine items), peer domain (seven items), and individual domain (twelve items) load on to (correlate with) the domain for which they were intended. Thus, there is evidence for the factorial validity of the ACE. In addition, because the items load onto the factors for which they were intended, there is also support for the ACE's content and construct validity.

A detailed description of factorial analysis and its uses in measurement construction are beyond the scope of this chapter. For a more detailed exposition on this topic, see additional resources (e.g., Abell et al., 2009; Kaplan & Succuzzo, 2009; Springer, Abell, & Hudson, 2002; Springer, Abell, & Nugent, 2002).

## INCREMENTAL VALIDITY

Incremental validity is a method of comparing standardized measures to determine whether data from one assessment instrument better predicts a criterion beyond what can be accomplished with other assessment efforts or instruments (Hunsley & Mash, 2003, 2007). The practical relevance of incremental validity for practice, in general, is to offer additional information (e.g. whether use of assessment procedure leads to better assessment and/or treatment outcomes) that helps practitioners decide among the large number of assessment instruments that are often available for the same purpose and population. According to Hunsley and Mash (2007), there are several questions related to incremental validity that play an essential role in guding evidence-based assessment and the development of EBA protocols. These questions ask whether it is worth it in terms of time and money to use a standardized measure, to obtain data on the same target using multiple methods, to collect parallel information from multiple informants, and to bother collecting assessment data beyond information related to diagnostic status, as most evidence-based interventions are targeted at a diagnosis.

When research has sufficiently answered all these questions, the sum of this information should provide a protocol for the most effective and clinically useful assessment procedures with certain problems and populations. Unfortunately, there has been little effort to date to establish incremental validity for most standardized assessment measures, although there are some indications that such research is increasing and becoming more relevant in providing the necessary information to guide clinical assessment decisions (Hunsley & Mash, 2007). It is likely that incremental validity will eventually become the gold standard of validity as the EBA movement grows and practitioners and researchers become more invested in identifying effective assessment protocols or processes for working with disparate populations.

### Validity Standards

A rule that has been proposed to interpret validity coefficients is to consider coefficients in the range of 0.40 to 0.60 as acceptable (see Downie & Heath, 1974). However, Springer, Abell, and Nugent (2002) caution against using a strict criterion to interpret validity coefficients. Validity coefficients for one scale must be viewed in the context of similar validity coefficients for other measures that measure the same construct and are intended for similar uses (e.g., clinical decision making with clients, research studies).

## NORMS, SCORING, AND INTERPRETATION OF MEASURES

Understanding normative measurement and its related scoring systems will help social work practitioners develop further competence in using measures. Norms provide information on the typical or average performance of a particular group of clients. They are needed because the raw scores of a measure do not reveal anything about what the client's score means. Norms are developed by administering the measure to a large, representative sample of clients with known characteristics. It is then possible to calculate the mean (average score) and standard deviation (deviation from the mean) for the sample. This allows the practitioner to compare the client with the norm group, and so aids in understanding what other similar individual client scores may mean.

To give further meaning to raw scores, they are statistically converted into derived, or standard, scores and compared with the normatization group (standardization sample). Standard scores are evenly distributed along the normal curve (see figure 3.1) and make it possible to determine the client's standing in relation to the norm group. It is therefore possible to determine whether the client is scoring in the average range. Standard scores make measurements possible across clients and even across measures (Warner, 2008). Some of the derived and standard scoring systems used in normative measurement include cutting points, z-scores, t-scores, percentile ranks, and stanines (Kaplan & Succuzzo, 2009).

Cutting points indicate when a client has moved from the normal to the critical range of performance on a measure. For example, on the Index of Self-Esteem (ISE), a measure introduced in chapter 2 and developed as part of the Clinical Measurement Package (Hudson, 1982), the cutting point is 30 (+5). This indicates that a client score of 30 or higher on this measure may indicate clinically significant problems in the area of self-esteem. Percentile ranks are based on derived scores that indicate a client's position relative to the standardization sample. They present the relative standing of a client in a given distribution. A percentile rank is the point in the distribution at or below which a percentage of the normalization group falls in comparison to the client.

Z-scores are derived scores that translate into standard scores. A z-score is a standard score with a mean of 0 and a standard deviation of 1. Frequently, z-scores are transformed into other standard score systems to eliminate the plus and minus signs. T-scores have a mean (average score) of 50 with a standard deviation of 10. According to the properties

**Figure 3.1**    Standard Scores

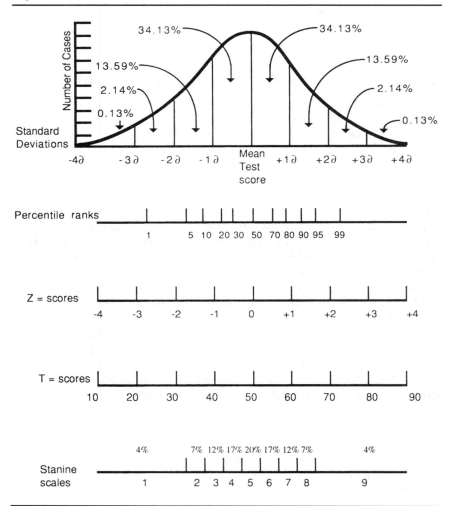

SOURCE: Adapted from Sattler (1988).

of the normal curve, two standard deviations above or below the mean is considered to deviate outside the normal range of functioning. Those clients scoring 70 or above or 30 or below deviate into the critical range. *T*-scores are popular standard scores used to interpret many psychological and clinical assessment measures. For example, the Minnesota Multiphasic Personality Inventory (MMPI; Hathaway & McKinley, 1943) is interpreted on the basis of *t*-scores. Stanines have a mean of 5 and a standard deviation of 2.

Several psychological and clinical measures are scored and interpreted using standard scoring systems based on properties of the normal curve. For example, the popular Wechsler Intelligence Scales (Wechsler Adult Intelligence Scale—Revised [WAIS-R] and Wechsler Intelligence Scale for Children—Revised [WISC IV]) are interpreted with a standard scoring system with a mean of 100 and a standard deviation of 15. The Stanford-Binet Intelligence Test is interpreted similarly with a mean of 100 and a standard deviation of 16. Figure 3.1 illustrates several standard scoring systems discussed in relationship to the properties of the normal curve.

Norms are essential to standardized measurement and the development of measurement tools and should be considered in relationship to the characteristics of your particular client. Sattler (2001) provides the following three guidelines for evaluating the norms of a measure:

1. *Representativeness:* Norms are useful only if they share the characteristics of the client. For example, if minorities of color are being assessed using a particular measurement instrument that included no minorities in its normative sample, the available norms are not appropriate for comparison with your client.

2. *Size:* The larger and more representative the norm group, the better. As a general rule, at least one hundred of your clients should be included in a norm group before it is appropriate to use the norms for comparison.

3. *Relevance:* It is important to determine how relevant a particular norm group is to your client. Because many standardized measures have several different norm samples grouped by client characteristics (e.g., age), it becomes important to choose the norm group that best characterizes your client.

## ASSESSMENT OF TREATMENT OUTCOME AND RAPID ASSESSMENT INSTRUMENTS

The fourth step of the EBP process requires that evidence-based practitioners monitor the effectiveness of the implemented practice decision, and this step of the process is consistent with much of what has been emphasized in the practice literature regarding the ongoing nature of assessment throughout the treatment process. Despite the fact that the evidence-based practitioner will select the intervention supported by the best-available evidence with the best fit for the client, it is impossible to be certain that the individual client will benefit from the intervention. There are several reasons a certain intervention may not work for a client—the practitioner may not deliver the intervention with the same fidelity or level of skill as those in the original research study; the client may differ from those in the research study in significant ways; and even if the client is similar to those in the research study, the client may be more like participants in the experimental group that did not benefit from the intervention. For this reason, it is essential that evidence-based practitioners engage in an ongoing assessment process of the client's functioning and response to treatment. This type of assessment is usually accomplished using a single-case design, in which the practitioner monitors an indicator of change over time, often daily or weekly, to determine whether there is improvement in targeted symptoms. Description of such designs is beyond the scope of this chapter, but additional reading on feasible ways to implement such designs within the context of evidence-based practice is found in Rubin (2008).

Although monitoring treatment outcome does not always necessitate the use of standardized instruments (often the frequency of behaviors, thoughts, and so on, may be more appropriate), there are several rapid assessment instruments (RAIs) that may be beneficial to use in a weekly and/or pretest-posttest manner. Key considerations in selecting a standardized instrument to monitor treatment outcome, in addition to the issues of psychometric adequacy listed earlier, include the following:

- The length and the amount of time required to complete the instrument. The treatment monitoring process should not place an undue burden on the client, and the client should ideally consider it a useful and exciting opportunity to become more engaged in the treatment process.

- The sensitivity of the measure to change. It is essential that the standardized instrument be able to pick up small changes that may be clinically important over the duration of treatment. If there is little change on a measure over time and the sensitivity of the measure is unknown, then it is difficult to know whether the problem of concern is truly not changing or whether the lack of change is an artifact of an insensitive measure. The sensitivity to change is often reported as the average effect size (or magnitude of change) from pretest to posttest that has been achieved in efficacy or effectiveness studies (Burlingame et al., 2005). For this reason, the effect size also provides a baseline with which to benchmark expectations for client gains based on a particular RAI.

Burlingame et al. (2005) offer a framework for selecting the most useful outcome assessment instruments in an agency. Although the focus of their article is primarily on the selection of instruments for inpatient clients with severe and persistent mental illness, the overall model appears useful for reducing the myriad standardized scales that are often available to those that are most suitable and useful for an identified client population. This model proposes five steps:

1. Identify the patient population targeted for outcome assessment.

2. Identify relevant outcome measures by tabulating those used in randomized clinical trials and effectiveness studies treating the targeted client population (and those summaries of such instruments available at the Web sites listed at the end of this chapter).

3. Identify a finite and manageable number of selection criteria focused on restrictions of the setting (e.g., resources), accuracy of the decision to be made, and target patient population.

4. Evaluate each outcome measure by using standards that match available resources.

5. Select one or more outcome measures.

## COMPUTER-ASSISTED ASSESSMENT TECHNOLOGIES

Research evidence from empirical studies demonstrates the lack of reliability and validity of practitioner-based assessments (Garb, 2000; Grove et al., 2000; Mash & Hunsley, 2005). Grove et al.'s (2000) meta-analysis of 162 studies on computers and prediction confirmed that computers perform well in making clinical judgments and setting tasks, and they usually outperform clinicians who perform such tasks. Computers still need to improve in the areas of developing well-validated algorithms for making diagnosis and treatment decisions (Wood, Garb, Lilienfeld, & Nezworski, 2002).

Studies have repeatedly shown, however, that computers perform just as well as or better than clinicians. The reasons for this are complex. First, practitioners lack the time and resources to check the reliability and validity of assessment information, to analyze the important variables, and to project their possible outcomes. Practitioners have to base their decisions on the information available at a given time, usually during the first or second contact with a client. Second, lack of standardization in the assessment process leads to inconsistencies in the data gathered and the conclusions drawn. Absence of standardized criteria for making assessment decisions prohibits setting priorities for treatment and development of normative data that may facilitate effectiveness in long-range treatment planning. In addition, a lack of criteria for organizing the existing data and making judgments about the available information makes it difficult for practitioners to accurately discriminate the critical from the less critical variables in making treatment decisions. The best practice wisdom must be relied on. Third, lack of knowledge concerning community resources, availability of those resources, and the criteria for admission into those programs interferes with appropriate treatment decisions and long-term planning.

With the advent of computer technology, a variety of computer-assisted assessment procedures and measurement instruments have been developed. The cost-effectiveness and speed of personal computers makes this technology readily available and useful to practitioners. Several psychological and clinical measures are available in software that may be purchased from its respective publishers and marketers. Some software examples are the Minnesota Multiphasic Personality Inventory (MMPI), a personality assessment measure that released its third and psychometrically improved version, the MMPI-2-RF, in July 2008; the Millon Clinical Multiaxial Inventory (MCMI, MCMI II, and the more recent MCMI III; Millon, 1977, 1982, 1994); personality assessment measures; and the Child Behavior Checklist, a behavioral assessment measure for children (Achenbach & Edelbrock, 1983).

These measures are administered, scored, and interpreted on the computer. Computer scoring and interpretation technologies produce client profiles based on the norms of the measure, narrative statements about client characteristics, and alternatives for treatment (for an example of a computer-generated profile, see figure 3.2; for an example of a computer-generated narrative from the MCMI, see appendix 3A).

The MCMI is a clinical personality assessment measure that parallels the *DSM*. The profile and narrative in the example are from the marital and family practice of one of the authors. The presenting problem of the assessed female client used in the example was marital distress. The client had also experienced a severe career setback and some interpersonal difficulties on her job. She sought treatment at the insistence of her husband. As the example illustrates, computer-generated assessments can provide comprehensive information concerning client characteristics and recommendations for treatment. One caveat of these measurement computer-generated profiles, however, is that the reports tend to be canned, and little attention has been given over the past decade to examining the validity and reliability of the computer-generated scoring algorithms and accompanying narrative reports for popular measures like the MMPI II and MCMI II personality assessment measures. Butcher, Perry, and Atlis (2000) reviewed the literature and found only four validity studies on the popular personality measures, and two of the studies showed negative findings. Fortunately, however, there are good computer algorithms for predicting violence, child abuse and neglect, and recidivism among juvenile offenders.

In addition to software, many test publishers provide computerized scoring services for measures they market. These measures are administered in the practitioners' office and mailed to the publisher for scoring, which takes a week or less. The cost varies according to the measure and quantity given. Some examples of measures for which computerized scoring is available are the McMaster Family Assessment Device, a measure

**Figure 3.2** Computer-Generated Profile

| Scales | Raw BR | | Profile of T Score 35 60 75 85 100 | DSM (Millon) Parallels |
|--------|-----|-----|-------------------------------------|-----------------------|
| 1 | 5 | 12 | | Schizoid (Asocial) |
| 2 | 3 | 15 | | Avoidant |
| 3 | 12 | 46 | | Dependent (Submis) |
| 4 | 18 | 82 | | Histrionic (Gregar) |
| 5 | 25 | 76 | | Narcissistic |
| 6 | 19 | 75 | | Antisocial (Aggressive) |
| 7 | 30 | 72 | | Compulsive (Confor) |
| 8 | 7 | 35 | | P. Aggressive (Negat) |
| S | 2 | 23 | | Schizotypal (Schiz) |
| C | 7 | 66 | | Borderline (Cycl) |
| P | 13 | 75 | | Paranoid |
| A | 9 | 87 | | Anxiety |
| H | 8 | 72 | | Somatoform |
| N | 18 | 58 | | Hypomania |
| D | 7 | 71 | | Dysthymia |
| B | 10 | 62 | | Alcohol Abuse |
| T | 19 | 71 | | Drug Abuse |
| SS | 5 | 55 | | Psychotic Thinking |
| CC | 4 | 49 | | Psychotic Depression |
| PP | 7 | 65 | | Psychotic Delusion |

NOTE: "BR" stands for base rate. The left-hand column beneath BR is the raw score; the right-hand column beneath BR is the T-score.

SOURCE: NCS Assessments, P.O. Box 1416, Minneapolis, MN 55440.

of family functioning (Epstein, Baldwin, & Bishop, 1982); the Hilson Adolescent Profile, a behavioral assessment measure for adolescents (Inwald, Brobst, & Morrissey, 1987); and the Couple's Pre-Counseling Inventory, a behavioral marital assessment measure (Stuart, 1987).

The trend in clinical assessment is to use such computer-assisted assessment technologies. These software programs are broader and more inclusive of intake and clinical assessment procedures than those described previously. For example, Walter Hudson has developed the Computer Assisted Social Services System (CASS), which includes a comprehensive assessment system for clients: social history forms, clinical questionnaires, mental status testing, unidimensional and multidimensional standardized measures, and more (Hudson, 1999; Nurius & Hudson, 1993). This program runs on a personal computer. The program administers measures to the client and scores them; most of the twenty-two scales in the CASS are scored in the same way and have the same clinical cutting score of 30. In addition, this program also graphs measurements taken on clients at different times and is compatible with single-subject design methodology (see chapter 11).

## Use of Computerized Databases in Assessment

The development of computerized technologies has moved practice agencies to link assessment activities with computerized database systems. A database system is a computerized information system that stores, organizes, and retrieves client information and the related information necessary for administrative office management. Such technologies help standardize assessment methods and improve program evaluation in practice agencies.

Databases are used to manage client information, produce agency reports, and evaluate programs. The database, for example, makes it possible to produce client profiles, lists of the services provided to clients, and information on the effectiveness of these services. The latter assessment becomes particularly important to database technologies because assessment measures are used to identify the problems of clients and to track their progress clients during and after interventions. This tracking allows practitioners, agency administrators, and program funders to see tangible evidence of the impact of their services on clients (the use of assessment measures to evaluate the progress of clients in treatment is explained in more detail in chapter 11).

Computerized database systems may further be used to develop standardized and more effective assessment systems that aid the treatment decisions of practitioners. Such assessment systems, for example, have been used to improve assessments in the field of children's services.

## Expert Systems and Computer-Assisted Statistical Decision Models

Computer-assisted assessment models and database systems have been suggested as methods to address the foregoing issues and to provide support to practitioners as they make treatment decisions (Baird & Wagner,

2000; Berger, 2006; Butcher, Perry, & Hahn, 2004; Sarrazin, Hall, Richards, & Carswell, 2002). Some studies have demonstrated the superiority of the computer over practitioners in making assessment and treatment decisions (for a fairly recent review, see Wood et al., 2002). The sum of these studies indicated that computers usually outperform practitioners by about 10 percent. It has been demonstrated, for example, that the use of computer-based clinical assessment does not compromise the validity of responses among clients receiving substance abuse treatment, even when pending legal issues exist (Sarrazin et al., 2002).

Expert systems and statistical decision models have been discussed for more than fifty years as important methods for improving assessment and treatment decisions, and the literature has also suggested the advantages of integrating these approaches (Berger, 2006; Butcher, Perry, & Hahn, 2004; Epstein & Klinkenberg, 2001). Most recent reviews of the use of such technology suggest three main areas of application that are becoming more common: computer-assisted interviewing (CAI), computer-assisted technology (CAT), and Internet surveys (Epstein & Klinkenberg, 2001). With Internet surveys, an organization's computer administers data collection through a Web site (online). These kinds of services are generally available on a pay-by-test basis as opposed to the purchasing of an entire software program. With the expansion of broadband computer networks and increased interest in increasing the availability of psychological assessment instruments online, this may become a more common way to purchase and administer clinical statistical decision models (Berger, 2006; Butcher et al., 2004). However, before such services become available online, Butcher et al. (2004) suggest that the following issues need to be further addressed: equivalence between response sets of the Internet-administered tests and tests administered in a standard format; assurance that test norms are appropriate for an Internet application though the collection of Internet-administered samples; and proper test security to prevent use by nonqualified persons or professionals, to protect sensitive information, and to prevent copyright infringement.

Recent work in the area of quality assurance and in child welfare settings demonstrates that statistical decision models may be combined with standardized measures to greatly improve treatment (Baird & Wagner, 2000; Wood et al., 2002).

## Computerized Quality Assurance Measures

Quality assurance measures are computerized and offer ongoing reports to the practitioner about the clinical outcomes of their clients. A special journal issue edited by Lambert (2001) discussed various quality assurance measures and reviewed the strengths and weaknesses of many of the well-known measurement systems (see Barkham et al., 2001; Beutler, 2001; Kordy, Hannover, & Richard, 2001). These measurement systems are being used in the United States and Europe to study the effectiveness of psychotherapy and as alternatives to group-oriented, outcome studies on psychotherapy effectiveness (e.g., efficacy and effectiveness studies). Quality assurance systems use individual client data to provide feedback to clinicians on the therapy outcomes. They combine many of the methods previously discussed in this chapter, such as computer algorithms, used with standardized measures and actuarial and statistical decision methods to evaluate the outcomes of individual clients. Sophisticated statistical procedures are used to make decisions about client data, such as probit analysis, survival analysis, and hierarchical linear modeling. These methods help researchers determine the progress and lack of progress of clients in treatment programs (Lambert, Hansen, & Finch, 2001). Similar to single-case designs, these procedures focus on individual clients, and clinicians can use them in practice to evaluate the effectiveness of their practices. These client- or patient-focused measurement systems answer questions that are of interest to practitioners, such as, Is my client getting better? Is it time to stop treatment? Should I refer this client to someone else? (Lambert et al., 2001).

Quality assurance systems improve practice by using norms and standardized measures to define clinically significant change and the need for further treatment, and they can feed this information back to clinicians. Table 3.1 offers a comparative review of several measures (for more information on the computerized quality assurance measures and a review of the Outcomes Questionnaire, 45.2, see chapter 7).

## LIMITATIONS IN STANDARDIZED ASSESSMENT MEASURES

Standardized assessment measures have many strengths: they are quick and efficient to use, they are easy to score and interpret, and they provide sources of data other than can be gained in a client interview in that they measure or screen for specific client problems or characteristics. Yet these measures do have some practical weaknesses other than possible limitations in their psychometric properties (e.g., validity, reliability, normalization). Five such limitations follow.

First, standardized assessment measures are subject to demand characteristics or social desirability. Clients may answer the questions on the measure to cast themselves in a favorable or unfavorable light. Clients may seek to please the social worker or give incorrect information on purpose. Some measures include lie scales or faking good scales to try to correct for this limitation. A lie scale is a set of items that tests for false responses on the measure. The Personal Experience Screen Questionnaire, which assesses substance abuse in adolescents, has such a subscale, for example (Winters, 1988).

**Table 3.1**   A Comparison of Five Computerized Quality Assurance Systems and Their Measures

| Dimensions | Stuttgart-Heidelberg System | OQ-45 | CORE-OM | COMPASS | Systematic Treatment Selection |
|---|---|---|---|---|---|
| Source of Information | Clinician and patient | Patient only | Patient only | Patient and four clinician questions | Clinician and patient |
| Length | Very long | Very short | Very short and Variable | Moderate | Variable |
| Flexibility of Questions | Very flexible | Nonflexible | Flexible | Nonflexible | Very flexible |
| Breadth | In-patient & out-patient | Out-patient | Out-patient | Out-patient | In-patient & Out-patient |
| Projected Response | Yes | Yes | No | Yes | Yes |
| Feedback | Graphic and narrative | Graphic and color codes | Graphic | Graphic | Graphic and narrative |
| Clinical Range | Yes | Yes | Yes | Yes (modified) | Yes |
| Signal Risk | Yes | Yes | Yes | Yes | Yes |
| Development and Availability | Center for Psychotherapy Research, Governmental agencies in Germany kordy@psyres-stuttgart.de | Brigham Young University, For fee, American Professional Credentialing Services www.oqfamily.com | Psychological Therapies Research Center, Leeds University, Public domain, United Kingdom m.barkham@leeds.ac.uk | Northwestern University, For Fee, lueger@Marquette.edu | Center for Behavioral Health Care Technologies STS4outcomes@aol.com |

SOURCE: Adapted from Beutler, L. (2001).

Second, measures present a narrow band of information; they are not able to assess the whole client picture. Some have criticized standardized assessment methods for being unable to assess dynamic interactions or the systems complexities of the real world of clients (Tzuriel, 2001). These critics assert that the measures have limited usefulness because they treat characteristics of clients as if they were static instead of forever changing in response to environmental contingencies. To these practitioners, the psychometric properties of the measures limit their usefulness. Many social workers who take this position object to trying to quantify client behavior. They believe that broader, qualitative methods are more useful for understanding the complexities of client behavior (qualitative assessment methods are covered in chapter 4). The argument that standardized measures cannot capture the complexities and dynamic, fluctuating interactions of client and environment appears to be true; such characteristics are beyond these measures' scope and current level of development.

Third, standardized measures have been criticized for focusing on client problems instead of strengths. In this regard, standardized methods are believed to pathologize clients without pointing to their unique motivation and capacities. Some assessment measures, however, have begun to include scales on coping abilities or problem solving. For example, the MMPI, the popular personality assessment measure, has an ego strengths subscale, and some family measures look at family strengths as well as problems. The Behavioral and Emotional Rating Scale, Second Edition (BERS-2, Epstein, 2004) is a notable exception. The BERS-2 is a strength-based battery of three instruments that measures functioning in youth across five different areas: interpersonal strength, family involvement, intrapersonal strength, school functioning, and affective strength. A key feature that distinguishes the BERS-2 from many other standardized tools is that it is truly based on a strengths perspective; the wording of the items reflects this perspective. The Teacher Rating Scale (TRS), summarized in box 3.1, has fifty-two items and is one of the three measures in the BERS-2 package. Some sample items are as follows:

- Maintains positive family relationships
- Accepts responsibility for own actions
- Pays attention in class
- Identifies own feelings

Fourth, standardized assessment measures have been criticized for their inability to directly link client problems to their interventions; that is, the measures do not prescribe a useful treatment plan, which is the main purpose of assessment (chapter 11 illustrates how to make decisions about treatment plans, based on assessments). Developing a treatment plan involves practitioners using their own cognitive abilities to map out

**BOX 3.1**
**Evaluation of the TRS**

**Name of measure:** Teacher Rating Scale (one of three batteries from the BERS-2)

**Authors:** Michael H. Epstein

**Purchase availability:** Pro-Ed, International Publisher, 8700 Shoal Creek Blvd., Austin, Texas 78757

**Availability of manual:** The manual is available from Pro-Ed and summarizes the following: description of the TRS, scoring and interpretation, reliability and validity, and its normatization.

**Cost:** $34.00 for TRS (includes examiner's manual and 25 summary/response forms).

**Time for administration:** approximately ten minutes.

**Ease of use:** The TRS contains 52 strength-based items. It is designed for use by teachers with knowledge of the child. Scoring is easy and guidelines are provided to assist in interpreting results.

**Clarity of directions:** Directions are brief and easy to understand.

**Scoring procedures:** Each of the five subscales produces a total raw score. These raw scores can then be converted into percentile ranks and to standard scores.

**Level of training needed:** Little training is needed for use.

**Purpose of the measure:** The instrument was developed to measure the personal strengths of children and adolescents ages 5 to 18 years. It measures functioning in five areas: interpersonal strength, family involvement, intrapersonal strength, school functioning, and affective strength. It also provides a cumulative strength quotient.

**Theoretical orientation:** Based on a strength perspective, which is reflected in the wording of the items.

**Standardization and appropriateness of norms:** Norms are based on a nationally representative sample. Two sets of normative data are provided. One is based on children not identified with emotional or behavioral disorders (NEBD sample, $N$ = 2,176) and one on children diagnosed with emotional or behavioral disorders (EBD sample, $N$ = 861). Standard score for the NEBD sample = 17. Standard score for the EBD sample = 20.

**Evidence for validity:** There is solid evidence for content validity. Criterion-related validity and construct validity: Known-instruments validity: When compared with several other measures of children's emotional and behavioral disorders (The Walker-McConnell Scale of Social Competence and School Adjustment-Adolescent Version; Self-Perception Profile for Children; and Achenbach's Teacher Report Form), the TRS had resultant coefficients large enough and in the direction hypothesized to demonstrate known-instruments validity. Mean standard scores and the ability of TRS to significantly discriminate between children with and without emotional and behavioral disorders demonstrate the known-groups validity of the TRS. Factorial validity is demonstrated as items load onto their respective domains.

**Evidence for reliability:** The TRS evidences a high degree of reliability. Coefficient alphas for the EBD sample on each domain are as follows: interpersonal strength (.92); family involvement (.89); intrapersonal strength (.85); school functioning (.85); affective strength (.84); overall strength quotient (.97). Coefficient alphas for the NEBD sample are even higher on average. Interrater reliability coefficients for each domain range from .83 to .96, with an interrater reliability coefficient of .98 for the overall strength quotient. The TRS possesses little test error as evidenced by low SEM values ranging from 0.8 to 2.6.

**Evidence for clinical utility:** The TRS is available at a reasonable cost and is easy to administer and score. It is able to distinguish between children and adolescents with and without emotional and behavioral disorders. The strength-based wording of the items makes it appealing to both parents and practitioners.

SOURCE: Review of TRS adapted from Epstein (2004).

a set of tasks to undertake with the client. As standardized assessment measures have been combined with computerized assessment technologies, however, these technologies have begun to produce narrative client reports that do make recommendations for treatment (for examples of a narrative report, see figure 3.2 and appendix 3A). Even so, they are still unable to present a complete treatment plan that is relevant to the client's unique experiences and environmental contingencies. The capabilities of standardized measures to help clinicians produce meaningful treatment plans is increasing with the use of the quality assurance measures and patient-focused measurement systems, as discussed earlier.

Fifth, standardized measures are subject to false positives and false negatives like any other standardized assessment procedure. For example, false positives and negatives are often found in tests used in medical practice. It may be necessary to give the test again to verify the results. Errors in the administration of the test, errors in the scoring and interpretation of the test, and measurement error inherent in the psychometric properties of the test can cause a false positive or negative. Researchers have focused on reducing and accounting for measurement error in a standardized assessment measure. In the next section, we discuss in detail measurement error and its implications for interpreting and reporting results on standardized assessment measures.

## MEASUREMENT ERROR

Unfortunately, there is no measurement instrument that can provide a perfect assessment of client characteristics. All measures, even computerized ones, are susceptible to certain errors that reduce their validity and reliability.

Reliability can be conceptualized as having two hypothetical components: a true score and an error score. Each person's observed score, O, contains both a true score, T, and a random error score, E. The following equation depicts this relationship (Nunnally & Bernstein, 1994):

$$O = T + E.$$

These random errors prevent us from knowing the "true" client score for characteristics that a measure assesses. Errors of measurement are always present—we never have perfect conditions. Another way to conceptualize this relationship is that a true score is that which reflects what the client is actually experiencing, and an error score is the gap between that actual experience and what is observed.

In this section, we discuss types of measurement error, common sources of error, and how to account for measurement error. Although it is impossible to know the client's true score on a measure, it is possible to know approximately how close we might be to the true score (Jordan et al., 2005).

## Types of Errors

Two major types of errors occur in measurement, systematic and random. Systematic error results in the measurements becoming biased in a singular or consistent direction. For example, the scores either become consistently higher or lower, and the error is essentially the same for each client.

A common cause of this type of error is clients' attempts to produce desirable answers on the measure. Clients often try to guess what the measure is developed to assess and choose answers that they think will show themselves in a more favorable light. This tendency of clients has been labeled "social desirability" (Crowne & Marlowe, 1964); clients consistently change their scores on the measure in a favorable direction. Social workers may also contribute to this type of error by using measures that cue clients about the construct and about the favorable direction of a measure. Social workers may also make erroneous judgments in observing behavior or interpreting a measure that makes the outcome correspond to their personal desires. For example, a social worker might provide a biased rating because of a desire to see improvement in the client.

Systematic error can be reduced by selecting measurement instruments that guard against social desirability; such measures have usually been well standardized. A technique to reduce error is to reverse items so that some items are worded in the positive direction and others are worded in the negative direction to guard against response set (i.e., a client answering all the items in the same direction). Some measures have actually been correlated with social desirability scales to evaluate their resistance to this construct. An example of such a measure is the Coopersmith Self-Esteem Inventory (Coopersmith, 1986), a standardized measure of self-esteem. In its development, this measure was administered along with a social desirability scale. The two measures were correlated to test the inventory's ability to measure the construct of self-esteem instead of social desirability. Other measures incorporate validity scales (items developed to detect lying or faking on the measure). Several standardized personality and behavioral measures have validity scales (e.g., the MMPI, the Hilson Adolescent Profile).

Social workers can further reduce systematic error by using standardized quality measures. An example of such measures developed by a social worker is the Hudson Clinical Measurement Package (Hudson, 1982). Through supervision of their observations and work, social workers can also reduce errors that originate from their own systematic biases.

Random error results in measurements becoming biased in a nonsystematic, fluctuating way. Some clients may score lower on the measure than their accurate score, whereas other clients score higher. The scores fall to either side of the range of the accurate score but in no predictable pattern. Random error may occur at any point of the measurement.

There are four common sources of error (Blythe & Tripodi, 1989; Guy et al., 1987). First, client characteristics like mood, reactions, and behavior may fluctuate day to day or even hour to hour. This sometimes makes it difficult to obtain a stable baseline measure of the client characteristics. Second, deficits in the measurement instrument always serve as the major contributor to error in any measurement situation. Measurements are essentially as accurate and reliable as the measures used. Selecting appropriate measures becomes the first rule for reducing measurement error. Third, a measure may be administered improperly; this can greatly reduce even an excellent measure's accuracy. Some important factors to remember in proper administration of measures are to present the exact instructions suggested in the measurement manual and to double-check that you are giving the right measure to the right client—some measures have several different versions, and not all versions are appropriate for all clients. Being completely familiar with the measure is mandatory to administering it properly. To familiarize yourself with measures, you must study the manual or other relevant research and instructions. This requires devoting a great amount of time and commitment to the assessment situation. It may also be necessary to practice several times before giving the instructions and administering the measure to a client.

Finally, personal and situational factors are an additional source of measurement error. Personal results when clients read and respond to questions carelessly (Jordan et al., 2005). Errors may result when clients are tired, hungry, distressed, sick, or malingering. Such personal factors may greatly decrease measurement accuracy and contribute to measurement error. Being attentive to possible client distress can help reduce such errors. Environmental factors also may contribute to measurement error. It is important to provide an appropriate environment in which to administer the measure. Noise, uncomfortable room temperatures, and distractions increase measurement error. Comfortable, quiet, and nondistracting surroundings are essential to the measurement situation. It is also important not to expect the client to respond to measures for overly long periods. Overwhelming the client with too many measures at once unnecessarily stresses the client and increases measurement error. The amount of time a client can respond to a group of measures without becoming stressed varies from client to client. As a general rule, however, extending assessment for longer than one to two hours is not recommended in most cases. Shorter periods are recommended when working with children or adolescents. Measurement error is an inevitable part of measuring client characteristics. In the next section, we discuss a way to systematically account for measurement error.

Measurement error is an inevitable part of the measurement process. Social work practitioners should do everything they can to reduce the sources of error. Thus far, we have been discussing technical considerations in measurement. The next section focuses on clinical and ethical uses of measures.

## ETHICAL USE OF STANDARDIZED MEASURES: ATTENDING TO CULTURE AND DIVERSITY

The assessment of and sensitivity to diversity issues in the assessment process is of central importance to evidence-based assessment and practice. Diversity issues encompass age, gender, race, ethnicity, culture, disability, sexual orientation, language, socioeconomic status, and any other unique characteristic that may bear on accurate assessment, appropriate choice of intervention, and sensitivity to differences during the treatment process. Of particular importance is attention to ethnic and cultural differences, as recent research has demonstrated that there is often both ethnic and cultural variability in symptom expression and the psychometric appropriateness of commonly used self-report measures (Achenbach & Edelbrock, 2003; Joneis, Turkheimer, & Oltmanns, 2000). Social workers have a long tradition of working with ethnically and culturally diverse client populations. Consistent with social work values and ethics, social workers should lead the way in ensuring that clinical assessments are not used to mislabel the attributes of ethnic minority clients. Standardized measurement instruments may be biased against certain ethnic and cultural groups. For example, Mercer (1979) has documented that African American children routinely scored ten points lower than European American children on the Weschler Intelligence Scale for Children, Revised (WISC IV). There appears to be cultural bias in the WISC IV and other normative-based standardized measures; they do not reflect the strengths of diverse populations. Mercer recommended applying a correction score to the WISC IV when administering it to African American children. Social workers should exercise cultural sensitivity in the selection and administration of measurement instruments and only administer measures that have been normed with those populations. In addition, social workers should be aware of any clinical caveats of a measure when applied to culturally diverse clients and make appropriate modifications, such as those described earlier.

Rubin (2008) provides some guidelines on what what to look for in determining whether a measurement instrument is culturally biased (if it was not originally normed with that specific population or culture). Basically, the researcher must make a case for measurement equivalence or a case that the standardized measure measures the same thing in terms of value and meaning with another culture as it did with the original culture or group with which it was normed. This is accomplished by demonstrating the following (Rubin, 2008):

*Linguistic equivalence:* This is important when a client speaks a different language from the one with which the original was constructed. It is essential that the questions are asked using the same or very similar wording so that there is no variation in what is being asked. To have confidence that the instruments are linguistically equivalent, the researcher should have worked with two bilingual persons, one of whom translated the instrument from the primary language to the new language and another who translated it back from the new language back to the primary language. If the back-translated version is similar to the original version, there is good evidence of linguistic equivalence.

*Conceptual equivalence:* This means that the questions, observed behaviors, or other components of the assessment mean the same thing across cultures. An example of an item that is likely not to have conceptual equivalence for many cultures is the use of the term *blue* from the Generalized Contentment Scale (GCS) to mean "sad." Conceptually, the statement "I feel blue" is likely to elicit much different responses from those in a culture that does not use this colloquialism.

*Psychometric equivalence:* This means that the scores are comparable across cultures and is most important in examining clinical cutoff scores (e.g., what score constitutes certain diagnoses, distress) and in comparing disparate cultures in research. Of course, an instrument cannot have psychometric equivalence if it is not first linguistically and conceptually equivalent.

When all these criteria are met, a practitioner can be more confident that the standardized measure is culturally valid and useful. Moreover, when culturally valid measures are integrated with a thorough cultural formulation of factors related to diagnosis, care, and client preferences (e.g, cultural identity, cultural beliefs regarding presenting problem and help seeking), then the assessment and treatment process is more congruent with the EBA model and culturally sensitive practice (Vergare, Binder, Cook, & Galanter, 2006; for additional information on using standardized measures with American minorities, see Chapter 10).

## ASSESSING COMORBIDITY

The assessment of comorbidity is a reality of clinical practice. It is quite common for people in real clinical settings to meet the diagnostic criteria for more than one disorder or to have symptoms across disorders (Kazdin, 2005). Recent research has shown that as many as 45 percent of people diagnosed with an anxiety, mood, impulse control, or substance abuse disorder also met criteria for one or two additonal diagnoses (Kessler, Chiu, Demler, & Walters, 2005). The assessment of comorbidity has been recognized as increasingly important, as research has shown that people with comorbid presentations are typically more severely impaired, have chronic mental health histories, and have more physical health problems (Bender, Springer, & Kim, 2006). Also, there is budding evidence that comorbidity may be at least partially linked to core pathological processes whose symptoms cut across disparate disorders (Krueger & Markon, 2006; Widiger & Clark, 2000).

To assess comorbidity, conceptualize the assessment process as having multiple, interdependent stages, with the initial stage addressing more general considerations such as a preliminary evaluation of symptoms and life context (Hunsely & Mash, 2007). To accomplish this, practitioners can use semistructured interviews (some are available for use with both adults and children), multidimensional screening tools and brief symptom checklists for disorders that are more frequently comorbid with the target disorder, and evaluation of common parameters or domains that cut across the comorbid conditions.

## CLINICAL UTILITY, COMPETENCY, AND APPROPRIATE USE

Earlier discussion in this chapter made clear that practitioners should choose standardized measures on the basis of their overall quality and purposes. In clinical practice, measures with excellent validity and reliability, sensitivity (when looking to assess over time), and appropriate norms should be selected. Beyond such technical considerations, the practitioner must also consider the clinical utility of the measure. Clinical utility refers to the practical advantages of using a measure to assess clients, to plan interventions, and to obtain accurate feedback (Fischer & Corcoran, 2007). For example, does the measure tap a clinically relevant problem? Is it easy to administer and score? Does it make sense in the particular practice situation? A measure may have excellent technical properties (e.g., validity, reliability) but be too lengthy to administer in a crisis clinic where clients need rapid assessments and immediate assistance—in such a situation, the measure does not have clinical utility.

Clinical utility also has to do with the degree to which using a measure in practice actually "makes a difference with respect to the accuracy, outcome, or efficiency of clincial actitvities" (Hunsley & Mash, 2007, p. 45). In other words, does using a particular standardized measure or protocol result in better assessment and treatment outcomes for clients? Research has shown that some of the most valid standardized measures may lack clinical utility. For example, a recent study by Lima et al. (2005) examined the clinical utility of the widely used MMPI-2 by randomly assigning patients who had been assessed with the MMPI-2 to a group of therapists who received feedback from the test results and a group of therapists who did not. The results of the study suggest that having the information from this measure did not add to the prediction of positive treatment outcome beyond what other measures in the setting would normally predict (a lack of incremental validity). For that reason, the authors concluded that the measure may not provide clincially useful information, although they suggested that replication of this study is necessary in other settings and with other populations before concluding that the measure truly lacks clinical utility. In contrast, the Outcome Questionnaire, 45 (OQ-45), which measures distress, interpersonal relations, and social functioning, has been shown to have excellent reliabilty, validity, and sensitivity (Vermeersch et al., 2004). In addition, the contribution of the OQ-45 to outcome has been assessed in a meta-analysis of three large scale studies in a similar manner as the MMPI-2 study mentioned previously, and the condition in which practitioners received the ongoing feedback from the OQ-45 over time ended up with 38 percent fewer clients deteriorating and 67 percent more clients improving, in comparison with the control condition that did not receive such feedback (Lambert et al., 2003). Although this provides good support for the clinical utility of the OQ-45, the measure remains clinically meaningful only if it taps into a clinically relevant problem for an individual client and is feasible to use.

For this reason, the practitioner should also weight the clinical benefits of the measure in relationship to its cost. In many instances, measures may prove cost effective and provide rapid and objective assessments of client attributes. This is especially true with the availability of computerized assessment and measurement technology. For example, we discussed earlier that statistical decision models and other computerized database systems are cost effective. The clinical benefits and utility of including standardized measures, however, should be considered in relationship to the needs of the client. Measurement should exist to serve the needs of the client. Does the standardized measure help assess and serve the client better? This should be the primary question all social work practitioners ask before including a measure in their assessment.

To determine the appropriateness, clinical utility, and benefits of a measurement instrument, the practitioner must carefully evaluate the instrument. The evaluation of the Teacher Rating Scale (TRS; Epstein, 2004) in box 3.1 serves as a form for evaluating measures for clinical practice.

Ethical considerations are relevant to the clinical utility of measures. For instance, social workers should use only measures that they are competent to administer. Social workers must be trained in the administration, scoring, and interpretation of the measures they use. This includes training in measurement theory and in evaluation of the quality of various measurement tools, as well as training in scoring and interpreting measures. This chapter has summarized several important issues related to measurement. However, social work practitioners may need additional training in the application of these concepts before they achieve competence in the administration of some measures.

Social workers receive training in measurement in their research courses, which cover issues such as validity, reliability, item development, and norms. In recent years, there has also been a trend toward training social workers to administer measures in their direct practice courses, in the context of using single-subject design methodology in practice settings (Fischer & Corcoran, 2007). The measurement training that most social workers receive is adequate for the administration of several measurement instruments. Unfortunately, some social workers receive only minimal training in tests and measurement, which precludes their use of many excellent assessment tools. Test publishers are unwilling to sell measurement instruments to unqualified users. Therefore, social workers who want to use such measures in practice may need to seek additional training. This training is indispensable to clinical practitioners who work in settings in which measures are often administered. Even if social workers do not administer measurement instruments themselves as a part of their assessments, it is important for them to understand tests and measurement so that they can evaluate other practitioners' work. In keeping with the current trends in clinical practice, social work programs undoubtedly need to provide additional training in measurement as a part of their assessment and practice courses.

A second ethical consideration concerns the responsible and appropriate use of measures. Measures should not be used as single indicators of client characteristics; rather, the use of multiple methods of assessment is recommended (Springer, Abell, & Nugent, 2002; Vergare, Binder, Cook, & Galanter, 2006). It is appropriate for social work practitioners to use measures along with other sources of assessment information. However, it is not appropriate to use a measurement instrument as a substitute for a clinical interview and other behavioral observations of the client; the practitioner should administer the instrument in conjunction with other clinical assessment techniques. Measures can facilitate good assessments, but they are not an end in themselves. They should be used cautiously, responsibly, and appropriately in service of the client.

A third ethical consideration is confidentiality. Social workers should assure clients of confidentiality of measurement scores in the same way that they hold other client information confidential. Social workers should be aware that scores on standardized measures may be used to negatively label clients (e.g., by other clinicans or school personnel). They may also be used politically or legally against clients who are involved with government agencies. In reporting measurement scores, practitioners should always consider other client information. In keeping with social work values, client strengths and resources should be focal to assessment reports.

In selecting standardized measures for use in practice, practitioners should consider the technical considerations of the measure. Equally important is the clinical utility of the measure and ethical considerations regarding its use.

## FINDING THE BEST STANDARDIZED MEASURE

In chapter 1, we talked about some general ways to located evidence-based assessment tools. In addition, a handful of Internet and published resources to support EBA are listed and described briefly here. Although many of the sources are well established, it is not uncommon for Web site addresses to change. If one of these sites has become outdated, try searching by the title of the site instead.

Some Web sites or sources provide access to general information to locate and or search for assessment instruments. For example, the APA FAQ/Finding Information about Psychological Tests Web site (www.apa .org/science/programs/testing/find-tests.aspx) provides general guidance on how to locate and stay abreast of most current published and unpublished psychological tests and measures. The Buros Institute of Mental Measurements (www.unl.edu/buros) provides a searchable database of a wide collection of standardized assessment measures. Information is provided on where to obtain the measure, but there is a fee to access the review of each measure's psychometric and clinical utility (Spies, Carlson, & Geisinger, n.d.). University libraries and sometimes public libraries provide free access. The site can be a useful first step to gain a sense of what measurement instruments are available for different assessment topics. The Tests or Measures in the Social Sciences Pages (http://libraries.uta.edu/helen/Test&Meas/testmainframe.htm) provides basic information on various measures but does not provide the actual instruments because of U.S. copyright laws. The local library or its interlibrary loan department may be useful in assisting in the location of hardcopies of potentially useful instruments from this site.

There are a variety of rapid assessment instruments or brief standardized assessment tools that can be used for assessment or monitoring practice outcomes on the Walmyr Publishing Scales Web site (www.walmyr .com/index.html). Information regarding the psychometric background of the available tests is provided, and links are available for viewing many of the scales. The Psychology Department at Muhlenberg College (www.muhlenberg.edu/depts/psychology/Measures.html) provides an eclectic collection of standardized measures informed by resources that psychology faculty and students have found. Several links are provided for viewing actual measures.

With regard to books, Fischer and Corcoran (2007) provide detailed information on more than four hundred rapid assessment instruments in *Measures for Clinical Practice: A Sourcebook*. Likewise, Maltby, Lewis, and Hill (2000) provide various psychological measures in *Commissioned Reviews of 250 Psychological Tests*.

The Alcohol and Drug Abuse Institute—Screening and Assessment Database (http://lib.adai.washington.edu/instruments/) is designed to help clinicians and researchers find instruments used for screening and assessment of substance use and substance use disorders. Some instruments are in the public domain and can be freely downloaded from the Web; others can be obtained from only the copyright holder. The site provides a searchable engine; a brief description of each scale and its intended use; a general description of its psychometric properties and supporting reference articles, cost, who it is normed on, and length of time required to administer the scale; and who to contact to obtain copies. The Health and Psychosocial Instruments (HaPI) Web site (www.ovid.com/site/catalog/DataBase/866.jsp) features information on unpublished information-gathering tools for clinicians that are discussed in journal articles, such as questionnaires, interview schedules, tests, checklists, rating and other scales, coding schemes, and projective techniques. The database contains several content categories—citations to actual test documents that copyright holders authorize Behavioral Measurement Database Services to share with the public, bibliographic citations to journal articles that contain information on specific test instruments, and a catalog of commercial test publishers and their available instruments. In addition to medical measurement instruments, HaPI presents tests used in medically related disciplines including psychology, social work, occupational therapy, physical therapy, and speech and hearing therapy.

Marianne Yoshioka (n.d.) developed the Psychological Measures for Asian-American Populations site (www.columbia.edu/cu/ssw/projects/pmap/) as a resource for practitioners and researchers working with Asian and Pacific Islander populations. The University of Miami College of Psychology (www.psy.miami.edu/faculty/ccarver/CCscales.html) provides several self-report scales for use in research and teaching applications, and some have been translated into Spanish. All are available without charge and without any need for permission.

The American Academy of Child and Adolescent Psychiatry (AACAP) (www.aacap.org/cs/root/member_information/practice_information/practice_parameters/practice_parameters) has published more than twenty-five practice parameters as official actions of the AACAP in *Journal of the American Academy of Child and Adolescent Psychiatry*. Summaries and full text parameters are available. The AACAP parameters are designed to assist clinicians in providing high-quality assessment and treatment that is consistent with the best-available scientific evidence and clinical consensus.

Finally, the National Center for PTSD—Department of Veteran Affairs (www.ptsd.va.gov/professional/pages/assessments/assessment.asp) provides information on many assessment instruments used to measure trauma exposure and posttraumatic stress disorder.

## MOVING FROM ASSESSMENT TO INTERVENTION: CASE EXAMPLES ON SELECTING STANDARDIZED MEASURES

### Case Study No. 1: Carlos

Carlos is a Hispanic fifteen-year-old who was recently arrested for grand theft auto and is awaiting a court hearing while being detained in juvenile hall. This is his eighth arrest in the past two years, and his prior charges include assault, petty theft, and cruelty to animals. According to his mental health records, he has a history of major depressive disorder, cannabis abuse, and conduct disorder, and he has taken psychotropic medication in the past while in juvenile detention to stabilize his mood and prevent suicide attemps (he attempted suicide the last time he was incarcerated). There is a need to conduct a current psychosocial assessment to establish both current symptomology and suicide risk, and to determine the level of mental health care necessary for Carlos while he is incarcerated.

Because Carlos is not able to use alcohol or drugs while in detention and a diagnosis of a mood disorder was made after Carlos had been detained in juvenile detention previously for five months (ruling out a substance-induced mood disorder), and because the diagnosis of conduct disorder is obviated given his prior arrest and juvenile justice history, the primary purpose for using a standardized assessment measure is to identify the current level of depression and, if possible, obtain additional information regarding suicide risk. The goals for identifying a standardized assessment instrument are the following: shows good psychometric properties; is brief, easy to score, and inexpensive; has been normed with the Hispanic adolescent male population; and provides a sense of the severity of depressive symptoms and need for additional evaluation and services. This information, coupled with a thorough suicide assessment and updated psychosocial assessment, should provide the necessary information for identifying the best intervention plan for Carlos and keeping him safe while he awaits his court date.

A search for brief assessment instruments that meet these qualifications was conducted to identify the best assessment instrument for Carlos and for future use in assessing depression among similar adolescents in the juvenile justice setting. The practitioner searched the following sites for information: the Mental Measurements Yearbook (accessed through public university Web sites or at the Web site of the Buros Institute) and the Fischer and Corcoran (2007) text noted previously (sample copies of the Generalized Conentment Scale (GCS) can be obtained at the Walmyr Web site), and was narrowed down to the following instruments:

- Reynolds Adolescent Depressive Scale, 2nd ed.
- Generalized Contentment Scale
- Beck Depression Inventory II

All these scales are relatively brief (requiring between five and ten minutes to self-administer) and have been normed on adolescent populations. They also have excellent psychometric qualitites or have been shown to constitute reliable and valid measures of depression. Of the three instruments, the Reynolds Adolescent Depressive Scale, 2nd ed., has been normed on the most ethnically and socioeconomically diverse adolescent population (including young men and young women), making this scale more applicable to both the larger juvenile justice population and individual use with Carlos. This scale has also been found to be useful for diagnosing depression and identifying the severity of adolescent depressive symptomology, as well as for monitoring the outcome of interventions over time. The drawback of the scale, however, in comparison with the other two scales, is that it is expensive—it may not be cost effective to purchase this scale for broad use in the juvenile justice mental health program.

Both the Beck Depression Inventory-II (BDI-II) and the Generalized Contentment Scale (GCS) were normed on primarily Caucasian populations, but both scale samples included adolescent males in their validation samples. The sample for the GCS appears to be more ethnically diverse, and this scale offers ease of administration and scoring, does not require training to administer, and is relatively inexpensive ($22.50 for fifty copies, with no required purchase of an introductory manual and the freedom to copy each scale for multiple use with each client). The GCS also offers clinically useful cutting scores, which indicate the severity of depression and the liklihood of suicidal ideation and suicidal behavior. Finally, the GCS has good sensitivity and was designed to monitor treatment outcomes (see box 3.2).

**Box 3.2**
**Generalized Contentment Scale (GCS)**

### GENERALIZED CONTENTMENT SCALE (GCS)

Name: _____    Today's Date: _____

This questionnaire is designed to measure the way you feel about your life and surroundings. It is not a test, so there are no right or wrong answers. Answer each item as carefully and as accurately as you can by placing a number beside each one as follows.

1 = None of the time
2 = Very rarely
3 = A little of the time
4 = Some of the time
5 = A good part of the time
6 = Most of the time
7 = All of the time

1. ____ I feel powerless to do anything about my life.
2. ____ I feel blue.
3. ____ I think about ending my life.
4. ____ I have crying spells.
5. ____ It is easy for me to enjoy myself.
6. ____ I have a hard time getting started on things that I need to do.
7. ____ I get very depressed.
8. ____ I feel there is always someone I can depend on when things get tough.
9. ____ I feel that the future looks bright for me.
10. ____ I feel downhearted.
11. ____ I feel that I am needed.
12. ____ I feel that I am appreciated by others.
13. ____ I enjoy being active and busy.
14. ____ I feel that others would be better off without me.
15. ____ I enjoy being with other people.
16. ____ I feel that it is easy for me to make decisions.
17. ____ I feel downtrodden.
18. ____ I feel terribly lonely.
19. ____ I get upset easily.
20. ____ I feel that nobody really cares about me.
21. ____ I have a full life.
22. ____ I feel that people really care about me.
23. ____ I have a great deal of fun.
24. ____ I feel great in the morning.
25. ____ I feel that my situation is hopeless.

5, 8, 9, 11, 12, 13, 15, 16, 21, 22, 23, 24.

The GCS is self-administered and has twenty-five items, all of which ask the client to rate a statement on a Likert scale from 1 ("none of the time") to 7 ("all of the time"). To score this scale, the items at the bottom left-hand corner are reverse scored (e.g., if someone answers 2, or "very rarely," to No. 5, this would be reverse scored to 6). Once the reverse scoring is completed, all the scores are summed up and substracted from the total number of completed items. That figure is then multiplied by one hundred and then divided by the number of items completed times six. This provides a range from 0 to 100, with higher scores indicating a higher magnitude of severity. Scores greater than 30 suggest the presence of a clinically significant problem, whereas scores greater than 50 often reflect some suicidal ideation and scores greater than 70 indicate severe distress and a clear possibilty that suicide is being considered (Fischer & Corcoran, 2007).

## Case Study No. 2: Eve

Eve is a twenty-eight-year-old pregnant Caucasian whose OB-GYN referred her for a substance abuse assessment, as Eve had disclosed that she was having difficulty in her efforts to stop drinking during her pregnancy. Eve has expressed a desire to stop drinking over the phone, especially after her doctor informed her of the risks of an alcohol-exposed pregnancy. She also disclosed that she has never been assessed for or received treatment for a substance abuse or mental health problem in the past. The goals for this initial asssessment are to assess whether Eve meets the criteria for a diagnosis of alcohol dependence and to conduct a psychosocial assessment to determine whether there is comorbidity or other issues that may be related to or affecting her drinking problem. The practitioner will use the information to determine the most effective treatment plan to help her meet her goal of avoiding drinking during her pregnancy.

To accomplish this aim, the practitioner completes a search to identify standardized assessment measures that briefly screen for and assess the severity of alcohol use to guide in the diagnosis of an alcohol problem and that ideally provides a broader picture of how alcohol use is affecting Eve's psychosocial functioning. A thorough psychosocial assessment will, of course, supplement this information. After a search for instruments at the University of Washington's Alcohol and Drug Abuse Institute Library and the Mental Measurements Yearbook, the practitioner identified three brief screening instruments that all have fairly good psychometric properties. The strengths and weaknesses of each are presented here:

- *Alcohol Dependence Scale (ADS):* The ADS provides a measure of the severity of alcohol dependence. This measure is completed in five to ten minutes, and it provides information that is clinically useful for matching clients to appropriate treatment and for evaluating the outcome of treatment. It also assesses the physical, social, and psychological consequences that drinkers report. The ADS has also been found to have excellent predictive value in making a *DSM* diagnosis and in indicating the presence and severity of a drinking problem (Connors, Young, Williams, & Ricciardelli, 2000)). This scale has been normed on adults, but reviews of the scale have not discussed whether it had been normed on a ethnically diverse sample. This scale is available from the Centre for Addiction and Mental Health and costs $9.95 for a package of twenty-five scales and $17.95 for the user's guide).

- *The Substance Abuse Subtle Screening Inventory-3 (SASSI-3):* The SASSI-3 offers a more comprehensive assessment of substance dependence disorder. This measure is self-administered (by either paper and pencil or computer) and takes approximately fifteen minutes to complete and two minutes to score. The inventory measures ten subscales: face valid alcohol, face valid other drugs, symptoms, obvious attributes, subtle attributes, defensiveness, supplemental addiction measure, family versus controls, correctional, and random answering pattern. Items are used that are designed to minimize suspicion and untruthful answers. In addition, the scale has been noted to be clinically useful for identifying defensiveness, insight and awareness of substance misuse, emotional pain, and relative risk of involvement with the legal system, and in Eve's case, it will identify whether she is using additional substances beyond alcohol (University of Washington Alcohol and Drug Abuse Institute, n.d.). The SASSI-3 can be obtained in both paper and computer administration versions from the SASSI Institute (http://sassi.com).

- *Michigan Alcoholism Screening Test (MAST):* This brief, twenty-five-item alcoholism screening instrument measures lifeitme alcoholism and alcohol-related problems (Conoley & Reese, 2001). It takes approximiately ten minutes to administer and five minutes to score. This screening tool is not intended for use as a diagnostic instrument for substance abuse or dependence but as a supplementory screening tool for alcoholism (Conoley & Reese, 2001). It also does not identify levels or intensity of substance abuse, as the previously mentioned instruments do (Conoley & Reese, 2001). In addition, studies have shown that women, regardless of their alcohol use, tend to score lower than men, which suggests that the measure may not be as useful for assessing substance use among women (Conoley & Reese, 2001). The MAST is of public domain and available free of charge (http://adai.washington.edu/instruments/pdf/Michigan_Alcoholism_Screening_Test_156.pdf; see also appendix 7D).

## SUMMARY

This chapter helped social work practitioners become informed consumers in the selection, use, and interpretation of standardized measurement instruments. We explored major issues involved in the development, evaluation, and interpretation of standardized measures, as well as applications of standardized assessment systems that use computer technologies. This chapter also defined and covered the process of evidence-based assessment. Evidence-based assessment incorporates theory and research to identify assessment targets, methods, and measures that maximize the effectiveness of the overall assessment process. In addition, EBA focuses on the most effective assessment processes that best fit the client's situation, culture, values, and preferences. Four major factors to consider when engaging in EBA include (a) psychometric adequacy of standardized instruments or assessment protocols, (b) diversity issues and the fit of the procedure with the individual client, (c) issues of comorbidity, and (d) clinical utility of the standardized instruments or assessment protocols. Many valuable resources, several of which are Web-based, have become available to support EBA. Finally, case examples showed how to move from assessment to intervention in the selection and use of appropriate standardized measures.

## STUDY QUESTIONS

1. What are the key features that distinguish standardized measures from nonstandardized measures?

2. What are the various methods of establishing the reliability and validity of a measure? In what ways are reliability and validity interrelated?

3. Choose a problem area that is of interest to you (e.g., depression, stress) and develop ten items that you think capture your construct of interest. Apply both the rational-intuitive method and the empirical method to examine the content validity of your new items. What advantages and disadvantages did you find for each approach?

4. What are the inherent advantages and challenges associated with practitioners using computer-assisted assessment technologies and standardized assessment measures?

5. Develop a case vignette in which a statistical decision model would potentially aid clinical decision making with a client system. Now develop a case vignette in which a statistical decision model would potentially hinder or complicate clinical decision making. Explore the advantages and disadvantages associated with practitioners using statistical decision models.

6. Your agency administrator has asked you to select a measure to monitor client progress. What criteria would you use to select a measure to aid clinical decision making in practice with clients? Some possible criteria include reliability and validity properties, norms, clinical utility, cost-effectiveness, and ethical considerations. Are any of these criteria more important to you than others? If so, which ones and why?

7. Why is incremental validity considered to be the highest form of validity?

8. Why does every measurement instrument have some measurement error? Come up with at least one example of systematic error and one example of random error that might occur in administering a measurement instrument in clinical practice.

9. Develop a case vignette in which you would use an assessment measure. Locate at least one measure for the vignette and evaluate it for its clinical utility, competency, and appropriateness to the situation.

## REFERENCES

Abell, N., Springer, D. W., & Kamata, A. (2009). *Developing and validating rapid assessment instruments*. New York: Oxford University Press.

Achenbach, T. M. (2005). Advancing the assessment of children and adolescents: Commentary on evidence-based assessment of child and adolescent disorders. *Journal of Clinical Child and Adolescent Psychology, 34*, 541–547.

Achenbach, T. M., & Edelbrock, C. S. (1983). *Manual for the child behavior checklist and revised child behavior profile*. Burlington, VT: Thomas M. Achenbach.

Baird, C., & Wagner, D. (2000). The relative validity of actuarial- and consensus-based assessment systems. *Children and Youth Services Review, 22*, 839–871.

Barkham, M., Margison, F., Leach, C., Lucock, M., Mellor-Clark, J., Evans, C., et al. (2001). Computer assisted clinical assessment. *Child and Adolescent Mental Health, 11*, 64–75.

Bender, K., Springer, D. W., & Kim, J. S. (2006). Treatment effectiveness with dually diagnosed adolescents: A systematic review. *Brief Treatment and Crisis Intervention, 6*, 177–205.

Berger, M. (2006). Computer assisted clinical assessment. *Child and Adolescent Mental Health, 11*, 64–75. doi: 10.1111/j.1475-3588.2006.00394.x.

Beutler, L. (2001). Comparisons among quality assurance systems: From outcome assessment to clinical utility. *Journal of Consulting and Clinical Psychology, 69*, 197–204.

Bloom, M., Fischer, J., & Orme, J. (2005). *Evaluating practice: Guidelines for the accountable professional* (5th ed.). Boston: Allyn and Bacon.

Blythe, B. J., & Tripodi, T. (1989). *Measurement in direct practice*. Newbury Park, CA: Sage.

Burlingame, G. M., Dunn, T. W., Chen, S., Lehman, A., Axman, R., Earnshaw, D., et al. (2005). Selection of outcome assessment instruments for inpatients with severe and persistent mental illness. *Psychiatric Services, 56*, 444–451.

Butcher, J. N., Perry, J. N., & Atlis, M. M. (2000). Validity and utility of computer-based test intervention. *Psychological Assessment, 12*, 6–8.

Butcher, J. N., Perry, J. N., & Hahn, J. (2004). Computers in clinical assessment: Historical developments, present status, and future challenges. *Journal of Clinical Psychology, 80*, 331–345.

Connors, J. P., Young, R. M., Williams, R. J., & Ricciardelli, L. A. (2000). Drinking restraint versus alcohol expectancies: Which is the better indicator of alcohol problems? *Journal of Studies on Alcohol, 61*, 352–359.

Conoley, J. C., & Reese, R. J. (2001). Michigan Alcoholism Screening Test (MAST). In J. C. Impara & B. S. Plake (Eds.), *The mental measurements yearbook* (14th ed., pp. 751–753). Lincoln, NE: Buros Institute of Mental Measurements.

Coopersmith, S. (1986). *The Coopersmith inventory.* Palo Alto, CA: Consulting Psychologist Press.

Cronbach, L. J. (1951). Coefficient alpha and the internal structure of tests. *Psychometrika, 16*, 297–334.

Crowne, D. P., & Marlowe, D. (1964). *The approval motive: Studies in evaluative dependence.* New York: Wiley.

Downie, N. M., & Heath, R. W. (1974). *Basic statistical methods* (4th ed.). New York: Harper and Row.

Epstein, J., & Klinkenberg, W.D. (2001). From Eliza to Internet: A brief history of computerized assessment. *Computers in Human Behavior, 17*, 295–314.

Epstein, M. H. (2004). *Behavioral and Emotional Rating Scale-2: A strength-based approach to assessment.* Austin, TX: PRO-ED.

Epstein, M. H., & Sharma, J. M. (1998). *Behavioral and Emotional Rating Scale: A strength based approach to assessment: Examiner's manual.* Austin, TX: Pro-Ed.

Epstein, N. B., Baldwin, M., & Bishop, D. S. (1982). *McMaster Family Assessment Device (FAD) manual (version 3).* Providence, RI: Brown University/Butler Hospital Family Research Program.

Fischer, J., & Corcoran, K. (2007). *Measures for clinical practice: A sourcebook* (2 vols., 4th ed.). New York: Oxford University Press.

Garb, H. N. (1998). Recommendations for training in the use of the Thematic Apperception Test (TAT). *Professional Psychology—Research and Practice, 29*, 621–622.

Garb, H. N. (2000). Computers will become increasingly important for psychological assessment: Not that there's anything wrong with that. *Psychological Assessment, 12*, 31–39.

Grove, W. M., Zald, D. H., Lebow, B. S., Snitz, B. E., & Nelson, C. (2000). Clinical versus mechanical prediction: A meta-analysis. *Psychological Assessment, 12*, 19–30.

Guttman, L. (1945). A basis for analyzing test-retest reliability. *Psychometrika, 10*, 255–282.

Guy, R., Edgley, C., Arafat, I., & Allen, D. (1987). *Social research methods.* Boston: Allyn and Bacon.

Hathaway, S., & McKinley, J. (1943). *The Minnesota Multiphasic Personality Inventory.* St. Paul: University of Minnesota Press.

Hodges, K. (2000). *The Child and Adolescent Functional Assessment Scale* (2nd rev.). Ypsilanti: Eastern Michigan University.

Hudson, W. W. (1982). *The clinical measurement package: A field manual.* Homewood, IL: Dorsey Press.

Hudson, W. W. (1999). *Measuring personal and social problems: Methods for scale development*. Unpublished manuscript. Tallahassee, FL.

Hunsley, J., & Mash, E.J. (2003). The incremental validity of psychological testing and assessment: Conceptual, methodological, and statistical issues. *Psychological Assessment, 15*, 446–455.

Hunsley, J., & Mash, E. J. (2005). Introduction to the special section on developing guidelines for the evidence-based assessment (EBA) of adult disorders. *Psychological Assessment, 17*, 251–255.

Hunsley, J., & Mash, E. J. (2007). Evidence-based assessment. *Annual Review of Clinical Psychology, 3*, 29–51.

Inwald, R. E., Brobst, K. E., & Morrissey, R. F. (1987). *Hilson adolescent profile*. Kew Gardens, NY: Hilson Research.

Joneis, T., Turkheimer, E., & Oltmanns, T. F. (2000). Psychometric analysis of racial differences on the Maudsley Obsessional Compulsive Inventory. *Assessment, 7*, 247–258.

Jordan, C., Franklin, C., & Corcoran, K. (2005). Measuring instruments. In R. M. Grinnell Jr. (Ed.), *Social work research and evaluation: Quantitative and qualitative approaches* (7th ed.). Itasca, IL: Peacock.

Kaplan, R. M., & Succuzzo, D. P. (2009). *Psychological testing: Principles, applications, and issues*. Belmont, CA: Wadsworth.

Kazdin, A. E. (2005). Evidence-based assessment for children and adolescents: Issues in measurement development and clinical applications. *Journal of Clinical Child and Adult Psychology, 34*, 548–558.

Kessler, R. C., Chiu, W. T., Demler, O., & Walters, E. E. (2005). Prevalence, severity, and comorbidity of 12-month *DSM*-IV disorders in the National Comorbidity Survey Replication. *Archives of General Psychiatry, 62*, 617–627.

Kordy, H., Hannover, W., & Richard, M. (2001). Computer assisted feedback driven active quality management for psychotherapy provision: The Stuttgart-Heidelberg Model. *Journal of Consulting and Clinical Psychology, 69*, 173–183.

Krueger, R. F., & Markon, K. E. (2006). Reinterpreting comorbidity: A model-based approach to understanding and classifying psychopathology. *Annual Review of Clinical Psychology, 2*, 111–133.

Kuder, G. F., & Richardson, M. W. (1937). The theory of the estimation of test reliability. *Psychometrika, 2*, 151–160.

Lambert, M. J. (2001). Psychotherapy outcome and quality improvement: Introduction to the special section on patient-focused research. *Journal of Consulting and Clinical Psychology, 69*, 147–149.

Lambert, M. J., Hansen, N. B., & Finch, A. E. (2001). Patient-focused research: Using patient outcome data to enhance treatment effects. *Journal of Consulting and Clinical Psychology, 69*, 147–149.

Lambert, M. J., Whipple, J. L., Hawkings, E. J., Vermeersch, D., Neilsen, S. L., & Smart, D. W. (2003). Is it time to track patient outcome on a routine basis? A meta-analysis. *Clinical Psychology: Science and Practice, 10*, 288–301.

Lima, E. N., Stanley, S., Kaboski, B., Reitzel, L. R., Richey, A., Castro, Y., et al. (2005). The incremental validity of the MMPI-2: When does therapist access not enhance treatment outcome? *Psychological Assessment, 17*, 462–468.

Maltby, J., Lewis, C. A., & Hill, A. (2000). *Commissioned reviews of 250 psychological tests* (2 vols.). Wales, UK: Edwin Mellen Press.

Mash, E. J., & Hunsley, J. (2005). Evidence-based assessment of child and adolescent disorders: Issues and challenges. *Journal of Clinical and Adolescent Psychology, 34*, 362–379.

Mercer, J. (1979). *System of multicultural pluralistic assessment manual.* New York: Psychological Corporation.

Millon, T. (1977). *Millon Clinical Multiaxial Inventory.* Minneapolis, MN: National Computer Systems.

Millon, T. (1982). *The Millon Clinical Multiaxial Inventory.* Minneapolis, MN: National Computer Systems.

Millon, T. (1994). *Millon Index of Personality Styles (MIPS) manual.* San Antonio, TX: Psychological Corporation.

Nunnally, J., & Bernstein, I. (1994*). Psychometric theory* (3rd ed.). New York: Mc-Graw-Hill.

Nurius, P. S., & Hudson, W. W. (1993). *Human services practice, evaluation, and computers: A practical guide for today and beyond.* Pacific Grove, CA: Brooks/Cole.

Proctor, E. K. (2004). Leverage points for the implementation of evidence-based practice. *Brief Treatment and Crisis Intervention, 4*, 227–242.

Quay, P. (1987). *The revised behavior problem checklist manual.* Miami, FL: University of Miami.

Rubin, A. (2008). *Practitioner's guide to using research for evidence-based practice.* Hoboken, NJ: Wiley.

Rubin, A., & Babbie, E. (2010). *Research methods for social work* (6th ed.). Belmont, CA: Thomson–Brooks/Cole.

Sackett, D. L., Straus, S. E., Richardson, W. S., Rosenberg, W. M. C., & Haynes, R. B. (2000). *Evidence-based medicine: How to practice and teach EBM* (2nd ed.). New York: Churchill Livingstone.

Sarrazin, M. S. V., Hall, J. A., Richards, C., & Carswell, C. (2002). A comparison of computer-based versus pencil-and-paper assessment of drug use. *Research on Social Work Practice, 12*, 669–683.

Sattler, J. M. (2001). *Assessment of children: Cognitive applications* (4th ed.). San Diego, CA: Author.

Spies, R. A., Carlson, J. F., & Geisinger, K. F. (Eds.) (n.d.). *The eighteenth mental measurements yearbook.* Retrieved on September 22, 2010, from Test Reviews Online, at www.unl.edu/buros.

Springer, D. W. (1998). Validation of the Adolescent Concerns Evaluation (ACE): Detecting indicators of runaway behavior in adolescents. *Social Work Research, 22*, 241–250.

Springer, D. W., Abell, N., & Hudson, W. W. (2002). Creating and validating rapid assessment instruments for practice and research: Part 1. *Research on Social Work Practice, 6*, 752–768.

Springer, D. W., Abell, N., & Nugent, W. R. (2002). Creating and validating rapid assessment instruments for practice and research: Part 2. *Research on Social Work Practice, 6*, 752–768.

Straus, S. E., Richardson, W. S., Glasziou, P., & Haynes, R. B. (2005). *Evidence-based medicine: How to practice and teach EBM* (3rd ed.). Edinburgh, UK: Elsevier Churchill Livingstone.

Stuart, R. (1987). *Couple's pre-counseling inventory*. Champaign, IL: Research Press.

Tzuriel, D. (2001). *Dynamic assessment of young children*. New York: Plenum.

University of Washington Alcohol and Drug Abuse Institute. (n.d.). *Screening and assessment database*. Retrieved September 22, 2010, from http://lib.adai.washington.edu/instruments/.

University of Miami, Department of Psychology. (n.d.). *Self-report measures available*. Retrieved September 22, 2010, from www.psy.miami.edu/faculty/ccarver/CCscales.html.

Vergare, M. J., Binder, R. L., Cook, I. A., & Galanter, M. (2006). *American Psychiatric Association practice guidelines, psychiatric evaluation of adults* (2nd ed.). Retrieved September 22, 2010, from http://psychiatryonline.com/pracGuide/pracGuide ChapToc_1.aspx. doi: 10.1176/appi.books.9780890423363.137162.

Vermeersch, D. A., Whipple, J. L., Lambert, M. J., Hawkins, E. J., Burchfield, C. M., & Okiishi, J. C. (2004). Outcome questionnaire: Is it sensitive to changes in counseling center cilents? *Journal of Counseling Psychology, 51*, 38–49.

Warner, R. M. (2008). *Applied statistics: From bivariate to multivariate techniques*. Thousand Oaks, CA: Sage.

Widiger, T. A., & Clark, L. A. (2000). Toward *DSM-V* and the classification of psychopathology. *Psychological Bulletin, 126*, 946–963.

Winters, K. (1988). *Personal experiences screen questionnaire (PESQ) manual*. Los Angeles: Western Psychological Services.

Wood, J. M., Garb, H. N., Lilienfeld, S. O., & Nezworski, T. M. (2002). Clinical assessment. *Annual Review of Psychology, 53*, 519–543.

Yoshioka, M. (n.d.). Psychosocial measures for Asian-American populations: Tools for direct practice and research. *Columbia University School of Social Work, Okura Mental Health Foundation*. Retrieved September 22, 2010, from www.columbia.edu/cu/ssw/projects/pmap/.

# CHAPTER 4

# Qualitative Assessment Methods

## Michelle S. Ballan, Cynthia Franklin, and Dorie J. Gilbert

### INTRODUCTION

Qualitative assessment methods are grounded in the need to understand and describe meaningful events in a client's life through words, observations, and graphical depictions rather than numbers. The need for practitioners to emphasize qualitative observations in addition to quantitative measures for client assessments has been a much-debated topic in the field of clinical assessment over the past fifty years (Groth-Marnat, 2000). Further, as with quantitative assessments, the clinician's choice of qualitative methods should be informed by evidence-based assessment (EBA), the use of research and theory to guide the selection of assessment targets, the methods and measures used in the assessment, and the assessment process itself (Hunsley & Mash, 2007) should guide the clinician's choice of qualitative methods. Evidence-based assessment not only involves the use of the best scientific information to inform clinician's decision making but also requires clinicians to incorporate the clients' preferences and values in applying that evidence. As such, focused qualitative methods are appropriate tools for identifying and addressing client priorities and for ensuring, most often along with conventional quantitative methods, a client-centered, evidence-based assessment.

In this chapter, we describe examples of qualitative assessment methods, including ways of interviewing, process recording, the use of case study methods, repertory grids, observational approaches, self-characterization methods, and portfolio assessments. In addition, we describe how both qualitative and quantitative assessment methods are complimentary and can be used together to improve clinical assessments. Finally, we illustrate qualitative assessment methods and how they benefit intervention plans with a case example of a portfolio assessment conducted in a school setting.

### DEFINITIONS AND DESCRIPTIONS

Qualitative assessment methods use words, pictures, diagrams, and narrative instead of numbers and quantitative approaches to understand clients. A clinician may describe the client verbally; use pictures or a dia-gram to demonstrate the client's life context; or use pictorial language, metaphors, or case-study methods to describe the client and his or her problems (Borden, 1992; Guba, 1990; Moon, Dillon, & Sprenkle, 1990; Neimeyer, 1993; Taylor, 1993). This rich, in-depth description, sometimes referred to as thick description, is used to provide enriching details about the client's experience to help clinicians gain a full understanding and ap-preciation for the complexity of a client's problem (Gilgun, Daly, & Han-del, 1992). Instead of relying on quantitative methods such as a measure-ment instrument to gather information about the client's problems, the social worker becomes the primary data gatherer when using a qualita-tive approach to assessment. For example, instead of labeling the client's marital arguments as severe because of a cutoff score on a quantitative measure or a record of the number of arguments a client has had in a week, the clinician would describe in detail using words, narrative, or pictures one or more of the arguments and expound on the impact of the fights on the couple's relationship. This is not to say that numbers cannot be used in a qualitative assessment to describe the client's experience. When numbers are used, however, they are viewed as another method of description, generally as anchors along a continuum that represents the client's experiences (Appendix 4A shows an excerpt from a narrative as-sessment report, including rich detail, pictorial language, and descriptive information).

## QUALITATIVE VERSUS QUANTITATIVE ASSESSMENT METHODS: DISTINCT BUT COMPLIMENTARY

In his fifty-year review of psychological assessment, Groth-Marnat (2000) notes the classic work of Hunt (1946), who emphasized that clinical prac-titioners "should pay more attention to qualitative behavior during the testing situation and rework tests to yield a maximum amount of rich qualitative responses" (p. 350). So, how does one decide whether to choose a quantitative or a qualitative assessment strategy? We support a synthesis approach and believe that there are many ways to know and empirically report a client's attributes and experiences. Various assess-ment strategies can provide worthwhile and useful knowledge. Neither qualitative nor quantitative approaches should be privileged, as both have their place in any assessment based on methodological pluralism. It should be noted, however, that regardless of whether the clinician obtains information qualitatively or quantitatively, the clinical judgment in as-sessment is ultimately a human qualitative judgment that involves sub-jective appraisal of all the evidence (Friedman & MacDonald, 2006).

The best assessments are a matter of the pragmatics and techniques of the assessment (i.e., what the practitioner does to gather information about the client). The axiom followed throughout this text is this: "if an assessment method is valid and reliable and helps you obtain the type of information needed to help a particular client, then use it!" From our perspective, practitioners can use all assessment methods, regardless of their distinct theoretical origins, conjointly to improve the data gathered for an assessment. Multiple methods usually enhance the reliability and validity of clinical information. In particular, qualitative methods add to the detail and thick description of a case assessment and may increase the clinician's understanding of the context and process in which problems occur. Qualitative methods can be used along with the quantitative methods described in chapters 2 and 3; when used together, they may improve our clinical assessments (Franklin, Cody, & Ballan, 2010).

## Unique Contributions of Qualitative Assessment

Qualitative assessment methods offer unique contributions to the assessment process. The ability of qualitative assessment methods to uncover personal perspectives is grounded in the flexibility and emphasis on the context and process that clients present in the therapeutic relationship. Qualitative assessments range from behavioral observations to verbal and written descriptions of a person's behavior or thoughts, biographical or autobiographical narratives, interviews, experiential exercises, and graphical depictions, all of which are well suited for developing a holistic understanding of the client. The unique contributions that qualitative assessment approaches bring to the assessment process and the helping relationship are discussed in the following sections.

**Ability to Uncover and Corroborate Client Viewpoints.**    A major contribution of qualitative assessment is its ability to uncover social meanings of everyday behavior, the symbolic significance of an individual's behavior. In addition, qualitative assessments are often needed to corroborate and further elucidate the context of quantitative findings. Layton and Lock (2001) provided an excellent example of this in demonstrating the need for qualitative approaches to fully assess and confirm learning disabilities in students with low vision. The authors point out that the standardized measures used to assess learning disabilities in children rely on intake visual functioning and cannot be reliable when low-vision students use adaptations for visual impairments; the measures have not been normed on a low-vision student population. Instead, the authors use qualitative methods (informal testing to determine strengths and weaknesses in specific learning areas, behavioral observations and intensive observations of psychologically based mental actions and operations, interviews with parents and teachers, and sampling of students' work over time and across different environments) to provide a picture of

students' daily performance. They then used the qualitative data to corroborate findings from the traditional, quantitative measure in what the
authors call a mixed methodology.

**Adaptability to Assessing Diverse Populations.**     Standardized instruments have been criticized for their limitations with people of color
and other nonmajority populations (Dana, 2000; Kutchins & Kirk, 1997).
Furthermore, attaining cultural sensitivity for quantitative evidence-
based assessments necessitates achieving an instrument's measurement
equivalence in other cultures (Rubin, 2008). In making assessments across
diverse populations, qualitative assessment measures have the advantage of being easily adapted to different populations that vary from the
mainstream in ethnic or cultural identity, presence of disabilities, and any
life experiences that separate them from the populations on whom tests
are usually normed. For example, some Native American tribes do not es-
pouse the concept of depression as a reaction to grief and loss; thus, a
standardized depression scale would not be appropriate with this population (Gilbert & Franklin, 2001). The open-ended, process-oriented style
of qualitative assessment provides social workers with a window on
clients' culturally based thinking and behaviors. Certain Eurocentric values, such as individualism and competition, which are central themes to
many dominant theoretical perspectives, directly conflict with values of
collectivism and cooperation that many populations of color hold. Qualitative assessments allow the social worker to explore cultural scripts and
cultural meanings that would not be apparent in standardized assessments. The knowledge gained helps place clients' experiences in a cultural context. This is especially important for identifying clients'
strengths, even when their behavioral norms or beliefs do not match the
values or norms of the majority culture.

**Promotion of the Social Worker's Self-Awareness.**     The human-to-
human interaction of a therapeutic relationship makes individualized assessment possible. The relationship further helps the social worker, as data
gatherer, capture unequivocal insights. Human-to-human assessments do
not allow the social worker to maintain the type of objectivity that one
might maintain in assessing a rock, for example (Peshkin, 1988). Rather,
human-to-human assessment is subjective and experiential. When we are
assessing our fellow humans, we are looking at ourselves. To understand
the subjective human experience, both the social worker's and the client's,
the social worker must develop a keen sense of self-awareness. Self-
awareness refers to the "therapists' momentary recognition of and attention to their immediate thoughts, emotions, physiological responses and
behaviors during a therapy session" (Williams & Fauth, 2005, p. 374).
Qualitative assessment requires social workers to be continuously

cognizant that their own biases and beliefs may influence their clinical judgment (Gilgun et al., 1992). By developing self-awareness, clinicians are able to discern the differences between their interpretations and those of the client. It is essential that clinicians not force their reality or values on a client, because this will lead to misunderstandings of the client's problem and hamper the assessment process.

**Importance of the Client–Social Worker Relationship.**   Qualitative assessment methods allow for a more holistic, intimate, and cooperative relationship between the client and the practitioner. For example, soliciting recollections about early childhood experiences as an assessment strategy actively engages the client in the counseling process and reduces defensiveness while allowing the practitioner to interact empathetically in the counseling process (Clark, 2001). When conducting quantitative assessment, it may be easy to ignore the reality of the effect of the social worker's presence on the client, even though quantitative approaches suggest that it is important to consider the impact of setting events and the reactions of clients on the results of measures. When using a qualitative approach to assessment, social workers must more readily accept that their presence does affect the client-problem context and that they cannot avoid this. On entering into a relationship with a client, the social worker becomes a part of the problem; only by skillfully comprehending the client's problem definition and unique context can the social worker become part of the solution. For example, clients are often more aware than social workers of how the social welfare system negatively affects the clients' lives. Thus, the social worker's inability to form an empathic relationship and to comprehend a client's context means that the social worker's role and the system in which he or she works may inadvertently maintain a client's problem. To understand the inner workings of the client, the social worker must use assessment methods that unravel human thought and experience and allow the client to become the key informant and primary expert concerning his or her own problems. Qualitative methods therefore call on social workers to have exceptional relationship management skills.

**Fit with Many Theoretical and Therapeutic Perspectives and Evidence-Based Standards.**   Qualitative assessment strategies are flexible to use with many theoretical perspectives and generally focus on understanding the meanings attributed to events, personal relationships, and private experiences (Duffy & Chenail, 2004). The diverse theoretical models that use qualitative methods range from family systems theories to ecological systems models, cognitive-constructivist therapies, and the strengths perspectives (for a brief review, see chapter 1). In addition, because qualitative methods emphasize process and preference

the experiences of the client, they also fit well with cross-cultural perspectives, feminist theory, and Africentric theory—all of which emphasize the contextualized experiences of the client over traditional quan-
tifiable ways of assessing a client (for a further discussion of how
qualitative methods aid the assessment of ethnic clients, see chapter 10).
Therapeutic approaches such as personal construct therapies, cognitive-
constructivist therapy, Adlerian therapy, and systemic family therapies
(Neimeyer, 2010) also make use of qualitative assessment strategies.
Having so strongly emphasized the unique contributions of qualitative
assessment methods, we reiterate that both qualitative and quantitative
assessment methods may be used together in clinical assessment, and
combining these approaches may increase the usefulness of the information gathered from clients.

Both qualitative and quantitative assessments play an important role
in developing and establishing evidence-based practice, and qualitative
research can inform evidence-based practice independent of other research methodologies. Guidelines for qualitative evidence are still evolving (Lincoln, 2002; Morse, Swanson, & Kuzel, 2001), but research evidence from the approach can be valid and reliable and even can add to
the development of quantitative assessment tools. Williams (2008), for example, used the qualitative reports of key informants to develop the Self-
Awareness and Management Strategies (SAMS) scales for therapists,
which has informed numerous interventions. Gilgun (2004) demonstrated in two case studies how qualitative methods can contribute to the
development and evaluation of clinical assessment tools and argues that
evaluations of clinical instruments are incomplete if they do not include
a qualitative component.

## QUALITATIVE ASSESSMENT METHODS

### Interviewing: Ethnographic Interviewing

Interviewing is the most frequently used method for assessing clients,
and the face-to-face interview has been the cornerstone of social work
practice. Qualitative assessment relies heavily on a form of interviewing
known as ethnographic interviewing (Berg, 2010). Ethnographic interviewing entails speaking face-to-face and mutual observation while also
providing an abiding respect for context, language, and meaning. Ethnographic interviewing takes place in the context of building a relationship
of mutual respect and cooperation with the client. Ethnographic interviewing also assumes a position of equality and collaboration among social worker and client, an approach clearly in accordance with the responsibility of practicing clinicians to modify their own behaviors and

therapeutic styles to meet the needs of underserved populations (Swartz et al., 2007).

Ethnographic interviewing is highly personal, interpretive, reflective, and elaborative. The interviewer tries to put away preconceived notions, diagnoses, and hunches about the client and starts out on a journey of understanding. To do so, social workers have to be reflective and in touch with their own feelings, biases, and thoughts about the client. Clients become like teachers telling the social worker about their personal reality. But as every student knows, learning is not totally dependent on the teacher; learners have to be open, flexible, and receptive as well. They also have to be willing to interpret the ideas communicated in the context of the teacher and the concepts being taught. For example, if a student is a behaviorist and decides to study psychoanalytic theories, it will be necessary for that student to interpret those theories within his or her own linguistic and conceptual frameworks. If the student tries to interpret the psychoanalytic theories according to the concepts of behaviorism, he or she will never really understand the theories. The same is true for the social worker conducting ethnographic interviews; interpretations must occur within the client's own framework or worldview, not within that of the social worker.

Ethnographic interviews may be structured, semistructured, or open ended (Berg, 2010), although the latter two approaches appear to be more suitable to the explorative nature of the ethnographic approach. A structured interview has a previously formulated set of questions that the social worker asks the client; social workers do not deviate much from their list of questions. Structured interviews are critical to best practices in mental health assessments. For example, Pettit and Joiner (2006) note that, although there is no one extant evidence-based assessment in the extensive and complex assessment of depression, the structured clinical interview approaches the ideal, particularly when incoporrated as an overall assessment strategy. Semistructured interviews have a previously formulated set of questions, but the social worker may veer from that list as information emerges. Widiger and Samuel (2005) recommend semistructured interviews in a two-stage process of evidence-based assessment of personality disorders. The first stage involves the administration of a self-report inventory; if the practitioner identifies maladaptive personality traits, a semistructured interview should follow to determine the presence, nature, and severity of any possible personality disorders. The use of established semistructured interviews allows clinicians to give careful attention to the influence of age, gender biases, cultural and ethnic factors, and probable inaccuracies in patient self-perception and presentation. Open-ended interviews have no previously formulated questions; the social worker just begins the interview and sees where it goes. Open-ended ethnographic questions are used both to encourage clients to tell their story and to uncover how clients integrate their beliefs and experiences to create a sense of meaning and coherence (Swartz et al., 2007). In all three types of interviews, a guiding purpose usually directs the interview, for example, to build rapport or to assess whether abuse has occured.

Within the structure of different ethnographic interviews, the clinician can use various types of questioning techniques to gather information from the client (Berg, 2010; Crabtree & Miller, 1999).

For example, descriptive questions are broadly open ended. Grand-tour descriptive questions attempt to elicit a rich story from the client (e.g., "Describe your experiences at the university after you became disabled," "Tell me about life on the reservation," "Describe your future"). Mini-tour descriptive questions elicit smaller units of experience (e.g., "How did your mother treat you after you began using a wheelchair? Your teachers? friends?" "Tell me about your final day of employment at the factory").

Structural questions are inclusive and expand the focus of experience (e.g., "Have you been married before?" "What does she do when she is feeling melancholy?")

Substituting frame questions take a term or phrase the client uses and substitute another question (e.g., social worker: "Tell me what your sister is like"; client: "She comes across like she is better than me and a know-it-all"; social worker: "What else does she come across like?")

Contrast questions are exclusive and expand experience (e.g., "You said that you and Yolanda had some good times together in the past; how has that changed now?" "You mentioned seeing a marital therapist in the past; how is your relationship different now?").

Rating questions ask clients to give differential meaning to their experience (e.g., "What is the best experience you have had since you have been divorced?" "What is the worst thing someone said since you lost your partner?").

Circular questions elicit information about transactions embedded in a system. They focus on the relationships among persons and among the beliefs and views held by indviduals (e.g., "How do Mom and Dad solve arguments between them?" "What do you think Brother would say when Dad doesn't pay attention to Mom?").

These types of questions are not used exclusively with ethnographic interviewing; they can be used in other forms of interviewing as well. In chapter 8, for example, we cover how systemic family therapists use circular questions and give examples of such questions in that chapter's appendix.

Clinicians may use ethnographic interviewing to discover the personal meaning clients attribute to their problems, the therapy process, relationship patterns, or any other intrapersonal or interpersonal process. For example, Todd, Joanning, Enders, Mutchler, and Thomas (1990) used ethnographic interviewing to discover how clients perceive the therapy process. A semistructured interview was conducted to keep the clients focused on their experience. Following are examples of questions used in the ethnographic interview and a sample dialogue from one of the interviews. Todd et al. (1990, p. 56) provide these examples of questions:

> How do you refer to this place? What do you call what is done here? What do you feel is the role of a counselor? It is important that the interviewer use the term used by the family (i.e., therapist, counselor, interviewer). Please describe the process you went through from the time you parked your car until now, please be as specific as possible. Does a "therapist" (whatever term the family uses) do the same things as other mental health professionals? What is the difference between mental health professionals such as therapists, counselors, psychologists, and psychiatrists? What makes a good "therapist"? (Use the term used by the family). How do you know if a "therapist" is or is not meeting your needs?

It must be remembered that the interviewer should adopt the language of the family. In the example questions, the term *therapist* was used, but if the family continually referred to the therapist as a counselor, the term *counselor* should be substituted. Furthermore, each question may facilitate a response from a family that the interviewer may want to investigate in more detail, and he/she should improvise and do so.

A case example of an ethnographic interview by Todd et al. (1990) follows:

> ETHNOGRAPHIC INTERVIEWER (EI): I would like to talk to you about what it is like for you to come into counseling. I would like to hear your perceptions, your story of what it is like to come here as if you were talking to another couple. . . . Fill me in briefly on what you would tell someone else about your experiences.
>
> PHILIP: To start with . . . a little scary . . . I didn't know what they would say about me, didn't know if I'd be judged wrong, everything I was doing and saying. I've gotten to the point where I'm not scared to come here and say what I'm feeling. If they want to knock, that's their privilege. I want to get off my chest what I'm feeling.
>
> EI: You moved from a place to come and be somewhat afraid because you might be blamed and jumped on to a place where you can get things off your chest?
>
> PHILIP: Yeah.
>
> EI (TO MARGE): OK, how about you?
>
> MARGE: I like having that third person out there that is supposedly trained to know . . . to be able to read between the lines instead of a friend who will either agree with you because they think that's what you want them to say or a family member who is too much involved in it or doesn't have an objective view.
>
> EI: Read between the lines? That part I was a little fuzzy.
>
> MARGE (pause): Well maybe like at the second session when the therapist said that he observed the anger and hurt going on . . . We might realize that but not understand it or maybe not want to admit it, and when a third person says it, you go, yeah that's what's going on.

 EI: The therapist helped you understand and admit things you felt?

MARGE: Yeah.

PHILIP: At home I see her get angry, but I don't realize that she was angry because she was hurt. At the time I felt she was mad at me and wanted revenge, but actually it's because she has been hurt and I know I do that too and she doesn't know I've been hurt.

EI: So being here has helped you see more clearly what you've been feeling?

MARGE AND PHILIP: Yeah.

(Later in the interview)

PHILIP: I think he's done a super job.

MARGE: He gets the idea going then backs off and lets you fill in the pieces.

PHILIP: Passes you the ball and lets you run with it.

EI: He gives you the ball to run with?

MARGE: He points things out, that's where reading-between-the-lines-type thing comes in.

EI: His role is to point things out, read between the lines, give you a ball to play with then get out of the way?

MARGE: To be there. (pp. 57–58)

As this example shows, ethnographic interviewing asks clients to explain in their own words the meanings that they ascribe to processes. Social workers listen intently and probe to understand in more depth what the client is saying. In addition, social workers adopt the language and the meanings of the client when communicating with the client. This aids in their mutual understanding of the world. Ethnographic interviewers know that there are multiple perspectives and that all clients communicate from their own unique social and cultural viewpoints. In a sense, every individual stands alone and speaks a unique language. Individuals from similar ethnicities, religions, cultures, or social classes have a long history of interaction, however, and have built similar realities; they speak the same type of language and may have had equivocal or similar experiences. Ethnographic interviewing is therefore particularly useful for understanding different ethnicities, religions, cultures, and classes. In every interview situation, the ethnographic interviewer becomes like an anthropologist seeking to discover the culture and personal frames of reference of the client. Clients become the key informants and teachers about their social realities.

Mutual understanding of different cultures and religious beliefs forms out of the negotiation and social consensus building that transpire as we openly encounter one another and find ways to communicate (for an example of a pretherapy assessment form used to assess a client's personal frames of reference in the context of solution-focused family therapy, see Box 4.1; de Shazer, 1985; Todd, 1993).

**Box 4.1**
**Pretherapy Assessment Form**

1. What makes you think your family needs our services?
2. What do you expect to happen here that will be helpful to your family?
3. What will convince you that your family does not need to come here?
4. How many days per week does the problem occur? (please circle)
   1   2   3   4   5   6   7
5. How many hours per day is the problem present?
6. Please place an X indicating the severity of the problem.
   1 .................................................. 5 .................................................. 10
   very mild                                                                    very severe
7. Who will be the first person to notice an improvement in the problem? What will he or she notice that will indicate an improvement?
8. What is one of the first things your family will be doing differently when they notice improvement?
9. When does your family NOT have the problem?
10. How do you explain when the problem does not happen?
11. How will you know when the problem is really solved?
12. What are you doing to keep things from getting worse?
13. What would tell you that things are getting better?

SOURCE: T. Todd. (1993). *Pretherapy assessment*. The Brief Therapy Institute of Denver. Westminster, CO: Author.

## Narrative Methods

A narrative can be communicated in verbal or written form. The client usually communicates the narrative in verbal form but may also do so in writing. The social worker usually captures in written form the essence of the narrative as the client reports but also may communicate the narrative in a verbal report, as at a case conference. Written narratives make it possible for social workers to record and reflect on the client's meanings and beliefs, as well as on their own responses to those private thoughts. Written narratives are also used to communicate to others the client's experiences in a manner that provides insight into human behavior and motivations. The following sections cover three narrative methods: process recording, case studies, and self-characterizations.

**Process Recording.**   Process or narrative recording is an intricately detailed and specialized type of written case recording in which social workers document the process of an interview with a client, including his or her actual words and behaviors. In addition, the process recorder identifies his or her feelings or personal reactions to what the client says. The process recording does not necessarily reflect objective events but instead constructions of the social worker and, indirectly, of the client (Gergen, 2003). A supervisor typically reviews the recording and makes other comments about the client-social worker interview (Wilson, 1976). Process recordings help teach social workers interviewing and assessment skills. They also bring to light many of the relational or process issues that might emerge in managing a case. Social workers may be able to observe from the process recording something they said wrong or how their attitudes or feelings toward the client caused them to misunderstand the client. As process recordings are germane to clinical assessment, social workers may be able to observe emerging themes or patterns in the interview that they might have missed if they had used a shorter, less process-oriented recording of the interview.

Despite its usefulness, process recording is time consuming and impractical for use in everyday practice. It is usually reserved for social work education. It may also be used in agency practice, in the context of educational supervision, when a clinician wants special help with a difficult or unusual case. Following are some guidelines for writing a process recording.

According to Wilson (1976, pp. 18–20), the following information should go into a process recording:

(1) Identifying information. The name of the worker or student, the date of the interview, and the client's name and/or identifying number are necessary. It may be helpful to state the number of the interview (such as "fourth contact with Mrs. Smith").

(2) A word-for-word description of what happened, as well as the student can remember. For example: I told Mr. Garcia, "In order to find out what kind of work you might be able to do, you will be seen by the psychiatrist as well as the physician." Mr. Garcia said, "Psychiatrist? What do you mean?"

This student had chosen to spell out "I told Mr. Garcia" and "Mr. Garcia said." An abbreviated style is preferred, using W for "worker" and C for "client." Quotation marks are not necessary:

W: In order to find out what kind of work you might be able to do, you will be seen by the psychiatrist as well as the physician.

C: Psychiatrist? What do you mean?

(3) A description of any action or nonverbal activity that occurred. For example:

C: I invited Mr. Garcia into my office and asked him to sit down. He did so slowly and just sat there staring at the floor.

W: How are you feeling today Mr. Garcia? It took him a long time to answer but he finally raised his head and looked at me and said:

C: I feel terrible.

W: Before I had time to say or do anything he rose up out of his chair, started pacing around the room and was shouting that there was nothing wrong with him mentally and that he "didn't need to see no psychiatrist."

(4) The student's feelings and reactions to the client and to the interview as it takes place. This requires that the recorder put into writing his unspoken thoughts and reactions as the interview is going on. In the interview with Mr. Garcia, for example, the next few sentences might read: "At this point I began to feel a little uneasy. Mr. Garcia seemed to be getting awfully upset and I didn't know why. I was a little frightened and wondered what he would do next and I didn't know what to say."

(5) The social worker's observations and analytical thoughts regarding what has been happening during the interview. "What should I do next? I wonder how it would affect the client if I said such-and-such? Why is he acting this way? I wonder what he really meant by that statement? That seems to contradict what he told me earlier. He said he felt happy but he certainly didn't look it." In process recording, all these silent thoughts are put into writing. If the example of the contact with Mr. Garcia were continued, the next few lines might read as follows:

I was a little puzzled and wondered what to de next. I didn't know whether I should let him shout and get it out of his system or whether I should try and calm him down. I was curious why he was getting so upset but I didn't dare ask him any questions because I was afraid of getting him even more upset. I finally decided I had better show some empathy since he would probably argue and disagree with most anything I said anyway about the psychiatrist.

W: I can see that something about the idea of going to a psychiatrist is very upsetting to you.

C: (Turning and looking straight at me): You bet it is. I've been to those headshrinkers before and I've had it with them.

As soon as Mr. Garcia said that a lot of questions came to my mind about his past history and I knew he had opened the door for me to talk with him about this.

Another example of the worker's analysis and observations during the process recording might be as follows:

I asked Mrs. Jones if she had any income other than what she gets from our financial assistance program. She said not. She seemed very nervous though as she told me this. She was sitting very uncomfortable on the edge of her chair; she had a scarf in her hands that she kept winding around her fingers and she couldn't seem to sit still. She seemed so nervous that it made me wonder if she was telling me the truth or not. I asked her again, "Are you sure you don't have any other income?"

(6) A "diagnostic summary" or paragraph on the "worker's impressions" at the end of the process recording. Here the worker should summarize his or her analytical thinking about the entire interview he has just recorded.

(7) A "social service plan," "casework plan," or "treatment plan" immediately following the diagnostic summary statement. It indicates the
worker's and client's goals for further social service contracts. (Wilson, 1976,
pp. 18–20)

Notice that, in the preceding guidelines, the process recording is very
relevant to assessing a case, and the information from the process recording is used to formulate an immediate intervention plan. Most process
recordings are set up in a column format that provides a place for the different aspects of the recording. Appendix 4B provides an example of a
process recording that a social work student, Teyla Haas, completed in an
educational setting at the School of Social Work, University of Texas at
Austin.

Black and Feld (2006) suggest a learning-oriented thematic approach
for the process recording, which affords social work interns an opportunity to analytically reflect or introspect on encounters in their field education setting. According to Black and Feld (2006), the following information should be included in a process recording:

1. Statement of Learning Themes and Purpose of the Encounter
   This section should be formulated prior to the actual client encounter and
   includes:
   A. Learning theme(s) (student learning objectives targeted by the student
      and the field instructor for educational attention)
   B. A succinct indication of the purpose of the encounter: Why is the
      client/client system being seen? What is hoped to be accomplished in
      this session?
2. Background Information
   This section offers a brief indication of the nature of the problem, those
   present at the session, the setting of the encounter and any other pertinent
   information not otherwise known to the field instructor that might orient
   him/her to the session.
3. Analysis of the Encounter
   What happened in the session? Description, reaction, reflection, and
   analysis. Within the framework of "beginning, middle, and end" of the encounter, the student describes what transpired sequentially in the session,
   using an "expansion/contraction format." [In contraction, the] student
   summarizes or bullets the main topics covered in the encounter. [For expansion, in] this core section of the recording, the student details sections
   of the encounter that relate to the established themes(s) selected for the
   session. Included is an account of what exactly occurred both verbally and
   nonverbally, approximating the client/worker dialogue to the extent possible. Interwoven throughout this presentation is an indication of the student's assessment of the emotional climate of the transaction in terms of
   associated feelings—the client's as well as the students.
      The student interjects analytical comments regarding the interaction re-
   lated to what the student was trying to accomplish in a particular exchange including hindsight as well as evaluative comments. Incorporated

are segments of the interview that the student can use to demonstrate application or evidence of the theme in operation. For example, this may be an instance of successful implementation of a particular skill or a situation in which the student retrospectively perceives that s/he "missed the boat" in relation to the targeted skill.
4. Evaluation
   A. Evaluation of learning theme(s) and the extent to which they were addressed
   B. Evaluation of client/client system purpose
5. Future Plans
   A. For self (learning themes for future attention)
   B. For client/client system
6. Supervisory Agenda (questions and issues to discuss with field instructor). (Black & Feld, 2006, pp. 146–147)

The learning-oriented thematic method provides structure but also encourages flexibility. The model further serves to promote student self-awareness and analytical thinking, as well as practice knowledge, values, and skills related to assessment.

**Case Studies.**   Another narrative method of recording and assessment, case studies, assists social workers in assessing different aspects of the client's functioning and related variables that may affect client functioning. A case study is a systematic organization and presentation of information about an individual case; it is typically undertaken to elucidate a particular clinical entity or problem requiring reflection or intervention (Trepper, 1990).

Case studies can be completed on individuals, families, groups, or organizations (Feagin, Orum, & Sjoberg, 1991; Yin, 2010). They make use of multiple sources of information, including interviews, social histories, life histories, and observations to investigate and communicate relevant clinical data concerning a certain aspect of the case (Yin, 2010). Usually the case study focuses on some descriptively relevant aspect of the case that the practitioner wishes to investigate. The practitioner organizes case information into a narrative summary, to explore or describe the client functioning along certain dimensions. For example, the case study might elucidate the impact of early developmental history on the client's current relationship functioning or discuss the impact of culture on the client's response to treatment.

Case studies have also been used to discuss treatment effectiveness and outcomes (Trepper, 1990). A practitioner may discuss or write a case study to demonstrate how a certain set of interventions led to the resolution of a client's problems.

Historically, case studies were the preferred method for clinical investigation in several fields, including social work (Trepper, 1990). The case study method, however, fell into clinical disrepute with the increased focus on empiricism in clinical science. Scientific control of explanatory variables became of great concern, and any treatment outcomes that could not be verified through quantitative measurement methods and statistical models were considered invalid. These attitudes led many to shy away from the case study as a useful method of inquiry (Trepper, 1990). Recent years have witnessed a resurgence of interest in the case study among clinical researchers and practitioners. For example, proponents of single-case-study designs brought a new empiricism to the case study (in chapter 11, we discuss the use of single-case designs). At the same time, other qualitatively oriented practitioners continued to see the usefulness of case studies and continued to use case study methodologies in their traditional forms (Crabtree & Miller, 1999; Gilgun et al., 1992).

Throughout the years, the case study has remained a favorite methodology among clinical practitioners. Case studies are presented at conferences in narrative form and on video and are frequently reported in journals and books to illustrate different aspects of clients' functioning and their responses to treatments. To present case studies that are rich in detail and filled with thick description, practitioners must take copious notes of their interviews and observations of the client (Crabtree & Miller, 1992; Yin, 2010). As they must with all qualitative assessment methods, practitioners creating case studies must make sure they are reporting the empirical processes that emerge from the client's case. In addition, it has been argued that the case study can serve as a prime source of evidence in developing evidence-based assessment methods (Stickley & Phillips, 2005).

Following are five guidelines for keeping detailed notes for a case study:

1. Record key pieces of information while interviewing and observing the client. These may be in the form of key words or jottings. Use exact phrases and differentiate clinical impressions from empirical observations when necessary.

2. Limit the time the practitioner comes into contact with the client. For example, limit home visits to one or two hours so that stimulus overload does not occur and you can keep track of the information.

3. Make notes about the sequence of events and context in which they occur.

4. Write up detailed case notes that include a narrative account of the interview, observations, and clinical impressions immediately after or as close as possible to the client contact.

5. Write your case notes before sharing details of the case or your clinical impressions with anyone, such as a colleague or supervisor.

Copious notes lead to case studies filled with thick description and clinically useful insights. Without detailed case notes, it is not possible to construct a meaningful case study. Once the case notes are written, the social worker must find a method for reflecting on them and interpreting them into the case study. The immersion and crystallization analysis method that is used in qualitative research is useful for examining the case notes to identify clinically relevant patterns and themes (Crabtree & Miller, 1992). Immersion and crystallization analysis comes from the heuristic paradigm in clinical research that emphasizes self-reflection in the research experience. Social workers using the immersion and crystallization analysis method take the following steps in analyzing the case notes. First, as interpreters and reflectors, social workers enter (read) the text (case notes) with the intent of empathetically immersing themselves, until an intuitive insight, interpretation, or crystallization of the text emerges. Second, social workers investigate and interpret the case notes through concerned reflection, intensive inner searching, and the yearning for insight. They rely on clinical intuition to gain insights into the clinical themes and patterns present in the case notes. Third, a cycle of empathic immersion with the case notes and crystallization is repeated until the social worker finds an interpretation. Finally, the results may be reported as a part of the case study (Appendix 4C presents an example of a case study on ethnic identity). This case study was presented to illustrate the response of an African American adolescent girl to a predominantly white social service delivery system. The case study illustrates the damage done to the adolescent's sense of self (Williams, 1987).

## Self-Characterizations

Self-characterizations is a self-recording method developed within personal construct theory. Another personal construct assessment method, the repertory grid, is described in the next section; however, an exhaustive discussion of personal construct psychology is beyond the scope of this text, and we refer readers to Neimeyer (2010) for a thorough investigation of the constructivist therapies. The self-characterization assessment technique asks clients to write a description of themselves as if they were a principal character in a play. In writing their description, they are instructed to take the position of an intimate friend or a personal and empathetic confidant. The primary purpose of this description is to assess how clients cognitively construct the world in relation to the roles they feel they must maintain. The unique cognitive structures of clients and the clients' social roles can then be explored and changed in therapy.

The written description of the self is extremely flexible and may be adapted in various ways to meet the particular assessment or therapeutic needs of the social worker. Therefore, the characterization can, for example, address a marriage (Kremsdorf, 1985), experience of loss or bereavement (Neimeyer, Keesee, & Fortner, 2000), a characterization of a child by his or her parents (Davis, Stroud, & Green, 1989) or of a family (Feixas,

Proctor, & Neimeyer, 1993). Feixas et al. (1993) give the following example of how practitioners can give an instruction to family members to gather a family characterization from them. The couple and family are asked to take about fifteen minutes to write a characterization of the family: "Write a brief character sketch of the family. Write it from the perspective of someone who knows the family intimately and sympathetically, perhaps better than anyone else knows the family. You should write in the third person. For example, begin by saying, I know the Smith Family" (p. 161).

## Repertory Grids

Repertory grids assess the personal meanings and cognitive constructions of clients along a particular dimension; they have become the most popular and best researched of the personal construct psychology assessment methods. The grid has appeared in more than one thousand studies, and some consider it to be the MMPI or Rorschach test of constructivist assessment (Neimeyer, 1993). Designed to assess personal meanings in relationship to personal construct theory, George Kelly developed repertory grids, which are the most widely known and widely used aspect of Kelly's (1955) personal construct theory. In their manual of repertory grid techniques, Fransella, Bell, and Bannister (2004) provide a systematic review of repertory grids, including specific theoretical rationale and logical structure of different repertory grid formats.

The repertory grid technique draws from an open interview procedure that requires clients to classify and evaluate elements in the environment. The repertory grid aims to identify client's constructs through a continuous comparison of the elements in a perceived field: the individuals' mental frame of reference and the unique meaning and significance individuals attach to their experiences (Borell, Espwall, Pryce, & Brenner, 2003). Repertory grids can be used as both as a quantitative and as a qualitative assessment tool. In this section, we explore their strengths as a qualitative method, yet considerable work has also been done to perfect the grid as a quantitative measure. Statistical analysis of the patterns in the repertory grid and computerization of the grid have progressed significantly in the past ten years (Sewell, Adams-Webber, Mitterer, & Cromwell, 1992). Repertory grids are an example of an assessment method that combines or integrates the qualitative and quantitative assessment paradigms much as the projective assessment measures discussed in chapter 3.

According to Neimeyer (1993), repertory grids may be defined procedurally as a method for eliciting a client's construction of some domain of experience. Typically, the client is asked to compare or contrast representatives from that domain (e.g., family members, possible careers) and then to systematically describe each of them on her or his own repertory of dimensions of evaluation, or personal constructs. The grid may be administered as a formal interview, as a written assignment, or on a computer. Sewell et al. (1992) review several computer programs that have been developed to obtain repertory grids from clients. Computer technologies for qualitative methods such as the repertory grid are on the increase (Fielding & Lee, 1992).

The following suggestions are adapted from Neimeyer (1993) and provide guidelines for developing a repertory grid. First, determine which of the client's experience (domain) to explore in depth; this, in turn, determines the elements used in the grid method. For example, does the social worker want to know about the client's relationship to the opposite sex? Parenting skills? Family relationships? Any element of experience can be used in the grid method as long as it comes from the same domain of experience. Different domains of experience must not be mixed, because the client may not construe them in the same way.

Second, after the elements are chosen, elicit from the client the constructs of the grid, that is, the items from the client's experience that are represented as a construct or a polar opposite for that realm or experience to generate many core constructs.

The practitioner can invite the client to compare or contrast elements. For example, if the elements on the grid were intimate relationships, the practitioner might ask questions such as, "How are your father and your mother alike?" "How are they different?" "How are you and your brother alike or different?" "How is your wife like your mother?" or "How are they different?"

Or, as another example, the practitioner might give the client a set of three elements on the grid and ask the client to compare two of the elements and contrast them with the third. Based on the answers to these questions, constructs would emerge that would represent polar opposite experiences, which the practitioner could be put on the repertory grid as representations of the client's constructs concerning intimate relationships. For example, if a client said that his mother and father differed in that one was lenient and easygoing and the other was strict and harsh, then these dimensions become polar opposites of relationship experiences on the grid.

Third, in keeping with the qualitative approach to the measurement of meaning, the therapist can use the client's own words and representations in developing the grid. The therapist can also develop constructs from the session material. For example, if the social worker had taken an extensive social and family history from the client, it might be possible to ascertain from that material some of the client's constructs. The therapist might also use standardized constructs to compare one client with a group of clients of similar characteristics. For example, it is believed that clients who have been sexually abused have similar psychological experiences, and much research literature is available to describe their experiences. It might be possible to describe the relationship experiences of a client from that material. For example, the practitioner might use control versus lack of control, trust versus mistrust, or manipulation versus honesty as constructs for the intimate relationship experiences of incest victims.

Fourth, after eliciting several constructs from the client, possibly up to ten or twenty, the practitioner can ask the client to compare, contrast, rank, order, or rate each element according to the construct dimensions (side or pole of a cognitive structure) elicited.

Fifth, the practitioner can interpret results of grid assessments by focusing on the content and the structure of the client's constructions. At the content level, grids can be analyzed in a qualitative or impressionistic manner by considering the patterns or unique constructions of the elements and constructs on the grid. At a formal level of content analysis, grids can be coded for their themes or intrapersonal or interpersonal content. For example, themes such as fear, forcefulness, violence, and dependency may emerge as clinically relevant material. The level of abstractness that suggests a client's cognitive abilities in construing others may also be considered in the content analysis. Analysis of themes or abstractness of content are similar methods of assessment, as described by the projective measures discussed in chapter 3. Such methods apprise clinicians of the latent, or hidden, psychological characteristics of a client's interpersonal experience.

At the structural level, grids can be analyzed using quantitative measurement methods, by concentrating on the degree of differentiation in the client's construct system or among the elements on the grid. Specifically, grid-scoring programs can assess relationships between the constructs and the elements and a host of subtler structural features. Many such computer programs provide interactive feedback during administration of the grid (Neimeyer, 1993). Figure 4.1 presents an example of a repertory grid constructed for the client Nadine. Nadine had a heterosexual relationship with Carl, who has now reentered her life. She is confused about her feelings and sexual orientation. Listed at the top are the elements of the grid (the persons); listed on the sides are the constructs elicited. The numbers in the boxes are Nadine's comparisons of elements and constructs: 1 means that the person is better described by the first pole, 2 means that the person is better described by the second pole, and 0 means that neither pole applies. Recall from earlier discussion that there is more than one method for the client to make comparisons of the elements and constructs on a repertory grid. The repertory grid can help access important information regarding individuals' perceptions and interpretations of reality. Such understanding better positions the practitioner to understand how and why clients may use specific coping strategies and, in so doing, offers potential pursuits for change to occur (Borell et al., 2003).

**Figure 4.1**   Repertory Grid

| | Mother | Father | Joe (brother) | Nancy (sister) | Nadine (self) | Paul (son) | Joy (former lover) | Beth (lover) | Carl (lover) | Therapist | |
|---|---|---|---|---|---|---|---|---|---|---|---|
| 1. Someone I am sexually attracted to | 0 | 0 | 0 | 0 | 0 | 0 | 0 | 2 | 1 | 1 | Less sexually attracted |
| 2. Feel commitment toward | 0 | 0 | 0 | 0 | 0 | 0 | 0 | 2 | 1 | 1 | Feel no commitment |
| 3. Committed to family and friends | 0 | 0 | 0 | 0 | 0 | 0 | 0 | 2 | 1 | 1 | Out for self |
| 4. Dependent | 0 | 0 | 0 | 0 | 0 | 0 | 0 | 2 | 1 | 1 | Self-reliant |
| 5. Smart | 0 | 0 | 0 | 0 | 0 | 0 | 0 | 2 | 1 | 1 | Average |
| 6. Introverted/shy | 0 | 0 | 0 | 0 | 0 | 0 | 0 | 2 | 1 | 1 | Outgoing/assertive |
| 7. Sexy and playful | 0 | 0 | 0 | 0 | 0 | 0 | 0 | 2 | 1 | 1 | Boring and serious |
| 8. Moves toward me when I hurt | 0 | 0 | 0 | 0 | 0 | 0 | 0 | 2 | 1 | 1 | Stays away when I hurt |
| 9. Intense | 0 | 0 | 0 | 0 | 0 | 0 | 0 | 2 | 1 | 1 | Emotional |
| 10. Meets my expectations for affection | 0 | 0 | 0 | 0 | 0 | 0 | 0 | 2 | 1 | 1 | Doesn't like to be close |
| 11. Successful in job | 0 | 0 | 0 | 0 | 0 | 0 | 0 | 2 | 1 | 1 | Dependent on me for support |
| 12. Always knows what wants | 0 | 0 | 0 | 0 | 0 | 0 | 0 | 2 | 1 | 1 | Indecisive |
| 13. Trustworthy | 0 | 0 | 0 | 0 | 0 | 0 | 0 | 2 | 1 | 1 | Mysterious |
| 14. Feel admiration for | 0 | 0 | 0 | 0 | 0 | 0 | 0 | 2 | 1 | 1 | Feel sorry for |

## Graphics Methods

Graphic assessment methods are qualitative assessment tools that make use of pictures, drawings, spatial representations, or images to assess the client. There are many graphic methods that can be used in social work assessment; full coverage of these methods is beyond the scope of this chapter. We summarize three graphic methods in this chapter and refer readers to Mattaini (1993) for more detailed coverage of the graphic methods of assessment.

One graphic method developed by a social worker to assess families is the ecomap (Hartman, 1978). Ecomapping (introduced in chapter 1) provides a pictorial representation of the family and its ecological context from a cross-sectional perspective. An advantage of this approach is that it maps the family and the relationships among family members, as well as the relationship of the family to other social systems, such as schools, social services, and work (for an example of an ecomap, see figure 1.2). Ecomaps are excellent tools for creating innovative approaches to assessment. For example, to assess African American spirituality, Hodge and Williams (2002) illustrate how a diagrammatic assessment instrument, a spiritual ecomap, can be used to explore and show spiritual strengths in a clinically useful manner. The spiritual ecomap depicts the existential relationships between the family or individual system and discrete spiritual systems (e.g., God, ritual, faith community, transpersonal encounters). These key spiritual systems are drawn as circles and placed in a radius around the center circle, which symbolizes the individual or family.

The social worker engages the client by exploring the nature and strength of these relationships through open-ended questions such as "Are there particular spiritual rituals that are important to you?" and "How does spirituality relate to your life's trials (blessings)?" Various lines represent relationships between the individual or family system and the spiritual systems. Thick lines represent stronger or more powerful relationships, a dashed line indicates tenuous relationships, and a jagged line denotes a conflicted relationship. Descriptive encapsulations and meaningful dates can be written alongside the lines for further context. The resulting visual depiction allows individuals, couples, or family systems to visualize their own and one another's often subjective spiritual strengths, demonstrates spirituality-related differences in family units, and assists the social worker in understanding the client(s) spiritual orientation. Although the spiritual ecomap was originally tailored to assess spirituality among African Americans, it can be easily modified to reflect the spiritual and cultural sensitivities of other populations.

Another type of graphic assessment technique is the problem, intervention, evaluation (PIE) method, which measures individuals' and family members' psychological commitment to the different roles in their lives. Cowan (1988) originally developed the PIE method. Initially, the method was used to assess a husband's and wife's feeling regarding their roles as they transitioned into parenthood, but the method can be applied to whole families. The PIE is easy to use. Each family member is given a page on which is drawn a circle with an eight-inch diameter (it looks like a pie, hence the name). Family members are asked to list the main roles in their lives, such as husband, wife, parent, son, friend, and student (Cowan, 1988). Family members are then asked to divide their PIE so that the different sections reflect the importance of each role to them. The different sections of the PIE can be measured to determine what percentage of the PIE is allocated to each role. These scores represent the psychological self of each family member.

The Self Concept and Motivation Inventory (SCAMIN), or "What face would you wear?," is a graphic method developed for use with small children. It involves showing children different drawings of faces: one face with a happy smile, a second with a straight line for a mouth, and a third with a down-turned mouth. Children are asked to mark the face that best depicts their feelings about certain conditions, such as how they feel at home (Farrah, Milchus, & Reitz, 1968). This method is best for understanding the feelings of young children and for assessing depression in particular. However, some clinicians have adapted the method for work with families by asking family members to draw one of the three faces for each family member. Extended family members can be included also. Younger children can be included in this assessment technique by asking them which face belongs to each family member (for an example of a family SCAMIN drawing by a female client, see figure 4.2).

## Observational Methods: Participant Observation

Qualitative assessment makes use of two specialized forms of observation: nonstructured and participant observation. Nonstructured observation allows the clinician to observe the client without having a specific preconceived plan to observe particular content. The clinician reflectively records information as it emerges in interactions with the client. This nonstructured method is in contrast to the structured behavioral observation methods described in chapter 2. Participant observation takes the nonstructured method a step further by encouraging the practitioner to purposefully observe the client in everyday life and even participate with the client in his or her daily routine, as nonintrusively as possible. This methodology, of course, requires clinicians to get permission from clients to observe them and assumes that the clinician has arranged for a prolonged period of observation.

Participant observation is a humanistic methodology that is excellent for studying processes and relationships among people (Jorgensen, 1989).

## Figure 4.2    Family SCAMIN

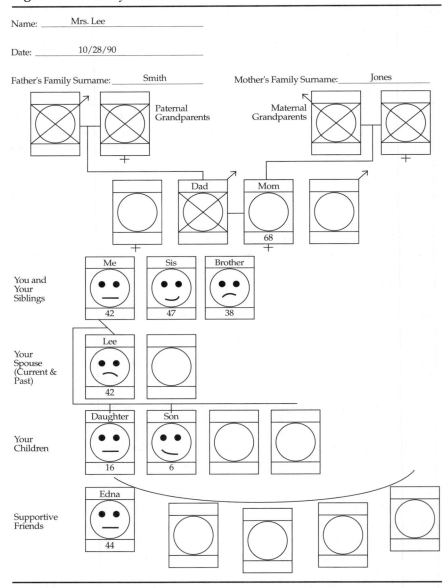

It is considered empowering for both those observed and for the practitioners, because of the ability to study behavior in its natural setting as it is. Participant observation contextualizes culture (Graue & Walsh, 1998) and responds to a variety of abilities (Ward, 1997). It also emphasizes the insider's viewpoint of the participant's everyday life experience. The participant observation methodology originated in the research of social and cultural anthropologists, and family therapists and other clinicians have adapted it to social work research (Gilgun et al., 1992). It also has clinical utility for social work assessment. Participant observation emphasizes the understanding of how the activities of groups and interactions of settings give meaning to certain behaviors or beliefs (Jorgensen, 1989).

Participant observation is most appropriate in the following situations:

- The problems are concerned with human meanings (e.g., beliefs, values), contexts, and interactions that are best viewed from an insider's perspective.
- What is being assessed is an everyday life situation in a setting in which the practitioner can observe or join the activities of the client (e.g., have dinner with the client's family, observe a student in class, participate in an activity at a day hospital).
- The practitioner is able to gain access to otherwise off-limits settings such as a crack or gang house.
- The practitioner is trying to perform an in-depth case study.
- The assessment information needed can be gained from the thick description obtained through the qualitative observation of clients.

As an assessment method, participant observation is especially useful when (a) the practitioner knows little about the client; (b) there are important difference between the outsider and insider view, as in the case of diverse cultures or economic conditions; (c) outsiders usually obscure the phenomenon, as in the case of family life; and (d) the phenomenon is intentionally hidden from public view, as in the case of illegal behaviors (Crabtree & Miller, 1992; Jorgensen, 1989).

The following are suggestions for conducting a participant observation. First, clinicians must gain permission to enter and observe the everyday life of the client. They must decide where to start observing the client and gain supporters from the client's social network who will also agree to the observation. Clinicians must be prepared to reassure clients about concerns regarding their presence in everyday activities. Second, clinicians must establish rapport and develop a trusting and cooperative relationship with those involved in observation. They must fit in with the client's everyday life, be unobtrusive, and play down their evaluative role as an expert. Reflective listening and genuineness are critical skills to be used to gain rapport in participant observation settings. Finally, clinicians should tell the truth about the purpose of their presence but not go into so much detail that they intimidate the client. The initial contact can make or break the observation period. Clinicians should try not to communicate the evaluative nature of their visits. They should, however, be honest if their observations could result in a decision or action that would affect the client's life, as in the case of an adoption study (Berg, 2010; Crabtree & Miller, 1992; Jorgensen, 1989).

Participant observation uses different types of observations. Descriptive observation is less systematic and represents a shotgun approach in which the clinician observes everything about clients and their situation to get an overall impression of client functioning. Focused observation is based on the specific interests of the assessor. For example, if the client's parenting style is of concern, the social worker might observe the client only in interactions with his or her children, perhaps at playtime, at dinnertime, or at bedtime. Selective observation enables clinicians to concentrate on specific characteristics or attributes. For example, if the social worker is interested in assessing only how the client disciplines his or her children, the social worker might observe specific situations between parent and child in which the parent disciplines the children (Crabtree & Miller, 1992; Jorgensen, 1989).

Clinicians who use participant observation use case notes to keep track of what they observe. A simple format will help the clinician keep case notes to aid in the understanding of client behavior and its context. Notes on observations should be able to answer the following questions:

- Who is present?
- What is happening?
- When does the activity or behavior occur?
- Where is the activity or behavior happening?
- Why is the activity or behavior happening?
- How is the activity or behavior organized? (Crabtree & Miller, 1992)

Recording structured case notes that answer the preceding questions will help clinicians draw on their observations to formulate meaningful client assessments. Keeping track of the sequence of events and the emotions expressed during these events may give clinicians further insights into what motivates the client.

Participant observations have many advantages over other qualitative assessment methods. As time passes in an observation in clients' everyday life, clients are less likely to alter their behavior because of the clinician's presence. Therefore, practitioners may gain a more accurate picture of clients' behavior in an observation than in an interview. The longer the clinician observes clients in their everyday life, the more likely it is for the clinician to accurately distinguish between real and perceived behavior. Also, participant observation methods help clinicians learn effective ways to communicate with the client and therefore assist in the reconstruction of client beliefs and behaviors (Crabtree & Miller, 1992; Jorgensen, 1989).

## Combining Qualitative Methods through Portfolio Assessment

Portfolio or performance-based assessments are multidimensional in nature and blend several types of evaluative approaches. These methods have been particularly popular in educational settings that employ school social workers, and they have many different applications (Johnson, Mims-Cox & Nichols, 2009). Wolf (1991) defines portfolio assessment as a "depository of artifacts" that at some point requires "a written reflection by the developer on the significance or contributions of those artifacts to the attributes of interest" (p. 36). The compilation of artifacts, or the portfolio, is an assortment of various documents, some of which may be paper-and-pencil tests or classroom observations; others may be projects, constructions, videotapes, audiotapes, poems, artwork, or stories by the student (Karoly & Franklin, 1996). Portfolios reflect a shift in assessment from a behaviorist framework of learning involving the acquisition of a sequence of component skills through drill and practice to a constructivist lens that regards learning as complex, contextual, and collaborative. Portfolio assessment is culturally sensitive in that it recognizes broad diversity in the pace and style of cognitive and learning development among children from various cultures.

Self-observation and reflection are a part of the portfolio process (Johnson et al., 2009). Reflections are most often written but can also be oral presentations, remarks, or ruminations supplemented by teacher annotations. Writing portfolio reflections is a meaning-making process, a way to help learners think critically about assignments they have completed and the relationship of assessments to those performances. It is a way to consciously call to mind effective and ineffective process strategies; to monitor performance objectives in terms of expectations; and to consider steps in the overall learning process that should be adopted, adapted, or eliminated (Fernsten & Fernsten, 2005). Done well, reflection promotes self-regulation and can help students learn to think strategically (Martin-Kniep, 2000). Two assumptions underlie the use of portfolio assessment in schools: (a) judgments based on portfolios are more reliable and valid because of the comprehensive and inclusive nature of the samples, and (b) portfolios, when used to supplement other methods of measuring learning, will improve the reliability and validity of the evidence (Karoly & Franklin, 1996).

Standards for evaluating performance-based assessments are usually developed after portfolio work has been systematically collected; this method is consistent with the qualitative approach to research and evaluation. This method is also in sharp contrast to traditional testing with standardized measures (discussed in chapter 3), which sets specific criteria or develops normative-based samples for comparison before students are evaluated. The rationale for portfolio assessment is that standards should be locally (and realistically) established only after student work has been gathered. Portfolios cannot be reduced to numeric grades; they must be approached qualitatively, through a multidimensional evaluation. The case study assessment at the end of this chapter further clarifies the usefulness of the portfolio or performance-based methods of assessment.

## Determining Validity and Reliability of Qualitative Information

Recall from our discussion in chapter 3 that validity and reliability refer, respectively, to the accuracy and consistency of the assessment information. The evaluation of the validity and reliability of qualitative assessment data rests on the credibility, thoroughness, completeness, and consistency of the information; how it is gathered and reported; and the logical inferences and conclusions that the clinician draws from this information about the client. Chapter 5 covers in even more detail the logic behind reliability and validity of assessment methods and emphasizes the need to ensure that any method used has reliability and validity—this criteria also applies to qualitative approaches to data gathering. It may not be possible to know from an assessment report whether the clinician is reporting the client's story accurately, but it is possible to view the information in the report, with knowledge of the manner in which it was gathered, and to evaluate the validity and reliability of the clinician's data gathering and the interpretations (Berg, 2010; Franklin, Cody, & Ballan, 2010). Seven suggestions for evaluating the reliability and validity of qualitative assessment information follow:

1. Does the information tell a complete story, and do the conclusions drawn make sense in relationship to the client's story, as told? For example, are there big gaps in the information? Is the information too sketchy? Does it skip around too much to make a clear connection with the clinician's interpretations?

2. Are there missing details or information that would put the clinician's interpretations in doubt? For example, does the clinician make a diagnosis that the data in the report do not support or fail to disqualify a differential diagnosis that is equally as plausible as the one given?

3. Are there any contradictions that may disqualify the clinical impressions—if so, does the clinician explain them in the interpretations? For example, if the clinician interprets that the client had a warm and secure upbringing, but the report gives only minimal information about the client's family history and specifically mentions that the family moved frequently because of personal and economic hardships, perhaps this interpretation should be questioned unless further explanation is provided.

4. Do the metaphors, pictures, or diagrams used make sense, and does the clinician interpret themes and patterns in them? All diagrams and pictures should be provided as part of the assessment report to give others an opportunity to verify the interpretations in the assessment. Although more than one clinical interpretation is possible using these methods, the clinical themes that the clinician interprets and reports should be easy to discern from the data.

5. Did the clinician collaborate with the client in formulating and interpreting the client's problems? Did the clinician check out his or her interpretations with the client? Qualitative assessment relies on the personal stories of clients and their private meanings. Clinicians should ensure the readers of the report that they are representing the client's life context appropriately and without undue interpretations or unsupported inferences. Clinicians should use the client's own language throughout and explicitly differentiate their interpretations from the client's report (see Appendix 4A).

6. Were multiple methods used to gather the information? Qualitative assessment relies on triangulation of data-gathering techniques (e.g., client's observation interview, client's and others' reports) is used to interpret assessment data. All methods and sources should be compared to determine whether they point to the same conclusion. Did the social worker's observations of the client agree with collateral sources' reports? If there was not agreement, was this inconsistency logically explained?

7. Has the clinician tried to disqualify his or her own interpretations? In qualitative assessment, clinicians should seek to prove themselves wrong by looking for other explanations for a client's behavior. For example, if the clinician believes a client has depression, he or she would look for disconfirming evidence to see whether the judgment holds up to further exploration and probing.

## MOVING FROM ASSESSMENT TO INTERVENTION: PORTFOLIO ASSESSMENT EXAMPLE

Qualitative assessment helps us move from assessment to intervention in that we can view the clinical processes through the thick descriptions that result from the many sources of qualitative data gathered from interactions with clients. In addition, qualitative information provides context and meaning with which to make clinical decisions and intervention plans. The following case study, taken from Karoly and Franklin (1996), illustrates the importance of qualitative assessment strategies in effective intervention planning. The sections that follow are from an authors' report on a portfolio assessment of an African American student in a school setting.

## Background Information

The associate psychologist (AP) working in the Judson School District (near San Antonio) in Texas, conducted a routine re-evaluation of a special education student, following the guidelines mandated by the Texas Education Agency (TEA). Essentially, TEA requires that school districts assess special education students in specified domains primarily with psychometric instruments. The student evaluated was a 10-year-old African American male, AM, who was being served in a self-contained Behavior Adjustment Class (BAC) for students with severe behavior problems. The evaluation included standard psychometric procedures including the Wechsler Intelligence Scale for Children, 3rd ed.; the Woodcock Johnson Psychoeducational Battery; the Holtzman Inkblot Technique; the Self-Report of Personality; and the Personality Inventory for Children. Additionally, the AP conducted a clinical interview and consulted teacher and parent information checklists developed by the school district.

AM had a long history of services in self-contained classrooms since the first grade for the purpose of managing his severe temper tantrums and aggressive behaviors. He was initially diagnosed by another school district as having dysthymia and overanxious disorder. After his placement in a self-contained classroom in the first grade, he was never assigned to a less restrictive mainstream setting with exposure to students who were not developmentally disabled. AM enrolled in the Judson School District in the middle of the 1992–1993 school year, where he was placed in a BAC class on his home elementary campus. He has an intact family, which includes his natural parents and two younger sisters. Both parents are blue-collar workers.

The results of the psychological assessment indicated that AM had average intellectual functioning and academic skills ranging from marginally average to below average. Information from this assessment identified specific deficits in AM's math and writing skills. Projective data suggested that AM perceives his environment as threatening, has difficulty with interpersonal relationships, and fantasizes excessively. There were some morbid themes in his inkblot responses including "evil people plotting to destroy the world," "evil fighting evil," and "people and animals who are dead or messed up." Parent and teacher checklists provided corollary information about AM, indicating frequent daydreaming, peer conflicts, periods of mood lability and explosive outbursts, and feelings of helplessness. The diagnoses of dysthymia and overanxious disorder were continued.

## Presenting Problem

When the AP met with the teachers to conduct a planning meeting for AM's individual education plan (IEP), the AP anticipated that she would spend an extensive amount of time developing a discipline plan and that it was unlikely that AM would be mainstreamed. Contrary to the expectations, AM had been mainstreamed extensively in the regular classroom and he was also doing very well. His teachers anticipated a full-time placement in the regular classroom within a month. They related that AM was making B's in all subjects and his behavior was appropriate in the regular classroom, although still aggressive and disruptive in the BAC class. His BAC teacher, Mr. St. Romain, and his regular education teachers Ms. Haushall and Ms. Pruitt, had been coordinating a plan to assist AM in the transition from the self-contained to the regular classroom. Because of the discrepancy between the findings from the standardized assessment data and teachers reports, a portfolio assessment was undertaken with the help of the teachers, and the consultation of a school social worker.

## Sources of Information

Three, ninety-minute observations were scheduled for AM, two in the regular classroom and one in the BAC classroom. Handwritten notes were taken during the observations, and field notes were later typed. Three, sixty-minute interviews were conducted with each of AM's teachers. These interviews were open-ended, loosely structured, and guided only by the topic of the student. The interviews were "conversational" and free flowing, encouraging the teachers to identify what they perceived as important issues about this student and his performance. The flexibility of the interviews facilitated the emergence of new and sometimes unanticipated information.

## The Portfolio Assessment

The portfolio consisted of three notebooks of documents and several individual products that AM had designed and constructed. One aspect of AM's development in which we could see a progression of skills was his written composition. Many of the documents included early and final drafts of essays, themes, stories, and research projects that he had completed. When we examined the range of his writing samples, it was obvious that AM's writing skills had evolved from constructing simple ungrammatical sentences, to composing sentences with correct usage that were more elaborate and descriptive, to organizing ideas with the same topic into paragraphs. AM's compositions included both compound and complex sentences with appropriate verb and pronoun agreement. This is in marked contrast to his writing samples on the Woodcock Johnson, some of which included sentence fragments.

Included in the portfolio were several constructed items, including a pyramid, an Indian village, a wooden stool, a weathervane, a small race car that ran on a battery, and a terrarium. Each of these products demonstrated a multiplicity of skills and was accompanied by a written narrative by AM, describing the item and how it was constructed. We noticed that to construct the wooden stool and the pyramid, AM was required to make many math computations, which he illustrated on diagrams. All of the computations were done by hand (Ms. Pruitt would not permit calculators) and were on an illustration drawn to scale. Besides the hand tools AM used, he also described the use of a protractor for the pyramid and a level for the stool. It did not appear that he had much difficulty applying multiplication and division skills to design these products. The written description of the car with the battery included a discussion of electromagnetic principles. Ms. Haushall reported that this project was actually not assigned, but that AM had requested to work on "something" in his free time when they were studying a unit on electromagnetic energy. Very quickly, she and the class became interested in his project. She noted that AM had taught the children better about the concept of electromagnetism than all of her class presentations had.

Several of the portfolio documents included both written and illustrated book reports. In some, AM had drawn pictures depicting scenes from the books. The illustrations were completed in great detail. For example, a watercolor portrait of a scene from a children's book about King Henry VIII included a drawing of the Tower of London and beside it a guillotine dripping with blood. With other book reports, AM had drawn a series of comic strips in crayon to show consecutive sequences of events in the stories. One comic strip included in the final frame a drawing of AM himself saying, "I'm a Caldecott winner!" (The actual illustrator of the book AM was describing was awarded a Caldecott medal for his work.)

Other entries in the portfolio included several photo displays. One in particular showed the different stages of construction of props used in a class play about the Alamo. AM had been the "project manager" in designing an Alamo backdrop task, which he organized very well. An Alamo profile, a barracks scene, and a small chapel were all developed by AM's team. AM's photo history of the props was an item of great interest to the other children. AM was the photographer for all of the pictures included in the portfolio.

Finally, there was an assortment of quizzes and major exams in the portfolio. AM's performance on these items was variable, ranging from A's and B's on social studies, science, reading, English and math word-problem tests to C's and D's on math calculation and English usage exams. It was interesting that on the samples where AM made good grades, the content was complex and required the application of skills. The documents with low grades were tests of isolated skills that were not linked to a larger project or product.

### Results of the Portfolio Assessment

AM's portfolio was evaluated jointly by the AP and the three teachers who gathered the samples. The products were judged using a hermeneutical framework grounded in a holistic interpretation by teachers who were familiar with the context in which the tasks were performed and whose interpretations evolved from a dialogue and debate among all of us. Therefore, unlike the psychometric evaluation, AM was truly being evaluated within the classroom milieu. True to the findings in the literature (Moss, 1994), there was some debate among us about the merits of certain products. All final decisions were the result of a consensus of the judgments of the four evaluators. Although, in contested cases, the opinions of the teachers usually prevailed because they were more familiar with the context in which the work was performed.

An interesting discovery that emerged from the observations and interviews conducted during the portfolio assessment concerned AM's fantasizing. AM's frequent fantasizing, which was regarded as pathological in the traditional assessment, was found to be an asset for him in his classroom. Ms. Haushall and Ms. Pruitt reported that AM usually "daydreams aloud" before his writing assignments. However, far from being off-task, this behavior seems to reflect his unique style of organizing a task and outlining his composition. Mr. St. Romain regards AM's rich fantasy life as a "coping" style for dealing with demands on him at school. AM keeps a journal in the BAC class that includes interesting anecdotes and reveals AM's internal reflections about important issues (e.g., Why do some kids hurt other kids' feelings? How come if someone hurts you, it's not OK to hurt him back? Mr. St. Romain and Ms. Pruitt reported that when AM is timed-out for misbehavior, he often "talks out" his problems aloud to characters in books, plays, and posters).

Another perceived strength of AM's is a combination of high intelligence and creativity. Despite the marginally average and below average scores AM earned on his Woodcock Johnson Psychoeducational Battery, AM is regarded by his teachers as above grade level and capable of producing unusual and high quality work. Ms. Haushall reported that AM earned a top rating on his TAAS writing sample (Texas Assessment of Academic Skills, a state-mandated achievement test) and described his compositions as full of elaboration and insight. For library week, he wrote a short story that was coherent and entertaining, and he has made numerous oral presentations in class about topics in social studies and science that were interesting and thorough.

Ms. Pruitt and Ms. Haushall both indicated that AM responds well to their correction in the classroom because he wants to "fit in" and "not stand out." All three of the teachers have observed that AM is also a "follower" who is greatly influenced by the peer models around him and who is highly susceptible to peer provocation. If others are working quietly and cooperatively, then he will follow suit. This observation was further supported by AM himself during a classroom observation in Ms. Pruitt's room when she was giving the students a fifteen-minute timed test in math. Aware that AM has difficulty sitting still and concentrating for fifteen sustained minutes, Ms. Pruitt quietly called AM to her desk and asked him whether he needed "more time" to complete his test. AM replied that he preferred to take the test in the fifteen-minute allotted period "just like everybody else." The two regular education teachers have also noted that the other students in AM's classes have extinguished some inappropriate behaviors simply by telling him to stop. This was evident during one observation in Ms. Pruitt's class when AM, while working in a group, got off-task and began drawing and coloring. A male classmate, who is a leader and an athlete, nudged him gently and said quietly, "Put that away and pay attention, man!"

All three teachers have built in both opportunities for movement for AM during their class periods and some choices about planning his work. They believe that both the movement and the power to make some decisions have made him more invested in his work at school. For behaviors that are very difficult for AM to demonstrate on a sustained basis (e.g., pay attention for the entire lesson, avoid impulsive comments), they ask for successive approximations of these behaviors such as attending for ten minutes and remaining quiet until the teacher stops talking. At the end of the day, both regular teachers "debrief" AM about the extent to which he has complied with their expectations.

## Recommendations for Intervention

Findings from the portfolio assessment indicate that AM must see the task as one that reflects his membership in a regular classroom and as one that is part of a larger integrated whole, rather than just an isolated drill. This was well evidenced by AM's desires to "fit in" and "not stand out" in the regular classroom. The portfolio particularly illustrated that AM does well on work that he sees as either directed toward a purpose or producing a product. The work had to be meaningful to him in some fashion. For those assignments in which he was unable to see an immediate goal or outcome (including drills of facts or computations), he was poorly motivated to do well.

AM's general academic functioning, as evidenced by the portfolio documents, is characterized by higher-level thinking skills, clear and coherent written expression, and an ability to read well and reflect on his readings. These results could not be identified by a psychometric assessment because it does not address contextual issues and is limited to sampling only isolated skills in a single session evaluation. (Karoly & Franklin, 1996, pp. 179–186).

## SUMMARY

In this chapter, we have discussed qualitative assessment methods, a distinct type set of assessment methods. We defined and illustrated several types of qualitative assessment methods, including ethnographic interviewing; narrative approaches, such as process recording, case studies and self-characterization; repertory grids; graphic methods; and participant observations. We also summarized the importance of validity and reliability in qualitative assessment and provided some guidelines for determining whether the information gathered in a qualitative assessment has credibility and consistency across data sources. Finally, we illustrated how the clinician can move from assessment to intervention by presenting a portfolio assessment conducted on a client in a school setting.

## STUDY QUESTIONS

1. What are some ways that qualitative assessment methods differ from quantitative assessment methods?
2. How do qualitative assessment methods complement quantitative approaches to assessment?
3. What are some benefits of case studies and how they have been used in clinical practice?
4. What are a few of the helpful elements of a process recording? How do such methods aid work with clients?
5. Write a client note following the elements of good note taking in participant observation.

## REFERENCES

Berg, B. L. (2010) *Qualitative research methods for the social sciences.* Boston: Allyn and Bacon.

Black, P., & Feld, A. (2006). Process recording revisited: A learning-oriented thematic approach integrating field education and classroom curriculum. *Journal of Teaching in Social Work, 26*(3–4), 137–153.

Borden, W. (1992). Narrative perspectives in psychosocial intervention following adverse life events. *Social Work, 27*(2), 135–141.

Borell, K., Espwall, M., Pryce, J., & Brenner, S. O. (2003). The repertory grid technique in social work research, practice and education. *Qualitative Social Work, 2,* 477–491.

Clark, A. J. (2001). Early recollections: A humanistic assessment in counseling. *Journal of Humanistic Counseling, Education, and Development, 40,* 96–105.

Cowan, C. P. (1988). Working with men becoming fathers: The impact of a couples group intervention. In P. Bornstein & C. P. Cowans (Eds.), *Fatherhood today: Men's changing role in the family* (pp. 276–298). New York: Wiley.

Crabtree, B. F., & Miller, W. L. (Eds.). (1992). *Doing qualitative research.* Newbury Park, CA: Sage.

Crabtree, B. F., & Miller, W. L. (Eds.). (1999). Doing qualitative research in primary care: Multiple strategies (2nd ed.). Newbury Park, CA: Sage.

Dana, R. (Ed.). (2000). *Handbook of cross-cultural and multicultural personality assessment.* Mahwah, NJ: Erlbaum.

Davis, H., Stroud, A., & Green, L. (1989). Child characterization sketch. *International Journal of Personal Construct Psychology, 2,* 323–337.

de Shazer, S. (1985). *Keys to solution in brief therapy.* New York: Norton.

Duffy, M., & Chenail, R. (2004). Qualitative strategies in couple and family assessment. In L. Sperry (Ed.), *Assessment of couples and families: Contemporary and cutting-edge strategies* (pp. 33–63). New York: Brunner-Routledge.

Farrah, G. A., Milchus, N. J., & Reitz, W. (1968). *The self-concept and motivation inventory: What face would you wear? SCAMIN manual of direction.* Dearborn Heights, MI: Person-O-Metrics.

Feagin, J. R., Orum, A. M., & Sjoberg, G. (Eds.). (1991). *A case for case study.* Chapel Hill: University of North Carolina Press.

Feixas, G., Proctor, H. G., & Neimeyer, G. J. (1993). Convergent lines of assessment: Systemic and constructivist contributions. In G. J. Neimeyer (Ed.), *Constructivist assessment: A case book* (pp. 143–178). Newbury Park, CA: Sage.

Fernsten, L., & Fernsten, J. (2005). Portfolio assessment and reflection: Enhancing learning through effective practice. *Reflective Practice, 6*(2), 303–309.

Fielding, N. G., & Lee, R. M. (Eds.). (1992). *Using computers in qualitative research.* Newbury Park, CA: Sage.

Franklin, C., Cody, P. A., & Ballan, M. (2010). Reliability and validity in qualitative research. In B. Thyer (Ed.). *The handbook of social work research methods* (2nd ed., pp. 355–374). Thousand Oaks, CA: Sage

Fransella, F., Bell, R., & Bannister, D. (2004). *A manual for repertory grid technique* (2nd ed.). Chichester, UK: Wiley.

Friedman, H. L., & MacDonald, D. M. (2006). Humanistic testing and assessment. *Journal of Humanistic Psychology, 46,* 510–529.

Gergen, K. (2003). *An invitation to social construction.* Thousand Oaks, CA: Sage.

Gilbert, D. J., & Franklin, C. (2001). Evaluation skills with Native American individuals and families. In R. Fong & S. Furuto (Eds.), *Culturally competent practice: Skills, interventions and evaluations* (pp. 396–412). Needham Heights, MA: Allyn and Bacon.

Gilgun, J. F. (2004). Qualitative methods and the development of clinical assessment tools. *Qualitative Health Research, 14,* 1008–1019.

Gilgun, J. F., Daly, D., & Handel, G. (Eds.). (1992). *Qualitative methods in family research.* Newbury Park, CA: Sage.

Graue, M. E, & Walsh, D. J. (1998). *Studying children in context.* London: Sage.

Grieg, A., & Taylor, J. (1999). *Doing research with children.* London: Sage.

Groth-Marnat, G. (2000). Visions of clinical assessment: Then, now, and a brief history of the future. *Journal of Clinical Psychology, 56,* 349–365.

Guba, E. G. (Ed.). (1990). *The paradigm dialogue*. Newbury Park, CA: Sage.

Hartman, A. (1978). Diagrammatic assessment of family relationships. *Social Casework, 59*, 465–476.

Hodge, D., & Williams, T. (2002). Assessing African American spirituality with spiritual ecomaps. *Families in Society: The Journal of Contemporary Human Services, 83*, 585–595.

Hunsley, J., & Mash, E. J. (2007). Evidence-based assessment. *Annual Review of Clinical Psychology, 3*, 29–51.

Hunt, W. A. (1946). The future of diagnostic testing in clinical psychology. *Journal of Clinical Psychology, 2*, 311–317.

Jorgensen, D. L. (1989). *Participant observation: A methodology for human studies*. Newbury Park, CA: Sage.

Johnson, R. S., Mims-Cox, J. S., & Nichols, A. R. (2009). *Developing portfolios in education: Reflection, inquiry and assessment*. Thousand Oaks, CA: Sage.

Karoly, J. C., & Franklin, C. (1996). Using portfolios to assess students' academic strengths: A case study. *Social Work in Education, 18*, 179–185.

Kelly, George (1955) *The Psychology of Personal Constructs*. New York: Norton.

Kremsdorf, R. (1985). An extension of fixed role therapy with a couple. In H. Kutchins & S. A. Kirk (1997). *Making us crazy: DSM—The psychiatric bible and the creation of mental disorders*. New York: Free Press.

Layton, C. A., & Lock, H. (2001). Determining learning disabilities in students with low vision. *Journal of Visual Impairment and Blindness, 95*, 288–296.

Lincoln, Y. S. (2002, November). *On the nature of qualitative evidence*. Paper presented at the meeting of the Association for the Study of Higher Education, Sacramento, CA.

Martin-Kniep, G. O. (2000). *Becoming a better teacher: Eight innovations that work*. Alexandria, VA: Association for Supervision and Curriculum Development.

Mattaini, M. A. (1993). *More than a thousand words*. Silver Spring, MD: National Association of Social Workers Press.

Moon, S. M., Dillon, D. R., & Sprenkle, D. H. (1990). Family therapy and qualitative research. *Journal of Marital and Family Therapy, 16*, 357–373.

Morse, J. M., Swanson, J. M., & Kuzel, A. J. (Eds.). (2001). *The nature of qualitative evidence*. Thousand Oaks, CA: Sage.

Moss, P. (1994). Can there be validity without reliability? *Educational Researcher, 23*, 5–12.

Neimeyer, R. A. (1993). Constructivist approaches to the measurement of meaning. In G. A. Neimeyer (Ed.), *Constructivist assessment: A case book* (pp. 58–103). Newbury Park, CA: Sage.

Neimeyer, R. A. (2010). *Constructivist psychotherapy: Distinctive features*. New York: Taylor and Francis.

Neimeyer, R. A., Keesee, N. J., & Fortner, B. V. (2000). Loss and meaning reconstruction: Propositions and procedures. In R. Malkinson, S. Rubin, & E. Witzum (Eds.), *Traumatic and non-traumatic loss and bereavement* (pp. 197–230). Madison, CT: Psychosocial Press.

Peshkin, A. (1988). In search of subjectivity: One's own. *Educational Researcher, 17*(7), 17–21.

Pettit, J. W., & Joiner, T. E. (2006). *Chronic depression: Interpersonal sources, therapeutic solutions.* Washington, DC: American Psychological Association.

Rubin, A. (2008). *Practitioner's guide to using research for evidence-based practice.* Hoboken, NJ: Wiley.

Sewell, K. W., Adams-Webber, J., Mitterer, J., & Cromwell, R. L. (1992). Computerized repertory grids: Review of the literature. *International Journal of Personal Construct Psychology, 5,* 1–23.

Stickley, T., & Phillips, C. (2005). Single case study and evidence-based practice. *Journal of Psychiatric and Mental Health Nursing, 12,* 728–732.

Swartz, H. A., Zuckoff, A., Grote, N. K., Spielvogle, H. N., Bledsoe, S., Shear, K. M., et al. (2007). Engaging depressed patients in psychotherapy: Integrating techniques from motivational interviewing and ethnographic interviewing to improve treatment participation. *Professional Psychology: Research and Practice, 38,* 430–439.

Taylor, J. B. (1993). The naturalistic research approach. In R. M. Grinnell Jr. (Ed.), *Social work research and evaluation* (4th ed., pp. 53–78). Itasca, IL: Peacock.

Todd, T. (1993). *Pretherapy assessment.* Westminster, CO: Brief Therapy Institute of Denver.

Todd, T. A., Joanning, H., Enders, L., Mutchler, L., & Thomas, F. N. (1990). Using ethnographic interviews to create a more cooperative client-therapist relationship. *Journal of Family Psychotherapy, 1*(3), 51–63.

Trepper, T. S. (1990). In celebration of the case study. *Journal of Family Psychotherapy, 1,* 5–13.

Ward, L. (1997). Seen and heard: Involving disabled children and young people in research and development projects. York, UK: York Publishing Services for the Joseph Rowntree Foundation.

Widiger, T. A., & Samuel, D. B. (2005). Evidence based assessment of personality disorders. *Psychological Assessment, 17,* 278–287.

Williams, B. E. (1987). Looking for Linda: Identity in black and white. *Child Welfare, 66,* 207–216.

Williams, E. N. (2008). A psychotherapy researcher's perspective on therapist self-awareness and self-focused attention after a decade of research. *Psychotherapy Research, 18,* 139–146.

Williams, E. N., & Fauth, J. (2005). A psychotherapy process study of therapist in session self-awareness. *Psychotherapy Research, 15,* 374–381.

Wilson, S. J. (1976). *Recording: Guidelines for social workers.* New York: Free Press.

Wolf, K. (1991). *The schoolteacher's portfolio.* Stanford, CA: Stanford University Press.

Yin, R. K. (2010). *Case study research: Design and methods.* Newbury Park, CA: Sage.

# CHAPTER 5

# Pseudoscience in Clinical Assessment

## Bruce A. Thyer and Monica Pignotti

The cure for the "pseudo-science of much of our present investigation" Richmond claimed, is *"more* investigation" and a willingness to use "our best brains, time and strength upon [the] delicate task of finding out the right thing to do"

—Agnew (2004, p. 106)

### INTRODUCTION

Clinical social workers make extensive use of a wide array of assessment methods, as the preceding chapters have illustrated. This array of approaches to assessment is itself dictated by the expansive meaning of the term *assessment*, which is defined as "the process of determining the nature, cause, progression, and prognosis of a problem and the personalities and situations involved therein; the social work function of acquiring an understanding of a problem, what causes it, and what can be changed to minimize or resolve it" (Barker, 2003, p. 30).

Each of these components in turn—nature, cause, progression and prognosis, personalities, and situations—is of itself a complex concept, and widely divergent methods have been developed to address each domain of assessment. Assessing personalities is considerably different from assessing social situations, which is in turn distinctive from arriving at a prognosis or prediction about the likely course of clients and their situations. Other definitions of assessment are equally broad in scope, such as the following: "Assessment is an ongoing process, in which the client participates, the purpose of which is to understand people in relation to their environment; it is a basis for planning what needs to be done to maintain, improve, or bring about change in the person, the environment, or both" (Coulshed & Orme, 2006, p. 21).

This chapter asserts that clients have a right to be provided with effective psychosocial assessment methods and interventions, when these are known to exist (Myers & Thyer, 1997). Clinical assessment methods should be based on credible, empirical research that shows both reliability and validity. Social workers who waste time and energy learning about and using approaches that lack evidence can harm clients. Using unreliable and invalid assessment methods can lead social workers to make ill-founded and possibly harmful conclusions about their clients, with corresponding negative effects of effective treatment. Social work's association with pseudoscientific assessment practices harms the profession and prevents the field from gaining respect as a legitimate helping profession that provides genuinely effective services to the public. In this chapter, we critique several assessment methods that do not have any research evidence to support their use or that have evidence to the contrary that shows that they are not effective.

This book teaches an evidence-based approach in which social workers seeking to learn about various methods of clinical assessment can and should be guided by existing published research addressing the merits of the assessment method in question. Regrettably, social work textbooks do not emphasize the research basis of practice methods enough. One survey of social work assessment texts found that, "while the notion of needing to base assessments on research and not just on unsubstantiated assumption is actively encouraged in a few textbooks . . . others include little or no explicit discussion of research evidence" (Crisp, Anderson, Orme, & Lister, 2006, p. 352). This leads social work students and practitioners vulnerable to adopting bogus or pseudoscientific assessment methods.

This chapter builds on the previous chapters by critiquing several bogus, unscientific assessment methods that have been used in clinical assessment. Assessment methods covered lack an adequate research basis and would not be selected if practitioners followed the steps of evidence-based practice as discussed in previous chapters. We critique popular clinical assessment methods such as anatomically correct dolls, applied kinesiology, personality typing and testing, facilitated communication, neurolinguistic programming, and the person-environment system. We believe this critique is a useful in helping practitioners become more evidence based in their approach to assessment. We further encourage students and practitioners to evaluate clinical assessment methods according to their scientific merits before adopting them into practice and to discontinue using assessment practices that may be questionable.

We believe this critique is overdue in social work—a focused critique here concerning the validity and reliability of some popular assessment tools may improve future social work assessments. In regards to our focus on the critique of assessment methods, we subscribe to the viewpoint that Pope Benedict XVI (2008, n.p.) recently expressed:

> In some circles to speak of truth is seen as controversial or divisive, and consequently best kept in the private sphere. And in truth's place—or better said its absence—an idea has spread which, in giving value to everything indiscriminately, claims to assure freedom and to liberate conscience. This we call relativism. But what purpose has a "freedom" which, in disregarding truth, pursues what is false or wrong?

# THE RELIABILITY AND VALIDITY OF
# SOCIAL WORK ASSESSMENT

Earlier chapters have discussed reliability, but we return to it here because reliability is of upmost importance to all the observations and information gathered about clients. In fact, reliability of observations is the very foundation of social work assessment and has been so since the field's inception. First, we note Richmond's (1917) emphasis on the reality and importance of objective facts: "The word *fact* is not limited to the tangible. Thoughts and events are facts. The question whether a thing be fact or not is the question whether or not it can be affirmed with certainty. The gathering of facts is made difficult by faulty observation, faulty recollection, and by a confusion between the facts themselves and the inferences drawn from them" (p. 63). Moreover, "no considerable group of social case workers . . . seem[s] to have grasped the fact that the *reliability* of the evidence on which they base their conclusions should be no less rigidly scrutinized that is that of legal evidence by opposing counsel" (Richmond, 1917, p. 39).

Years later, the social worker Mary Macdonald (1953) stressed that "the essence of research is that the findings relate to that which is observed, and not the individual observer. This is the criterion of objectivity, or reliability. . . . In research the burden of proof is on the investigator, and he is expected to show that his results are not the matter of personal whim" (p. 136).

Stressing the importance of obtaining factual and reliable evidence in social work assessment does not imply ignoring the client's subjective experiences, only that attempting to undertake solely a subjective accounting of the client-in-situation is an incomplete appraisal at best. Inferences, however, are best kept to a minimum in most respected approaches to social work assessment. Social workers should ask a series of simple questions about any assessment method they propose to use with clients, and one of the most fundamental questions is, Is there good evidence that the assessment method yields reliable results?

Reliability is important to the evaluation of all types of assessment methods and is a cardinal principle in evidence-based practice when selecting different methods. Reliability refers to the consistency of the results obtained by using the assessment method, and there are different types of reliability, such as test-retest and interobserver (or interrater) reliability. High reliability does not mean that the conclusions are accurate, only that they are consistent, but without consistency in results, no assessment measure can be said to be valid.

If the assessment involves the client's completion of a pencil-and-paper scale, internal consistency, another form of reliability, might be important. If you are contemplating using a particular method of clinical assessment, determine whether considerations such as test-retest reliability, interrater agreement, or internal consistency are important (they usually are). Try to locate information on the reliability of the measure you are considering in published reports. If reliability is too low, then reconsider using the measure.

If the assessment method you want to adopt is satisfactorily reliable, then the next question to ask is, Is there good evidence that the assessment method yields valid results? Different kinds of validity are necessary for establishing good measurement instruments. Among the several types of validity are face validity (whether the measure, at least superficially, appears to assess a certain factor), content validity (whether the measure does a comprehensive, or at least adequate, job of assessing the construct under consideration), concurrent validity (whether the measure correlates highly with known or accepted measures of the construct being assessed), and predictive validity (whether knowledge of the results of the assessment enable you to accurately predict the client's situation at some point in the future).

The next question is, If the assessment method is theoretically based (e.g., clearly derived from one or more formal psychosocial or other etiological or causal theories), is the theory a sensible one supported by adequate empirical evidence? The research basis for the assessment methods derived from diverse theories may be credible only if an underlying theory has sufficient empirical evidence. However, there are many nontheoretical assessment methods. A structured interview designed to assess a client's eligibility to receive certain social or health-care benefits (an eligibility determination) is a clear example of a nontheoretical assessment method. Some structured interviews used to arrive at diagnostic determinations (e.g., a *DSM* diagnosis) are also nontheoretical in that they convey no etiological assumptions as to the nature of the client's presumptive problem. One may use such an interview protocol to determine whether a client meets the formal criteria for a particular diagnosis. The series of questions asked and the diagnostic criteria found in the *DSM* are generally theoretically neutral, not based on any etiological assumptions (e.g., the problem has a biological or psychosocial or familial etiology), and are more focused on simple descriptive features.

Conversely, several clinical assessment methods clearly derive from one or more theories. Often these are theories of the mind or of intrapersonal dynamics, or sometimes of forces external to the individual. Certain forms of assessment have as their default assumptions the hypothesis that dysfunctional family dynamics underlie psychopathological behavior of individuals. Projective tests such as the inkblot test or the house-tree-person test, which asks clients to draw a house, a person, and a tree, clearly derive from psychodynamic theory, as do assessment methods based on the clinician's inferences of what clients say about their own dreams. The Myers-Briggs Personality Type Indicator is a measure of the human personality based on the psychodynamic psychology of Carl Jung, and a social worker's use of her hands to supposedly sense distortions in a client's purported energy field can be based on various theories of energy therapy (e.g., Feinstein, 2008). Behavioral assessment has as its base theory the hypothesis that environmentally based contingencies of reinforcement or punishment can cause a client's dysfunctional actions.

It is important to ascertain whether a given assessment method clearly derives from one or more formal theories, because even if an assessment method possesses adequate reliability and validity, if the underlying theory the method is based on is erroneous, then any conclusions, however reliable and valid, drawn from an assessment method based on that theory are likely invalid. Thus, well-trained clinicians seek out credible information pertaining to the degree of empirical support behind any theories undergirding a given assessment method. If the evidence seems sufficient and the method possesses adequate reliability and validity, then there are firmer grounds for adopting the method in your practice. If the evidence is credible but largely negative (i.e., the theory has been proved incorrect), then the use of any assessment method derived from that theory, even if reliable and valid, is difficult to justify according to the principles of evidence-based practice. If the available evidence is insufficient, or entirely absent (unhappily not an infrequent occurrence), caution is warranted before enthusiastic adoption of the assessment method. It is certainly good to be open to underresearched practices, but one need not be so open that one's brains fall out! What follows is an example of being too open.

Therapeutic touch (TT) is a theoretical approach to assessment and treatment of mental, emotional, and physical ailments and is premised on the theory that the human body is surrounded by an invisible energy field unknown and thus far undetectable by conventional science. Distortions or perturbations in this energy field supposedly cause human distress and illness. Therapists (e.g., nurse, social worker, psychologist) can allegedly be trained to detect these invisible energy misalignments by moving their hands over a client's body without touching the client. When the therapist intuits or senses a distortion adjacent to a particular point on the client's body, the therapist can "realign" the distorted energy field, thus providing relief and restoring health (Sayre-Adams & Wright, 1995).

Some clinical social workers have adopted TT, which has been around for a long time. In considering the validity of TT, it is important for a clinical social worker to appraise whether the human energy fields can be detected at all. If the answer is no, then the whole TT enterprise is founded on a spurious claim. And if they cannot be detected, how could a clinical social worker possibly use TT? A search of the literature will find only one well-controlled study investigating whether experienced

TT practitioners could blindly determine which of their two hands was closest to the investigator's hand (behind a screen and randomly alternated). The evidence was crystal clear: they could not (Rosa, Rosa, Sarner, & Barrett, 1998). This is not to say that TT may not possess beneficial effects plausibly attributable to placebo influences and comforting human interaction, only that the approach is not one that the evidence-based practitioner should offer clients.

Figure 5.1 presents factors that serve as warning signs that a given assessment may be a bogus or pseudoscientific approach to clinical measurement. No single one of the factors can be considered damning, but the more the elements are associated with a given assessment method, the more cautious clinical social workers need to be before devoting extensive time to learning about or using a method in practice. The following sections cover some methods that some clinical social workers have used to assess client functioning and change, but these generally lack credible evidence of reliability or validity.

**Figure 5.1**   Warning Signs That an Assessment Method Is Pseudoscientific or Bogus

---

- Claims that the assessment method yields exceedingly remarkable and effective results
- Someone who is making large sums of money from selling the method, providing training in it, or lecturing about it
- Someone who is receiving significant personal or professional recognition or accolades as an expert in a novel training method
- Requirement that practitioners trained in the method sign pledges of secrecy or promise not to teach others the method
- Use of too-good-to-be-true language in claims (e.g., unbelievable, incredible)
- Complaints that the "establishment" or mainstream is ignoring the method
- Use of neologisms, or new words coined to describe the method and how it works
- Inappropriate application of genuine scientific terminology to describe the use or application of the method (e.g., quantum, chaos theory, neurolinguistic programming)
- Failure to conduct and publish research on the method's reliability and validity in independent peer-reviewed journals
- Overreliance on anecdotal claims and testimonial evidence of the method's usefulness
- Overreaching claims that the method is remarkably effective for assessing an array of often unrelated problems
- Invocation of theological or religious language (e.g., chakras, Reiki, angels)
- Claims of assessing nonreligious but otherwise metaphysical forces or energy fields unknown to science (e.g., auras, bioenergetic fields, meridian points)

---

*Note:* No single warning sign brands a method as pseudoscientific or bogus, but generally, the more of these features that characterize a method, the greater is the likelihood of it being hucksterism.

## ANATOMICALLY CORRECT DOLLS

Anatomically correct dolls (ACD; dolls with secondary sexual character-istics) are sometimes used in clinical assessment to ascertain whether a child has been sexually abused. The use of such dolls seems to have some face validity (i.e., it makes sense), and they are comparatively widely used in the field of child protective services and in clinical social work in particular (e.g., Faller, 2005). The implications of a false positive (i.e., er-roneous conclusion that a child had been sexually abused) or false nega-tive (i.e., erroneous conclusion that a child had not been sexually abused) finding of sexual abuse are enormous, with grave ramifications for a fam-ily. Despite the widespread use of ACDs, the available research does not encourage reliance on them. For example, Cronch, Viljoen, and Hansen (2006) concluded: "Overall, research in this area indicates that anatomi-cally detailed dolls should be avoided with preschool children, due to the suggestibility and lack of self-representational skills found in this age group. . . . Anatomically detailed dolls should be used cautiously, should be avoided with very young children, and should be introduced to obtain further details only after the child has already disclosed" (pp. 201–205; see also Aldridge, 1998; Thierry, Lamb, Orbach, & Pipe, 2005). Anatomi-cally correct dolls are not to be used casually or as a strong indicator of abuse (or its absence) among small children. Social workers employ such methods at their peril, as well as that of their clients.

## APPLIED KINESIOLOGY AND OTHER BIOENERGETIC ASSESSMENT METHODS

The chiropractor George Goodheart (1975) invented applied kinesiology (AK), a procedure that tests the strength of a person's muscles (usually by applying pressure to an outstretched arm) to supposedly provide feed-back about various aspects of bodily or emotional functioning.

The psychologist Roger Callahan applied AK to the treatment of emotional problems and used it in conjunction with thought field therapy (TFT; Callahan & Trubo, 2001), which he invented. Thought field therapy is based on the idea of stimulating acupressure meridian points while a client thinks about an upsetting issue. Callahan uses an AK-based proce-dure that he calls causal diagnosis (TFTDx) to determine a prescribed, in-dividualized sequence of meridian points on the body to be stimulated, usually by finger tapping. It has been claimed that TFTDx has a 95 per-cent success rate (Callahan & Trubo, 2001). Another form of TFT is voice technology, an assessment procedure carried out over the telephone that is claimed to have a 97 percent success rate. Several licensed clinical so-cial workers provide TFTDx (Pignotti, 2005a). Moreover, a licensed clini-cal social worker recently recommended TFT to members of the House Veteran Affairs Committee on Posttraumatic Stress Disorder (Bray, 2007), and a top-ranked social work school has taught variants of TFT (Pignotti, 2007b). Some social workers have offered voice technology to clients (Pignotti, 2007a; Callahan Techniques, n.d.). However, a controlled study conducted by a licensed social worker revealed that no differences existed between the sequences of tapping points identified by voice technology and randomly identified ones (Pignotti, 2005b), thus showing the theoretical foundations of TFT to be false. Furthermore, there are no existing credible studies that support the efficacy of any form of TFT diagnosis or treatment.

## Other Energy Therapy Assessment Methods

Licensed clinical social workers have developed and are practice several offshoots of TFT diagnosis and assessment, such as energy diagnostic and treatment methods (EDxTM; Philips, n.d.). There are no published studies to support any claims of these offshoots.

Another form of assessment and treatment involves the chakras, a proposed energy system in which points on the body represent various organs (based on Hinduism). An MSW developed the Seemorg matrix method, recently renamed advanced integrative therapy (AIT), which is described as "an amalgam of approaches from eastern spirituality, western psychology, and psychoneuroimmunology" (Clinton, 2005, p. 1). In AIT, the practitioner asks the client to move his or her hand down a series of chakras on the body while repeating a verbal phrase connected with a certain trauma. This is believed to move the trauma through the chakras and produce healing. The main Web site for AIT claims that it provides "lasting relief from a range of intractable psychological disorders, physical diseases, allergenic symptoms and spiritual impasses" (Seemorg Matrix Work, n.d., para. 2). These extraordinary claims appear to be based primarily on testimonials.

## Personality Typing and Testing

**The Enneagram.**    The enneagram is a system of nine personality types developed by Oscar Ichazo and the Chilean psychiatrist Claudio Naranjo. Some say that the theological teachings of George Gurdjieff's fourth way influenced the creation of the enneagram, whereas others maintain that the teachings of the ancient Sufis were influential (Riso, 1990). The nine personality types represent different fixations of the ego that limit a person from developing and realizing his or her full potential as a human being. For example, type 1 represents a person who has a fixation on perfection, order, and intolerance; type 8 represents a person who has a fixation on power, aggression, and being dictatorial. No one type is considered superior to any other type, and each type has its strengths and its weaknesses.

A search of the PsycINFO database reveals scant evidence of any formal psychometric analysis of the enneagram. Only one refereed publication contained preliminary psychometric analyses of the Riso-Hudson Enneagram Type Indicator (Newgent, Parr, Newman, & Higgins, 2004). However, the authors did not conduct an exploratory or confirmatory factor analysis, and the reliability (alpha) coefficients produced mixed results, with two types having unacceptably low reliability. Although several other enneagram assessments appear in popular books, they have not undergone any peer-reviewed, published psychometric analyses.

An Internet search on "enneagram" and "LCSW" revealed that a number of LCSWs use the enneagram in their practices, and a recent search of the PsycINFO database found half a dozen references that included "social work" and "enneagram." This method of assessment does seem to be penetrating the world of practice to some extent. One licensed clinical social worker wrote that, although she was initially skeptical, after investigating enneagrams, she found their "description of personality styles to be subtle, complex and useful" (Bartlett, 2005). She found enneagrams helpful in her own relationship with her husband, so she decided to use them in her professional practice. An international study of more than 4,900 psychotherapists, including social workers, found that personal and clinical experience was a more important influence than research the use of particular approaches in psychotherapy based on personal and clinical experience rather than empirical evidence (Orlinsky, Botermans, & Ronnestad, 2001).

**The Myers-Briggs Type Inventory.**    The Myers-Briggs Type Inventory (MBTI) is a widely used personality test based on the personality theories of Carl Jung (1921/1971; see also Myers & Myers, 1995). Katherine Briggs and her daughter Isabel Briggs-Myers developed the MBTI— but neither of them had any formal psychological training. They developed the MBTI by testing out their notes from library research on close friends and acquaintances whose type they felt that they already knew— later they tested out the types on college and medical students (Myers and Briggs Foundation, n.d.). The first three dimensions of the MBTI derive directly from Jung; the MBTI's developers added the fourth:

1. *Introversion (I) versus extraversion (E)*: extraverts are said to be energized by interactions with others and the outside world, whereas introverts draw their energy from time spent in solitude.

2. *Sensing (S) versus intuition (N)*: S types mainly focus on tangible, concrete details, whereas N types focus more on abstract concepts and the big picture.

3. *Thinking (T) versus feeling (F)*: This dimension pertains to how people make decisions. T types make decisions based on principles of logic and reason, whereas F types make decisions based on personal values.

4. *Judging versus perceiving*: J types prefer to schedule and plan their time in advance, whereas P types prefer to live in a more open-ended and unplanned manner.

According to Jung, these personality traits are set at birth and do not change. The types are not intended to be indicative of pathology but are said to be normal, healthy personality differences—there are no good or bad types.

The MBTI classifies the test taker as one of each of the four types, for sixteen possible type combinations. For example, INTJ indicates a preference for introversion, intuition, thinking, and judging. The ability to administer the MBTI is not limited to psychologists. Anyone can be trained under the auspices of the Center for Applications of Psychological Type (CAPT), which owns the right to the MBTI, though the costs of the training are considerable. Several licensed clinical social workers have received this training and use the MBTI in their practice.

The CAPT Web site claims that the MBTI is "based on well-researched and validated personality theory with proven applications in a variety of fields" (CAPT, 2008, para. 1). However, CAPT's own journal has published many of the studies on the MBTI, and reviews of the MBTI literature have revealed serious problems with reliability and validity (Hunsley, Lee, & Wood, 2003; Pittenger, 2005).

In agency settings, clinical social workers should refrain from using MBTI results to provide career advice because of the lack of sound evidence for the validity of the sixteen types and scant evidence for a link between type and job suitability (Pittenger, 2005). Some social work educators recommend that the MBTI be used to facilitate social work field education by using it with students, faculty, and field instructors (Moore, Dietz, & Dettlaff, 2004). We believe that such claims are premature, and until this assessment method accumulates stronger evidence of its validity, its use is not recommended except for research purposes.

## Electronic or Mechanical Assessment Devices

Some practitioners have an affinity for employing gizmos, "a mechanical device or procedure for which the clinical benefit in a specific clinical context is not clearly established" (Leff & Finucane, 2008, p. 1830), perhaps because the use of such devices somehow conveys an aura of more scientific analysis or enhanced credibility. Here are a few examples of social work assessment methods using gizmos:

• *Radionics:* This method uses a device claimed to be able to diagnose and heal people and animals from a distance (Frank, n.d.). Proponents believe that the equipment broadcasts energy patterns similar to those claimed to be in homeopathic remedies and that distance assessment and healing can occur if one has something from the person's body, such as a lock of hair, in the presence of the machine. Some licensed clinical social workers have used this method.

- *QXCI, EPFX, or Scio:* These devices are biofeedback devices that claim to be able to "detect reactions to things like stress, viruses, deficiencies, allergies and food sensitivities" (Hamilton, 2006) and to measure various biological processes in the body. Several licensed clinical social workers have used these devices—one has offered workshops in using the devices for couples (Benoit & Neander, 2008).

- *Clarity Meter or E-Meter:* Proponents of traumatic incident reduction, an offshoot of Dianetics and Scientology, use this device to measure electrical resistance on the surface of the skin. A drop in skin resistance is believed to indicate an emotionally charged area.

- *Gentle Wind Project Instruments:* These instruments—promoted by an MSW and former LCSW—claim to assess for a client what "GWP-given personality traits have been assigned to him or her by the 'spirit world'" (Bergin & Garvey, 2004).

## Other Examples of Pseudoscience

There are a plethora of other methods of social work assessment that are pseudoscientific or bogus, and such methods particularly abound in the fields of developmental disabilities and clinical psychology (see Jacobson, Foxx, & Mulick, 2006; Lilienfeld, Lynn, & Lohr, 2003). Here we cover just a few:

- Facilitated communication, which enjoyed widespread popularity in the 1990s, involves more accurately assessing the cognitive abilities of people with serious intellectual impairments by having a trained "facilitator" hold the person's hand over a keyboard. Those people, with no previous knowledge of the alphabet, could then answer questions, compose poetry, and so on. However, well-controlled studies clearly demonstrated that facilitators were unwittingly guiding clients; in essence, facilitated communication is an elaborate Ouija board (Jacobson et al. 2006).

- Neurolinguistic programming (NLP) is an approach to psychosocial assessment and treatment developed by Richard Bandler and John Grinder and derived in part from the theories of social worker Virginia Satir. According to Barker (2003), "Major components of the model are 'neuro' (the processing of information perceived through the five senses by the nervous system), 'linguistic' (the system of verbal and nonverbal communication that organize the neural representations into meaningful data), and 'programming' (the ability to organize the neurolinguistic systems to achieve specific outcomes" (p. 294). It has modestly penetrated the clinical social work literature (e.g., Angell, 1996). A review of seventy articles on NLP found that proponents' claims of being able to conduct assessments based on eye movements and representational systems (e.g. visual, auditory, kinesthetic) were not supported; no further evidence to support NLP theories has since materialized (Heap, 1988). Social workers can become licensed practitioners of NLP by attending expensive weeklong training workshops and can earn approved continuing education credits by attending lectures on the topic.

- Reiki is a Japanese variant of the laying on of hands (similar to therapeutic touch). Several licensed clinical social workers have incorporated Reiki into practice (for a description of Reiki, see Jackson, 2004). The University of Maryland School of Social Work has provided continuing education workshops in Reiki taught by a social worker, and it is said to be useful for such varied issues as the labored breathing of dying cancer patients, decreasing stress, and improving sleep. However, a systematic review of randomized controlled trials showed that Reiki has no effects (Lee, Pittler, & Ernst, 2008).

- Person-in-environment is a social work effort to describe, classify, and code client problems and psychosocial functioning; in other words, it is an assessment method (Karls & Wandrei, 1992; Williams, Karls, & Wandrei, 1989). A recent literature search found that nothing has been published related to the system's reliability and validity.

- Genograms and ecomaps and are widely taught as clinical assessment methods in schools of social work and are believed to be useful in family therapy practice to help practitioners conceptualize family organization and dynamics (Jantzen, Harris, Jordan, & Franklin, 2006). However, we found no published studies on the reliability or validity of these tools.

## SUMMARY

We encourage practitioners to discontinue the use of pseudoscientific methods and to instead use the principles of evidence-based practice to select reliable and valid assessment methods. We wrap this chapter up with another pertinent quote from Mary Richmond (1917), lest the criticisms of this chapter cause others to view us as professional misanthropes: "No one will accuse me of disloyalty to the group with which I have been identified so long because I have not hesitated to point out its present weaknesses on the diagnostic side. My task was undertaken because there are weaknesses, but it could not have been pushed forward if many social case workers had not been doing effective and original work, though often under great difficulties" (p. 11).

## STUDY QUESTIONS

1. How can social workers recognize pseudoscientific assessment methods?

2. Select one specific assessment method of interest to you. Investigate what is published regarding its reliability and validity. Report what you learned in class, including a recommendation that the approach does or does not seem adequately empirically supported.

3. Why may the use of unreliable or invalid assessment methods in social work practice harm clients and, more broadly, the profession?

## REFERENCES

Agnew, E. N. (2004). *From charity to social work: Mary Richmond and the creation of an American profession.* Urbana: University of Illinois Press.

Aldridge, N. C. (1998). Strengths and limitations of forensic child sexual abuse interviews with anatomical dolls: An empirical review. *Journal of Psychopathology and Behavioral Assessment, 20,* 1–41.

American Psychiatric Association. (2000). *Diagnostic and statistical manual of mental disorders* (4th ed., text rev.). Washington, DC: Author.

Angell, G. B. (1996). Neurolinguistic programming theory and social work treatment. In F. J. Turner (Ed.), *Social work treatment* (4th ed., pp. 480–502). New York: Free Press.

Associated Press. (2006). Gentle Wind Project drops lawsuit against whistle-blowers. Retrieved on July 9, 2008 from http://www.boston.com/news/local/maine/articles/2006/11/10/gentle_wind_project_drops_lawsuit_against_whistle_blowers/.

Barker, R. L. (Ed.). (2003). *The social work dictionary* (5th ed.). Washington, DC: National Association of Social Workers Press.

Bartlett, C. (2005). *The enneagram field guide.* Retrieved on June 22, 2008, from http://www.insightforchange.com/EnneagramFieldGuide.html.

Benedict XVI (2008, April 19). *Meeting with young people and seminarians, Address of His Holiness Benedict XVI.* St. Joseph Seminary, Yonger, NY. Retrieved October 5, 2010, from http://www.vatican.va/holy_father/benedict_xvi/speeches/2008/april/documents/hf_ben-xvi_spe_20080419_st-joseph-seminary_en.html.

Benoit, V., & Neander, S. E. (2008, February 23). *Relationship intention to improve your partnership.* Presentation at a virtual conference of the Repatterning Practitioners Association. Retrieved June 22, 2008, from http://www.repatterning.org/conferencedetails1.htm#SECTION_B.

Bergin, J. (2008). *Inside the Gentle Wind Project: A husband's perspective.* Retrieved July 9, 2008, from http://www.windofchanges.org/Husbandsperspective.html.

Bergin, J., & Garvey, J. (2004). *The Gentle Wind Project: Insider stories.* Retrieved July 9, 2008, from http://www.cs.cmu.edu/~dst/Gentle-Wind/documents/GWP-Insiders.pdf.

Bray, R. L. (2007). *House Veteran Affairs Committee symposium on PTSD*. Retrieved June 22, 2008, from http://rlbray.com/.

Callahan, R. J., & Trubo, R. (2001). *Tapping the healer within*. Chicago: Contemporary Books.

Callahan Techniques. (n.d.). *VT diagnostic support and consultations*. Retrieved June 22, 2008, from http://www.tftrx.com/vt_schenck.html.

Center for Applications of Psychological Type. (2008). *The MBTI qualifying program*. Retrieved July 8, 2008, from http://www.capt.org/training-workshops/MBTI-Training-qualifying.htm.

Clancy, F., & Yorkshire, H. (1989, February–March). The Bandler method. *Mother Jones*, 63–64.

Clement, M. J. (n.d.). *EPFX = QCXI + SCIO (biofeedback)*. Retrieved June 22, 2008, from http://www.bold-eagle.com/home/epfxqxciscio.html.

Clinton, A. (2005). *The theoretical basis of Seemorg matrix*. Retrieved June 22, 2008, from http://www.seemorgmatrix.org/ArticlesPDF/Article.4.pdf.

Coulshed, V., & Orme, J. (2006). *Social work practice* (4th ed.). Basingstoke, UK: Palgrave Macmillan.

Crisp, B. R., Anderson, M. R., Orme, J., & Lister, P. G. (2006). What can we learn about social work assessment from the textbooks? *Journal of Social Work, 6,* 337–359.

Cronch, L. E., Viljoen, J. L., & Hansen, D. J. (2006). Forensic interviewing in child sexual abuse cases: Current techniques and future directions. *Aggression and Violent Behavior, 11,* 195–207.

Faller, K. C. (2005). Anatomical dolls: Their use in assessment of children who may have been sexually abused. *Journal of Child Sexual Abuse, 14*(3), 1–21.

Feinstein, D. (2008). Energy psychology: A review of the preliminary evidence. *Psychotherapy: Research, Practice, Training, 45,* 199–213.

Frank, S. (n.d.). *Homeopathy, radionics, counseling, naturecure*. Retrieved October 4, 2010, from http://www.luizart.net/stephenfrank.html.

Goodheart, G. (1975). *Applied kinesiology 1975 workshop procedure manual* (11th ed.). Detroit, MI: Author.

Hamilton, A. (2006). *We hear a lot about energetic medicine—so what is it?* Retrieved June 22, 2008, from http://www.worldwidehealth.com/article.php?id=391&categoryID=61.

Heap, M. (1988). *Neurolinguistic programming: An interim verdict*. New York: Croom Helm.

Hunsley, J., Lee, C. M., & Wood, J. M. (2003). Controversial and questionable assessment techniques. In S. O. Lilienfeld, S. J. Lenn, & J. M. Lohr (Eds.), *Science and pseudoscience in clinical psychology* (pp. 39–76). New York: Guilford Press.

Jackson, K. (2004). Reiki: Rising star in complementary care. *Social Work Today, 4*(3), 28–29.

Jacobson, J. W., Foxx, R. M., & Mulick, J. A. (2006). *Controversial therapies for developmental disabilities: Fad, fashion, and in science in professional practice*. Mahwah, NJ: Erlbaum.

Jantzen, C., Harris, O., Jordan, C., & Franklin, C. (2006). *Family treatment: Evidence-based practice with populations at-risk.* Pacific Grove, CA: Brooks/Cole.

Johnson, C. (2006). Couple: Maine lawsuit vindicates our claims. *Foster's Sunday Citizen.* Retrieved July 9, 2008, from http://www.windofchanges.org/Couple_-_Maine_Lawsuit_Vindicates_Our_Claim_-_Fosters_7-23-06.pdf.

Jung, C. G. (1971). *Collected works of C. G. Jung: Vol. 6. Psychological types* (H. G. Baynes, Trans., revised by R. F. C. Hull). Princeton, NJ: Princeton University Press. (Original work published 1921)

Karls, J. M., & Wandrei, K. E. (1992). PIE: A new language for social work. *Social Work, 37,* 80–85.

Karls, J. M., & Wandrei, K. E. (Eds.). (1994). *Person-in-environment system: The PIE classification system for social function problems.* Washington, DC: National Association of Social Workers Press.

Lee, M. S., Pittler, M. H., & Ernst, E. (2008). Effects of Reiki in clinical practice: A systematic review of randomized clinical trials. *International Journal of Clinical Practice, 62,* 947. doi:10.1111/j.1742-1241.2008.01729.x.

Leff, B., & Finucane, T. E. (2008). Gizmo idolatry. *Journal of the American Medical Association, 299,* 1830–1832.

Lilienfeld, S. O., Lynn, S. J., & Lohr, J. M. (2003). *Science and pseudoscience in clinical psychology.* New York: Guilford Press.

Macdonald, M. E. (1953). Some essentials in the evaluation of social casework. *Journal of Psychiatric Social Work, 22,* 135–137.

Moore, L. S., Dietz, T. J., & Dettlaff, A. J. (2004). Using the Myers-Briggs Type Indicator in field instruction supervision. *Journal of Social Work Education, 40,* 337–349.

Myers and Briggs Foundation. (n.d.). *Original research.* Retrieved July 7, 2008, from http://www.myersbriggs.org/my-mbti-personality-type/mbti-basics/original-research.asp.

Myers, I. B., & Myers, P. B. (1995). *Gifts differing: Understanding personality type.* New York: Davies-Black.

Myers, L. L., & Thyer, B. A. (1997). Should social work clients have the right to effective treatment? *Social Work, 42,* 288–298.

Newgent, R. A., Parr, P. E., Newman, I., & Higgins, K. K. (2004). The Riso-Hudson enneagram type indicator: Estimates of reliability and validity. *Measurement and Evaluation in Counseling and Development, 36,* 226–237.

Orlinsky, D. E., Botermans, J., & Ronnestad, M. H. (2001). Towards an empirically grounded model of psychotherapy training: Four thousand therapists rate influences on their development. *Australian Psychologist, 36,* 139–148.

Philips, M. (n.d.). *Dr. Maggie Phillips, Ph.D. Referrals and Links.* Retrieved June 22, 2008, from http://users.lmi.net/mphillips/links.html.

Pignotti, M. (2005a). Thought field therapy in the media: a critical analysis of one exemplar. *Scientific Review of Mental Health Practice, 3*(2), 60–66.

Pignotti, M. (2005b). Thought field therapy voice technology vs. random meridian point sequences: A single-blind controlled experiment. *Scientific Review of Mental Health Practice, 4*(1), 38–47.

Pignotti, M. (2007a). Thought field therapy: A former insider's experience. *Research on Social Work Practice, 17,* 392–407.

Pignotti, M. (2007b). Questionable interventions taught at top-ranked school of social work. *Scientific Review of Mental Health Practice, 5*(2), 78–80.

Pittenger, D. J. (2005). Cautionary comments regarding the Myers-Briggs Type Indicator. *Consulting Psychology Journal: Practice and Research, 57,* 210–221.

Richmond, M. (1917). *Social diagnosis.* New York: Russell Sage Foundation.

Riso, D. R. (1990). *Understanding the enneagram: The practical guide to personality types.* New York: Houghton Mifflin.

Rosa, L., Rosa, E., Sarner, L., & Barrett, S. (1998). A close look at therapeutic touch. *Journal of the American Medical Association, 279,* 1005–1010.

Sayre-Adams, J., & Wright, S. G. (1995). *The theory and practice of therapeutic touch.* New York: Churchill-Livingstone.

Seemorg Matrix Work. (n.d.). *Seemorg matrix work: The new transpersonal energy psychotherapy.* Retrieved June 22, 2008, from http://www.seemorgmatrix.org/.

Thierry, K. L., Lamb, M. E., Orbach, Y., & Pipe, M-E (2005). Developmental differences in the function and use of anatomical dolls during interviews with alleged sexual abuse victims. *Journal of Consulting and Clinical Psychology, 73,* 1125–1135.

Williams, J. B., Karls, J. M., & Wandrei, K. (1989). The person-in-environment (PIE) system for describing problems of social functioning. *Hospital and Community Psychiatry, 40,* 1125–1127.

Winds of Change. (2008). *Gentle Wind Project morphs to Family Systems Research Group (FSRG).* Retrieved July 9, 2008, from http://www.windofchanges.org/GWPconnections.html.

# Developing Clinical Assessment Methods for Practice

Special populations have unique issues that can and should be addressed during assessment. Part III identifies these issues for children, adults, and families. Chapter 6, "Children and Adolescents," acknowledges childhood experts' disagreement on the appropriate method of diagnosing children's problems and discusses different diagnostic methods. It also reviews multicultural issues of child assessment. Chapter 7, "Adults," summarizes types of questions and assessment methods that practitioners can use to gain information from adults at different ages and stages of life. Chapter 8, "Family Systems," reviews and summarizes selected assessment and developmental frameworks for understanding the normative characteristics of families, as well as methods that can be used as family information-gathering techniques. Chapter 9, "Assessing Families Who Are Multistressed," reviews families experiencing stressors, including families of gay and lesbian persons and families experiencing child maltreatment.

# CHAPTER 6

# Children and Adolescents

## Catheleen Jordan, Linda Openshaw, and Janie Hickerson

## INTRODUCTION

The special issues of child and adolescent populations are the focus of this chapter, which reviews assessment and measurement techniques and presents a case example. The important environmental interactions for this group occur in the school, at home, and with peers.

Before conducting a formal assessment with a child, it is important to understand the factors that have caused and that are contributing to the child's problem. A thorough assessment requires an understanding of the child's age, culture, race, gender, socioeconomic status, family background, personality, and intellectual capacities. In assessing a child or adolescent, it is "critical to consider the child holistically (i.e., thought, affect, behavior, culture, race/ethnicity, spirituality)" (Yalof & Abraham, 2007, p. 19).

Assessment should not be confused with testing, however. Testing uses an instrument or procedure to measure the magnitude of a variable. Assessment is a problem-solving process in which the assessor uses tests as a tool in combination with his or her knowledge, skill, and experience and in the context of historical information, referral information, and behavioral observations to arrive at a "cohesive and comprehensive understanding of the person being evaluated" (Handler & Meyer, 1998, pp. 4–5). An assessment that considers all aspects of a child's life provides information that aids clinicians in developing an appropriate intervention and treatment plan (Yalof & Abraham, 2007).

Childhood experts disagree on the appropriate method of diagnosing children's problems; thus, the following sections discuss different diagnostic methods and the multicultural issues of child assessment.

## DIAGNOSIS

There are three perspectives on child diagnosis: categorical, empirical, and behavioral (Bornstein & Kazdin, 1985; Harper-Dorton & Herbert, 1999).

## Categorical Diagnosis

The most widely used categorical system for diagnosing children is the *Diagnostic and Statistical Manual of Mental Disorders* (*DSM-IV-TR*; American Psychiatric Association, 2000). As discussed in chapter 1, the categories in this type of system are clinically derived and based on the judgment of those thought to be experts in the field.

Categorical diagnosis describes client symptoms and features such as age at onset, predisposing factors, and prevalence. It also provides diagnostic criteria, such as key symptoms, duration of dysfunction, and so on, which are based on clinical judgment. In general, corrections are made as new data become available. Furthermore, categorical diagnosis is multiaxial; that is, it takes into account the presenting problem and related issues. Box 6.1 lists the most often used categories for describing problems of children and adolescents.

An advantage of categorical diagnosis is that it considers multiple aspects of the problem. For example, if a child is being diagnosed for a language or speech disorder, categorical diagnosis considers the child's articulation as well as expressive and receptive language. Another advantage is that the system gives child helpers a common language for discussing child problems.

Limitations of categorical diagnosis include the continual addition of categories with no supporting empirical evidence. The *DSM-IV-TR* has been criticized for overstepping its boundaries and diagnosing child problems not traditionally considered in the psychiatric domain, such as developmental delays. The low reliability of the categories has also been criticized; research to date on childhood diagnostic categories has not been positive. Other criticisms suggest that the duration of dysfunction or age of onset for some disorders was included in the *DSM* in some instances when there was either no evidence, or conflicting evidence, for such inclusions. In addition, the *DSM* does not give children's social functioning enough attention. Finally, there is no system for prioritizing problems for children who experience multiple problems.

## Empirical Diagnosis

The development of empirically tested measures to diagnose child problems is called empirical diagnosis. Statistical procedures, such as correlational analysis and factor analysis, are used to identify the important features that should be included for a specific diagnostic category or concept. For example, three factors have emerged as significant predictors of child problematic behavior: conduct problems, personality problems, and inadequacy or immaturity (Quay & Peterson, 1987).

**BOX 6.1**
**Child/Adolescent Disorders**

### Mental Retardation (Axis II)

317.00  Mild mental retardation
318.00  Moderate mental retardation
318.10  Severe mental retardation
318.20  Profound mental retardation
319.00  Unspecified mental retardation

### Learning Disorders

315.00  Reading disorder
315.1   Mathematics disorder
315.2   Disorder of written expression
315.9   Learning disorder NOS

### Motor Skills Disorder

315.4   Developmental coordination
        disorder

### Communication Disorders

315.31  Expressive language disorder
315.31  Mixed receptive-expressive
        language disorder
315.39  Phonological disorder
307.0   Stuttering
307.9   Communication disorder NOS

### Pervasive Developmental Disorders (Axis I)

299.00  Autistic disorder
299.80  Rett's disorder
299.10  Childhood disintegrative
        disorder
299.80  Asperger's disorder
299.80  Pervasive developmental
        disorder NOS

### Attention-Deficit and Disruptive Behavior Disorders (Axis I)

314.    Attention-deficit/hyperactivity
        disorder
314.01  Combined type
314.00  Predominantly inattentive type
314.01  Predominantly hyperactive-
        impulsive type
314.9   Attention-deficit/hyperactivity
        disorder NOS
312.8   Conduct disorder
        Specify type:
        childhood-onset type/
        adolescent-onset type
313.81  Oppositional defiant disorder

### Feeding and Eating Disorders of Early Childhood

307.52  Pica
307.53  Rumination disorder
307.59  Feeding disorder of infancy or
        early childhood

### Tic Disorders (Axis I)

307.23  Tourette's disorder
307.22  Chronic motor or vocal tic
        disorder
307.21  Transient tic disorder
        Specify: single episode or
        recurrent
307.20  Tic disorder NOS

### Elimination Disorders

        Encopresis
787.6   With constipation and
        overflow incontinence
307.7   Without constipation and
        overflow incontinence
307.6   Enuresis (not due to a general
        medical condition)
        Specify type: nocturnal only/
        diurnal only/nocturnal and
        diurnal

### Other Disorders of Infancy, Childhood, or Adolescence (Axis I)

313.23  Selective mutism
313.89  Reactive attachment disorder
        of infancy or early childhood
        Specify type: inhibited type/
        dishibited type
307.30  Stereotype/movement disorder
        Specify: if with self-injurious
        behavior
309.21  Separation anxiety disorder
        Specify: if early onset
313.9   Disorder of infancy,
        childhood, or adolescence
        NOS

**NOS = Not Otherwise Specified**

In addition to identifying groupings of symptoms or syndromes that have been empirically derived, empirical diagnosis uses multivariate classification (use of several different measures) to diagnosis a problem. Reviews of these multivariate studies show similarities.

Advantages of empirically derived diagnosis include evaluating the child across all areas (factors) included in the empirically derived test. Because testing provides an empirically derived score, children's problems can also be prioritized, an advantage over the *DSM*). Finally, because tests provide interpretive data that enable comparison of the child's score with a normative group, empirically derived tests help establish how children compare with their peers.

Limitations of empirically derived testing include variation in a given analysis resulting from such factors as rater reliability, appropriateness of the clinical sample, and item content. Furthermore, data collected are often from parent or teacher reports rather than observations of behavior. Such reports are not always verified by comparison with direct observation of the problem behavior.

Finally, parents may suffer from their own marital or individual problems that influence the ratings.

### Behavioral Diagnosis

Characteristics of behavioral diagnosis include emphasis on a functional analysis of behavior rather than reliance on a categorical system such as the *DSM*. Functional analysis seeks to identify or operationalize children's specific problematic behaviors and the controlling conditions that continue or promote those behaviors. The behaviors, in turn, are targeted for modification. A behavior observation that measures the frequency of specific behaviors in a given time is a prerequisite to a functional analysis. The behavior observation provides data to conduct a functional analysis of a child with problems in the classroom. For example, a behavior observation may reval that a child initiates conversations with other children and leaves his seat without permission approximately three times per half hour of observation period. A functional analysis reveals that these incidents occur only in reading class, where the teacher has a somewhat authoritarian disciplinarian style that seems to elicit disruptive behavior from the child. A second characteristic of behavioral diagnosis is the classification of behavior into broad categories, such as excesses and deficits. In the foregoing example, the child is excessively out of his seat. Third, behavioral diagnosis relies on direct measurement of the specific problem behavior. The teacher might measure or count the number of incidents of disruptive behavior (e.g., number of times child left seat).

One advantage of behavioral diagnosis is that it is highly individualized. It provides an in-depth analysis of a specific child's problematic behavior, the controlling conditions, and the modifications necessary for change. Behavioral diagnosis provides information on specific problems targeted for change, which facilitates an easy transition from assessment to treatment.

Limitations of behavioral diagnosis relate to the lack of a classification system, which hampers accumulation of knowledge. Also, because behavioral diagnosis is oriented toward assessing the problem in the present rather than looking into the past, relevant historical factors (e.g., onset, depth of dysfunction) may be overlooked. The behavioral literature does not reflect what types of clients have which types of problems.

In contrast to classifying children's problems according to diagnostic or other criteria, psychological theories explain how children acquire behavior, problematic or otherwise. The next section reviews prominent child developmental theories.

In summary, a child assessment that includes all three types of diagnosis—categorical, empirical, and behavioral—is the strongest assessment. Using all three methods together, the social worker can get a complete picture of the child's problems and strengths. Theories of child development guide the social worker's selection of assessment tools.

## PSYCHOLOGICAL THEORIES

Barth (1986) suggests that children's problems may be time limited, because children often outgrow their problems. Stage theories of development, such as the theories of Piaget (2001) and Erikson (1993), suggest that children go through fixed developmental stages. Given more credence in recent years, however, are theories that show the developmental process to be more flexible; that is, children must have the maturational readiness and learning opportunities in the environment before they can move ahead. Therefore, children develop at different rates. This also implies that all children can learn and change. The major child developmental theories can be categorized as cognitive, affective, or learning (Bloom, 1984).

### Cognitive Theories

The cognitive theories of Kohlberg (1981) and Piaget (2001) describe development from the perspective of how one's mental processes perceive and affect one's experience in the world. The development of mental processes or structures is the focus of the theory. Information is believed to be assimilated into existing mental structures, which are represented as schemata; integration of new experiences occurs by accommodation. Piaget (2001) described four discrete stages to explain this development.

The first stage, the sensorimotor period, describes cognitive development from birth to two years of age. During this period, an infant's contact with the world is through the senses, that is, by sucking, tasting, touching, hearing, and seeing. Piaget describes the essential tasks that infants have during this period: differentiation of self from others, or object permanence; recognition that external people or objects can be experienced through more than one sense; and beginning formation of cognitive schemata through interaction with others or objects.

The second stage, the preoperational period, occurs from ages two to seven and is composed of two phases, egocentric and intuitive. Egocentricism describes the child who is more attentive to current experiences and environment but, through language development, begins to develop more symbolic processing. This symbolic processing is continued in the intuitive phase.

The third stage, the period of concrete operations, lasts from ages seven to eleven. The development of logical thinking, classification, seriation, and conservation charactize this stage, as does what Piaget calls decentering, or moving away from the previous egocentric view of the world.

The fourth stage is the period of formal operations and lasts from ages eleven to fifteen. In this, the highest form of cognitive development that Piaget described, children develop the ability to logically reason, both inductively and deductively.

Piaget described children's moral development as occurring in two stages: heteronomy and autonomy. Children's adherence to the fixed rules of others, particularly the parents, characterizes the first stage. Children gradually move into the second phase, which is characterized by rules that can be negotiated and changed by mutual consent.

Kohlberg (1981) furthered the discussion of children's moral development by describing three levels of moral development: premoral, conventional, and postconventional. Each level has two stages that describe the choices individuals have at each level.

The premoral phase coincides with the preoperational stage of cognitive development. The two stages are punishment and obedience, in which the child obeys the rules to avoid being punished, and instrumental behavior, in which the child obeys to be rewarded.

The conventional phase is reached after the period of concrete operations begins. The two stages are conformity, in which the child seeks approval and tries to avoid disapproval from others, and law and order, in which the child obeys because of a respect for law and order.

The postconventional level is reached after the formal operations stage. The two stages are social contracts, in which the child makes rational decisions but the law is the final word, and the perception of universal ethical principles, in which the child bases moral decisions on his or her conscience.

The strongest research support for the cognitive model appears to be for the substages in the sensorimotor stage and for the concrete operational stage. Findings from studies on the other stages are less clear cut. Both Piaget and Kohlberg have been criticized for the difficulty of replicating their research findings and by critics who believe that their view minimizes the role of the environment.

## Affective Theories

Numerous theorists and practitioners concerned with personality development from the affective perspective have extended the work of Sigmund Freud. The affective perspective of child development is concerned primarily with the role of feelings in human behavior rather than the rate of thought, as with the cognitive theories described previously. Freud's work is described in five dimensions: dynamic, genetic, topographical, structural, and economic.

The dynamic dimension describes psychological energy located in the instincts, innate structures that direct behavior (e.g., the libido, an unconscious force that is expressed sexually). Freud also described the pleasure principle, a child's tendency to seek pleasure and avoid painful experiences or tensions.

The genetic or developmental dimension describes stages or periods that Freud felt to be a part of every individual's history. First, the oral period is represented by the infant's mouth and the taking in of food, and symbolically the taking in of other nourishment such as warmth. The developing child then faces the challenge of toilet training, which leads to the second stage, which Freud called the anal stage. The child's ability to exert control over his or her bodily functions, and perhaps to be in conflict with parental demands, may contribute to problems that continue in the individual's adult life. The third stage is referred to as the phallic period and involves the child's developing awareness of his or her genitalia. The next stage, the latency period, is a time when sexual issues are suppressed by the child's entering school and becoming refocused on other issues. However, in the genital period, which begins in puberty, sexual issues again become important to the developing child. Children are believed to need to achieve mastery in each of these stages before they can successfully move on to the others. If children do not achieve mastery, they can become fixated at any one point and will display signs of this lack of resolution.

In the topographical or depth dimension, Freud described three personality components believed to account for behavior: the unconscious, the conscious, and the preconscious. The unconscious component is outside of the person's awareness and believed to be mostly composed of the id. The conscious component is a smaller area of awareness, focused on something in the present. The preconscious is outside current awareness but accessible. The material in the unconscious is believed to be accessible only through mechanisms such as a slip of the tongue or somatically as in the case of phobias.

The structural dimension describes the personality, as divided into id, ego, and superego. The id is believed to be unconscious and represents the primitive portion of the personality, which operates on the basis of the pleasure principle. The ego develops next and is the rational portion of the personality. It seeks to express id impulses in a more rational fashion. Finally, the superego is composed of the ego ideal, that is, the information about good and bad that the child learns from the parents, the conscience, and the information about good and bad that the child learns from the parent's actions.

The economic dimension describes how children use their inherent energy. Psychic investment toward a specific object is called cathexis. External conditions may prohibit expending energy toward an object, which is anticathexis; in this case, the child forms internal mechanisms to block or delay the energy.

Erikson (1993) described eight psychosocial developmental issues: trust, autonomy, initiative, industry, identity, intimacy, generativity, and integrity. These issues correspond to eight stages of the life span, from infancy and early childhood to old age. As did Freud, Erikson postulated that the child had to resolve the tasks of one stage before moving onto the tasks of the next stage.

Affective theories have been criticized for their lack of empirical evidence and for the difficulty involved in operationalizing the concepts. However, recent attempts to study psychoanalytic theory have provided some support for some of the concepts.

## Learning Theories

So far, we have reviewed thinking and feeling theories of child development. Learning theories focus on acting, which is behavior itself. Three learning models are discussed here: respondent conditioning, operant conditioning, and social learning theory. These models share the common idea that behavior is learned.

Pavlov's (1927/1960) respondent, or classical, conditioning model illustrates the learning process as follows. Pavlov found that food (a natural or unconditional stimulus) elicited a salivation response. He paired the natural stimulus with another stimulus, a bell. This second stimulus, after repeated pairings with the natural stimulus, also elicited the salivation response without the presentation of the food. The second stimulus is now called the conditioned stimulus and has the power to condition other stimuli. This conditioning process occurs with objects, persons, and verbal behavior as well; for example, a baby is comforted by his or her baby blanket, which was conditioned by pairings with mother and feedings.

Skinner's (1972) operant conditioning model proposes that behavior is learned as a consequence of the rewards or punishments that follow the behavior. If the behavior is positively reinforced, it is more likely to occur again; it is less likely to occur again if an aversive experience follows the behavior. If the parent or teacher gives attention only when a child acts disruptively at home or in class, the child will continue to be disruptive. Schedules or contingencies of reinforcement determine how quickly behavior is learned and how well established it will be. Continuous reinforcement encourages behavior to be emitted more quickly, whereas intermittent reinforcement establishes behavior at a slower rate. Behavior reinforced intermittently maintains longer after cessation of reinforcement than does behavior reinforced continuously. For example, if a child is rewarded with candy every time she carries her dishes to the sink, she will learn this behavior quickly but stop quickly if the reward is stopped. A child rewarded only some of the time will take longer to learn the behavior; however, once the child learns the behavior, he or she will maintain it for a longer time, because the child thinks a reward is forthcoming.

Bandura's (1977) social learning theory elaborates on learning by respondent or operant mechanisms, which contributes the idea of vicarious learning; that is, learning may occur by observation of a model and by observation of the consequences of the model's behavior. Bandura's studies on the vicarious development of aggressive social behavior has contributed to the debate on causes of aggressive behavior in children and others. Bandura showed that children viewing adults modeling aggressive behavior were more likely to exhibit the same aggressive behavior than children who did not view these adult models.

Learning theorists have contributed more empirical research to support their theoretical views than have cognitive or affective schools of thought. Bloom (1984) recommends, however, that "until such time as enough of the evidence is in to maintain or to discontinue use of one or another theory, the student is probably most wise to study their major representatives and try to become facile in all of them" (p. 312). The following sections review social theories, familial and environmental.

## Social Theories

Child problems are a symptom not of individual pathology but of a malfunctioning ecosystem, according to some (Barth, 1986; Harper-Dorton & Herbert 1999; Janzen, Harris, & Jordan, & Franklin, 2005). These researchers assert that positive changes are longer lived when children's problems are assessed and treated in the broader context of the family and the environment. Next, we review issues related to familial and environmental theories that affect child problems.

## Familial Theories

Children's problems are related to the number of stressful events the family experiences. Also, as children grow, their normal developmental changes may lead to maladjustment. Isolated families and those living in rural settings often have limited resources to help them adjust to developmental changes (Barth, 1986). Family isolation with limited access to resources and supportive extended family members can be a stress factor for both parents and children (Openshaw & Halvorson, 2005).

Physical or mental issues, or parent or family morale problems, may affect children (Jordan & Hoefer, 2002). Domestic violence, either a single incident or long-term violence, affects a child's emotional state and development. The more intense and long lasting the exposure, the more severely the child is affected. Direct exposure to violence, such as when the child is hit, or indirect exposure, such as when the child merely hears parents fighting, both have devastating effects on children (Openshaw & Halvorson, 2005). Likewise, child abuse and neglect influence the child's development. Early trauma or emotional neglect interferes with the brain's development of explicit memory and the capacity for empathy and modulation of impulses. Continued trauma may also affect cognitive and social development. Persistent and severe abuse may result in pervasive developmental delays (Davies, 2004; Nelson & Carver, 1998; Perry, 1997).

Trauma that results from abuse, neglect (e.g., removal from the home or foster care placement), and exposure to violence may interfere with a child's cognitive development. According to Perry (2002), trauma can create a lifetime loss of potential. Accordingly, assessment of cognitive abilities must consider exposure to trauma.

Family changes or transitions cause stress (Jordan & Cobb, 2001). The traditional family that consists of a father who goes out to work and a mother who stays home with the two kids is virtually nonexistent. New family styles, such as dual working couples, single-parent families, and remarried or blended families all have associated stressors. Other family transitions, such as the birth of a sibling or children leaving for college, can also cause stress on the family system. Any family change may be expected to cause at least temporary discomfort for the parents and children, and any loss of money or status can be extremely devastating.

Although more and more mothers work outside the home and share the role of provider, women still do the majority of the housework, with resultant fatigue, morale problems, and resentment. A mother's working outside the home may benefit the family by helping her feel better about herself and by enhancing the family income. Problems may arise, however, when family members move from work or school to home life. Other parental job factors that may affect children's adjustment include parental job loss or transfer. Parent psychopathology, divorce, or spouse abuse can also affect children.

## Environmental Theories

Parents' friendships and other external relationships define their perception of their children's adjustment (or lack of it) (Barth, 1986). Parents learn what is "normal" and how their children stack up to other children by comparing them with others in their neighborhood. Parents' social supports, friends, family, and neighbors all informally support parenting efforts. Some communities have more formal support systems, such as parenting classes and alcoholic support groups for parents.

The primary settings in which children are expected to perform are the home and the school (Barth, 1986). Studies show that children's personalities and environments determine their behavior. Some studies find that children behave differently at home than at school, but others find that children's behavior is consistent across settings. Children need social, cognitive, and self-management competencies to be successful at home and at school.

Social competencies include the ability to accept influence, exert influence, learn from models, accept reprimands, negotiate with others, protect oneself from others, groom oneself, engage the company of others and avoid isolation, and resolve conflicts with strategies such as problem solving.

Cognitive competencies include cognitive skills for solving interpersonal problems: identifying the problem, generating alternative solutions, seeing the other party's viewpoint, seeing the consequences of the alternative solutions, evaluating the consequences, and choosing the best solution.

Self-management competencies include commitment, goal setting, arousal management, self-monitoring, evaluation, and self-administration of consequences (self-reinforcement).

Individual factors, such as social competencies, cognitive abilities, and self-management skills, contribute to a child's ability to thrive in difficult situations. Likewise, the child's family and environment may aid the child's normal development. Family factors that encourage the child's normal development include secure attachment with a positive and warm parental relationship, parental support during stress, parental marital stability, structure, and high parental expectations. Environmental factors that aid a child's normal development include middle class and above socioeconomic status, available health care and social services, consistent parental employment, adequate housing, family religious participation, good schools, and supportive adults outside the family (Davies, 2004).

The child's level of motivation—the interaction between individuals and their environments—is an important part of the environmental picture. A lack of motivation indicates that social or material incentives should be considered for the child. For example, parents can reward the child for completing homework assignments with a point system. The child can then exchange points for toys, privileges, and so forth.

Finally, the child's culture is an important part of assessing the child's environment. It is important to know how the members of the child's culture and ethnic background define child problems, child discipline, and so forth, as discussed in the following section on children of color.

## CHILDREN OF COLOR

Children and families of color require special consideration and should be assessed as framed by Erikson's (1993) developmental stages, ecological systems, and with a cross-cultural perspective (Gibbs & Huang, 2003; Janzen et al., 2005). Canino and Spurlock (2000) discuss a multiaxial approach to assessment and intervention with children of color; this approach should be spearheaded by a culturally competent practitioner who is willing to consider ethnicity and immigration status in assessment and who is willing to advocate for change in larger systems, such as school and community, as part of the intervention process.

### Psychosocial Adjustment

Individual psychosocial adjustment includes several special considerations. Low-income minority children may suffer from the effects of malnutrition, which leads to lack of energy and stunted growth; therefore, a physical exam may be indicated. Children's affect may be a product of cultural variation; for example, not making eye contact may indicate respect for adults rather than lack of respect. Particular ethnic groups may differently define self-esteem, interpersonal competence, achievement, and attitudes toward autonomy; therefore, it is important to check one's assumptions and determine the norms for ethnic groups. Ethnicity and culture affect all aspects of a child's life. Migration and acculturation experiences vary among minorities and can be stressful events, especially if a youth emigrates from a war-torn country. Psychosocial adjustment should be carefully assessed in this context (Guarnaccia & Lopez, 1998). Achievement might be defined in ways other than the traditional majority-culture definition of educational achievement (Nurmi, 1993); if so, assessment should focus on the child's success in other areas, such as sports or music. Beliefs about development and behavior vary widely cross-culturally. Even the emergence of language is regarded uniquely according to ethnicity. Some cultures value characteristics such as dependence and passivity, whereas others prize independence and assertiveness (Johnson-Powell, Yamamoto, & Arroyo, 1997). Ethnic groups have different methods of teaching children how to manage aggression and control impulses. Some may use guilt, and others, shame. Finally, coping and defense mechanisms to protect the child from anxiety may be either externalizing (e.g., acting out, yelling) or internalizing (e.g., withdrawing from social situations).

## Relationships with Family

A second area for assessment is family relationships. Ethnicity and social class influence family size, structure, traditions, and so forth, all of which influence the child's role in the family. Some important characteristics that may prescribe norms or expectations for children include age, sex, birth order, physical characteristics, and personality traits. Families also differ in terms of parental authority, disciplinary practices, communication styles, and language fluency, all of which should be topics in the assessment. Recognizing the family beliefs, the level of acculturation and the degree of involvement in neighborhood and community can provide important information in assessment, as can religion. In some cases, religion plays an important role in health issues as well as in the family value system. Acknowledging not only the parents but also extended family, and significant adults such as "healers" and religious leaders, can improve the prospects for successful intervention (Barona & de Barona, 2000; Canino & Spurlock, 2000).

## School Adjustment and Achievement

School adjustment and achievement should be assessed from four perspectives: psychological adjustment, behavioral adjustment, academic achievement, and relationships with peers. Children from low-income minority families sometimes have difficulty making the transition to school environment from homes that are different from the societal norm. Families may lack education and view the educational system negatively, they may be unfamiliar with school requirements, or they may have language and other difficulties. Therefore, a review of records, sensitive interviews with parents and children, and interviews with teachers can establish rapport and enlist needed support for intervention. Furthermore, expectations and cultural norms can emerge to direct the clinician in interpreting the assessment in the appropriate ethnic context. When assessing or testing a minority child, the practitioner may want to suspend some procedures. For example, use of time-limited standardized tests may work unnecessarily against the child (Gopaul-McNicol & Armour-Thomas, 2001).

Adolescents may fear school or fear the rejection they may suffer from being different. Minority children account for a proportion of students with behavior problems that result from their propensity to solve problems or to cope with the environment by acting out. Behavior problems, however, may be symptoms of other, more worrisome problems, such as poor health from inadequate nutrition or health care. In addition, the social pressures of being a minority, of feeling disempowered, of chronic poverty and anxiety predispose these children and adolescents to depression (Roberts & Chen, 1995; Siegel, Aneshensel, Taub, Cantwell, & Driscoll, 1998). Minority students do not generally do as well in school as white students and have more problems with dropping out and with expulsion and suspension. Some of the problems may lie with inappropriate testing procedures; IQ and achievement tests may not be culturally sensitive. Also, children may have motivational deficits or lack of parental support. Study skills should also be assessed.

## Peer Relationships

Peer relationships are an indicator of the minority child's well-being. Peer interactions, or lack thereof, and degree of involvement may indicate the child's perception of self in relation to the larger society. Peer-group assessment should be done at the school and community level, as the child may have different experiences in the two settings. Peer interactions, and particularly opposite-sex relationships, may be an issue for biracial youths.

## Adaptation to the Community

The child's overall community relationships should be assessed, as these may indicate the child's adjustment. Specific areas to look for include the child's group and community involvement, as well as special interests or abilities that could help the child develop a sense of competence. Gibbs and Huang (2003) stress that these assessment guidelines should serve as general guides to assessing children in their unique culture. They point out that there is variation within ethnic groups and that one should consider the uniqueness of each child.

One must always, also, be aware of the conditions by which the child arrived in the mainstream culture. Immigrant children have different issues, such as the trauma of hurriedly leaving a country torn by war or political upheaval, whereas children of color who were born into minority status may be fully acculturated. In all cases, children may experience a sense of belonging to both cultures (the minority and the majority cultures) or of belonging to neither culture. In assessing this factor, clinicians should consider, too, how willing the majority culture has been to confer equal status on these children and their families (Canino & Spurlock, 2000).

In summary, a complete childhood assessment should address four broad areas: diagnosis, psychological issues, social issues, and issues of children of color. The following section reviews methodologies available to aid the assessment process.

## ASSESSMENT METHODS

This section reviews some of the many assessment tools currently available to assist in the assessment of children. These tools can be categorized as global techniques and rapid assessment scales. To be valid, an assessment must consider the individual's unique experience and research specific to the individual's problem. Global techniques, such as ecomaps or genograms (qualitative), help the social worker get a big picture of how the child is functioning and in which areas problem exist. For instance, a genogram may reveal a family history of depression, which helps explain the child's behavioral symptoms. This can guide the social worker to then use a self-report (quantitative) instrument to explore and measure the child's depression. Further, measurement of depression may use a depression instrument that focuses on cognitive, affective, or behavioral symptomatology according to the manner in which the child expresses his or her depression.

### Evidence-Based Assessment

Relevant research consists of a combination of cross-sectional and longitudinal surveys, experimental research, and case studies. Relevant and sound research findings provide base-rate estimates (incidence and prevalence) of specific problems in the community, estimate the rates of co-occurring problems, and identify key risk and resiliency factors (both developmental and current) that are expected to contribute to the client's problems or predict recovery. Research also provides estimates for the relative strength of risk and resiliency factors, explains the multidimensional nature of the individual's problems, supports or invalidates theories, and provides an empirical and theoretical basis for testing (O'Hare, 2005). Practitioners must review the professional literature for studies that measure the effectiveness of various assessment tools to select the one that is most appropriate for each client. Many assessment tools may be found on Web sites, some of which list articles that provide evidence of the effectiveness of that assessment tool.

## Global Techniques

Global techniques for assessing children help obtain a global picture of children's functioning and the problems they encounter. The three qualitative techniques mentioned here are interviews, play, and sculpting or other family techniques.

**Interviews.** Inteviews are the most effective qualitative assessments. "To conduct an informed qualitative assessment, practitioners must choose a human behavior model that is relevant to the client's presenting problems and based on research specific to the relevant problem area" (O'Hare, 2005, p. 15; see also Wakefield, 1996). Interviews are the most commonly used technique for assessing children, parents, and teachers (Hughes & Baker, 1991; McConaughy, 1996). Sattler (1988) reviewed the use of interviews for gleaning information from children and their parents. Goals for the interview include establishing rapport, understanding the presenting problem, and obtaining information from a broad range of perspectives. In addition to the guidelines presented in chapter 1 for the integrative skills protocol, important areas to include in the assessment interview of children are interests, school, peers, family, fears or worries, self-image, mood or feelings, somatic concerns, thought disorders, aspirations, expectations, and fantasies. Additional topics for adolescents include heterosexual or homosexual relationships, sexual activity, and drug or alcohol usage.

Structured and semistructured interviews can elicit this wide range of information. Some structured interviews require lengthy time to administer and, in some cases, extensive training for the clinician; laypersons can conduct and score others. Examples of structured interviews that do not require specialized training include the Diagnostic Interview Schedule for Children, Version 2.3 (Schaffer, 1992) and the Diagnostic Interview for Children and Adolescents—Revised (Reich & Welner, 1990). These instruments yield information that is easily codified for data analysis and for diagnosing mental disorders in children and adolescents. However, these instruments may not be as flexible as semistructured interviews, which provide not only standardized questions but also some adaptability for the age and personality of the child.

The Semistructured Clinical Interview for Children and Adolescents (SCICA) (McConaughy & Achenbach, 2001) was specifically designed for use with children aged six to eighteen years. This instrument allows the interviewer to adjust the order of questions to the natural order of the discussion with the child; it also provides information about a variety of facets in the child's life, including peer group and school, not just mental health status. The SCICA shows moderate to good test-retest reliability (0.54 to 0.89) for all of its subscales and generally good concurrent validity (McConaughy, 1996). Social workers should be mindful that the reliability of all interviews rests solidly with the interviewer, in how careful the interviewer is to follow testing protocol, how prepared the interviewer is to work with the child, and how conscientiously the interviewer scores the data. In general, the reliability of interviews across time and sometimes across subjects (child and parent) can be questionable, particularly structured interviews with children younger than twelve.

Interviewing parents generates essential information in the assessment of and intervention with children and adolescents. Barkley (2005) recognized parent interviews not only as a source for diagnosis but also as the primary way to gauge the level of family distress and to understand more about the child's problems with relationships. In addition, interviewing the parents gives them the chance to express their concerns, their frustrations, and their systems for coping with the child's problems. This process establishes rapport with the parent that is fundamental to successful intervention or treatment later on (Jenson & Potter, 1990).

The practitioner should ask parents about the referral problem; the ways they have attempted to deal with the problem; the child's medical, developmental, educational, and social history; family history; prior treatment for the problem; results of past treatment; and expectations about the evaluation. As with child interviews, parents can provide more comprehensive information through semistructured interviews that may include standardized rating scales such as the Child Behavior Checklist (CLBC; Achenbach, 1991) or the Basic Assessment System for Children (BASC; Reynolds & Kamphaus, 2003). A primary goal of interviews with parents is to define the child's problems in observable, discreet behaviors that facilitate targeted intervention and measurable progress.

Teachers should also be interviewed when appropriate. It is appropriate to involve teachers when the child's problem is exhibited in the school setting. They should be asked about their view of the referral problem, the antecedents and consequences of the problem, any attempts that have been made to solve the problem, how others (teachers and students) react to the problem, school academic performance, their view of the family, and their expectations and suggestions for school-based interventions (McConaughy, 1996). Standardized teacher rating scales include the BASC (Reynolds & Kamphaus, 2003) and the Behavior Evaluation Scale-2 (McCarney & Leigh, 1990). More-specific problems, such as attention and hyperactivity or social skills difficulty, are addressed by scales like the Conners' Teacher Rating Scale (Conners, 2008) and the School Social

Behavior Scales (Merrell, 1993, 2007). Of course, personal interviews with teachers are useful, as well, and can uncover any negative feelings the teacher has toward the child or any underlying reasons for referral.

The family may also be interviewed as a whole. Information about the following subjects can be obtained from the social worker's observation of the family or through direct questioning: each member's view of the child's problem(s); family interactional patterns; family communication patterns; family social and cultural norms and values; and child's behavior individually, as compared with child's behavior in the family group. The Darlington Family Assessment System (Wilkinson, 2000) presents a thorough method for describing and assessing families by providing information from the child's point of view, the parents' point of view, and the total family point of view. This framework offers a semi-structured interview and rating scale with explicit directions about how to implement the system in clinical work with children and families. A fundamental advantage to this model is its adaptability to a variety of families and theoretical approaches.

Sattler (1988) gives guidelines for interpreting the assessment data and sharing it with the child and parents. Before practitioners meet with the child and parents, they should synthesize the data gathered from the interview and evaluate their own feelings about it; look for common patterns or themes; try to account for any discrepancies they may find; look for indicators of the child's strengths and weaknesses, as well as resources for change or for coping. Then practitioners should meet with the child to provide reassurance, verify their hypothesis about the problem(s), and present findings. The practitioner can meet with the parents to describe the child's problems and the plan for treatment and to address any parental issues or problems that may affect the child. Practioners should be sensitive to the parents' feelings while also protecting the child's right to confidentiality.

**Play.**    With younger children, the social worker can gather information during games or other play activities more efficiently than in a formal interview session. Asking children to engage in unstructured play, such as drawing pictures of themselves or their family and then telling about what they've drawn or making models of themselves out of clay, may help the social worker establish rapport and learn valuable information. More structured therapy games are also available (e.g., the Thinking, Feeling, Doing Game, 1973) and may serve the same purpose.

Sattler (1988) offers guidelines for interpreting children's unstructured play. These include how the child enters the room, initiates play activities, expends energy while playing, moves while manipulating the play materials, paces self during play, moves his or her body in play, verbalizes while playing, integrates play activities, exhibits creativity, uses products, and reflects attitudes about adults during play. Other important considerations in assessing children's play are the age appropriateness of the child's play, as well as the tone of play (e.g., hostile, impatient). Cross-culturally, children's play mirrors social role and family structure and may display symptoms of family problems such as uninvolved or neglectful parenting (Berk, 2007).

**Sculpting or Other Family Techniques.**     Older children may be assessed in the context of the family system by using techniques such as sculpting (Frieson, 1993) or ecomapping (Sheafor, Horejsi, & Horejsi, 1988). These qualitative techniques also can help establish rapport with an older child who may be reluctant, at first, to sit down and participate in a formal interview. Sculpting requires the child or other family member to address family members as if they were made of clay and mold them accordingly. The social worker might request that the child mold the family to depict a typical family scenario, such as when they have supper together. The child then places members in relation to one another and molds their faces to convey moods. The child would also place him- or herself in the picture. Then the family would be asked to talk about how it felt to be in the scene and whether they agreed with the depiction. Other members might then remold the family as they see it.

Ecomapping depicts the family in the larger community or societal system. It is done with paper and pencil and requires family members to identify external, environmental issues that affect each member (see figure 1.2). This form of assessment not only sets up collaboration between the clinician and the family but also encourages interaction among family members that may facilitate needed change. In addition, ecomapping allows parents to view their families more objectively, which may obviate defensiveness and resistance (Miley, O'Melia, & DuBois, 2006).

Frieson (1993) describes other family techniques that might be helpful to children and their families. The family may be asked to construct a family floor plan. Each member draws his or her house floor plan and then answers questions about each room: What is the mood of the room? Smells, sounds, colors? Is there a special room? Are there issues of closeness or privacy in the house? How does the house fit in with the neighborhood? Frieson also discusses using metaphors (e.g., animals, objects) to describe oneself or other family members.

## Self-Report Techniques and Scales

Self-report techniques give children the opportunity to give information about themselves and their problems after rapport has been established using the qualitative methods described in the preceding section. The measures described here include standardized instruments, self-anchored and other rating scales, and self-observation. Because evaluating children is typically a multiaxial process, many standardized instruments have companion scales for parents and teachers. Obtaining multiple views of the child's problem helps provide a more complete picture of the situation.

**Standardized Instruments.**    The Depression Self-Rating Scale, identified by Corcoran and Fischer (2000; see figure 6.1), was designed by P. Birleson to measure the extent and severity of depression in children ages seven to thirteen. The scale asks questions about children's mood and thoughts, as well as physiologic or somatic problems. The test has fair reliability (alpha = 0.86 and 0.73, test-retest = 0.80) and good validity (correlation = 0.81) with the Children's Depression Inventory. The Children's Depression Inventory (CDI; Kovacs, 1992) was created to determine depressive symptoms in children ages seven to seventeen. Based on the

**Figure 6.1**    Depression Self-Rating Scale

Please answer as honestly as you can by indicating at left the number that best refers to how you have felt over the past week. There are no right answers; it is important to say how *you* have felt.

$$1 = \text{Most of the time}$$
$$2 = \text{Sometimes}$$
$$3 = \text{Never}$$

_____ 1. I look forward to things as much as I used to.
_____ 2. I sleep very well.
_____ 3. I feel like crying.
_____ 4. I like to go out to play.
_____ 5. I feel like running away.
_____ 6. I get tummy aches.
_____ 7. I have lots of energy.
_____ 8. I enjoy my food.
_____ 9. I can stick up for myself.
_____ 10. I think life isn't worth living.
_____ 11. I am good at things I do.
_____ 12. I enjoy the things I do as much as I used to.
_____ 13. I like talking with my family.
_____ 14. I have horrible dreams.
_____ 15. I feel very lonely.
_____ 16. I am easily cheered up.
_____ 17. I feel so sad I can hardly stand it.
_____ 18. I feel very bored.

SOURCE: Used with permission of Peter Birleson, Royal Children's Hospital, Fleminton Road, Parkville, Victoria 3052, Australia.

Beck Depression Inventory, the CDI requires that children identify statements that characterize themselves over the course of the previous two weeks on a scale of 0 to 2. Although the test-retest reliability of the CDI is moderate (0.38–0.87), it has shown good internal consistency (Cronbach's alpha of 0.80), and it was normed on a sample of more than 1,200 boys and girls from various ethnic and socioeconomic backgrounds.

The Hare Self-Esteem Scale, another commonly used scale, measures children's self-esteem in three settings: at home, at school, and with peers. Each of the three subscales comprises ten items; a total score is computed, and higher scores indicate higher self-esteem. Reliability for the general scale is 0.74; validity was 0.83 with both the Coopersmith Self-Esteem Inventory and the Rosenberg Self-Esteem Scale (Corcoran & Fischer, 2000). The population sampled to norm the measures was fifth- and eighth-grade students including 41 blacks and 207 whites, 115 boys, and 137 girls. The Multidimensional Self-Concept Scale (MSCS; Bracken, 1992) was designed for use with children age nine to nineteen. Comprising 150 items, this four-point Likert scale contains six subscales: social, compentence, affect, academic, family, and physical. The MSCS shows test-retest reliability coefficients ranging from 0.85 to 0.97 in the subscales, with higher coefficients for the total scale ranging from 0.97 to 0.99. In addition, concurrent validity of 0.69 to 0.83 has been established with the Coopersmith Self-Esteem Inventory.

The Assessment of Interpersonal Relations (AIR; Bracken & Kelley, 1993) was constructed to evaluate the interpersonal relationships between children and their peers, parents, and teachers. Children are asked to rate their level of agreement with the same thirty-five statements as they pertain to all three groups. Normed on 2,501 U.S. children and adolescents aged nine to nineteen, the AIR displays high test-retest reliability (0.93–0.96) and good discriminant validity across the subscales. This multidimensional instrument yields comprehensive information about the quality of relationships from the child's perspective.

The Impulsivity Scale (figure 6.2) was designed by Hirschfield, Sutton-Smith, and Rosenberg and measures the child's tendency toward restlessness, rule breaking, and indulgence in horseplay. Reliability was good (test-retest = 0.85), and criterion-referenced validity was established by significant correlations with teacher ratings of children. The test was normed on 127 fifth and sixth graders.

Other children's scales include the Children's Action Tendency Scale, by Deluty; the Children's Cognitive Assessment Questionnaire, by Asher; the Common Belief Inventory for Students, by Hooper and Layne; and the Compulsive Eating Scale, by Kagan and Squires (see Corcoran & Fischer, 2000). In their review of clinical measures for social workers, Corcoran and Fischer (2000) also included a number of family relationship scales appropriate for children to complete. The best

**Figure 6.2** Impulsivity Scale

---

Decide whether each statement is true as applied to you or false as applied to you. If a statement is True or Mostly True as applied to you, circle T. If a statement is False or Mostly False as applied to you, circle F.

T F 1. I like to keep moving around.
(I don't like to keep moving around.)

T F 2. I make friends quickly.
(I don't make friends quickly.)

T F 3. I like to wrestle and to horse around.
(I don't like to wrestle and to horse around.)

T F 4. I like to shoot with bows and arrows.
(I don't like to shoot with bows and arrows.)

T F 5. I must admit I'm a pretty good talker.
(I must admit that I'm not a good talker.)

T F 6. Whenever there's a fire engine going someplace, I like to follow it.
(If there's a fire engine going someplace, I don't usually like to follow it.)

T F 7. My home life is not always happy.
(My home life is always happy.)

T F 8. When things get quiet, I like to stir up a little fuss.
(I usually don't like to stir up a little fuss when things get quiet.)

T F 9. I am restless.
(I am not restless.)

T F 10. I don't think I'm as happy as other people.
(I think I'm happy as other people.)

T F 11. I get into tricks at Halloween.
(I don't get into tricks at Halloween.)

T F 12. I like being "it" when we play games of that sort.
(I don't like being "it" when we play games of that sort.)

T F 13. It's fun to push people off the edge into the pool.
(It's not fun to push people off the edge into the pool.)

T F 14. I play hooky sometimes.
(I never play hooky.)

T F 15. I like to go with lots of other kids, not just one.
(I usually like to go with one kid, rather than lots of them.)

T F 16. I like throwing stones at targets.
(I don't like throwing stones at targets.)

T F 17. It's hard to stick to the rules if you're losing the game.
(It's not hard to stick to the rules even if you are losing the game.)

T F 18. I like to dare kids to do things.
(I don't like to dare kids to do things.)

T F 19. I'm not known as a hard and steady worker.
(I'm known as a hard and steady worker.)

---

SOURCE: Used with permission of Paul Hirschfield, Hirschfield and Associates, 529 Pharr Road, Atlanta, GA 30305.

**Figure 6.3**    Children's Self-Anchored Anxiety at Bedtime Scale

1 .......... 2 .......... 3 .......... 4 .......... 5 .......... 6 .......... 7
Least Anxiety          Mid-level Anxiety          Most Anxiety

| | | |
|---|---|---|
| Relaxed, sleeps peacefully through the night. | Falls asleep, wakes 1–2 times during the night, reports bad dreams in the morning. | Trouble falling asleep, sleeps fitfully, nightmares/wakes up screaming. |

example is the Hudson Family Scale Package, which measures the child's relationship with mother, father, and siblings, as well as the child's overall family satisfaction.

**Self-Anchored and Other Rating Scales.**    Children can rate the intensity of problems such as depression or anxiety on self-anchored scales (figure 6.3). Children may be asked, for example, to develop anchors for a one- to seven-point scale describing their depression from the lowest to the highest they could possibly imagine. Anchors are the specific behavioral indicators of depression for that child.

Another type of self-rating scale used with children measures their anxiety on a one-hundred-point scale (Jordan, Franklin, & Corcoran, 2010). The scale can be drawn to look like a thermometer, with a red center that moves up and down. When children push the red part all the way up (scale reads one hundred points), they are told this indicates that they are the most anxious they could ever imagine. When they lower the reading to zero, they are told that they are not anxious at all. Children are then instructed to move the red center to indicate their current amount of anxiety.

**Self-Observation.**    Children may be asked to observe their own behavior. One format is to make a simple problem checklist that asks children to check off the specific problems for which they would like help. This type of checklist can be made to reflect the types of problems for which the agency can provide services. An example of such a checklist developed for completion by children receiving social work services in a school setting appears in figure 6.4. Children may also be asked to collect data on their own or other's behavior using simple data collection methods. For example, children can staple a three-by-five card to the inside of their school folder and keep a tally of the number of times they talk in class or the number of times they get out of their chair. Children may be asked to record information about family members or peer interactions using similar methods.

**Figure 6.4**    Problem Checklist

---

Name _____    Age _____    Grade _____

Who referred you to the social worker? _____

The following list are problems about which other kids at school have talked to the social worker. **Please check all of the following that are problems for you.**

____ New student adjustment
____ Failing grades
____ Lack of motivation in class
____ Disruptive classroom behavior
____ Truancy
____ Problems with a teacher
____ Excessive tardiness
____ Drug policy violation
____ Organization skills
____ Problems with peers
____ Conflicts with siblings-parents
____ Low self-concept
____ Poor social skills
____ Concern about friend
____ Depression
____ Withdrawn and isolated
____ Aggressive behavior
____ Failure to serve detention
____ Overweight or other physical problems
____ Physical abuse by parents
____ Other (please specify) _____

---

## Ratings by Others

Parents and teachers are frequently asked to provide information about children's problems. Sometimes other professionals are asked to help in the assessment. One popular instrument is the Achenbach Child Behavior Checklist (CBCL; Achenbach & Edelbrock, 1983). This is perhaps the most frequently used scale of its type. It has been shown to provide less accurate results for children who are mildly retarded, but it has demonstrated clear accuracy for children of color when used in translation, identifying not only the impairment but also its severity (Bird, Gould, Rubio-Stipec, Staghezza, & Canino, 1991; Embregts, 2000). The CBCL was used to analyze premorbid behavioral differences among young adults diagnosed with schizophrenia and to analyze behavior functioning for children in foster care (Armsden, Pecora, Payne, & Szatkiewicz, 2000; Rossi, Pollice, Daneluzzo, Marinangeli, & Stratta, 2000).

Functional behavioral assessments are conducted in schools to determine the antecedents and consequences of specific behaviors. A behavior observation monitors an individual's actions by visual or electronic means while recording quantitative and/or qualitative information about those actions (Cohen & Swerdlik, 2005). "A functional assessment of behavior asks what the behavior is, when it occurs, what the activating events are, and what happens as a result of the behavior both positive and negative" (Openshaw, 2008, p. 39; see also Boys Town, 1989).

Derived from the CBCL, the Child Behavior Checklist Depression Scale (CBCL-D) (Clarke, Lewinsohn, Hops, & Seeley, 1992) was designed to identify symptoms of depression as noted by both adolescents and parents. Each checklist has fifteen items. Although it possesses adequate criterion-related validity with diagnoses of depression from psychiatrists and acceptable concurrent validity with other measures of depression, the CBCL-D has demonstrated only moderate ranges of reliability (test-retest = 0.20–0.57; interrater = 0.35–0.59). It remains useful, however, as a general index of depression and for its adaptability across sources.

The Inventory of Children's Individual Differences (ICID; Halvorson et al., 2003) provides researchers with an age- and culture-neutral instrument designed specifically to assess the five-factor model (FFM) of personality in children and adolescents ages two to fifteen using parental, nonparental, or self-reports (Deal, Halvorson, Martin, Victor, & Baker, 2007).

Another frequently used instrument is the Hilson Adolescent Profile (Inwald, Brobst, & Morrisey, 1988). Appendix 6A presents a copy of the computer-generated report provided when the test is sent in for computer scoring. In addition to these specially designed instruments, parents, teachers, or other significant people in the child's environment may fill out the same self-report measures mentioned in the previous section. For example, if the child is asked to complete the Hare Self-Esteem Scale, the parent is also asked to fill out the measure for the child. This way, the social worker has two different perspectives on the child's self-esteem.

Parents and teachers, as well as social workers, may do direct observation and recording of children's behavior. Four types of recording are recommended. Narrative recording is a qualitative recording of an event. Special attention is given to the behavior and to the setting in which the behavior occurs. For example, a child may be observed while interacting in the classroom. The social worker might look for specific behaviors to occur, such as getting out of one's seat. Other, external conditions that might affect the child would also be observed and noted, such as actions of the teacher, actions of other students, and distracting aspects of the classroom setting itself. Interval recording is continuous, direct observation of the child during specified time periods divided into equal intervals. For example, the social worker may look to see whether a child got out of his seat during a given interval. Frequency recording notes each occurrence of the behavior. For example, each occurrence of the child getting out of his seat would be counted. Duration recording is concerned with the length of each occurrence of the behavior, for example, how long the child was out of his seat.

Child protective services caseworkers may record information about children in a form such as the Children's Restrictiveness of Living Environments Instrument (figure 6.5). This instrument provides an indicator of factors related to out-of-home placement (Thomlison & Krysik, 1992). Magura and Moses (1985) have developed a set of scales to measure outcomes for child welfare services.

**Standardized Tests.**    Quantitative data derived from some of the tests used with children are designed to measure intelligence, achievement, or special problems or abilities. Social workers do not usually administer these tests but refer children to other trained personnel when appropriate. Social workers may administer screening inventories such as the Attention Deficit Hyperactivity Disorder Rating Scale (DuPaul, 1992) or the Conners' Continuous Performance Test II (CPT IIV.5), but comprehensive evaluations for ADHD or other complicated disorders require specialized training and skill (for a listing of some of the commonly used tests of this type, see appendix 6B). When referring a child for testing, the social worker should follow these guidelines: have a specific reason for referring a client; explain to the psychologist what questions you want answered; provide information you have collected to the psychologist; prepare the client for what to expect at the psychologist's office; do not have unrealistic expectations of what the testing will provide, because testing is only one tool for assessing the client; and ask the psychologist to explain any limitations of the specific tests that your client has been given (Sheafor et al., 1988). To further promote the process, social workers can learn more about testing instruments, their interpretation, and implications. Social workers can also help other professionals understand the parameters of social service and child welfare systems (Kayser & Lyon, 2000).

As a response to federal initiatives to improve education, such as No Child Left Behind and the 2004 Individuals with Disabilities Education Improvement Act (IDEIA) revisions, many states and school districts are adopting a cross-battery assessment system. The cross-battery approach (XBA) provides a conceptual model for measurement and interpretation of cognitive abilities. The cross-battery approach gives educators the means to "make systematic, valid, and up-to-date interpretations of intelligence batteries, and to augment them with other tests (e.g., academic ability tests) in a way that is consistent with the empirically supported Cattell-Horn-Carroll (CHC) theory of cognitive abilities" (Flanagan, Ortiz & Alfonso, 2007, p. 1).

**Figure 6.5**   Children's Restrictiveness of Living Environments Instrument

Children's Restrictiveness of Living Environments

Instructions for calculating the restrictiveness of children's living environments:
A. Complete the child and rating information.
B. On the right side of the items in column B, number the child's placements in sequential order and record the corresponding number of days in each placement, e.g., (1,30) indicates first placement, 30 days.
C. Record the corresponding Restrictiveness Score for each placement into the Restrictiveness Formula in column C, i.e., $R_{p1}$, represents the restrictiveness score of the child's first placement. Calculate the totals.
D. Record the corresponding per diem cost and the number of days in each placement in column D. Calculate the totals.

A. Child Name: _____        Rater Name: _____

Child Birthdate: _____/_____/_____     Date Completed: _____/_____/_____
                  (year) (month) (day)                       (year) (month) (day)

Child Identification: _____

| B. Restrictiveness Scores | C. Restrictiveness Equation |
|---|---|
| 1.51 Self-maintained residence | |
| 2.10 Private boarding home | |
| 2.18 Home of child's friend | $R_{p1}$_____ − $R_{p2}$_____ = _____ |
| 2.33 Home of family friend | $R_{p2}$_____ − $R_{p3}$_____ = _____ |
| 2.40 Home of relative | $R_{p3}$_____ − $R_{p4}$_____ = _____ |
| 2.45 Home of biological parent | $R_{p4}$_____ − $R_{p5}$_____ = _____ |
| 2.60 Homeless | |
| 2.66 Adoptive home | |
| 2.75 Supervised independent living | |
| 3.09 Independent living prep. group home | Total _____ |
| 3.13 Regular foster care home | |
| 3.38 Family emergency shelter | |
| 3.48 Receiving foster care | **D. Cost Equation** |
| 3.57 Treatment foster family care home | |
| 3.58 Special needs foster home | |
| 3.61 Long-term group home | $T_{p1}$_____ × $C_{p1}$_____ = _____ |
| 3.85 Youth emergence shelter | $T_{p2}$_____ × $C_{p2}$_____ = _____ |
| 3.86 Receiving group home | $T_{p3}$_____ × $C_{p3}$_____ = _____ |
| 4.00 Medical hospital | $T_{p4}$_____ × $C_{p4}$_____ = _____ |
| 4.14 Private residential school | $T_{p5}$_____ × $C_{p5}$_____ = _____ |
| 4.18 Wilderness camp | |
| 4.45 Ranch-based treatment center | |
| 4.60 Open youth correction facility | |
| 4.62 Adult drug/alcohol rehab. center | |
| 4.63 Cottage based treatment center | Total # Days                Total Cost |
| 4.85 Psychiatric group home | in Placement ___        of Placement ___ |
| 4.97 Youth drug/alcohol rehab. center | |
| 5.13 Armed services base | |
| 5.40 Young offender group home | |
| 5.50 Psychiatric ward in a hospital | |
| 6.10 Psychiatric institution | |
| 6.40 Closed youth correction facility | |
| 6.56 Adult correction facility | |
| 6.58 Secure treatment facility | |

SOURCE: Used by permission of Barbara Thomlison (1992), Faculty of Social Work, The University of Calgary.

The psychometrically and theoreticaly defensible XBA principles and procedures represent an improved method of measuring cognitive abilities (Carroll & Kaufman 1998; Kaufman, 2000; Flanagan, Ortiz & Alfonso 2007). In a cross-battery assessment, "many scale and composite measures on intelligence are mixed containing excess reliable variance with a construct irrevelant to the one intended for measurement and interpretation. The cross-battery approach ensures that assessments include composites or clusters that are relatively pure representations of CHC broad and narrow abilities, allowing for valid measurement and interpretation of muliple unidimensional constructs" (Flanagan et al., 2007, p. 3).

The use of new testing procedures in the schools ensures that children and adolescents are labeled accurately and, when needed, correctly placed in programs that provide the types of assistance students need to thrive in school.

## MOVING FROM ASSESSMENT TO INTERVENTION

The following case example illustrates the various systemic factors and personal difficulties that families face today. The case example is used to illustrate how to apply the correct assessment tools for the child.

## CASE STUDY

### Identifying Information

*Name:* Anthony Estrada
*Date of Birth:* 11/09/2000
*Address:* 1112 N. Clement Street, Mayfield, TX
*Phone:* 555.123.4567 (home), 555.890.1112
*Family members living in the home:*

| Anthony Estrada | Client | Male | 8 y.o. | Hispanic | 2nd grader |
|---|---|---|---|---|---|
| Robert Estrada | Brother | Male | 10 y.o. | Hispanic | 3rd grader |
| John Estrada | Brother | Male | 11 y.o. | Hispanic | 5th grader |
| Lydia Estrada | Sister | Female | 6 y.o. | Hispanic | 1st grader |
| Hector Estrada | Father | Male | 35 y.o. | Hispanic | Construction |
| Alina Estrada | Mother | Female | 30 y.o. | Hispanic | Classroom Assistant |

*Family income:* The family income is $3,500 and $4,000 per month, depending on the mother's employment. She works part time at the elementary school during the school year.

*Presenting problem:* Anthony has been suspended from school for hitting a teacher while on the playground. He did not want to go inside at the end of recess and struck her in his frustration. His teacher complains that he's had a "bad attitude" all year, and the principal is suggesting placement for him in an alternative school.

*Previous counseling:* None.

*Source of data:* In-office assessment visit with Anthony and his parents. Additional information from the pediatrician, the teachers, and the school counselor.

### Nature of Presenting Problem

In the past two years, Anthony has changed from an energetic, loving child to a moody, irritable child. Although Anthony has always been "busy and active," his mother reports that he has become more competitive with his older brothers and that he is easily frustrated if he cannot beat them at sports or other games. She reports that if Anthony loses a board game, he will sulk and say that he is "stupid" or that his brothers cheated. Often, he will cheat, himself, in an attempt to win. About a month ago, as the boys were playing soccer in their backyard, Anthony became so upset that he began to scream at his brothers and say that he wished he were dead. Shocked by this outburst, the mother tried to comfort Anthony, but she said that he resisted her effort and finally only calmed down at the urgings of his oldest brother. Since that incident, the family has tried to avoid making Anthony too angry.

Despite their efforts to mollify him, however, the mother reports that Anthony has become "sassy" and that, increasingly, she must discipline him for hitting his siblings and for not obeying her. She attempts to spank him, but she says that when she does that, he only tries to hit her back. More often, now, she sends him to his room. Although he obeys his father, who uses corporal punishment, Anthony seems to ignore his mother's requests that he pick up his clothes and toys and that he complete his homework for school. She says that he is difficult to get up in the mornings and that he dawdles rather than dressing himself and gathering his supplies for school as his brothers do. She finds that she must spend as much time helping Anthony get ready in the mornings as she does his younger sister. Sometimes, they are all late for school because of Anthony's dilatory actions or because of one of his angry outbursts, when he feels that everyone is pushing him and causing him to be late.

With incomplete homework and, sometimes, incomplete work in school, Anthony's grades have suffered this year. The teacher says that Anthony is inattentive at school and that he bothers other children, often distracting them from their work and provoking them into confrontations with him. She believes that Anthony is smart enough to learn the material but that he doesn't seem to want to. She reports that his work is careless and that he often leaves worksheets partially blank. In her exasperation, she enlisted help from the school counselor, who assisted her in setting up a classroom behavior management plan of rewards and consequences for directing Anthony's behavior. Although Anthony responds to this system, the teacher says that the time she must spend managing Anthony's behavior takes away from class time that would normally be devoted to all of the children. She believes that Anthony should be transferred to a class for "emotionally disturbed" children, where his behavior can be monitored more closely in a smaller class of students.

The teacher reports that Anthony is able to play with peers most of the time, but she notes that his angry behavior alienates some children. In all competitive instances, he becomes frustrated and aggressive if he is unable to win or to perform as well as he wants to. The day of the playground incident, Anthony was playing in a group of children who were divided into teams for kickball. Anthony's team was behind, and when the teacher said that recess was over, Anthony was upset because he wanted to continue playing until his team could catch up. When the teacher refused to extend recess, he hit her in the back with his fist. She immediately took him to the principal, who called Anthony's mother and suspended Anthony from school for three days. During the suspension, the principal and the teacher arranged to meet with Anthony and his parents to discuss appropriate ways to help him control his behavior and be more successful in school. The school social worker was asked to attend this meeting.

Anthony has several strengths. His parents are devoted to their family and are genuinely concerned for their son. They are willing to participate in recommended plans for intervention both at school and at home, but they strongly advocate for their son's continued placement in a regular classroom. Anthony's personal strengths include his ability to maintain focus on certain types of projects in school, his apparent ability to master second-grade work, and a stated understanding of why he has been suspended. He says that he is sorry for hitting his teacher.

The school prioritizes the problems (with 1 being the most severe) in the following order: (1) aggressive behavior, (2) distracting other students, (3) being unable to focus on schoolwork. The parents prioritize the problems similarly: (1) angry behavior, (2) being argumentative, (3) making poor grades.

## Client Interpersonal Issues

**Cognitive Functioning.**    Anthony's school achievement tests indicate that he is capable of mastering second grade. He consistently scores in the fiftieth percentile, but his teacher thinks that he is capable of more. Neither his pediatrician nor his parents report any type of cognitive developmental delay. In fact, when he was young, his mother thought that he was exceptionally bright, because he could figure out how to get out of his crib and how to take apart most toys. Anthony has mastered all developmental tasks at age-appropriate times. The teacher reports that if she works with Anthony individually, he can learn anything, but he becomes easily distracted when she works with students as a group or when he must work alone.

**Emotional Functioning.**   During the assessment visit, Anthony seemed like a quiet child. He sat between his parents, closer to his mother, during most of the interview, showing appropriate anxiety about being in a meeting with adults. He warmed up quickly, however, to the interviewer and answered questions easily, although he did show some discomfort while discussing the playground incident. Only after about thirty minutes did he begin to fidget by swinging his legs against the chair, finally standing up and walking around the room as the adults continued to talk.

**Behavioral functioning.**   Anthony exhibited no unusual behaviors during the assessment session. His impatience and need to move after thirty minutes were within normal limits for his age. In fact, he asked his father if he could stand up before he began to walk around. He sighed occasionally to display his boredom, but he did not interrupt the conversation by talking. His parents reported that Anthony has never enjoyed paperwork such as drawing and coloring; he prefers to climb, run, and jump. His parents recounted several events of inappropriate angry behavior over the past six months, but Anthony did not exhibit such behavior in this session. In fact, his behavior in this session indicated some strength in self-control and coping. His weakness in this area seems to be with coping in the classroom environment.

**Physiologic functioning.**   Anthony's medical records reveal basically normal development. Anthony is in the fiftieth percentile for both height and weight, his immunizations are up to date, and he currently takes no medication. His illness history is not remarkable, although he did require minor surgery for repeated ear infections and ear tubes when he was three years old. Since that time, he has shown no delay in speech or hearing. He has only had minor colds and infections that have responded to conservative medical intervention. Although teachers complain about Anthony's handwriting, he does not demonstrate any unusual deficit in fine-motor skills. His drawings are not detailed, but they are not immature for his age. Anthony can dribble a basketball and throw a baseball within the appropriate range for his age. Neither the pediatrician nor the PE teacher reports any physical limitations, although the PE teacher says that he seems clumsy at times and that he needs to "run off steam" in PE.

**Developmental considerations.** Developmental milestones have been met within normal time ranges. Anthony's birth history reveals that he was delivered spontaneously and without complications at forty-one weeks gestation with an Apgar rating of nine, as reflected by the parents and the medical record. He weighed seven pounds, ten ounces.

## Client Interpersonal Issues: Family

Anthony resides with his parents, his two older brothers, and his younger sister in a modest home in Mayfield. Anthony's parents are first-generation Mexican Americans. Both sets of grandparents immigrated to Texas from northern Mexico. Anthony's mother grew up in a small border town, where she says that she liked school but often missed class to babysit for her younger siblings while her mother worked. She dropped out of high school in eleventh grade because she was somewhat behind in her studies, and she had found a good job as a seamstress. She later acquired her GED by studying at night in an adult education class before her first child was born. Having the GED allows Mrs. Estrada to work as a classroom assistant for the elementary school Anthony attends. Anthony's father grew up in the same small border town, where he worked in fields from the time he was a boy. He reports that school was boring for him and that he preferred the physical activity of the fields but that he stayed in school until high school. He dropped out after two years. He says that teachers sometimes called him inattentive and disruptive, too, because he found it hard to pay attention to things that did not matter to him. He currently works as a foreman for a local construction company. He says that he has always preferred being outdoors and working with his hands.

Mrs. Estrada has learned behavioral disciplining techniques, such as time-out, in her job, and she thinks these techniques work with her children when she is not too stressed to employ them. Mr. Estrada thinks these techniques are fine, but he prefers corporal punishment because he thinks that it works best and that children should have a "healthy fear" of their parents. Mr. Estrada leaves much of the discipline to his wife, because she is with the children more than he is; but when he is home, he intervenes if he finds that the children are not responding appropriately to him or to their mother. He says that he has had to spank Anthony more than the other children lately, and he admits that the spankings seem to escalate Anthony's anger.

The other Estrada children, John, Robert, and Lydia, are healthy and developing normally. As a fifth grader, John makes good grades and is well liked by his peers. He is in the highest performance groups for reading and math. Schoolwork appears to come easily for him, but his passion is baseball, where he is demonstrating talent as a pitcher. He is a confident and bright boy. Anthony seems closer to him than he is to Robert, who is only eighteen months older than he is. Robert is described as the "squeaky wheel" of the family. Like John, Robert performs well in school, but his parents and teachers describe him as competitive and whiny, although he has never displayed the anger problems that Anthony has. Robert excels in art. His drawings show dimensional depth and detail that are unusual for his age. Lydia is in first grade, where she seems to be on level. She is described as quiet and the "baby" of the family. The parents insist that the boys protect her and not tease or aggravate her.

Mrs. Estrada is with the children most of the time because her job allows her to leave for school and return with her children. In good weather, Mr. Estrada works many evenings and weekends. When he is home, he is often too tired to play with the children, but sometimes he throws the ball with the boys. Mrs. Estrada reports that all of the children want to spend more time with their father. Because the family depends heavily on Mr. Estrada's income, however, she acknowledges that he must work hard to maintain his job.

## Client Interpersonal Issues: School

The school counselor reports that she observed Anthony's behavior in the classroom on several occasions, at the request of his teacher. The counselor found that Anthony was often off-task, playing with his pencil or talking to classmates, and that he seemed unable to follow directions that were spoken to the entire class. At times, the more he was corrected by the teacher, the more disruptive Anthony became.

The school counselor reports that Anthony responded well to the token economy system she set up for improving his focus in the classroom. She says that he was willing to work for the tokens and stayed on task better when he knew that his teacher would reward him. This focus, in turn, reduced his disruptive behavior with his peers and seemed to improve his schoolwork. Reviewing his test scores, she reported that she could see some disparity between Anthony's ability and performance scores, a disparity that continues in the classroom. She expresses some concern that if his school problems continue, he will fall behind in his schoolwork and lose interest completely. She recognizes that he must gain some control of his temper and his attention span if he is to succeed in the classroom.

## Client Interpersonal Issues: Peers

Anthony and his parents report that he has some friends, but that sometimes people do not like to play with him because he gets so angry. The counselor reports that students in second grade try to stay out of trouble, and they fear that Anthony will get them in trouble with the teacher. Anthony is signed up for soccer this year, but the soccer season has not begun. His parents hope that sports will give him an outlet for his energy and that he will make friends.

## Context and Social Support Networks

The family has been somewhat isolated since their move from the border two years ago, where they left behind both sets of grandparents and a large extended family of aunts, uncles, and cousins. Mrs. Estrada stays busy with her work, her home, and her children. She does enjoy her colleagues at work, but she is busy the rest of the time meeting the needs of four active children. With his long work hours, Mr. Estrada is not often available to help with family and housekeeping tasks. He is, himself, exhausted with his labors. The children are each expected to do chores, but Mrs. Estrada admits that sometimes she does the work herself to ensure that it is done well and in a timely manner.

The family does attend a Catholic church nearby, but they have not become active in the church community, though all of their children have participated in first communion and will likely continue all of their religious education through confirmation.

Mr. and Mrs. Estrada are happy with their family and their circumstances. They believe that they have provided well for their children. Although they miss the support of extended family, they believe that the move has been beneficial financially and that they and their children will have more opportunity in Mayfield than in their home town.

## Measurement

**Individual Functioning: Assess for Depression.**    Evidence-based support for assessment with Anthony should include the use of a multidimensional functional assessment. Because children often mask depression with anger, multiple observations should be conducted under different situations, and data should be obtained from multiple informants (O'Hare, 2005). The assessment should cover three modes of expression: (a) Anthony's cognitive appraisial of the events in his life; (b) physiological symptoms, such as somatic complaints; and (c) behaviors associated with depression (O'Hare, 2005). Tools to be used should include the Children's Depression Inventory, (Kovacs, 1992), the Depression Self-Rating Scale (Birleson, Hudson, Buchanan, & Wolff, 1987), and the Children's Depression Rating Scale (Poznanzski, Cook, & Carroll, 1979).

**Assess anger and noncompliance.**    Evidence-based support for assessment includes a functional analysis of Anthony's angry outbursts and noncompliance. This analysis would delineate the patterns and sequencing of the antecedents and consequences of his negative behaviors (O'Hare, 2005). His teacher should conduct behavior observations throughout the school day to see when the behavior occurs, and what consequences follow it. Likewise, Mrs. Estrada should design a daily behavioral checklist and record the number of Anthony's noncompliances, compliances, and angry outbursts. Instruments that could assist in the analysis include the Revised Behavior Problem Checklist (Quay, 1983), the Eyberg Child Behavior Inventory (Eyberg & Robinson, 1983), and the New York Teacher Rating Scale (Miller et al. 1995, O'Hare, 2005).

**Family functioning.** Administer the Hudson Index of Family Relations (Inwald et al., 1988) to assess overall family functioning and the Family Adaptability and Cohension Evaluation Scales, which is in its fourth revision and measures cohesiveness and flexibility in family functioning (Franklin, Streeter, & Springer, 2001, O'Hare, 2005; Olsen, Russell, & Sprenkle, 1989).

---

**BOX 6.2**
**Treatment Plan:** Anthony Estrada

---

**Problem:** Child behavior problems; parental lack of skills

**Definitions:** Distractibility, inattentiveness, angry outbursts, and occasional aggression for child. Have skills deficit in parenting and use corporeal punishment instead of positive discipline, such as rewards.

**Goals:** 1. To improve attentiveness at home and at school
2. To eliminate angry outbursts and aggression
3. Improve overall parent-child relationship

| Objectives: | Interventions: |
|---|---|
| 1. Parents learn how to help Anthony stay on task, as measured by behavioral checklist. | 1. Teach parents use of a reward system for child's staying on task. Teach parents to redirect inappropriate behaviors. Refer child for ADHD test. |
| 2. Anthony learns to control his anger as measured by behavioral checklist. | 2. Teach Anthony anger management skills, such as time-out, breathing, and focusing. |
| 3. Improve family relationships, as measured by the Index of Family Relationships | 3. Teach family to have family meetings and outings. |

**Diagnosis**: Consider 314.01 Attention-Deficit/Hyperactivity Disorder, Combined Type

## SUMMARY

This chapter described assessment of children and adolescents. The special issues important in assessing this population are diagnosis, psychological and social theories, and ethnicity. Childhood diagnosis is done from three different perspectives: categorical, empirical, and behavioral. Psychological theories explain child development from cognitive, affective, and learning perspectives. Development is assumed to occur at different rates for different children, depending on maturational readiness and environmental opportunities. Social theories explain children's behavior in the broader context of family and society. Issues that influence assessment of children of color include psychosocial adjustment, relationship with family, school adjustment and achievement, peers, and community.

Measures available for assessment of children and adolescents should be empirically supported with evidence-based outcome research. Measures should include global techniques such as interviews, use of play, and sculpting and other family techniques. Self-report measurement techniques include standardized instruments, self-anchored and other rating scales, self-observation, and ratings by others. Finally, the chapter presented the case of Anthony, an eight-year-old boy with problems including distractability, inattentiveness, angry outbursts, and social aggression.

## STUDY QUESTIONS

1. Use psychological, social, and color guidelines from the chapter to assess a child you know. What are the strengths and weaknesses of each approach?

2. Using the same case example as in question 1, design a measurement system that includes both qualitative (play or sculpting) and quantitative (standardized measures, self-anchored scales) techniques.

3. Review the Web sites of assessment tools listed at the end of this chapter. Which assessment tools are evidence-based and which are not? What is the most effective way to ensure that an assessment tool is effective?

## WEB SITES

### Evidence-Based Assessment Materials

*American Psychiatric Association*
http://www.psych.org/psych_pract/treat/ppg/prac_guide.cfm
*Campbell Collaboration*
http://www.campbellcollaboration.org/c1_protocol_guidelines%20doc
    .pdf
*Cochrane Collaboration*
http://www.cochrane.org/colloquia/agstracts/melbourne/P-069.htm

## Various Assessments of Children

### Child Abuse and Neglect
http://nccanch.acf.hhs.gov/index.cfm
http://www.state.sd.us/social/CPS/Services/signs.htm

### Anatomically Detailed Dolls
http://www.ipt-forensics.com/library/special_problems5.htm

### Learning
http://www.pearsonassessments.com/tests/vmi.htm (for the Beery VMI, ages 2–18, includes helpful information about the test and developmental learning materials)

### Social-Emotional
*Children's Depression Inventory, ages 7–17*
https://www.mhs.com/index.htm
*Reynolds Adolescent Depression Scale (ages 11–20, includes critical items)*
http://www3.parinc.com/

### Emotional-Behavioral Screening
*Behavior Assessment System for Children (different forms cover ages 2.5–18)*
http://www.agsnet.com/
*Child Behavior Checklist (ages 1.5–18)*
http://www.aseba.org/

### Personality-Projective Tests
*Children's Apperception Test (covers ages 3–10)*
http://portal.wpspublish.com

### Intellectual Assessments
*Wechsler Preschool and Primary Scale of Intelligence, 3rd ed. (covers ages 2–3)*
http://harcourtassessment.com/haiweb/cultures/en-us/product detail.htm?pid=015-8989-317

### Achievement Tests
*Woodcock Johnson III (measures academic achievement, ages 2 and up)*
http://www.cps.nova.edu/~cpphelp/WJIII-ACH.html

## REFERENCES

Achenbach, T. M. (1991). *Manual for the youth self report and 1991 profile.* Burlington: University of Vermont, Department of Psychiatry.

Achenbach. T. M., & Edelbrock, L. (1983). *Manual for the Child Behavior Checklist and revised child behavior profile.* Burlington, VA: Queen City Printers.

American Psychiatric Association. (2000). *Diagnostic and statistical manual of mental disorders* (4th ed., rev.). Washington, DC: Author.

Armsden, G., Pecora, P. J., Payne, V. H., & Szatkiewicz, J. P. (2000). Children placed in long-term foster care: An intake profile using the child behavior checklist/4-18. *Journal of Emotional and Behavioral Disorders, 8,* 49–64.

Bandura, A. (1977). *Social learning theory.* Englewood Cliffs, NJ: Prentice Hall.

Barkley, R. (2005). *Attention deficit hyperactivity disorder: A handbook for diagnosis and treatment* (2nd ed.) New York: Guilford Press.

Barona, A., & de Barona, M. S. (2000). Assessing multicultural preschool children. In Bracken et al. (Eds.), *The psychoeducational assessment of preschool children* (pp. 282–297). Boston: Allyn and Bacon.

Barth, R. (1986). *Social and cognitive treatment of children and adolescents.* San Francisco: Jossey-Bass.

Berk, L. E. (2007). *Infants, children and adolescents* (6th ed.). Boston: Allyn and Bacon.

Bird, H. R., Gould, M. S., Rubio-Stipec, M., Staghezza, B., & Canino, G. (1991). Screening for childhood psychopathology in the community using the child behavior checklist. *Journal of the American Academy of Child and Adolescent Psychiatry, 30,* 116–123.

Birleson, P., Hudson, I., Buchanan, D. G., & Wolff, S. (1987). Clinical evaluation of a self-rating scales for depressive disorder in childhood (Depression Self-Rating Scale). *Journal of Child Psychology and Psychiatry, 28,* 43–60.

Bloom, M. (1984). *Configurations of human behavior.* New York: Macmillan.

Bornstein, P., & Kazdin, A. (1985). *Handbook of clinical behavior therapy with children.* Homewood, IL: Dorsey Press.

Boys Town. (1989) *Working with Aggressive Youth.* Boys Town, NE: Boys Town Press.

Bracken, B. A. (1992). *Multidimensional self concept scale: Examiner's manual.* Austin, TX: PRO-ED.

Bracken, B. A., & Kelley, P. (1993). *Assessment of interpersonal relations.* Austin, TX: PRO-ED.

Canino, I. A., & Spurlock, J. (2000). *Culturally diverse children and adolescents: Assessment, diagnosis, and treatment* (2nd ed.). New York: Guilford Press.

Carroll, J. B., & Kaufman, A. (1998). Foreword. In K. S. McGrew & D. P. Flanagans, *The intelligence test desk reference (ITDR): GF-Gc cross-battery assessment* (pp. xi–xii). Boston: Allyn and Bacon.

Clarke, G. N., Lewinsohn, P. M., Hops, H., & Seeley, J. R. (1992). A self- and parent-report measure of adolescent depression: The Child Behavior Checklist depression scale. *Behavioral Assessment, 14,* 443–463.

Cohen, R. J., & Swerdlik, M. E. (2005). *Psychological testing and assessment: An introduction to tests and measurement* (6th ed.). Boston: McGraw-Hill.

Conners, K. C. (2008). *Conners' rating scales manual* (3rd ed.). North Tonawanda, NY: Multihealth Systems.

Corcoran, K., & Fischer, J. (2000). *Measures for clinical practice.* New York: Free Press.

Davies, D. (2004). *Child development: A practitioner's guide* (2nd ed.) New York: Guilford Press.

Deal, J. E., Halvorson, C. F., Jr., Martin, R. P., Victor, J., & Baker, S. (2007). The inventory of children's individual differences: Development of validation of a short version. *Journal of Personality Assessment, 89,* 162–166.

DuPaul, G. J. (1992). How to assess attention deficit hyperactivity disorder within school settings. *School Psychology Quarterly, 7,* 60–74.

Embregts, P. (2000). Reliability of the child behavior checklist for the assessment of behavioral problems of children and youth with mild mental retardation. *Research in Developmental Disabilities, 21,* 31–41.

Erikson, E. (1993). *Childhood and society.* London: Norton.

Eyberg, S. M., & Robinson, E. A. (1983). Conduct problem behavior: Standardization of a behavioral rating scale with adolescents. *Journal of Clinical Child Psychology, 12,* 347–357.

Flanagan, D., Ortiz, S. O., & Alfonso, V. C. (2007). *Essentials of cross-battery assessment* (2nd ed.). Hoboken, NJ: Wiley.

Franklin, C., Streeter, C., & Springer, D. (2001). Validity of the FACES IV family assessment measure. *Research on Social Work Practice, 11,* 576–596.

Frieson, J. (1993). *Structural-strategic marriage and family therapy.* New York: Gardner.

Gibbs, J., & Huang, L. (2003). *Children of color.* San Francisco: Jossey-Bass.

Gopaul-McNicol, S., & Armour-Thomas, E. (2001). *Assessment and culture: Psychological test with minority populations.* San Diego, CA: Academic Press.

Guarnaccia, P. J., & Lopez, S. (1998). The mental health and adjustment of immigrant and refugee children. *Child and Adolescent Psychiatric Clinics of North America, 7,* 537–553.

Halverson, C. F., Havil, V., Deal, J. E., Baker, S., Victor, J., & Pavlopoulos, V. (2003). Personality structure as derived from parental ratings of free descriptions of children: The Inventory of Child Individual Differences. *Journal of Personality, 71,* 995–1026.

Handler, L., & Meyer, G. J. (1998). The importance of teaching and learning personality assessment. In L. Handler & M. J. Hilsenroth (Eds.), *Teaching and learning personality assessment.* Mahwah, NJ: Erlbaum.

Harper-Dorton, K., & Herbert, M. (1999). *Working with children and their families* (2nd ed.). Chicago: Lyceum Books.

Hughes, J., & Baker, D. B. (1991). *The clinical child interview.* New York: Guilford Press.

Inwald, R. E., Brobst, K. E., & Morrisey, R. F. (1988). *Hilson adolescent profile.* Kew Gardens, NY: Hilson Research.

Janzen, C., Harris, O., Jordan, C., & Franklin, C. (2005). *Family treatment: Evidence-based practicer with populations at risk* (4th ed.) Belmont, CA: Brooks/Cole.

Jenson, B. F., & Potter, M. L. (1990). Best practices in communicating with parents. In A. Thomas & J. Grimes (Eds.), *Best practices in school psychology II* (pp. 183–193). Washington, DC: National Association of School Psychologists.

Johnson-Powell, G., Yamamoto, J., & Arroyo, W. (1997). *Transcultural child development*. New York: Wiley.

Jordan, C., & Cobb, N. (2001). Competency-based treatment for persons with marital discord. In K. Corcoran (Ed.), *Structuring change* (2nd ed.). Chicago: Lyceum Books.

Jordan, C., Franklin, C., & Corcoran, K. (2010). Development of measuring instruments. In R. Grinnell (Ed.), *Social work research and evaluation* (pp. 196–215). New York: Oxford University Press.

Jordan, C., & Hoefer, R. (2002). Work versus life: Family friendly benefits in nonprofit organizations. *National Social Science Journal, 17*, 16–25.

Kaufman, A. S. (2000). Foreword. In D. P. Flanagan, I. S. McGrew, & S. O. Ortiz (Eds.), *The Wechsler intelligences scales and GF-Gc theory: A contemporay approach to interpretation* (pp. xiii–xv). Boston: Allyn and Bacon.

Kayser, J. A., & Lyon, M. A. (2000). Teaching social workers to use psychological assessment data. *Child Welfare, 79*, 197–222.

Kohlberg, L. (1981). *Essays on moral development, Vol. 1: The philosophy of moral development*. San Francisco: Harper and Row.

Kovacs, M. (1992). *Children's depression inventory*. Los Angeles: Multi-Health Systems.

Magura, S., & Moses, B. (1985). Outcome measures for child welfare services. Washington, DC: Child Welfare League of America.

McCarney, S. B., & Leigh, J. E. (1990). *Manual for the behavior evaluation scale 2*. Columbia, MO: Educational Services.

McConaughy, S. H. (1996). The interview process. In M. Breen & C. Fiedler (Eds.), *Behavioral approach to assessment of youth with emotional/behavioral disorders: A handbook for school-based practitioners*. Austin, TX: PRO-ED.

McConaughy, S. H., & Achenbach, T. M. (2001). *Manual for the semistructured clinical interview with children and adolescents*. New York: Guilford Press.

Merrell, K. W. (2007). *Behavioral, social, and emotional assessment of children and adolescents* (3rd ed.). Hillsdale, NJ: Erlbaum.

Merrell, K. W. (1993). Using behavior rating scales to assess social skills and antisocial behavior in school settings: Development of the School Social Behavior Scales. *School Psychology Review, 22*, 115–133.

Miley, K. K., O'Melia, M., & DuBois, B. (2006) *Generalist social work practice: An empowering approach*. Boston: Allyn and Bacon.

Miller, L. S., Klein, R. G., Piacentini, J., Abikoff, H., Shah, M. R., Samoilov, A., et al. (1995). The New York Teacher Rating Scale for disruptive and anti-social behavior. *Journal of the American Academy of Child and Adolescent Psychiatry, 34*, 359–370.

Nelson, C. A., & Carver, L. J. (1998). The effects of stress and trauma on brain and memory: A view from developmental cognitive neuroscience. *Development and Psychopathology, 10*, 793–809.

Nurmi, J. E. (1993). Adolescent development in an age graded context: The role of personal beliefs, goals, and strategies in the tackling of developmental tasks and standards. *International Journal of Behavioral Development, 16*, 169–189.

O'Hare, T. (2005). *Evidence-based practices for social workers: An interdisciplinary approach.* Chicago: Lyceum Books.

Olsen, D. H., Russell, C., & Sprenkle, D. (1989). *FACES III manual.* St. Paul: University of Minnesota Press.

Openshaw, L. (2008). *Social work in schools: Principles and practice.* New York: Guilford Press.

Openshaw, L., & Halvorson, H. (2005). The co-occurrence of intimate partner violence and child abuse. In L. H. Ginsberg (Ed.), *Social work in rural communities* (4th ed., pp. 207–221). Alexandria, VA: Council on Social Work Education.

Pavlov, I. P. (1960). *Conditional reflexes.* New York: Dover. (Originally published 1927.)

Perry, B. D. (1997). Incubated in terror: Neurodevelopment factors in the cycle of violence. In J. D. Osofsky (Ed.), *Children in a violent society* (pp. 124–149). New York: Guilford Press.

Perry, B. D. (2002). Helping traumatized children: A brief overview for caretakers. In *Parent and Caregiver Education Series of the Child Trauma Academy.* Retrieved from http://www.childtrauma.org.

Piaget, J. (2001). *Psychology of intelligence.* Florence, KY: Routledge.

Poznanzski, E. O., Cook, S. C., & Carroll, B. J. (1979). A depression rating scale for children. *Pediatric, 64*, 442–450.

Quay, H. C. (1983). A dimensional approach to behavior disorder: The Revised Behavior Problem Checklist. *School Psychology Review, 12*, 244–249.

Quay, H., & Peterson, D. (1987). *Manual for the revised behavior problem checklist.* Coral Gables, FL: Author.

Reich, W., & Welner, Z. (1990). *Diagnostic interview for children and adolescents-revised.* St. Louis, MO: Washington University, Division of Child Psychiatry.

Reynolds, C. R., & Kamphaus, R. W. (Eds.) (2003). *The handbook of psychological and educational assessment of children. Vol. 1: Aptitude and achievement.* New York: Guilford Press.

Roberts, R. E., & Chen, Y. W. (1995). Depressive symptoms and suicidal ideation among Mexican-origin and Anglo adolescents. *Journal of the American Academy of Child and Adolescent Psychiatry, 34*, 81–90.

Rossi, A., Pollice, R., Daneluzzo, E., Marinangeli, M. G., & Stratta, P. (2000). Behavioral neurodevelopment abnormalities and schizophrenic disorder: A retrospective evaluation with childhood behavior checklist (CBCL). *Schizophrenia Research, 44*, 121–128.

Sattler, J. (1988). *Assessment of children* (3rd ed.). San Diego, CA: Author.

Schaffer, D. (1992). *NIMH Diagnostic interview schedule for children, version 2.3.* New York: Columbia University, Division of Child and Adolescent Psychiatry.

Sheafor, B., Horejsi, C., & Horejsi, G. (1988). *Techniques and guidelines for social work practice*. Newton, MA: Allyn and Bacon.

Siegel, J. M., Aneshensel, C. S., Taub, B., Cantwell, D. P., & Driscoll, A. K. (1998). Adolescent depressed mood in a multi-ethnic sample. *Journal of Youth and Adolescence, 27*, 413–427.

Skinner, B. F. (1972)*Beyond freedom and dignity*. New York: Bantam Vintage.

The thinking, feeling, and doing game. (1973). Cresskill, NJ: Creative Therapeutics.

Thomlison, B., & Krysik, J. (1992). The development of an instrument to measure the restrictiveness of children's living environments. *Research on Social Work Practice, 2*, 207–219.

Wakefield, J. C. (1996) Does social work need the eco-systems perspective? *Social Service Review, 70*, 1–32.

Wilkinson, I. (2000). The Darlington Assessment System: Clinical guidelines for practitioners. *Journal of Family Therapy, 22*, 211–224.

Yalof, J., & Abraham, P. (2007). Personality assessment in schools. In S. R. Smith & L. Handler (Eds.), *The clinical assessment of children and adolescents: A practitioner's handbook*. Mahwah, NJ: Erlbaum.

# CHAPTER 7

# Adults

**Elizabeth C. Pomeroy, Lori K. Holleran, Cynthia Franklin, Jeremy Goldbach, and Katherine Sanchez**

## INTRODUCTION

Social workers assess clients across the life cycle from the cradle to grave and frequently work with adult clients at different ages and stages of life. This chapter discusses a different perspective for how to assess adult clients incorporating examples across the life cycle that highlights different problem areas that adults may experience. The chapter also offers further suggestions for the types of assessment methods that practitioners can use when assessing adults. We summarize several methods for assessing adult clients that are consistent with the types of assessment and measurement techniques described in chapters 2, 3, and 4, including interview questions, diagnostic systems like the *DSM*, mental status interviews, the use of standardized measures and quality assurance systems, and other rating scales. Finally, a case study offers an opportunity for readers to practice moving from assessment to intervention planning.

## ASSESSMENT METHODS

### Interview Questions

While social workers are examining aspects of the adult client's functioning, they must also keep in mind the complex interplay among the various personal issues being presented. For example, clients' culture and ethnicity have pervasive implications throughout all aspects of the client's life experience and can affect their ability to obtain adequate mental health care (Snowden, 2003). Although some factors distinguish adult assessment from assessment of children and adolescents, it is important to note that, in cases of serious mental illness, boundaries may be blurred depending on the client's level of functioning. In general, when assessing adults, it is important to recognize that there is normally an extensive history of life experiences that affect the client's presentation, coping mechanisms are more solidified and complex and often less mutable, and there are additional areas for inquiry based on adult functioning and interactions. The goal of an assessment with an adult client is to gain a comprehensive profile of the client's present functioning in all areas of life.

The following is a list of questions (box 7.1) that a social worker can use depending on the particular needs of an adult client. These questions are designed to guide social workers in developing their own questions to ask the client; that is, social workers do not simply ask the client these questions—rather, they carefully choose wording that is sensitive, culturally appropriate, and at the client's developmental and intellectual level.

---

**Box 7.1**
**Interviewing Questions**

---

**Appearance:**
How is the client dressed (e.g., neatly, professionally, disheveled, colorfully, coordinated)?
What is the client's level of personal hygiene?
What is the client's physical appearance (e.g., overweight, underweight, marked physical anomalies)?

**Biomedical/Organic:**
What is the client's medical history?
What is the family medical history?
Are there any physical disabilities or limitations?
Are there any cognitive disabilities or limitations (such as, aphasia, ataxia, echolalia)?
Does the client take any prescribed drugs?
What are the client's eating patterns?
What are the client's sleeping patterns?
Has the client experienced any exposure to chemical or environmental toxins that may produce behavioral abnormalities?
How does the client describe his or her recent general state of health?
Has the client discovered any solutions to these concerns?
What is the impact of the above concerns regarding family, friends, school/work, or community?

**Developmental Issues/Transitions:**
Is the client experiencing any developmental or life transitions (such as, adolescent individuation, marriage, birth of a child, divorce, death of a family member, aging, retirement)?
How is the client being affected by the current life cycle tasks and demands?
Does the client have support systems available to help in these transitions?
Has the client discovered any solutions to these concerns?
What is the impact of the above concerns regarding family, friends, school/work, or community?

**Box 7.1**
**Interviewing Questions**—(*Continued*)

**Problem Solving/Coping Skills:**
What type of coping styles does the client demonstrate (e.g., problem solving, relational, avoidance, emotion-focused, task-focused)?
What type of coping skills does the client employ?
Does the client feel that his or her coping mechanisms are effective in dealing with problems?
Does it appear that the client's coping mechanisms are problematic?
Has the client discovered any solutions to these concerns?
What is the impact of the above concerns regarding family, friends, school/work, or community?

**Stressors:**
What are the primary stressors in the client's current life situation?
How long have these stressors been affecting the client?
Are the stressors internal or situational?
Is there a pattern of stress in the client's life (examples include, chronic, occupational, or relational problems)?
Are there any environmental or cultural stressors (such as, neighborhood violence, acculturation issues, minority status)?
Has the client discovered any solutions to these concerns?
What is the impact of the above concerns regarding family, friends, school/work, or community?

**Relationship and Social Capacities:**
Who are the client's significant others? With whom does he or she reside?
What are client's communication skills?
In what activities outside the home does the client participate?
How does the client perceive his or her level of social support?
Are there noteworthy relationship patterns?
Does the client appear to have the ability to form lasting relationships?
Does the client have the capacity for empathy toward others?
Does the client experience significant stress, fear, or anxiety concerning interpersonal contacts?
Is the client currently experiencing any relationship difficulties?
Has the client discovered any solutions to these concerns?
What is the impact of the above concerns regarding family, friends, school/work, or community?

**Behavioral Functioning:**
Does the client display any unusual behavioral characteristics (such as, tics, tremors, violence, hyperactive movements, responding to unobserved stimuli)?

**Box 7.1**
**Interviewing Questions—**(*Continued*)

Does the client appear to behave appropriately in the interview?
How comfortable is your interaction with the client?
Does the client report problems in psychosocial functioning because of be-
  havioral issues?
Has the client discovered any solutions to these concerns?
What is the impact of the above concerns regarding family, friends,
  school/work, or community?

**Sexual Functioning:**
Does the client report any sexual difficulties?
If so, are the problems emotional, physical, or cultural in origin?
What is the duration of these problems?
Have the problems affected other areas of functioning?
Has the client discovered any solutions to these concerns?
What is the impact of the above concerns regarding family, friends,
  school/work, or community?

**Cognitive Functioning:**
(Use the Mini-Mental State Exam that follows to determine the possibility
of cognitive impairment.)

What are the results of the mental status exam?
What is the client's intellectual capacity and level of education?
Is there a history of cognitive/neurological problems in the client system?
Does the client display or report any delusional thinking (such as, para-
  noid ideations, grandiosity, delusions of reference)?
Does the client use bizarre expressions?
Is the client able to use language to express him- or herself clearly?
Does the client appear to have good judgment or "common sense" (i.e.,
  has a realistic plan for his or her life, recognizes risks and consequences
  of decisions, and is able to choose appropriate solutions to problems)?
Has the client discovered any solutions to these concerns?
What is the impact of the above concerns regarding family, friends,
  school/work, or community?

**Emotional Functioning:**
What is the client's general affective presentation (is it flat, manic, sad,
  content, anxious)?
Is the client's mood or affect stable or labile?
Is any lability situation-related?
Is the client's mood or affect appropriate to his or her current circumstances?
Is the client's mood or affect creating problems in his or her psychosocial
  functioning?

**Box 7.1**
**Interviewing Questions—**(*Continued*)

If so, what is the duration of these problems?
Has the client discovered any solutions to these concerns?
What is the impact of the above concerns regarding family, friends,
    school/work, or community?

**Self-Concept:**
Does the client view him- or herself as a valuable, worthwhile individual?
Does the client see him- or herself as competent?
Does the client have a reality-based perception of self?
Does the client report any problems with self-concept or self-esteem?
If so, has the client discovered any solutions to these concerns?
What is the impact of the above concerns regarding family, friends,
    school/work, or community?

**Motivation:**
Does the client report a desire to change?
How strong is the client's motivation to make changes?
What are the external and internal motivators?
Does the client have goals for him- or herself?
Can the client imagine ways of changing and visualize improvement?
What is the impact of the above concerns regarding family, friends,
    school/work, or community?

**Culture and Ethnic Identification:**
Does the client identify with particular cultural and/or ethnic group(s)?
Does the client gain strength from the identification(s)?
Does the client experience conflict related to his or her ethnic/cultural
    identity?
Does the client feel oppressed by membership in this group or population?
What cultural barriers are experienced by the client?
Has the client discovered any solutions to these concerns?
What is the impact of ethnic and cultural identity with regard to family,
    friends, school/work, or community?

**Role Functioning:**
What roles does the client currently fulfill?
How were these roles acquired (voluntarily or involuntarily)?
Is the client having difficulty with any of these roles or balancing these
    roles?
Has the client discovered any solutions to these concerns?
What is the impact of the above concerns regarding family, friends,
    school/work, or community?

---

**Box 7.1**
**Interviewing Questions—(***Continued***)**

---

**Spirituality and Religion:**
Does the client adhere to a particular spiritual belief system or religion?
Does the client view his or her spiritual or religious orientation as a
    strength?
Does the client view his or her spiritual or religious orientation as a prob-
    lem?
If so, has he or she sought and/or discovered any solutions to these con-
    cerns?
What is the client's sense of life purpose?
Do the client's beliefs hinder his or her psychosocial functioning in any
    way?
What is the impact of the above concerns regarding family, friends,
    school/work, or community?

**Other Strengths:**
Does the client identify any other strengths or talents?

---

## Using the *DSM* to Diagnose Problems

Psychiatric classifications and assessment tools assess various psychopathologies and are useful for determining whether a client has one
or more major mental disorders. So it is important for the social work
practitioner to have a thorough grounding in nosological assessment systems, such as the *Diagnostic and Statistical Manual for Mental Disorders* (4th
ed., text revision; *DSM-IV-TR*) and its forthcoming release, *DSM-V*, and
to learn how to give a client a mental status exam to assess the client's
current functioning and make an accurate diagnosis of a mental disorder,
when appropriate to do so.

The *DSM-IV-TR* provides criteria that help practitioners decide
whether a client has one or more of mental disorders, which is very important to clinical practice. Even in a brief interview, for example, it is important to find out about the presenting problems of clients and to assess
clients for serious mental illnesses, such as psychosis, mood disorders,
anxiety disorders, and substance abuse. The practitioner must be aware
of serious impairments, such as psychosis and suicidal behavior, which
put the client and others at significant risk of harm. Extreme moods, hallucinations, delusions, and other signs of thought disorders are major
concern and the *DSM* criteria can help us sort through the myriad symptoms and presentations of different problem areas.

There are several other advantages to being trained in using the *DSM*.
For example, *DSM* diagnostic criteria are widely accepted in practice settings, descriptive in nature, and not tied to any particular theoretical

frameworks. The manual is organized according to mental and emotional disorders found in children, adolescents, and adults. Diagnoses are made according to five axes: axis I, primary clinical disorder; axis II, personality disorder or mental retardation; axis III, medical problems; axis IV, psychosocial issues; and axis V, global assessment of functioning (for an outline of the five axes in the *DSM-IV-TR*, see Appendix 7A). Although some mental disorders such as Alzheimer's disease require medical evaluation by a neuropsychologist and other doctors, most others can be assessed by master's-level social workers who have a license to practice clinical social work.

## Specific Criticisms of the *DSM* for Social Work Practice

The *DSM* is first and foremost a psychiatric textbook for diagnosing clients, and its credibility and use are somewhat controversial among professionals (Bentall, 2006). As discussed in chapter 1, for example, practitioners trained in the strengths perspective do not prefer the use of diagnostic labels because they may marginalize the client. Other practitioners, such as those trained in solution-focused brief therapy and behavioral perspectives, prefer more empirical and functional ways to describe the problems of clients over diagnostic labels. Practitioners also believe that the diagnostic labels used in the *DSM* pathologize clients instead of empowering them to overcome their psychosocial problems. Diagnostic labels, in fact, may be used by some clients to disempower, excuse dysfunctional behavior, and remove the personal incentives and self-determination necessary to change. Many therapists, including family therapists and others practicing from the systems perspectives, brief therapists, cognitive constructivist therapists, and behaviorist practitioners, express some skepticism about the usefulness of *DSM* nosological system. They do not see diagnostic labels as helpful because they do not describe the specific behaviors of the client that are a problem for them and others, for example. Neither do they specify change goals that are necessary for the client to solve his or her presenting problems.

Beyond the critiques offered by social work practitioners and therapists working from differing models, the *DSM* has also been criticized for its lack of research into the validity and reliability of its diagnostic categories. It is necessary for a measurement instrument or an assessment tool to demonstrate validity and reliability before it is useful to practitioners (Kendell & Jablensky, 2003). The social work researchers Kutchins and Kirk (1997) have offered some of the most compelling criticisms of the research for the manual, showing that the categories lack reliability. Other practice researchers have pointed to the political and social constructivist nature of the diagnoses in the *DSM*. These researchers demonstrate that the diagnoses are maintained or deleted from the manual based on social political processes such as associations of pharmaceutical industries to the *DSM* instead of empirical research (Cosgrove, Krimsky, Vijayaraghavan, & Schneider, 2006; Neimeyer & Raskin, 2000). Some social constructivists and advocates for the oppressed groups of mental health patients go so far as to say that the *DSM* is neither valid nor helpful to clients, but serves instead to maintain the power of an elite group of psychiatrists and therapists. The social work profession in general does not prefer the categorical, noncontextual view of human behavior of the *DSM*.

Because of these criticisms, the National Association of Social Workers responded by publishing its own diagnostic assessment system, the person-in-environment (PIE) system (Karls & Wandrei, 1994). Unfortunately, however, the PIE approach to assessment has not yet completed the necessary studies to show that it has validity and reliability, which limits its usefulness to clinical practice.

## Improving the *DSM* for Social Workers

Over the years, the developers of the *DSM* have worked to address criticisms of it; the current *DSM* offers more of a person-in-environment assessment for making a diagnosis. This is accomplished through the axial system; in particular, axis IV addresses psychosocial stressors. The manual also currently integrates more material on culture and ethnicity. Future additions of the *DSM* are likely to continue to address criticisms. Prospective reviews of the *DSM-V* on what the future manual might look like suggest a major overhaul of the *DSM*. Diagnosis is likely to become less categorical, for example, and to reflect more of a continuum or dimensional view of mental disorders (Widiger & Clark, 2000). It is not likely, however, that any revision will totally satisfy practitioners who have theoretical or epistemological concerns about the helpfulness of psychiatric diagnosis.

## Importance of Using *DSM*

Despite the limitations of the *DSM-IV-TR*, its current version at the time of this writing, it is important for social workers to learn to use the *DSM*. The *DSM* is the most frequently used diagnostic system in mental health assessment.

One national survey conducted by the Substance Abuse and Mental Health Services Administration (SAMHSA) board found that social workers outnumber psychiatrists and psychologists two to one in the mental health practice field. The majority of practicing social workers are employed in mental health or school mental health services (O'Neil, 1999; Whitaker, Weismiller, & Clark, 2006). The manual is constantly used in health and mental health services and in work with clients and insurance reimbursement, and other mental health professionals consider it the state of the art in mental health assessment. Because social workers often collaborate with other health-care professionals, they need to be familiar with the content of the *DSM* to communicate effectively about their clients with other professionals. The *DSM* delineates the symptoms, cultural factors, differential diagnoses, and prevalence rates that must be examined thoroughly in a complete psychosocial assessment. For this reason, this chapter also uses the diagnostic categories and their measurements when discussing assessment methods for adult clients.

## ASSESSING MAJOR MENTAL ILLNESSES IN ADULTS

Social workers assess adult clients with major mental illnesses, such as schizophrenia and bipolar illnesses, and serious neurological symptoms, such as delirium and dementia. It is important that practitioners be astute in diagnosing these symptoms in clients to ensure that clients get the proper help and care. The mental status exam has long been used to help examine current mental functioning and to assess serious mental disorders (for a list of criteria for diagnosing schizophrenia and other psychotic behaviors, bipolar disorder, delirium, and dementia in clients, see Appendix 7B). Depression, anxiety disorders, and substance abuse are covered later in this chapter.

### Mini-Mental State Exam

The Mini-Mental State Examination (MMSE), published by Folstein, Folstein, and McHugh (1975), is a frequently used assessment tool designed to evaluate the mental state of clients in both clinical and research settings (Crum, Anthony, Bassett, & Folstein, 1993; Molloy & Standish, 1997). It assesses cognitive impairments like dementia, delirium, and other thought disorders. The MMSE consists of brief and basic items that allow for a time-efficient and effective evaluation of various cognitive domains, including orientation, encoding, attention, recall, language, reading, writing, and drawing (Folstein et al., 1975). The eleven-item scale has a possible total of thirty points and requires less than ten minutes to administer. The MMSE has been widely used to detect cognitive difficulties in special populations, such as the elderly, head-injured clients, and individuals with severe mental illness (Lezak, 1995).

When using the MMSE, a cutoff score of twenty-three or twenty-four is generally accepted in order to separate patients with cognitive impairment from those who are cognitively intact (Anthony, LeResche, Niaz, von Korff, & Folstein, 1982; DePaulo, Folstein, & Gordon, 1980). Research indicates that a cutoff score of twenty-three for clients with mental health issues is acceptable (Folstein et al., 1975). However, some studies have suggested a lower sensitivity level for those clients with less education, clients of certain ethnicities, or older clients (Fillenbaum, Heyman, Willians, Prosnitz, & Burchett, 1990; Launer, Dinkgreve, Jonker, Hooijer, & Lindeboom, 1993; Murden, McRae, Kaner, & Bucknam, 1991).

The MMSE is published in the *Journal of Psychiatric Research*; thus, it is in the public domain. The following sections describe the procedure for using the MMSE in practice.

**Orientation.**    Orientation refers to individual's grasp of time and place. By asking the client to note the year, season, day, or month, the social worker can ascertain the client's level of temporal awareness. Then, by asking about location, such as state, county, or agency, the worker can assess the client's spatial awareness. Clients who are disoriented as to time and/or place may need further evaluation for serious cognitive impairment.

**Registration.**    This section evaluates how much repetition is necessary for a client to recognize and understand (i.e., register) a concept. If a client takes considerable time or cannot register concepts, this may indicate a thought disorder or organic illness.

**Attention and Calculation.**    By asking a client to count backward in intervals of seven, a social worker can assess the person's ability to focus and reformulate a concept. This indicates a level of reasoning ability that is necessary for normal cognitive functioning.

**Recall or Memory.**    By asking the client to recall three items identified earlier in the exam, the social worker can assess the client's ability to retain information. If the client is not able to remember, this may indicate a cognitive deficit associated with such disorders as amnesia, stroke conditions, dissociative disorders, head trauma, dementia, or other neurological conditions.

Amnesia, the absence of memory, can be partial or complete, or it can have an emotional or organic basis. Disassociative amnesia is a highly selective loss of memory involving emotionally charged events (e.g., a childhood sexual assault, ritualistic abuse, other trauma). In the case of a stroke, anterograde amnesia, or loss of memory for recent events, is usually progressive and somewhat characteristic of arteriosclerotic cerebral degeneration (hardening of the arteries). Retrograde amnesia involves long-past events and is usually not progressive. A fugue state is a severe and abrupt personality dissociation involving amnesia and actual physical flight (during the period of amnesia) from the area of ostensible psychological conflict. Assumption of a new identity during the fugue is common.

**Language.**   The language portion of the exam determines a client's capacity and fluency with verbal expression, literacy, and writing skills. For example, can the client write a simple sentence that is orally administered. It also assesses the client's ability to comprehend and follow instructions and to make the complex series of recognitions necessary to complete a simple task (e.g., "Take a paper in your right hand, fold it in half, and put it on the floor"). Thus, the social worker can concurrently assess motor tasks and cognitive understanding.

This section also elucidates bizarre thinking patterns and disruptions in communication. For example, punning and rhyming to an extreme can occur in those with mania and occasionally in those with schizophrenia (disorganized type). Mutism (refusal or simply the inability to speak) frequently accompanies severe psychosis. Verbigeration (word salad), the stringing together, in a seemingly meaningless way, of words and phrases repetitively occurs in certain kinds of schizophrenia (notably disorganized type, occasionally other types). Aphasia (loss of some faculty for language comprehension or production) may indicate lesions in certain parts of the brain.

**Use of MMSE in Concert with Other Information.**   The Structured Clinical Interview for *DSM-IV* (SCID) (First, Spitzer, Gibbon, Williams &, 1997) is the most common clinical interview used with adults with mental disorders. It is a comprehensive assessment that is based on the *DSM-IV* decision tree. The SCID requires a fair degree of clinical judgment and includes several open-ended questions that help account for self-report. The SCID is an extensive tool that can be used to diagnose for many disorders.

## RAPID ASSESSMENT OF COMMON PROBLEMS IN ADULT CLIENTS

Two of the most prominent types of problems that adult clients experience are depression and anxiety. Other frequent problems are substance-related disorders. To develop accurate assessments of these disorders, a social worker can use a set of rapid assessment instruments specific to the particular diagnoses. The following sections introduce some of the prominent rapid assessment tools recommended for assessment purposes. Recall from chapter 3 that these standardized measures are meant to offer quick, valid, reliable assessments of a client's characteristics. As screening tools, rapid assessment measures can provide one part of the information necessary to make a diagnosis. If the client scores are clinically significant on one of these rapid assessment measures, the practitioner can follow up with more thorough diagnostic interviews and procedures to determine whether the person qualifies for the diagnosis. The measures are also helpful in outcomes monitoring (for more ideas about measuring outcomes, see chapter 11).

## Major Depressive Disorder

In practice, a social worker is likely to encounter clients with a variety of mood disorders. According to the *DSM-IV-TR*, there are several basic types of depression in adults. Major depressive disorder is characterized by one or more depressive episodes over a two-week period, which are evidenced by five or more of the following symptoms nearly every day:

- Depressed mood most of the day
- Diminished interest or pleasure in activities
- Significant weight loss or gain
- Insomnia or hypersomnia nearly every day
- Psychomotor agitation or retardation
- Fatigue
- Feelings of worthlessness or inappropriate guilt
- Diminished ability to concentrate or think
- Recurrent thoughts of death

Dysthymic disorder, in contrast, is defined as a protracted, less severe form of depression that is characterized to a lesser extent by many of the same symptoms as major depressive disorder. These include poor appetite, insomnia or hypersomnia, low energy, low self-esteem, poor concentration, and feelings of hopelessness (American Psychiatric Association [APA], 1994). For a diagnosis of dysthymia, the symptoms must be present most of the time over a two-year period.

Depression may be an accompanying symptom with other disorders (e.g., adjustment disorder with depressed mood). Although the use of clinical tools for the assessment of depression may be necessary, self-report instruments are also valuable. With regard to suicidal ideations, patient self-report can be more useful than clinical judgment (Jobes, Jacoby, Cimbolic, & Hustead, 1997). The following sections cover some examples of appropriate screening instruments to appropriately diagnose major depression and dysthymia.

**Beck Depression Inventory.**   The mostly widely known and extensively used assessment instrument for ascertaining depressive symptomatology in adults is the Beck Depression Inventory II (BDI-II) (Beck, Steer, & Brown, 1996). First developed in 1961 by Aaron Beck, the Beck Depression Inventory consists of twenty-one items rated on a four-point scale (0–3) to assess the intensity of depression in adult clients. The current version, the

BDI-II, was revised from earlier versions to be congruent with the *DSM-IV-TR*. The self-administered instrument takes between five and ten minutes to complete and should be filled out in the presence of a doctoral-level clinician trained in the use of the instrument. It has excellent reliability with a test-retest coefficient of 0.90. Hundreds of research studies have been conducted using the BDI over the past forty years, which attests to its concurrent and criterion validity. A score of 0–13 indicates normal levels of depressive symptoms, 14–19 indicates mild to moderate levels of depression, 20–28 indicates moderate to severe levels of depression, and 29–63 indicates extremely severe levels of depression. The social worker needs to be able to comprehend these scores provided by the doctoral-level administrator to facilitate treatment strategies for the client.

**The Hamilton Rating Scale for Depression.**    The Hamilton Rating Scale for Depression (Hamilton, 1967), unlike the Beck Depression Inventory, is an assessment instrument that the interview completes. It is normally used when the interviewer has some knowledge of the client's affective status and strong evidence of symptoms of depressive disorder. The scale has eighteen items measured on a five-point Likert scale. It addresses the issues of depressed mood, suicide, anxiety, general somatic symptoms, and loss of interest in work and recreational pursuits. It has been widely used in clinical research studies and in practice with adult populations, including the elderly, adults with HIV/AIDS, adults with sexual disorders, and adults with minor depressive disorders.

**Center for Epidemiological Studies—Depression Scale, Revised (CES-D-R).**    Another commonly used instrument to assess depression is the Center for Epidemiologic Studies—Depression Scale (CES-D) (Radloff, 1977). This self-report scale consists of twenty items. The scale has been found to be highly reliable with populations of varying ages, ethnicities, and cultures (Beals, Manson, Keane, & Dick 1995; Garrison, Addy, Jackson, McKeown, & Waller, 1991; Joiner, Pfaff, & Acres, 2002; Radloff, 1977; Radloff & Terri, 1986). However, some studies have found the CES-D may not be as valid an instrument when administered to minority clients (Prescott et al., 1998). Studies using this scale have confirmed the finding that women report depressive symptoms more frequently than men do in the general population in the United States (Berganza & Aguilar, 1992; Radloff & Rae, 1981; see also Gjerde, Block, & Block, 1988; Kessler et al., 1994).

## Anxiety Disorders

In addition to depression, clients often encounter problems with anxiety. There is growing evidence of a strong relationship between depression and anxiety disorders. The genetic causes of depression and generalized anxiety disorder (GAD) have striking similarities (Kendler, Neale, Kessler, & Heath, 1992). Clients often qualify for both diagnoses, for example. The *DSM-IV-TR* defines an anxiety disorder as worry and "apprehensive expectation" most of the time during a six-month period (APA, 2000). Other symptoms might include restlessness, concentration difficulties, sleep problems, tension, and irritability. According to the *DSM-IV-TR*, the variety of anxiety disorders includes panic disorder, agoraphobia, obsessive-compulsive disorder (OCD), posttraumatic stress disorder (PTSD), phobias, and anxiety disorders of varied etiologies (e.g., from a general medical condition, substance induced). Anxiety can be assessed using multiple methods, including standardized measurement tools. The following sections discuss some examples (see Appendix 7B for criteria for assessing anxiety disorders using the *DSM-IV-TR*).

**State Trait Anxiety Inventory.**    The State Trait Anxiety Inventory (STAI) is a standardized two-part, self-report instrument. Both the state and trait sections contain twenty items, which the respondent rates from "not at all" to "very much so" on a scale of 1 to 4. The scale has been validated and shown to have coefficient alpha reliability coefficients ranging from 0.86 to 0.95 (Spielberger, 1983). Several of the items are reverse scored. Examples of items include "I feel tense," "I feel upset," and "I feel secure."

**Trauma Symptom Checklist.**    The Trauma Symptom Checklist (TSC-33), a thirty-three-item instrument, has been used in clinical research as a measure of traumatic effect (Briere & Ruentz, 1989). It has been used relative to the long-term effects of childhood physical and sexual abuse. It can be used in the assessment of PTSD in adults. The scale has been shown to have internal consistency with an alpha of 0.89 (Briere & Ruentz, 1989). The respondent rates a list of thirty-three items (from 0 = never to 3 = very often). Examples of the items include "insomnia," "feeling isolated from others," and "trouble getting along with others."

**Fear Questionnaire (FQ).**    The Fear Questionnaire (FQ) is a twenty-four-item instrument designed to assess symptoms for treatment with phobic individuals (Fischer & Corcoran, 1994). In addition to general fears, the scale can target specific phobias. The instrument includes fifteen questions and has subscales that assess agoraphobia, blood injury phobia, and social phobia. Items are rated from 1 to 8 with higher scores reflecting greater severity of symptoms. The instrument has an alpha of 0.82 for the three subscales and 0.92 for the main target phobia. Some examples of the scale items include "going into crowded shops," "going into large spaces," and "speaking or acting to an audience."

**Panic Attack Symptoms Questionnaire (PASQ).** The Panic Attack Symptoms Questionnaire (PASQ) is a thirty-three-item instrument measuring the severity of symptoms the client experiences during a panic attack (Clum, Broyles, Borden, & Watkins, 1990; Fischer & Corcoran, 1994). Items are rated from 0 to 5, where 0 = "Did not experience this" and 5 = "protractedly (1 day to 2 days or longer)." The instrument has good reliability, with an alpha of 0.88. The scale can be used to differentiate between individuals who have panic attacks and those who do not have panic attacks.

## Personality Disorders

Clients with personality disorders often have difficulty functioning in work and social settings. Some examples from the *DSM-IV-TR* include antisocial personality disorder, paranoid personality disorder, borderline personality disorder, and obsessive-compulsive personality disorder. These disorders tend to require extensive therapeutic intervention, and clients may be at risk for harming themselves and others, as is the case with clients who have antisocial and borderline diagnoses. A social worker needs to be careful not to fall into the trap of labeling confusing clients with certain personality diagnoses without also validating the disorder with standardized measurement instruments and appropriate developmental history. One method a social worker can use to ensure an appropriate diagnosis is to rely on standardized, structured interviews for assessing psychopathology. Interviews such as the Structured Clinical Interview for Diagnosis (SCID-II) can improve the reliability and validity of diagnosis among clinicians (see, e.g., Garb, 1998). In a review of this literature, Wood, Garb, Lilienfeld, and Nezworski (2002) report that numerous studies that compare clinician-alone diagnosis to structured interviews indicate that practitioners both overrate and underrate diagnoses in clients and that clinical judgment in general does not perform as well as standardized, structured interviews.

A social worker can also use other standardized measures to assess a client's personality, such as a personality assessment measure. The client may be referred to a psychologist for a more-formal personality assessment if there is a suspicion that the person may have some underlying personality disorder. Psychologists may administer objective and projective measures such as the Millon and Rorschach inkblot tests. When social workers make referrals to a psychologist, it is best that they choose one that uses more objective forms of personality assessment and has considerable experience with personality disorders.

Standardized measures, covered in chapter 3, are among the best self-report assessment tools for measuring personality functioning. Personality assessment measures, such as the Minnesota Multiphasic Personality Inventories (MMPI and MMPI II), are based on the original work of Hathaway and McKinley (1943). In recent years, the MMPI II was updated with the help of James Butcher and others (Butcher, 2004; Butcher, Graham, Williams, & Ben-Porath, 2007; Butcher, Williams, & Fowler, 2000). The short version of the MMPI II includes 370 items; the measure also offers longer versions with additional scales for assessing clients in forensic and correctional populations (for a list of the scales of the MMPI II, see Appendix 7C).

The MMPI and MMPI II are some of the most popular measures in psychology practice and have held this position for decades (for more information, see http://assessments.ncspearson.com/assessments/tests/mmpi_2.htm).

Psychologists, clinical social workers, and other clinicians can also use other standardized personality assessment measures, such as the Millon Clinical Multiaxial Inventory III (Millon, 1997) and the California Psychological Inventory (McAllister, 1996). The Millon assessment was discussed and illustrated in chapter 2. More information about the Millon and how to purchase the instrument can be obtained from the NCES Assessments Web site (http://assessments.ncspearson.com/assessments/tests/mcmi_2.htm). Another measure that helps diagnose antisocial personality and predict the aggression and violence these individuals are at risk of committing is the Hare Psychopathy Checklist-Revised (Hare, 1991; Hemphill, Hare, & Wong, 1998). This measure is helpful for use in forensic settings, in which clinicians are asked to diagnose antisocial personality and psychopathy, and to present and predict a person's profile for violence. The original version of the Hare is a long instrument to use, as it takes two to three hours. There is, however, a shorter screening version of the measure that reduces the time to ninety minutes (for more information, see the Web site for Psychological Assessment Resources, at www.parinc.com/product.cfm?ProductID=324). To use personality assessment measures, the practitioner should have adequate training in testing and measurement and should be familiar with the scoring and interpretation of the particular measure being used.

Some advocates for the unstructured clinical interview cite the use of the Shedler-Westen Assessment Procedure-200 (SWAP-200). The SWAP-200 is a clinician ranking of two hundred items, identified through personality disorder and psychotherapy literature, which relies heavily on the "empathically attuned and dynamically sophisticated clinician" (Shedler, 2002; Westen & Shedler, 1999; for more information on the SWAP-200, see www.swapassessment.com/).

## Substance-Related Disorders

When assessing adults, it is important to consider the possibility of substance-related disorders and the severity of substance use. This chapter does not detail individual substances; however, for many years, professional medical organizations have recognized alcoholism as a distinct, primary, chronic, progressive, and often fatal disease. The Substance Abuse and Mental Health Services Administration (SAMHSA, 2006) also reports that about 54 million (23 percent) of Americans binge drink (i.e., five or more drinks in the past month), which puts many adults at risk for alcohol-use disorders. The *DSM-IV-TR* offers a detailed way to diagnose alcoholism, various drug dependencies, and polysubstance (at least three of the eleven substances in a twelve-month period) dependencies. This aspect of adult diagnosis is extremely tricky, because it is hard to differentiate chemically induced symptoms from symptoms of mental illness, many clients have dual diagnoses, and a major presenting issue of substance abuse is denial (i.e., a mechanism for minimizing and avoiding an issue). This section explores these complications and provides mechanisms for accurately diagnosing substance disorders.

First, as noted, the symptoms of substance use and abuse often mimic symptoms of other mental illnesses and vice versa. For example, almost all addicts have mood swings between periods of elation and apparent depression (e.g., restlessness, irritability, discontent); however, only some addicts may actually be diagnosed with bipolar disorder.

Many adults with diagnoses other than addiction use substances as a mechanism of self-medication. Still others can be diagnosed with concurrent illnesses. Such comorbidity is also referred to as dual diagnoses and, in twelve-step recovery realms, as double trouble. Dually diagnosed individuals have complicated, multiproblem presentations in treatment; such individuals may require inpatient and longer-term services.

The other major complicating factor in diagnosing substance problems is the tendency for the user to minimize and deny the problems. Chemically dependent individuals are often aware that their use and subsequent behaviors are socially unacceptable. Therefore, they often become adept at hiding their use and at manipulating and lying to cover up their actions. They also may try to minimize consequences and find ways to deceive others, especially the people who care about them, who, in turn, enable or perpetuate the problem through caretaking.

Substance abuse is a pattern of substance use that results in recurrent and significant adverse consequences associated with the frequent use of substances. A repeated pattern of self-administration usually results in tolerance, withdrawal, and compulsive drug use.

Substance abuse causes a wide variety of medical and psychiatric symptoms and diseases. Therefore, all patients presenting to the healthcare system should be considered for the diagnosis. However, certain organ systems and problems have such a high prevalence of underlying substance abuse that they must be viewed with an even higher index of suspicion.

Common medical symptoms of substance abuse include vitamin deficiency, malnutrition, dyspepsia, upper gastrointestinal problems, peptic ulcer, hepatitis, pancreatitis, hypertension, new-onset arrhythmia, cardiomyopathy, seizures, peripheral neuropathy, and HIV/AIDS. Trauma of any kind should arouse suspicion during an interview, especially accidents at work, single-car crashes, and domestic violence. Substance abuse also manifests in the following behavioral, emotional, and cognitive problems: stress, insomnia, anxiety, depression, suicidal ideation, acute psychotic states, impaired cognition, and violent behavior. Perhaps the subtlest aspects of substance abuse are the associated social problems. Substance abusers are at high risk of marital and family problems, legal difficulties, loss of employment, and financial deterioration. Special consideration should be given to patients who are homeless, involved in prostitution, and those in the criminal justice system.

People who abuse substances are at particularly high risk for HIV/AIDS. During the course of an assessment, social workers must be alert to symptoms that may be related to HIV infection (Fisher & Harrison, 2000). According to Barthwell and Gilbert (1993), these signs and symptoms may include complaints of swollen lymph nodes, severe abdominal pain, diarrhea, visual changes, and severe dermatological conditions or rashes. In addition, a mental status exam may reveal HIV/AIDS-related cognitive impairments.

## How to Determine Severity of Substance Use

The primary distinguishing characteristics between a person who uses substances and one who abuses or is dependent on a substance overlap with one another. In the *DSM-IV-TR*, criteria abuse and dependence were separate diagnosis and were distinguished mainly by physiological characteristics as follows: the phenomenon of craving, which is a psychological and biological drive that addicts experience to use more substances regardless of consequences; the need for more or stronger substances for the same effect; progression, or increasing problems and consequences of use over time; and eventual fatality if untreated. These aspects are the grounds for the characterization of substance abuse and dependence as separate disease. However, the *DSM-V* work groups have suggested dropping substance dependence and abuse as a separate diagnosis and subsuming both under a diagnosis of substance-related disorders. According to the research findings of the *DSM* work group that covered substance related disorders, a "large body of literature on the structure of abuse and dependence criteria in clinical and general population samples suggests that the *DSM*-IV abuse and dependence criteria can be considered to form a unidimensional structure, with abuse and dependence criteria interspersed across the severity spectrum" (www.dsmv.org). What this means is that both abuse and dependence have many similarities, and determining which substance-related disorder a client may be experiencing is more of a matter of severity than of deciding on a distinct and different diagnosis (for a further review of the changes suggested for the *DSM-V*, see www.dsm5.org).

## ASSESSMENT INSTRUMENTS FOR SUBSTANCE-RELATED DISORDERS

There are a variety of assessment instruments that social workers can use to determine the presence, nature, and treatment directions with regard to clients with potential substance abuse problems. For an extensive list of assessment tools, clinicians can visit the Internet site of the National Institute on Alcohol Abuse and Alcoholism (NIAAA). The updated 2005 edition of the clinicians guide *Helping Patients Who Drink Too Much: A Clinician's Guide* can assist with collecting sensitive information by providing tools for assessment and intervention, patient education materials, and other useful clinical support. The guide is available free online and contains printable materials for use in the clinical setting (see http://pubs.niaaa.nih.gov/publications/Practitioner/Clinicians-Guide2005/clinicians_guide.htm).

There is a wealth of validated screening and assessment tools to determine the severity and extent of substance use, as well as the impact of substance abuse on an individual's functioning. The following sections present three of the most commonly used and widely accepted assessment tools used to guide the clinical interview.

### CAGEii

The CAGEii test (CAGE stands for cut, annoyed, guilty, eye opener) was developed by John Ewing, founding director of the Bowles Center for Alcohol Studies, at the University of North Carolina at Chapel Hill (Mayfield, McLeod, & Hall, 1994). The CAGE test is an internationally used assessment instrument for identifying alcoholics and other substance abusers. It is particularly popular with primary caregivers, and the test has been translated into several languages. The patient is asked four questions:

1. Have you ever felt you ought to cut down your drinking (or drug use)?
2. Have people annoyed you by criticizing your drinking (or drug use)?
3. Have you ever felt bad or guilty about your drinking (or drug use)?
4. Have you had a drink (or used drugs) first thing in the morning (eye opener) to steady your nerves or get rid of a hangover?

Affirmative answers to two or more questions is a positive screen and should prompt further history.

## The Alcohol Use Disorders Identification Test

The Alcohol Use Disorders Identification Test (AUDIT) was developed from a six-country World Health Organization collaborative project as a screening instrument for hazardous and harmful alcohol consumption. It is a ten-item questionnaire that covers the domains of alcohol consumption, drinking behavior, and alcohol-related problems. Responses to each question are scored from 0 to 4, with a maximum possible score of 40. An AUDIT score of 8 or more indicates hazardous or harmful alcohol use. The AUDIT provides a simple method for early detection of harmful alcohol use (Saunders, Aasland, Babor, Delafuente, & Grant, 1993). The AUDIT is available in both English and Spanish. It takes only about five minutes to complete, has been tested internationally, and has high levels of validity and reliability (for a downloadable version complete with scoring instructions, see www.niaaa.nih.gov/guide; see also table 7.1).

## The Michigan Alcohol Screening Test

The Michigan Alcohol Screening Test (MAST, see Appendix 7D; Selzer, 1971) is a written, twenty-five-item screening test that may be given to a patient initially or in follow-up to another screening test, such as CAGEii. Its brevity makes it useful as an outpatient screening tool. Cutoff scores correlate well with more extensive diagnostic tests for alcohol disorders. The MAST has been modified for drug abuse (i.e., Drug Alcohol Screening Test).

## Other Resources

In addition, the following instruments are also useful for a comprehensive assessment with substance abusing clientele and are available online at such sites as the National Library of Medicine (www.ncbi.nlm.nih .gov/books/bv.fcgi?rid=hstat5.section.72871):

- TWEAK (i.e., Tolerance, Worried, Eyeopener, Amnesia, and Kut-down)—initially designed for use with pregnant women (Russell et al., 1991)
- Addiction Severity Index (McLellan et al., 1980) (www.tresearch.org; www.niaaa.nih.gov/publications/asi.htm)
- Substance Use Disorders Diagnostic Schedule (Harrison & Hoffmann, 2001) (www.evinceassessment.com/product_sudds.html)

In summary, substance abuse disorders are complex problems with a variety of etiologies and outcomes. Social work practitioners can use the previously noted assessment tools to assess substance abuse disorders. If you, as a social worker, have a large clientele of substance users or abusers, special training will be valuable and important.

**Table 7.1**   AUDIT Assessment Instrument

| Questions | 0 | 1 | 2 | 3 | 4 |
|---|---|---|---|---|---|
| 1. How often do you have a drink containing alcohol? | Never | Monthly or less | 2 to 4 times a month | 2 to 3 times a week | 4 or more times a week |
| 2. How many drinks containing alcohol do you have on a typical day when you are drinking? | 1 or 2 | 3 or 4 | 5 or 6 | 7 to 9 | 10 or more |
| 3. How often do you have five or more drinks on one occasion? | Never | Less than monthly | Monthly | Weekly | Daily or almost daily |
| 4. How often during the last year have you found that you were not able to stop drinking once you had started? | Never | Less than monthly | Monthly | Weekly | Daily or almost daily |
| 5. How often during the last year have you failed to do what was normally expected of you because of drinking? | Never | Less than monthly | Monthly | Weekly | Daily or almost daily |
| 6. How often during the last year have you needed a first drink in the morning to get yourself going after a heavy drinking session? | Never | Less than monthly | Monthly | Weekly | Daily or almost daily |
| 7. How often during the last year have you had a feeling of guilt or remorse after drinking? | Never | Less than monthly | Monthly | Weekly | Daily or almost daily |
| 8. How often during the last year have you been unable to remember what happened the night before because of your drinking? | Never | Less than monthly | Monthly | Weekly | Daily or almost daily |
| 9. Have you or someone else been injured because of your drinking? | No | | Yes, but not in the last year | | Yes, during the last year |
| 10. Has a relative, friend, doctor, or other health care worker been concerned about your drinking or suggested you cut down? | No | | Yes, but not in the last year | | Yes, during the last year |

*Total*

NOTE: Instructions for patients are as follows: "Because alcohol use can affect your health and can interfere with certain medications and treatments, it is important that we ask some questions about your use of alcohol. Your answers will remain confidential, so please be honest." To reflect standard drink sizes in the United States, the number of drinks in question 3 was changed from six to five. A free AUDIT manual with guidelines for use in primary care settings is available online at www.who.org. Reprinted with permission from the World Health Organization.

## SPECIAL ISSUES IN WORKING WITH OLDER ADULTS

With increasing advances in medical technology during the past two decades, there has been a corresponding increase in the number of older persons in the population. Nearly one-third of the population today is older than sixty-five years old. Older adults experience many of the same emotional problems that younger adults experience. For example, older adults can be diagnosed in any of the adult categories for mental disorders found in the *DSM*. In contrast, depression and dementia are two psychobiological and emotional problems that are prevalent in the older adult population. In addition, medical or physical problems may be confounding factors for older adults and may mask emotional symptoms such as depression that older adults experience. In the older adult population, it is also important to be able to differentiate between an emotional or medical problem and a normal result of aging. Therefore, assessment instruments that specifically focus on the problems confronting older adults have been developed to address the psychological and medical issues that are prevalent in this population.

One of the most common emotional disorders experienced by older adults is depression. As do other adults, older persons display symptoms of sadness, hopelessness, fatigue, loss or increase of appetite, difficulty sleeping, and other symptoms outlined in the *DSM*. However, in addition to those symptoms, older adults may also experience memory loss and cognitive impairment when depressed. These symptoms mimic dementia, and practitioners can often confuse them with more serious cognitive impairment when, in fact, the problem is depression (Mitchell, Mathews, & Yesavage, 1993; Saez-Fonseca, Lee, & Walker, 2007; Yesavage et al., 1983). This condition is known as pseudodementia. Other symptoms that may be present in depressed, younger adults, such as a decline in sexual interest and other somatic complaints, may be normal signs of aging in older adults and not an indication of depression. Because of these differences in psychological symptomatology among older adults, specific scales have been designed to measure depression in the elderly, such as the Geriatric Depression Scale (GDS).

The GDS is a well-known instrument designed to assess depressive symptoms in older adults (Brink et al., 1982). It is available in a thirty-item version and a highly correlated fifteen-item shorter version. The GDS has high internal consistency and has been validated in many studies (Burns, Lawlor, & Craig, 2002). Because depression in older adults is often first assessed in a physician's office, it is helpful to have a questionnaire that requires only a short time to complete. The GDS is often used as an initial screening tool to diagnose depressive symptoms in the elderly. If an elderly person scores above the cutoff point on this scale, it is likely that a significant depressive symptomatology exists, and the practitioner should pursue a fuller assessment. Social workers who have elderly clients can use this instrument during an initial interview or at any time the client appears to be displaying depressive symptoms. Box 7.2 presents the original version of the long form of the scale and instructions for scoring. The scale is in the public domain, can be used by practitioners without

---

**Box 7.2**
**Geriatric Depression Scale (Long Form)**

1. Are you basically satisfied with your life?
2. Have you dropped many of your activities and interests?
3. Do you feel that your life is empty?
4. Do you often get bored?
5. Are you hopeful about the future?
6. Are you bothered by thoughts you can't get out of your head?
7. Are you in good spirits most of the time?
8. Are you afraid that something bad is going to happen to you?
9. Do you feel happy most of the time?
10. Do you often feel helpless?
11. Do you often get restless and fidgety?
12. Do you prefer to stay at home, rather than going out and doing new things?
13. Do you frequently worry about the future?
14. Do you feel you have more problems with memory than most?
15. Do you think it is wonderful to be alive now?
16. Do you often feel downhearted and blue?
17. Do you feel pretty worthless the way you are now?
18. Do you worry a lot about the past?
19. Do you find life very exciting?
20. Is it hard for you to get started on new projects?
21. Do you feel full of energy?
22. Do you feel that your situation is hopeless?
23. Do you think that most people are better off than you are?
24. Do you frequently get upset over little things?
25. Do you frequently feel like crying?
26. Do you have trouble concentrating?
27. Do you enjoy getting up in the morning?
28. Do you prefer to avoid social gatherings?
29. Is it easy for you to make decisions?
30. Is your mind as clear as it used to be?

This is the original scoring for the scale: One point for each of these answers. Cutoff: normal-0–9; mild depressives-10–19; severe depressives-20–30.

| | | | | | |
|---|---|---|---|---|---|
| 1. no | 6. yes | 11. yes | 16. yes | 21. no | 26. yes |
| 2. yes | 7. no | 12. yes | 17. yes | 22. yes | 27. no |
| 3. yes | 8. yes | 13. yes | 18. yes | 23. yes | 28. yes |
| 4. yes | 9. no | 14. yes | 19. no | 24. yes | 29. no |
| 5. no | 10. yes | 15. no | 20. yes | 25. yes | 30. no |

SOURCE: Yesavage, J. A., Brink, T. L., Rose, T. L., Lum, O., Huang, V., Adley, M., & Otto, V. (1982). Development and validation of the Geriatric Depression Screening Scale: A preliminary report. *Journal of Psychiatric Research, 17*(1), 37–49.

permission from the authors, and is available in the short or long version with scoring instructions (www.stanford.edu/~yesavage/GDS.html).

## Functional Status of Older Adults

Another important factor to consider in assessing older adults is their functional status. Functional status refers to the person's ability to take care of him- or herself, to perform physical activities, and to participate in activities of daily living. Older adults who have difficulties in their functional status may require additional community resources, such as home health services, delivered meals, visiting nursing services, or housekeeping assistance. Elderly persons can range from mildly to severely impaired in their ability to perform functional activities. Current recommendations from the U.S. Preventive Services Task Force suggest that early recognition of cognitive impairment, in addition to helping make diagnostic and treatment decisions, enables clinicians to anticipate problems the patients may have in understanding and adhering to recommended therapy (Berg et al., 2003). This information may also be useful to the patient's caregiver and family members in helping anticipate and plan for future problems that may develop as a result of progression of cognitive impairment. Clinicians should assess cognitive function whenever they suspect cognitive impairment or deterioration, through direct observation; patient report; or concerns that family members, friends, or caretakers raise. One evidence-based tool that clinicians and gerontologists have widely used is the Functional Activities Questionnaire (FAQ; available with scoring guidelines at (www.hospitalmedicine.org/geriresource/toolbox/pdfs/function _status_questionnai.pdf). We describe the FAQ and its usage in more detail in the following section.

## FAQ: Administration and Scoring

The FAQ is a ten-item scale that assesses shopping; handling finances; preparing a meal; traveling; remembering appointments; and paying attention to, understanding, and discussing television, a book, or a magazine (Pfeffer, Kurosaki, Harrah, Chance, & Filos, 1982). The total score ranges from 0 (independent) to 30 (dependent), with a cutoff of 9 (i.e. dependent in three or more activities) signifying impairment. An informant, such as a spouse, a child, a relative, or a close friend, completes the FAQ (Burns, Lawlor, Craig, & Coen, 2004). The FAQ is an informant-based measure of functional abilities. Informants provide performance ratings of the target person on ten complex, higher-order activities.

Individual items of the FAQ include the following:

1. Writing checks, paying bills, balancing checkbook
2. Assembling tax records, business affairs, or papers

3. Shopping alone for clothes, household necessities, or groceries

4. Playing a game of skill, working on a hobby

5. Heating water, making a cup of coffee, turning off stove

6. Preparing a balanced meal

7. Keeping track of current events

8. Paying attention to, understanding, discussing television, book, magazine

9. Remembering appointments, family occasions, holidays, medications

10. Traveling out of neighborhood, driving, arranging to take buses

The levels of performance assigned range from dependence to independence and are rated as follows:

- Dependent = 3
- Requires assistance = 2
- Has difficulty but does by one's self = 1
- Normal = 0

Two other response options can also be scored:

- Never did [the activity] but could do now = 0
- Never did and would have difficulty now = 1

A total score for the FAQ is computed by simply summing the scores across the ten items. Scores range from 0 to 30. A cutoff of 9 (dependent in three or more activities) is recommended (Pfeffer et al., 1982).

### Quality Assurance and Brief Assessment Screening and Outcome Measures for Adults

Rapid assessment tools like the ones covered in the sections on depression and anxiety provide a general screening for specific problem areas. More comprehensive assessment measures like the MMPI II covered in the section on personality disorders provide a comprehensive screen of major mental health diagnosis and psychological characteristics but are time consuming and expensive to use in practice. In today's fast-paced, managed-care, practice settings it is not always desirable or cost effective to perform a comprehensive assessment or to give a client a long measure like the MMPI II or the Millon measure described earlier. In fact, surveys of psychologists indicate that the whole field of psychological assessment is being challenged to change and is evolving because of managed care. Psychologists are using standardized measures less and less for traditional psychological assessment batteries (Wood et al., 2002). Standardized brief screening and outcomes measurement instruments, as well as quality assurance systems that provide specific feedback on individual clients for treatment planning and outcomes monitoring, are replacing traditional psychological assessment batteries (Beutler, 2001). Chapter 3 introduced computerized quality assessment systems and their measures. Such measurement systems are able to assess client functioning quickly (as are rapid assessment instruments) but include several problem areas instead of one specific area like depression. They also give specific feedback on high-risk areas, such as suicide and violence, and provide both graphic and narrative reports that practitioners can use in treatment planning and outcome monitoring.

When used in quality assurance systems, brief screening instruments can assess several problem areas and measures, either by acting as a screen of several different areas or by making it possible for clinicians to combine rapid assessment questions as needed from different test-item banks or measurement tools. Some systems even allow the clinician to add client data from more traditional instruments such as the MMPI or Millon. The latter choices give clinicians more flexibility in assessment and can be individualized for client need. Quality assurance measurement systems generally provide the following:

- A screen of several problem areas that is completed in a short time and directly linked with treatment planning
- Clinically significant scores based on normative data
- A risk assessment profile
- A projection for client outcome
- An ongoing monitor of treatment effectiveness through the completion of repeated measures
- A signal for the practitioner if treatment is not progressing
- A clinical change score and reliability of change index for showing client improvement
- Graphic displays and/or narratives that the practitioner can use (for a review of several quality assurance systems and their measures, see table 3.1).

These types of measurement tools meet all the criteria and common themes that chapter 1 identified as important for social work assessment. Problem identification, task planning, and treatment monitoring, for example, are inherent in these quality assurance measurement systems. These types of measurement systems are also easy to use in single-case designs and practice evaluation, as discussed in chapter 11. One shortfall of many of the quality assurance measurement systems, however, is that they often rely exclusively on client self-reports. Recall from earlier chapters that it is usually important to include more than one source of data in building valid and reliable assessments of clients. Some quality assurance systems correct for this possible information bias by including the practitioner's and other persons' perspectives as well.

One of the most popular measures is the Outcome Questionnaire (OQ-45.2). The OQ-45.2 is a computerized, self-report measure belonging to a family of outcomes measures. The measure is available online and is instantly scored (www.oqsystems.com). The OQ-45.2 has a clinical support technology known as a signal-detecting device, which can alert clinicians to treatment progress or failure. We describe in the signal-detecting device in more detail here (for a copy of the measure, see chapter 3).

The OQ-45.2 is a brief, forty-five-item, self-report outcome and tracking instrument designed for repeated measurement of client progress through the course of therapy and following termination. It can be completed in five minutes and is inexpensive to use, which makes it cost effective and suitable for agency-based practice. It offers measures of social functioning and appears to have excellent potential for social work practice.

The OQ-45.2 measures functioning in three domains—subjective distress or symptom dysfunction (items loaded for depression and anxiety); interpersonal functioning; and social role—which enables the practitioner to assess functional level and change over time. The OQ-45.2 contains risk assessment items for suicide potential, substance abuse, and potential violence at work. This questionnaire is available in Windows-based and Web-based versions, and it graphically reports treatment progress in real time. It has decision support features and numerous standard reports. Each item on the measure is rated on a five-point Likert scale (0 = never, 1 = rarely, 2 = sometimes, 3 = frequently, and 4 = almost always). The overall score is recommended for tracking progress in treatment because the number of items on the individual scales is small.

The OQ-45.2 provides a signal-detecting system that alerts clinicians to the status of the client's treatment and the need to adjust the treatment plan. Feedback dots appear on the report. White feedback indicates that the client is functioning in the normal range and may be ready for termination. Green feedback suggests that the change the client is making is in the normal range and everything is OK; no change in treatment plan is needed. Yellow feedback indicates that the change the client is making is less than expected and that some adjustment in treatment plan is needed. Red feedback tells the practitioner that the client is not making progress and may terminate prematurely with no benefit from therapy.

The validity and reliability of the OQ-45.2 are acceptable, and it is one of the better measures in the quality assurance area. It has a large national normative base and good internal consistency reliability ($r = 0.93$). The test-retest reliability after three weeks ($r = 0.84$) is acceptable. The measure has also demonstrated construct validity in factor-analytic studies showing a three-factor solution. Studies into concurrent validity have been done with acceptable results, and it has been shown to be sensitive to clinical change. A reliable change index has also been calculated: fourteen points. Clients whose scores change by fourteen points or more are regarded as having made reliable change during treatment (Lambert, Hansen, & Finch, 2001).

The OQ-45.2 is among the first quality assurance measures to demonstrate in research that feeding back outcome information to practitioners can make a difference in the treatment outcomes of clients (Lambert et al., 2001; Lambert, Gregersen, & Burlingame, 2004).

Recent experimental design studies indicate that, when combined with other clinical support tools such as empirically derived problem-solving tools, an alliance measure, and a measure of social support, the OQ-45.2 and its signal-detecting device is effective at improving treatment outcomes (e.g., Harmon et al. 2007; Slade, Lambert, Harmon, Smart, & Bailey, 2008; Whipple et al., 2003).

To further improve their evidence-based practices, social work clinicians and administrators should consider the benefits of using quality assurance systems that produce client-focused feedback in real time using empirically derived feedback systems like the OQ-45.2 and its associated clinical support tools.

## MOVING FROM ASSESSMENT TO INTERVENTION

Several other chapters in this book provide examples of assessment reports and intervention plans. This chapter gives each reader a chance to practice developing an intervention plan. In the case example that follows, we encourage readers to practice deciding what diagnosis, assessment tools, and treatment goals are appropriate. You may wish to consult chapters 6, 8, and 9 for examples of completed assessments to help you answer the questions, but use the case study as a learning tool to reflect on and answer the following questions:

- Develop a *DSM-IV-TR* diagnosis based on the information presented in the case.
- What is this client's current mental status?
- Which measures covered in this chapter are most suitable for this client?
- Develop an intervention plan by identifying symptoms that may require referral to other professionals (e.g., physician, psychologist, psychiatrist, career counselor) and by identifying availability of client resources (e.g., social support systems, transportation, housing, finances, recreational outlets).

- What are the most pressing issues for this client? What needs to be done first to help? Second? Third?
- What types of treatment goals might you be able to form with this client? How might the client suggest his or her main goals?
- Which measurement tools will you use in outcomes monitoring?

## CASE STUDY

Christopher T. Hager, a sixty-two-year-old Caucasian man, appeared for the first interview wearing a wrinkled cardigan, blue jeans, and plaid shirt. He was unshaven and appeared to have just gotten out of bed. His hair was uncombed, and he had dark circles under his eyes. Chris was slightly underweight and had a subtle tremor in his hands.

When asked about his medical history, he reported that he recently had gone to the doctor for headaches. Chris reported that the doctor found no physiological reason for the pain he was experiencing. He also remarked, "My headaches really made it hard to eat, so I've lost some more weight. I think I really need to gain a few pounds." Chris stated that there had been no prominent family history of illness, although he noted having an uncle who had committed suicide. He reported having tried Advil, Tylenol, and aspirin for the headaches but has taken no other pre-scribed medication on a regular basis to alleviate the chronic pain. He also stated that he sometimes has a "nightcap" to help him fall asleep, which has become more difficult lately.

The client was referred to this behavioral health center by his family physician, who felt that he needed a psychological assessment. Chris readily agreed to make an appointment at the center because his twenty-four-year-old daughter, a graduate student in social work, supported the physician's recommendation.

Chris was employed for thirty years at a well-known, high-tech computer corporation as an electronics engineer. He recently took early retirement because of the company's employee layoffs and their offer of a compelling severance package. Chris stated that he missed the routine of getting up and going to work every morning, although he did not miss the pressure of trying to "keep up with young, new college grads."

Chris noticed that, after being out of work for approximately one month, he felt more lethargic and was having difficulty pursuing activities that he normally enjoyed. He mentioned that he often felt bored and "didn't know what to do with myself at times." Another difficulty that he encountered was that he no longer saw friends from work—for lunch or for weekend activities. When asked about solutions to this problem, he said, "I don't really have the energy to make plans with the guys." He reported that his daughter, Catherine, has been urging him to get out of the house and socialize. However, Chris stated that he "just can't get going on anything these days."

Throughout the course of this assessment, Chris seemed to be using avoidance coping strategies to deal with his current problems. Rather than asserting himself on his own behalf, Chris tends to passively wait for others to initiate activities and solutions. When asked whether he felt his coping mechanisms are effective, he answered, "No, but I don't know what else to do."

In addition to his headaches and the loss of his job, Chris stated that he was divorced from his wife, Connie, approximately five years ago and that he is still disturbed by the divorce. When the social worker probed further, Chris revealed that his wife had left him after twenty-eight years of marriage. He stated angrily, "She was fed up with the whole thing." He also felt that Catherine had been caught in the middle, which prompted her to go to school in another state. Following the divorce, Chris moved from his comfortable, four-bedroom home in the suburbs to a small apartment downtown. Despite the manageable size of his present residence, he reportedly still has difficulty adjusting to taking care of the apartment and with other skills of daily living (e.g., laundry, cleaning, self-care).

Chris has weekly phone contact with Catherine. She is his only child. He no longer is in contact with his former wife, except on rare occasions. His primary companion is his bloodhound named Blue. Chris is quite committed to his dog, as he spoke at length about Blue's pedigree and how he takes Blue for long walks late at night. He constantly made references to Blue throughout the conversation (e.g., "Blue and I had macaroni and cheese for dinner," "Blue and I like to walk to the grocery store and get coffee in the mornings").

Chris noted that "in his day," he was an eloquent speaker, a member of a large social network (primarily through playing golf), and a good communicator. However, he lamented that he no longer felt like he part of a community, as he was when he was working. He stated that he lost many of his golfing partners, because they were guys at work and they would make plans to golf at the end of the day. He also said that he was a member of several engineering organizations but that he'd lost interest in those functions since he left his job. He also indicated that he used to play a lot of bridge when he was married but that, since the divorce, he had no one to partner with. He said he was embarrassed to go to bridge tournaments by himself. Chris stated that he not only felt like he was robbed of his professional title but also lost his role as a husband. He stated that he had been married for so long that he didn't know how to function as a single person. He did, however, mention one person, Mack, who played golf with him occasionally and who also went out to dinner with him at times.

Throughout the interview, Chris appeared sad when discussing his divorce and job loss. He seemed engaged in the conversation and showed no signs of psychotic behavior. He did appear to have a slight trembling in both hands but made no mention of this problem during the session.

When asked about romantic interests, Chris laughed and responded: "Are you kidding? I haven't even looked at a woman since my wife left me." On inquiry, Chris noted that, although his first few years married to his wife were "romantic and fun," approximately five years before his wife left, the couple began sleeping in separate rooms. He noted in a defensive tone, "I snore pretty loudly." Chris was vague in response to questions about his sex life, but he did add, "I'm not what I used to be, if you know what I mean."

The social worker administered the Mini-Mental State Exam to Chris before the interview. Chris scored in the normal range on the scale. He showed no signs of cognitive impairment, loss of memory, or thought disorder. He reported no history of cognitive problems. His thinking appeared to be clear, focused, and well organized, and he had no difficulty engaging in conversation with the social worker. Although he seemed to have some difficulty finding solutions to his present life problems, he appeared to have good judgment and decision-making capacities.

Chris consistently had flat affect during the assessment. Even his sporadic laughter at his own jokes was forced. He has a tendency toward sarcasm and a pessimistic attitude, as evidenced by his statement: "Even though I want things to be different, I am what I am. Guess you can't expect me to change after all these years." When asked whether he has times when he feels good, he stated, "There are times when I feel a bit better or worse, but I don't really ever feel like myself since my wife left." He added that retirement is a challenge to a "workaholic like me." When asked about the impact of his mood on others, he expressed the belief that his daughter avoids spending time with him because she feels frustrated about his situation.

Although it was apparent that Chris viewed himself as a valuable worker and father, his self-esteem seems to have diminished since he left his job. His relatively recent divorce also seems to have deflated his sense of self-worth. Although he did not offer a great deal of information about his marriage or causes of the divorce, it was evident that the divorce was a traumatic event in his life. He appeared to be feeling somewhat hopeless about developing new relationships with others. His low self-esteem also seems to be preventing him from seeking out friends and other social supports with whom he could be involved.

Although Chris's low self-esteem and sadness appear to be preventing him from finding solutions to his present difficulties, he verbally expressed a strong desire to make changes in his life. For example, he stated, "I just don't want to continue living this way," and "Something's got to change in my life." Catherine seems to be strong support and motivator for Chris to resolve his feelings of loss. He obviously respects her opinions and acknowledged that she "knows a whole lot more about this type of thing [feelings] than I do." When the social worker asked about any goals he might have for the future, Chris stated that it is all he can do to get through a day and that he doesn't think beyond that very much. However, he stated that he used to always set goals and was a fairly "driven" person when employed. When the social worker asked whether he could imagine ways that things could improve, Chris stated that he thought he might be drinking more than usual and that he needed to cut down on his alcohol consumption. "I think it may be clouding my vision right now." Chris exhibits some ambivalence about the work involved in making some of these changes. "One day I tell myself I'm going to stop drinking and start finding some healthy outlets for myself, and the next day, I can't get out of bed. Two days last week, I never got out of my pajamas and Blue and I just spent the day watching videos and eating popcorn."

When asked about his culture and ethnicity, Chris reported that he is "Irish-Catholic." He jokes, "No wonder I am the way I am, right?" When asked to elaborate, he noted that he comes from a long line of "stoic, hard-working, hard-drinking" men. He stated that his grandparents came to the United States when his parents were children. He did not know any more details about the family history. When asked about strengths and solutions that have come from his ethnic culture, he noted that he attributes his sense of humor, determination, and "realistic expectations" to his Irish heritage.

As referred to earlier, Chris considers himself Catholic. He reported that he used to go to church, at least on holidays, but that he has not gone since his divorce. He believes that God punishes people for "sins." Through further inquiry, it became clear that Chris feels that because of his divorce, drinking, and his perception of a lack of contribution to society, there is "no way I can squeeze my way through the 'pearly gates.'" When asked about his life purpose, Chris responded, "At this point, just getting through the day." When pressed, he noted gaining strength from his belief that "I'm really Blue's 'higher power,' I suppose. He needs me."

Chris is apparently experiencing some role transition and confusion. He has lost his former roles of professional and husband. He has been having a great amount of difficulty transitioning to other roles in his life. He seems to enjoy the role of caretaker for his dog; however, he appears to need other roles to gain a sense of self-fulfillment. It does not appear that Chris is ready to accept the role of retired person and may need to find another part-time position or volunteer in the nonprofit sector to gain a sense of self-worth.

When asked whether he had anything to add to the assessment, he noted that he used to be an avid woodworker. He told the social worker that he made much of the furniture in his home. He expressed some pride in his work but noted that it has been so long since he has done such work that he does not even know where his tools are.

## SUMMARY

This chapter described how to assess adult clients at different points in the life cycle and with diverse problem areas, as well as several methods of assessing adults using interview questions, *DSM* diagnosis, standardized assessment measures, and other rating scales. A case study provides an opportunity for the reader to practice moving from assessment to intervention with an actual client situation. Assessment of adults from a strengths-based systems perspective is a crucial component in the social worker's repertoire of skills. Learning how to make accurate diagnoses and how to use different methods that aid assessment with adults can improve social workers' assessment skills.

## STUDY QUESTIONS

1. How is the *DSM* used in practice?
2. What are three criticisms of the *DSM*?
3. What are three measures for depression and anxiety? Describe them.
4. What are two specific considerations in assessing older adult clients?
5. What are nine characteristics of quality assessment measurements used in managed care?

## WEB SITES

*Campbell Collaboration*
www.campbellcollaboration.org
*Cochrane Collaboration*
www.cochranecollaboration.org
*Psych Web*
www.psychweb.com
*DSM-V Prelude Project*
www.dsm5.org

## REFERENCES

American Psychiatric Association. (1994). *Diagnostic and statistical manual of mental disorders* (4th ed.). Washington, DC: Author.

American Psychiatric Association. (2000). *Diagnostic and statistical manual of mental disorders* (4th ed.). Washington, DC: Author.

Anthony, J. C., LeResche, L., Niaz, U., von Korff, M. R., & Folstein, M. F. (1982). Limits of the mini-mental state as a screening test for dementia and delirium among hospital patients. *Psychological Medicine, 12*, 397–408.

Barthwell, A. G., & Gilbert, C. L. (1993). *Screening for infectious diseases among substance abusers* (Treatment Improvement Protocol Series, No. 6). Rockville, MD: U.S. Department of Health and Human Services.

Beals, J., Manson, S. M., Keane, E., & Dick, R. W. (1995). Factorial structure of the Center for Epidemiologic Studies Depression Scale among American Indian college students. *Psychological Assessment, 3*, 623–627.

Beck, A. T., Steer, R. A., & Brown, G. K. (1996). *Manual for the Beck Depression Inventory* (2nd ed.). San Antonio, TX: Psychological Corporation.

Bentall, R. (2006). Madness explained: Why we must reject the Kraepelinian paradigm and replace it with a "complaint-orientated" approach to understanding mental illness. *Medical Hypotheses, 66*, 220–233.

Berg, A. O., Allan, J. D., Frame, P., Homer, C. J., Johnson, M. S., Klein, J. D., et al. (2003). Screening for dementia: Recommendation and rationale. *Annals of Internal Medicine, 138*, 925–926.

Berganza, C. E., & Aguilar, G. (1992). Depression in Guatemalan adolescents. *Adolescence, 27*, 771–782.

Beutler, L. (2001). Comparisons among quality assurance systems: From outcome assessment to clinical utility. *Journal of Consulting and Clinical Psychology, 69*, 197–204.

Briere, J., & Ruentz, M. (1989). The TSC (TSC-33): Early data on a new scale. *Journal of Interpersonal Violence, 4*, 151–163.

Brink, T. L., Yesavage, J. A., Lum, O., Heersema, P., Adley, M. B., & Rose, T. L. (1982). Screening tests for geriatric depression. *Clinical Gerontologist, 1*, 37–44.

Burns, A., Lawlor, B., & Craig, S. (2002). Rating scales in old age psychiatry. *British Journal of Psychiatry, 180*, 161–167.

Burns, A., Lawlor, B. A., Craig, S., & Coen, R. (2004). *Assessment scales in old age psychiatry* (2nd ed.). London: Martin Dunitz.

Butcher, J. N. (2004). *A beginner's guide to the MMPI-2* (2nd ed.). Washington, DC: American Psychological Association.

Butcher, J. N., Graham, J. R., Williams, C. L., & Ben-Porath, Y. S. (2007). *Development and use of the MMPI-2 content scales* (3rd ed.). Minneapolis: University of Minnesota Press.

Butcher, J. N., Williams, C. L., & Fowler, R. D. (2000). *Essentials of MMPI-2 and MMPI-A interpretation* (2nd ed.). Minneapolis: University of Minnesota Press.

Clum, G. A., Broyles, S., Borden, J., & Watkins, P. L. (1990). Validity and reliability of panic attack symptoms and cognition questionnaire. *Journal of Psychopathology and Behavioral Assessment, 12*, 233–245.

Cosgrove, L., Krimsky, S., Vijayaraghavan, M., & Schneider, L. (2006). Financial ties between DSM-IV panel members and the pharmaceutical industry. *Psychotherapy and Psychosomatics, 75*, 154–160.

Crum, R. M., Anthony, J. C., Bassett, S. S., & Folstein, M. F. (1993). Population-based norms for the mini-mental state examination by age and education level, *Journal of the American Medical Association, 18*, 2386–2391.

DePaulo, J. R., Folstein, M. F., & Gordon, B. (1980). Psychiatric screening on a neurological ward. *Psychological Medicine, 10*, 125–132.

Fillenbaum, G., Heyman, A., Willians, K., Prosnitz, B., & Burchett, B. (1990). Sensitivity and specificity of standardized screens of cognitive impairment and dementia among elderly black and white community residents. *Journal of Clinical Epidemiology, 43*, 651–660.

First, M. B., Spitzer, R. L., Gibbon, M., & Williams, J. B. W. (1997). *Structured clinical interview of DSM-IV axis I disorders: Clinicians' version.* Washington, DC: American Psychiatric Press.

Fisher, J., & Corcoran, K. (1994). *Measures for clinical practice: A sourcebook* (2nd ed.). New York: Free Press.

Fisher, G. L., & Harrison, T. C. (2000). *Substance abuse: Information for school counselors, social workers, therapists, and counselors.* Needham Heights, MA: Allyn and Bacon.

Folstein, M. F., Folstein, S. E., & McHugh, P. R. (1975). Mini-mental state: A practical method for grading the cognitive state of patients for the clinician. *Journal of Psychiatric Research, 12*, 189–198.

Garb, H. N. (1998). *Studying the clinician: Judgment research and psychological assessment.* Washington, DC: American Psychological Association.

Garrison C. Z., Addy A., Jackson K. L., McKeown R., & Waller J. L. (1991). The CES-D as a screen for depression and other psychiatric disorders in adolescents. *Journal of the American Academy of Child and Adolescent Psychiatry, 30*, 636–641.

Gjerde P. F., Block J., & Block J. H. (1988). Depressive symptoms and personality during late adolescence. *Journal of Abnormal Psychology, 97*, 475–486.

Hamilton, M. (1967). Development of a rating scale for primary depressive illness. *British Journal of Social and Clinical Psychology, 6*, 278–296.

Harmon, S. C., Lambert, M., Smart, D. M., Hawkins, E., Nielson, S., Slade, K., et al. (2007). Enhancing outcome of potential treatment failures: Therapist-client feedback and clinical support tools. *Psychotherapy Research, 17*, 379–392.

Hare, R. (1991). *Manual for the revised psychopathy checklist.* Toronto: Multihealth Systems.

Harrison, P. A., & Hoffmann, N. G. (2001). *SUDDS: Substance Use Disorder Diagnostic Schedule administration guide.* Smithfield, RI: Evince Clinical Assessments.

Hathaway, S. R., & McKinley, J. C. (1943). *Minnesota Multiphasic Personality Inventory.* Minneapolis: University of Minnesota Press.

Hemphill, J. F., Hare, R., & Wong, S. (1998). Psychopathy and recidivism: A review. *Legal Criminologist Psychologist, 3*, 139–170.

Jobes, D. A., Jacoby, A. M., Cimbolic, P., & Hustead, L. A. T. (1997). Assessment and treatment of suicidal clients in a university counseling center. *Journal of Counseling Psychology, 44*, 368–377.

Joiner, T. E., Jr., Pfaff, J., & Acres, J. (2002). A brief screening tool for suicidal symptoms in adolescents and young adults in general health settings: Reliability and validity data from the Australian National General Practice Youth Suicide Prevention Project. *Behaviour Research and Therapy, 40,* 471–481.

Karls, J. M., & Wandrei, K. E. (1994). PIE as a new tool for more effective case management. In J. M. Karls & K. E. Wandrei (Eds.), *Person-in-environment system: The PIE classification system for social functioning problems* (pp. 151–157). Washington, DC: National Association of Social Workers Press.

Kendell, R., & Jablensky, A. (2003). Distinguishing between the validity and utility of psychiatric diagnoses. *American Journal of Psychiatry, 160*(1), 4–12.

Kendler, K. S., Neale, M. C., Kessler, R. C., & Heath, A. C. (1992). Major depression and generalized anxiety disorder: same genes (partly) different environments? *Archives of General Psychiatry, 49,* 716–722.

Kessler, R. C., McGonagle, K. A., Zhao, S., Nelson, C. B., Hughes, M., Eshleman, S., et al. (1994). Lifetime and 12 month prevalence of *DSM* III-R psychiatric disorders in the United States. *Archives of General Psychiatry, 51,* 8–19.

Kutchins, H., & Kirk, S. A. (1997). *Making us crazy—DSM: The psychiatric bible and the creation of mental disorders.* New York: Free Press.

Lambert, M. J., Gregersen, A. T., & Burlingame, G. M. (2004). The Outcome Questionnaire-45. In M. E. Mariush (Ed.), *The use of psychological testing for treatment planning and outcomes assessment* (3rd ed., pp. 191–234). Mahwah, NJ: Erlbaum.

Lambert, M. J., Hansen, N. B., & Finch, A. E. (2001). Patient-focused research: Using patient outcome data to enhance treatment effects. *Journal of Consulting and Clinical Psychology, 69,* 147–149.

Launer, L. J., Dinkgreve, M. A., Jonker, C., Hooijer, C., & Lindeboom, J. (1993). Are age and education independent correlates of the Mini-Mental State Exam performance of community-dwelling elderly? *Journal of Gerontology, 48,* 271–277.

Lezak, M. D. (1995). *Neuropsychological assessment* (3rd ed.). New York: Oxford University Press.

Mayfield, D., McLeod, G., & Hall, P. (1994). The CAGE questionnaire: Validation of a new measure. *American Journal of Psychiatry, 131,* 1121–1123.

McAllister, L. W. (1996). *A practical guide to California Psychological Inventory interpretation.* Palo Alto, CA: Consulting Psychologist Press.

McLellan, A. T., Luborsky, L., Woody G. E., & O'Brien, C. P. (1980). An improved diagnostic evaluation instrument for substance abuse patients. *Journal of Nervous and Mental Disease, 168,* 26–33.

Millon, T. (1997). *The Millon inventories: Clinical and personality assessment.* New York: Guilford Press.

Mitchell, J., Mathews, H. F., & Yesavage, J. A. (1993). A multidimensional examination of depression among the Elderly. *Research on Aging, 15,* 198–219.

Molloy, D. W., & Standish, T. I. (1997). A guide to the standardized Mini-Mental State Examination. *International Psychogeriatrics, 9,* 87–94.

Munson, C. E. (2000). *The mental health diagnostic desk reference.* Binghamton, NY: Haworth Press.

Murden, R. A., McRae, T. D., Kaner, S., & Bucknam, M. E. (1991). Mini-Mental State Exam scores with education in blacks and whites. *Journal of the American Geriatrics Society, 43,* 138–145.

O'Neil, J. V. (1999). Profession dominates in mental health. *NASW News, 44*(1), 8.

Neimeyer, R. A., & Raskin, J. D. (2000). *Constructions of disorder: Meaning-making frameworks for psychotherapy.* Washington, DC: American Psychological Association.

Pfeffer, R. I., Kurosaki, T. T., Harrah, C. H., Chance, J. M., & Filos, S. (1982). Measurement of functional activities in older adults in the community. *Journal of Gerontology, 37,* 323–329.

Prescott, C. A., McArdle, J. J., Hishinuma, E. S., Johnson, R. C., Miyamoto, R. H., Andrade, N., et al. (1998). Prediction of major depression and dysthymia from CES-D scores among ethnic minority adolescents. *Journal of the American Academy of Child and Adolescent Psychiatry, 37,* 495–503.

Radloff, L. S. (1977). The CES-D scale: A new self-report depression scale for research in the general population. *Applied Psychological Measurement, 1,* 385–401.

Radloff, L. S., & Rae, D. S., (1981). Components of the sex difference in depression. *Residential Community Mental Health, 2,* 111–137.

Radloff, L. S., & Terri, L. (1986). Use of the Center for Epidemiological Studies-Depression Scale with older adults. *Clinical Gerontologist, 5,* 119–136.

Russell, M., Martier, S. S., Sokol, R. J., Jacobson, S., Jacobson, J., & Bottoms, S. (1991). Screening for pregnancy risk drinking: TWEAKING the tests. *Alcoholism: Clinical and Experimental Research, 15*(2), 638.

Saez-Fonseca, J. A., Lee, L., & Walker, Z. (2007). Long-term outcome of depressive pseudodementia in the elderly. *Journal of Affective Disorders, 101,* 123–129.

Substance Abuse and Mental Health Services Administration. (2006). *Results from the 2005 National Survey of Drug Use and Health: National findings* (NSDUH Series H-30, No. (SMA) 06-4194m). Rockville, MA: Author.

Saunders, J. B., Aasland, O. G., Babor, T. F., Delafuente, J. R., & Grant, M. (1993). Development of the Alcohol Use Disorders Identification Test (Audit)—WHO collaborative project on early detection of persons with harmful alcohol consumption. *Addiction, 88,* 791–804.

Selzer, M. L. (1971). The Michigan Alcoholism Screening Test: The quest for a new diagnostic instrument. *American Journal of Psychiatry, 127,* 89–94.

Shedler, J. (2002). A new language for psychoanalytic diagnosis. *Journal of the American Psychoanalytic Association, 50,* 429–456.

Slade, K., Lambert, M. J., Harmon, S. C., Smart, D. W., & Bailey, R. (2008). Electronic feedback and revised clinical support tools. *Clinical Psychology and Psychotherapy, 15,* 287–303.

Snowden, L. R. (2003). Bias in mental health assessment and intervention: Theory and evidence. *American Journal of Public Health, 93,* 239–243.

Spielberger, C. D. (1983). *Manual for the State-Trait Anxiety Inventory*. Palo Alto, CA: Consulting Psychologist Press.

Westen, D., & Shedler, J. (1999). Revising and assessing axis II—Part I: Developing a clinically and empirically valid assessment method. *American Journal of Psychiatry, 156*, 258–272.

Whitaker, T., Weismiller, T., & Clark, E. (2006). *Assuring the sufficiency of a frontline workforce: A national study of licensed social workers*. Washington, DC: National Association of Social Workers.

Whipple, J. L., Lambert, M. J., Vermeersch, D. A., Smart, D. W., Nielson, S. L., & Hawkins, E. J. (2003). Improving the effects of psychotherapy: The use of early identification of treatment failure and problem solving strategies in routine practice. *Journal of Counseling Psychology, 50*, 59–68.

Widiger, T. A., & Clark, L. A. (2000). Toward *DSM* V and the classification of psychopathology. *Psychological Bulletin, 126*, 946–963.

Wood, J. M., Garb, H. N., Lilienfeld, S. O., & Nezworski, T. M. (2002). Clinical assessment. *Annual Review of Psychology, 53*, 519–543.

Yesavage, J. A., Brink, T. L., Rose, T. L., Lum, O., Huang, V., Adey, M., et al. (1983). Development and validation of a geriatric depression screening scale: A preliminary report. *Journal of Psychiatric Research, 17*, 37–49.

# CHAPTER 8

# Family Systems

## Cynthia Franklin and Laura Hopson

## INTRODUCTION

This chapter provides several methods for conducting a family assessment and summarizes key concepts and issues to consider in the evaluation of family systems. We review and summarize selected assessment and developmental frameworks for understanding families, as well as techniques for gathering information on families. Specifically, we briefly review empiricially derived family assessment models, standardized measures, interviewing techniques, family-task observations, family goal recording, graphic problem-oriented and specific methods for assessing family strengths. Finally, this chapter shows how to move from assessment to intervention by providing family assessment report illustrating how to integrate multiple sources of information into a family assessment and how to create an intervention plan from that information.

## KEY CONCEPTS AND ISSUES OF FAMILY SYSTEMS

The focus of family practice has been on the assessment and treatment of families as a system. This grounding in systems theory helps us understand a family as a whole functioning entity. A family system is made up of a group of individuals who are interconnected and interdependent. These individuals are related to one another in a stable manner over time, and each individual's behavior influences the behavior of the others. Thus, mutual causality of interactions can be assumed (Buckley, 1967). All the members interrelate; together, they create interactive and reactive behavioral sequences, which may be viewed as a family drama, dance, or game.

Thinking about families from a systems perspective focuses our attention on the way the family functions as an entity rather than on the individual behavior or attributes of one of its members. Systems theorists have often used the description "the whole is greater than the sum of its parts." Wholeness or whole-systems functioning means that the family system is not just the sum of its parts viewed separately; the family members' interactions produce a unique type of behavior pattern all its own (Foley, 1989; Grotevant & Carlson, 1989). These interactions are often referred to as systemic patterns. We cannot truly understand a family's systemic functioning until we understand how all the parts function together to make up the behavior of the whole.

The converse is also true: we cannot understand the individual behavior of a family member unless we understand how that behavior relates to the functioning of the whole family. For example, we cannot understand the behavior of a child experiencing separation anxiety unless we also understand how the child's behaviors relate to the functioning of the family. The child's family may have experienced a disruption or recent loss (e.g., death, divorce). The child's anxious and clinging behavior may be a response to the distress of one or both parents. The anxious and avoidant behavior of the child may serve to pull a distant and conflicted parental relationship together by allowing the couple to mutually focus on the behavior of the child.

As another example, the passive and persistently nonassertive behavior of a female client cannot be understood outside the context of her relationship with her partner. It may be that the partner is an assertive, take-charge person and prefers to be in control of the direction of their relationship. At the same time, the client may encourage this type of relationship through passiveness and lack of assertiveness. Their relationship therefore is one of complementarity, so it may be necessary for the partner to change his behavior for the client to accomplish meaningful change and vice versa. The consequence of changing one without changing the other would throw the couple system out of balance. It is also true, however, that changing the behavior of either person can produce change in the couple system.

Family researchers and practitioners developed several models for helping us understand and evaluate how families function and change. Several family systems models emerged: structural, strategic, behavioral-functional, psychodynamic-transgenerational, experiential, and communication. Other more recent, strengths-based models have also been developed, such as postmodern, brief solution focused, narrative, feminist, and multicultural. A comprehensive discussion of these models is beyond the scope of this chapter (for a review, see Franklin & Jordan, 1999).

In recent years, family practitioners have expanded their emphasis on assessing family systems to understanding broader ecological systems such as the school and neighborhood (Franklin & Jordan, 2002). The family in context is the main concern of family practitioners. Although systems theory is the most widely used theory in family assessment and practice, postmodern approaches, feminist, multicultural, narrative therapy, and brief solution-focused therapy have become popular alternatives for the practice of family therapy. These newer approaches developed in reaction to traditional systems models; each model disavows allegiance to the family systems theory (Franklin & Jordan, 2002). Brief solution-focused therapy, for example, does not emphasize presenting problems as a basis for assessing and helping families. Instead, the practitioner assesses exceptions to the problems and co-constructs with the client a set of goals and new behaviors. In the narrative model, the social worker assesses the restraining aspects of the client's narrative construction of the self and helps the client challenge constraining and oppressive narratives that he or she has internalized from societal discourses.

Assessing families from postmodern viewpoints emphasizes the constructed nature of reality and the need for collaborative relationships between client and therapist. Postmodern family therapists examine sociocultural issues, such as how client problems and beliefs become socially constructed, the need for empowerment of marginalized clients, the political nature of therapy, and a need for social justice (Franklin & Jordan, 2002). The postmodern perspective appears to prefer qualitative methods to quantitative methods because of their emphasis on individuality and context. Standardized methods and any approach to assessment that seeks to categorize and marginalize are not believed to be very helpful to clients.

Multicultural perspectives emphasize race and culture and how these things affect the presenting problems of clients. Multicultural, postmodern, narrative, and solution-focused practices share an emphasis on nonpathological, antidiagnostic approaches to client assessment. Instead, the models have a functionalist and contextual orientation to assessment. These family assessors share similar beliefs to those discussed in chapter 10 concerning the assessment and measurement of multicultural clients. Normative approaches to assessment may not be the best way to describe clients or to help them solve their problems. Contextual methods that are congruent with the clients' culture and unique context are the best way to assess clients of any background. Clinicians should use multiple methods and should always include the opinions and viewpoints of the clients involved in the assessment. The strengths and resources of the family are always at the forefront of assessments.

In summary, family therapists practice from the perspective that problems must be understood as resulting from the relationship patterns in a family and broader ecological system. Understanding individual family members without understanding the whole family system and its relationship to other systems is like trying to understand a concert by listening to the instruments one by one. Synchronization of all the instruments, with their own unique chords, rhythms, and arrangements, is what makes the music. Similarly, the way families synchronize as a group accounts for the functional and dysfunctional behavior patterns of their members.

Practicing therapists often use a combination of traditional systems theory, postmodern, and solution-focused approaches in assessing families. Integrationism and technical eclecticism are the preferred ways to practice family therapy (Franklin & Jordan, 2002). In this chapter, we selectively borrow relevant concepts from across family therapy models.

From a family systems perspective, several qualities of family functioning are important to evaluate in a family assessment. The list of qualities we briefly describe here is not comprehensive; it does not include every possible aspect of family life that can be considered in an assessment. Rather, the qualities mentioned are practical guidelines for practitioners to use when conducting a family assessment.

## Family Strengths

Strengths encompass both individual and environmental factors. The individual factors are often referred to as resilience, whereas the environmental factors are referred to as protective. Some examples of resilience include social skills and competencies, as well as the ability to set goals and to have a future orientation. Protective factors include characteristics of the environment, such as having a caring family or other adults, safe schools, and parental monitoring. A strengths perspective assumes that clients who come for help are more than their problems and circumstances dictate. All clients have competencies, knowledge, hidden resources, and resilience that they can use to reverse the misfortunes of their life struggles. Therapists practicing from a strengths perspective are convinced that clients have aspirations, motivation, untapped goals, and spiritual fortitude that they can muster against the impossible odds of their disabilities and social environment. Clients have self-determination and are able to resist and shape their environments and can use hidden resources in their environments (Franklin, 2002).

Many popular and effective approaches to martial and family therapy (including brief solution-focused, narrative, and multisystemic models) use client strengths in therapy. This idea can be traced back to the early foundations of the profession in strategic and structural models through concepts like Erickson's utilization principal (Franklin & Jordan, 1999). Psychotherapy research indicates that positive belief and expectation for client change is a prerequisite for effective therapy, regardless of the model used. Practicing from a strengths perspective incorporates a value system that encompasses beliefs in the dignity and worth of individuals, their self-determination, and the transformative power of humans and human relationships. Regardless of the model the practitioner uses, practicing with clients from a strengths perspective means viewing them through a humanistic lens that assumes that all clients can grow and change (Franklin, 2002; for a case study on the importance of assessing client strengths, see box 8.1).

**Box 8.1**
**The importance of a strengths based assessment**

A CASE STUDY

Venetia is a sixteen-year-old African-American female. She has a son, Charles, age four months. Venetia dropped out of high school after she was five months pregnant. Prior to dropping out, she was in trouble with school authorities for skipping school and failing several of her classes. Her teachers suspected that Venetia was using drugs and said that she was known to "hang out" with some of the older gang boys. Venetia was ordered to see a therapist at the student assistance program at the school. She saw the therapist only once before quitting school. During a home visit, the school's truant officer encountered an elderly woman who said she was Venetia's grandmother and that Venetia no longer lived with her but was staying with her boyfriend. She did not know the address.

Venetia currently lives with her maternal aunt in public housing in a small one-bedroom apartment in an extremely poor, ethnic minority neighborhood. Her aunt has limited resources but offers Venetia and her son a place to live. Venetia's mother has a crack addiction and lives down the street with her maternal grandmother. Venetia sees her mother and her grandmother approximately twice a week. Her grandmother's eyesight is failing and she is also hard of hearing and can offer little support to Venetia. Venetia's father is in prison for murder and armed robbery, and she has not seen him in over eight years. Venetia anticipates that he may get parole in a few years. The baby's father is an African-American man named Charles who is approximately eight to ten years older than Venetia. After her pregnancy, Charles disappeared, though Venetia has not seen him since three months prior to her son's birth.

**Adding Strengths to the Case**

Venetia is attractive, verbal, and intelligent—slender, introverted girl who liked arts and math in school. She was a good to average student (earning Bs and Cs) until one year before she became pregnant. Venetia liked music and sang in the school choir for two years. She had several friends and one best friend, Latisha. Together, they sang in the church choir at the African-Zion Baptist Church. When Venetia was thirteen, she went on tour with the choir and performed in several African-American churches across the south. Venetia's childhood dream is to be in a singing group with her soul sister, Latisha (who is also a pregnant and parenting mom who attends an alternative school to finish her education). Venetia stopped taking drugs when she found out she was pregnant. Since Venetia had her baby, her aunt and mother have spoken and been in each other's house for the first time in ten years. Venetia's father writes from prison three to four times a year and, in his latest letter, he encouraged Venetia to finish high school and not to let her motherhood stop her from singing in the choir. Venetia says she wants to finish her education and get more instruction in music. She has an interest in attending the alternative school where Latisha is enrolled. The school offers childcare and special groups for pregnant and parenting teens.

SOURCE: C. Franklin. (2002). Becoming a strengths fact finder. *AAMFT Magazine*. Washington, DC: The American Association of Marital and Family Therapists.

### Ethnicity, Culture, and Gender

The behaviors, expectations, and prescribed roles that emerge from clients' social class, ethnicity, culture, and gender roles are sometimes outside their awareness; at other times, clients' awareness of these viewpoints may restrict or oppress them so that they feel that they have limited options. For example, after facing incidences of discrimination in trying to find housing in middle-class areas, African American clients may feel that their options have been limited because of race and then transfer these feelings to other areas of their life or even have similar experiences that validate these social realities.

As another example, a woman may experience depression because she feels trapped in a unhappy marriage with a domineering husband. She may be unaware, however, that the gender roles of each partner are partly responsible for this dilemma. Both she and her husband have internalized culturally prescribed roles for how men and women are to behave in relationship to each other. She wants more intimacy, and he has difficulty sharing feelings, for example.

As a part of the assessment process, the practitioner assesses a person's culture, ethnicity, and social class and develops and understanding of strengths and resources, as well as the effects of social oppression. To understand a client's culture and ethnic experiences, it is important to use interpersonal skills and cultural sensitivity to form a helping relationship with a client (Grier, Morris, & Taylor, 2001). Some strategies that can facilitate the relationship-building and assessment process include the following:

- Remain open and nonjudgmental to alternative life styles. Clearly communicate to clients that you know there are many different ways of living and doing things. Cite examples and initiate conversation into an area so that the client will feel comfortable talking to you about his or her family and life situation.

- Disclose patterns and ways of doing things in your family and culture, and ask the client to describe how things are handled in his or her family and culture. A comparison conversation may facilitate information exchange and mutual understanding.

- Ask, "How do you do that in your family or culture?" Or, "What does this mean in your culture?"

- Be self-aware and explore possible cultural biases with a supervisor.

- Ask and accept feedback from the client about your level of cultural knowledge and sensitivity. Tell clients what you are thinking, and ask them to comment on whether your thoughts and beliefs are accurate from their viewpoint.

## Family Structure

Family structure relates to the way family members organize themselves into interactional patterns (Minuchin, 1974; Minuchin & Fishman, 1982). It also includes the family constellation, which describes the nature of the family (e.g., single parent, intact family) and number of family members. For example, a recently divorced father is depressed over his divorce and fears that it will damage his two teenage sons and complicate his already-strained relationship with them. The father attempts to form a blended family in which the father and his two children cohabitate with the father's new partner. The following structural interactional pattern emerges: The father doesn't enforce the rules because he is used to a mother figure assuming the discipline of the children. When the partner therefore attempts to step in and enforce the rules, the children resist the discipline because she is not "their mother." The partner and the children get into a screaming match, and the father becomes involved and tries to negotiate. The children refuse to obey the father because he is siding with the partner against them. This angers the father, who threatens the children with a severe punishment (taking their transportation away) but then changes his mind after further argument, in exchange for the boys' halfhearted compliance. By that time, however, everybody is mad at everybody else, including the father and his partner.

If this type of structural interactional pattern occurs over time, it becomes well rehearsed and well known. This behavior pattern involves every member of the family and composes part of the structural, interactional sequences of the family system. Such interactional sequences are circular in nature rather than linear. Systems explanations for human behavior are contextual; no simple, linear cause-and-effect relationships exist. That is, A and B coexist and cause each other, rather than A causing B or B causing A (Goldenberg & Goldenberg, 1990). In this example, it is impossible to identify a simple cause-and-effect relationship for the dysfunctional pattern of this family. Causes and effects feed into one another to produce complex and interactive behavioral chains (e.g., partner looks to father to intervene with children, partner intervenes, father reacts to screaming, children resist, father chastises children, children comply, father backs down, partner looks to father to intervene). For questions that you can use to assess family structure, see the section on interviewing in this chapter and review the information on circular questions in appendix 8A.

## Subsystems

Subsystems are smaller parts of the systemic arrangement of the family and are important to the organization of the family (Aponte & Van Dusen, 1981; Minuchin, 1974). The main subsystems in a family are the couple subsystem, parental subsystem, sibling subsystem, and parent-child sub-system (Janzen, Harris, Jordan, & Franklin, 2005). The practitioner should evaluate each subsystem in the family carefully to determine whether it is carrying out its appropriate function. For example, in the couple subsys-tem, the two individuals involved should have a satisfactory relationship that is mutually beneficial. The couple subsystem is one of the most im-portant because it provides for the direction and health of the family (Beavers & Hampson, 1990). Two individuals join (i.e., create a couple sub-system) to form a family, and it is important for each to accommodate the other in a complimentary way. For example, the unconditional giving of pleasing behaviors to each other is important to marital adjustment and satisfaction (Stuart, 1980). At the same time, the couple must keep indi-vidual autonomy so that each can act independently and continue his or her own individual development. A healthy couple subsystem is sine qua non for a healthy family organization (Beavers & Hampson, 1990; Janzen et al., 2005). For this reason, practitioners may choose to evaluate the cou-ple subsystem separately from the other subsystems in a family assess-ment. Social workers may talk to the couple privately about issues related to their personal relationship (e.g., time spent together, quarrels, sex life, financial management).

The practitioner should also evaluate the parental subsystem to de-termine how the couple handles parenting responsibilities. Do both have adequate parenting skills and social support necessary to be effective par-ents? In a healthy parental subsystem, the parents lead the family and hold most of the power (Beavers & Hampson, 1990; Brock & Barnard, 1988). The notion of a hierarchy of the subsystems becomes extremely im-portant to well-functioning families; parents must maintain their adult roles and appropriate control of the direction of the family (Haley, 1990; Minuchin, 1974).

Hierarchy across generations (e.g., parents and children, parents and grandparents) must be maintained in a functional family system. The parental subsystem works out complementary ways of handling the de-mands of parenting and the roles between and across generations. The availability of such social supports as mother's and father's day out, child care, nurturing extended family relationships, and supportive in-teractions with other parents help parents fulfill their parenting responsi-bilities without becoming exhausted, frustrated, and lost.

The practitioner should evaluate the sibling subsystem to determine how the siblings get along together. What is the nature of their relation-ship? Is the relationship conflicted, competitive, approving, or similar to that of best friends? In a healthy family, there are strong emotional bonds between individuals in the sibling subsystem, and they share information and commonalities that are unique to that bond (Brock & Barnard, 1988). The practitioner should also explore the parent-child subsystem. How do the children get along with their parents? Are their any prolonged parent-child coalitions in which a child and parent form a power alliance against another parent or another child?

It is important for subsystems to maintain their own unique roles, identities, and boundaries. Some examples of subsystem dysfunction that social workers frequently encounter in their work with families include a child taking sides with one parent against another parent; children providing ongoing nurturing, emotional support, and parenting to a parent; parents being overly intrusive into the private lives of their children; parents asking their children to take sides in an argument between them; adults in one generation forming a prolonged coalition with a member of another generation against particular family members (e.g., parent and grandparent against a spouse, grandparent and grandchild against parents); parents refusing to interact with or negotiate with their children; children shutting themselves off from guidance, interactions, and relationships with their parents; and parents forming a prolonged coalition against a child or children forming a prolonged coalition against parents.

Such breakdowns in the integrity and interactions between subsystems are common in dysfunctional families (for a visual representation of the family system and its various subsystems, and some of the important roles that the different subsystems fulfill, see figure 8.1).

**Figure 8.1**   Family Systems

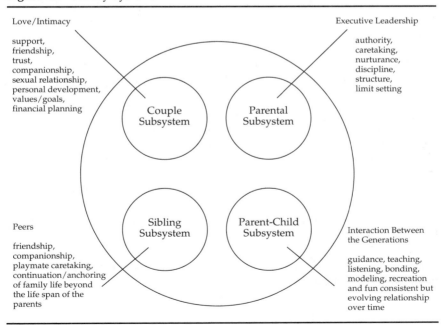

## Boundaries

Boundaries are the demarcations that distinguish one system or subsystem from another (Minuchin, 1974). The terms *disengagement* and *enmeshment* describe boundary traits or specific situational interactions of a family. They usually describe a family trait that defines specific characteristics concerning the structure, communication, and interpersonal involvement of family members (Brock & Barnard, 1988). Boundaries can be rigid and tightly drawn, which results in disengagement, or loose and diffuse, which results in enmeshment in families.

Members of disengaged families are uninvolved with one another and tend to be self-absorbed. These families have low cohesion, appear to lack appropriate bonding, and are therefore slow to respond to the emotional needs of family members. In fact, it may take a serious crisis before members of such families come to the aid of one another; even then, they may resent the demands the others place on them. Such families value individual freedom and personal autonomy. They are highly tolerant of differences among family members, and their members are oftentimes more involved with people outside their own family.

Enmeshment is overinvolvement and a lack of appropriate boundaries in a family. Enmeshed families usually have high cohesion and family loyalty. Such families demand consensus from their members and are intolerant of them having views that differ from the family norms. In the extreme example of this type of family, individual autonomy and growth are stifled. Enmeshed families are family absorbed and not open to outsiders. They may have many family secrets, hidden agendas, and secret power alliances in the family. Because enmeshed families are invested in keeping an image of agreement and alliance, they are often resistant to exploring conflict and possible differences that may exist between the members.

Some family therapists believe that when the transactions in a family system cause a family to take on the characteristics of either extreme (disengagement or enmeshment), the family becomes dysfunctional (Olson, 1985). Other family therapists believe there is more of a continuum and that families relate in competent or less competent ways, depending on degrees of cohesion and their ability to maintain clear boundaries (Beavers & Voller, 1983).

Regardless of a practitioner's theoretical views, if a family tends to have rigid boundaries, communication across the subsystems may be extremely difficult, which results in impaired relationship functioning. Conversely, if boundaries are too loose in a family, there may be inappropriate transactions between subsystems.

In assessing characteristics of families, it is critical to consider the many cultural variations in family functioning. No behavior pattern should be considered dysfunctional if it is culturally prescribed or satisfactory and functional for those involved (Minuchin, 1974; Olson et al., 1985), which means that it is the responsibility of the practitioner to find out what cultural considerations occupy the family spaces (for descriptions of different ethnic and cultural patterns in families, see chapter 11. Families in each different ethnic and cultural community have unique ways of thinking and behaving. These patterns are normative for that particular culture, and practitioners should assess families from the perspective of that culture. The ethnographic assessment methods described in chapter 4 offer suggestions for how to gain an inside understanding of cultural variations in families.

## Homeostasis, Information, and Feedback

Family systems are dynamic systems, constantly changing, simultaneously pursuing their goals, and responding to outside information. Family homeostasis is the self-regulating mechanism of a family system, the proclivity for members of a family to maintain a steady state in their relationships (Janzen et al., 2005). Families develop recurring patterns of interaction that maintain the stability of the family system (Becvar & Becvar, 1988). Thus, family therapists have observed that if a disturbed child is removed from the family system, another child in that family will develop disturbed behaviors. In such a family system, the child's disturbed behavior is believed to serve as a homeostatic mechanism. It may be that the child's parents have a severe marital conflict that might lead to divorce, but they rely on the misbehavior of the child to keep them focused on a common goal that keeps the family together.

All systems seek to maintain themselves, and they regulate the flow of information from inside and outside of the system to this end. Family systems that allow a free flow of information are known as open systems; those that restrict the flow of information are known as closed systems. Families with open systems are often highly visible in the community and are involved in numerous civic and recreational activities. Families with closed systems are more exclusionary and totally rely on their internal resources to sustain them (Janzen et al., 2005).

Regulation of information by a system occurs through feedback loops, circular mechanisms that return to input information about the system's output, to correct and ultimately manage the system's functioning (Goldenberg & Goldenberg, 1990). Feedback provides information that helps a system guard against too much fluctuation and govern itself in a way that will promote its longevity. Negative or attenuating feedback is self-corrective and allows for the deviation in a system to be corrected so that the system can maintain its steady state (Constantine, 1986). An example of a negative feedback mechanism in a family is a battering husband's plea for forgiveness. By pleading for forgiveness and promising to never hit his wife again, the husband may convince the wife to give the marriage another try, thus returning the system to its former steady state.

Positive or amplifying feedback does the opposite; it accelerates the deviation in a system. If the woman in our previous example comes to a battered women's shelter and insists that unless her husband gets help, she will end the marriage, the system will not be allowed to return to its former steady state, and further change in the system will be initiated. Positive feedback forces the system to change; the ultimate outcome of positive feedback if unregulated may be destruction of the system (divorce).

From the systems perspective, for example, an affair may be considered a positive feedback loop and the reconciliation of the married couple and discontinuation of the affair a negative feedback loop. Both positive and negative feedback processes operate at the same time to regulate the flow of information, change, and homeostasis in a family system. Questions that help social workers track the circular feedback sequences in a family system are known as circular questions. This interviewing technique and examples of questions used to elicit systemic information are described in the section on interviewing methods later in this chapter.

## Communication and Relationships

In family assessment, a view of pathology is ecological in perspective, and the focus shifts from healing pathology in the individual to correcting dysfunctional roles and relationships. Social workers must gain an understanding of the health of dyads and triads in the family. Dyadic relationships function most harmoniously when those involved function in a complementary pattern rather than a symmetrical one. Complementary patterns denote reciprocal interaction and inequality of responses. Symmetrical patterns are equal and may lead to competition (Watzlawick, Beavin, & Jackson, 1967).

For example, in a couple's relationship, one may be assertive and domineering, whereas the other is passive and submissive. When they disagree, the submissive partner may defer to the more assertive one. Such reciprocal interaction is characterized as complementary. Another couple may both be assertive and, during disagreements, find themselves in an argument over who is right. The second couple's relationship is symmetrical, and although it is more equal, it is also more at risk for escalations, quarrels, and competition.

Triadic relationships in families are especially important to observe. In family systems, the triad (triangle) is believed to be the basic building block of family relationships (Bowen, 1978). Triangulation is a common occurrence and happens when any two members of a family experience too much stress between them. These two members may pull a third member into their relationship, thus regulating the stress between them. Another way to think about a triad is in terms of its ability to defocus conflict. An example of this process, known as detouring, is when parents focus on a child's behavior instead of their own issues (Minuchin, 1974). Family relational processes often consist of a series of interlocking triangles that may extend across generations and that lend stability to the system but also cause family dysfunction (Bowen, 1978). Social workers assessing such processes must evaluate the nature of these triangles to understand the network of relationships in the family system.

Communication is important to the competent functioning of family systems. For communication to be effective between family members, it must be open, direct, clear, and congruent at different levels, such as the tone and content of one's message. People communicate at three basic levels: verbal, nonverbal, and metacommunication. Verbal communication refers to the words and content of the message; nonverbal communication refers to the body posture and subtle innuendoes sent with a message; and metacommunication (communication about communication) refers to the context of the communication, such as voice tone, tenor, and timing (Janzen et al., 2005).

In most dysfunctional families, members have difficulty communicating with one another. It is common to observe members of such families sending messages through a third party (e.g., the daughter tells the father why the mother is mad at him). Dysfunctional families also withhold information or send confusing and double-binding messages to one another. Here is an example of a double-binding message: A mother says to her daughter that she can confide in the mother about her relationship with her boyfriend (content level) and that the mother will be accepting and not upset (voice rising sharply and arms crossed at nonverbal level) if she confides that she has chosen to have sex with the boyfriend.

### Rules and Myths

Families are rule-governed systems, and rules define the relationship agreements among family members (Janzen et al., 2005). Some rules are explicit and clearly stated (e.g., this family goes to church every Sunday). Other rules are implicit or covert and may not be as clearly stated. For example, it may be an implicit rule that a family does not talk about sex in front of members of the opposite sex or that the family does not discuss Grandpa's drinking problem at all. Rules dictate much of the family members' behavior toward one another.

Family myths, like rules, contribute considerably to a family's behavior. Myths, here, are family members' shared beliefs and expectations concerning one another (Janzen et al., 2005). A family may develop a type of shared mythical reality concerning the behavior of one of its members. For example, the highly successful, artistic son of a conventional, enmeshed family may receive the label "queer" or "deviant." The family may view him as inadequate, even though he wins a scholarship to study art at a prestigious university and later establishes a successful art gallery. Such an inadequate view of an obviously creative and successful young man is a family myth that serves an important function in that family.

## Problem Solving, Negotiation, and Decision Making

Functional family systems have good problem-solving skills. They do not get lost in the process or stuck in a power struggle. Effective families are able to brainstorm solutions and come to agreement about how to proceed to solve a problem. Families that can effectively solve problems may have special times to meet to discuss problems and come up with solutions (e.g., a weekly family gripe session). They may also have a way to monitor the progress of proposed solutions, such as a daily report card or a meeting to discuss outcomes (Dinkmeyer & McKay, 1983).

Like problem solving, negotiation is important to the functioning of family systems. Couples in particular must learn to negotiate roles and power between them and model those behaviors to their children. The adage goes "the two shall be one," but the ultimate task may be to negotiate which one. Families work out different ways to negotiate for the things that each member wants. For example, some couples work out relationship agreements in which one member exchanges something for something else. In this bargaining type of relationship, the wife may be willing to do the husband's laundry if he washes her car, or each may care for the children one night in exchange for a free night out. These are sometimes referred to as quid pro quo relationships (Stuart, 1980). Other families take a more giving attitude in which members go out of their way to please one another. Members of such families behave similarly toward one another. Some families have difficulty negotiating their relationships; the result may be endless and relentless power struggles and conflict.

Decision making, like negotiation, is central to the functioning of a family system. Who makes the decisions and how they do so are critical determinants of how the family operates. Equally important is who appoints the decision maker. Observing the pattern of decision making is important to understanding a family. In some families, for instance, one person (e.g., the father) makes major decisions. Other families make decisions in an egalitarian, democratic fashion. In most families, the patterns of decision making shifts from situation to situation or role to role. For example, the mother may be responsible for making major decisions about the home and the father about the finances. Some families delegate decision making to the members most proficient in those tasks, whereas others rigidly follow the terms established in their family of origin. Some families have difficulty deciding who will make the decisions and how they will be made. Such families may argue over decisions or shift responsibility for making the decisions from one person to another in a chaotic manner. As part of a family assessment, social workers need to become acquainted with the problem-solving and negotiation skills, as well as the decision-making processes of the family.

## Individual Dynamics and Biological Systems

Thus far, this review of major concepts for understanding families has focused on families as a social system. In keeping with the holistic view of systems theory, social workers also need to assess psychological and biological competencies and vulnerabilities of families (Brill, 1988; Hepworth & Larsen, 1989; Johnson, 1987; Simon, McNeil, Franklin, & Cooperman, 1991). There is increasing evidence that major mental disorders like schizophrenia and major depression have biological determinants that may be biochemical. In addition, there is other evidence suggesting genetic links and biological vulnerabilities for problems such as attention deficit/hyperactivity disorder and alcoholism. It is impossible for social workers to effectively treat such disorders in families until there have been interventions in the biological system. Family assessments need to identify or rule out psychological or biological dysfunctions.

Teamwork and collaboration with medical professionals need to be a routine part of a family assessment for high-risk families. For example, a family brings a hyperactive child with severe behavior problems to a social worker for treatment. In this case, there is a repeated family history of alcoholism, mood disorders, and psychotic reactions. As a part of a good social work assessment, the social worker should refer and consult with medical professionals to establish a proper diagnosis and identify the appropriate combination of medical and family interventions for the child and family (for examples of questions for assessing the individual and biological aspects of children and adults, see chapters 6 and 7).

Thus far in this chapter, we have summarized some major concepts important for understanding how families function as a system and family assessment considerations. Next, we review developmental frameworks and empirical assessment models that help us better understand the normative characteristics of families.

## DEVELOPMENTAL LIFE CYCLE STAGES OF FAMILIES

Developmental frameworks for understanding families have emerged from research and theoretical explorations of the passage of families through life-cycle stages and from therapeutic work with them. In this section, we discuss the life-cycle stages of families as depicted by Carter and McGoldrick (2005).

Families, like individuals, are believed to pass through developmental life-cycle stages. Each life-cycle stage is believed to have its own accompanying set of tasks to be accomplished for families to make successful transitions from one stage to the next. Families tend to consult social workers for help during periods of difficult transition. It is, therefore, important for family practitioners to evaluate where families are in their life cycle and to be cognizant of any difficulties that the families may be experiencing in accomplishing the tasks that are essential at different points in their life-cycle development.

Family cohesion and the ability to maintain family get-togethers and rituals are important to the adjustment of families throughout the life cycle. Life-cycle transitions sometimes require families to renegotiate rituals to maintain these important family connections. For example, when an adult child moves away from home, the family may need to establish a new tradition of spending Christmas together. Table 8.1 describes the normal life-cycle development of an intact nuclear family; tables 8.2 and 8.3 show the additional tasks that must occur in a divorced, single-parent, or blended family.

## Evidence-Based Assessment Models

As discussed throughout this book, evidence-based practice involves a process of applying the best-available research evidence, clinical judgment, and client feedback in selecting, implementing, and evaluating family interventions (Gambrill, 2006). The growing emphasis on evidence-based practice means that practitioners will feel greater pressure to use evidence-based assessment models and standardized measurement instruments in evaluating their practice. In this section, we discuss empirically derived family assessment models and their measures. Such models, based on systems theory, demonstrate how families work and develop over their life cycles, which provides perspective for judging when families are working well and when they are not. Evidenced-based assessment models derive from research on the classification and assessment of family functioning and from clinical work with families.

## Olson Circumplex Family Model

The Olson Circumplex Family Model derives from systems theory. It provides a classification schema for understanding marital and family functioning, which provides a typology of family functioning along three important dimensions: cohesion (emotional bonding), adaptability or

**Table 8.1**  Life-Cycle Stages for Intact Majority American Families

| Family Life-Cycle Stage | Emotional Process of Transition | Developmental Tasks |
|---|---|---|
| 1. Leaving home: single young adults | Accepting emotional and financial responsibility for self | a. Differentiating self in relation to family of origin<br>b. Developing intimate peer relationships<br>c. Establishing self through work and financial independence |
| 2. The joining of families through marriage: the new couple | Committing to new system | a. Forming marital system<br>b. Realigning relationships with extended families and friends to include spouse |
| 3. Families with young children | Accepting new members into the system | a. Adjusting marital system to make space for child(ren)<br>b. Joining in child-rearing, financial, and household tasks<br>c. Realigning relationships with extended family to include parenting and grandparenting roles |
| 4. Families with adolescents | Increasing flexibility of family boundaries to include children's independence and grandparents' frailties | a. Shifting parent-child relationships to permit adolescent to move in and out of system<br>b. Refocusing on mid-life marital and career issues<br>c. Beginning shift toward joint caring for older generation |
| 5. Launching children and moving on | Accepting a multitude of exits from and entries into the family system | a. Renegotiating marital system as a dyad<br>b. Developing adult-to-adult relationships between grown children and their parents<br>c. Realigning relationships to include in-laws and grandchildren<br>d. Dealing with disabilities and death of great grandparents |
| 6. Families in later life | Accepting the shifting of generational roles | a. Maintaining own and couple functioning and interests in face of physiological decline; exploration of new familial and social role options<br>b. Supporting a more central role of middle generation<br>c. Making room in the system for the wisdom and experience of the elderly, supporting the older generation without overfunctioning for them<br>d. Dealing with loss of spouse, siblings, and other peers, and preparation for own death; life review and integration |

SOURCE: B. Carter & M. McGoldrick. (1988). *The changing family lifecycle: A framework for family therapy* (2nd ed., p. 15). New York: Gardner.

**Table 8.2**  Dislocations in the Family Life Cycle Requiring Additional Steps to Restabilize and Proceed Developmentally

| Phase | Emotional Process of Transition | Developmental Tasks |
|---|---|---|
| | *Divorce* | |
| 1. The decision to divorce | Accepting inability to resolve marital tensions sufficiently to continue relationship | Accepting one's own part in the failure of the marriage |
| 2. Planning the breakup of the system | Supporting viable arrangements for all parts of the system | a. Working cooperatively on problems of custody, visitation, and finances<br>b. Dealing with extended family about the divorce |
| 3. Separation | a. Willingness to continue cooperative coparental relationship and joint financial support of children<br>b. Working on resolution of attachment to spouse | a. Mourning loss of intact family<br>b. Restructuring marital and parent-child relationships and finances; adaptation to living apart<br>c. Realigning of relationships with extended family; staying connected with spouse's extended family |
| 4. The divorce | Working further on emotional divorce: overcoming hurt, anger, guilt, etc. | a. Mourning loss of intact family; giving up fantasies of reunion<br>b. Retrieving hopes, dreams, expectations from marriage<br>c. Staying connected with extended families |
| | *Postdivorce family* | |
| Custodial single parent | Willing to maintain financial responsibilities, continue parental contact with ex-spouse, and support contact of children with ex-spouse and his or her family | a. Making flexible visitation arrangements with ex-spouse and his or her family<br>b. Rebuilding own financial resources<br>c. Rebuilding own social network |
| Noncustodial single parent | Willing to maintain parental contact with ex-spouse and support custodial parent's relationship with children | a. Finding ways to continue effective parenting relationship with children<br>b. Maintaining financial responsibilities to ex-spouse and children<br>c. Rebuilding own social network |

SOURCE: B. Carter & M. McGoldrick. (1988). *The changing family lifecycle: A framework for family therapy* (2nd ed., p. 22). New York: Gardner.

**Table 8.3**    Remarried Family Formation

| Step | Prerequisite Attitude | Developmental Issues |
|---|---|---|
| 1. Entering the new relationship | Recovery from loss of first marriage (adequate "emotional divorce") | Recommitting to marriage, to forming a family, and dealing with complexity and ambiguity |
| 2. Conceptualizing and planning new marriage and family | a. Acceptance of one's own fears and those of new spouse and children about remarriage and forming a stepfamily<br>b. Acceptance of need for time and patience to adjust to complexity and ambiguity of: (i) Multiple new roles; (ii) Boundaries of space, time, membership, and authority; and (iii) Affective issues of guilt, loyalty conflicts, desire for mutuality, and unresolvable past hurts | a. Working on openness in the new relationships to avoid pseudomutality<br>b. Planning for maintenance of cooperative financial and co-parental relationships with ex-spouses<br>c. Planning to help children deal with fears, loyalty conflicts, and membership in two systems<br>d. Realigning relationships with extended family to include new spouse and children<br>e. Planning maintenance of connections for children with extended family of ex-spouse(s) |
| 3. Remarriage and reconstruction of family | a. Final resolution of attachment to previous spouse and ideal of "intact" family<br>b. Acceptance of a different model of family with permeable boundaries | a. Restructuring family boundaries to allow for inclusion of new spouse-stepparent<br>b. Realigning relationships and financial arrangements throughout subsystems to permit interweaving of several systems<br>c. Making room for relationships of all children with biological (noncustodial) parents, grandparents, and other extended family<br>d. Sharing memories and histories to enhance stepfamily integration |

SOURCE: B. Carter & M. McGoldrick. (1988). *The changing family lifecycle: A framework for family therapy* (2nd ed., p. 24). New York: Gardner.

flexibility (degree of change in family rites and structure), and communication (facilitative dimension). The communication dimension is important for establishing appropriate levels of the other two dimensions. Through research on more than one thousand families over the past decade, Olson et al. (1985) developed several empirically derived family inventories that measure these three dimensions of family life. Family assessment instruments, including the Family Satisfaction Inventory and the Family Crisis Oriented Personal Evaluation Scales (F-COPES), have been developed for the model.

The most famous of the self-report measures is the Family Adaptability and Cohesion Scale (FACES III), which measures the first two dimensions of the Circumplex Model: cohesion and adaptability and flexibility. The third dimension, communication, can be assessed using other inventories the authors have developed (e.g., the Parent and Adolescent Communication Form). The FACES III measure is a twenty-item, normative-based, paper-and-pencil, self-report inventory that operationalizes the Circumplex Model. The original Circumplex Model posits a curvilinear understanding of family functioning that emphasizes the need for balance in family relationships. Families that fall along extreme dimensions of functioning in cohesion, adaptability and flexibility, or communication are believed to be at risk of dysfunction. Those that fall into balanced or midrange dimensions are believed to be better adjusted.

For example, in the cohesion dimension, families characterized at the two extremes of enmeshed or disengaged are both considered at risk for dysfunction, whereas those characterized as balanced between the two extremes are considered to function well. The same idea applies to the adaptability and flexibility (change) dimension. Families characterized at the extremes of chaotic (too much flexibility and random change) or rigid (not enough flexibility and change) are at risk of dysfunction; those characterized as balanced between the dimensions function well (Olson, 1986; Olson, Sprenkle, & Russel, 1979).

The FACES III measure categorizes families into sixteen types, from lowest to highest, on four categories each of the cohesion and adaptability dimensions (see figure 8.2). They form a helpful typology for understanding how a family functions regarding cohesion and adaptability and flexibility. In addition, FACES III provides a reference for understanding what types of families may have dysfunctional characteristics; the ones falling into the extreme dimensions on the model (e.g., chaotically disengaged, chaotically enmeshed) tend to have greater dysfunction. The real key to family functioning, however, is not in the classification per se but in the amount of family life satisfaction that the family members participating in the various family types experience. If individuals in the family are satisfied with a chaotic or rigid family structure, the type is considered functional for the individuals involved in that type of relational patterns. Fortunately, the FACES III instrument provides a way for family practitioners to calculate a family satisfaction score that makes it possible to determine the amount of family satisfaction that family members derive, thereby adding to the clinical utility of the model for a wider variety of families from different cultures.

Thomas and Olson (1993) found considerable research support for the curvilinear Circumplex Model using the Clinical Rating Scale (CRS)

**Figure 8.2**  FACES III

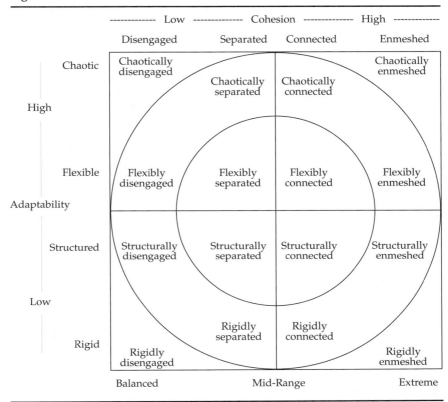

SOURCE: D. H. Olson. (1986). Circumplex Model VII: Validation studies and FACES III. *Family Processes, 26,* 337–351.

with sixty clinical families and sixty control families. Less support has been found for FACES III (Green, Harris, Forte, & Robinson, 1991). In response to criticisms concerning the validity of the FACES III measure, Olson (1991) reconceptualized the Circumplex Model as the Three-Dimensional (3-D) Circumplex Model. The 3-D model is linear, and FACES III, when used in conjunction with this model, is believed to provide a valid assessment of family functioning (Olson, 1991). The researchers and developers of the instrument instructed practitioners to use the 3-D model for their clinical assessments (for a depiction of the FACES 3-D model, see figure 8.3).

As the evidence on this measure continued to cumulate, however, Franklin and Streeter (1993) found support for the full 3-D Circumplex Model but found that the adaptability dimension lacked validity; they questioned whether the introduction of the 3-D model had been an

**Figure 8.3**    Three Dimensional (3-D) Circumplex Model

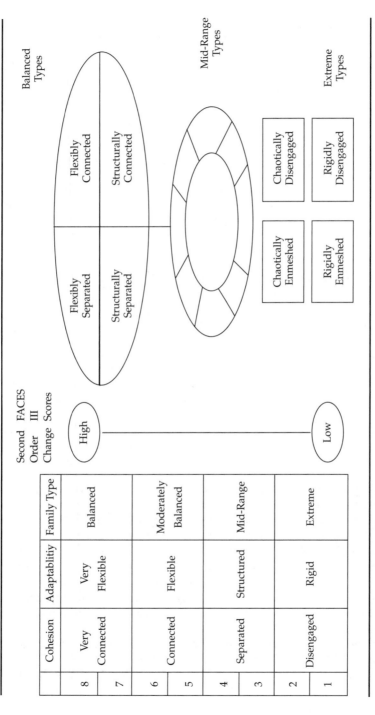

SOURCE: D. H. Olson & J. Tiesel. (1991). *FACES III: Linear scoring and interpretation.* St. Paul: University of Minnesota, Family Social Science.

improvement. Another study, by Thomas and Zechowski (2000), challenged the validity of FACES III as a means to operationalize the curvilinear dimension of the Circumplex Model constructs. The authors cite numerous studies to support their conclusions that two central concepts of the model—cohesion and adaptability—appear to be linear rather than curvilinear in relating to family functioning. Thomas and Zechowski (2000) advise that the Clinical Rating Scale (CRS) rather than FACES should be used to test the central hypotheses of the model, which include the following:

- Direct effects of cohesion and adaptability on family functioning
- Direct effects of communication on cohesion and adaptability
- Indirect effect of communication on family functioning through its facilitation of cohesion and adaptability
- Orthogonal relationship between cohesion and adaptability

Thomas and Zechowski's (2000) research supported a direct relationship between cohesion and family functioning, communication, and adaptability. Their findings suggest that therapists should help families raise levels of communication to promote healthy family cohesion. This is consistent with other popular models of marital and family therapy, such as emotionally focused marital therapy, integrative couple therapy, and functional family therapy.

In response to the criticisms of the previous FACES measures, Olson (1991) developed FACES IV in hopes of contributing a reliable and valid, self-report measure for assessing the original Circumplex Model (for more information about FACES IV, see www.facesiv.com/home.html). Similar to its predecessors, FACES IV is a self-administered, pencil-and-paper, rapid assessment instrument. The current measure contains twenty-four items measured on a five-point Likert scale to assess four dimensions (chaotic, disengaged, enmeshed, and rigid) that represent the extremes of the Circumplex Model. The constructs cohesion (enmeshed, disengaged) and flexibility (chaotic, rigid) are inferred from the four subscales as the higher-order dimensions of the four subscales (Franklin, Streeter, & Springer, 2001).

Previous empirical research showed that attempts to change the response format of the measure to enhance its ability to capture the extremes of the model failed to demonstrate an advantage. For this reason, FACES IV follows the same rationale and response format as previous versions of the measure, except that the items are worded in an extreme manner in an effort to assess dysfunction in the families who fell into the upper extremes of the model. However, FACES IV continues to be a leader in its ongoing empirical work to establish a useful measure for family practice (Olson, Gorall, & Tiesel, 2007). Recent work on the measure, for example, shows that there is a relationship between extreme scores on the dimensions of the model and family dysfunction, which shows the clinical usefulness of the Circumplex Model (Craddock, 2001). Researchers currently use FACES to assess family cohesion in studies investigating a range of topics, including the effects of trauma (Lohan & Murphy, 2007; Uruk, Sayger, & Cogdal, 2007), eating disorders (Franko, Thompson, Bauserman, Affenito, & Striegel-Moore, 2008), and ethnic differences (Baer & Schmitz, 2007). More than 250 studies using FACES measures and several studies using the Clinical Rating Scale support the major hypotheses of the Circumplex Model (Olson, 2000).

### Beavers Systems Model

The Beavers Systems Model, originally called the Beavers Timberlawn Family Evaluation Scales, developed over twenty-five years from clinical observations of both dysfunctional and healthy, competent families in treatment and research settings. From this work, three assessment instruments have been developed: the Beavers Interactional Scales, the Family Competence and Style Scales, and the Self-Report Family Inventory. The first two scales are observational clinical rating scales. The third is a self-report instrument completed by family members (Beavers & Hampson, 2000; Olson & Tiesel, 1993). Multiple studies by the Beavers research team have documented the reliability and validity of the measures (Beavers & Hampson, 2000).

The Beavers Systems Model (Beavers, 1981, 1982; Beavers & Hampson, 2000; Beavers & Voller, 1983) integrates family systems theory and developmental theory and is widely used in clinical practice. It seeks to understand the health and competence of families in relationship to their ability to produce healthy and competent children. This model classifies families on the axes of family competence and family style. The competence axis classifies families into types that fall along a continuum according to their level of functioning: optimal, adequate, midrange, borderline, and severely disturbed. The style axis classifies families according to their quality of interaction: centripetal and centrifugal. Centripetal families turn inward and seek pleasure and gratification from within the family. Centrifugal families turn outward and seek fulfillment in relationships outside the family. Both family competence and style converge to produce levels of family functioning, which are believed to have implications for the types of difficulties children may have, as defined by psychiatric categories. Figure 8.4 is a visual representation of the Beavers Systems Model.

Figure 8.5 shows the areas of family life used to obtain an assessment of the family competence and style dimensions on the Beavers Systems Model as described by Beavers (1982). When the two dimensions of the

**Figure 8.4**   Beavers Systems Model

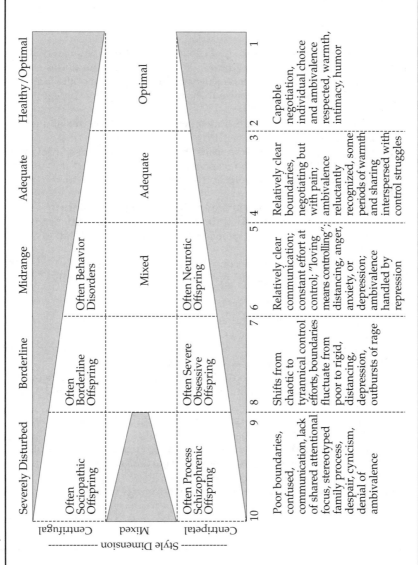

**Figure 8.5**    Assessing Family Competence and Style Dimensions,
Beavers System Model

---

I. Structure of the family
   A. Overt power: chaotic vs. egalitarian
   B. Parental coalition: parent-child coalitions vs. strong parental coalition
   C. Closeness: indistinct boundaries vs. close, distinct boundaries
II. Mythology: congruent vs. incongruent reality perception of the family
III. Goal-directed negotiation: efficient vs. inefficient problem solving
IV. Autonomy
   A. Clarity of expression: directness of expression of thoughts and feelings,
      from less clear to clear
   B. Responsibility: voicing responsibility for personal actions, from taking
      responsibility to taking no responsibility
   C. Permeability: open vs. unreceptive to statements of others.
V. Family affect
   A. Range of feelings: broad range vs. limited range of feelings
   B. Mood and tone: open and optimistic vs. cynical and pessimistic
   C. Unresolvable conflict: chronic underlying conflict vs. ability to
      resolve conflict
   D. Empathy: empathic vs. inconsiderate of individual feelings
VI. Global health pathology scale: optimal/adaptive (1) vs. severely
    dysfunctional (10)
VII. Family style
   A. Dependency needs: discouraged/ignored vs. encouraged
   B. Adult conflict: quite open vs. indirect, covert, hidden
   C. Proximity: all members give and expect lots of room between members
      vs. all members stay physically close with much touching
   D. Social presentation: try hard to appear well behaved and to make a
      good impression vs. seem unconcerned with appearances and social ap-
      proval
   E. Expression of closeness: consistently emphasize that they are close
      vs. deny that they are close
   F. Assertive/aggressive qualities: discourage aggressive or disruptive
      behavior and expressions vs. solicit or encourage assertive, even
      aggressive behavior and expressions
   G. Expression of feelings: express positive feelings more often vs.
      express negative feelings more often
   H. Global centripetal/centrifugal style: total inward oriented vs. total out-
      ward oriented

---

Beavers Systems Model, family competence and family style, are combined, nine distinct family groups diagrammatically emerge on the basis
of clinical observation and empirical research. Three of the groups are
considered functional, whereas six are problematic and require clinical
intervention (Beavers & Hampson, 2000; for a description of the characteristics of each grouping, see figure 8.6).

**Figure 8.6**   Beavers Systems Model of Family Functioning Dimensions of Competence and Style Characteristics of Nine Family Groupings

GROUP 1.  Optimal families
Optimal families serve as the model for effective functioning. The families have a systems orientation, with equality, respect, group problem-solving skills, individuation, and clear boundaries. Conflicts are easily and quickly resolved.

GROUP 2.  Adequate families
Adequate families are more control oriented than systems oriented, attempting to resolve conflict with fear and intimidation. Although this type of parental control exerting more overt power tends to achieve results, these families have less intimacy and trust and there is greater role stereotyping and greater power differentiation.

GROUPS 3, 4, & 5.  Midrange families
In midrange families, the children tend to be more vulnerable and parents susceptible to psychological problems. The families are very concerned with power and control, and negotiating of discipline is not allowed. These families do not have boundary problems, scapegoating is a common method, favorite children apparent, hostility, blame, and attack are frequent responses to familial conflict.

GROUPS 6 & 7.  Borderline families
Borderline families present with frequent ineffective struggles to maintain power. Parents express anger openly, and children learn manipulation early. Chaotic is used to describe the often-stormy and intense battles for dominance.

GROUPS 8 & 9.  Severely dysfunctional families
Severely dysfunctional families have almost total breakdown of communication, which means a limited ability to resolve conflict. Family members lack a shared focus, children are often seen as emotionally delayed. There is an insistence within the family system to maintain togetherness and extreme loyalty.

Development of the model, as with all assessment models, is ongoing. The recent introduction of a self-report version of the family assessment instrument has added to the clinical utility of the model. The Self-Report Family Inventory (SFI) measures two dimensions of family functioning (Beavers & Hampson, 2000).

## McMaster Family Model

The McMaster Family Model (Epstein, Baldwin, & Bishop, 1982) is another widely used family assessment model that evolved from clinical practice. The model was developed over a fifteen years with families in the Brown University and Butler Hospital Family Research Program. This model assesses whole-systems functioning of the family and evaluates family structure, organization, and transactional patterns that distinguish healthy from unhealthy families. Two assessment instruments have emerged from this work: the McMaster Clinical Rating Scale and a self-report family measure, the McMaster Family Assessment Device (FAD), version 3.

These scales assess seven dimensions of family functioning: problem solving, communication, roles, affective responses, affective involvement, behavior control, and overall family functioning. The following sections describe the subscales of the measure.

**Family Problem Solving.** Family problem solving refers to how families solve both instrumental (e.g., financial) and affective (e.g., social support and nurturance) problems. Families are considered most effective when they follow seven steps in their problem-solving efforts:

1. Problem identification
2. Communication of the problem to the appropriate family members
3. Development of a plan and subsequent alternatives (brainstorming)
4. Commitment to a plan
5. Action on that plan
6. Accountability and monitoring of the action
7. Outcome evaluation

Families are considered least effective in their problem solving if they cannot accomplish the first step.

**Communication.** Families with effective communication use a clear, direct style. Those with the least effective communication have a masked, indirect style. For example, a husband might say, "It really bothers me when you don't call before you come home if you are going to be late," rather than not speaking to his wife all evening because she was late.

**Roles.** Roles refer to how the family assigns instrumental, affective, and mixed-dimension (e.g., system maintenance, teaching independent living skills) role functions and how it handles accountability for those functions. Families are considered to have effective role assignments when all the necessary family functions have been clearly allocated to appropriate family members and when some form of monitoring and accountability takes place. Least effective role functioning occurs when the necessary family functions are not addressed or when accountability for those functions is not maintained.

**Affective Responsiveness.** Affective responsiveness refers to how families respond to crises and the degree to which emotional responses are aimed at the well-being of family members. Families are considered to have appropriate affective responses when they can demonstrate a full range of emotional responses that are consistent in degree and congruent with context. Families are least effective when the type and severity of emotional responsiveness is incongruent with context.

**Affective Involvement.**   Affective involvement refers to a range of emotional involvement, from absence of involvement to symbiotic involvement. Families are considered most effective when they express empathic involvement and least effective when they express an absence of involvement.

**Behavior Control.**   A range of styles from rigid to chaotic. Control of behavior is assessed in three areas: dangerous or threatening situations, meeting and expressing of family members' needs and drives (e.g., eating, sleeping, sex), and monitoring of interpersonal socializing both inside and outside the family. Flexible behavior control is assessed to be most effective and chaotic least effective.

Although there has been some debate over the past few years about whether the FAD scoring procedures should be reorganized to reflect higher-order factors from self-report measures (Ridenour, Daley, & Reich, 2000), Miller, Ryan, Keitner, Bishop, and Epstein (2000b) argue that the overall ecological validity of the scale, with the backing of numerous studies, suggests an absence in the utility of higher-order factors. In addition, Miller et al. (2000a) suggest that the most important issue regarding any scale is its clinical utility and validity, which the FAD has demonstrated repeatedly.

## Moos Family Environment Scales

The Moos Family Environment Scales (FES) (Moos & Moos, 1986; Moos & Spinrad, 1984) evolved from research on social climates, the unique personality or attributes of social environments. The FES is a self-report measure that assesses whole-family functioning and is compatible with social and systems ecological theory. It has been widely used in both clinical research and practice and has been demonstrated to be an effective outcome measure. The FES evaluates families' perceptions of their social or interpersonal climate along three dimensions: interpersonal relationships, personal growth, and systems maintenance. Each dimension comprises subscales that evaluate diverse areas of family functioning.

**Relationship Dimensions.**   The first three dimensions measured by FES assess how involved people are in their family and how openly they express both positive and negative feelings in a bipolar dimension of cohesion versus conflict, and then in a unipolar dimension of organization versus control.

The cohesion subscale measures the degree of commitment, help, and support family members provide for one another (e.g., the way they support one another, the amount of energy they put into what they do at home, how much feeling of togetherness there is in the family).

The expressiveness subscale taps the extent to which family members are encouraged to act openly and to express their feelings directly (e.g., how openly family members talk around home, how freely they discuss their personal problems, how often they just pick up and go if they feel like doing something on the spur of the moment).

The conflict subscale measures the amount of openly expressed anger, aggression, and conflict among family members (e.g., frequency of fights, whether family members sometimes get so angry that they throw things, how often they criticize each other).

**Personal Growth Dimensions.**    The personal growth, or goal orientation, subscales make up another set of FES dimensions. This set focuses on the family's goals by tapping the major ways in which a family encourages or inhibits personal growth.

The independence subscale measures the extent to which family members are assertive and self-sufficient and make their own decisions (e.g., how strongly family members are encouraged to be independent, how much they think things out for themselves, how freely they come and go in the family).

The achievement orientation subscale taps the extent to which activities, such as school and work, are cast into an achievement-oriented or competitive framework (e.g., how important they feel it is to do their best and to get ahead, how much they believe in competition).

The intellectual-cultural orientation subscale assesses the degree of interest in political, social, intellectual, and cultural activities (e.g., how often family members talk about political or social problems; how often they go to the library; how much they like music, art, and literature).

The active-recreational orientation subscale taps the extent of participation in social and recreational activities (e.g., how often friends come over for dinner or to visit; how often family members go out; how often family members go to movies, sports events, camping).

The moral-religious subscale measures the degree of emphasis on ethical and religious issues and values (e.g., how frequently family members attend church, synagogue, or Sunday school; how strict their ideas are about right and wrong; how much they believe there are some things that must be taken on faith).

**Systems Maintenance Dimensions.**    The last set of dimensions the FES measures assesses the family's emphasis on clear organization, structure, rules, and procedures in running family life.

The organization subscale measures the importance of clear organization and structure in planning family activities and responsibilities (e.g., how carefully activities are planned, how neat and orderly family members are, how clearly each person's duties are defined).

The control subscale assesses the extent to which set rules and procedures are used to run family life (e.g., how much one family member makes the decisions, how set the ways of doing things are at home, how much emphasis is on following rules in the family).

Even though the FES is one of the most popular environmental measures in clinical and family research, Chipuer and Villegas (2001) and others have found a potential problem with using the three-factor structure of the FES across different groups of respondents. In particular, their study of wives' and husbands' responses to the perceptions of their family environment did not support the Moos and Moos (1986) three-factor model. Rather, they found evidence supporting a two-factor solution— cohesion versus conflict and organization versus control. They recommend using the two-factor, second-order solution to compare perceptions of spouses and to provide the best fit across data for wives and husbands (Boake & Salmon, 1983; Chipuer & Villegas, 2001).

## Family Assessment Measure

The Family Assessment Measure (FAM; Skinner, Steinhauer, & Sitarenios, 2000) is based on the process model of family functioning, which describes how to conduct family assessments based on seven dimensions: affective involvement, control, task accomplishment, role performance, communication, affective expression, and values and norms. Each dimension is measured at three levels: whole-family systems, dyadic relationships, and individual functioning.

> *Affective involvement*: Assesses how much interest and concern family members show. There are five types: uninvolved, interest and devoid of feeling, narcissistic, empathic, and enmeshed.

> *Control*: Assesses how family members influence each other's behavior, their techniques and strategies. These include rigidity, flexibility, laissez-faire, and chaotic.

> *Task accomplishment*: Assesses three types of family tasks, which are defined in a cultural context: basic tasks, developmental tasks, and crisis tasks.

*Role performance*: Tied to task accomplishment and assesses three distinct operations: each family member's assigned role, the agreement of each family member to accept his or her role, and actually enactment of those roles and behaviors.

*Communication*: Assesses how affective role performance and tasks are accomplished. Three forms of communication are assessed: affective, instrumental, and neutral.

*Affective expression*: Assesses the content, intensity, and timing of affective expression. This is considered the most important form of communication for the family system in how it expresses itself.

*Values and norms*: Assesses basic family processes in terms of values and norms. The focus is on whether family rules are explicit or implicit, how free family members are to determine and express their own attitudes, and whether the family values and norms are consistent with those in the society at large.

The FAM, following twenty years of work in developing the measure, has four self-report components, including the general scale, which has fifty items and nine subcales; the dyadic relationship scales, with forty-two items and seven subscales; the self-rating scale, with forty-two items and seven subscales; and the brief FAM with fourteen items. The measure has demonstrated good reliability and discriminant validity (Skinner, Steinhauer, & Santo-Barbara, 1983; for guidelines for using the FAM, see figure 8.7).

**Figure 8.7**    Clinical Guidelines for Using the Family Assessment Measurement (FAM)

---

1) According to the authors, this is a good instrument for obtaining an overall index of family functioning, especially in time-limited situations (Skinner et al., 2000)
2) This instrument helps to pinpoint gaps in the assessment
3) This instrument helps identify areas of confusion where family members' perception of a situation is quite different
4) This instrument provides an independent and objective validation of the clinical assessment
5) This instrument identifies a starting point for circular questioning
6) This instrument allows the nonverbal members of the family a forum for expressing themselves
7) This instrument provides good visual representation of the strengths and weaknesses of the family
8) This instrument helps both the therapist and family members define treatment goals
9) This instrument shows a quantitative measure of change in response to treatment

---

## ASSESSMENT METHODS

### Global Assessment of Relational Functioning

The Global Assessment of Relational Functioning (GARF) is the first family assessment measure recognized in the *Diagnostic and Statistical Manual of Mental Disorders* (*DSM*). The *DSM*, published by the American Psychiatric Association, classifies mental disorders and provides diagnostic criteria for each. The GARF is a clinical rating scale that is typically completed by clinicians, although there is a version that clients can complete themselves. The GARF is considered a reliable and valid measure of relationship functioning, including the stability of relationships in a family (Hilsenroth et al., 2000).

A clinician can use the GARF to rate relationship functioning in the following areas:

- Problem solving, which includes skills in communication, negotiating routines, coping with stress, and conflict resolution
- Organization, which includes an ability to maintain family roles and boundaries
- Emotional climate, which involves the level of caring, empathy, involvement, and attachment (American Psychiatric Association, 1994)

Using the GARF, a family's functioning is rated on a hundred-point scale, with higher scores indicating better functioning. A score of 1–20, for example, indicates high levels of dysfunction, whereas a score of 41–60 indicates that the family often functions well but that there are frequent periods of dysfunction (American Psychiatric Association, 1994).

### Standardized Measures: Problem-Oriented Measures

It is important to point out that the assessment models discussed in the previous section, including standardized observational measures and self-report inventories, are all standardized methods of assessment. Those standardized measures represent the state of the art in objective assessment of families; practitioners are urged to become skillful in one or more of the models and to learn how to administer and score the various assessment measures. As was discussed in some detail in chapter 3, standardized measures are an important tool for conducting evidence-based practice. They have established reliability and validity and have been used in multiple studies. Comprehensive reviews of available measures for family assessment have been provided by Fredman and Sherman (1987), Grotevant and Carlson (1989), and Toulitas, Perlmutter, and Straus (2000). Darro et al. (1990) also provided a helpful review of measures associated with parenting, and Corcoran and Fischer (2007) provided a review of several rapid assessment instruments that can be used to assess marital and family systems. Recall from the discussion on standardized measures in chapter 3 that several different types of standardized measures exist, ranging from global, multidimensional ones to specific, unidimensional problem inventories. Standardized measures are most effective when administered as part of a comprehensive clinical assessment and evaluation. Using standardized clinical measures in any other way to diagnose a client or client system is ineffective clinical practice.

This section mentions a few problem-oriented measures to provide practitioners with an understanding of the breadth of the available standardized measures that are helpful in the assessment of families. We discuss problem-oriented standardized measures here because they are important to assessing clinical outcomes and because they differ from the whole-system functioning measures discussed in the earlier section on empirical assessment models. In addition, we discuss social support and network measures because they seem especially relevant to social work's approach to understanding the impact of broader systems on family functioning.

Problem-oriented measures are particularly useful because they are more specific than whole-system measures. These measures focus on a particular problem area for a family (e.g., parenting). They are especially useful to social work practitioners because they help assess clients at risk of a particular problem behavior and provide feedback concerning that client's improvement in this area. It may, for example, be important to learn that a family is less chaotic and enmeshed (whole-systems measure), but the questions funding sources and clients may want answered is, "Does Ms. Jones know how to parent her children better?" or "Have the violent arguments stopped?" Chapter 11 discusses in more detail how to assess change and the outcomes of clients during treatment. Problem-oriented standardized measures may help in tracking outcomes.

As the first example, several measures of parenting effectiveness are available for use in social work practice. For example, the Parenting Stress Index (PSI) is a 101-item self-report measure that identifies families at risk of dysfunctional parenting and psychopathology. The measure is useful for screening, diagnostic assessment, and practice evaluation (Abidin, 1983). Social workers assessing families under stress and believed to be at risk of dysfunctional parenting may find this measure helpful to their assessment protocol. Another useful problem-oriented measure is the Battering Severity Index, a measure aimed to identify women at risk of being battered. Although this measure was developed to assess at-risk behaviors in women, it may be useful in family practice insofar as battering is understood to be related to dysfunctional family dynamics and individual pathology. Another useful measure for assessing battering in families is the Abusive Behavior Inventory (Shepard &

Campbell, 1992). This thirty-item, self-report measure has both psychological and physical abuse items. Victims of domestic violence or their partners can complete the inventory (for a copy of the Abusive Behavior Inventory, see appendix 8B).

Some other measures that may be helpful to social workers include those that assess the levels of stressors that families encounter. For example, the Family Inventory of Life Events and Changes (FILE) is a seventy-one-item self-report measure that assesses the accumulation of normative and nonnormative life events and changes that a family experienced over the previous year.

Social support and social network measures also have special significance to social work family practice. Social workers know a family does not exist in a vacuum—the level of capacity to solve problems inside the family is tied to resources outside the family—and vice versa. Resolving family problems therefore is intricately tied to the social context in which the family lives. Social support resources are essential to a family's well-being. These become especially important to families who have multiple problems (Tracy & Whittaker, 1990; Wood & Geismar, 1989; for a detailed discussion on assessing families with multiple problems, see chapter 9.

Social support resources range from emotional support to material assistance. Measures are available for several types of social support. Social support measures assess both perceived support (cognitive appraisal of support) and enacted support (support actually given) of family members and their social network (Streeter & Franklin, 1992). For example, the Perceived Social Support Scale, a twenty-item self-report measure, assesses the extent to which individual family members perceive that their families meet their needs. This scale also measures perceived support from friends (Procidano & Heller, 1983). The Inventory of Socially Supportive Behavior (Barrera, Sandler, & Ramsey, 1981) and the Social Support Behavior Scales (Vaux, 1982) both have the capacity to measure actual social support received. Social network measures one's social network identifying its strengths and weaknesses. Social networks may include one's family but also expand to neighborhood, community, friends, and work relationships. Tracy and Whittaker (1990) developed the Social Network Map, a social network measure for use in clinical practice.

Social support and network measures are useful in understanding the broader context of the family environment. Social support has been shown to be an important predictor of individual health and well-being (Vaux, 1988; for reviews of the available social support and network measures, see Barrera, 1986; Darro et al., 1990; Vaux, 1988; for a review of eight social support network measures that are applicable to clinical practice, see Streeter & Franklin, 1992).

## OTHER FAMILY ASSESSMENT METHODS

Even though standardized family assessment measures are useful, practitioners should not exclusively rely on such models or measures—there are many other methods for assessing family functioning (Holman, 1983; Jacob & Tennenbaum, 1988). As discussed throughout this book, it is important for practitioners to use multiple methods of assessment. This section covers some of the other methods—ones that are consistent with the types of assessment methods summarized in chapter 2 on quantitative assessment and in chapter 4 on qualitative assessment—specifically, interviewing techniques, family-task observations, family goal recording, graphic problem-oriented, and standardized measures. The assessment methods presented here are not comprehensive but provide practitioners with several useful techniques for collecting assessment information on families.

### Interviewing Techniques

Social workers frequently rely on talking with family members as their primary way of gathering assessment information. Interviewing is one of the most important social work practice skills to acquire (Compton & Galaway, 1989; Garrett, 1991). Throughout this chapter, we provide several examples of questions to guide social workers through the interview and to aid in gathering pertinent information concerning family process and behavior. Practitioners can interview family members together or apart, depending on the type of information the social worker is seeking. For example, in exploring problems such as family roles or rules, the social worker may include everyone because such issues affect the entire family; however, the social worker would interview only the parents when exploring problems in the couple's sexual relationship.

Regardless of how many family members practitioners interviews at one time, they should remember that the members being interviewed are part of a larger family system. In essence, when interviewing families, social workers always have two clients: the family as a system and the individual members of that system (Schulman, 1992). This makes interviewing families complex and calls the social worker to engage all family members, to observe their interactions, and to assess the family at different levels. For example, the social worker may need to assess the behavior of an individual family member, such as the eight-year-old boy Chad, who has disruptive behavior. Chad started rocking back and forth on a chair in the social worker's office, distracting his parents from the meeting. The social worker not only recognized the disruptive behavior but also assessed a parental subsystem interaction—the parenting-skills deficits of the parents, who are unable to set appropriate limits on the boy's behavior. In addition, the social worker noted a systems-level interaction—Chad's behavior of jumping on the chair started immediately after the parents made critical remarks about his poor school performance and compared it with the superior performance of his twelve-year-old brother, Chip.

The social worker then observed the following interactional sequence: The father yells for the boy to stop his behavior of jumping on the chair (parent-child subsystem interaction). The older brother, Chip, joins in the interaction by calling Chad stupid for acting the way he does (sibling subsystem interaction and parent-child coalition). The social worker observed this interaction so that she can see the interactional functioning. The mother intervened and told Chip not to call his brother stupid (parental subsystem interaction). She also told the father not to raise his voice to Chad (parent-child coalition). The father told the mother to stop interfering in his discipline and stated that she is too easy on Chad (parental subsystem interaction). At the same time, Chad jumped out of the chair, sat in another chair near the mother, and began to pick a fight with his older brother. They exchanged a few putdowns (sibling subsystem interaction). Chip asked the parents to stop Chad from picking on him (parent-child subsystem interaction). The parents then united and told Chad to stop picking on Chip, and the mother stated that they both owe each other an apology (parental subsystem interaction). Chip said angrily, "You always take up for Chad" and pouted, refusing to apologize (parent-child subsystem interaction). Chad went and sat away from the family in the chair in which he was rocking back and forth before he moved to taunt his brother (individual member interaction).

Both parents turned to the social worker and denied that they give preferential treatment to one child over the other. Chip shook his head no. The father looked at the social worker and said that it is difficult to have peace in the family when Chad throws such fits. The mother agreed that there is much tension in the family but added that it is not all Chad's fault. The father added that Chad wears his feelings on his sleeve and does not cooperate. Chad started rocking the chair again (systems/contextual level).

In such a scenario, the social worker uses the face-to-face interview to observe the multiple interactions of the family. Interviewing in this context requires expert observation skills and the ability to engage the family verbally. It might be helpful, at this point, to refer back to the assessment protocol in chapter 1 and review some of the important information on family functioning that can be gathered during a comprehensive assessment.

As has been emphasized throughout this chapter, it is important to assess the family as a system and to understand how all the members' separate behaviors fit together into the complex, circular behavioral chain known as systemic functioning. One interviewing technique that helps assess the complexities of how families work as systems is circular questioning. Circular questions provide a structure for eliciting information from various family members about the transactions and operations embedded in the family system. The structure of circular questions is nonthreatening to the family because the questions generally ask family members to comment on the family process from the viewpoint of a different family member. Thus, a father might be asked to comment on how he believes a son is responding to the behavior of the mother or a sister might be asked how she believes her brother might be feeling in response to his mother.

Circular questions can be divided into categories of information-eliciting probes. O'Brien and Bruggen (1985) offer five categories for organizing different types of circular questions:

1. *Relationship to others:* These questions may refer to the relationship between two people in a family (e.g., "How do your mom and dad solve disagreements between them?").

2. *Relationship to events in family life:* These questions refer to how people organize meanings around events or time (e.g., "When Mom comes home late from work, what does Dad do?").

3. *Ranking behavior in the family:* Actual or hypothetical situations can be used (e.g., "Who is most strict, your mother or your father?" "Pretend for a moment that I am a magic fairy with the powers to send you on a vacation to an adventurous island—who in your family would you take with you?").

4. *Relationships to time:* Both events in time and specific points in time may be used (e.g., "How was your husband different before you moved to this city?" "How were things different between you a year ago?").

5. *Eliciting information from the perspective of the silent member:* This may include members not present at family sessions or those who will not talk. Examples include ("If your father were here in the session, what do you think he might say about your family?" "If your brother were to answer my question, what do you think he might say?").

Fleuridas, Nelson, and Rosenthal (1986) offer a more-detailed categorization for understanding different types of circular questions, as presented in appendix 8A. The ethnographic interviewing covered in chapter 5 also provides important interviewing techniques for gathering information from the insider perspective of a family system.

## Family-Task Observations

Observations of family members undertaking structured tasks provide an important way for social workers to observe and assess family functioning. Such tasks as playing a game, planning a vacation, solving a problem, and making a decision have been used. As an example of making a decision, the social worker may ask families to decide on their main issue in therapy while the social worker observes them from the corner of the room or through a one-way mirror. Observing families in such a task allows the social worker to view many aspects of family functioning, such as roles, power, communication, and decision-making processes.

Enactment is a structured family task in which the family is instructed to role-play or act out a previous situation in the family. For example, the practitioner might ask a couple who complains that they argue about how to spend their free time on weekends to reconstruct or reenact the argument in the office while the practitioner observes. The practitioner might instruct a wife who complains that she cannot talk to her husband to tell her husband those feelings in the session and to talk to him about them. Enactments help social workers understand both the strengths and the weaknesses of family process and provide meaningful information on which the social workers may base their interventions.

Family sculpting is an experiential task in which the social worker asks an individual family member to place other family members in stationary positions that represent what the family is like from that individual's perception. The individual places him- or herself among the family members. Significant therapeutic information is believed to emerge from the sculpting. For example, a woman sculpting her family placed herself on the floor with her husband's foot on top of her. From a family sculpture, social workers can assess such family dynamics as power, cohesion, affective responses, coalitions, and triangles. The experiential aspects of the sculpture also serve as a powerful tool that may help family members gain insight into the interactions in their own family.

## Family Goal Recording

Family goal recording (FGR) was adapted from goal attainment scaling, a method of assessment and measurement that has been used in more than 150 mental health settings since 1968 (Fleuridas, Rosenthal, Leigh, & Leigh, 1990; for a summary of goal attainment scaling, see chapter 3). Fleuridas et al. (1990) developed the FGR method at the University of Iowa's Marriage and Family Clinic. They conceptualized this method as contextually relevant and as possessing sensitivity to the uniqueness of each client's or program's needs. As does the goal attainment method, FGR provides a therapeutic tool for helping social workers select and define desirable outcome goals for clients. It further provides a scaling and weighing system in which the outcomes can be measured relative to the degree of change achieved toward the desired goals and weighted according to the importance of the problem to the family.

The scaling system requires social workers to solicit information from families that will help objectively and quantifiably understand the current base rate of a presenting problems. When the base rate of presenting problems is defined, the social worker and family determine a desired, achievable level of change within a given period. They also determine levels of change to mark whether the situation deteriorates during the same period. For example, a family agrees that one of their problems is that there are verbal arguments involving everyone in the household at least three or four times a week. This serves as the base rate for the problem the family is seeking to change. The family may agree that decreasing the arguments to one or fewer a week would be their desired level of positive change. They may also agree that if the situation at home were to deteriorate, if they increased their arguments to five or more a week, for example, the family might split up as a result of their persistent fighting. Social workers guide family members in defining outcome goals such as these for each presenting problem. Outcome goals would be scaled between +1 and –1. In such a mathematical system, the base rate is 0.00 (for an example of FGR, see appendix 8B).

Because individual family members often define family difficulties differently, several goals may be established that represent the different concerns of each family member. When possible, social workers should mediate these different perceptions and help family members come to agreement concerning some goals of mutual interest. Fleuridas et al. (1990) suggest that goals may first be defined according to the interests of individual family members and later classified as they relate to the different subsystems or whole systems functioning in a family (for an example of FGR classification schema, see appendix 8B).

Classifying goals according to the different subsystems makes it possible for family therapists to monitor how change in one part of the family system may affect change in another part. Assigning weights to the different goals takes this method a step further, thus making it possible for social workers to mathematically calculate a level of change score for each family. In this mathematical system, the goals for subsystem areas are weighted according to their significance to the family. All the cumulative weights for each area must add up to 100 percent (see appendix 8B). The change score is calculated by multiplying progress or deterioration on the levels scale by the weight given to that particular goal (for a more detailed explanation, see Fleuridas et al., 1990; Kiresuk & Sherman, 1968; Kiresuk, Stelmachers, & Schultz, 1982).

To use the FGR approach, social workers must objectively identify the specific problem areas and desired level of changes. This means, for example, that if the mother of a thirteen-year-old son complains that he is slovenly and rebellious, the social worker would help the mother be more specific about what behaviors her son is demonstrating that make her believe that he is slovenly and rebellious. *Slovenly* may come to mean that the boy does not clean his room, leaves dirty dishes in the living room, and leaves his dirty underwear on the bathroom floor. Rebellious may come to mean that he does not help with the dishes when asked and refuses to turn off the television at his designated bedtime. When the problems are clearly defined, the social worker can proceed to find a base rate of how often the behaviors occur and can determine what connotes a reasonable amount of positive change as well as definitions of deterioration. Finally, the social worker can work with the family to prioritize the goals and assign the appropriate weights to each area.

The FGR approach has been shown to be a valid and reliable method for the assessment and measurement of family functioning. Like its progenitor, goal attainment scaling, the method is believed to enhance assessment and treatment effectiveness.

## Graphic Measures

Family therapists have developed several pictorial and graphic methods for assessing family functioning (on graphic methods, see chapter 5). One of the most popular graphic methods is the genogram, which was popularized through the Bowenian approach to family therapy (Bowen, 1976). The genogram provides an assessment of the family from an intergenerational context and provides a map of the family from a longitudinal perspective across three generations. Symbols are used to depict the types of family members and different aspects of family functioning. For example, a square symbolizes males and a circle symbolizes females. A horizontal line symbolizes a marriage and a vertical line, offspring. The genogram also provides a method for gathering psychosocial information from the family. Such information as family members' cultural and ethnic backgrounds, socioeconomic status, religions, dates of marriage, dates of birth, birth order, dates of divorce, deaths, amounts of contact with and social support from family members, and other significant events (e.g., serious illnesses, abortions, personal tragedies) can be recorded on the genogram. Some social workers also record personal information about family members, such as descriptions of personality characteristics and personal and emotional problems. The genogram can provide a wealth of assessment information, and it is not unusual for transgenerational patterns of a certain type of family difficulty to emerge.

Another important graphic assessment method developed by the systemic family therapists is the film strip (Fisch, Watzlawick, & Segal, 1982; Watzlawick, Weakland, & Fisch, 1974). The film strip is used to identify the sequences of behavior that occur before and after a problem behavior. The film strip also helps social workers assess the full context in which the behavior occurs. In assessment, social workers tell the family that they would like to see a film of their problem. The social worker proceeds to interview the family to gather information for the film strip. A film strip can be drawn on a piece of paper, blackboard, or flip chart.

Usually, the clinician draws two vertical lines with several horizontal lines making up "frames," up and down the vertical lines; when the drawing is complete, it looks like a ladder. Then the family therapist writes the problem in one of the blocks (usually near the middle) and proceeds to find out more about the context of the problem. For example, the therapist may ask, "Who was there when the problem occurred? What were they doing? Where in the house did it happen?" After the family therapist has fully identified the context of the problem and has a clear picture of what was happening at the time it occurred, the family may be asked for assistance with filling in the frames before the problem happened.

Usually, the frames are broken into blocks that represent five or ten minutes to track the antecedents and context of a problem. For example, the therapist will ask, "What were you doing just five minutes before the problem occurred? Who was doing what and where were you in the house? Who was gone and who was present?" In this manner, the therapist can develop a clear and descriptive assessment of the behavior of the family just before the occurrence of the problem. When this information is recorded on the film-strip drawing, the family therapist proceeds to track what happened after the problem occurred. Again, in gathering this information, the frames on the graphic film strip represent small sequences of behavior of five to ten minutes.

Information is usually gathered in successive five- and ten-minute increments, until there is some type of resolution to the problem or standoff in which nothing else seems to be happening, as when people just elected to go away from each other or forget it. The social worker should always seek to know how the event depicted in the film strip ended. Gathering information in this manner helps the social worker track a problem and provides useful information for knowing when, how, and where to make changes in the family system.

We have discussed several different methods for assessing families. All of them are useful in helping social workers learn about family functioning. It is not practical, however, for social workers to use all these methods in an assessment situation with a family, because different families may respond to some techniques better than others. For example, Ho (1986) indicates that Hispanic families may respond favorably to the genogram technique because of their multigenerational family orientation. Individual social workers may also find a certain set of techniques more effective in helping them assess family processes. Social workers must choose among the assessment options and use knowledge of their clientele and practice wisdom to help them decide which methods to use in a family assessment. Social workers are encouraged to develop their own personal assessment outline that may guide them in practice. Chapter 3 provides guidelines for using multiple methods for assessing clients; it is important to remember these guidelines in assessing families.

## Assessing Family Strengths

Family researchers and practitioners have also developed specific methods for assessing family strengths. Early (2001), for example, reviews several measures that have been developed to assess family strengths and have been modified for those purposes by practitioners. Gilgun (2001) has also developed the Clinical Assessment Package for Assessing Client Risks and Strengths (CASPARS). This measurement package was developed for use in children's mental health and child welfare services, such as foster care and in-home services with families. The CASPARS specifically includes two measures that relate to the family: scales for family relationships and family embeddedness in the community (for a list of strengths-oriented family measures, see box 8.2).

Graybeal (2001) discusses ways that social workers can include strengths in traditional psychosocial assessments by using the ROPES interviewing approach. The acronym ROPES reminds the practitioner to consider all the following approaches:

*Resources*: Personal, family, social environment, organizational, community

*Options*: Present focus, emphasis on choice: What can be accessed now? What is available and hasn't been tried or used?

*Possibilities*: Future focus, imagination, creativity, vision of the future, play: What have you thought of trying but haven't tried yet?

*Exceptions*: When is the problem not happening? When is the problem different? When is part of the hypothetical future solution occurring? How have you survived, endured, thrived?

*Solutions*: Focus on constructing solutions, not solving problems. What's working now? What are your successes? What are you doing that you would like to change?

The ROPES interviewing approach encourages practitioners to think about strengths in areas they already assess. For example, they assess exceptions to the problem when collecting information about presenting problems or list resources when describing the family and social environment of clients.

---

**Box 8.2**
**Strengths-Based Measures for Families and Children**

---

**Family Functioning Style Scale (FFSS):** Measures family strengths and capabilities.

**Family Support Scale (FSS):** Assesses the degree to which potential sources of social support have been helpful to families.

**Family Resource Scale (FRS):** Measures tangible and intangible resources that are considered important for families with young children. The FRS can be used to identify areas in which the family is successfully meeting needs and for identifying goals.

**Family Empowerment Scale (FES):** Measures empowerment in families with children with emotional disorders.

**School Success Profile (SSP):** Measures protective and risk factors in the areas of neighborhood, school, friends, and family.

**Social Skills Rating System (SSRS):** Measures skills in children and adolescents in the areas of cooperation, assertion, responsibility, empathy, and self-control.

**Clinical Assessment Package for Assessing Client Risks and Strengths (CASPARS)** Five scales that measure risk and protective factors: Family Relationships, Family Embeddedness in Community, Peer Relationships, and Sexuality.

SOURCES: T. J. Early. (2001). Measures for practice with families from a strengths perspective. *Families in Society: The Journal of Contemporary Human Services, 82*(3), 225–232.
J. F. Gilgun. (2001). CASPARS: New tools for assessing client risks and strengths. Families in society. *The Journal of Contemporary Human Services 82*, 450–459.

---

The ROPES approach can also be used in the following other areas, in a traditional assessment of clients:

*Presenting problems*: Add exceptions, solutions, and options to your assessment.

*Background information*: Add resources and options to your social assessment.

*Goal setting*: Add exceptions, and co-constructed options and possibilities to your set of goals for the client change.

*Intervention plan*: Add possibilities and solutions to the set of recommendations for your assessment report.

## MOVING FROM ASSESSMENT TO INTERVENTION

What follows covers a family assessment completed by a social worker practicing in a juvenile justice setting. The report illustrates how to use the multiple sources of information gathered during an assessment to develop an assessment report on a client, including how to integrate standardized family assessments into the assessment report. In addition, the assessment report illustrates how to use assessment information to develop an intervention plan. It is important to note that, even though this is an actual assessment report on a client, the identifying information has been changed to protect the confidentiality of the clients.

Peggy Weeks, MSSW, is a social worker employed in a youth shelter for juvenile offenders. She frequently conducts family assessments to make recommendations to the court concerning youths who are brought to the shelter. Weeks employs several of the assessment methods discussed previously in her data-gathering process. She usually relies on interviews with family members, family-task observations, and standardized measures. The major purpose of an assessment is to make decisions about treatment. Weeks used multiple methods in her assessment; interviews, task observations, and a standardized measure guided her decision about what she would recommend to the court concerning the youth she was working with, Madie Williams.

For example, from her family assessment information, she was able to conclude that Madie's family had many strengths. They were loving and supportive, and capable of providing the structure and guidance that Madie needed. In contrast, the family had experienced many stressors and had some significant cross-generational conflicts that needed resolution. These stressors, however, did not appear to interfere with Mr. and Mrs. Williams' functioning as parents. Therefore, the social worker concluded that they were competent parents and able to provide a good home for Madie.

The social worker's assessment uncovered many emotional and psychological issues contributing to Madie's behavior problems. She was able to use this information to make a clinical judgment concerning what types of issues should be addressed in a treatment plan. Thus, in the recommendation section of the assessment report, Weeks outlined Madie's emotional issues (i.e., loss, depression, anger) and suggested that these issues be addressed in therapy. She also interpreted those emotional issues in relationship to Madie's adolescent developmental issues. She further looked at the severity of her behavior problem (e.g., running away) and inferred that Madie would need a fairly intensive treatment program that provided additional supports and structures besides those her family could provide. The social worker, therefore, recommended the day treatment program as an intervention for Madie.

The information uncovered in the assessment and written in the report was used to develop the recommendations section of the assessment report. The recommendations section is the first step toward developing a treatment plan for a client. Treatment plans generally flow out of and are the next step to be completed after the assessment (see chapter 11).

The process by which Weeks used the assessment information to create her recommendations for Madie is complex; she drew on her knowledge of child development, psychopathologies, and family practice theories, as well as her clinical experiences with adjudicated youths; that is, she used her clinical expertise to infer from the assessment information and make decisions about needed treatments.

All practitioners must rely on their clinical judgment when they move from assessment to intervention; this is not a completely objective nor a linear process but it is a process that can follow the steps of evidence-based practice described in previous chapters of this book.

Here are some guidelines for using the assessment information to construct treatment recommendations. Begin by reviewing information on the presenting problems. Focus on resolution of the presenting problems (in Madie's case, running away). Next, focus on resolving associated problems (in Madie's case, depression and identity disturbance). Ask yourself what interventions are needed to resolve these problems. Focus on the other dimensions (e.g., developmental context of the client's life, history, family situation) and decide what is affecting the presenting problems and how that needs to be considered in the treatment process. Consider all the assessment information in terms of resolving the problems, and then construct a set of recommendations.

## ASSESSMENT REPORT: THE WILLIAMS FAMILY

The Williamses are an African American family of four: Will (father), Lisa (mother), Tiffany (daughter), and George (son). They reside at 1200 Wagon St., Hays, Texas.

The following assessment information is based on two interviews with the parents on February 7 and 9; one interview with the whole family on February 11; and two separate interviews with the daughter, Tiffany, while she was in detention on February 6 and 7 at the youth shelter of Travis County. Behavioral observations of the family carrying out a task and scores from the administration of the family environment scales, a standardized measure, were also used to determine the family's overall level of functioning. All interviews took place in the shelter except for one of the parental interviews, which took place in the family home.

### Presenting Problem

Tiffany Williams, a fourteen-year-old female detained at the shelter for stealing two packs of cigarettes and awaiting a detention hearing, was assigned to the social worker, Peggy Weeks. On February 6, 1991, Judge Lyndon L. Roberts ordered Weeks to assess the family and be prepared to recommend placement in the best interest of Tiffany Williams, a juvenile.

### Individual Characteristics

Tiffany Williams, a fourteen-year-old African American female, is the older child in a family of two children. She is in the eighth grade at Johnson High School. Mrs. Williams reports that Tiffany has never failed a grade or had any significant academic problems. She has consistently been on the honor roll at school. There are no reports of significant behavior problems until age twelve, when Tiffany became openly defiant of authority and began to lie persistently and be truant from school. Mr. and Mrs. Williams also stated that Tiffany's "feelings are easily hurt, and that in the past she has allowed herself to be easily taken advantage of by friends just so she wouldn't lose them." Mrs. Williams believes that Tiffany became "depressed" about age thirteen and began stealing at about age fourteen. Tiffany reportedly has run away from home overnight on two occasions since age thirteen. At age fourteen, she left home with a boyfriend for five days. Police picked her up, she returned home, and she promised not to leave again.

From reports of both parents, the onset of Tiffany's behavior problems at age twelve occurred when she found out from the Jeffersons, Mrs. Williams' parents, that Lisa Williams was not Tiffany's biological mother. This incident was reported to have happened during a family argument where some "pretty mean things were said." Madeline Jones is Tiffany's biological mother. Her whereabouts are unknown, and she has not been heard from since she left Tiffany at the age of eighteen months with her father, Mr. Williams. Less than a year after Tiffany found out about the identity of her biological mother, she allegedly started a fire in her grandmother's house that destroyed the house and injured her grandmother and her brother.

Lisa Williams is a thirty-six-year-old African American female. She is both verbal and intelligent. She is stepmother to Tiffany and biological mother of George, Tiffany's brother. Mrs. Williams has cared for Tiffany since she was eighteen months old, and she states that she "loved her like her own." Williams works as an assistant at the Austin library and is the primary financial support for the family. She reports that she is currently estranged from her family, the Jeffersons, in Dallas because of the fire at her parent's house, their negative comments, and their attitude toward Tiffany and Will. She states that those family relationships are very stressful, but she truly believes her mother and father have misjudged the situation and that the fire was started by accident because Tiffany was trying to hide her smoking from them. Mrs. Williams graduated from high school and attended college, where she met her husband.

Will Williams is a highly articulate, thirty-five-year-old African American. He is the biological father of both Tiffany and George. Williams graduated from high school and attended college. He played football through college and for eight years as a professional for the L.A. Bulldogs. Williams has worked only part-time outside the home in the past five years. He provides child care and attends to the needs of the family at home. He began his current job as a part-time night stocker at a grocery store six months ago.

George Williams is an eleven-year-old African American male. He is in the fifth grade at Travis Elementary School, is consistently on the honor roll, and has won several trophies for his athletic abilities in baseball. He has a speech impediment, a stutter, which his parents report he has always had. He receives speech therapy at his school. He also reports feeling very close to his sister and being worried that she "may be in very big trouble."

### Family Background and History

Mr. and Mrs. Williams met in Dallas, Texas, nineteen years ago while attending Dallas College. They have been married for thirteen years. Mr. Williams was previously involved in a relationship with Megan Jones, with whom he fathered one child, Tiffany, in 1977. When Tiffany was eighteen months old, Megan Jones disappeared, leaving Tiffany in the care of her father, who subsequently married Lisa Jefferson shortly thereafter. The family moved to Los Angeles in 1979, after Mr. Williams was recruited out of college to play football for the L.A. Bulldogs, a semiprofessional team. Their son was born one year later, in 1980. Mrs. Williams worked as an assistant in a library while Mr. Williams played football for eight years. As a result of numerous knee injuries, Mr. Williams was dropped from the team in December 1988, and the family moved to Dallas, Texas, where they lived with Mr. and Mrs. John Jefferson, Mrs. Williams's parents. Mr. Williams held odd jobs, mostly as a security guard, and Mrs. Williams worked at a Dallas library.

Nine months after moving in with the Jeffersons, a fire burned the house completely down. Mrs. Jefferson and George were injured in the fire but recovered in a few weeks. Tiffany was arrested, placed on probation for arson, and sent to Buckner Children's Home for two weeks. Tiffany appears to have been arrested because the fire was started in or near her room, and the Jeffersons believed that she had set the fire with a lighter later found on her person. Tiffany and her parents maintain that she did not start the fire on purpose but that it did result from her smoking in her room. Relations between the Williamses and the Jeffersons deteriorated, and one year after moving to Dallas, the family decided to move to Hays. Mr. Williams moved first and found a job at a grocery store. He later took a similar job at another grocery chain. Lisa, Tiffany, and George followed three months later, after Lisa was able to get a job at the Hays library.

## Social Support and Current Living Arrangements

The Williamses live in a single-family home that they own. The home is spacious, with three bedrooms and two baths, and the social worker noted that it is tidy and well kept. Both Tiffany and George have their own rooms, and the home is enriched with music, art, and literature that Mrs. Williams provides. The family home is located in a middle-class neighborhood with parks and recreational facilities. The neighborhood is well integrated ethnically, and the family reports that the neighbors are friendly with one another. Mr. and Mrs. Williams socialize with one couple in the neighborhood and know several others. Both Tiffany and George state that they have friends that live on their street.

The family is very involved in the local Protestant church, and the parents state that religion is important to the family life. Mr. Williams says the minister had been a comfort to them during this "trial with Tiffany" and that several people in the church had offered emotional support to them.

Both Mr. and Mrs. Williams are involved in several civic and recreational groups. They belong to and attend meetings at the neighborhood association. Mr. Williams belongs to a fraternity and frequently plays sports with a "few of the men" from that group. Mrs. Williams loves African art and serves on the committee of the local art museum. Both children have been active in sports; George is especially involved in baseball and Tiffany in track. Family members report that they have been satisfied with the quality of their social relationships and that they like their neighborhood.

Both Mr. and Mrs. Williams have expressed regret, however, that they were not close to their extended family members and hope that something could be done about the problem between Mrs. Williams and her parents in the future.

The family at this time has adequate financial resources and expressed no concern for their financial well-being. Mr. Williams, however, expressed a concern that he should make plans to develop a new career now that he has left football.

## Results of the Family Environment Scale

The Family Environment Scale (FES), a standardized measure, was used to assess the family's social climate as it compares with a normative group. The social worker administered the measure to each family member during the family interview on February 11. The results from appear to be valid and consistent with the social worker's observations of the family (tables 8.4 and 8.5, figure 8.8).

According to the FES scores, this is a relationship-oriented family that also encourages personal growth. They also scored above average in

**Table 8.4**   FES Raw Scores on Subscales

|  | Mother | Father | Daughter | Son |
|---|---|---|---|---|
| **Relationship Dimensions** | | | | |
| Cohesion (C) | 9 | 8 | 8 | 9 |
| Expressiveness (Ex) | 3 | 5 | 6 | 5 |
| Conflict (Con) | 1 | 4 | 2 | 1 |
| **Personal Growth Dimensions** | | | | |
| Independence (Ind) | 5 | 8 | 4 | 7 |
| Achievement Orientation (AO) | 7 | 9 | 7 | 6 |
| Intellectual-Cultural Orientation (ICO) | 7 | 9 | 9 | 7 |
| Achievement-Recreational (ARO) | 8 | 7 | 7 | 8 |
| Moral-Religious Emphasis (MRE) | 7 | 6 | 5 | 6 |
| **System Maintenance Dimensions** | | | | |
| Organization (Org) | 8 | 5 | 7 | 7 |
| Control (Ctl) | 5 | 8 | 7 | 7 |
| Family Incongruence Score: 13.66 | | | | |

**Table 8.5**   FES Raw Scores on Subscales

|  | Mrs. Williams | Mr. Williams | Madie | Player |
|---|---|---|---|---|
| C | 90 | 80 | 80 | 90 |
| Ex | 30 | 50 | 60 | 50 |
| Con | 10 | 40 | 20 | 10 |
| Ind | 50 | 80 | 40 | 70 |
| AO | 70 | 90 | 70 | 60 |
| ICO | 70 | 90 | 90 | 70 |
| ARO | 80 | 70 | 70 | 80 |
| MRE | 70 | 60 | 50 | 60 |
| Org | 80 | 50 | 70 | 70 |
| Ctl | 50 | 80 | 70 | 70 |

achievement and support orientation. The family incongruence score indicates that they are a highly congruent family; they answered fifty-two questions out of ninety exactly the same. Given the results, the below-average score for Tiffany on the independence subscale can be explained as normal for an adolescent trying to master developmental goals of separation and individuation.

All family members' scores indicate a high degree of cohesiveness. They appear to be very committed to and supportive to one another. Their feelings of togetherness as a family are above average. Mr. Williams described his family as his "heartbeat." When he said this, the whole family embraced one another.

**Figure 8.8** FES Scores Graphed

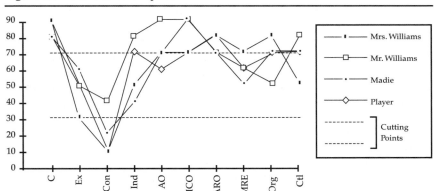

Mr. Williams and both children report an average feeling of openness; they can express their feelings openly and discuss their personal problems. Mrs. Williams, however, scored considerably below average on the expressiveness subscale, which is consistent with her observed quieter demeanor; she was the least outspoken and did not offer any information without being asked a direct question. Mrs. Williams and both children scored below average on the conflicts subscale, which indicates a lack of aggression or fighting in the family. All members agreed that "if there's a disagreement in our family, we try hard to smooth things over and keep the peace"; that they "do not fight a lot in our family"; that "family members do not get so angry that they throw things"; and that "family members do not hit each other." This family appears to show a preference for conflict avoidance and agreement. The social worker also observed these patterns during the family interview; family members were quick to come to the aid and defense of one another.

Except for the independence subscale, this family measured above average in encouraging personal growth. The family measured well above average on the achievement orientation subscale. Their dedication to school and sports clearly illustrates this pattern. They all report that it is important to be the best at whatever they do, and "work before play is the rule in our family." Given these results, the below-average score for Tiffany on the independence subscale may be related to her own personal turmoil over her identity and recent psychosocial stressors. It may also reflect Tiffany's own sense of powerlessness over the situation and her level of depression.

The family scores were average for the intellectual and cultural orientation subscale, which is consistent with the social worker's observations of their experience. The Williamses are very culturally aware and proud of their African heritage. They report that they have been discriminated against because of their race but continue to encourage their children to be proud of and to preserve their African heritage. Their political and social interests, however, do not go much beyond their immediate life. The average subscale measure is consistent with the social worker's own observations and conversations with them. The Williamses are heavily involved in their children's athletic activities, which is indicated in the above and well above average active recreational orientation subscale measures. Mr. Williams reports that he is Tiffany's trainer for track.

The Williamses range from average to well above average on the moral-religious Emphasis subscale. The family attends church on a regular basis and reports that they say prayers and believe that sin will be punished and that there is a heaven and hell.

This family is highly organized and structured. Their activities and responsibilities are planned and clear. The social worker's observation while in their home on one occasion is consistent with these outcomes. Their home is neat and orderly, as are their persons. When Mr. Williams observed his daughter being escorted from detention to the courtroom, his first comment to her was, "Baby, look at your hair—why didn't you comb it?"

The measures on the control subscale also fell into the well-above-average range. Mr. Williams, who is clearly the head of the house, scored above average on this subscale. The score appears to reflect both his cultural and religious beliefs concerning the gender roles of men in a family. All family members agreed that Mr. Williams makes most of the final decisions. They agreed that there are set ways of doing things at home and that there is a strong emphasis on following rules in the family.

## Recommendation to the Court

The social worker recommends that Tiffany be returned to her family. They are able to and have in the past provided needed support and structure for her. Tiffany's decline can be traced directly to several major events in her life: at the age of ten, she and her family moved from Los Angeles to Dallas, a major disruption that required a great deal of adjustment. At that time, Tiffany also discovered that Lisa Williams was not her biological mother, which caused a major shift in her self-image and in their relationship. She subsequently developed several behavior problems. Next, her grandparents' house burned down, injuring her grandmother and her brother. Tiffany was arrested, charged with arson, placed on probation, and briefly removed from her home when she was sent to the Buckner Children's Home. These events confirmed Tiffany's distorted beliefs that the Jeffersons were correct: "she wasn't good enough to be Lisa's daughter." To complicate matters, Tiffany entered adolescence at this time.

It is believed that Tiffany may suffer from depression associated with these stressors. Tiffany will benefit from individual and family counseling that helps the family better address her behavior problems. She needs a safe place to explore and talk about her feelings of loss at suddenly becoming a stepchild, anger toward her parents for keeping her ignorant of her biological mother, anger about the events that occurred in Dallas, and shame over her behavior in the past two years. It is believed that the family also needs help in adjusting to their stresses, their extended family conflicts, and the issues regarding Tiffany's runaways, stealing, and identity problems. To facilitate Tiffany's adjustment in the home, the social worker also recommended that she attend an alternative school or day treatment program so that she can receive the extra support and the structure needed to resolve her difficulties. She can do this best with the loving support of her family.

## SUMMARY

This chapter has reviewed several methods for conducting a family assessment and has summarized key concepts and issues to consider in evaluating family systems. We discussed selected assessment and developmental frameworks for understanding the normative characteristics of families, as well as techniques for gathering information on families. Specific assessment methods covered include empricially derived family assessment models, standardized measures, interviewing techniques, family-task observations, family goal recording, graphic problem-oriented, and specific methods for assessing family strengths. Finally, this chapter demonstrated how to move from assessment to intervention by providing family assessment report, which illustrated how to integrate multiple sources of information into a family assessment and how to create an intervention plan from this information.

## STUDY QUESTIONS

1. What are five key characteristics of family systems?
2. How does whole-systems measurement instruments help family practitioners?
3. Develop a family genogram on yourself or a friend.
4. Where are you presently in the family life cycle and what is the next stage of development for you and your family?

## WEB SITES

*American Association of Marriage and Family Therapy*
www.aamft.org

*Savannah Family Institute*
www.difficult.net
*Minuchin Center for Family Therapy*
www.minuchincenter.org/

## REFERENCES

Abidin, R. R. (1983). *Parenting stress index manual*. Charlottesville, VA: Pediatric Psychology Press.

American Psychiatric Association. (1994). *Diagnostic and statistical manual of mental disorders*. Washington, DC: Author.

Aponte, H., & Van Dusen, J. M. (1981). Structural family therapy. In A. S. Gurman & D. P. Knirsken (Eds.), *Handbook of family therapy* (pp. 45–72). New York: Brunner/Mazel.

Barrera, M., Jr. (1986). Distinctions between social support concepts, measures, and models. *American Journal of Community Psychology, 14*, 413–416.

Barrera, M., Jr., Sandler, I. N., & Ramsey, T. B. (1981). Preliminary development of a scale of social support: Studies on college students. *American Journal of Community Psychology, 9*, 435–447.

Baer, J. C., & Schmitz, M. F. (2007). Ethnic differences in trajectories of family cohesion for Mexican American and non-Hispanic white adolescents. *Journal of Youth and Adolescence, 36*, 583–592.

Beavers, W. R. (1981). A systems model of family for family therapists. *Journal of Marital and Family Therapy, 7*, 229–307.

Beavers, W. R. (1982). Healthy, midrange, and severely dysfunctional families. In F. Walsh (Ed.), *Normal family processes* (pp. 00–00). New York: Guilford Press.

Beavers, W. R., & Hampson, R. B. (1990). *Successful families: Assessment and intervention*. New York: Norton.

Beavers, W. R., & Hampson, R. B. (2000). The Beavers Systems Model of family functioning. *Journal of Family Therapy, 22*, 128–133.

Beavers, W. R., & Voller, M. N. (1983). Family models: Comparing the Olson circumplex model with the Beavers systems model. *Family Models, 22*, 85–98.

Becvar, D. S., & Becvar, R. J. (1988). *Family therapy: A systemic integration*. Needham Heights, MA: Allyn and Bacon.

Boake, C., & Salmon, P. G. (1983). Demographic correlates and factor structure of the Family Environment Scale. *Journal of Clinical Psychology, 39*, 95–100.

Bowen, M. (1976). Theory in the practice of psychotherapy. In P. J. Guerin (Ed.), *Family therapy: Theory and practice* (pp. 24–90). New York: Gardner.

Bowen, M. (1978). *Family therapy in clinical practice*. New York: Aronson.

Brill, N. (1988). *Working with people* (3rd ed.). New York: Longman.

Brock, G. W., & Barnard, C. P. (1988). *Procedures in family therapy*. Needham Heights, MA: Allyn and Bacon.

Buckley, W. (1967). *Sociology and modern systems theory*. Englewood Cliffs, NJ: Prentice Hall.

Carter, B., & McGoldrick, M. (2005). *The expanded family lifecycle: Individual, family and social perspectives*. Boston: Allyn and Bacon.

Chipuer, H. M., & Villegas, T. (2001). Comparing the second-order factor structure of the Family Environment Scale across husbands' and wives' perceptions of their family environment. *Family Process, 40,* 187–199.

Compton, B., & Galaway, B. (1989). *Social work process* (4th ed.). Belmont, CA: Wadsworth.

Constantine, L. L. (1986). *Family paradigms: The practice of theory in family therapy*. New York: Guilford Press.

Corcoran, K., & Fischer, J. (2007) *Measures for clinical practice and research—A source book: Couples and families*. New York: Oxford University Press.

Craddock, A. E. (2001). Relationship between family structure and family functioning: A test of Tiesel and Olson's Circumplex Model. *Journal of Family Studies, 7,* 29–39.

Darro, D., Abrahams, N., Casey, K., Rose, S., McCurdy, K., & Brown, L. (1990). *Parent program evaluation manual*. Chicago: National Committee for Prevention of Child Abuse.

Dinkmeyer, D., & McKay, G. D. (1983). *Systematic training for effective parenting: The parents' guide*. St. Paul, MN: American Guidance Service.

Early, T. J. (2001). Measures for practice with families from a strengths perspective. *Families in Society: The Journal of Contemporary Human Services, 82,* 225–232.

Epstein, N. B., Baldwin, L. M., & Bishop, D. S. (1982). *McMaster family assessment device (FAD) manual (version 3)*. Providence, RI: Brown University/Butler Hospital Family Research Program.

Fisch, R., Watzlawick, P., & Segal, L. (1982). *The tactics of change*. San Francisco: Jossey-Bass.

Fleuridas, C., Nelson, T. S., & Rosenthal, D. M. (1986). The evolution of circular questions: Training family therapists. *Journal of Marital and Family Therapy, 12,* 113–127.

Fleuridas, C., Rosenthal, D. M., Leigh, E. K., & Leigh, T. E. (1990). Family goal recording: An adaption of goal attainment scaling for enhancing family therapy assessment. *Journal of Marital and Family Therapy, 16,* 389–406.

Foley, V. D. (1989). Family therapy. In R. J. Corsini & D. Welding (Eds.), *Current psychotherapies* (4th ed., pp. 455–502). Itasca, IL: Peacock.

Franklin, C. (2002). Becoming a strengths fact finder. *American Association of Marital and Family Therapists Magazine*.

Franklin, C., & Jordan, C. (1999). *Family practice: Brief systems methods for social work*. Pacific Grove, CA: Brooks/Cole.

Franklin, C., & Jordan, C. (2008). Effective family therapy: Guidelines for practice. In A. R. Roberts & G. J. Greene (Eds.), *Social workers desk reference* (pp. 256–262). New York: Oxford University Press.

Franklin, C., & Streeter, C. L. (1993). Validity of the 3-D circumplex model for family assessment. *Research on Social Work Practice, 3*, 258–275.

Franklin, C., Streeter, C. L., & Springer, D. W. (2001). Validity of the FACES IV family assessment measure. *Research on Social Work Practice, 11*, 576–596.

Franko, D. L., Thompson, D., Bauserman, R., Affenito, S. G., Striegel-Moore, R. (2008). What's love got to do with it? Family cohesion and healthy eating behaviors in adolescent girls. *International Journal of Eating Disorders, 41*, 360–367.

Fredman, N., & Sherman, R. (1987). *Handbook of measurements for marital and family therapy.* New York: Brunner/Mazel.

Gambrill, E. (2006). Evidence-based practice and policy: Choices ahead. *Research on Social Work Practice, 16*, 338–357.

Garrett, A. (1991). *Interviewing: Its principles and methods* (3rd ed.). Milwaukee, WI: Family Service America.

Gilgun, J. F. (2001). CASPARS: New tools for assessing client risks and strengths. *Families in Society: The Journal of Contemporary Human Services, 82*, 450–459.

Goldenberg, I., & Goldenberg, H. (1990). *Family therapy: An overview.* Pacific Grove, CA: Brooks/Cole.

Graybeal, C. (2001). Strengths-based social work assessment: Transforming the dominant paradigm. *Families in Society: The Journal of Contemporary Human Services, 82*, 233–242.

Green, R. G., Harris, R. N., Forte, J. A., & Robinson, M. (1991). Evaluating FACES III and the Circumplex Model: 2,440 families. *Family Process, 30*, 55–73.

Grier, R., Morris, L., & Taylor, L. (2001). Assessment strategies for school-based mental health counseling. *Journal of School Health, 71*, 467–469.

Grotevant, H. D., & Carlson, C. I. (1989). *Family assessment: A guide to methods and measures.* New York: Guilford Press.

Haley, J. (1990). *Problem solving therapy.* San Francisco: Jossey-Bass.

Hepworth, D. H., & Larsen, J. A. (1989). *Direct social work practice* (3rd ed.). Belmont, CA: Wadsworth.

Hilsenroth, M. J., Ackerman, S. J., Blagys, M. D., Baumann, B. D., Baity, M. R., Smith, S. R., et al. (2000). Reliability and validity of *DSM*-IV axis V. *American Journal of Psychiatry, 157*, 1858–1863.

Ho, M. (1986). *Family therapy with ethnic minorities.* Newbury Park, CA: Sage.

Holman, A. M. (1983). *Family assessment: Tools for understanding and intervention.* Beverly Hills, CA: Sage.

Jacob, T., & Tennenbaum, D. L. (1988). *Family assessment: Rationale, methods, and future directions.* New York: Plenum.

Janzen, C., Harris, O., Jordan, C., & Franklin, C. (2005). *Family treatment in social work practice* (3rd ed.). Itasca, IL: Peacock.

Johnson, H. C. (1987). Biologically based deficit in the identified patent: Indications for psychoeducational strategies. *Journal of Marital and Family Therapy, 13*, 337–348.

Kiresuk, T. J., & Sherman, R. E. (1968). Goal attainment scaling: A general method for evaluating community mental health programs. *Community Mental Health Journal, 4,* 443–453.

Kiresuk, T. J., Stelmachers, E. T., & Schultz, S. K. (1982). Quality assurance and goal attainment scaling. *Professional Psychology, 13,* 145–1522.

Lohan, J. A., & Murphy, S. A. (2007). Bereaved mothers' marital status and family functioning after a child's sudden violent death: A preliminary study. *Journal of Loss and Trauma, 12,* 333–347.

Miller, I. W., Ryan, C. E., Keitner, G. I., Bishop, D. S., & Epstein, N. B. (2000a). Factor analyses of the family assessment device, by Ridenour, Daley, & Reich. *Family Process, 39,* 141–145.

Miller, I. W., Ryan, C. E., Keitner, G. I., Bishop, D. S., & Epstein, N. B. (2000b). Why fix what isn't broken? A rejoinder to Ridenour, Daley. *Family Process, 39,* 381–385.

Minuchin, S. (1974). *Families and family therapy.* Cambridge, MA: Harvard University Press.

Minuchin, S., & Fishman, H. C. (1982). *Family therapy techniques.* Cambridge: Harvard University Press.

Moos, R. H., & Moos, B. S. (1986). *Family environment scale manual* (2nd ed.). Palo Alto, CA: Consulting Psychologist Press.

Moos, R. H., & Spinrad, S. (1984). *The social climate scales: An annotated bibliography.* Palo Alto, CA: Consulting Psychologist Press.

O'Brien, C., & Bruggen, P. (1985). Our personal and professional lives: Learning positive connotation and circular questioning. *Family Process, 24,* 311–322.

Olson, D. H. (1985). Commentary: Struggling with congruence across theoretical models and methods. *Family Process, 24,* 203–207.

Olson, D. H. (1986). Circumplex model VII: Validation studies and FACES III. *Family Process, 26,* 337–351.

Olson, D. H. (1991). Commentary: Three-dimensional (3-D) circumplex model and revised scoring of FACES III. *Family Process, 30,* 74–79.

Olson, D. H. (2000). Circumplex model of marital and family systems. *Journal of Family Therapy, 22,* 144–166.

Olson, D. H., Gorall, D. M., & Tiesel, J. W. (2007). Faces IV manual. Minneapolis, MN: Life Innovations.

Olson, D. H., McCubbing, H. I., Barnes, H., Larsen, A., Muxen, M., & Wilson, M. (1985). *Family inventories: Inventories in a national survey of families across the family life cycle* (rev. ed.). St. Paul: University of Minnesota, Family Social Science.

Olson, D. H., Sprenkle, D. H., & Russel, C. S. (1979). Circumplex model of marital and family systems: Cohesion and adaptability dimensions, family types and clinical applications. *Family Process, 18,* 3–28.

Olson, D. H., & Tiesel, J. (1993). *FACES III: Linear scoring and interpretation.* St. Paul: University of Minnesota, Family Social Science.

Procidano, M., & Heller, K. (1983). Measures of perceived social support from friends and from family: Three validational studies. *American Journal of Community Psychology, 11,* 1–24.

Ridenour, T. A., Daley, J. G., & Reich, W. (2000). Further evidence that the family assessment device should be reorganized: Response to Miller and colleagues. *Family Process, 39,* 375–381.

Schulman, L. (1992). *The skills of helping individuals and groups.* Itasca, IL: Peacock.

Shepard, M., & Campbell, J. A. (1992). The abusive behavior inventory: A measure of psychological and physical abuse. *Journal of Interpersonal Violence, 7,* 291–305.

Simon, C. E., McNeil, J. S., Franklin, C., & Cooperman, A. (1991). The family and schizophrenia: Toward a psychoeducational approach. *Families in Society, 72,* 323–334.

Skinner, H., Steinhauer, P., & Santo-Barbara. (1983). The family assessment measure. *Canadian Journal of Community Mental Health, 2,* 91–105.

Skinner, H., Steinhauer, P., & Sitarenios, G. (2000). Family Assessment Measure (FAM) and process model of family functioning. *Journal of Family Therapy, 22,* 190–210.

Streeter, C. L., & Franklin, C. (1992). Defining and measuring social support: Guidelines for social work practitioners. *Research on Social Work Practice, 42,* 81–98.

Stuart, R. B. (1980). *Helping couples change: A social learning approach to marital therapy.* Champaign, IL: Research Press.

Thomas, V., & Olson, D. H. (1993). Problem families and the Circumplex Model: Observational assessment using the clinical rating scale (CRS). *Journal of Marital and Family Therapy, 19,* 159–175.

Thomas, V., & Zechowski, T. J. (2000). A test of the circumplex model of marital and family systems using the clinical rating scale. *Journal of Marital and Family Therapy, 26,* 523–534.

Toulitas, J., Perlmutter, B. F., & Straus, M. A. (2000). *Handbook of family measurement techniques.* Thousand Oaks, CA: Sage.

Tracy, E. M., & Whittaker, J. K. (1990). The social network map: Assessing social support in clinical practice. *Families in Society, 71,* 461–470.

Uruk, A. C., Sayger, T. V., & Cogdal, P. A. (2007). Examining the influence of family cohesion and adaptability on trauma symptoms and psychological well-being. *Journal of College Student Psychotherapy, 22,* 51–63.

Vaux, A. (1982). *Measures of three levels of social support: Resources, behaviors and feelings.* Unpublished manuscript, Southern Illinois University.

Vaux, A. (1988). *Social support: Theory, research and intervention.* New York: Praeger.

Watzlawick, P., Beavin, J. H., & Jackson, D. D. (1967). *Pragmatics of human communication.* New York: Norton.

Watzlawick, P., Weakland, J., & Fisch, R. (1974). *Change: Principles of problem formation and problem resolution.* New York: Norton.

Wood, K. M., & Geismar, L. L. (1989). *Families at risk: Treating the multiproblem family.* New York: Human Science Press.

# CHAPTER 9

# Assessing Families
# Who Are Multistressed

## Catheleen Jordan, Ski Hunter, Joan Rycraft,
## Vikki Vandiver, and Iran Barrera

## INTRODUCTION

This chapter addresses families involved with oppressive situations, multiple systems and environmental stress. Families reviewed here include families of gay and lesbian persons, as well as families experiencing child maltreatment and those experiencing health problems. Commonalities between these seemingly diverse populations include external stressors that impinge on individuals and their families. This chapter summarizes the issues and external stressors and facing gay and lesbian persons, as well as the stressors and experiences of families with child maltreatment and health challenges. We also describe specific assessment methods that a practitioner can use when working with these groups.

## GAY AND LESBIAN FAMILIES

Gay and lesbian families are defined as including at least one lesbian or gay adult or two or more adults with a same-sex orientation who are rearing a child. The current knowledge focuses on couples' friendship and on lesbian and gay couples with children (Allen & Demo, 1995).

### Friendships and Couples

Although they are members of families of origin and extended families, gay and lesbian persons claim other families composed of friends and partners. These families, also called "created families" (Weinstock, 1998) or "chosen families" (Weston, 1997), develop through voluntary choice and love. Although they are the major support system for most gay and lesbian persons, racial and ethnic group members may not place as much value on others who are outside their biological families (D'Augelli & Garnets, 1995). Families of choice typically provide benefits that families of origins do: protection, socialization, belongingness, a source for self-esteem, and a sense of identity (Matthews & Lease, 2000).

After self-identifying as lesbian, gay, or bisexual (LGB) and establishing friendships with LGB persons, individuals usually begin to seek involvement in same-sex or bisexual relationships, sometimes referred to in the literature as linkups. *Linkup* refers to the desire to be linked with someone of the same sex and a deepening commitment to a new identity (Savin-Williams, 1998). Gay and lesbian couples include persons who are emotional and usually sexual partners. Partners are also most likely the central focus of one's chosen family (James & Murphy, 1998).

Gay and lesbian couples are diverse. For example, some persons participate in more than one couple link at a time and make a distinction between primary and nonprimary links (Hostetler & Coher, 1997). Some couples may participate in a public "marriage" and some in a private commitment ceremony. Some couples wear rings or show their commitment in other ways or in no way. Variable close-couple configurations exist, including partners who commit to each other but do not live with each other, partners who consider themselves as a couple but have more than one significant partner, or partners who coexist with heterosexual marriages (James & Murphy, 1998). Shernoff (1995) reported that the diverse patterns in gay couples include those who are sexually exclusive; primarily sexually exclusive; sexually nonexclusive but in an unacknowledged, open relationship; sexually nonexclusive but in an acknowledged, open relationship; and linked with nonsexual lovers.

Given the diversity among same-sex couples, asking couples to define their configuration is the best way to know what it is (Hostetler & Coher, 1997). Another source of diversity is what gay and lesbian couples call themselves (e.g., partners, lovers). It is also best to ask each individual couple what they prefer to call themselves (Berger, 1990).

**Satisfaction and Other Positive Characteristics of Same-Sex Couples.** Being in a couple provides benefits for gay and lesbian persons including increased self-esteem and a sense of well-being (Wayment & Peplau, 1995). Many studies have reported no discrepancies between lesbian and gay couples and heterosexual couples in quality (Kurdek, 1994, 1995), closeness, adjustments (Kurdek, 1995), or satisfaction (Kurdek, 1994). In some studies, gay and lesbian couples experienced higher levels of functioning than did heterosexual couples (Kurdek, 1995). Lesbian couples in particular reported higher levels of cohesion, adaptability, equality, and satisfaction than did heterosexual couples (Rosenbluth & Steil, 1995).

Bryant and Demian (1994) reported that, compared with gay men, more lesbians rated the quality of their link at the highest level (47 percent versus 36 percent). Lesbian couples, compared with gay couples, also reported stronger liking for their partner; greater satisfaction, trust, and shared decision making; stronger intrinsic desire for involvement in their link; and less external motivations for involvement in their link

(Kurdek, 1988). Several studies also showed that satisfaction was higher in lesbian couples than in gay couples because of the higher value lesbians attributed to their relationships or to the rewards attained from them (Kurdek, 1991). Kurdek (1988) thought that the high ratings of lesbians for interpersonal factors such as caring and sensitivity to the needs and feelings of their partners might also partly account for their higher satisfaction levels.

**Duration of Same-Sex Links.** Without marriage and divorce records on lesbian and gay couples, the longevity of most of their links is not determinable (Peplau, 1993). From the few studies that have reported on longevity, the best information on breakup rates comes from the Blumstein and Schwartz (1983) landmark study of 3,574 married couples, 642 cohabiting couples, 957 gay couples, and 772 lesbian couples. When the survey began, all groups had comparable expectations of staying together; over eighteen months, one in five couples broke up. The percentage of breakups by group were highest among lesbian couples (22 percent), compared with gay (16 percent), cohabiting heterosexual (17 percent), and married heterosexual (4 percent) couples. Several other studies also reported a higher rate of breakups for lesbian couples. The Teichner Poll (Results, 1989) reported a median duration of 2.5 years for gay couples, compared with 1.8 years for lesbian couples. Weinberg, Williams, and Pryor (1994) also found that lesbian linkups were shorter in duration than other linkups (heterosexual, bisexual, and gay). Kurdek (1997) reported that, over a five-year period, breakup rates were comparable to those found by Blumstein and Schwartz (1983): 7 percent for heterosexual couples, 14 percent for gay couples, and 16 percent for lesbian couples. Kurdek (1997) also pointed out, however, that over the five years of study, 86 percent of gay couples and 84 percent of lesbian couples were still together. Several studies found lesbian and gay couples together for ten years or longer (e.g., Berger, 1996). Older lesbian and gay persons reported in anecdotal accounts linkups of twenty to thirty years' duration or longer (Clunis & Green, 2000).

**Breakups of Couples.** Every couple is vulnerable to an eventual breakup, and internal, interpersonal, and external factors may play a role in any breakup. Internal factors such as personality and maturity and interpersonal factors such as sexual incompatibility and arguments about money can contribute to difficulties for any couple. External factors, that is, those in the wider social context beyond the individual and interpersonal contexts, also can affect couples (Kitzinger & Coyle, 1995). An example of such a factor is the intrusion of work responsibilities. Lesbian and gay couples, however, face additional, unique external challenges to their links.

**External Challenges.**    There are many external challenges to gay and lesbian couples, including heterosexism. Lesbian and gay couples exist in a climate of heterosexism, defined as "the ideological system that denies, denigrates, and stigmatizes any nonheterosexual form of behavior, identity, relationship, or community" (Herek, 1995, p. 321). Society condemns the love the couple members have for each other, their sexuality, and their partnerships (Kitzinger & Coyle, 1995). If the couple expresses affection openly, they risk harassment that ranges from minor but humiliating insults (e.g., name-calling) to threats of death (James & Murphy, 1998). The first private company to offer employees domestic partnership benefits was the *Village Voice*, in 1982, and Berkeley, California, was the first city to do so, in 1984. Vermont was the first state to extend domestic partnership benefits to its public employees in 1995, and Hawaii extended these rights to all the state's same-sex couples in 1997. Now many states offer domestic partnership benefits to state employees, and a handful of other states offer domestic partnership registration to same-sex couples (see http://www.nolo.com/legal-encyclopedia/article-29916.html).

Lack of support from families and heterosexual friends is a second external challenge. A married heterosexual couple can usually count on congratulations, blessings, presents, and other tangible and intangible support from families and friends, beginning at the time they declare themselves as a serious couple. Lesbian and gay couples rarely receive anything close to the same degree of support. If they announce their partnership to their families, the reaction is often one of overt hostility (Bryant & Demian, 1994). Instead of celebrating the link, families often deny or trivialize it (Serovich, Skeen, Walters, & Robinson, 1993). Lesbian couples in most racial and ethnic communities experience a collusion of silence, ambivalence, and denial (Greene & Boyd-Franklin, 1996). If a lesbian or gay couple is in trouble, neither families nor heterosexual friends are likely to encourage the couple to work out the problems (Greene, 1997).

Hindrances in lesbian and gay communities pose another external challenge. Although friendships and support in the lesbian and gay community are valuable resources for couples (Weston, 1997), the community can also pose a threat to them. Couples in the San Francisco sample studied by Weinberg et al. (1994) did not view the lesbian and gay community as promoting long-term linkups. In Meyer's (1990) study of gay couples, many men reported that they limited contact with bars and other aspects of the gay community because the primary support available is for individuals not couples. Blumstein and Schwartz (1983) observed that the more a lesbian couple was involved in the community, the more often they broke up because of the availability of alternative partners.

**Consequences of External Obstacles for Couples.**    The external obstacles discussed previously can create internal difficulties for lesbian and gay couples that interfere with, if not destroy, happiness. Hiding and passing and internalization of negative beliefs and images are two behaviors that contribute to such difficulties.

Hiding and passing is one strategy couples use. Many lesbian and gay couples make no public disclosures because of anticipated hostile responses. Instead, they engage in various subterfuges to hide their links such as not talking about their personal life, introducing partners as "friends," changing pronouns when talking about with whom they did things over the weekend, talking as if they were going out on heterosexual dates, inventing (if not acquiring) a fiancé (or fiancée) or spouse, and sleeping in different rooms when parents visit (Kitzinger & Coyle, 1995). Although hiding may not affect a couple's satisfaction directly (e.g., Eldridge & Gilbert, 1990), it is an endless struggle for the couple.

Caron and Ulin (1997) found that relationship quality was higher when both partners were open about their link, especially with their families of origin. There also were positive effects on couple satisfaction when families took such actions as asking the partner to family events and accepting the display of affection between the partners. Closeting exceedingly limits the potential social support available from one's family, as well as from friends and work associates. In response, the couple may intensify their dependency on each other (Patterson & Schwartz, 1994). Isolation from other lesbian and gay persons also means that there are no models to observe for alternate and more satisfying couple behaviors and maintenance. Partners can also experience a sense of unreality about their couple status because the link is real only to them (Patterson & Schwartz, 1994).

Negative cultural beliefs and images saturate the lives of lesbian and gay persons. They may be internalized to the point that couples conjecture that they cannot form enduring, happy linkups or that their linkups do not compare favorably to heterosexual linkups (Bryant & Demian, 1994). Same-gender couples also may play out negative expectations (Bryant & Demian, 1994) and experience guilt, fear, self-hatred, hatred of the partner, failing satisfaction, and painful endings (Murphy, 1994).

Some of the same external factors delineated here can be obstacles with similar consequences in gay and lesbian families with children. A brief summary of these families, their children, and the challenges they face is presented in the following section.

## Lesbian and Gay Couples with Children

Many lesbian and gay persons create and maintain a family life with children; however, it is impossible to know the number of such families (as well as of couples without children). Recent estimates suggest a range from 2 million to 8 million in the United States (Hare, 1994). These rates could result in 4 million to 14 million children being raised in same-sex households (Patterson, 1995).

Formerly, most children of gay or lesbian parents probably resulted from heterosexual unions; that is, the parents today probably married, had children, and later divorced. Today, there are more options such as foster care, adoption, surrogacy, and donor sperm insemination (McLeod & Crawford, 1998). For example, in the context of a same-gender linkup, lesbians may conceive children with donor sperm contributed by a friend, relative, or acquaintance or by an unknown person through a sperm bank. Lesbians might also conceive a child through planned sexual intercourse with a consenting male who may or may not play a part in the child's upbringing. Gay men may become fathers to children through sexual intercourse with a woman with whom they have agreed to share the parenting role. This could mean entering a parenting arrangement with a lesbian friend who gives birth to a child conceived with the gay man's sperm. Alternatively, arrangements could be made that include a lesbian and a gay man or a lesbian couple and a gay couple who agree to joint biological or custodial parenting. Gay men may also use paid surrogacy arrangements, but this route can often entail legal and moral dilemmas (McLeod & Crawford, 1998).

Lesbian and gay persons may also become parents through adoption or foster care (Patterson, 1992). However, state foster-care and adoption policies, regulations, and practices often either forbid or discourage gay and lesbian parenting or at least accord it low priority (Leiter, 1997). The exception may involve the placement of adolescents identified as gay or lesbian with gay or lesbian couples; however, the agencies' motives for this are ambiguous. Do they do this to provide support and role models for the child or to avoid placing any adolescent not identified as gay or lesbian in these homes? Even if successful with the foster home or adoptive course, a gay or lesbian couple cannot officially enter such an arrangement. Instead, the partners must negotiate which partner will be the foster or adoptive parent of record (Appleby & Anastas, 1998).

Although lesbian and gay couples experience many issues that heterosexual couples experience when pursuing options to have children, they face an additional set of issues because of their sexual orientation. This variable does not affect everything, but it can lead to different types of stressors for gay and lesbian families.

**Stressors.**   To bear and rear children, gay and lesbian persons must overcome many obstacles, the overriding obstacle being heterosexism. Gay and lesbian persons experience no validation for their families because of disapproval of their sexual orientation and coupling. They face beliefs that they should have no association with children and that they are unfit to raise children. Further, the belief is that their children, if they do raise them, will be psychologically and socially maladjusted, will suffer social stigmatization (Matthews & Lease, 2000), will be negatively affected in the development of their gender identity, or will turn out as gay or lesbian themselves (Shapiro, 1996). On a practical and economic level, the parents cannot procure insurance or file income tax as a family, and their children cannot receive social security benefits from both parents. In many states, lesbian and gay sexual partners violate laws and are highly vulnerable to negative outcomes in courts if there is a challenge to the custody of their children (Segal-Sklar, 1996). Because of these and many other outcomes of the heterosexist ideology, gay and lesbian persons may come to believe themselves that they are not fit for parenting (Matthews & Lease, 2000).

Once a lesbian couple decides to have a child, the issue arises of which partner will become pregnant and what will be the role of the partner who does not. The next big issue is how to achieve a pregnancy: The heterosexual sex way? The gay-friend donor way? The medical system way? For this last option, one hopes to find affirming health care providers, but this may not be an easy thing to do in many parts of the country. If a couple uses assisted insemination, other questions arise: Will the sperm donor be anonymous? Is there any future possibility of legal or social connection with the donor? Gay men are unlikely to experience these kinds of issues because they often know the women giving birth.

For gay and lesbian persons who have custody of their children, one of the biggest stressors they experience is the fear that, because of their social orientation, they will lose custody of or contact with their children (Bigner, 1996). This is a realistic fear, as many gay and lesbian parents are denied visitation with or custody of their biological children (Patterson, 1992). In many jurisdictions, court decisions have awarded custody to the heterosexual parent or even to other persons in the extended family such as biological grandparents (Hartman, 1996).

If custody is granted to a gay or lesbian parent, there may be a requirement that the parent not live with a same-sex partner or associate in any way with other gay or lesbian persons (McLeod & Crawford, 1998). In some states, if a mother sharing a household with a lesbian partner does not receive custody of her children, she may be permitted visitation but only outside her home and nowhere else in the presence of the partner (Segal-Sklar, 1996).

The general assumption underlying much of the decision-making process regarding custody is that gay and lesbian parents have adverse effects on the social and psychological development of their children (Patterson, 1992). The related judicial assumption is that the best interests of a child require being reared by heterosexual parents instead of by gay or lesbian parents. As more lesbian and gay persons have had children, however, and as national attention to this phenomenon continues increasing, there has been more variation in court decisions. Cohn (1995) reported that, although five state supreme courts had ruled against a gay or lesbian parent, eight other state supreme courts ruled against automatic denial of custody to a gay or lesbian parent. In other words, some judges now take the stance that same-sex sexual orientation alone does not necessarily render a parent unfit to raise children (Rosenblum, 1991). The National Association of Social Workers (NASW), the American Psychological Association (APA), and other professional and human services organizations and associations likewise support the position that a person's sexual orientation should have no effect on child custody cases or in determining whether a person qualifies to be a foster or adoptive parent (Benkov, 1994). This line of thinking has resulted from consistent research findings that the developmental outcomes for children reared by lesbian or gay parents are as good or better when compared with children reared in comparable heterosexual households.

All studies to date also have found that lesbian and gay persons function just as well as parents as do their heterosexual counterparts (Tasker & Golombok, 1997). Compared with heterosexual mothers, lesbian mothers are as knowledgeable about effective parenting skills, and they demonstrate equal abilities to identify critical issues in child care situations and to formulate suitable solutions to the problems encountered with their children. Similarly, the parenting styles and attitudes of gay fathers are more similar than different from those of nongay fathers (Bigner & Jacobsen, 1992). No discrepancies in these two father groups occurred in the extent of involvement in their children's activities or in the recreational activities provided for their children. Further, there are no differences in intimacy with children or in problem solving regarding childrearing issues (Bigner & Jacobsen, 1992).

**Disclosures to the Children and to Others.**    Because of the fear of losing custody and of other potential harms, gay and lesbian parents may keep their sexual orientation secret (Patterson & Chan, 1996). Fredriksen (1999) found that three-fourths of the gay and lesbian persons with children she studied had experienced harassment because of their sexual orientation: verbal (88 percent), emotional (50 percent), physical (9 percent), and sexual (9 percent). Parents want to protect their children as well from possible discrimination because they have parents with a same-sex orientation. Yet secrecy can be a stressor and contribute to relationship difficulties, especially if partners disagree about the need for secrecy. It can limit support from others and leave a family with no one with whom to share celebrations (Matthews & Lease, 2000).

The available research also suggests that there is an association between psychological health and openness regarding one's sexual orientation (Rand, Graham, & Rawlings, 1982). Rand et al. (1982) found a positive link between a lesbian mother's sense of psychological well-being and the extent to which she is accepting of and open about her lesbian identity. Secrecy with the children limits both intimacy between parents and children (Rohrbaugh, 1992) and openness in addressing family issues (Patterson & Chan, 1996).

Partners who wish to disclose their link to children may have to negotiate how and when to do it (Bigner, 1996). When they do make the disclosure, it is a complex and delicate task, because it may entail discussing the children's origins and include such issues as alternative insemination or why they do not have a dad or mom (Segal-Sklar, 1996). If a partner enters a family where the other partner already has children, the presence, role, and meaning of the new same-sex partner also requires explanation. Many gay, lesbian, and bisexual parents who do not live with or have custody of their biological children may also face disclosure issues, such as tempering the reactions of the custodial parent or members of the child's extended family who can have influence on the continuation of contact with the child (Appleby & Anastas, 1998).

How do children react to the knowledge of their parent's sexual orientation? The reactions of most children are positive (Bigner, 1996); they respond with a sense of protectiveness toward their parents (O'Connell, 1993). They may indicate that the information makes no difference or that they already knew it (Turner, Scadden, & Harris, 1990). Even so, this does not mean that the children will have no questions. Generally, children will need to engage in continued discussion (Patterson, 1992).

Other children may react with distress, anxiety, anger, and sorrow and may make deprecating statements to the parents. However, it is unlikely that this will be the only response or an enduring one. Other issues such as divorce can also influence negative responses (Appleby & Anastas, 1998). The ages of the children also may make a difference. Children first told of their parents' gay or lesbian sexual orientation in early adolescence, as opposed to at younger or older ages, may have a more difficult time adjusting (Patterson, 1992). Moreover, those who came from heterosexual marriages and later live with lesbian and gay parents may suddenly worry about their peers viewing them differently (Hargaden & Llewellin, 1996). Adolescents do not like to feel different, and the disclosure of the parents' stigmatized sexual identity may lead to such negative feelings (O'Connell, 1993). Cramer (1986) reported that, compared with younger children of lesbian mothers who rarely recalled facing harassment from peers, adolescent children were more likely to receive negative messages from peers concerning their parents' sexual orientation. Older children, who likely make their own decisions about disclosure concerning their parents, may decide against it because they do not want to risk being singled out by peers (Matthews & Lease, 2000).

Some parents may caution their children to keep their parents' sexual orientation secret (Crawford, 1987). Yet even if the children want to keep the information to themselves, the secrecy can then create anxiety about discovery for the children (Baptiste, 1987; Crawford, 1987). The parents as well may fear that the children will accidentally reveal the information or out them (Segal-Sklar, 1996).

Parents also have to decide if they will disclose to a variety of people involved in a child's life, such as medical staff, child-care workers, school officials, and the children's peers and parents. How open will they be both as a family and as gay or lesbian parents when dealing with these individuals and groups? Are they going to cross out "Father" or "Mother" on forms and put in "Other Mother" or "Other Father" or "Parent/Parent"? (Segal-Sklar, 1996). Fredriksen (1999) found that most parents were open in at least some settings: 51 percent were out to all coworkers, 58 percent to medical service providers, 65 percent to school personnel and 34 percent to neighbors. Parents must also make endless decisions in ordinary encounters in the world. For example, how will they talk about who is the mother or the father of their child if someone inquires? (Martin, 1993).

**The Coparent.**    The coparent in a gay or lesbian family is the nonbiological parent of a child born into a lesbian link or the nonadoptive parent in a gay or lesbian couple. The presence of this person can provide both support and stress. For lesbian mothers, a partner who is a coparent can provide considerable support as a full partner with a child born or adopted into their link. In contrast, with blended families, or those in which a partner takes a parenting role in a relationship with a person who was already a parent, there can be more variation in the coparent's role (Appleby & Anastas, 1998). Coparents in gay male relationships also provide benefits; for example, inclusion of gay father's partners and the quality of the partner's relationships with the children is associated with happiness with family life.

However, the presence of a coparent can be a unique stressor because usually only one person is the legal parent or parent of record. It is the coparent who has no legal rights regarding a child. Rarely are both parents' names included on the birth certificate. It is also rare for the nonbiological parent to win the right to adopt the child (Segal-Sklar, 1996). If the partners break up, there is no legal protection of the link between the nonbiological, or nonlegal, parent and the child. If a custody fight ensues with the biological mother, the nonlegal mother has no grounds for a case. If the biological parent becomes incapacitated or dies, custody may be granted to the biological father, to other relatives, or to the state (Segal-Sklar, 1996).

If the couple wants several children, one solution is that parents can take turns in childbearing (Appleby & Anastas, 1998). Another solution is for the coparent to adopt a child born to or adopted by the other (Shernoff, 1996), but only a few states have granted this legal recourse, or second-parent adoption. This solution may more often be successful when pregnancy happened through donor insemination and the biological father was unknown or when there was a legal adoption in which both biological parents relinquished rights to the child.

It is prudent for parents to seek assistance from legal advocacy groups. Practitioners also need to know both the legal status of LGB families in their community and state, as well as attorneys who are themselves knowledgeable and affirmative. The Web page for the National Gay and Lesbian Task Force (http://www.ngltf.org) provides a starting point for an overview of state laws and assistance in reaching LGB-affirmative lawyers and lawmakers (Matthews & Lease, 2000).

**Ambiguity of Parenting Models.**   A lack of parenting models for gay and lesbian families may create difficulties. In particular, having a family with one legal parent and a coparent with no legal rights can make the definition of parenting roles for a couple ambiguous (Patterson, 1995). What are the parents of the same gender to be called? Will "Mom" refer only to the birth mother? Will the names be the same inside and outside the home? Will the child use only one surname or both? (Appleby & Anastas, 1998).

A benefit for these families is that there is the opportunity to create new parenting models (Weston, 1994). Because society does not recognize these families, it is especially important for these families to develop rituals, traditions, and ways to celebrate their family successes, whatever model they choose to use.

**Less Support from Family of Origin, Formal Systems, and the Gay and Lesbian Community.**   Even when one's family of origin is somewhat accepting or tolerant of one's sexual orientation and the couple's relationship, reactions may change if the couple decides to raise children. Members of one's family of origin might act on the myths about psychological and social difficulties the children may experience (Matthews & Lease, 2000). Gay and lesbian parents also face many health-care, legal, financial, social, and emotional hurdles, including lack of support from formalized support systems that assist heterosexual couples during parenthood (Patterson, 1995). Further, gay and lesbian families usually receive less support from their community than do heterosexual families, partly because the lesbian and gay community is not as structured around children as the heterosexual community is. In a comparison of lesbian and heterosexual parents, Stiglitz (1990) discovered that when heterosexual mothers experienced the arrival of a child, they felt more integrated into the community and more satisfied with emotional support from family, whereas lesbian mothers felt more isolated or more like a separate family. Not being able to reach out to support systems can be especially isolating for lesbian and gay individuals or couples who are first-time parents. However, because of the increase of lesbian and gay couples who are parents, support systems for them are expanding (Scrivner & Eldridge, 1995).

**Impact on Children.** The children of gay and lesbian parents do not differ from children of heterosexual parents in overall social (interpersonal relations) or psychological adjustment (emotional health) (Golombok & Tasker, 1996). They may experience greater acceptance of their sexuality, greater empathy for others, and greater tolerance of alternative viewpoints (Patterson, 1992). They are also no more likely to be gay than are children of heterosexual parents, nor do they differ in gender identity, gender role behavior, or sexual orientation (Golombok & Tasker, 1996). The children of lesbian parents do not lack male role models. In fact, they are more likely to have contact with their fathers than are children of divorced heterosexual mothers. They also have more male friends and relatives involved in their lives than do children of heterosexual mothers (Golombok, Spener, & Rutter, 1983). Greene, Mandel, Hotvedt, Gray, and Smith (1986) found no differences in the ways that lesbian and heterosexual mothers rated the social skills and popularity of their children; moreover, the children did not rate themselves differently in their popularity among peers whether with the same or the other sex. As indicated earlier, adolescent children may experience a difficult adjustment to their parents' sexual orientation, but on the whole, the children of gay and lesbian parents do not experience the expected downfalls that heterosexist beliefs suggest.

## Assessment Tools for Families of Gay and Lesbian Persons

As the current knowledge focuses on couples' friendship and on lesbian and gay couples with children, assessment techniques may be specified for each area. Appropriate measures for this population evaluate individual issues and characteristics, as well as measures of the quality of family relationship and satisfaction (see table 9.1).

**Table 9.1**    Assessment Tools for Families of Gay and Lesbian Persons

| *Measures for Individuals* | *Measures for Couples and Families* |
| --- | --- |
| Index of self-esteem | Index of marital satisfaction |
| Social support inventory | Index of family relationship |
| Loneliness | Child's attitude toward parent |
| Beck Depression Inventory | Parent's attitude toward child |

**Assessment—Couples' Friendship.** Social workers can use ecomaps to assess the community in which the individual or couple lives. Social support may be of particular interest. Measures of individual functioning include depression, loneliness, or self-esteem (Corcoran & Fischer, 2000). Couples may also benefit from a relationship measure such as Hudson's Index of Marital Satisfaction (Corcoran & Fischer, 2000).

**Assessment—Lesbian and Gay Couples with Children.** Bigner and Jacobsen (1992) found no differences in gay and heterosexual fathers' parenting styles with standardized parenting inventories. Standardized parenting inventories of child's attitude toward parent and parent's attitude toward child, along with other parenting inventories, can be found in Corcoran and Fischer (2000).

See table 9.1 for examples of measures to be used for assessing the issues mentioned above for individuals and families of gay and lesbian persons.

## CHILD MALTREATMENT IN FAMILIES

Child maltreatment is a pervasive problem in our society that families of all races, income status, beliefs, and structures experience. Causal indicators include individual characteristics of parents and children, familial factors, community environment, culture, and societal values (Pecora, Whittaker, Maluccio, & Barth, 2000). The most commonly recognized form of child maltreatment is familial abuse and neglect. Nearly 3.5 million incidents of child maltreatment are reported annually to child protection agencies. Following evidentiary investigation, slightly less than 1.5 million of the reports are confirmed (U.S. Department of Health and Human Services, 2006). This section reviews types of maltreatment, risk assessment, and cultural sensitivity.

### Types of Maltreatment

The four major types of familial child maltreatment include physical abuse, sexual abuse, physical neglect, and psychological maltreatment. Although states have varying definitions of specific categories of child maltreatment, the universal definition is found in the Federal Child Abuse and Prevention and Treatment Act of 1974 (Public Law 93-237): the physical or mental injury, sexual abuse, or negligent treatment of a child younger than the age of eighteen by a person who is responsible for the child's welfare under circumstances that would indicate that the child's health or welfare is harmed or threatened thereby.

Several perspectives on the etiology of child maltreatment should be used to inform assessment strategies. These perspectives cover the range of specific personality traits of caregivers, social factors such as attitudes toward violence and living conditions, child characteristics, and parent-child interaction. On the basis of findings from numerous studies, Pecora et al. (2000) note specific parent, child, and family causal factors identified across the different types of child maltreatment (see table 9.2).

Child maltreatment is a complex phenomenon requiring a multidimensional assessment to determine appropriate interventions; singularly, the various perspectives individually fail to adequately address the cause of child maltreatment. The more contemporary theoretical framework is based on an ecological perspective that views the cause of child maltreatment as multifaceted and as resulting from the interface of parent and child traits and relationships, environmental stressors, cultural beliefs and practices, and societal norms (Belsky, 1980; Belsky & Vondura, 1989).

Families experiencing child maltreatment typically come to the attention of child protective services (CPS) agencies. If the report of alleged abuse or neglect is determined to warrant intervention, an initial assessment will be conducted. The purpose of this initial assessment is

**Table 9.2**    Types of Child Maltreatment

| Physical Abuse | Sexual Abuse |
|---|---|
| Children with disabilities | Parental substance abuse |
| Premature births | Family violence |
| Children with behavioral problems | Parental history of maltreatment |
| Domestic violence | Low income |
| Marital conflict | Low educational level of mother |
| Parental history of maltreatment | Stepfather in the home |
| Family social isolation | Absent or ill mother |
| Low income | Weak bonds with mother |
| Lack of social supports | Social isolation |
| Lack of knowledge of | Few friends during childhood |
| child development |  |
| Parental substance abuse |  |
| *Psychological Maltreatment* | *Neglect* |
| Parental substance abuse | Loneliness |
| Parental history of maltreatment | Social isolation |
| Lack of parenting skills | Disorganization |
| Adolescent parent | Lack of social supports |
| Social isolation | Apathy |
|  | Family size |
|  | Parental substance abuse |
|  | Low income |
|  | Low education |

to verify whether child maltreatment has occurred and, if so, the likelihood that it may happen again, who was involved in the maltreatment, and what should happen as a result of the maltreatment. This initial assessment of child maltreatment has three possible outcomes: the report is considered unsubstantiated if there is no evidence that abuse or neglect occurred; the report is ruled inconclusive, which means that, although there are indicators that maltreatment has occurred, the evidence is lacking and statements cannot be corroborated; or the report is substantiated based on strong evidence that the maltreatment occurred or the caregiver admits to the abuse or neglect (Wiehe, 1992).

The primary mandate of child protection agencies is to ensure no further harm to children who are reported as alleged victims of child abuse and neglect. Child protection agencies use a systematic collection of data to determine the degree of potential harm to a child at some future point in time (Doueck, English, DePanfilis, & Moote, 1993). Across the nation, the prevailing approach is to combine practice wisdom and risk assessment instruments to create a risk assessment model. In addition to predicting risk of potential maltreatment, such models assist in prioritizing cases (English & Pecora, 1994; Fanshel, Finch, & Grundy, 1994; Jagannathan & Camasso, 1996) and in developing individualized treatment plans based on individual case levels of risk (English & Pecora, 1994). The risk assessment model provides a framework for case assessment, and documentation and is used as the foundation for case planning and service delivery.

## FAMILY OR CAREGIVER STRESS AND MENTAL ILLNESS

Caring for a relative with mental illness creates special stressors for family members and or caregivers. Many issues involve control and independence, conflicting family roles, caregivers' emotional overinvolvement, culture clashes with ethnically diverse families, and psychiatric illnesses experienced by more than one family member (Leff, 2005). In addition, providers who are treating an ill person do not always recognize that person's family and caregivers as a resource. The result is that many family members feel isolated and multistressed. This section overviews factors that affect families who care for a relative with mental illness: stress (e.g., stigma, lack of provider respect) and family experience (e.g., parents, siblings, and adult children caring for mentally ill parent and spouses.

### Family Stress

Research has identified three key areas of societal and or environmental stress that experienced by family members and caregivers who have a mentally ill relative in treatment: stigma, lack of provider respect, and organizational cultural competence.

**Stigma.**    Stigma is a cluster of negative attitudes and prejudicial beliefs (World Health Organization, 2001), a pervasive reality for people with mental illness and their families, and a leading factor in discouraging both from getting the services they need (Warner, 2005). Family members report difficulties with accessing mental health services, either on behalf of their family member who has a mental illness or because of their own need, such as respite from the freedom of care giving for a parent, child, or sibling with a mental illness (Drapalski et al., 2008). Some parents, for example, report having been forced to relinquish custody to obtain needed mental health services for their children
(Substance Abuse and Mental Health Service Administration, 2005). Others describe experiences in which they perceive mental health workers as blaming them for family problems and refuse to deal with their grief issues (New Freedom Commission on Mental Health, 2003). Stigma also plays a role in the underuse of mental health services by family members from ethnic communities. Recent immigrants are often reluctant to use mainstream health, mental health, or social services because of stigma-related concerns, including feelings of personal shame about mental illness and social embarrassment for one's family or community.

**Provider respect.**    Family members often play a dominant role in health-seeking behaviors and compliance with treatment. Despite providing information and playing a pivotal role in guiding their family members' health-care decisions, family members describe feeling disrespected when providers exclude them from sessions that involve the family member who has the mental illness (Vandiver, Jordan, Keopraseuth, & Yu, 1995). Some providers may still operate from the old family therapy paradigm of schizophrenia as a functional by-product of disturbed family dynamics and consequently disregard the supportive role of family members.

**Organizational cultural competence.**    An additional concern of family members has to do with the cultural competence of providers and organizations. Health-care and social service providers often refer family members from ethnically diverse communities to mainstream mental health settings. However, the referred clients perceive many of the available services as inadequate or inappropriate. Family members from non-English-speaking communities express difficulty with mental health organizations that rely heavily on English-only versions of health-care information. Because a great deal of health and mental health information is organized around the assumption of English-language literacy, some non-English-speaking family members express concern that they cannot participate or even comprehend important treatment information presented in English-only pamphlets, manuals, or even prescription directions (Institute of Medicine, 2002).

## Family Experience of Caring for Mentally Ill Relative

Here we look closer at some of the differential issues associated with family and caregiver stress: the family experience of parents, siblings' relationships, children caring for adult parents with mental illness, and spouses caring for spouses. These distinctions are important, particularly in trying to set up targeted programs based on the needs and role of the family member or caregiver. Understanding these distinctions can also assist in the development of mental health promotion strategies that are unique to the life stage and role of the caregiver.

**Family Members' Lack of Experience and Knowledge.** Research into the experiences of family members or caregivers who have a relative with mental illness report that families often provide care with little to no information or training about mental illness; problem-solving strategies; how to cope with the ongoing physical and emotional stressors of caring for an ill relative; and resources for social service, health benefits, or psychiatric services. In terms of parental caregivers, research suggests that mothers tend to take on most caregiving responsibilities, and they report that they often feel unsupported and unprepared to care for their ill relative (Pickett-Schenk, 2003). Lefley (1996) has written extensively on the challenge of parents providing care to an adult child with mental illness. These burdens include the stressors of providing continuous instrumental support (e.g., financial assistance, transportation, housing) and subjective feelings of guilt, depression, anger and grief. When education and support programs are offered for families, most participants are women (51 percent to 96 percent) who report caring for an adult male relative (57 percent to 90 percent) (Pickett-Schenk, 2003).

**Sibling Caregivers.** Siblings' relationship also plays a role in caregiving. Studies have found that adult sisters are more likely to report greater feelings of stigma; to have frequent contact; and to offer emotional, caregiving, and direct support to their mentally ill sibling than are non-ill adult brothers. Sister siblings were also more likely to assume future care for an ill sister but not a brother (Greenburg, Kim, & Greenley, 1997; Greenburg, Seltzer, Krauss, & Kim, 1999).

**Adult Children Caregivers.** With regard to adult children caring for a mentally ill parent, Marsh et al. (1993) found that adult children of parents with mental illness report a variety of psychological experiences, ranging from low self-esteem, resentment, sense of robbed childhood, fear of intimacy, and unresolved grief to increased levels of compassion and empathy. In both groups, adult children expressed a need for concrete information and explanations, as well as coping strategies to help improve their emotional well-being.

**Spouse Caregivers.**   Spouses experience distress in much the same way as parents, except that issues of loss and grieving are more for the loss of the adult relationship. Often these losses are economic, as when the primary wage earner becomes ill or, in contrast, when the primary wage earner has to assume full care for an ill spouse or partner. The marital relationship is even more distressed when one spouse may initiates court-ordered hospitalization proceedings for the ill spouse to receive needed help.

In summary, as research suggests, family stress is quite extensive for family members who care for an ill relative. The stress is experienced not only in the social environment (i.e., via stigma, provider relationships, and organizational issues) but also through multiple layers of family roles (i.e., from parents to siblings to spouses). By providing a thorough assessment of the societal, environmental, and differential issues affecting families and caregivers, social workers can identify interventions that reduce stressors.

### Assessment Tools for Child Maltreatment and Risk Assessment

**Child Assessment—Risk Assessment.**   Cash (2001) defines risk assessment as "the systematic collection of information related to the future abuse or neglect of a child" (p. 811). Camasso and Jagannathan (2000) state that the purpose of a risk assessment is "to determine the likelihood that a child will be maltreated at some future time" (p. 874). Pecora et al. (2000) classify the various risk assessment models into four types: matrix, empirical predictor, family assessment scales, and the child-at-risk field (CARF). The matrix model was one of the first types developed. It uses a table of between sixteen and thirty-two factors relating to severity of potential risk to the child. The empirical predictor model focuses on the identification of the small set of risk factors most predictive of child maltreatment. The family assessment scales use behaviorally anchored scales to assess child and family functioning levels and to identify areas of concern. The child-at-risk field is based on the ecological approach and uses open-ended questions and anchored scales to identify risk indicators present in the case.

Although several evaluative studies have been conducted on the various types of risk assessment models, debate continues regarding their accuracy, validity, and predictability. Critics of currently used risk assessment models find that workers receive little training on their use (English, Aubin, Fine, & Pecora, 1993; Gelles, 1996; Wald & Woolverton, 1990). In addition, factors included on many risk assessment instruments neither predict nor correlate with future abuse and neglect (Lyons, Doueck, & Wodarski, 1996), and they do not have significant predictive validity

(English et al., 1993). Throughout the studies, methodological problems have also been documented on risk assessment, including small sample sizes, ungeneralizable findings, and threatened statistical conclusion validity (DePanfilis, 1995). Other weaknesses noted are a lack of cultural sensitivity (English et al., 1993) and a predominant focus on deficits rather than on family strengths (Wald & Woolverton, 1990). Recognizing the potential utility of these models for improving child protection practices and outcomes, child welfare scholars and practitioners have issued a call for more empirical validation of these approaches (Lyons et al., 1996).

Morton and Browne's (1998) questions respond to all child maltreatment reports and assessments. They posit that the criminal justice model should be used in those instances in which facts substantiate violation of criminal statutes. However, they also argue that a safety or risk-of-harm standard should focus on the child rather than on blaming family members, thus determining which families are in need of services without labeling them with the stigma of child maltreatment (Morton & Browne, 1998). This more positive approach is based on the premise that "use of the strengths perspective rather than the deficit model reframes the nature of the intervention relationship from an involuntary one to a partnership with the child and family" (Holder & Lund, 1995, p. 21).

Following this approach, many child protection agencies have developed a safety assessment to determine the appropriate intervention for those children and families who have been identified as needing services. The safety assessment identifies the strengths of individuals and of the family as a whole that may help protect the child from future harm. In addition, the safety assessment determines areas in which supportive services are needed to ensure continued safety of the child. These safety assessments are in the initial stages and have yet to be evaluated for accurate outcomes.

Further, there are increased mandates for greater accountability and results in the child welfare system's response to child maltreatment. To meet these demands, it is crucial that the system develop an effective assessment framework for interventions with families experiencing child maltreatment. In response, the Child Welfare League of America, with support from the Edna McConnell Clark Foundation, has proposed the development of an "assessment tool kit" that would include the following: screening tools; safety assessment tools; risk assessment tools; and tools and processes that identify family connections, resources, and capacity to care for children (Day, 1999). LeVine and Sallee (1999) suggest that assessments of families engaged in the child welfare system include the family life cycle, the stage of family development, identification of internal and external stressors, a critical analysis of present functioning, and the strengths and challenges of the family members.

Table 9.2 describes types of child maltreatment and table 9.3 describes risk assessment measures. Baird, Wagner, Healy, and Johnson (2001) studied three risk assessment instruments, two consensus based and one actuarial. Case information from four different jurisdictions was collected along with outcome information and eighteen-month follow-up data. The researchers concluded that the actuarial approach more accurately classified cases to different risk levels and thus had superior potential to improve decision making in child welfare programs.

Further, the Colorado Department of Public Safety provides instruments for assessing actuarial risk and sex offender risk online (http://dcj.state.co.us/ors/risk_assessment.htm).

Table 9.3.    Assessment Tools for Families at Risk of Child Maltreatment

| Author and Year | Work | Annotation |
| --- | --- | --- |
| Abidin, R. R. (1990) | *Parenting Stress Index* (3rd ed.). Charlottesville, VA: Pediatric Psychology Press | Covers parent-child domains of stress vs. general life stress |
| Magura, S., Moses, B. S., & Jones, M. J. (1987) | *Assessing risk and measuring change in families: The Family Risk Scales.* Washington, DC: Child Welfare League of America. | A standardized measure of a child's risk of entering substitute care, consisting of 26 individual scales that apply to a full range of risk situations that bring families into the child welfare system. |
| Magura, S. & Moses, B. S. (1986) | *Outcome measures for child welfare services.* Washington, DC: Child Welfare League of America. | Provides several instruments for assessing individuals and families dealing with child abuse and neglect. |
| Milner, J. S. (1986). | *The Child Abuse Potential Inventory: Manual* (2nd ed.). Webster, NC: Psytec. | Psytec is a 160-item self-report instrument designed to identify and individual's potential for physical abuse. |
| National Committee for Prevention of Child Abuse (n.d.) | *Parenting program evaluation manual.* Chicago: Author. | Contains information on more than 50 instruments that can be used in assessment of individuals and families experiencing child abuse and neglect. |
| Children's Division of the American Humane Association (n.d.) | *The Family Activities Inventory: A tool for assessing family strengths.* Denver, CO: Author. | A strengths-based inventory of parenting skills, beliefs, and practices designed for home visitation services to parents of children (birth through age 3). |

**Child Assessment—Cultural Sensitivity.** A major challenge to the development of a comprehensive assessment package is the assurance of cultural sensitivity. According to Lewis-Fernandez and Kleinman (1995), culture should be viewed as a dynamic process influenced by differences in gender, ethnicity, age, class, and race. Building on this definition, Canino and Spurlock (2000) make a cogent plea for the "in-depth understanding of patients' lives, their family myths, and cultural mores—essential if we hope to help troubled children and adolescents" (p. viii).

Although children and families of color have always been disproportionately represented in reports of child maltreatment, Caucasians predominate the child protection workforce. To address cultural sensitivity, it is essential that Caucasian practitioners in particular have a keen cultural self-awareness and awareness of others' cultures. A culturally sensitive assessment of families experiencing child maltreatment should take into account cultural influences on the following areas: expectations of child development and behavior, attitudes toward health practices, child-rearing practices (sex education, sex roles and expectations, discipline, and social skills development), and family history (role of the extended family, family values, level of acculturation and adaptation to the community, and religion) (Canino & Spurlock, 2000).

A comprehensive, culturally sensitive assessment is crucial to appropriate interventions and positive outcomes for families experiencing child maltreatment. Practitioners in all fields of practice who provide services to abused and neglected children and their families should be familiar with and have access to a cadre of empirically tested assessment tools. Although a number of such tools are currently available, in the field of child protection, there is great need for improved assessment instruments and models. To combat the dearth of culturally sensitive assessment instruments and models, practitioners should research the latest effective strategies in working with diverse families. For example, Ayon and Lee (2005) found that family preservation services may be a more appropriate intervention to meet the needs of diverse populations. In summary, they state, "Workers need to take ethnicity into account as culturally sensitive and community-based programs, such as [family preservation], may be more effective when serving ethnic or racial minority groups" (p. 265).

### Assessment Tools for Families and Caregivers of People with Mental Illness

Appropriate measures for families and caregivers of people with mental illness include those that measure personal stress, adaptability, and flexibility. Table 9.4 describes the most common assessment instruments used to assess family and caregiver stress.

**Table 9.4**   Assessment Measures for Health Problems

| Measures | Sources |
|---|---|
| Perceived Stress Scale (PSS) | Cohen & Williamson, 1988 |
| Family Adaptability and Cohesion Evaluation Scale (FACES-III) | Olson, 1986 |
| Family Attachment and Changeability Index 8 (FACI-8) | McCubbin et al., 1996 |
| Family Assessment Device (FAD) | Epstein et al., 1983 |
| Family Crisis Oriented Personal Evaluation Scales (F-COPES) | McCubbin et al., 1991 |

**Assessment of Stress.**   Measures of perceived stress (Cohen & Williamson, 1988) are helpful in determining the level of stress that the family or caregiver is experiencing. Other similar stress inventories may be found in Corcoran and Fischer (2000).

**Assessment of Caregivers.**   Flexibility is an important trait in families coping with the stress of a mentally ill member and may be measured by an index such as Olson's (1986) Family Adaptability and Cohesion Evaluation Scale, which is widely used. Family attachment and crises oriented evaluation can be measured with instruments from McCubbin, Patterson, and Wilson (1991) and McCubbin, Thompson, and McCubbin (1996).

## MOVING FROM ASSESSMENT TO INTERVENTION: CASE EXAMPLE

### Identifying Information

*Name*: Emily Parker
*Date of Birth*: 3/16/92
*Address*: 1201 Fair Avenue, Oakdale
*Phone*: 555.765.4321 (home), 555.211.1098
*People living in the home:*

| | | | | | |
|---|---|---|---|---|---|
| Emily Parker | Client | Female | 10 y.o. | Anglo | 4th grader |
| Brad Hunt | Brother | Male | 6 y.o. | Anglo | 1st grader |
| Susan Blake | Mother | Female | 30 y.o. | Anglo | Secretary |
| Renee Lewis | Mother's Partner | Female | 36 y.o. | Anglo | Cook |
| Eddie Cantrell | Renee's Son | Male | 12 y.o. | Anglo | 6th grader |
| Jessica Cantrell | Renee's Daughter | Female | 6 y.o. | Anglo | 1st grader |

### Family Income

The family income is between $2,000 and $3,000 per month, depending on the collection of child support from fathers. Some months, the child support checks are delayed or remain uncollected.

## Presenting Problem

Emily is crying uncontrollably at times, both at home and at school. The teacher complains that Emily sometimes becomes so upset that she must go to the nurse's office. When asked why she is crying, Emily says that she's just sad and doesn't know why. Recently, Emily has begun having nightmares and has expressed anxiety about being separated from her mother. She is having "stomachaches" and does not always want to eat at school.

## Previous Counseling

There has been none for Emily, but her mother, Susan, and her mother's partner, Renee, have attended counseling as a couple. In addition, Susan reports that she is being treated for bipolar disorder and that both she and Renee have sought counseling separately for substance abuse issues.

## Source of Data

In-office assessment visit with Emily and her mother. Additional information was obtained from the other children in the home, the pediatrician, the school nurse, teachers, and the school counselor.

## Nature of Presenting Problem

In the six months since school started, the teacher has observed a decline in Emily's schoolwork. She says that Emily seems tired and unfocused; she says that Emily is listless in class and often prefers sitting with the teacher during recess instead of playing with the other children. At times, when she looks into the classroom, the teacher sees Emily sitting at her desk with her head down, crying softly. At these times, the teacher tries to comfort Emily, but she says that Emily is not always consolable. If the crying becomes distracting for the class, the teacher sends Emily to the nurse's office. Some days, Emily asks to go to the nurse's office because she has a stomachache. The teacher is not sure if Emily has a real stomachache or if something else is bothering her. The teacher worries that Emily is not getting enough rest or that something unusual is happening at home. She has called Emily's mother to report these concerns.

Emily's mother reports similar behavior at home. She says that Emily seems to be having trouble sleeping—that Emily goes to sleep at around 9 p.m. but is often awake again around midnight for an hour or more. She comes to her mother in the night and asks her mother to sleep with her. Emily's mother usually just takes Emily back to bed and spends a few minutes with her before returning to her own bed. She says that on many mornings Emily is so tired that she is hard to wake up for school. Emily tells her mother that she "can't think" at school. She expresses worry about her schoolwork, saying that she is too tired to do her homework and that it is boring anyway. About the stomachaches, Emily says that she has them after she eats. She cannot tell what causes them, but sometimes she skips lunch at school to avoid having a stomachache afterward. Emily's mother thinks that because Emily goes all day without eating, her stomach is upset by dinner, too. Often Emily eats very little of what is prepared for her.

Emily's mother reports, too, that Emily cries for no apparent reason. When she arrives home from work, she will find Emily on her bed crying. When she asks Emily what is wrong, Emily says that she doesn't know. Her mother reports that she spends extra time to console Emily, but she admits that the problem is not improving. Emily's brother and the other children in the home are beginning to ask what is wrong with her. Emily has been asked by her mom if the other children are mean or if things are going badly at school, but Emily always responds no and that she is just sad. Until now, Emily's mother has regarded this problem as a "phase." She says that Emily has always been a sensitive child and that she has always cried easily if teased or in trouble. However, this spontaneous crying is new. She says that she took Emily to the pediatrician a week ago to see if anything was wrong physically. After a full checkup, the doctor could not find anything seriously wrong, though he did prescribe some medication for Emily's stomachaches.

Emily's teacher reports that Emily has many friends at school. She says that Emily is generally easygoing. In fact, she believes that, at times, Emily does not stand up for herself, that she will allow other girls to take advantage of her rather than cause a conflict. Nevertheless, Emily plays appropriately and displays appropriate empathy and social skills among her peers. The teacher added that Emily's early performance in class was much better than her current work. The teacher believes that this decline is the result of whatever stress Emily is enduring and not the result of increasing difficulty of the work. She believes that Emily is capable of performing well in school.

The school nurse reports that when Emily comes to her office, she is often too busy to devote much individual time to her. On those occasions, Emily just lies on a cot for a while and cries. After about thirty minutes, she will get up, clean her face, and return to class. If the nurse has the time, they talk together about what is happening in the classroom and at home. Emily says everything is all right, but she does complain of stomachaches. The school nurse says that she contacted Emily's mother to report the stomachaches and that her mother agreed to bring some antacid tablets to school to see if these would alleviate the symptoms. The nurse expresses concern that Emily is under stress that she is unable to talk about. She contacted the school counselor about her concerns just this week.

The school counselor says that she has met with Emily only once so far, but she has observed her in class on two occasions. She plans to see her weekly during the next several weeks to see if Emily is appropriate for group work.

Emily demonstrates several strengths. Despite her lack of sleep, her stomachaches, and her tearfulness, she is able to maintain a B average. In addition, she has many friends whom she claims to enjoy. Her mother seems genuinely concerned for her and says that she will work with the school to help Emily overcome her difficulties.

The school prioritizes the problems (with 1 being the most severe) in the following order: (1) excessive crying or sadness, (2) time away from the classroom and in the nurse's office, (3) inability to focus on school-work. Emily's mother prioritizes the problems similarly: (1) sadness, (2) being unable to sleep, (3) stomachaches.

## Client Intrapersonal Issues

**Cognitive Functioning.**   Emily's school achievement tests indicate that she is capable of high classroom achievement. She consistently scores in the ninetieth percentile in language and math. Neither her pediatrician nor her mother reports any type of cognitive developmental delay. In fact, she has always made mostly As in school. Her cumulative file reveals that she might be eligible for the talented and gifted program if her performance in fourth grade is good enough. According to her mother, Emily achieved most developmental milestones ahead of schedule; for example, she was able at one year old to say two-and three-word sentences. The teacher reports that Emily is capable of working independently in all subjects and that she will help her classmates with their work if she has finished her own. Sometimes she even works ahead in math, though she has stopped doing that lately.

**Emotional Functioning.**   During the assessment visit, Emily was attentive and polite. She sat very close to her mother, seeming rather shy, but she answered all questions directed to her clearly and without hesitation. She displayed no disturbance or inappropriate affect. When asked why she had been crying so much, she just looked at the floor and shrugged. She said that her stomach is better, so she thinks the medicine is helping. At one point, she mentioned that she did not want her mother to worry about her.

**Behavioral Functioning.**    Emily's mother reports that Emily has always been easy to discipline and easy to direct. She says that Emily does her homework without prompting and that she helps out with her younger brother and with Renee's daughter, Jessica, by helping them get dressed and by playing with them while her mother cooks dinner. At those rare times when Emily needs correction, her mother reports that she is always remorseful and worried that she has been "bad." Emily's mother says that Emily may, in fact, be "too good," that is, more responsible than is typical of her age. Until now, however, Emily has never displayed any problems coping with her responsibilities. Emily expresses some worry that if she continues to cry at school, the other children may not want to play with her. Someone has already called her a "baby."

**Physiologic Functioning.**    Emily's medical records reveal basically normal development. Emily is in the fiftieth percentile for height and the seventy-fifth percentile for weight, which is not unusual for girls this age. Her immunizations are up to date, and she currently takes only Nexium to help settle her stomach. Her illness history is not remarkable, although she did have a broken arm that required setting when she was five years old. The injury was caused from falling out of a tree, and her arm seems to have healed without incident. Emily has had only chicken pox and minor colds and infections that have responded to conservative medical intervention. Emily's fine motor skills appear to be advanced in that she writes in cursive exclusively and legibly. She is not as adept with gross motor skills. Never an athlete, Emily is awkward in sports and prefers to avoid them; she has not even learned to ride a bike. Her mother reports that Emily prefers writing and drawing to being outside. She has attributed this to the tree accident, believing that Emily fears getting hurt again. The PE teacher reports that Emily is never chosen first in team sports but that she does participate, and she is typically chosen early because the children like her. She says that Emily's awkwardness in gross motor skills would likely disappear with more activity in sports.

**Developmental Considerations.**    All developmental milestones have been achieved within normal time ranges; some have been reached early, such as speech and fine motor development. Emily's birth history reveals that she was delivered spontaneously and without complications at thirty-nine weeks gestation and weighed seven pounds, four ounces.

**Client Interpersonal Issues: Family.**    Emily resides in a three-bedroom apartment with her mother, her younger brother, her mother's partner, and the partner's two children. The boys sleep in one room, the girls in another, and the mothers in a third. Emily's mother reports that she finished high school in a small town and married her high school sweetheart, Emily's father, Van Parker. She says that they were already separated when Emily was born two years later. She says that she and Van were too young to be married and that they argued all the time. She sought counseling at this time and was referred to a psychiatrist who diagnosed her with bipolar disorder. In the past ten years, she has been hospitalized three times with symptoms from this disorder—once when Emily was a baby, again when Emily was three, and again when Emily was five. Mr. Parker does not see Emily regularly, but his paycheck is garnished for child support, and his parents see Emily for two weeks each summer. They live on a farm, and Emily seems happy to go there to visit. She is already worrying, however, about having to go this summer, saying that she does not want to leave her mother.

Emily's mother says that she left the small town after her first "breakdown" to get away from her former husband and her own family. She moved to Oakdale because she thought that she would have better opportunities for work. She has worked as a clerk and is now a secretary for a home mortgage company. She and Emily lived alone, until they met Barry Blake, whom Emily's mother married when Emily was almost two. Emily's mother admits that she married for security but quickly found that life with Barry was anything but secure. They fought physically and drank heavily in their time together; she was hospitalized once during this time for depression and alcohol abuse. She finally moved away from Barry when Emily was five, but she says that he continued to harass her until her new boyfriend, Bob Hunt, threatened him one evening. She and Hunt dated for only a short time before she discovered that she was pregnant with her second child, Brad. At this time, she sent Emily to live with her paternal grandparents and spent about six weeks in a private psychiatric hospital.

Because Emily's mother never married Hunt, she became the single mother of two children. About three years ago, she met Renee Lewis and fell in love. They moved in together after dating for two months. Apparently, all of the children get along well, and both women love all the children as their own. Even so, Emily's mother admits that things are not perfect. She says that Lewis also has a history of emotional problems and that they argue and fight physically at times. She says that she is concerned about Lewis's drug and alcohol problems but that she is able to control her own impulses with alcohol because she can see that drinking makes the fights worse. Recently, she and Lewis have talked about separating; however, they are dependent on one another financially and for help with the children. Lewis is able to be home when the children come home from school, and Emily's mother is able to stay with them at night while Lewis works. Their combined income barely meets all of the expenses.

Emily's younger brother, Brad, is healthy and developing normally, although he is not as advanced as Emily. He struggles with reading in first grade but remains on level. Teachers report that he is easily frustrated with schoolwork and sometimes demonstrates angry, even somewhat aggressive, behavior toward classmates. They add, however, that he responds well to discipline and shows some remorse for his actions. If he continues to struggle with reading and language, teachers say that they will ask the school diagnostician to test him for possible learning disabilities. When asked about his sister, Brad openly admits that he loves her and thinks she is a good big sister.

The other children in the home, Eddie and Jessica, attend the same school. They do not display major difficulties, though Eddie has been diagnosed with ADHD, and Jessica is described as shy. Teachers say that Eddie can be difficult to control if he is not taking his medication and that they often must remind his mother to send his medication to school. Without the medication, Eddie cannot focus on work and he finds it hard to sit still in class. Jessica displays no symptoms of ADHD. Instead, she seems overly quiet, often avoiding other children. She prefers to play with one person at a time and seems overwhelmed by rambunctious playground activities. Since school has started, though, she is showing increasing tolerance for the active school environment. Teachers believe that she will achieve normally in school, even if she remains somewhat socially immature. All of the children speak of one another as if they are siblings, and all speak highly of Emily. Jessica notes that Emily is sad much of the time. She says this makes her sad, too.

Emily's mother and Lewis evenly divide parenting responsibilities. Even though Lewis works on weekends, she works in the evenings and devotes much of her day to activities with the children. All the children express affection for both women, yet all of the children report that the two women fight a lot. Emily's mother admits that the stress of her job, her finances, the children, her own struggles with mental health, and her fights with Lewis interfere with her ability to parent well. She is close to Emily, and she tries to provide security for her, but she worries that Emily's crying may be the result of their tumultuous home life.

**Client Interpersonal Issues: School.** Emily says that she likes school. She enjoys learning about new things and thinks that she is a good student. The school counselor reports that she has observed Emily on two occasions. On the first occasion, she noticed that Emily worked independently and easily on her schoolwork. She seemed focused and confident. On finishing her work, she sat at her desk reading a book until the class was ready to move on to the next assignment. From this observation, the counselor found Emily to be bright and mature.

The second observation was surprising to the counselor. She said that Emily was simply staring at her paper, making no attempt to work the problems. As she sat at her desk, Emily began to cry, tears slipping over her cheeks. Eventually, she put her head on the desk and began to sob. When the teacher came to her, Emily spoke with the teacher briefly before getting up to go to the nurse's office. The counselor walked to the nurse's office with Emily, patting her on the back and asking her what was wrong. Emily just replied that she did not know. The counselor thinks that Emily is a bright child who copes well in general with schoolwork and with peers, but she finds Emily's tearfulness disturbing and, perhaps, an indication of deeper problems either emotionally or at home.

**Client Interpersonal Issues: Peers.**    Emily says that she has lots of friends. She can name three "best" friends, but she adds that she likes other people, too. Teachers confirm that Emily plays well with other children and often assumes the role of peacemaker in disputes. They say that she enjoys the quieter play of girls but that she will participate with large group activities of boys and girls on the playground. The teachers also say that some children rely on Emily to help them with their work, and Emily is willing and able to provide this support.

**Context and Social Support Networks.**    This family is isolated from the support of extended family. Neither partner maintains close contact with her own parents and siblings. Emily's mother has sought some help from her family, but she says that they do not approve of her lifestyle and will not acknowledge Lewis as her partner. She says that she has never met Lewis's family. Because of their busy schedules, they also do not have a large network of friends. They have met some people in the apartment complex; and these neighbors have, at times, intervened in their fights, sometimes taking the children away from the conflict. Overall, however, they do not have a well-defined social network.

Both women have friends and acquaintances at work, but Emily's mother is not "out" at work. Her friends there believe that Lewis is simply a roommate who helps with expenses. Lewis's friends at work are aware of the nature of the relationship, but they do not socialize with the couple.

Emily's mother expresses her desire to make this family work, but she admits that she is tired of the conflict and that she is not sure she can continue with things as they are. She loves Lewis's children, but she says that even the burden of extra children makes her life harder. She has no plan for supporting herself and her children without the help and financial resources Lewis provides. She worries that she may have another "breakdown" if her life does not improve.

**Measurement: Family Functioning.**    Administer the Hudson Index of Family Relations (Hudson, 1982) to assess overall family function and an anger diary to monitor parental fighting.

**Measurement: Individual Functioning.**    First, design a daily log for Emily's mother and her teachers to determine the triggers for Emily's crying episodes, when they occur, and how long they last. Second, design a similar log to track stomach problems, noting what Emily eats and what occurs before each stomachache, to determine whether the attacks are related to food or to emotions. Third, administer the Child Depression Scale to determine the level of Emily's depression.

## SUMMARY

This chapter discussed families who are multistressed by external sources: gay and lesbian families, families experiencing child maltreatment, and families with health problems. For gay and lesbian families, the couple's friendship and couples with children were the two assessment areas reviewed. Families experiencing child maltreatment have been categorized according to type of maltreatment: physical, sexual, or psychological, or physical neglect abuse. Important areas for assessment for this group are risk assessment and cultural sensitivity. We discussed caregiver stress in families with a member diagnosed with mental illness and reviewed advantages of psychoeducational assessment and intervention reviewed.

We suggested assessment techniques for each of the three areas. Measurement is similar for these families as for families described in preceding chapters. Finally, we presented a case example using the integrative skills assessment protocol and treatment plan presented earlier in the text.

## STUDY QUESTIONS

1. Discuss the assessment issues for the multistressed family populations presented in this chapter. What are the similarities and differences in assessment method for each of the three groups presented here?

2. Consider the case of Emily, presented at the end of this chapter. Suppose her mother had divorced and moved in with a male partner. How would the assessment have been different?

3. Choose a family you know that is experiencing one of the problems described in the chapter and write an assessment using the integrative skills assessment protocol. Design a comprehensive measurement and treatment plan. Describe any difficulties you encountered.

## WEB SITES

### Resources for Enhancing Cultural Competence

*National Center for Cultural Competence*
http://www11.georgetown.edu/research/gucchd/nccc/

### Resources for Caregivers

*U.S. Department of Health and Human Services, Office on Women's Health.*
http://www.womenshealth.gov/faq/caregiver-stress.cfm

## REFERENCES

Allen, K. R., & Demo, D. H. (1995). The families of lesbians and gay men: A new frontier family research. *Journal of Marriage and the Family, 57,* 111–127.

Appleby, G. A., & Anastas, J. W. (1998). *Not just a passing phase: Social work with gay, lesbian, and bisexual people.* New York: Columbia University Press.

Ayon, C., & Lee, D. C. (2005). A comparative analysis of child welfare services through the eyes of African American, Caucasian, and Latino parents. *Research on Social Work Practice, 15,* 257–266.

Baird, C., Wagner, D., Healy, T., & Johnson, K. (2001). *Risk assessment in child protective services: Reliability of consensus and actuarial models.* Madison, WI: National Council on Crime and Delinquency, Children's Research Center.

Baptiste, D. A., Jr. (1987). Psychotherapy with gay/lesbian couples and their children in "stepfamilies": A challenge for marriage and family therapists. *Journal of Homosexuality, 14,* 223–238.

Belsky, J. (1980). Child maltreatment: An ecological integration. *American Psychologist, 35,* 320–335.

Belsky, J., & Vondura, J. (1989). Lessons from child abuse: The determinants of parenting. In D. Cicchetti, & V. Carlson (Eds.), *Child maltreatment: Theory and research on the causes and consequences of child abuse and neglect* (pp. 153–202). New York: Cambridge University Press.

Benkov, L. (1994). *Reinventing the family: The emerging story of lesbian and gay partners.* New York: Crown.

Berger, R. M. (1990). Men together: Understanding the gay couple. *Journal of Homosexuality, 19,* 31–49.

Berger, R. M. (1996). *Gay and gray: The older homosexual man* (2nd ed.). Binghamton, NY: Haworth.

Bigner, J., & Jacobsen, R. B. (1992). Adult responses to child behavior and attitudes toward fathering: Gay and nongay fathers. *Journal of Homosexuality, 23,* 99–112.

Bigner, J. (1996). Working with gay fathers. In J. Laird & R. Green (Eds.), *Lesbians and gays in couples and families* (pp. 370–403). San Francisco: Jossey-Bass.

Bigner, J. J., & Jacobson, R. B. (1992). Adult responses to child behavior and attitudes toward fathering: Gay and nongay fathers. *Journal of Homosexuality, 23,* 99–112.

Blumstein, P., & Schwartz, P. (1983). *American couples.* New York: Morrow.

Bryant, S., & Demian. (1994). Relationship characteristics of American gay and lesbian couples: Findings from a national survey. *Journal of Gay and Lesbian Social Services, 1,* 101–117.

Camasso, J. M., & Jagannathan, R. (2000). Modeling the reliability and predictive validity of risk assessment in child protective services. *Children and Youth Services Review, 22,* 873–896.

Canino, I. A., & Spurlock, J. (2000). *Culturally diverse children and adolescents: Assessment, diagnosis, and treatment* (2nd ed.). New York: Guilford Press.

Caron, S. L., & Ulin, M. (1997). Closeting and the quality of lesbian relationships. *Families in Society: The Journal of Contemporary Human Services, 78,* 413–419.

Cash, S. J. (2001). Risk assessment in child welfare: The art and science. *Children and Youth Services Review, 23,* 811–830.

Clunis, D. M., & Green, G. D. (2000). *Lesbian couples: A guide to creating healthy relations* (2nd ed.). Seattle, WA: Seal.

Cohen, S., & Williamson, G. (1988). Perceived stress in a probability sample of the United States. In S. Spacapan & S. Oskamp (Eds.), *The social psychology of health: Claremont symposium on applied social psychology* (n.p.). Newbury Park, CA: Sage.

Cohn, D. (1995, May 9). Courts send mixed messages in custody cases. *Washington Post,* 87.

Corcoran, K., & Fischer, J. (2000). *Measures for clinical practice: A sourcebook* (3rd ed., Vols. 1 & 2). New York: Free Press.

Cramer, D. (1986). Gay parents and their children: A review of research and practical implications. *Journal of Counseling and Development, 64,* 504–507.

Crawford, S. (1987). Lesbian families: Psychosocial stress and the family-building process. In Boston Lesbian Psychologies Collective (Eds.), *Lesbian psychologies* (pp. 195–214). Urbana: University of Illinois Press.

D'Augelli, A. R., & Garnets, L. D. (1995). Lesbian, gay, and bisexual communities. In A. R. D'Augelli & C. J. Patterson (Eds.), *Lesbians, gay, and bisexual identities over the lifespan* (pp. 293–320). New York: Oxford University Press.

Day, P. (1999). Rethinking assessment in an evolving child welfare system. *Protecting Children, 15,* 19–20.

DePanfilis, D. (1995). *The epidemiology of child maltreatment recurrences.* Unpublished doctoral dissertation, University of Maryland.

Doueck, H. J., English D. J., DePanfilis, D., & Moote, G. T. (1993). Decision-making in child protective services. *Social Service Review, 65,* 112–132.

Drapalski, A., Marshall, T., Seybolt, D., Medoff, D., Peer, J., Leith, J., et al. (2008). Unmet needs of families of adults with mental illness and preferences regarding family services. *Psychiatric Services, 59,* 655–662.

Eldridge, N. S., & Gilbert, L. A. (1990). Correlates of relationship satisfaction in lesbian couples. *Psychology of Women Quarterly, 14,* 43–62.

English, D. J., Aubin, S. W., Fine. D., & Pecora, P. J. (1993). *Improving the accuracy and cultural sensitivity of risk assessment in child abuse and neglect cases.* Seattle: University of Washington, School of Social Work.

English, D. J., & Pecora, P. J. (1994). Risk assessment as a practice method in child protective services. *Child Welfare, 73,* 451–473.

Fanshel, D., Finch, S. J., & Grundy, J. F. (1994). Testing the measurement properties of risk assessment instruments in child protective services. *Child Abuse and Neglect, 18,* 1073–1084.

Fredriksen, K. I. (1999). Family caregiving responsibilities among lesbian and gay men. *Social Work, 44,* 142–155.

Gelles, R. J. (1996). *The book of David: How preserving families can cost children's lives.* New York: Basic Books.

Golombok, S., Spener, A., & Rutter, M. (1983). Children in lesbian and single-parent households: Psychosexual and psychiatric appraisal. *Journal of Child Psychology, 24,* 551–572.

Golombok, S., & Tasker, F. (1996). Do parents influence the sexual orientation of their children? Findings from a longitudinal study of lesbian families. *Developmental Psychology, 32,* 3–11.

Greenburg, J. S., Kim, H. W., & Greenley, J. R. (1997). Factors associated with subjective burden in siblings of adults with severe mental illness. *American Journal of Orthopsychiatry, 67,* 231–241.

Greenburg, J. S., Seltzer, M. M., Krauss, M. W., & Kim, H. (1999). Siblings of adults with mental illness or mental retardation: Current involvement and expectation of future caregiving. *Psychiatric Services, 50,* 1214–1219.

Greene, B. (Ed.). (1997). *Ethnic and cultural diversity among lesbians and gay men.* Thousand Oaks, CA: Sage.

Greene, B., & Boyd-Franklin, N. (1996). African American lesbian couples: Ethnocultural considerations in psychotherapy. *Women and Therapy, 19*(3), 49–60.

Greene, B., Mandel, J. G., Hotvedt, M. E., Gray, J., & Smith, L. (1986). Lesbian mothers and their children: A comparison with solo parent heterosexual mothers and their children. *Archives of Sexual Behavior, 15,* 167–184.

Hargaden, H., & Llewellin, S. (1996). Lesbian and gay parenting issues. In D. Davies & C. Neal (Eds.), *Pink therapy: A guide for counselors and therapists working with LGB clients* (pp. 116–130). Philadelphia: Open University Press.

Hare, J. (1994). Concerns and issues faced by families headed by a lesbian couple. *Families in Society, 75,* 27–35.

Hartman, A. (1996). Social policy as a context for lesbian and gay families: The political is personal. In J. Laird & R. J. Green (Eds.), *Lesbians and gays in couples and families* (pp. 69–850). San Francisco: Jossey-Bass.

Herek, G. (1995). Psychological heterosexism in the United States. In A. D'Augelli & C. Patterson (Eds.), *Lesbian, gay, and bisexual identities over the lifespan: Psychological perspectives* (pp. 321–346). New York: Oxford University Press.

Holder, W., & Lund, T. R. (1995). Translating risks to positive outcomes: Outcome-oriented case management from risk assessment information. *APSAC Advisor*, *8*(4), 20–24.

Hostetler, A. J., & Coher, B. J. (1997). Partnership, singlehood, and the lesbian and gay life course: A research agenda. *Journal of Gay, Lesbian, and Bisexual Identity*, *2*, 199–230.

Hudson, W. (1982). *The clinical measurement package: A field manual*. Chicago: Dorsey.

Institute of Medicine. (2002). Speaking of health: Assessing health communication strategies for diverse populations. Washington, DC: National Academy Press.

Jagannathan, R., & Camasso, M. J. (1996). Risk assessment in child protective services: A canonical analysis of the case management function. *Child Abuse and Neglect*, *20*, 599–612.

James, S. E., & Murphy, B. C. (1998). Gay and lesbian relationships in a changing social context. In C. J. Patterson & A. R. D'Augelli (Eds.), *Lesbian, gay, and bisexual identities in families: Psychological perspectives* (pp. 99–121). New York: Oxford University Press.

Juliet, C. R. (2008). Cultural competence in process and practice: Building bridges. Boston: Pearson Education.

Kitzinger, C., & Coyle, A. (1995). Lesbian and gay couples: Speaking of difference. *Psychologist*, *8*, 64–69.

Kurdek, L. A. (1988). Perceived social support in gays and lesbians in cohabiting relationships. *Journal of Personality and Social Psychology*, *54*, 504–509.

Kurdek, L. A. (1991). Correlates of relationship satisfaction in cohabiting gay and lesbian couples: Integration of contextual, investment, and problem-solving models. *Journal of Personality and Social Psychology*, *61*, 910–922.

Kurdek, L. A. (1994). The nature and correlates of relationship quality in gay, lesbian, and heterosexual cohabiting couples: A test of the contextual, investment, and discrepancy models. In B. Greene & G. M. Herek (Eds.), *Lesbian and gay psychology: Theory, research, and clinical applications* (pp. 133–135). Thousand Oaks, CA: Sage.

Kurdek, L. A. (1995). Developing changes in relationship quality in gay and lesbian cohabiting couples. *Developmental Psychology*, *31*, 86–94.

Kurdek, L. A. (1997). Relation between neuroticism and dimensions of relationship commitment: Evidence from gay, lesbian, and heterosexual couples. *Journal of Family Psychology*, *11*, 109–124.

Leff, J. (2005). *Advanced family work for schizophrenia: An evidence-based approach*. London: Gaskell.

Lefley, H. (1996). *Family caregiving in mental illness*. Thousand Oaks, CA: Sage.

Leiter, R. A. (1997). *National survey of state laws*. Detroit, MI: Gale Research.

LeVine, E. S., & Sallee, A. L. (1999). *Child welfare: Clinical theory and practice*. Dubuque, IA: Bowers.

Lewis-Fernandez, R., & Kleinman, A. (1995). Cultural psychiatry: Theoretical, clinical, and research issues. *Psychiatric Clinics of North America*, *18*, 433–448.

Lyons, P., Doueck, H. J., & Wodarski, J. S. (1996). Risk assessment for child protective services: A review of the empirical literature on instrument performance. *Social Work Research, 20*, 143–155.

Marsh, D. T., Dickens, R. M., Koeske, R. D., Yackovich, N. S., Wilson, J. M., Leichliter, J., et al. (1993). Troubled journey: Siblings and children of people with mental illness. *Innovations and Research, 2*(2), 13–23.

Martin, A. (1993). *The lesbian and gay parenting handbook.* New York: HarperCollins.

Matthews, C. R., & Lease, S. H. (2000). Focus on lesbian, gay, and bisexual families. In R. M. Perez, K. A. DeBord, & K. J. Bieschke (Eds.), *Handbook of counseling and psychotherapy with lesbian, gay, and bisexual clients* (pp. 249–273). Washington, DC: American Psychological Association.

McCubbin, H., Patterson, J., & Wilson, L. R. (1991). *Family inventory of life events and changes.* Baltimore: Williams and Wilkins.

McCubbin, H., Thompson, M., & McCubbin, M. (1996). *Family assessment: Resiliency, copying and adaptation: Inventories for research and practice.* Madison: University of Wisconsin-Madison.

McLeod, A., & Crawford, I. (1998). The postmodern family: An examination of the psychosocial and legal perspectives of gay and lesbian parenting. In G. M. Herek (Ed.), *Stigma and sexual orientation: Understanding prejudice against lesbians, gay men, and bisexuals* (pp. 211–222). Thousand Oaks, CA: Sage.

Meyer, J. (1990). Guess who's coming to dinner this time? A study of gay intimate relationships and the support for those relationships. *Marriage and Family Review, 14*, 59–82.

Morton, N., & Browne, K. (1998). Theory and observation of attachment and its relation to child maltreatment: A review. *Child Abuse and Neglect*, 1093–1104.

Murphy, B. C. (1994). Difference and diversity: Gay and lesbian couples. *Social Services for Gay and Lesbian Couples, 1*, 5–31.

New Freedom Commission on Mental Health. (2003). *Achieving the promise: Transforming mental health care in America: Final report* (DHHS Publication No.SMA-03-3832). Rockville, MD: Department of Health and Human Services.

O'Connell, A. (1993). Voices from the heart: The developmental impact of a mother's lesbianism on her adolescent children. *Smith College Studies in Social Work, 63*, 281–299.

Olson, D. (1986). Circumplex model VII: Validation studies and FACES III. *Family Process, 25*, 337–351.

Patterson, C. J. (1992). Children of lesbian and gay men. *Journal of Sex Research, 30*, 62–69.

Patterson, C. J. (1995). Lesbian mothers, gay fathers, and their children. In A. R. D'Augelli & C. J. Patterson (Eds.), *Lesbian, gay, and bisexual identities over the lifespan: Psychological perspectives* (pp. 262–290). Oxford: Oxford University Press.

Patterson, C. J., & Chan, R. W. (1996). Gay fathers and their children. In R. P. Cabaj & T. S. Stein (Eds.), *Textbook of homosexuality and mental health* (pp. 371–393). Washington, DC: American Psychiatric Press.

Patterson, D. G., & Schwartz, P. (1994). The social construction of conflict in intimate same-sex couples. In D. D. Cahn (Ed.), *Conflict in personal relationships* (pp. 3–26). Hillsdale, NJ: Erlbaum.

Pecora, P. J., Whittaker, J. K., Maluccio, A. N., & Barth, R. P. (2000). *The child welfare challenge* (2nd ed.). New York: Aldine de Gruyter.

Peplau, L. A. (1993). Lesbian and gay relationships. In L. D. Garnets & D. C. Kimmel (Eds.), *Psychological perspectives on lesbian and gay male experiences* (pp. 395–419). New York: Columbia University Press.

Pickett-Schenk, S. (2003). Family education and support: Just for women only? *Psychiatric Rehabilitation Journal, 27*, 131–139.

Rand, C., Graham, D. L., & Rawlings, E. (1982). Psychological health and factors the court seeks to control in lesbian mother custody trials. *Journal of Homosexuality, 8*, 27–39.

Results of poll. (1989, June 6). *San Francisco Examiner*, A-19.

Rohrbaugh, J. (1992). Domestic violence in same gender relationships. *Family Court Review, 44*, 287–299.

Rosenblum, D. M. (1991). Custody rights of gay and lesbian parents. *Villanova Law Review, 36*, 1665–1696.

Rosenbluth, S. C., & Steil, J. M. (1995). Predictors of intimacy for women in heterosexual and homosexual couples. *Journal of Social and Personal Relationships, 12*, 163–175.

Savin-Williams, R. C. (1998). *". . . and then I became gay": Young men's stories*. New York: Routledge.

Scrivner, R., & Eldridge, N. S. (1995). Lesbian and gay family psychology. In R. H. Mikesell & D. D. Lusterman (Eds.), *Integrating family therapy: Handbook of family psychology and systems theory* (pp. 327–345). Washington, DC: American Psychological Association.

Segal-Sklar, S. (1996). Lesbian parenting: Radical or retrograde? In K. Jay (Ed.), *Dyke life: A celebration of the lesbian experience* (pp. 174–191). New York: Basic Books.

Serovich, J. M., Skeen, P., Walters, L. H., & Robinson, B. E. (1993). In-law relationships when a child is homosexual. *Journal of Homosexuality, 26*, 57–75.

Shapiro, J. (1996). Custody and conduct: How the law fails lesbian and gay parents and their children. *Indiana Law Journal, 71*, 623–621.

Shernoff, M. (1995). Male couples and their relationship styles. *Journal of Gay and Lesbian Social Services, 2*, 43–57.

Shernoff, M. (1996). Gay men choosing to be fathers. In M. Shernoff (Ed.), *Human services for gay people: Clinical and community practice* (pp. 41–54). Binghamton, NY: Harrington Park.

Stiglitz, E. (1990). Caught between two worlds: The impact of a child on a lesbian couple's relationship. *Women and Therapy, 10*, 99–116.

Substance Abuse and Mental Health Service Administration. (2005). *National Survey on Drug Use and Health: National findings*. Retrieved from http://www.drug abusestatistics.samhsa.gov/NSDUH/2k5NSDUH/2k5results.htm.

Tasker, F. L., & Golombok, S. (1997). *Growing up in a lesbian family: Effects on child development.* New York: Guilford Press.

Turner, P. H., Scadden, L., & Harris, M. B. (1990). Parenting in gay and lesbian families. *Journal of Gay and Lesbian Psychotherapy, 1,* 55–66.

U.S. Department of Health and Human Services, Administration on Children, Youth and Families. *Child Maltreatment 2006.* Washington, DC: U.S. Government Printing Office, 2007. Retrieved April 12, 2008, from http://www.acf.hhs.gov/programs/cb/pubs/cm06/chapter2.htm.

Vandiver, V., Jordan, C., Keopraseuth, K., & Yu, M. (1995). Family as educator: Cross-cultural approaches for integrating family knowledge with psychosocial rehabilitation programs. *Journal of Psychosocial Rehabilitation, 19*(1), 47–54.

Wakefield, P., Williams, R., Yost, E., & Patterson, K. (1996). *Couple therapy for alcoholism: A cognitive behavioral treatment manual.* New York: Guilford Press.

Wald, M. S., & Woolverton, M. (1990). Risk assessment: The emperors new clothes. *Child Welfare, 69,* 483–511.

Warner, R. (2005). Local projects of the world psychiatric association to reduce stigma and discrimination. *Psychiatric Services, 56,* 570–575.

Wayment, H., & Peplau, L. A. (1995). Social support and well-being among lesbian and heterosexual women: A structural modeling approach. *Personality and Social Psychology Bulletin, 21,* 1189–1199.

Weinberg, M. S., Williams, C. J., & Pryor, D. W. (1994). *Dual attraction: Understanding bisexuality.* New York: Oxford University Press.

Weinstock, J. S. (1998). Lesbian, gay, bisexual, and transgendered friendships in adulthood. In C. J. Patterson & A. R. D'Augelli (Eds.), *Lesbian, gay, and bisexual identities in families: Psychological perspectives* (pp. 122–153). New York: Oxford University Press.

Weston, K. (1994). Building gay families: In G. Handlel & G. G. Whitechurch (Eds.), *The psychosocial interior of the family* (4th ed., pp. 525–533). New York: Aldine de Gruyter.

Weston, K. (1997). *Families we choose* (2nd ed.). New York: Columbia University.

Wiehe, V. R. (1992). *Working with child abuse and neglect.* Itasca, IL: Peacock.

World Health Organization. (2001). *Mental health, new understanding, new hope.* Retrieved from http://www.who.int/whr/2001/en/index.html.

World Health Organization. (2002). *Atlas: Mental health resources in the world.* Geneva: World Health Organization.

World Health Organization. (2006). *Epidemiological fact sheets on HIV/AIDS and sexually transmitted infections, United States of America, update 2006.* Washington, DC: U.S. Government Printing Office, 2006. Retrieved April 12, 2008, from http://www.who.int/globalatlas/predefinedReports/EFS2006/EFS_PDFs/EFS2006_US.pdf.

# Assessing Special Populations in Social Work Practice

Part IV moves from child, adolescent, and family populations to a discussion of special issues. Chapter 10, "Multicultural Assessment," covers the limitations of assessment methods and provides an overview of ethnic-sensitive assessment strategies for four groups (American Indians/Alaska Natives, African Americans/Blacks, Hispanics/Latinos, and Asian Americans). Chapter 11, "Linking Assessment to Outcome Evaluation: Using Single-System and Group Research Design," emphasizes the importance of clinical social workers systematically appraising the outcomes of their own practice and integrates this long-standing tradition with the newer initiative called evidence-based practice, which is currently infusing the social work field and has been discussed previous chapters.

CHAPTER 10

# Multicultural Assessment

## Dorie J. Gilbert

## INTRODUCTION

Diverse value orientations, life experiences, and worldviews are all implicit in the term *multiculturalism*. In our increasingly multicultural society, social work practitioners are challenged to demonstrate an understanding of how factors like race or ethnicity, gender, sexual orientation, age, and different physical and mental abilities affect our practice with clients. This chapter focuses on the influence of race/ethnicity or ethnocultural factors on a client's assessment. Wong (2000) noted almost a decade ago that as practitioners are being asked more frequently to evaluate clients who are of different ethnic, cultural, or language backgrounds than themselves, they are "finding few resources to aid them" (p. 43). Today, practitioners remain challenged in availing themselves of the most relevant resources for culturally competent assessment. Further, professional standards also dictate that assessment be integrated with evidence-based practice (EBP), or the use of empirically tested and verified knowledge in practice decision-making (Rosen, Proctor, & Staudt, 2003). Yet the applicability of standardized measures and clinical diagnostic categories for multicultural assessment has been brought into question in numerous critiques of standardized assessment practices (Dana, 1998, 2000, 2005). Procedures for EBP require practitioners to engage in "complex and conscientious decision-making based not only on the available evidence but also on patient characteristic, situations and preferences" (McKibbon, 1998, p. 396). As such, cultural differences should be a key component in determining the best assessment and intervention alliance to optimize the client's outcome.

However, the ethnocentrism of the U.S. majority culture creates a situation in which assessment procedures and measurement instruments do not fully consider culturally based ways of thinking, feeling, and behaving that may be outside of the majority (Eurocentric) perspective. The historical misdiagnosis and distortion of ethnic and racial populations based solely on a Euro-American worldview has been called "cultural malpractice" (Hall, 1997) and "occurs as a result of unintentional, often unconscious, but unremitting bias from a variety of sources" (Dana, 2000,

p. xiii). The goal of multicultural assessment training is to increase the practitioner's ability to conduct assessments using culturally congruent techniques, methods and clinical conceptions, without which the most well-intentioned practitioners act unethically.

Toward this goal, this chapter covers the limitations of assessment methods and provides an overview of ethnic-sensitive assessment strategies for four groups (American Indians/Alaska Natives, African Americans/Blacks, Hispanics/Latinos, and Asian Americans). These groups have been historically overrepresented in receiving inaccurate and culturally biased assessments, diagnosis, and interventions. The chapter includes a tabular guide for identifying examples of specific measures, by ethnicity, that are recommended for use with specific clients. Finally, a case study illustrates a culturally grounded assessment approach.

## BACKGROUND ON ETHNIC-MINORITY CLIENTS

Racial/ethnic trends in the United States point to a society that is increasing in ethnic diversity and developing a growing awareness of ethnic identity. By the year 2050, racial and ethnic minorities will represent nearly 49.9 percent the population (U.S. Census Bureau, 2004). At the same time, many whites are starting to gain increased understanding of their own ethnic ancestry as it may be linked to various heritages, such as Italian American or Irish American (Waters, 2001), and thereby are creating a new entity in the history of American ethnic groups, referred to as Euro-Americans (Rubin, 2001). As Lum (2004) notes, ethnic groups who are able to blend into the white-dominated society of Anglo-Saxon and European groups have successfully assimilated into the mainstream of American society and power. However, the color factor has been a barrier to African Americans, Latinos, Asian Americans, and Native Americans. Thus, groups of color, while increasing in numbers, remain a minority because of a lack of economic, political, and social power (Feagin & Feagin, 2003; Lum, 2004). The social construction of race in our society means that most ethnic-minority individuals continue to contend with societal stigma and negative outcomes perpetuated by the biased majority culture. This chapter outlines the basic demographic, sociocultural experiences of the four groups and briefly discusses relevant group-related factors that contribute to group-level differences and may influence a client's clinical presentation at assessment. A comprehensive description of each group addressed is beyond the scope of this chapter; thus, practitioners are advised to consult other works for detailed discussions of histories, cultural norms and practices, and salient intragroup differences for each group and its corresponding subgroups.

## American Indians and Alaska Natives

The term *Native Americans* can be extended to include all descendants of the pre-Columbian inhabitants of North America, including American Indian, Alaska Native, and Canadian, and Mexican Indian people (Paniagua, 2005). There is an enormous amount of diversity both within and between each of these subgroups. Today, this group numbers slightly more than 4.1 million and account for 1.5 percent of the U.S. population; but it is one of the fastest-growing groups in the United States, given increased birthrates, decreased infant mortality, and an increased willingness to report American Indian ancestry (U.S. Census Bureau, 2004). There are more than 550 federally recognized American Indian tribes and Alaska Native village groups in the United States (Russell, 2006).

The land, language, religion, and culture of Native peoples were nearly destroyed by the colonialization practice of the Europeans and today Native peoples remain one of the most disadvantaged groups in the United States. Their strengths are grounded in Native cultural values, which often conflict with those of the majority culture (Weaver, 2008; Yellowbird, 2001). Weaver (2008) describes values and norms associated with traditional native culture, including but not limited to a fluid sense of time, with the view of being ruled by a clock as unhealthy and unnatural; a sense of spirituality that incorporates guidelines for behavior; a collective identity strongly linked to family, clan, and nation; a deep respect for elders' knowledge and wisdom; leaders' willingness to sacrifice on behalf of the communities; and the view of children as the future of Native nations.

Among individuals treated by the Indian Health Service (IHS), mental health and social problems were associated with one-third of requests for services, and mental health was identified as the top health problem by ten of twelve IHS areas and the Urban Indian Health Programs in fiscal year 2001. Native populations primarily seek professional psychological services for substance abuse, anxiety, depression, and adjustment-related problems, which can be associated with a historical trauma response to the genocide of Native peoples and the population's unresolved grief from those historical traumas (Brave Heart, 2001).

## African Americans and Blacks

African Americans make up 13 percent of the U.S. population. The more than 33 million individuals constituting this group include people with roots in Africa and the African diaspora, including the West Indies, South America, and the Caribbean (Feagin & Feagin, 2003). In addition, the number of immigrants from African countries is increasing because of large numbers of immigrants from Nigeria, Ghana, and Ethiopia (Dhooper & Moore, 2001).

The major strengths of American Blacks have been tied to the premise that African Americans, for the most part, survived historically based on Africentric worldviews and African values and traditions (Karenga, 1996). Africentric values and traditions include unity (striving for unity in family, community, and race), self-determination (defining, naming, and creating for ourselves), collective work and responsibility (building and maintaining community and solving problems together), cooperative economics (building and maintaining an economic base of community), purpose (restoring people to their original traditional greatness), creativity (enhancing the beauty and benefits of self and community), and faith (belief in righteousness of the black struggle). Although African Americans are diverse and vary in terms of the extent to which they endorse these principles, these values reinforce positive mental and physical health (Morris, 2000).

At the same time, African Americans lead the nation across a number of current mental health and health disparities. As a group, they are often at a socioeconomic disadvantage in terms of accessing both medical and mental health care, and more than 20 percent of African Americans are uninsured. The Office of Minority Health Disparities (2008) reports that African Americans experience disproportionately high rates of death from heart diseases, stroke, cancer, diabetes, HIV/AIDS, and homicide. Mental health disparities include depression, substance abuse, and suicide. Across a recent fifteen-year span, suicide rates increased by 233 percent among African Americans aged ten to fourteen, compared with a 120 percent increase among Caucasians in the same age group. More than 25 percent of African American children exposed to violence meet criteria for posttraumatic stress disorder. As is the case for Native Americans, many current problems of African Americans can be traced to their historical trauma experience of slavery and genocide, referred to as the *maafa* (a Kiswahili word for "great disaster and destruction beyond comprehension") (Parham, 1995).

### Hispanics and Latinos

*Hispanic* is an ethno-cultural label for a heterogeneous constituency of people of Mexican, Dominican, Puerto Rican, and Cuban descent, as well as of individuals from Central and South America. However, many in the group prefer the term *Latino*. Mexican Americans, who reside primarily in the western and southwestern United States, comprise almost two-thirds of Latinos. The actual number of Latinos in the United States is probably greater than official data indicate as a result of undocumented immigrants being missed by the census. Although this population represents the largest racial and ethnic minority in the United States, it still faces multiple challenges that continue to affect quality of life, including chronic and infectious diseases and limited access to health care (National Council of La Raza, 2008).

Although there are differences among and within subgroups, Latino values include the important role of godparenthood (*compadres*), a deep sense of family obligation (*familismo*), social engagement and avoidance of interpersonal conflict (*simpatía*), and emphasis on spritiual beliefs, as well as the Spanish language, which helps preserve cultural identity (Dhooper & Moore, 2001). Conceptions of mental health, health, and illness among Latinos vary according to different theories of various subgroups. According to Guinn (1998), studies of health conceptions of Mexican Americans in the Southwest reveal salient cultural beliefs that can be traced to both a traditional Mexican belief in supernatural sanctions and a tendency toward fatalistic acceptance. For example, the cause of an illness may be believed to be beyond realm of human forces. Although Catholicism is relatively common among this group, many Latinos may simultaneously practice other forms of religion or healing, such as spiritism in Puerto Rico and Santeria in Cuba and seek help from from folk healers such as *curanderos* and herbalists who play roles similar to that of psychotherapists (Dhooper & Moore, 2001).

Findings suggest that Hispanics have similar rates of psychiatric disorders as non-Hispanic whites, but as a group, they underuse the mental-health-care system, which may be partly because of the lack of bilingual and bicututural professionals. Among Hispanic Americans with a mental health disorder, fewer than one in eleven contact mental health specialists (U.S. Department of Health and Human Services, 2008a). According to the Office of Minority Health and Health Disparties (2008), Hispanic women tend to suffer from depression more than Hispanic men, and studies have found that Hispanic youths experience more anxiety related issues and delinquency problem behaviors than non-Hispanic white youths. Regarding older Hispanic Americans, one study found that more than 26 percent of the group members were depressed, and depression was related to physical health (U.S. Department of Health and Human Services, 2008a).

## Asian and Pacific Islander Americans

One of the fastest-growing racial-ethnic groups in the United States, Asian and Pacific Islander Americans are expected to account for nearly 8 percent of the U.S. population by the year 2050 (U.S. Census Bureua, 2004). Currently, they constitute about 3 percent of the population and reside primarily in California, New York, and Hawaii. This group represents extremely diverse ethnic backgrounds, including Japanese, Chinese,

Filipinos, Koreans, Vietnamese, Hmong, Laotians, Cambodians, Asian Indians, Native Hawaiians, Samoans, Tongans, Fijians, and Chamorros (Guamanians). There are multiple and complex reasons for the diversity among the subgroups of Asian and Pacific Islander Americans, and practitioners should be able to recognize the distinctions among the various groups and subgroups to ensure appropriate assessments (Wong & Fujii, 2004). In addition, immigrants and refugees are a growing population in this group with vast differences among the incoming subgroups. Asian Americans and Pacific Islanders place a high value on harmony in relationships, mutual dependency rather than individual dependency, and important cultural values (Chow, 2001). These values include filial piety, modesty, respect for authority, and communal responsibility. Similar to other ethnic-minority groups, Asian Americans and Pacific Islanders are more group oriented than self-oriented and have histories of discrimination and continued oppression in this country.

The myth of the group as a monlithic model minority creates the belief that Asian Americans have their own resources to succeed and overcome discrimination and prejudice, which in turn results in denial of their vulnerability and need for mental health services (Dhooper & Moore, 2001). This label masks the struggles among some of the subgroups, thereby causing the plight of many subgroup members to go unrecognized. For example, Native Hawaiians are known to have disproportionately high rates of cancer, diseases of the heart, and diabetes mellitus (Mokuau, Garlock-Tuiali'i, & Lee, 2008). Moreover, the most recent surgeon general's report notes that Asian American women have the highest suicide rate of all women older than sixty-five in the United States. As a agroup, Asian Americans are 25 percent as likely as whites and 50 percent as likely as African Americans and Hispanics to seek outpatient mental health care and less likely than whites to receive inpatient care. When they do seek care, they are more likely to be diagnosed as "problem free" (U.S. Department of Health & Human Services, 2008b).

## CONSIDERATIONS IN ASSESSING ETHNIC-MINORITY CLIENTS

The concepts of emic and etic functioning underlie the notion of culturally competent assessment practice. Some aspects of functioning are unique to the client's culture (emic); others are common across many cultures (etic). Eurocentric (or majority) culture assumes an etic position, which is detrimental for members of ethnic minority groups. When practitioners approach assessment from the assumption that all individuals should be treated the same (e.g., with the same assessment instruments, the same assumptions about mental health), they are likely to misdiagnose clients who do not identify with mainstream culture. Inasmuch as the initial assessment phase determines the course of treatment, it is important that practitioners avoid the tendency to gloss over cultural components when assessing clients (Draguns, 2002).

The lack of culturally competent assessment centers on three main issues: (a) practitioners' bias and/or lack of awareness of cultural differences, (b) reliance on stereotypes or overgeneralizations for assessment strategies, and (c) culturally biased measurement and assessment instruments.

## Practitioners' Bias and/or Lack of Awareness of Cultural Differences

The dominant cultural standards (i.e., white, middle-class, heterosexual, male) have tended to result in more diagnoses of mental disorders and pathology among those who are outside the dominant culture than in it (Snowden, 2003). The literature contains numerous examples of misdiagnoses and differential assessment outcomes for ethnic-minority clients. Uomoto and Wong (2000) also express concern that "patients from certain ethnic backgrounds who may be exhibiting common behavioral/cognitive sequelae of certain types of brain injuries, such as restlessness, agitation, or disinhibition following frontal lobe damage, may be suspected of having premorbid personality problems" (p. 163). Research over the decades has documented evidence that African Americans receive more severe diagnostic labels than whites, have higher than expected rates of diagnosed schizophrenia and lower rates of diagnosed affective disorders, and that diagnostic testing is used less frequently with African American clients even when they have insurance; Snowden, 2003). When African Americans do seek mental health care, they often are prescribed higher doses of psychiatric medication,which may result in increased side effects and decreased medication compliance (Office of Minority Health Disparities, 2008). Moreover, African American men are sometimes subjected to an assumed and unverified history of drug abuse during assessments and intake procedures (Uomoto & Wong, 2000).

These differences point to ways in which clinicians indeed are biased in the course of routine practice. Further, a recent Institute of Medicine report on racial and ethic disparities documented mounting evidence that racial-ethnic minorities receive lower-quality health care than whites do, even when insurance status, income, age and severity of conditions are comparable, and that practitioner providers' attitudes, communication with persons of color, and lack of cultural competence are factors not only in maintaining these disparities but also in exacerbating them (Smedley, Stith, & Nelson, 2003).

Lack of awareness of culture-based symptoms is also a factor. Culture-bound syndromes can result in misdiagnosis. For example, Hispanics may experience *ataque de nervios* with such symptoms as screaming uncontrollably, crying, trembling, verbal and physical aggression, dissociative experiences, fainting episodes, and suicidal behaviors (U.S. Department of Health and Human Services, 2008a). Latino and other clients who believe in the supernatural and believe that fate or a deceased person is in control of their lives may be diagnosed as psychotic. Another example is the common practice of ancestor veneration (Grills, 2002), the practice of some African-descent people to call on ancestors as part of a coping strategy, whereas "talking to ancestors" might be misdiagnosed as hallucinating and psychotic.

To be aware of the cultural differences that can affect the assessment process means that practitioners must first be aware of their own cultural orientation to understand how they may potentially impose their own values or worldviews on others. Social workers, regardless of their ethnocultural background should engage themselves in a self-assessment process as the first step toward cultural competence self-assessments to determine their own cultural orientation and how their culture and values may interact with clients from diverse backgrounds. Pedersen and Ivey (1993) sagely remind us that ignoring the influence of our own and others' culturally learned assumptions "is a little like speeding in a car down a busy street without having your hands on the steering wheel" (p. 1). Thus, self-assessment is a crucial tool by which practitioners can understand culturally learned meanings behind their own and others' behavior. In addition, it is important to note that ethnic-minority practitioners also face challenges with internalized oppression and horizontal prejudices against subgroups in ethnic-minority communities or may have a cultural "blind spot," whereby they perceive those who share their cultural identity as just like themselves and ignore the uniqueness of clients (Pinderhughes, 1989).

### Reliance on Stereotypes or Overgeneralizations for Assessment Strategies

A common mistake practitioners make in their attempt to master culturally sensitive assessment is to apply stereotypes and overgeneralizations about a client's racial/ethnic group during the assessment process. For example, a practitioner conducting an assessment with an Asian American female client may notice the client's quiet, withdrawn behavior and assume that this is a "normal" demeanor of Asian American women. The practitioner therefore may not explore other reasons for the observed behavior or investigate the specific beliefs and norms of the client's subgroup (e.g., Chinese, Filipino). An erroneous assumption that some practitioners make in assessing ethnic-minority clients is that racial/ethic status is the equivalent construct of culture, a concept Trimble (1995) refers to as ethnic glossing. Although this glossing may be acceptable for broad classifications and policy making, Oetting, Swaim, and Chiarella (1998) warn against equating culture with racial/ethnic status: "Professionals need to use special care in defining what is meant by culture in different contexts and situations. Culture can, under certain circumstances, still serve to define at least some of the characteristic attitudes, beliefs, and behaviors of a group of people that share a commonly perceived cultural identity. The extent to which a person conforms to those culturally determined behaviors, however, depends on both cultural identity and the level of identification with that culture" (p. 132).

Oetting et al. (1998) define cultural identity as a person's affiliation with a specific group, for example a person's membership in an ethnic group. In contrast, cultural identification is a personal trait; it is the extent to which individuals view themselves as involved with an identifiable group along with their investment or stake in that particular culture. Thus, the first step in any assessment involves determining the client's ethnic-group schematicity, or the extent to which the client's culture, derives from his or her ethnic group. There is substantial intragroup differences among the four major groups addressed here. Cultural orientations vary within each of the ethnic-minority groups, particularly as an increasing number of people identify with multiple ethnicities or choose not to define themselves by racial/ethnic categories at all. A good example is the use of the term *Hispanic* to describe a large, ethnically diverse group of people who differ regarding a number of demographic variables. However, Hispanic groups are often aggregated when examining drinking patterns, for example. Epstein, Botvin, and Diaz (2001) examined the roles of Hispanic group identification (Puerto Rican versus Dominican) and gender in alcohol use among inner-city youths. Sixth and seventh graders in twenty-two New York City schools who identified themselves as Puerto Rican or Dominican completed self-report questionnaires at two assessments. The questionnaires showed that Dominican adolescents generally engaged in more alcohol use than Puerto Rican adolescents. Gender also played a role in drinking patterns for Dominican adolescents. Specifically, Dominican boys reported greater use than Dominican girls, but use was similar across gender for Puerto Rican adolescents. These findings highlight the importance of considering Hispanic group and gender when examining adolescent drinking. Moreover, the study underscores the need to consider multiple variables, not just broad categories of race/ethnicity, in assessment of clients.

Furthermore, in addition to cultural orientation that centers around racial/ethnic status, individuals in any group differ with regard to a number of other variables (e.g., class, gender, age, religion, recency of immigration, sexual orientation, educational level), all of which challenges the myopic notion of the monolithic group. Each client is unique and must be encountered without prejudgement and assumptions. Ethnic identity is one component of our sense of self. The Multigroup Ethnic Identity Measure (MEIM; Phinney, 1992) measures attitudes, behaviors, practices, and belongingness to assess the concept we have of ourselves as a member of a racial/ethnic group. Considering the range of cultural orientations, practitioners should first determine the level of acculturation and ethnic group orientation and identity (Dana, 1993, 1998) before proceeding to administer assessment instruments. Ethnic identity also varies with acculturation, the extent to which racial and ethnic subpopulations adapt to language, identity, behavior patterns, and preferences to those of the majority society. For example, the MEIM has been used to explore relationship between ethnic identity and acculturation.

### Culturally Biased Measurement and Assessment Instruments

Practitioners must also select assessment measures and strategies in the context of cultural norms and values. Although most practitioners embrace the valuing of diversity, they also fall prey to conformity in their adherence to dominant cultural standards and the judgment of what constitutes an objective assessment. Standardized measures are usually the first choice for social work practitioners in conducting assessments; however, most of these measures have been constructed on the basis of the majority culture and with little attention to the values, attitudes, and life experiences of individuals from nonmainstream cultures. Dana (2005) refers to this as "imposed etics" in describing the way in which all instruments in the United States "are still assumed to be etic in nature, or universal, rather than emic" (n.p.). As society becomes more diverse, there is a recognized shortage of cross-culturally validated assessment instruments. Although standardized measures may pass the test of high reliability and stability, they can be culturally biased when used with ethnic-minority groups (Aponte & Crouch, 2000; Dana, 1993, 1998; Paniagua, 2005). In some instances, important emic-assumed mental-health-related concepts lack true equivalents in languages and cultural interpretations other than English, which opens the way to misunderstanding of complaints. When faced with standardized assessment procedures, for example, some Asian Americans approach the very task of responding with tendencies different from those assumed by developers of the procedures (Snowden, 2003). Other research suggests that older Caribbean people might use terms for emotional distress that differ from those found in standard screening instruments (Abas, Phillips, Richards, Carter, & Levy 1996).

Jones (1996) states that the bias inherent in standardized measures is multifacted: the content of the items constituting the measure; the administration of the measure by a person unfamiliar with the language, behavior, or culture of the person being given the measure; and the validation and norming of measures without consideration of diverse cultures. Paniagua (2005) ranked measurement instruments on the basis of the level of cultural bias. Highly biased instruments include clinical interviews (e.g., the mental status examination), trait measures, self-report psychopathology measures (e.g., Minnesota Multiphasic Personality Inventory, referred to as MMPI and MMPI2; Beck Depression Inventory, BDI), and the Rorschach test (Dana, 1993). For example, compared to the BDI, the Center for Epidemiologic Studies Depression (CES-D) scale contained a number of items that were more likely to be endorsed by Chinese Americans regardless of their level of depression. In another example, Reid et al. (1998) explored the extent to which the ADHD Rating Scale-IV (School Version) differed across male white and African American five-to eighteen-year-old students. Teachers rated African American students higher on all symptoms across age groups, and analyses indicated that the scale does not perform identically across groups.

Similarly, the *DSM-IV* has been criticized for its lack of cultural validity and absence of commitment to culturally sensitive assessments (Dana, 1998, 2000; Kutchins & Kirk, 1997). In an effort to improve the measure, Mezzich et al. (1999) outline significant changes to the *DSM-IV*, including an introductory statement about cultural considerations for the use of diagnostic categories and criteria, a glossary of culture-bound syndromes and idioms of distress, and an outline for a cultural formulation. Because the *DSM-IV* is commonly used, social workers must commit to incorporating the guidelines presented by the cultural formulation. These include the consideration of cultural identity, cultural explanations of illness, cultural factors and psychosocial environment, and cultural factors in the clinical relationship. Brave Heart (2001) presents a detailed discussion of how to incorporate the cultural formulation guidelines with American Indians (specifically the Lakota tribe), and practitioners should employ a similar strategy with other ethnic-minority groups.

Despite the significant changes to the *DSM-IV* however, several authors also point to the need for further contextualization of illness, diagnosis, and care (Dana, 1998; Kutchins & Kirk, 1997; Mezzich et al., 1999). Furthermore, the *DSM-IV* does not include disorders resulting from oppression (e.g., racism as a trauma) and does not explicitly label oppression-induced conditions (Dana, 1998). Fabrega (1992) recommends including a cultural axis among several possible avenues to resolve the conflict between disease and cultural viewpoints. Dana (1998) notes that, "in the absence of basic DSM changes, assessment of culturally diverse groups, therapeutic assessment, and assessment as a precursor to interventions by psychologists [and other counseling practitioners] could become increasingly medicalized under managed mental health auspices with implications for quality of care" (p. 7).

With such noted disappointments in the culturally appropriate utility of both the *DSM-IV* and commonly used standardized instruments, practitioners will undoubtedly feel caught between two conflicting professional demands when conducting assessments. On the one hand, practitioners are accountable to institutionalized mental health guidelines that specify the use of standardized and widely used measurement tools and diagnostic procedures. On the other hand, practitioners are required to conduct culturally competent assessments for clients who may not be appropriately served—and may even be harmed—by such "objective" measures and procedures. So, how are practitioners to proceed in resolving this assessment dilemma? The recent assessment literature points to three new directions as alternative or mixed models of assessment with ethnic-minority clients: assessment of cultural identity, assessment of acculturative stress and responses to oppression, and the use of pictorial tests.

## ASSESSMENT METHODS FOR MULTICULTURAL PRACTICE

Table 10.1 includes a selected list of measures for the four ethnic groups covered in this chapter and information on how to obtain those measures. The measures presented reflect the four recommended alternatives discussed here.

### Alternative 1: Use of Revised Tests and Newly Devised Ethnic Specific Tests

Revised tests are instruments that have been developed and validated to tap the emic-based cultural contexts of mental health issues; they include translations of commonly used tests. Examples include the Chinese Depression Symptom Scale and the Vietnamese adaptation of the MMPI-2 (Tran, 1996). Whenever possible, practitioners should use tests that have been normed on the client's ethnic population in assessments; however, such tests are few and far between, and their development lags behind revisions of the original test. As Okazaki and Sue (2000) note, "Often, by the time individual researchers have conducted cross-cultural adaptation studies with a given assessment instrument, the revised version of the same instrument may well be under development" (p. 278).

In contrast, some researchers question whether the areas of needed assessment are the same for Euro-Americans as they are for ethnic-minority

**Table 10.1**  Selected List of Measures for Four Ethnic Groups

| Racial/Ethnic Group | Measure | Measure Characteristics | Reliability/Validity | Where to obtain |
|---|---|---|---|---|
| **American Indians/ Alaska Natives** | **Cultural Involvement and Detachment Anxiety Scale (CIDAQ)** Promising measure for examining culturally related anxiety in American Indian and Alaska Natives, particularly in college counseling and behavioral health care centers | Scale contains 3 factors measuring anxiety about (1) social involvement w/National American and cultural knowledge, (2) economic issues, and (3) social involvement with majority culture | High levels of item-total reliability, internal consistency, and convergent and divergent validity. Cronbach's alpha .92 for total scale. | Daniel W. McNeil Dept. of Psychology West Virginia University, Anxiety, Psychophysiology, and Pain Research Laboratory P. O. Box 6040 Morgantown, WV 26506-6040 Email: dmmcneil@wvu.edu |
| | **Native American Addictions Severity Index (ASI) Adult Version** Customized for Native Americans; assesses chemical dependency and behavioral health concerns | The ASI (developed by S. M. Manson) is a comprehensive survey-type questionnaire that assesses a range of areas that could be affected by respondent's substance abuse (legal status, employment, family and social relationships, etc.) | The ASI has been found to be reliable and valid over the past 12 years across various populations. The Native American version is available for both adults and adolescents. | Computerized programs: Accurate Assessments 1823 Harney Street, Suite 101 Omaha, NE 68102 (402) 341-8880 (800) 324-7966 |

**Table 10.1**    Selected List of Measures for Four Ethnic Groups—*(continued)*

| Racial/Ethnic Group | Measure | Measure Characteristics | Reliability/Validity | Where to obtain |
|---|---|---|---|---|
| | **Tribe-Specific Thematic Apperception-Type (TAT) Tests** Developed by Dana, (1982) to assess emotional themes, conflicts, and concerns unique to Lakota culture. | Tests use picture story techniques; assessors and interpreters should be familiar with specific culture, history, philosophy, healing practices, and language of the population. | In the absence of adequate validity research for most standardized instruments with American Indians/Alaska Natives, local adaptations of TAT tests can provide valuable emic-based alternatives (Allen, 1998). | Richard H. Dana, Ph.D. Regional Research Institute Portland State University P. O. Box 751 Portland, OR 97207 (503) 725-4040 |
| **African Americans/Blacks** | **Optimal Extended Self-Esteem Scales (OESES)** Instruments for assessing the extended self-concepts for African Americans' racial/cultural identity and values based on Africentric principles. | Separate scales are developed for children, adolescents, and adults. Items on each scale vary according to developmental level. | Cronbach alpha coefficients were .82 and .76 for the OESES-Adolescent and the Rosenberg Self-Esteem, respectively ($n = 95$ males and 95 females adolescents). | Seward E. Hamilton, Jr. Ph.D. Gore Education Complex-Building–C, #305 Dept. of Psychology Florida A & M University Tallahassee, FL 32307 |

**Table 10.1**  Selected List of Measures for Four Ethnic Groups—*(continued)*

| Racial/Ethnic Group | | | | |
| --- | --- | --- | --- | --- |
| | Measure | Measure Characteristics | Reliability/Validity | Where to obtain |
| | **Index of Psychological Well-Being among African Americans** A 23-item index constructed from 40 items in the National Survey of Black Americans interview schedule. | Factors analysis revealed 7 factors: 10 happiness, self-esteem (positive), blame for bad job, self-esteem (negative), economic well-being, role performance, and interpersonal relations. | Reliability coefficients for the scale range from .59 to .70. | Anderson Franklin, Ph.D. Psychology Dept. The City College of New York Convent Ave. @ 138th Street New York, NY 10031 Ajfcc@cunyvn.cuny.edu |
| | **The Perceived Racial Stress and Coping Apperception Test (PRSCAT)** Designed to elicit child and adult conceptualizations of race-related stressors and the racial coping strategies available to cope with those stressors. | The PRSCAT consists of 5 picture cards for which the respondent tells a story and offers an explanation of what he/she would do. Responses are coded from 0 to 4 depending on the intensity of the racial conflict expressed by the respondent. | Interrater reliability coefficients for racial conflict ratings and racial coping strategies were .83 and .75 respectively. | Deborah J. Johnson, Ph.D. Dept. of Child and Family Studies 1430 Linden Drive University of Wisconsin-Madison Madison, WI 53706 (608) 263-4066 |

**Table 10.1**  Selected List of Measures for Four Ethnic Groups—*(continued)*

| Racial/Ethnic Group | Measure | Measure Characteristics | Reliability/Validity | Where to obtain |
|---|---|---|---|---|
| | **Scale for Racial Socialization for Adolescents (SORS-A)** (Stevenson, 1994) A 45-item scale designed to assess the degree of acceptance of racial-socialization attitudes and race-related messages of childrearing within African-American culture. | The SORS-A has 4 subscales: spiritual and religious coping, extended family caring, cultural pride reinforcement, and racism awareness teaching. | Initially normed with 236 inner-city African American adolescents, the SORS-A has fair reliability with an alpha of .75 for the total scale. Factors analyses suggest racial socialization has 2 dimensions: proactive and protective, regarding adolescents' perceptions of racial socialization. | Dr. Howard C. Stevenson, Jr. University of Pennsylvania Graduate School of Education, School, Community and Child Psychology 3700 Walnut St., Philadelphia, PA 19104 |
| **Hispanic/Latino Americans** | **Children's Health Locus of Control** A 20-item measure that has been suggested as appropriate for cross-cultural use with Mexican-American youth. | Scale determines the extent to which respondent believes that one has control over the status of one's health, ranging from belief in self-control (Internal), control by someone more powerful (Powerful Other) or uncontrollable factors (Chance). | Two studies by Guinn (1998) using the scale with Mexican-American youth reported alpha reliabilities of .76 for Internal, .72 for Powerful Others, and .80 for Chance (Study 1, 1997) and .78 for Internal, .75 for Powerful Others, and .81 for Chance (Study 2). | Parcel, G., & Meyer, M. (1978). Development of an instrument to measure children's health locus of control. *Health Education Monographs, 6,* 149–159. |

**Table 10.1** Selected List of Measures for Four Ethnic Groups—(*continued*)

| Racial/Ethnic Group | | | | |
|---|---|---|---|---|
| | Measure | Measure Characteristics | Reliability/Validity | Where to obtain |
| | **Spanish Version Expectations About Counseling Questionnaire (EAC-B)** Based on research documenting the relationship between ethnicity and counseling expectations and Hispanics' unmet expectations of counselors and the counseling process. | Questionnaire is composed of 53 items constituting 17 scales grouped into 4 general expectance factors: personal commitment, facilitative conditions, counselor expertise, and nurturance. | All scales correlated above .60, the criterion proposed for translated instruments. Results suggest that the Spanish version of the EAC-B is a reliable and valid translation for students and nonstudents from a variety of Hispanic populations. | Robin A. Buhrke School of Education 312 Merrick University of Miami Coral Gables, FL 33124 |
| | **Simpatica Scale (SS)** The SS is a 17-item scale developed to measure the concept of simpatia, the Hispanic cultural script that denotes the general tendency to avoid interpersonal conflict. | The concept of simpatica is often cited as potentially important for Hispanics in drug treatment. | SS has good construct validity and good internal consistency with alpha of .80 for the overall scale. | Dr. James D. Griffith Institute of Behavioral Research Texas Christian College Fort Worth, TX 76129 |

**Table 10.1** Selected List of Measures for Four Ethnic Groups—*(continued)*

| Racial/Ethnic Group | Measure | Measure Characteristics | Reliability/Validity | Where to obtain |
|---|---|---|---|---|
| **Asian Americans/ Pacific Islander Americans** | **Hawaiian Culture Scale-Adolescent Version** To assess the degree to which adolescents know of, believe in, value, and practice elements of traditional Hawaiian culture and to delineate the biological (i.e., blood quantum) and sociocultural factors shaping ethnic identification. | The 50-item inventory (7 subscales) measures the source of learning the Hawaiian way of life, how much the maintaining of Hawaiian beliefs is valued, Hawaiian blood quantum, and specific cultural traditions. | Cronbach alpha ranged from .82 to .96 for Hawaiian adolescents and from .76 to .96 for non-Hawaiian adolescents. These coefficients indicate satisfactory internal consistency. | Earl S. Hishinuma, Dept. of Psychiatry, Native Hawaiian Mental Health Research Development Program, 1356 Lusitana St., 4th Floor, John A Burns School of Medicine University of Hawaii at Manoa, Honolulu, HI 96813 earlhish@aol.com |
| | **Suinn-Lew Asian Self-Identity Acculturation Scale (SL-ASIAS)** To assess self-identity and level of acculturation among Asian Americans. | Scale has been used in conjunction with MMPI-2 with Asian Americans; less acculturated Asian Americans scored in the most disturbed direction on MMPI-2. | Researcher reported Cronbach's alpha for internal consistency of .88 and .91 from two studies. Scale has been widely used in the last 10 years in spite of limited research. | Suinn, R. M., Rikard-Figueroa, K., Lew, S., & Vigil, P. (1987) The Suinn-Lew Self-Identity Acculturation Scale: Concurrent and factorial validation. *Educational and Psychological Measurement, 52,* 1041–1046. |

**Table 10.1**  Selected List of Measures for Four Ethnic Groups—(*continued*)

| Racial/Ethnic Group | Measure | Measure Characteristics | Reliability/Validity | Where to obtain |
|---|---|---|---|---|
| **Cross-cultural measures for Ethnic Minority Children and Families** | **Kaufman Assessment Battery for Children (K-ABC)** (Kaufman & Kaufman, 1983) and **Kaufman Adolescent and Adult Intelligence Test (KAIT)** (Kaufman & Kaufman, 1993). | K-ABC is an individually administered assessment battery that measures achievement and intelligence in children. The KAIT is designed to assess cognitive functioning and may be useful when working with culturally diverse persons 11–85. (Russo & Lewis, 1999). | Research suggests that the measure is useful for Mexican-American assessment and may be useful for general cross-cultural assessment. Scales are currently undergoing revisions and norming with widely diverse populations. | American Guidance Service 4201 Woodland Rd. Circle Pines, MN 55014-1796 1-800-328-2560 |

**Table 10.1** Selected List of Measures for Four Ethnic Groups—*(continued)*

| Racial/Ethnic Group | | | |
|---|---|---|---|
| | Measure | Measure Characteristics | Reliability/Validity | Where to obtain |
| | The **Dominic** (Valla, Bergeron, Berube, & Gaudet, 1994; Valla, Bergeron, Bidaut-Russell, St. Georges, & Gaudet, 1997) is a cartoon-based questionnaire designed to study the mental health status of children age six to eleven. | Drawings convey situations based on symptoms of 7 more prevalent diagnoses in the *DSM-III-R* Axis I: Attention Deficit Hyperactivity Disorder (ADHD), Conduct Disorder (CD), Oppositional Defiant Disorder (ODD), Major Depressive Disorder/ Dysthymia (MDD), Separation Anxiety Disorder (SAD), Over-Anxious Disorder (OAD), and Simple Phobia (SPh). | The Dominic/Dominique character was designed to be interpreted as either a boy or a girl and also includes racially appropriate pictures of the characters. Internal consistency for each of the subscales ranged from .62 to .88 (Valla et al., 1994). | Jean-Pierre Valla, Ph.D. Hospital Riviere-des-Prairies 7070 Boulevrad Perras Montreal, Quebex H1E 1A4 Canada (514) 323-7260, ext. 2281 Fax (514) 323-4163 Jpvalla@sympatico.ca |

**Table 10.1**    Selected List of Measures for Four Ethnic Groups—*(continued)*

| Racial/Ethnic Group | | | |
|---|---|---|---|
| | Measure | Measure Characteristics | Reliability/Validity | Where to obtain |
| | **Family Pressures Scale-Ethnic (FPRES-E)** (McCubbin, Thompson, & Elver, 2000) is a 64-item measure designed to be inclusive of the life experiences of families of color. | Adapted from the Family Inventory of Life Events and Changes, this scale obtains an index of the severity of culturally sensitive pressure in the family system, especially in Native-American families, including families of Hawaiian descent. | The FPRES-E has excellent internal consistency with an alpha of .92. Scale was normed on 174 families of Native Hawaiian ancestry and was found to be the strongest predictor of family distress among this study population. | In H. I. McCubbin, A. I. Thompson, & M. A. McCubbin (1996). *Family assessment: Resiliency, coping, and adaptation: Inventories for research and practice.* Madison: University of Wisconsin, 227–236. The book provides instructions for permission to use the instrument. |
| | **Multigroup Ethnic Identity Measure (MEIM)** (Phinney, 1992) Designed to measure ethnic identity, particularly among adolescents across multiple ethnic groups. | | The MEIM has good internal consistency with alphas above .80 for subscales across a range of ethnic groups. There is evidence of some degree of concurrent validity between the MEIM and the Rosenberg Self-Esteem Inv. for Minority Students. | Jean S. Phinney, Ph.D. Department of Psychology California State University Los Angeles, CA 90032 |

groups. For example, traditional psychology assesses such attributes as IQ, cognitive functioning, personality, and achievement. However, Africentric theorists challenge the appropriateness of such measures to understand African American behaviors and functioning. Instead, these researchers recommend perceptions of racism, responses to racism, acculturation, identity development and formulation, and self-consciousness as crucial constructs to be assessed with African American clients. The *Handbook of Tests and Measurements for Black Populations* contains more than one hundred instruments and approaches for assessing black clients (Jones, 1996). Some of the tests represent traditional constructs such as self-esteem, stress, coping, and social support (e.g., Optimal Extended Self-Esteem Scale), whereas other measures are unique to assessing the impact of societal oppression on psychological functioning (e.g., Scale for Racial Socialization for Adolescents). Another example of culture-specific constructs for assessment included in table 10.1 is the Simpatía Scale. This was developed to measure the concept of *simpatía*, the Hispanic cultural script that denotes the general tendency to avoid interpersonal conflict.

Advocating that both traditional and ethnic-based constructs are important, Lindsey (1998) argues that "we have to create African-American norms for the existing instruments being used. . . . [A]t the same time, we must continue to develop instruments from the Africentric perspective" (p. 46). More research is needed to establish psychometric properties for ethnic-based, revised, standardized norms and newly devised, ethnic-specific measures; some of this work is under way. Noting that Asian Americans have been severely underrepresented in validation studies, Okazaki and Sue (2000) advocate for test revisions with cross-cultural validation with Asian Americans and other heterogeneous groups. They cite the recent publication of the Hmong adaptation of the MMPI-2 (Dienard, Butcher, Thao, Vang, & Hang, 1996) as an example of collaborative test development between mainstream (majority-culture) test developers and ethnic-minority researchers.

### Alternative 2: Assessment of Cultural and Ethnic Identity, Acculturation, and Acculturative Stress as Moderators of Standardized Tests

In discussing the development of the Hawaiian Culture Scale, Hishinum et al. (2000) note that the first step in discerning the role of ethnicity is to develop valid measures; the second step is to determine the association of ethnic constructs in indicators of psychological adjustment. There is some evidence that ethnic-identity measures offer some assistance in interpreting problematic standardized instruments. As a first step toward culturally competent assessment, practitioners should assess the client's cultural identity as a moderator variable and administer appropropriate measures as part of the assessment interview with the client. Measures used to examine the client's "culture self" can provide critical information on clients' cultural identity, which may be a precondition for mental, physical, and spiritual well-being (Dana, 1998). In a study to identify the relationship between reference-group labels and characteristics of personality such as self-esteem and social competence, Rotheram-Borus (1990) identified the reference labels of "mainstream," "bicultural," and "ethnically identified." She studied 330 black, Hispanic, Asian, and white high school students to determine the extent to which subjects identified with the dominant culture. The study showed that reference-group labels were consistently associated with differences in ethnic-group values, attitudes, and behaviors. Thus, understanding the cultural orientation of the client, beyond racial/ethnic categorizing, is a crucial step toward culturally competent assessment. Among those scales measuring cultural orientation, Walters's (1999) Urban American Indian Identity Scale measures four dimensions of identity attitudes: internalization, marginalization, externalization, and actualization.

Acculturation (low to high) has been studied extensively among ethnic-minority populations and has mental health implications. For example, acculturation has been linked to anxiety responding in American Indian and Alaska Natives (McNeil, Kee, & Zvolensky, 1999). A number of scales are designed to explore the level of acculturation of ethnic minorities. The Native American Cultural Involvement and Detachment Anxiety Questionnaire (CIDAQ) was developed by McNeil, Porter, Zvolensky, Chaney and Kee (2000) to assess acculturation anxiety in American Indian and Alaska Natives. Moreover, a growing body of assessment research focuses on the inclusion of acculturative stress and racism-based trauma as part of a holistic assessment procedure with ethnic-minority clients, given their exposure to racism, discrimination, and poverty. Choney, Berryhill-Paapke, and Robbins (1995) report that some native peoples experience clinical levels of stress-related responsivity (termed *intergenerational posttraumatic stress disorder*) (Choney et al., 1995) or historical trauma and unresolved grief (Brave Heart, 2001) associated with decades of cultural abuses against Native peoples. Similarly, others advocate for recognition of race-based traumatic injury diagnostic category in the *DSM* (Bryant-Davis & Ocampo, 2005). The Social, Attitudinal, Familial, and Environmental Acculturative Stress Scale (SAFE) (Padilla, Wagatsuma, & Lindholm, 1985) assesses acculturative stress in social, attitudinal, and familial and environmental contexts.

For information on some cultural-specific rapid assessment instruments in the area of cultural identity and acculturation, Corcoran and Fischer's (2007) most recent volumes of *Measures for Clinical Practice and Research: A Sourcebook* contain new scales and material, including the Acculturation Rating Scale for Mexican Americans—II, the Scale of Racial

Socialization—Adolescent Version, the Orthogonal Cultural Identification Scale, and the Multigroup Ethnic Identity Scale.

## Alternative 3: Use of Thematic Apperception-Type Tests

Increasingly, debates exists about whether projective measures are inherently based on Eurocentric assumptions and should thus be summarily dismissed with ethnic-minority clients or whether there is some value in emic-based adaptations (Allen, 1998; Dana, 1998, 2000; Okazaki & Sue, 1995). With respect to American Indians and Alaska Natives, Allen (1998) recommends that, in the absence of adequate validity research for most standardized tests, adaptations of thematic apperception-type tests can provide valuable emic-based alternatives with depictions created to cultural specifications. Several picture story tests have been developed over the years targeting various populations, including Lakota adults (Dana, 1982), Hispanic children (Malgady, Costantino, & Rogler, 1984), and African American children and adults (Johnson, 1996). The Tell-Me-a-Story test is the only comprehensive assessment instrument constructed for ethnic minority and nonminority children and adolescents with established reliable and valid scoring systems for the emic-based picture story techniques with Hispanic, black, Asian, and white children (Constantino, Dana, & Malgady, 2007).

When assessing mental health outcomes, picture-type assessments may be more appropriate for some use or for mixed assessment use with children of color. For example, Murphy et al. (2000) report that the pictorial approach (using the Dominic mental health assessment measure; Valla, Bergeron, Berube, & Gaudet, 1994; Valla, Bergeron, Bidaut-Russel, St. Georges, & Gaudet, 1997) may be more effective than a written version in assessing anxiety and depression in children. The Dominic is a cartoon-based questionnaire designed to study the mental health status of children aged six to eleven. The drawings convey situations based on symptoms of the seven prevalent diagnoses in the *DSM-III-R* axis I: attention deficit/hyperactivity disorder (ADHD), conduct disorder (CD), oppositional defiant disorder (ODD), major depressive disorder/dysthymia (MDD), separation anxiety disorder (SAD), overanxious disorder (OAD), and simple phobia (SPh). Children are shown a series of ninety-seven cartoon drawings. In eighty-nine of the drawings, a child, Dominic, is depicted exhibiting ninety-five symptoms covering sixty-two of the sixty-six *DSM-III-R* criteria included in the diagnoses. Mixed in with these are eight pictures of a smiling Dominic enjoying various activities. Children are asked to respond yes if they are like Dominic or no if they are not. The Dominic/Dominique character was designed to be interpreted as either a boy or a girl and also includes racially appropriate pictures of the characters.

### Alternative 4: Qualitative Assessment and Triangulated Assessment Approaches

Paniagua (2005) suggests that the least-biased assessment approaches involve self-monitoring (e.g., client's own records of thoughts, behaviors, feelings) and self-report individualized rating scales, which can accurately capture a client's interpretations and beliefs about behavior. Culture-specific measures, such as life histories and interviews, can be used to elicit assessment information (Dana, 1993). A mapping technique is especially appropriate for ethnic-minority families with language barriers, and it is more visual and activity oriented (Jordan & Franklin, 1995).

In addition, whenever possible, the practitioner should use more than one assessment strategy. Often this requires combining qualitative and quantitative assessment techniques or using multiple standardized instruments. For example, practitioners working with a Native population at the Eagle Lodge Behavioral Health Treatment Center use extensive psychosocial qualitative assessment interviews in conjunction with the Traumatic Symptoms Inventory Index. Stephens, Kiger, Karnes, and Whorton (1999) advise that a single test also does not suffice when assessing economically and culturally diverse children for academic giftedness. The researchers used the Culture-Fair Intelligence Test, the Raven Standard Progressive Matrices, and the Naglieri Nonverbal Abilities Test to assess 189 third through eighth graders who attended a rural elementary school and who were underrepresented in gifted student programs. Together, the three tests identified twenty-six students who merited additional consideration for gifted programs.

Combining measures can also be useful when assessing mental health in ethnic-minority groups. Multiple screenings were used to determine that the Center for Epidemiologic Studies—Depression Scale (CES-D), a ten-item scale that takes about two minutes to administer, is a useful tool for identifying Puerto Rican patients in need of in-depth mental health evaluation in a primary care setting. To assess convergent validity, Robison, Gruman, Gaztambide, and Blank (2002) compared multiple versions of four depression screening tools (CES-D, Geriatric Depression Scale, Yale one-question screen, and PRIME-MD two-question screen) to the Composite International Diagnostic Interview (CIDI), the World Health Organization's diagnostic interview, which has been validated in adult Latino populations. The study involved 303 Puerto Rican primary care patients age fifty and older who completed all screens and the CIDI in a face-to-face interview. Between 34 percent and 61 percent of patients screened positive for depression, depending on the measure, with 12 percent meeting *DSM-IV* criteria for major depression (CIDI). The researchers report that the ten-item CES-D worked best to identify major depression in this population, with a sensitivity of 84 percent and specificity of 64 percent using a cutpoint of three (instead of the conventional cutpoint of four), which is recommended for optimal sensitivity and specificity.

In addition to the recommended alternatives, social work practitioners are encouraged to use Jordan and Franklin's Integrative Skills Assessment Protocol, a detailed guide for conducting a comprehensive assessment framework (see chapter 1). This protocol focuses on assessing the client in an environmental context, and it uses an integrative assessment approach that borrows from several assessment models. General guidelines from this protocol are used in presenting the following case study and in discussing how the assessment guided the intervention.

## MOVING FROM ASSESSMENT TO INTERVENTION: BRIEF ASSESSMENT CASE STUDY

### Client Identifying Information

Janet is a nineteen-year-old, African American female attending a small community college in a large, predominantly Euro-American metropolitan area about an hour away from her hometown community, an inner-city urban environment.

### Nature of Presenting Problem

Although Janet had a successful first semester in the community college, during the beginning of her second semester, she began to have difficulty passing her exams and feels that she is "falling apart." Janet has experience increased anxiety about school and her surroundings. She described herself as "just moving on" with her life, which she defines as getting an education and getting away from her inner-city upbringing.

### Family and Social History

Janet is from a lower-middle-class, urban background. Janet's parents divorced when she was thirteen, and she and her brother lived with her mother but had regular contact with their father. Janet's parents argued often, with a major conflict centering around the father's bouts with unemployment as a security guard. Janet's mother is a nurse. After the divorce, Janet's brother, Derek, began having problems at home and at school. He became defiant with his mother, started skipping school, and has spent some time in jail for possession of marijuana. Over the past year, Janet has drifted away from her family. Janet was extremely frustrated with "not being able to get through" to her brother. Janet's parents are also very concerned about Derek, but as Janet put it, "they are caught up in their own problems" from the divorce. For the past seven months, Janet has worked part-time at a popular chain restaurant, which is where she met Sam, her boyfriend whom she has been dating for five months. Sam is an African American student who was born and raised in an upper-middle-class, predominantly white environment. Sam is supportive but feels that Janet's recent problems with her schoolwork will pass and that she is "trying too hard to prove herself" in her new college environment. Janet has not made many friends at her college. At first she felt that she was going to be fine and fit in, but once she started to develop her social life, Janet became distressed in the predominantly white university environment.

**Racial and Ethnic Considerations.**    Janet comes from an inner-city neighborhood, but she has not been part of that community for nearly a year. Janet came from a predominantly African American community and has not had very much exposure to a large, predominantly Euro-American metropolitan school or community. Considering her ethnicity and non-Eurocentric background, it is necessary to assess Janet's racial/ethnic identity and cultural orientation.

## Measurement

As recommended in this chapter, the first step in multicultural assessment strategy is to access the cultural orientation of clients and their level of acculturation by identifying client's attitudes.

**Multigroup Ethnic Identity Measure (MEIM).**    The MEIM (Phinney, 1992) is a 14-item ethnic identity scale that measures ethnic attitudes, behaviors, practices, and belongingness. The scale has also differentiated two unique types of bicultural adolescents (i.e., blended and alternating) and a third group of predominantly African American adolescents who were not bicultural (i.e., separated) and had strong sense of African American identity (Phinney & Devich-Navarro, 1997). Janet's score indicated she is strongly centered in her ethnic group identity and has a more separated than bicultural identity.

Next, two standardized clinical scales were used to assess Janet's anxiety level and her degree of psychological splitting.

*Measure: Clinical Anxiety Scale (Thyer, 1992):* This twenty-five-item scale measures the amount, degree, or severity of clinical anxiety. Sample scale items are "I feel afraid without good reason" and "I feel generally anxious." Janet scored 40, which exceeds the clinical cutoff score of 30, thus indicating that that she is experiencing anxiety in the clinical range.

*Measure: Splitting Scale (Gerson, 1984):* This fourteen-item scale assesses symptoms of splitting, the psychological defense mechanism used to keep ambivalence at bay. This scale has been normed on female and male psychology students, as well as on a sample from an urban health clinic; it has moderate to good reliability and validity. Sample scale items are "When I'm with someone really terrific, I feel dumb" and "I often feel I can't put the different parts of my personality together so that there is one 'me.'" Janet scored 60, reflecting moderately high characterological use of splitting.

Next, an ethnic specific test was employed to assess Janet's behavior in the context of her cultural orientation.

*Measure: Social, Attitudinal, Familial, and Environmental Acculturative Stress Scale (Padilla, Wagatsuma, and Lindholm, 1985):* This is a twenty-four-item scale that assesses acculturative stress in social, attitudinal, and familial and environmental contexts, including perceived discrimination, perceived barriers to adaptation, negative reactions of family members to one's desire to adapt, feelings of isolation, difficulties in communication. Participants rate each item on a scale of one (not stressful) to five (extremely stressful). Reasonable reliability of the scale has been extablished with a diverse sample, including African American college students on both predominatly white and historically black college campuses (Joiner & Walker, 2002). Janet scored well above the mean score for samples on which the scale was normed.

## How the Assessment Guided the Intervention Plans

The intervention selected for Janet should address each of the concerns identified in the assessment, with specific attention to the presence of acculturative stress, anxiety, and splitting. Given Janet's ethnic considerations and the timing of the onset of her anxiety, it appears that acculturative stress plays a substantial role in her presenting problem. Culture-based assessments provide valuable information not always evident in standardized measures. For example, studies on acculturative stress show that recent immigrants have stronger acculturative stress than the children and grandchildren of immigrants, and African Americans on a predominantly white campus have higher acculturative stress than those in a predominantly black college setting (Joiner & Walker, 2002). Thus, the treatment would include interventions to reduce acculturative stress. Practitioners should be knowledgeable about how risks to the psychosocial well-being of people of color are often rooted in collective and historical disenfranchisement and contemporary challenges associated with loss of traditional culture and identity. Strong family and community bonds; wisdom and guidance of elders; and positive cultural practices, traditions, and strong ethnic identity are among the recognized strengths and buffers that should be incorporated into culturally congruent interventions for youths and adolescents of color. Treatment techniques that infuse traditional values and group-based interventions are components to established intervention practices when working with historically oppressed youths of color (Gilbert & Sims, 2006). Infusion of Africentric values has been associated with decreased depression, lowered anxiety, and increased competitiveness in academic achievement (Constantine, Alleyne, & Wallace, 2006). Once acculturative stress is reduced, similar effects would be expected in the areas of clinical anxiety and characterological splitting. In addition, reduction in acculturative stress should allow Janet to concentrate on her schooling and career plans.

## SUMMARY

Evidence-based, culturally sensitive assessment practices are still in development. In ensuring a do-no-harm assessment approach, social work practitioners are encouraged to probe, question, and make changes in any cases where there is a possibility that standardized assessment techniques may not be culturally appropriate for a client assessment. Once an individual is labeled with an invalid assessment or inaccurate pathological diagnosis, intervention and evaluation of the client's progress are no longer valid. This chapter has discussed in detail several alternative assessment approaches for use in multicultural assessment and encouraged practitioners to adopt those into practice.

## STUDY QUESTIONS

1. How has the ethnocentrism of the U.S. culture affected assessment procedures and measurement instruments for nonmajority (i.e., ethnic-minority) clients?

2. The special concerns about assessing ethnic minority clients center around three main issues. List and define those three issues.

3. What are some of the criticisms about the *DSM-IV* with respect to assessing ethnic minority clients?

4. The chapter states that "practitioners feel caught between two conflicting professional demands for conducting assessments." Explain these two conflicting professional demands.

5. What are the recommended alternative or mixed models for multicultural assessment? List alternative models applied in the case study?

## WEB SITES

*Assessments.com*
www.assessments.com/default.asp
*Multicultural Family Institute*
www.multiculturalfamily.org
*National Center for Cultural Competence*
www.georgetown.edu/research/gucchd/nccc/

## REFERENCES

Abas, M., Phillips, C., Richards, M., Carter, J., & Levy, R. (1996). Initial development of a new culture-specific screen for emotional distress in older Caribbean people. *International Journal of Geriatric Psychiatry, 11*, 1097–1103.

Allen, J. (1998). Personality assessment with American Indian and Alaska Natives: Instrument considerations and service delivery style. *Journal of Personality Assessment, 70*, 17–42.

Aponte, J. F., & Crouch, R. T. (2000). The changing ethnic profile of the United States. In J. F. Aponte, R. Y. Rivers, & J. Wohl (2nd ed.), *Psychological interventions and cultural diversity*. Boston: Allyn and Bacon.

Brave Heart, M. Y. H. (2001). Clinical social work assessment with Native clients. In R. Fong & S. Furuto (Eds.), *Culturally competent practice: Skills, interventions, and evaluations* (pp. 163–195). Boston: Allyn and Bacon.

Bryant-Davis, T., & Ocampo, C. (2005). Racist incident-based trauma. *Counseling Psychologist, 33*, 479–500.

Choney, S. K., Berryhill-Paapke, E., & Robbins, R. R. (1995). The acculturation of American Indians: Developing frameworks for research and practice. In J. G. Ponterotto, J. M. Casas, L. A. Suzuki, & C. M. Alexander (Eds.), *Handbook of multicultural counseling* (pp. 73–92). Thousand Oaks, CA: Sage.

Chow, J. C. (2001). Assessment of Asian American/Pacific Islander organizations and communities (pp. 211–224). In R. Fong & S. Furuto (Eds.), *Culturally competent practice: Skills, interventions, and evaluations* (pp. 163–195). Boston: Allyn and Bacon.

Corcoran, K., & Fischer, J. (2007). *Measures for clinical practice and research: A sourcebook* (4th ed., Vols. 1 & 2). New York: Oxford University Press.

Constantine, M. G., Alleyne, V. L., & Wallace, B. C. (2006). Africentric cultural values: Their relation to positive mental health in African American adolescent girls. *Journal of Black Psychology, 32*, 141–154.

Costantino, G., Dana, R. H., & Malgady, R. G. (2007). *TEMAS (Tell-Me-a-Story) assessment in multicultural societies*. Mahwah, NJ: Erlbaum.

Dana, R. H. (1982). *Picture-story cards for Sioux/Plains Indians*. Fayetteville: University of Arkansas.

Dana, R. H. (1993). *Multicultural assessment perspectives for professional psychology*. Needham Heights, MA: Allyn and Bacon.

Dana, R. H. (1998). *Understanding cultural identity in intervention and assessment* (Multicultural aspects of Counseling Series, Vol. 9). Thousand Oaks, CA: Sage.

Dana, R. (Ed.). (2000). *Handbook of cross-cultural and multicultural personality assessment*. Mahwah, NJ: Erlbaum.

Dana, R. H. (2005). *Multicultural assessment principles, applications, and examples*. Mahwah, NJ: Erlbaum.

Dhooper, S. S., & Moore, S. E. (2001). *Social work practice with culturally diverse people*. Thousand Oaks, CA: Sage.

Dienard, A., Butcher, J. N., Thao, U. D., Vang, S. H. M., & Hang, K. (1996). Development of a Hmong translation of the MMPI-2. In J. N. Butcher (Ed.), *International adaptations of the MMPI-2* (pp. 194–205). Minneapolis: University of Minnesota Press.

Draguns, J. G. (2002). Universal and cultural aspects of counseling and psychotherapy. In P. B. Pedersen, J. G. Graguns, W. L. Lonner, & J. E. Trimble (Eds.), *Counseling across cultures* (pp. 29–50). Thousand Oaks, CA: Sage.

Epstein, J. A., Botvin, G. J., & Diaz, T. (2001). Alcohol use among Dominican and Puerto Rican adolescents residing in New York City: Role of Hispanic group and gender. *Journal of Developmental and Behavioral Pediatrics, 22*, 113–118.

Fabrega, H., Jr. (1992) Commentary. Diagnosis interminable: Toward a culturally sensitive *DSM*-IV. *Journal of Nervous and Mental Disease, 180*, 5–7.

Feagin, J. R., & Feagin, C. B. (2003). *Racial and ethnic relations* (7th ed.). Upper Saddle River, NJ: Prentice Hall.

Gerson, M.-J. (1984). Splitting: The development of a measure. *Journal of Clinical Psychology, 40*, 157–162.

Gilbert, D. J., & Sims, G. (2006). Working with American Indian Students and Families. In C. Franklin, M. B. Harris, & P. Allen-Meares (Eds), *The school social work and mental health worker's training and resource manual* (pp. 811–818). New York: Oxford University Press.

Grills, C. (2002). African-centered psychology: Basic principles. In T. A Parham (Ed.) *Counseling persons of African descent* (pp. 10–24). Thousand Oaks, CA: Sage.

Guinn, B. (1998). Acculturation and health locus of control among Mexican American adolescents. *Hispanic Journal of Behavioral Sciences, 20*, 492–499.

Hall, C. I. J. (1997). Cultural malpractice: The growing obsolescence of psychology with the changing U.S. population. *American Psychologist, 52*, 642–651.

Hishinuma, E. S., Andrade, N. N., Johnson, R. C., McArdle, J. J., Miyamoto, R. H., Nahulu, L. B., et al. (2000). Psychometric properties of the Hawaiian Culture Scale-Adolescent Version. *Psychological Assessment, 12*, 140–157.

Johnson, D. J. (1996). The perceived racial stress and coping apperception test. In R. L. Jones (Ed.), *Handbook of tests and measurements for Black populations* (pp. 231–244). Hampton, VA: Cobb and Henry.

Joiner, T. E., & Walker, R. L. (2002). Construct validity of a measure of acculaturative stress in African Americans. *Psychological Assessment, 14*(94), 462–466.

Jones, R. L. (1996). *Handbook of tests and measurements for Black populations* (Vols. 1 & 2). Hampton, VA: Cobb and Henry.

Jordan, C., & Franklin, C. (1995). *Clinical assessment for social workers: Quantitative and qualitative methods*. Chicago: Lyceum Books.

Karenga, M. (1996). The *nguzo sabe* (the seven principles): Their meaning and message. In M. K. Asante & A. S. Abarry (Eds.), *African intellectual heritage: A book of sources* (pp. 543–554). Philadelphia: Temple University Press.

Kutchins, H., & Kirk, S. A. (1997). *Making us crazy—DSM: The psychiatric bible and the creation of mental disorders.* New York: Free Press.

Lindsey, M. L. (1998). Culturally competent assessment of African American clients. *Journal of Personality Assessment, 70,* 43–53.

Lum, D. (2004). *Social work practice and people of color: A process-stage approach* (5th ed.). Belmont, CA: Brooks/Cole.

Malgady, R. G., Costantino, G., & Rogler, L. H. (1984). Development of thematic apperception test (TEMAS) for urban Hispanic children. *Journal of Consulting and Clinical Psychology, 52,* 986–996.

McKibbon, K. A. (1998). Evidence based practice. *Bulletin of the Medical Library Association, 86,* 396–401.

McNeil, D. W., Kee, M., & Zvolensky, M. J. (1999). Culturally related anxiety and ethnic identity in Navajo college students. *Cultural Diversity and Ethnic Minority Psychology, 5,* 56–64.

McNeil, D. W., Porter, C. A., Zvolensky, M. J., Chaney, J. M., & Kee, M. (2000). Assessment of culturally related anxiety in American Indian and Alaska Natives. *Behavior Therapy, 31,* 301–325.

Mezzich, J. E., Kirmayer, L. J., Kleinman, A., Fabrega, H., Parron, D. L., Good, B. J., et al. (1999). The place of culture in *DSM-IV. Journal of Nervous and Mental Disease, 187*(18), 457–464.

Mokuau, N., Garlock-Tuiali'i, J., & Lee, P. (2008). Has social work met its commitment to Native Hawaiians and other Pacific Islanders? A Review of the periodical literature. *Social Work, 53,* 115–121.

Morris, E. F. (2000). Africentric perspective. In R. Dana (Ed.), *Handbook of cross-cultural and multicultural personality assessment* (pp. 17–41). Mahwah, NJ: Erlbaum.

Murphy, D. A., Cantwell, C., Jordan, D. D., Lee, M., Cooley-Quille, M. R., & Lahey, B. B. (2000). Test-retest reliability of Dominic anxiety and depression items among young children. *Journal of Psychopathology and Behavioral Assessment, 22,* 257–270.

National Council of La Raza (2008). *Hispanic health data.* Retrieved from www.nclr.org/content/programs/detail/25670.

Oetting, E. R., Swaim, R. C., & Chiarella, M. C. (1998). Factor structure and invariance of the orthogonal cultural identification scale among American Indian and Mexican American youth. *Hispanic Journal of Behavioral Sciences, 20,* 131–154.

Office of Minority Health and Health Disparities. (2008). *Eliminate disparities in mental health.* Retrieved from www.cdc.gov/omhd/AMH/factsheets/mental.htm.

Okazaki, S., & Sue, S. (1995). Methodological issues in assessment research with ethnic minorities. *Psychological Assessment, 7,* 367–376.

Okazaki, S., & Sue, S. (2000). Implications of test revisions for assessment with Asian Americans. *Psychological Assessment, 12,* 272–280.

Padilla, A. M., Wagatsuma, Y., & Lindholm, K. J. (1985). Acculturation and personality as predictors of stress in Japanese and Japanese Americans. *Journal of Social Psychology, 125,* 295–305.

Paniagua, F. A. (2005). Assessing and treating culturally diverse clients: A practical guide (3rd ed.). Thousand Oaks, CA: Sage.

Parham, T. A. (1995). American violence: Our challenges. *Psych Discourse, 26*(3), 7–9.

Pedersen, P. B., & Ivey, A. (1993). *Culture-centered counseling and interviewing skills: A practical guide.* Westport, CT: Praeger.

Phinney, J. S. (1992). The multigroup ethnic identity measure: A new scale for use with diverse groups. *Journal of Adolescent Research, 7,* 156–176.

Phinney, J. S., & Devich-Navarro, M. (1997). Variations in bicultural identification among African American and Mexican American adolescents. *Journal of Research on Adolescence, 7,* 3–32.

Pinderhughes, E. (1989). *Understanding race, ethnicity, and power: The key to efficacy in clinical practice.* New York: Free Press.

Reid, R., DuPaul, G. J., Power, T. J., Anastopoulos, A. D., Rogers-Adkinson, D., Noll, M., et al. (1998). Assessing culturally-different students for attention deficit hyperactivity disorder using behavior rating scales. *Journal of Abnormal Child Psychology, 26,* 187–198.

Robison, J., Gruman, C., Gaztambide, S., & Blank, K. (2002). Screening for depression in middle-aged and older Puerto Rican primary care patients. *Journals of Gerontology, 57A,* M308–M314.

Rosen, A., Proctor, E., & Staudt, M. (2003). Targets of change and interventions in social work. An empirically based prototype for developing practice guidelines. *Research on Social Work Practice, 13,* 208–233.

Rotheram-Borus, M. J. (1990). Adolescents' reference-group choices, self-esteem, and adjustment. *Journal of Personality and Social Psychology, 59,* 1075–1081.

Rubin A. (2001). Is this a white country or what? In M. L. Andersen & P. H. Collins (Eds.), *Race, class, and gender: An anthology* (4th ed., pp. 430–438). Belmont, CA: Wadsworth.

Russell, C. (2006). *Racial and ethnic diversity: Asians, Blacks, Hispanics, Native Americans, and Whites* (5th ed.) Ithaca, NY: New Strategist.

Smedley, B. D., Stith, A. Y., & Nelson, A. R. (Eds.). (2003). *Unequal treatment: Confronting racial and ethnic disparities in healthcare.* Washington, DC: National Academic Press.

Snowden, L. R. (2003). Bias in mental health assessment and intervention: Theory and evidence. *American Journal of Public Health, 93,* 239–243.

Stephens, K., Kiger, L., Karnes, F. A., & Whorton, J. E. (1999). Use of nonverbal measures of intelligence in identification of culturally diverse gifted students in rural areas. *Perceptual and Motor Skills, 88,* 793–796.

Thyer, B. A. (1992). Clinical Anxiety Scale (CAS). In W. W. Hudson (Ed.), *The Walmyr Assessment Scale scoring manual.* Temple, AZ: Walmyr.

Tran, B. N. (1996). Vietnamese translation and adaptation of the MMPI-2. In J. N. Butcher (Ed.), *International adaptation of the MMPI-2* (pp. 175–193). Minneapolis: University of Minnesota Press.

Trimble, J. E. (1995). Toward an understanding of ethnicity and ethnic identity, and their relationship with drug use research. In G. J. Botvin, S. Schinke, & M. A. Orlandi (Eds.), *Drug use prevention with multiethnic youth* (pp. 3–27). Thousand Oaks, CA: Sage.

Uomoto, J. M., & Wong, T. M. (2000). Multicultural perspectives on the neuropsychology of brain injury assessment and rehabilitation. In E. Fletcher-Janzen, T. L. Strickland, & C. R. Reynolds (Eds.), *Handbook of cross-cultural neuropsychology* (pp. 169–184). New York: Plenum.

U.S. Census Bureau. (2004). *U.S. interim projections by age, sex, race and Hispanic origin.* Retrieved from www.census.gov/ipc/www/usinterimproj/.

U.S. Department of Health and Human Services, Office of the Surgeon General (2008a). *Surgeon General's Report: Fact sheet for Latinos/Hispanic Americans.* Retrieved from http://mentalhealth.samhsa.gov/cre/fact3/asp.

U.S. Department of Health and Human Services, Office of the Surgeon General (2008b). *Surgeon General's Report: Fact sheet for Asian Americans/Pacific Islanders.* Retrieved from http://mentalhealth.samhsa.gov/cre/fact2/asp.

Valla, J. P., Bergeron, L., Berube, H., & Gaudet, N. (1994). A structured pictorial questionnaire to assess *DSM-III-R* based diagnoses in children (6–11): Development, validity and reliability. *Journal of Child Psychology, 22,* 404–423.

Valla, J. P., Bergeron, L., Bidaut-Russell, M., St. Georges, M., & Gaudet, N. (1997). Reliability of the Dominic-R: A young child mental health questionnaire combining visual and auditory stimuli. *Journal of Child Psychology and Psychiatry, 38,* 717–724.

Walters, K. (1999). Urban American Indian identity attitudes and acculturation styles. *Journal of Human Behavior in the Social Environment, 2,* 163–178.

Waters M. C. (2001). Optional ethnicities: For whites only? In M. L. Andersen & P. H. Collins (Eds.), *Race, class, and gender: An anthology* (4th ed., pp. 430–438). Belmont, CA: Wadsworth.

Weaver, H. (2008). Native Americans. In G. C. Gamst, A. Der-Karabetian, & R. Dana (Eds.), *Readings in multicultural practice* (pp. 217–239). Thousand Oaks, CA: Sage.

Wong, T. M. (2000). Neuropsychological assessment and intervention with Asian Americans. In E. Fletcher-Janzen, T. L. Strickland, & C. R. Reynolds (Eds.), *Handbook of cross-cultural neuropsychology* (pp. 43–53). New York: Plenum.

Wong, T. M., & Fujii, D. E. (2004). Neuropsychological assessment with Asian Americans: Demographic factors, cultural diversity, and practice guidelines. *Applied Neuropsychology, 11,* 23–36.

Yellowbird, M. (2001). Critical values and First Nations peoples. In R. Fong & S. Furuto, *Culturally competent practice: Skills, interventions, and evaluations* (pp. 61–74). Boston: Allyn and Bacon.

# CHAPTER 11

# Linking Assessment to Outcome: Evaluation Using Single-System and Group Research Designs

## Bruce A. Thyer and Laura L. Myers

## INTRODUCTION

The social work profession has long paid attention to the importance of conducting empirical evaluations of the outcomes of clinical services. For example, more than eighty years ago one of the founders of social casework, Mary Richmond (1917/1935), claimed, "Special efforts should be made to ascertain whether abnormal manifestations are *increasing* or *decreasing* in number and intensity, as this often has a practical bearing on the management of the case" (p. 435). Individual clinical social workers are concerned with evaluating the outcomes of their own practice with clients, not only to help build on the evidence-based foundations of social work knowledge but also to use feedback in continuing work with clients, small groups, couples, or families. This is why, for example, the Code of Ethics of the National Association of Social Workers (NASW) mandates that "social workers should monitor and evaluate policies, the implementation of programs, and practice interventions. Social workers should promote and facilitate evaluation and research to contribute to the development of knowledge. Social workers should . . . fully use evaluation and research evidence in their professional practice" (NASW, 1999, section 5.02).

Relatedly, the NASW Standards for the Practice of Clinical Social Work clearly states that "clinical social workers shall have . . . knowledge about and skills in using research to evaluate the effectiveness of a service" (NASW, 1989, p. 7). The NASW Standards for School Social Work Services further claim that "all school social work programs, new or long standing, should be evaluated on an ongoing basis to determine their relevance, effectiveness, efficiency, and contributions to the process of educating children" (NASW, 1992, p. 16). We have recently reviewed some additional historical and ethical positions that emphasize the importance of clinical social workers' systematic appraisal of the outcomes of their own practice and integration of this long-standing tradition with the newer initiative of evidence-based practice, which is currently infusing our field (Thyer & Myers, 2007a).

Empirical research on the outcomes of clinical services can be roughly divided into two major categories. Efficacy studies are tightly designed experimental investigations that usually use carefully screened clients who meet certain inclusion criteria, specially trained and supervised therapists, interventions delivered in accordance with a treatment manual or other structured protocol, and the repeated administration of reliable and valid outcome measures. Effectiveness studies attempt to replicate the positive findings obtained through prior efficacy studies in practice contexts in contexts that more closely approximate the real world of clinical services. Effectiveness studies involve the type of heterogeneous clientele seen at community mental health agencies (as opposed to volunteers treated at specialized university-based clinics), clients with multiple diagnoses (as opposed to only one diagnosis), more complex problems (e.g., serious mental disorders complicated by psychosocial difficulties such as abuse or poverty), naturally occurring treatment groups (clients with similar problems seen at two different agencies using differing interventions, as opposed to random assignment to different treatment conditions), and the more usually encountered clinicians (most often with a master's degree rather than a doctorate in medicine, psychology, or social work).

It is a particular strength of the clinical social work profession, which is the largest provider of mental health services in the United States, that the bulk of practitioners are engaged in agency-based practice in public or not-for-profit private agencies. Thus, we are ideally positioned to collaborate with other disciplines in the design and conduct of effectiveness research. According to Mullen (1995), "Social work has no more important use of research methods than assessment of the consequences of practice and policy choices . . . [S]mall scale, agency-based studies are worthwhile if they succeed in placing interest in effectiveness at the center of agency practice and when they create a critical alliance between practitioners and researchers" (pp. 282–283).

Katherine Ell (1996), past executive director of the Institute for the Advancement of Social Work and Research, similarly pointed out that "studies are needed on the effectiveness of psychosocial intervention, including interventions previously tested under ideal controlled conditions, in real-world health care systems" (p. 589). And as early as 1965, the late Harold Lewis commented on the importance of agency-based research being conducted by social workers: "Some would reject agency-based research as inconsequential because it is directed to immediate practice ends rather than on development of theory. Others deny the value of agency-based research in helping clairify and add to significant problems encountered in day-to-day practice. Both represent attitudes that can, and often do, prove the costly of all causes of 'waste' in the utlization of the efforts of the research worker" (p. 24).

If social work is to continue to enjoy substantial amounts of financial support from local, state, and federal sources, it is imperative that social workers be able to demonstrate, with legitimate data that are credible to others, that they are genuinely capable of helping the clients they serve. Similarly, clinical social workers whose services are reimbursed via third-party payers are under considerable pressure to empirically document client changes. Among some managed-care firms, actual reimbursement can be contingent on the clinical social worker being able to provide such information.

Evaluating the outcomes of clinical social work services is a specialized form of research inquiry. It is so specialized that some have argued that outcome studies not be considered research at all, given their focus on individual clients or specific programmatic services and the traditional construction of research as an effort to build theory and to contribute to generalizable knowledge. One may construe evaluation studies as either being a legitimate component of the broader field of scientific research or as having a more limited role best described by terms such as *quality assurance study*, *clinical evaluation*, or *outcome assessment*. However, the field of evaluation, clinical or programmatic, does make use of the same methods of inquiry as mainstream scientific investigations. The clinical social worker attempting to undertake an empirical evaluation of services should be thoroughly familiar with and comfortable in using those methods. But fear not: the actual design and conduct of evaluation studies is not as complex and intimidating as it may appear, and the balance of this chapter attempts to bear out this claim. An elaboration of the research methods descibred in this chapter can be found in our recent book *A Social Worker's Guide to Evaluating Practice Outcomes* (Thyer & Myers, 2007b).

Evaluation of the outcomes of clinical social work generally makes use of two major forms of inquiry—single-system designs and group designs. Both rely on certain fundamental prerequisites. First, the clinical social worker must have available a practical, reliable, inexpensive, and valid outcome measure for use in evaluating results. Second, it must be possible to administer the outcome measure with clients on at least two, and ideally more, occasions.

If social workers can accomplish the foregoing, with some modest efforts, they are well on their way to designing empirical evaluations of the results of clinical social work practice. This may include practice conducted on a variety of levels, such as one-to-one therapy, group work, marital or family counseling, or the treatment of couples. In principle and in fact, these methods also can be used in the design and conduct of social work outcome studies of organizational, community, and policy practice, as well, but such endeavors are outside the scope of the present chapter.

We now review the basic principles of the design and conduct of single-system designs, as used in the evaluation of clinical social work. We then similiarly explain the use of simple group designs for the same purpose.

## THE DESIGN AND CONDUCT OF SINGLE-SYSTEM DESIGNS

Other chapters in this text have reviewed the factors involved in selecting reliable and valid quantitative and qualitative outcome measures for use in clinical assessment (see also Hudson & Thyer, 1986). The distinction between assessment and screening measures that are suitable for arriving at, perhaps, a formal diagnosis of a mental disorder or other baseline or pretreatment assessment of client status or functioning has also been made. Throughout the text, readers have been encouraged to use measures that are sensitive to the types of important changes in client functioning that may occur during clinical social work. Please note that the application of the methods of single-system designs (SSDs) may be undertaken in the context of virtually any model of social work assessment and treatment. If you anticipate that your clinical services will affect client functioning in meaningful ways, then SSDs can be useful ways to document this. In general:

> *Axiom 1:* If something exists (e.g., a client problem or strength), it is potentially measurable.

> *Axiom 2:* If you measure client functioning, you are in a better position to treat client functioning.

> *Axiom 3:* If you measure client functioning, you are in a better position to evaluate clinical outcomes.

We refer to these three simple axioms as Thyer's axioms, which are an extension and somewhat of a softening of the late Walter Hudson's (1978) first axioms of treatment, which created quite a stir when they were first published (see Hudson, 1978, and subsequent commentaries in later issues of the same journal (e.g., Neisser, Taubman, Levitt, Brown, & Gingerich, 1978). There is now some preliminary evidence supporting the hypothesis that the clients of social workers who evaluate their practice using SSDs have more improved clinical outcomes than clients whose social workers do not use SSRs to evaluate their practice (see Faul, McMurtry, & Hudson, 2001; Slomin-Nevo & Anson, 1998).

In the context of SSDs, clinical social workers attempt to empirically measure client functioning repeatedly over time. This can be done before, during, and/or after intervention. Measures taken before formal treatment begins are the baseline of client functioning. How many measures are enough to constitute a credible baseline? There is no simple answer to this. One is better than none, two are better than one, at least three are necessary to ascertain a real trend in the data (because any two data points can be linked to form a straight line), four are better than three, and so forth. Ideally, baseline data, when graphed, should appear relatively stable to you and. "Stable: means that one would answer no to the questions "Are the data clearly increasing?" and "Are the data clearly decreasing?" This is a rather conservative test because fairly unambiguous trends in the data are required for visual detection.

Data can also be gathered during the course of actual clinical social work intervention, in the treatment phase, or after treatment has been discontinued, in the follow-up phase.

The experimental logic behind SSDs is relatively simple. The baseline data phase is an operational manifestation of the hoary (but most certainly valid) social work precept "begin where the client is at." If you carefully select your outcome measure to be reliable and valid, you may be able to augment your clinical judgment that the client is getting worse, getting better, or staying the same during the assessment process. You may, therefore, be able to go to your supervisor or managed-care utilization reviewer, and, in addition to your personal and professional powers of persuasion, display a graph justifying the need for intervention.

Next, continue the process of assessment/measurement during treatment using the same methods and measures you employed during the baseline. If you get immediate and dramatic improvements, this too is good and is consistent with the hypothesis that your intervention caused the improvements. Note the careful wording here: "consistent with the hypothesis that treatment caused the improvements." This is a more cautious and conservative interpretation than "My services caused the client to improve." In most circumstances, your clinical assessment of outcomes may justify the former conclusion, but it is a very rare practice situation indeed that enables you to embrace the latter. According to a recent analysis of social work outcome studies by Rubin and Parrish (2007), a large proportion of such studies reported causal conclusions (e.g., treatment caused improvements), even though design limitations precluded such strong statements from being made. Rubin and Parrish recommended that social workers be more circumspect in the claims they make when drawing inferences from outcome studies. We urge readers of this chapter to be similarly cautious. We use some examples of the use of SSDs to evaluate the outcome of clinical social work to illustrate the scope and flexibility of these evaluation methods.

## The A-B Design

The A-B design is among the simplest forms of SSD and involves the social worker taking a baseline measure of client functioning before and during intervention. Krista Barker, an MSW student, used this approach in her practicum setting at a vocational rehabilitation program for persons with disabilities. One client, John (a pseudonym), was a twenty-three-year-old African American man with moderate mental retardation and a seizure disorder. While in the program, John displayed numerous inappropriate behaviors such as taunting peers, throwing objects, threatening violence, demonstrating physical aggression against staff and peers, and making inappropriate sexual advances. The severity and frequency of John's inappropriate behavior were placing him in danger of imminent discharge from the vocational rehabilitation program.

Barker developed a way to reliably observe and count John's inappropriate behavior; she did this for five consecutive workdays. She then implemented a simple reward program wherein John could earn reinforcers (augmented opportunities for socialization) based on appropriate behavior. She used the plan over the following seven days, and it seemed to result in a considerable reduction in John's inappropriate behavior (see figure 11.1). The data in figure 11.1 suggest but do not prove that the reward program Barker developed caused the improvements in John's behavior—there are too many other explanations that could account for the changes. However, the data certainly suggest, and at the very least reveal, that the plan did not seem to result in any exacerbation of inappropriate

**Figure 11.1**    Daily Number of Aggressive Behaviors Displayed by John. Reproduced from Barker and Thyer (2000, p. 40) with permission

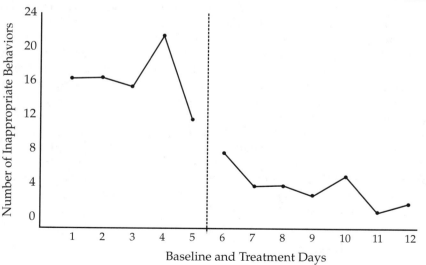

Baseline and Treatment Days
Total Number of Inappropriate Behaviors From 9:00AM - 2:00PM
Daily number of aggressive behaviors displayed by John

behavior. The agency staff were very impressed with the apparent results of Barker's program, which, it should be noted, focused on strengthening positive behaviors via rewards and made no use of punishment. Barker and Thyer (2000) provide addition details about this case.

In preparing this chapter, we conducted a search of the PsycINFO database, using "AB design" or "A-B design" as our search terms, and searching for these terms in journal abstracts published between 2005 and 2008. We found more than forty citations describing the the use of this design in a wide array of clinical situations, including providing cognitive therapy to patients with Alzheimer's disease, improving childrens' academic skills, evaluating the use of Ritalin to treat adults with ADHD, decreasing no-shows in appointments, reducing self-harm, enhancing the social skills of youths with autism, evaluating animal-assisted therapy provided to the elderly, evaluating family therapy for a child with Asperger's syndome, evaluating speech therapy, reducing aggression in a psychiatric patient, and providing therapy to stroke patients. The A-B design is a theory-free approach (in that it can be applied to evaluate the outcomes of practice using diverse interventive models) that is relatively simple and remains widely used.

## The A-B-A Design

The A-B-A design is simply the continued collection of data after the discontinuation of the social work intervention. the MSW student Susan Massa used this approach at a senior citizens' center that served a daily hot meal at lunchtime. In Florida in the late 1980s, there was no law requiring safety-belt use among automobile drivers, and Susan wanted to see whether she could get senior citizens to use their safety belts more frequently. She developed a reliable method of using independent observers stationed outside the senior citizens' center parking lot to record the over-the-shoulder use of safety belts by exiting drivers. This was baselined for seven consecutive days (the first A phase). The intervention consisted of having an MSW student stand at the exit to the parking lot after lunch and display to the departing elderly drivers a printed sign reading "Please Buckle Up—I Care" on one side and "Thanks for Buckling Up!" on the other side. The observer displayed the first side to unbuckled exiting drivers, and flipped the sign over if the observer saw them buckling up. The second side was displayed if the driver was already buckled as he or she left. Independent observers collected data on safety-belt use during the two-week implementation of the intervention (the B phase). Use of the sign was then halted, but data continued to be collected for another six consecutive days (the second A phase).

Figure 11.2 depicts the data from this A-B-A study (see also Thyer, Thyer, & Massa, 1991). The baseline data showed that, on average, about

**Figure 11.2**    Daily Percentages of Observed Safety Belt Use. Reproduced from
Thyer, Thyer, and Massa (1991, p. 128) with permission.

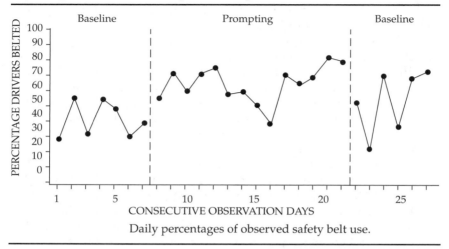

Daily percentages of observed safety belt use.

42 percent of exiting drivers were using their safety belts. This increased to
about 60 percent during the intervention phase and dropped to about 48
percent during the second A phase. Data from the first A phase are fairly
stable, and the magnitude of the change between the first A phase and the
B phase suggests that a real change occurred—certainly an 18 percent increase in safety-belt use is a meaningful one. The immediate decline in belt
use after the intervention favors the hypothesis that the display of the sign
actually caused more frequent safety-belt use. Further, because there are
two changes in the outcome measure corresponding to the introduction
and removal of the intervention, the A-B-A design can be a methodologi-
cally stronger SSD than the A-B design alone, which allows for only one
such possible shift in the data. Therein is the experimental logic behind the
stronger SSDs, that is, those that may permit causal inferences.

Faced with an A-B design like Krista Barker's described earlier, the
skeptic could claim that something else may have happened at the same
time treatment was implemented and that the observed changes were
due to that other factor, not to the introduction of social work intervention. Indeed, the skeptic is correct to raise this reasonable caveat. However, with the results of the A-B-A design Susan Massa used, the skeptic
would have to argue for two successive, coincidental changes—one that
happened to occur when treatment began and the second that happened
to occur when treatment was halted! Here one's skepticism must weaken.
Perhaps, just perhaps, social work intervention really did cause the observed changes. What seems more plausible? Either there is a real func-

tional relationship between social work and outcomes, or there is no such relationship; it is merely a coincidence. Of course, such a judgment needs to take into account the nature of the client problem or situation, its duration and severity, and the quality and magnitude of any observed changes. Nevertheless, you can appreciate the logic at work. You will appreciate it even more in the next design.

## The A-B-A-B Design

By now you have figured out where this is going. The A-B-A-B design involves the collection of reliable and valid data over a first baseline phase, then during an initial treatment phase, then over a second baseline phase during which treatment is halted, and then during a second treatment phase when treatment is reinstated. A clear example of this type of design was used at an elementary school to evaluate a simple intervention designed to reduce school violence (Murphy, Hutchison, & Bailey, 1983). Before the school opened at 8:45 a.m., arriving children went to a playground for free play. One to three teachers' aides monitored the playground, and there were more than 220 children at play. Playground violence was common—interpersonal physical aggression, property abuse, and so forth. A reliable and valid way to measure violent acts was developed, and baseline assessments were gathered for twelve mornings (first A phase). The first intervention period involved the introduction of organized games that the teachers' aides mediated and had a brief time-out contingency for particularly dangerous behaviors; this was implemented for seven days (first B phase). Four days of baseline conditions (second A phase) followed, and then six days of the same intervention (second B phase; see figure 11.3). The average number of violent acts observed during the first A phase was 212; during the first B phase, 91; during second A phase, 191; and during the second B phase, 97. The clarity of the data argue strongly in favor of the hypothesis that introducing structured games actually caused the observed reductions in violence and aggression. The skeptic would be hard pressed to argue that anything except the psychosocial intervention was causally responsible for the changes, because there are three consecutive alterations in the data clearly associated with the introduction or removal of the intervention. This is quite compelling visually, so much so that there is no need to use inferential statistics to help the reader make a conclusion. The data almost hit you between the eyes. Given the paucity of intervention research that tries to reduce school violence (as opposed to simply studying it using descriptive or correlational methods), this study by Murphy, Hutchison and Bailey (1983) is all the more compelling, despite the elegant simplicity of its research design.

**Figure 11.3**   Frequency of Incidents Recorded during the 20-min Morning
Observation Periods in the Play Group. Reproduced from Murphy, Hutchison,
and Bailey (1983, p. 33) with permission.

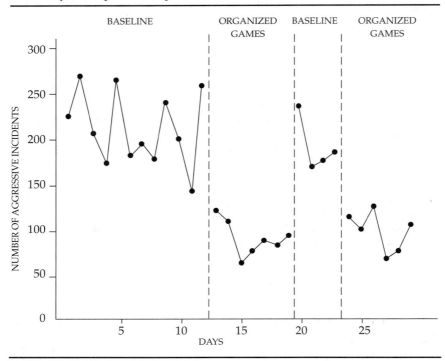

We conducted a further search on PsycINFO using "ABAB design"
and "A-B-A-B design" as our search terms and found a body of literature
similar in size to that we found in reviewing the use of the A-B design,
and also covering a diverse array of interventions and clinical problems.
Social workers have used single-system research designs to evaluate their
practice since the late 1960s, and examples of clinical assessment and
evaluation using these methods have been published in every major social work journal (see Thyer & Thyer, 1992). Mainstream social work research textbooks include these methods as a viable and practical approach to clinical assessment (e.g., Royse, Thyer, Padgett, & Logan, 2006;
Rubin & Babbie, 2008; Thyer 2001a, 2001b), and they can be creatively
employed in the evaluation of social work practice that is derived from
all theoretical orientations. Although originating in the traditions of
quantitative research that emphasizes reliable, valid, and objective measurement of clinical phenomena and other aspects of clients' lives, SSDs
lend themselves nicely to integration with qualitative research methods.
For example, they are readily integrated with narrative case histories as a

research method. They are also well positioned to be of use in the evaluation of community, organizational, and other forms of macro social work practice (Thyer, 1998), as well as of use in clinical supervision (Artelt & Thyer, 1998). Social workers and other human service professionals have also used them in many countries, which suggests that the evaluation approach has applicability across national boundaries (Thyer, Artelt, & Shek, 2003; Kazi & Wilson, 1996).

## THE DESIGN AND CONDUCT OF GROUP RESEARCH

You have undoubtedly been exposed to the general principles behind the design and conduct of group research designs, also called nomothetic research designs. Rather than relying on many consecutive measurements taken from one or a small number of clients (as in single-system designs), group designs typically rely on few (usually two or three) repetitions of measurement on larger groups of clients.

Group designs typically use inferential statistics such as *t*-tests, analysis of variance, or chi-square assessments to aid the practitioner-researcher in making reliable judgements as to whether change has really occurred. Single-system designs usually rely on the visual inspection of graphically presented data to infer the existence of reliable changes in client functioning. Each approach has its strengths and limitations, indications, and contraindications. If you are employed in an agency where relatively few clients with a particular problem seek assistance, it will be very difficult to conduct a credible group research design to evaluate the outcomes of social work services. In such circumstances, single-system designs may be applicable. If, however, you have access to large numbers of clients and/or multiple repeated measurement of client functioning is not possible, then a nomothetic approach is the way to go. It is definitely not the case that one method is intrinsically superior to the other.

The inferential statistical methods used to evaluate changes in average scores for group designs are very good at detecting reliable but small effects, especially if your sample sizes are large. This is good if you spend a lot of time studying interventions of modest to minimal effectiveness. Making inferences about changes by visually inspecting graphically presented data is not very good for detecting small (but reliable and statistically significant) changes. This means that you could potentially overlook an intervention that is only modestly effective and learn only about treatments that produce whopping effects. Claiming that an effect is present when it is not (for all practical purposes) is known in research as a type I error. This kind of error is more likely when using inferential statistics. Claiming that an effect is not present when it really is (though it is a small change) is known as a type II error and is more likely when to occur when visually analyzing data. We tend to side with those who claim that in the field of evaluation research, committing a type II error is less damaging to good science than a type I error: you learn about fewer (weaker) interventions, but the ones you end up studying are only those that are quite powerful. This is an arguable point, and as it is not central to this chapter, we do not pursue it further here.

Nomothetic designs used in evaluation research can be hierarchically ranked in terms of their strength or potential for yielding internally valid conclusions. A common system is to categorize them as preexperimental, quasi-experimental, and truly experimental (see Royse et al., 2006; Thyer, 2001a; Thyer & Myers, 2007b); we follow this convention here.

## Preexperimental Group Research Designs

Perhaps the simplest outcome study used in clinical assessment is the posttest-only group design, wherein a group of clients is formally assessed after having received a social work intervention. Consider the following scenario: In our hometown, once or twice a year, an entreprenurial hypnotist (let us call him Professor Marvel) rents a hotel meeting room and offers a one-session smoking cessation program involving so-called group hypnosis. He takes out a large advertisement in the local paper, charges a modest fee, packs the room with his gullible clients, and does his group hypnosis. He might even sell booster treatments on cassette tapes for an extra charge. Even if a few clients are unhappy at the end of the evening's session and demand their fees back, Professor Marvel does well enough out of this night's work to make a profitable living.

It is conceivable for a clinical social worker to attend one of Marvel's hypnotic workshops and, as clients exit the meeting room at the end of the session, to distribute a stamped, self-addressed postcard asking participants to mail it in a month to the social worker, perhaps anonymously, indicating whether or not they are smoking. The outcome measure can be the percentage of those who are still smoking. Assuming that all participants accepted the postcard, returned it after one month, and reported their smoking behavior honestly, this would be an instructive evaluation of Professor Marvel's hypnosis workshops. If 100 percent of participants claimed that a month later they were still smoking, we could be fairly sure that Marvel's intervention was not really helpful in quitting smoking. If 100 percent claimed that they were not smoking, this would be evidence corroborative (but not conclusive) of Marvel's claim to be able to help people quit smoking. In the arcane symbolism of group designs, this study could be labeled an X-O study, with X representing exposure to the intervention and O representing some reliable and valid assessment of client function.

Myers and Rittner (1999, 2001) provide a realistic example of the X-O design; they used a convenience sample of about one hundred adults who had been raised in a traditional, old-fashioned orphanage. Many years after these people had left the orphanage, Myers and Rittner contacted them and asked them to complete some standardized assessments about their psychosocial functioning, including such issues as family and interpersonal relationships, educational attainment, employment history, emotional or mental disorders, quality of life, life satisfaction, and so on. In this way, the social workers were able to determine that adults who had been raised in an orphanage enjoyed fairly positive lives, with generally good incomes, interpersonal relationships, life satisfaction, educational attainment, and quality of life.

A stronger form of preexperimental group design systematically assesses client functioning before social work intervention, and then again using similar methods after treatment. This design can be diagrammed as an O-X-O design. A recent example of this design in the evaluation of clinical practice was conducted by the MSW student Wendi Schwartz, who was interning at a psychiatric hospital in Atlanta. Schwartz was assigned to a partial hospitalization program wherein depressed or substance-abusing clients spend time from 9:00 a.m. to 3:00 p.m., Monday through Friday, in a structured hospital setting, receiving psychotherapy, group work, family therapy, vocational services, and other interventions. Partial hospitalization is much less expensive than inpatient treatment. Schwartz found that there were few studies that had examined the outcomes of partial hospitalization services. She was able to work with her field instructor and hospital administrators to administer to all newly admitted depressed patients a rapid assessment instrument called the Generalized Contentment Scale (GCS), which is a measure of depression. Then, just before discharge, Schwartz asked the patients to complete the GCS again. During the course of her internship, Schwartz obtained admission and discharge GCS scores from a total of nine clients—the mean score at admission was about 60, and the discharge score averaged 43.

A t-test found this reduction (lower scores mean less depression) to be statistically significantly different. Did Schwartz show that partial hospitalization caused the clients to improve? By no means. There are too many alternative explanations for the improved scores to permit her to draw such a conclusion. However, the data are consistent with the hypothesis that the program is effective; the data are also consistent with the hypothesis that the clients are not getting worse. Most psychiatric programs lack even this minimal level of evaluation data, and in this limited sense, Schwartz's study was a useful undertaking in programmatic assessment. More details can be found in Schwartz and Thyer (2000).

## Quasi-Experimental Group Research Designs

Quasi-experimental group research designs are characterized by their use of some sort of control group, that is, a number of people who receive no social work treatment, alternative social work or other treatment method, or (more rarely) placebo social work treatment. The logic being that if improvements are seen in a group of clients who receive an active social work intervention and no changes or only small effects are seen in the control group, then there is tentative evidence (evidence consistent with the hypothesis) that social work caused improvements.

Tracey Carpenter-Aeby, a school social worker, helped conduct a quasi-experimental evaluation of alternative schooling provided to disruptive middle and high school youths. The school administrators wanted to compare the results of a standard alternative school program to the regular alternative school combined with an intensive family intervention component. In lieu of complete suspension (with its deleterious academic effects), behaviorally disruptive youths are placed in alternative schools (AS) that provide a much more structured and disciplined school environment. The standard AS program was provided to 95 youths during the 1994–1995 school year, and the same AS program plus a program of intensive family involvement was provided to 120 youths during the 1995–1996 school year. The school staff wanted to test the hypothesis that augmenting AS with intensive family work (largely provided by the AS school social worker) would help the students make greater academic and disciplinary gains than those achieved through the standard AS program. Outcome measures included standardized measures of self-esteem, depression, locus of control (all assessed before and after AS), academic grades, and school attendance achieved. These areas were assessed in the home school during the terms before and during the terms after placement in the AS. This design is a bit more complicated to diagram and looks like this:

|                                                      | 1994–1995 | 1995–1996 |
|------------------------------------------------------|-----------|-----------|
| Year 1 (standard AS program)                         | O-X-O     |           |
| - - - - - - - - - - - - - - - - -                    |           |           |
| Year 2 (standard AS with intensive family involvement) |           | O-Y-O   |

The X refers to the standard program, and the Y refers to the standard program plus intensive family involvement. The dashed line separating the two groups means that they were not constructed using random assignment (more on this later). Obviously, the school administration could not preselect or randomly assign school-aged children to the AS in given years—hence the mandated use of a nonrandom comparison group. Inferential statistics were used to look at group scores both before and after the youths' entry into the AS program (within-group changes) and between the two groups at the beginning and end of the program (between-group changes). Although the overall results were mixed, students who received the AS program with added family involvement demonstrated greater improvements in locus of-control, grades, and attendance; a smaller proportion of kids dropped out of school as well. Aeby, Manning, Thyer, and Carpenter-Aeby (1999) can be consulted to learn more details about this quasi-experimental study.

Social worker Betsy Vonk used a similar design to compare the clinical outcomes at a student counseling center. Vonk was employed at this center and arranged for all college students seeking counseling services to complete the Symptom Checklist 90 (SCL 90), a rapid assessment instrument that measures multiple psychiatric symptoms like anxiety and depression. In the normal course of the center's operation, not all students seeking counseling could be immediately accommodated and were instead placed on a waiting list. Some time later they were recontacted, readministered the SCL 90, and scheduled for counseling. All clients were then readministered the SCL 90 when counseling was terminated. This structure lent itself to the naturalistic construction of the following quasi-experimental group design:

Immediate Treatment Group ($N = 41$)          O-X-O
------------------------------

Delayed Treatment Group ($N = 14$)                   O O-X-O

Here both groups of college students received the same treatment (counseling provided by licensed mental health professionals, including clinical social workers), but the second group received delayed treatment. This delay was noncontrived, having been dictated by the exigencies of agency resources and staff availability. Inferential statistics were used to examine pre- versus posttreatment mean scores on various psychiatric symptoms both within the groups over time and between the groups at pre- and posttreatment. On the initial assessment, the groups had essentially equivalent levels of symptoms. After counseling, the immediate treatment group's symptoms were greatly reduced. However, after a time, when the delayed treatment group was reassessed (without having had any formal treatment), their scores were found to have not changed. When the delayed treatment group subsequently received counseling, they improved to an extent similar to those seen among the immediate treatment group. This creative study produced data consistent with the hypothesis that the services at the counseling center were followed by symptomatic improvements among the students and that the improvements were unlikely due to the simple passage of time, because the delayed treatment group experienced no change between their first and second evaluations. Given the few published studies that empirically evaluate the clinical outcomes of college-based student counseling centers, Vonk's study was a very useful contribution to the literature (for more details, see Vonk & Thyer, 1999).

Johnson and Stadel (2007) used a posttest-only quasi-experimental design to determine which of two methods of encouraging patients scheduled for surgery was more effective in getting them to complete a health care proxy. A health-care proxy form designates someone to make decisions on a patient's behalf if the patient becomes incapacitated or incompetent. Thirty-six patients were given written information only about the need to designate a health-care proxy, and twenty-one received the same written information, as well as one-to-one social work counseling on the need for advanced directives. The availability of the author to conduct patient interviews determined whether a patient received standard intervention or the augmented version. It was nonrandom but not obviously biased. The design can be expressed as follows:

Standard intervention ($n$ = 36)                                                    X – O
Standard intervention plus social work counseling ($n$ = 21)       Y – O

The primary outcome measure was the number and percentage of patients who completed the health-care proxies. It turned out that 43 percent (nine of twenty-one) did so, who received the social work counseling, versus only 6 percent (two of thirty-six) who received only the written information. The differences were statistically significant, favoring the social work counseling group. This is a simple demonstration evaluating the outcomes of hospital social work practice, useful to the hospital, and perhaps to the evidence-based foundations of social work practice in health-care settings. It is not a perfect study, but nevertheless very helpful to the profession. We searched PsycINFO using "quasi-experimental" and "social work" as abstract search terms, covering 2005–2008 and found more than thirty references, including several social work dissertations, so it would appear that these (stet) designs too are not uncommon in the field.

## Experimental Group Research Designs

True experiments involve the random assignment of clients to different conditions, a new social work intervention, to standard care, to some other alternative service, to placebo treatment, or to no treatment whatsoever. There are considerably fewer opportunities to conduct genuine experimental group research designs to evaluate clinical social work practice, but occasionally circumstances do permit their use. True experiments have much higher levels of internal validity, allowing stronger inferences about whether social work treatment caused any observed improvements. This is why our research textbooks stress their value.

Schoolsocial worker Rufus Larkin was employed as an elementary school social worker, and a large number of behaviorally disruptive children were referred to him each year. He used a structured group-work treatment program using cognitive behavioral methods to try to help the children. Larkin could not always accommodate his referrals immediately, and he had to place some children on a waiting list before he could place them in a new group. To be fair to all the children, Larkin tossed a coin to determine which children entered group intervention immediately and which began group work later. This process naturally generated a genuinely random waiting list comparison group and enabled him to develop the following experimental design:

Immediate Treatment Group ($N = 31$)               R O-X-O-O
Delayed Treatment Group ($N = 21$)                 R-O-O-X-O

The prefix R before each group indicates that random assignment was used to create the two groups. The O indicates some type of standardized assessment, and X stands for receiving the cognitive behavioral group therapy. The outcome measures included student self-control, self-esteem, and reliable assessments of in-class behavior, and the data were examined using inferential statistics. The results provided answers to the following questions: "Did children who entered group work have improved self-esteem, self-control, and behavior?" Yes. "Were these improvements due to simply being assessed?" No. "Were the improvements caused by the group work?" Yes. "Were the improvements maintained over a fairly long period of time after the social work intervention was completed?" Yes. The clinical social worker who can provide data-based answers to such questions is indeed in an enviable position. Larkin and Thyer (1999) provide more details about this experimental evaluation of clinical social work practice.

If you can use random assignment to create sufficiently large groups (more than twenty), a pretreatment assessment is not necessary to be fairly sure that the groups are equivalent. Some genuine experiments make use of the approach of posttest-only control-group design to evaluate the outcomes of social work. The MSW student Kelly Canady did this to determine whether he could promote voting behavior among low-income African American residents of a small Georgia community. A few months before the presidential election of 1988, Canady went to the voting office and obtained the names and addresses on mailing labels for all registered voters in the poorest voting precinct in his town. This precinct contained a large number of public housing projects and was more than 90 percent African American. Canady randomly picked four hundred voters from the list of 2,500 names and randomly assigned each to one of four different experimental conditions. Those assigned to group 1 received a letter signed by the local chairs of the Democratic and Republican parties urging the citizen to be sure to vote in the upcoming presidential election. They received the letter about three days before the election. Those assigned to group 2 received the same letter twice, about

a week before and again about three days before, the election. Those assigned to group 3 received the letter three times—two weeks, one week,
and a few days before the election. Voters randomly assigned to group 4
received no reminder letters.

Canady hypothesized that a higher proportion of those receiving the
letter would vote, relative to those who did not get the letter, and that the
more letters a voter received, the more likely a voter would be to vote.
After the election, Canady went back to the voting registrar's office for a
printout of who among his four hundred voters actually voted. This information did not reflect how they voted but simply whether they actually cast a ballot (this is publically available information). He was able to
use simple inferential statistics to determine whether the groups reliably
differed in terms of the proportion that voted. This experimental strategy
can be diagrammed as follows:

| Group 1 (1 letter) | R | W | O |
|---|---|---|---|
| Group 2 (2 letters) | R | X | O |
| Group 3 (3 letters) | R | Y | O |
| Group 4 (no letter) | R | | O |

Again, R indicates that the group was formed on the basis of random
assignment; W, X, and Y refer to the experimental treatment condition;
and the gap in group 4's diagram signifies no intervention (for the results,
see Canady & Thyer, 1990).

As demonstrated in the preceding examples, clinical social workers
have a wide array of preexperimental, quasi-experimental, and experimental group research designs that they can use to evaluate practice outcomes. Practicality and internal validity are almost inversely propor-
tional. The designs that are easiest to implement in real-life practice are
usually the weakest ones. Those with the highest levels of internal validity may be too difficult to implement in agency-based or private practice
settings.

## WHAT ABOUT EXTERNAL VALIDITY?

You have no doubt been exposed to the concept of external validity,
which refers to the extent that a researcher (or reader of a research study)
can generalize the findings of a given study to similar clients or groups.
There are two basic methods for demonstrating the external validity of a
given study. The first approach (the most widely taught but all too rarely
employed) involves obtaining a sample of clients that is genuinely representative of the larger universe of individual with similar problems.
The method used to approximate a representative sample involves randomly choosing a subset of clients to participate from the larger sample
of such persons. A randomly chosen sample can be confidently viewed

as legitimately representative of the larger group from which they were chosen. Therefore, a finding from a truly randomly selected sample of clients can be legitimately generalizable. For example, consider the problem of determining the average age of all clients, about four thousand of them, currently receiving services at a large agency. You could manually extract the information from every chart. However, this would be a lot of unnecessary work because you can obtain virtually the same result by randomly sampling a much small subset of charts from your entire set of patient records, perhaps as few as a few hundred records. There are some handy tables in some research books (e.g., Royse et al., 2006) that tell you what size sample you need to randomly select from a given population to have a fairly accurate estimate of the real statistic you are interested in. Using the same statistical logic, following elementary probability theory, if you find through a suitably rigorous research design that a randomly selected sample of clients genuinely benefited much more from treatment A than from treatment B, then you can infer that treatment A is very likely better than treatment B for the others in the universe of clients you sampled from. Thus, all things being equal (e.g., cost, social validity, ethical appropriateness), treatment A should be offered in lieu of treatment B to members of that group. So far so good, but here is where we come up abruptly against the practical realities of agency-based clinical research: we can almost never obtain a randomly chosen sample of clients from the larger universe of clients we wish to generalize to.

The truth of the matter is that field research usually employs convenience samples of clients, that is, persons chosen on the basis of their availability, ability, and willingness to provide informed consent, among other variables. Even client groups obtained through some approximation of random sampling are usually compromised because of patient mortality (dropping out of the study), inability to locate clients posttreatment or at follow-up, refusal to continue participation in the study, or other detrimental developments. As soon as any of the initially randomly selected clients begin dropping out of your study for any reason, the representativeness of your sample is compromised and external validity becomes suspect.

Therefore, our advice to clinical social workers evaluating their own practice and to novice program evaluators valiantly trying to determine whether clients are getting better is simply this: accept from the outset that your findings may well end up not being generalizable and that you are not capable of conducting a study with strong external validity. This is unfortunate when measuring your study against the idealized canons of ivory-tower science, but it need not be a source of embarrassment, so long as you are modest in your initial goals. Do not claim that you will determine whether assertive community treatment for persons with bipolar disorder is better than, say, interpersonal psychotherapy for such persons, as a general rule. It is ill advised to conduct such a study to yield generalizable knowledge applicable to all persons meeting the *DSM* criteria for bipolar disorder. Instead, be more modest in your aspirations: "Do the clients at our agency do better with assertive community treatment than those clients receiving interpersonal psychotherapy?" Note the subtle distinction. You can accomplish the latter goal at your agency, whereas it is extremely unlikely that with modest resources you would be able to satisfactorily answer the former question. It is perfectly legitimate and desirable to find out whether your clients are getting better and to leave the development of generalizable knowledge to others better equipped via training and resources. It is unfortunate that many clinical social workers, imbued with the mistaken notion that the only scientifically acceptable finding is one obtained from a randomly selected sample, abandon any efforts at empirically evaluating the outcomes of their work because the findings may not be generalizable. Remember that small scale, locally conducted, unfunded, less-than-perfectly-designed evaluation studies are an exceedingly valuable undertaking and should not be dismissed.

But how will the profession ever develop generalizable knowledge? The answer is replication. Replication can be accomplished in many ways. Let's say that Dr. Faust at XYZ agency made the following finding: drug-abusing clients randomly assigned to receive reinforcers, contingent on submitting drug-free urine screens, were more drug abstinent than clients who submitted similar urine specimens but did not receive reinforcement for abstinence. Faust can replicate this finding at the same agency at a later time with a different group of similar clients. If the same result emerges, then our confidence in this approach to treating drug abusers is somewhat strengthened. Or, Faust can try to replicate his study at another agency with similar clients. Or, other researchers at different agencies (perhaps in different parts of the country), independent of Faust, can use this approach to see whether they obtain similar outcomes. Or, other independent researchers at different agencies in other parts of the country can try to replicate Faust's findings with different clients. If the effect was first obtained using samples of only men, then researchers could see if it holds up with samples of women. If it was first demonstrated with white clients, researchers could look for similar in samples of African Americans or Hispanics.

You can see the value in this approach—science via creeping incrementalism it could be called. Rather than conducting one massive study that controls for all possible threats to internal and external validity, more limited investigations can approach solving a given problem in a more piecemeal manner. Such lofty aspirations are out of reach for most agency-based clinical social workers, who are concerned not with building the edifice of scientific knowledge but with obtaining credible data regarding the outcome of their own efforts. This, too, is a noble endeavor and should not be dismissed as trivial. Indeed, it can be argued that localized efforts by clinical social workers are more relevant to practice and evaluation concerns than are grandiose megastudies.

## SUMMARY

The social work profession has a long history of recognizing the importance of clinical practice evaluation. The two major forms of inquiry for evaluating social work outcomes are single-system designs and group designs. With single-system designs, the clinician measures a single client's (or small group's) functioning before, during, and after intervention, whereas with group designs, social workers use inferential statistics to look at outcomes on larger groups of clients. This chapter reviewed different models of each design and the issues of external validity, as well as generalizability of results.

## STUDY QUESTIONS

1. Think of a client you have seen in your field placement. Design a single-system study to evaluate client outcomes. Include problem, measurement, and goal/objective. Present your expected findings on a graph.
2. Now consider your field placement agency. Design a group study to help the agency look at its client outcomes. What design would be best? What measures? What would you expect to find?
3. Considering Questions 1 and 2, speak to the issue of generalizability (external validity). How could you improve the external validity of your designs?

## REFERENCES

Aeby, V. G., Manning, B. H., Thyer, B. A., & Carpenter-Aeby, T. (1999). Comparing outcomes of an alternative school program offered with and without intensive family involvement. *School Community Journal, 9,* 17–32.

Artelt, T., & Thyer, B. A. (1998). Empirical approaches to social work supervision. In J. S. Wodarski & B. A. Thyer (Eds.), *Handbook of empirical social work practice. Volume II: psychosocial problems and practice issues* (pp. 413–431). New York: Wiley.

Barker, K. L., & Thyer, B. A. (2000). Differential reinforcement of other behavior in the treatment of inappropriate behavior and aggression in an adult with mental retardation at a vocational center. *Scandinavian Journal of Behaviour Therapy, 29,* 37–42.

Canady, K., & Thyer, B. A. (1990). Promoting voting behavior among low-income black voters using reminder letters: An experimental investigation. *Journal of Sociology and Social Welfare, 17*(4), 109–116.

Ell, K. (1996). Social work research and health care policy and practice: A psychosocial research agenda. *Social Work, 41*, 583–592.

Faul, A. C., McMurtry, S. L., & Hudson, W. W. (2001). Can empirical clinical practice techniques improve social work outcomes? *Research on Social Work Practice, 11*, 277–299.

Hudson, W. (1978). First axioms of treatment. *Social Work, 23*, 65.

Hudson, W., & Thyer, B. A. (1986). Research measures and indices in direct practice. In A. Minahan (Ed.), *Encyclopedia of social work* (pp. 487–498). Washington, DC: National Association of Social Workers Press.

Johnson, Y. M., & Stadel, V. L. (2007). Completion of advanced directives: Do social work preadmission interviews make a difference? *Research on Social Work Practice, 17*, 686–696.

Kazi, M. A. F., & Wilson, J. (1996). Applying single-case evaluation methodology in a British social work agency. *Research on Social Work Practice, 6*, 5–26.

Larkin, R., & Thyer, B. A. (1999). Evaluating cognitive-behavioral group counseling to improve elementary school students' self-esteem, self-control, and classroom behavior. *Behavioral Interventions, 14*, 147–161.

Lewis, H. (1965). The use and place of research in the administration of the social agency. *Child Welfare, 44*, 21–25.

Mullen, E. J. (1995). A review of *Research Methods for Generalist Social Work. Social Work, 40*, 282–283.

Murphy, H. A., Hutchison, J. M., & Bailey, J. S. (1983). Behavioral school psychology goes outdoors: The effect of organized games on playground aggression. *Journal of Applied Behavior Analysis, 16*, 29–35.

Myers, L. L., & Rittner, B. (1999). Family functioning and satisfaction of former residents of a non-therapeutic residential care facility: An exploratory study. *Journal of Family Social Work, 3*(3), 53–68.

Myers, L. L., & Rittner, B. (2001). Adult psychosocial functioning of children raised in an orphanage. *Residential Treatment for Children and Youth, 18*(4), 3–21.

National Association of Social Workers. (1989). *NASW standards for the practice of clinical social work.* Washington, DC: Author.

National Association of Social Workers. (1992). *NASW standards for school social work services.* Washington, DC: Author.

National Association of Social Workers. (1999). *Code of ethics.* Washington, DC: Author.

Neisser, M., Taubman, S. B., Levitt, J. L., Brown, L., & Gingerich, W. J. (1978). Responses to Hudson's "First Axioms of Treatment" (letter). *Social Work, 23*, 249–252.

Richmond, M. (1935). *Social diagnosis.* New York: Russell Sage Foundation. (Original work published in 1917).

Royse, D., Thyer, B. A., Padgett, D. K., & Logan, T. K. (2006). *Program evaluation: An introduction* (4th ed.). Belmont, CA: Brooks/Cole.

Rubin, A., & Babbie, E. (2008). *Research methods for social work* (6th ed.). Pacific Grove, CA: Brooks/Cole.

Rubin, A., & Parrish, D. (2007). Problematic phrases in the conclusions of published outcome studies: Implications for evidence-based practice. *Research on Social Work Practice, 17,* 334–347.

Schwartz, W. L., & Thyer, B. A. (2000). Partial hospitalization treatment for clinical depression: A pilot evaluation. *Journal of Human Behavior in the Social Environment, 3*(2), 13–21.

Slomin-Nevo, V., & Anson, Y. (1998). Evaluating practice: Does it improve treatment outcome? *Social Work Research, 22,* 66–74.

Thyer, B. A. (1998). Promoting research on community practice: Using single-system research designs. In R. H. MacNair (Ed.), *Research strategies in community practice* (pp. 101–113). Binghamton, NY: Haworth.

Thyer, B. A. (2001a). Single system designs. In B. A. Thyer (Ed.), *The handbook of social work research methods* (pp. 239–262). Thousand Oaks, CA: Sage.

Thyer, B. A. (2001b). Single system designs. In R. M. Grinnell (Ed.), *Social work research and evaluation: Quantitative and qualitative approaches* (pp. 455–480). Itasca, IL: Peacock.

Thyer, B. A. (2008). *Preparing research articles.* New York: Oxford University Press.

Thyer, B. A., Artelt, T., & Shek, D. (2003). Using single system research designs to evaluate practice: Potential applications for social work in Chinese contexts. *International Social Work, 46,* 163–146.

Thyer, B. A., & Myers, L. L. (2007a). Research in evidence-based social work. In T. Ronen & A. Freeman (Eds.), *Cognitive behavior therapy in clinical social work* (pp. 45–66). New York: Springer.

Thyer, B. A., & Myers, L. L. (2007b). *A social worker's guide to evaluatng practice outcomes.* Alexandria, VA: Council on Social Work Education.

Thyer, B. A., & Thyer, K. B. (1992). Single system research designs in social work practice: A bibliography from 1965–1990. *Research on Social Work Practice, 2,* 99–116.

Thyer, B. A., Thyer, K. B., & Massa, S. (1991). Behavioral analysis and therapy in the field of gerontology. In P. K. H. Kim (Ed.), *Serving the elderly: Skills for practice* (pp. 117–135). New York: Aldine de Gruyter.

Vonk, E. M., & Thyer, B. A. (1999). Evaluating the effectiveness of short-term treatment at a university counseling center. *Journal of Clinical Psychology, 55,* 1095–1106.

# Cassata History Questionnaire

Date: _____

*General Information:*

Name:                                          Age:
Address:                                       Soc. Sec. #
City:                                          Zip:
Home phone:                                    Work phone:

Ethnic background:    ___White      ___American Indian    ___Black
                      ___Oriental   ___Hispanic           ___Other, specify
Sex:      ___Male    ___Female

*Educational History:*

School last attended: _____
Highest grade completed: _____    Grade average: _____
Are you interested in school now?    ___Yes   ___No
If not enrolled in school, how long have you been out?    ___months

*Check* reason(s) you left school:
___  Failing
___  Learning problems
___  Suspended for aggressive behavior (ex., fighting, hitting teachers, vandal-
     ism, etc.)
___  Truancy
___  Ran away
___  Drug/alcohol problem
___  Pregnancy
___  Took a full time job
___  Couldn't get along with school authorities (ex., argued with teachers or prin-
     cipal)
___  Family problems
___  Got in trouble with police (ex., was arrested for stealing, drug possession,
     etc.
Other (please specify) _____

Starting with elementary school, how many schools have you attended in your
lifetime?
___(give number)

How did you hear about Cassata? _____
Why do you want to enroll in Cassata? _____

*Employment History:*

Are you working?     ___Yes     ___No
Where: _____     How long? _____
How many hours a week do you usually work? _____
What shift or work schedule do your work? _____

*Past Employment*

| Employer | From/To | Reason for leaving |
|---|---|---|
| 1. | | |
| 2. | | |
| 3. | | |

*Family History:*

MOTHER: ___living ___deceased   If deceased give your age at time of death. ___

Mother's name:                              Age:
Address:                                    Home phone:
Occupation:                                 Work phone:

*Circle* highest grade completed by Mother:

| | | | | | | | | |
|---|---|---|---|---|---|---|---|---|
| Grade School: | 1 | 2 | 3 | 4 | 5 | 6 | 7 | 8 |
| High School: | 1 | 2 | 3 | 4 | | | | |
| College: | 1 | 2 | 3 | 4 | | | | |
| Graduate School: | 1 | 2 | 3 | 4 | | | | |

Marital Status of Mother:

___Married              ___Separated              ___Common law
___Single              ___Divorced              ___Widowed

Write in number of times your Mother has been married? _____

FATHER: ___living ___deceased   If deceased give your age at time of death. ___

Father's name:                              Age:
Address:                                    Home phone:
Occupation:                                 Work phone:

*Circle* highest grade completed by Father:

| | | | | | | | | |
|---|---|---|---|---|---|---|---|---|
| Grade School: | 1 | 2 | 3 | 4 | 5 | 6 | 7 | 8 |
| High School: | 1 | 2 | 3 | 4 | | | | |
| College: | 1 | 2 | 3 | 4 | | | | |
| Graduate School: | 1 | 2 | 3 | 4 | | | | |

Marital Status of Father:

___Married              ___Separated              ___Common law
___Single              ___Divorced              ___Widowed

Write in number of times your Father has been married? _____

Your parents are currently:

___Married  ___Separated  ___Divorced  ___Never been married

SIBLINGS:

Number of brothers:                    Ages:
Number of sisters:                     Ages:

*PERSONAL INFORMATION*

Rate your ability to get along with other people. *Circle* one:

1. *Poor*          2. *Fair*          3. *Not sure*          4. *Good*          5. *Excellent*

What is the current state of your health? *Circle* one:

1. *Poor*          2. *Fair*          3. *Not sure*          4. *Good*          5. *Excellent*

Do you have any medical or physical disabilities?   ___Yes  ___No
If yes, please specify: _____

CASSATA believes in helping people deal with problems that keep them from accomplishing their goal of finishing school.

*Check* those which apply to you:

| | |
|---|---|
| ___ Low self-image | ___ Afraid |
| ___ Inconsiderate of others | ___ Nervous |
| ___ Authority problems | ___ Withdrawal |
| ___ Lead others into trouble | ___ Concentration difficulties |
| ___ Easily led into trouble by others | ___ Sad |
| ___ Aggravate others | ___ Suicidal attempt |
| ___ Easily angered | ___ Strange thoughts |
| ___ Stealing | ___ Hear voices |
| ___ Alcohol or drug problem | ___ Learning difficulties |
| ___ Lying | ___ Family problems |
| ___ Fronting (always putting on an act) | ___ Aggressive behavior (fighting, property destruction, etc.) |

With whom have you lived most of your life?

| | |
|---|---|
| ___ Both parents | ___ Mother and Stepdad |
| ___ Mother | ___ Father and Stepmom |
| ___ Father | ___ Grandparents |

If other, please specify: _____

What are your goals in life?

_____
_____

Where do you want to be in five years? (career, school, other)

_____
_____

List current activities, interests and hobbies:

_____

_____


*Financial Information*

CASSATA has scholarships available to students who qualify. Documentation of income will be required to prove eligibility. *Check* all that apply to you and your family:

___ AFDC recipient
___ Food stamp recipient
___ Supplemental Security income recipient
___ Foster child
___ Employed full time for last six months
Number of family members who live with you _____
What is your gross family income per year? (Include income of all family members) _____
Other income: _____


*Present living arrangement:*

Where do you live now?

___ With both parents               ___ With Mother
___ With Father                     ___ With Mother and Stepdad
___ With Father and Stepmom         ___ With grandparents
___ Live independently and support self


*Treatment/Counseling History:*

I have received counseling and/or treatment for a drug-alcohol problem.
___ Yes  ___ No

*Please check one of the following:*

___ I *was* in the hospital for treatment for a drug-alcohol problem.
___ I *was not* in the hospital for treatment for a drug-alcohol problem.
I have sought help from a professional person about my emotions (ex., depression, fear, suicide, anger).  ___Yes  ___No

*Please check one of the following:*

___ I *was* in the hospital for treatment of my emotions.
___ I *was not* in the hospital for treatment of my emotions.
I have been to family counseling.  ___Yes  ___No
I have been counseled or tutored for a learning problem.  ___Yes  ___No
I have been told I have an attention problem (attention deficit disorder, hyperactivity) by a doctor or therapist.  ___Yes  ___No
I have been in some type of counseling or treatment. (Please check the one that is true for you):
___Not at all ___1 time ___2–3 times ___4 times ___5 times or more

*Check the one that is true for you:*

I feel that my participation in counseling or treatment

___ made me worse
___ didn't help at all
___ helped a little
___ helped me a lot
___ helped me to make a complete change

Please list the doctors or therapists you have seen and dates:
(Please begin with the most recent)

*Agency seen for counseling*          *Name of Doctor or Therapist*          *Dates seen:*

# Sample Clinician Report for the Youth Outcome Questionnaire 2.0 (YOQ)

## Assessment: Clinician Report

DOB: 1/1/1992
Date of Assessment: 1/8/2008

Gender: Female
Date Report Created: 8/7/2008

## Youth Outcome Questionnaire 2.0 (YOQ)

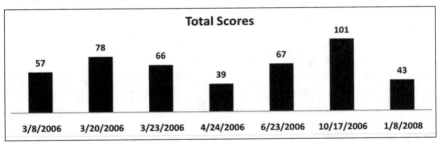

**Total Scores**

| Date | 3/8/2006 | 3/20/2006 | 3/23/2006 | 4/24/2006 | 6/23/2006 | 10/17/2006 | 1/8/2008 |
|------|----------|-----------|-----------|-----------|-----------|------------|----------|
| Score | 57 | 78 | 66 | 39 | 67 | 101 | 43 |

| Date | Total Score | ID | S | IR | SP | BD | CI |
|------|-------------|-----|---|-----|-----|-----|-----|
| 3/8/2006 | 57 | 36 | 7 | 0 | −1 | 11 | 4 |
| 3/20/2006 | 78 | 40 | 8 | 9 | 7 | 9 | 5 |
| 3/23/2006 | 66 | 40 | 7 | 5 | 0 | 10 | 4 |
| 4/24/2006 | 39 | 16 | 1 | 5 | 7 | 7 | 3 |
| 6/23/2006 | 67 | 28 | 1 | 9 | 2 | 21 | 6 |
| 10/17/2006 | 101 | 36 | 5 | 19 | 6 | 22 | 13 |
| 1/8/2008 | 43 | 22 | 5 | 5 | 3 | 4 | 4 |

### Item Analysis

| Item | Response | Comments |
|------|----------|----------|
| 1. Wants to be alone more than other children of the same age | Never or almost never (0) | |
| 2. Complains of dizziness or headaches | Rarely (1) | |

| | | |
|---|---|---|
| 3. Doesn't participate in activities that were previously enjoyable | Never or almost never (0) | |
| 4. Argues or is verbally disrespectful | Rarely (1) | |
| 5. Is more fearful than other children of the same age | Sometimes (2) | |
| 6. Cuts school or is truant | Rarely (1) | |
| 7. Cooperates with rules and expectations | Sometimes (0) | (R) Relative strength |
| 8. Has difficulty completing assignments, or completes them carelessly | Rarely (1) | |
| 9. Complains or whines about things being unfair | Sometimes (2) | |
| 10. Experiences trouble with bowels, such as constipation or diarrhea | Rarely (1) | |
| 11. Gets into physical fights with peers or family members | Rarely (1) | |
| 12. Worries and can't get certain ideas off his or her mind | Never or almost never (0) | |
| 13. Steals or lies | Never or almost never (0) | |
| 14. Is fidgety, restless or hyperactive | Rarely (1) | |
| 15. Seems anxious or nervous | Rarely (1) | |
| 16. Communicates in a pleasant and appropriate manner | Rarely (1) | (R) |
| 17. Seems tense, easily startled | Sometimes (2) | |
| 18. Soils or wets self | Rarely (1) | |
| 19. Is aggressive toward adults | Rarely (1) | |
| 20. Sees, hears, or believes things that are not real | Rarely (1) | Critical item endorsed |
| 21. Has participated in self-harm (e.g., cutting or scratching self, attempting suicide) | Never or almost never (0) | |
| 22. Uses alcohol or drugs | Sometimes (2) | |
| 23. Seems unable to get organized | Rarely (1) | |
| 24. Enjoys relationships with family and friends | Sometimes (0) | (R) Relative strength |
| 25. Appears sad or unhappy | Rarely (1) | |
| 26. Experiences pain or weakness in muscles or joints | Rarely (1) | |
| 27. Has a negative, disrespectful attitude toward friends, family members, or other adults | Rarely (1) | |
| 28. Believes that others are trying to hurt him or her even when they are not | Rarely (1) | Critical item endorsed |
| 29. Threatens to or has run away from home | Never or almost never (0) | |
| 30. Experiences rapidly changing and strong emotions | Never or almost never (0) | |
| 31. Deliberately breaks rules, laws, or expectations | Never or almost never (0) | |

| | | |
|---|---|---|
| 32. Appears happy with her- or himself | Sometimes (0) | (R) Relative strength |
| 33. Sulks, pouts, or cries more than other children of the same age | Sometimes (2) | |
| 34. Pulls away from family or friends | Sometimes (2) | |
| 35. Complains of stomach pain or feeling sick more than other children of the same age | Never or almost never (0) | |
| 36. Doesn't have or keep friends | Never or almost never (0) | |
| 37. Has friends of whom I don't approve | Never or almost never (0) | |
| 38. Believes that others can hear his or her thoughts, or that she or he can hear the thoughts of others | Never or almost never (0) | |
| 39. Engages in inappropriate sexual behavior (e.g., sexually active, exhibits self, sexual abuse towards family members of others) | Never or almost never (0) | |
| 40. Has difficulty waiting his or her turn in activities or conversations | Rarely (1) | |
| 41. Thinks about suicide, says she or he would be better off if dead | Never or almost never (0) | |
| 42. Complains of nightmares, difficulty getting to sleep, oversleeping, or waking up from sleep to early | Never or almost never (0) | |
| 43. Complains about or challenges rules, expectations, or responsibilities | Never or almost never (0) | |
| 44. Has times of unusual happiness or excessive energy | Rarely (1) | Critical item endorsed |
| 45. Handles frustration or boredom appropriately | Frequently (−1) | (R) Relative strength |
| 46. Has fears of going crazy | Never or almost never (0) | |
| 47. Feels appropriate guilt for wrongdoing | Sometimes (0) | (R) Relative strength |
| 48. Is unusually demanding | Never or almost never (0) | |
| 49. Is irritable | Rarely (1) | |
| 50. Vomits or is nauseous more than other children of the same age | Rarely (1) | |
| 51. Becomes angry enough to be threatening to others | Rarely (1) | Critical item endorsed |
| 52. Seems to stir up trouble when bored | Rarely (1) | |
| 53. Is appropriately hopeful and optimistic | Rarely (1) | (R) |
| 54. Experiences twitching muscles or jerking movements in face, arms, or body | Never or almost never (0) | |
| 55. Has deliberately destroyed property | Never or almost never (0) | |

| | | |
|---|---|---|
| 56. Has difficulty concentrating, thinking clearly, or attending to tasks | Never or almost never (0) | |
| 57. Talks negatively, as though bad things are all his or her fault | Rarely (1) | |
| 58. Has lost significant amounts of weight without medical reason | Never or almost never (0) | |
| 59. Acts impulsively, without thinking of the consequences | Never or almost never (0) | |
| 60. Is usually calm | Sometimes (0) | (R) Relative strength |
| 61. Will not forgive her- or himself for past mistakes | Sometimes (2) | |
| 62. Lacks energy | Sometimes (2) | |
| 63. Feels that he or she doesn't have any friends, or that no likes him or her | Sometimes (2) | |
| 64. Gets frustrated and gives up, or gets upset easily | Rarely (1) | |

## General Interpretation Guidelines

*Cutoff.* Total Scores of 46 or more are in the clinical range.
*Reliable Change Index (RCI).* A difference of 13 points or more (RCI) between two total scores is clinically significant.

## Youth Outcome Questionnaire 2.0 (YOQ), 1/8/2008

Total score is the total of the following six subscales. High scores reflect endorsement of a large number of items, indicating distress in the intrapersonal, somatic, interpersonal, social, and behavioral domains. Scores equal to or greater than 46 are in the clinical range:

- Intrapersonal distress assesses emotional distress, including anxiety, fearfulness, hopelessness, and thoughts of self-harm. Scores equal to or greater than 16 are in the clinical range.

- Somatic assesses somatic distress, including symptoms typical in emotionally disturbed children and adolescents, such as headaches, dizziness, stomachaches, nausea, bowel difficulties, and pain or joint weakness. Scores equal to or greater than 5 are in the clinical range.

- Interpersonal relations assesses issues relevant to relationships with parents, other adults, and peers. Items cover attitude toward others, communication and interaction with friends, cooperativeness, aggressiveness, arguing, and defiance. Scores equal to or greater than 4 are in the clinical range.

- Social problems assesses problematic behaviors that are socially related, including truancy, sexual problems, running away, destruction of property, and substance abuse. Similar to the interpersonal relations subscale, this subscale also addresses aggressiveness. However, the aggressive content found here is more severe, typically involving the breaking of social mores. Scores equal to or greater than 3 are in the clinical range.

- Behavioral dysfunction assesses the ability to organize tasks, complete assignments, and concentrate. It measures inattention, hyperactivity, and impulsivity. Scores equal to or greater than 12 are in the clinical range.
- Critical items assesses paranoia, obsessive-compulsive behaviors, hallucinations, delusions, suicidal ideation, mania, and eating disorders. Scores equal to or greater than 5 are in the clinical range.

## Note

An automated screening is not a substitute for a complete evaluation or clinical judgment but can contribute to formulation of a diagnosis and planning treatment. Alert reports assess the significance of clinical change. They are derived from statistical comparison of individual patient's progress with normative groups of patients with similar levels of initial severity. Progress expectations and predictions for any particular patient must be based on the totality of clinical and psychometric data available.

# Sample Biofeedback Profile

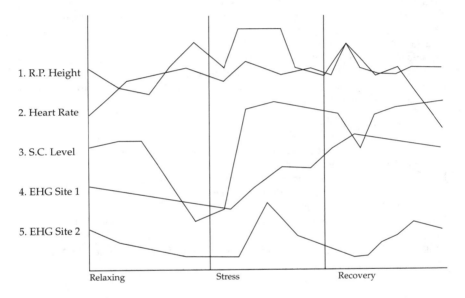

1. R.P. Height

2. Heart Rate

3. S.C. Level

4. EHG Site 1

5. EHG Site 2

Relaxing            Stress            Recovery

Brief Psychophysiological Stress Analysis (PSA)

Individual Tested: I. M. Stressed        Testing Date: 26 July 1989        Time: 10:18
Plethysmograph Site: left forefinger            EMG Site 1: right trap
SCL Site:            left middle finger        EMG Site 2: forehead

This procedure sampled levels of physiological activity during a brief guided relaxation condition, in response to the stress of a short test, and for a second guided relaxation condition. Each condition was approximately one minute in duration and consisted of five ten-second periods.

A photoelectric plethysmograph was used to detect the peripheral blood volume pulse. Changes in pulse height (PH) indicate changes in peripheral blood flow. Increases in PH generally correspond to vasodilatation, and decreases to vasoconstriction. The PH units are relative and have no absolute value. A peripheral vasoconstriction change index (PCI) is calculated that represents the change in PH relative to the mean PH for the initial relaxation condition. In the presence of stable or increasing cardiac output, increasing PCI values (i.e., lower PH) indicates an increase in peripheral resistance. The actual relationship between changes in PH or PCI values and peripheral resistance cannot be assumed to be linear.

The interval between pulse wave peaks is equivalent to the interbeat interval (IBI) of the cardiac cycle. Heart rate (HR) is derived from IBI using the formula HR=(1/mean IBI) x 60. Because PCI and heart rate are derived from PH and IBI respectively, standard deviation values are provided only for the latter. Electrodermal activity (EDA) and muscle activity(EMG) from two sites were also measured.

An analysis of the PSA results should take into account the initial level for each measure, the magnitude of the response of each measure to the stress of the short test, and the extent to which each measure returns to the starting level. This procedure was designed specifically to be used as part of an initial work-up or as a screening device. An extended evaluation should be considered for individuals showing high initial levels, minimal recovery, or atypical patterns such as a general decrease in arousal across the three conditions. The latter pattern is usually associated with high arousal relating to the testing procedure that overwhelms the modest stress of the short test.

*PHYSIOLOGICAL MEASURES:*

| | |
|---|---|
| PCI | peripheral vasoconstriction change index |
| HEART RATE | beats per minute |
| EDR | Electrodermal activity in micrOmhos |
| EMG | muscle activity in microvolts |
| PULSE HEIGHT | peripheral blood volume pulse in relative units |
| IBI | interbeat interval of cardiac cycle in seconds |

SOURCE: BRIEF PSA version 2. Released by Biobehavioral Associates for MEDAC 3000.

# Computer-Generated Millon Clinical Multiaxial Inventory Narrative

MCMI narratives have been normed on patients experiencing either genuine emotional discomforts or social difficulties and who are currently engaged in the early phases of assessment or psychotherapy. Respondents who do not fit this normative population or who have inappropriately taken the MCMI for nonclinical purposes may have distorted reports. Based on theoretical inferences and probabilistic data from actuarial research, MCMI report statements cannot be judged definite and must be viewed as only one facet of a comprehensive psychological assessment. The report should be appraised in conjunction with other clinical data such as current life circumstances, observed behavior, biographic history, interview responses, and information from other tests. To avoid possible misconstrual or misuse, computer-based test interpretations should be evaluated by mental health clinicians who are thoroughly trained in recognizing the strengths and limitations of psychological test data. This report should not be shown to patients or their relatives.

This female patient showed no unusual characterological or test-taking attitudes that may have distorted her MCMI results.

## Axis II: Personality Patterns

The following pertains to the enduring and pervasive characterological traits of this woman that underlie her personal and interpersonal difficulties. Rather than focus on currently distinct but essentially transitory symptoms, this section concentrates on her habitual, maladaptive methods of relating, behaving, thinking, and feeling.

There is evidence of a moderate level of pathology in the overall personality structure of this woman. She is likely to have a checkered history of disappointments in her personal and family relationships. Deficits in her social attainments may be notable, as is a tendency to precipitate self-defeating vicious circles. Earlier hopes for herself may have met with frustrating setbacks, and efforts to achieve a consistent niche in life may have failed. Although she is frequently able to function on a satisfactory ambulatory basis, she may evidence a persistent emotional discontrol with periodic psychotic episodes.

This woman has been typified by a social undependability and a tendency to exploitation, capriciousness and irresponsible behavior, a glib social style, the persistent seeking of excitement, and frequent seductive and self-dramatizing behavior. Interpersonal relationships are characteristically shallow or tense, and she appears indifferent to the welfare of others. Praise and approval are actively solicited by immature and histrionic demands for attention. She is easily excited and quickly bored. Although willing to expend effort to achieve something for herself, she is difficult and resistant about carrying out what others ask of her Intolerance of inactivity and an inability to delay gratification are associated with her impulsiveness, short-sighted hedonism, and her minimal regard for the consequences of her behavior, which may lead to difficulties with legal authorities.

Her judgment is typically undependable and highly erratic, and her surface affability is often punctuated with abrupt and angry outbursts. She may appear charming to casual acquaintances, but those with more enduring relationships with her are likely to see her testy, irritable, flippant, and manipulating side. Notable also is that her energies may be devoted to clever deceptions designed to seduce others into supporting her immature or irresponsible excesses. An exploitive pattern, often characterized by a history of disregarded agreements may be seen in her family and work settings. She will typically offer only fleeting and superficial displays of affection in return for meeting her demands. Her inability to sustain meaningful and trustworthy relationships with others may have recently disrupted her characteristically unruffled composure. Current difficulties may stem from family problems or legal entanglements resulting from impulsive and immature behavior. These difficulties are likely to shake her illusion of omnipotence only briefly. Accustomed to viewing herself as the center of attention and an admired figure in a select group, she will not likely tolerate a lessened role for too long.

Her habitual exploitation of others and careless disregard for social conventions may not be overtly hostile or malicious in intent. Rather, they appear to derive from her attitude of omnipotent self-assurance and her indifference to the rights of those she uses to enhance and indulge her desires. Only when her manipulative skills falter, as when she may be faced with legal difficulties or disruptive family tensions, is she likely to recognize her personal deficiencies. During these times, her moods may range from giddy elation to desperate unhappiness to being caustic and vindictive. Troubled by mounting and inescapable evidence of inadequacy and failure, she may not only disown these objectionable traits, but project them onto her accusers. This not only absolves her of fault, but justifies her resentment and anger, at least in her own eyes.

## Axis I: Clinical Syndromes

The following distinctive clinical disorders are notable. They may be of brief duration, arise in response to external precipitants, and accentuate the more persistent features of her basic personality.

This woman feels apprehensive and restless and may complain of distressful phobias, recurrent indecisiveness over picayune matters, and acute physical discomforts such as insomnia, muscular tightness, headaches, tremors, and cold sweating.

These symptoms are an extension of her basic personality style although she has recently felt subjected to unjust social condemnation or the constraints of a routine and boring life pattern. Unable to tolerate humiliation and failure or withstand the restraints of tiresome pursuits, she may act out somewhat irresponsibly or unconventionally, with periodic outbursts of hostility.

## Noteworthy Responses

The following statements were answered by the patient in the direction noted in the parentheses. These items suggest specific problem areas that may deserve further inquiry on the part of the clinician.

*Health Preoccupation*

73. I have a very tight feeling in the pit of my stomach every few days or so (T)

*Interpersonal Alienation*

No items.

*Emotional Discontrol*

No items.

*Self-Destructive Potential*

54. I have begun to feel like a failure in recent weeks (T).

## Parallel *DSM-III* Multiaxial Diagnoses

Although the diagnostic criteria utilized in the MCMI differ somewhat from those in the *DSM-III*, there are sufficient parallels to recommend consideration of the following assignments. More definitive judgment should draw upon biographic observation, and interview data in addition to self-report inventories such as the MCMI.

*Axis I: Clinical Syndrome:*

The major complaints and behaviors of the patient parallel the following Axis I diagnoses, listed in order of their clinical significance and salience.

*300.02 Generalized Anxiety Disorder*

*Axis II: Personality Disorder:*

A deeply ingrained and pervasive pattern of maladaptive functioning underlies the Axis I clinical syndrome picture. The following personality diagnoses parallel the most salient features that characterize the individual.

*301.89 Mixed Personality; histrionic, antisocial and borderline traits (provisional; rule out paranoid traits).*

*Course:*

The major personality features described previously reflect long-term or chronic traits that are likely to have persisted for several years prior to the present assessment.

The clinical syndromes described previously tend to be relatively transient, waxing and waning in their prominence and intensity depending on the presence of environmental stress.

## Axis IV: Psychological Stressors

The report on personality traits and current symptomatology suggest the following complicating factors may be exacerbating the present emotional state. They are listed in order of probable applicability. The listings should be viewed as a guide for further investigation by the clinician and should not be assumed to be definite factors in the case.

Recent life changes.

Family tensions; work upsets; authority difficulties.

*Severity of Disturbance:*

On the basis of the test data it may be reasonably assumed that the patient is experiencing a moderately severe mental disorder. Further professional study is justified to assess the appropriateness of clinical care.

## Therapeutic Implications

The following considerations are likely to be of greater utility and accuracy during early treatment planning than in later management phases.

This patient is not likely to have sought therapy voluntarily and may be convinced that, if let alone, self-resolutions will suffice. If treatment was self-motivated, it probably followed a period of prolonged and unaccustomed social humiliations or achievement failures. Complaints are likely to take the form of vague feelings of boredom, restlessness, and discontent. Her tendency to avoid major problems by wandering from one superficial topic to another or to dramatize minor issues should be monitored and prevented. She may view the therapist in the early stages of treatment as a person possessing extraordinary powers. This enthusiasm will be short-lived because she is likely to become extremely uncomfortable following intensive therapeutic probing. Treatment may be best geared to short-term goals, such as re-established psychic balance and strengthening previously adequate coping behaviors.

# Narrative Assessment Report

## Identifying Data and Background Information

Juanita Crosby is a thirty-eight-year-old working-class female of Hispanic origin. She is of average height and build, and her weight appears normal. She appears to be of average intelligence and is verbal. Juanita dropped out of high school to get married but later obtained her GED. She is in her second marriage and has four children: son Jose, age fourteen; daughter Julia, age twelve; daughter Monica, age seven; and son Peter Jr., age four. The two oldest children are by a previous marriage and the two youngest by her present marriage. The client is a waitress at a local bar and grill, where she works rotating shifts that may vary from month to month. She is currently working mostly weekends and evening shifts. Her husband, Pete, an Anglo male, works at a local factory on the "graveyard" shift (11:00 P.M. to 7:00 A.M.). The client wants help but is extremely reluctant to come to the Mental Health Center (MHC) because she fears that her family will find out and will only serve to confirm their belief that she is "crazy." She expressed similar fears regarding people at her place of employment finding out. She also stated that she would not be "locked up" and she knew that "Doctors at the MHC like to lock people up."

## Presenting Problem

Juanita was referred to a social worker at the local community mental health center by her priest, to whom she had confided that she was subject to intense "fits" in which she screamed at her children and threw things at her husband; sometimes she needed to be physically restrained by her family. The client reported that for approximately the last two years, these fits happened about every three to five weeks and lasted several hours. The client further reported that the frequency of the fits had remained fairly constant but the intensity had grown considerably worse, especially in the past six months. The client stated she did not understand these fits or why she was getting worse. The social worker identified these fits as fits of rage, and the client agreed with this description. From the report of the client, in the last fit of rage, which occurred about one month ago, she actually smashed several pieces of furniture and dishes in their home before she gained control of herself. Her husband and she usually engage in a"big fight"

SOURCE: Franklin, C. (1993). *Case Assessment.* Unpublished manuscript, University of Texas, School of Social Work, Austin.

about one of these fits of rage. The client stated that these big fights could be about almost anything (e.g., money, sex, the children). When asked by the social worker what the big fights are mostly about, however, the client responded "keeping the house."

The social worker identified the following context for a fit of rage to happen Juanita comes home from work and the chores are not done, "Pete's beer cans are on the floor and table in the living room." She is "fed up" with doing the work. She cleans up and goes to bed around 2:00 A.M. without eating or relaxing. Juanita described herself as having a "fitful" sleep, tossing and turning. She gets up about 6:00 or 6:30 A.M. to help get the children off to school. Pete arrives home around 7:30 or 7:45 A.M. She gives him a "mean stare." He asks where his breakfast is? She says, "Fix your own. I am tired of waiting on you hand and foot." They start arguing, and he will go to bed. She mops and does various chores throughout the day. The children arrive home around 3:00 P.M., and Pete gets up right before she goes to work. They either don't speak or "light into each other." When they "light into each other a fit will usually come on." According to the client, Sunday is the "big fight day" at their house.

At least once every two months the fights between the client and her husband end in them exchanging physical blows with their hand and fists, and she has also struck her husband with other physical objects such as a lamp. She stated, however, that he did not "hit her back" with anything except his hands on most occasions and usually was "acting in self-defense." The client admitted on at least one occasion pulling a weapon, a butcher knife, on her husband, but she stated her oldest child became involved, telling her to put the knife down. The client then reportedly became ambivalent about using the knife, and the husband was able to take it out of her hand.

When asked by the social worker, the client admitted that the children were present many times during the "fits of rage" and sometimes became involved by siding with one of the parents, usually the father, when the arguments between she and her husband were intense. This was especially true of the two oldest children. Most of the time, though, the children had learned to run off to their rooms and lock their doors when she begins to "rant and rave." She would scream such things at them as, "did you do your homework" and "look at this messy house." She also would call them names like "stupid," "dumb ass," and "lazy," along with many other obscenities. Juanita further admitted that during one of her episodes of rage she stood one of the children, the seven-year old daughter Monica, in the corner of the room and screamed vulgarities such as, "you no good mother fucker" for at least twenty minutes. The child reportedly hovered in the corner and begged, "please don't hurt me mommy." This incident raises a great concern for the social worker that the client's behavior may be out of control in relation to her family members. The incident with Monica occurred about one month ago and has been a major precipitant for the client to seek help. She denies ever striking the children or using physical force against them.

The client reported that she believes her fits have caused "her family to hate her." She has overheard her children referring to her as "crazy mommy." Her husband also would not talk to her for several days after one of these incidents and has threatened to leave her but has never followed through on his threats. The social worker noticed that the client herself appears to feel very guilty and ashamed following one of the episodes and tries hard to make up with her children and husband. She reports being "extra nice." Juanita does not know what brings on these fits of rage and was unable to identify any specific insights regarding her severe behavior problems. Detailed questioning by the social worker, however, revealed that the last episode was apparently associated with the client "sneaking a few drinks" of whiskey from a bottle she kept hidden from her husband in the trunk of her car. The client denied that her rages occurred every time she drank the whiskey, which was about two or three times a week or whenever she felt "bad at Pete." She also denied getting drunk.

# APPENDIX 4B

# Process Recording

| | | |
|---|---|---|
| Worker: Teyla Haas | Client: Sarah Duncan Shareka and Roderick Trotter | Date of Session: 2/19/93 |
| Date turned in: 2/23/92 | Place: Their home, East Austin | |

Client System (including age/sex/ethnicity): Sarah Duncan: African American woman, late 60s; Shareka Trotter: African American girl, five years old; Roderick Trotter: African American boy, eight years old.

Present Problem: Adoption.

Goals for the Session: Explain my role, the lifebooks, and the process of adoption. Also, begin lifebooks and start to build rapport.

| Content | Worker's Feelings | Analytical Comments | FI/Liaison Comments |
|---|---|---|---|
| ME: How long have Shareka and Roderick lived with you? | Feeling comfortable | | |
| SARAH: I have taken care of them almost their whole life. Let's see, they have lived with me for about three years, but when they was little, I always lived real close to them and took care of them. Their mother— she treat them real bad. | | | |

SOURCE: Haas, Tayla. (1993). Process Recording. University of Texas at Austin, School of Social Work.

| Content | Worker's Feelings | Analytical Comments | FI/Liaison Comments |
|---|---|---|---|
| ME: Yes, that is what I heard. | | | A response such as "she treated them real bad?"—a minimal encouragement would have been appropriate. However, Sarah did go on to provide specifics. |
| SARAH: She used to throw them up against the wall all the time, and she would tie them up and gas them up. | Feeling uncomfortable and somewhat sad. | | |
| ME: What does "gas them up" mean? | Feeling confused about what "gas them up" meant. | | Nice pursuit. |
| SARAH: She would turn on the gas on the stove and leave it on, to try to kill them. Then, I would come in and find them. I take them home with me after that and take care of them. | Feeling sad about this child abuse, but feeling glad that she felt comfortable enough to talk to me about this. | This sounds like a situation that could cause Sarah to feel afraid, angry, or sad. I was wondering what her emotions were about this. I also wanted to attend to her feelings because this sounded like a very painful event for her. | Nice sensitivity on your part. |
| ME: How did you feel about this? | | | |
| SARAH: I felt real sad. I still do. It's just not right. | | | |
| ME: I can see the sadness on your face as you talk about this. You look like this is very painful for you. | I feel sad because she looked so hurt. Her facial expression displayed a great deal of pain. | | |

| Content | Worker's Feelings | Analytical Comments | FI/Liaison Comments |
| --- | --- | --- | --- |
| SARAH: It is, very painful.<br>    Roderick, he don't want to see his mother no more. I used to take him to visit her, but he would always say, Granny, I don't want to go. So I wouldn't make him.<br>    Sometimes, I try to talk to him about the way his mother treated him, but he won't talk about it. He won't talk to the people at Day-Glo about it either. | | | |
| ME: It sounds like he has a lot of hurt and anger toward his mother. | Feeling sad. | | |
| SARAH: Yes, a lot of anger. He has had such a hard life, so has Shareka. I try not to be too hard on them. Their mother, she used lots of drugs when she had them—lots of drugs. That is why they hyper like they are right now. | I was glad that she seemed to be very understanding of Shareka and Roderick. | I wanted to communicate this to her. | |
| ME: I think that Shareka and Roderick are very lucky to have a grandmother as kind and understanding as you to take care of them. | | | |

# Case Study on Ethnic Identity

## The Dream

Linda was upset. The houseparent told the social worker at the Home that Linda seemed distracted, out of sorts, and "not her usual cheerful, well organized self" that morning. Before school she requested an interview later in the day with the social worker because she had something "very important" to discuss, so it was no surprise when Linda appeared mid-afternoon in the clinical director's office, having left school early. But the purpose of Linda's session was a surprise. She wanted to talk about a dream she had had the previous night—a very disturbing dream, like none she had had before, or at least none that she remembered. In fact, she had taken time to write the dream down during a lull at school, so that she would not forget any part of it (although at this time she felt it was unforgettably seared in her brain).

This was the dream:

It all started the summer before (according to Linda's dream). She met a nice boy at the beach. The other kids at the Home, the houseparents, the directory, really liked her new boyfriend. The couple went everywhere together, and she felt the "world smiling" on them as they fell in love. Although she knew that she was going to miss the Home, with the staff's blessing she decided to marry him in the fall. It was a happy marriage, with Linda learning to cook, keep house, and do "wifely" things. Everything was wonderful except she knew that her family would not approve of him, so she put off telling them of the marriage. Then she discovered she was pregnant. From the beginning she had mixed feelings about the pregnancy and found herself sad and happy at the same time. The husband seemed completely happy, but she just couldn't seem to reconcile herself to the approaching birth. The crux of the dream came when she was about six months pregnant and showing quite a bit. It was early in the morning and her young husband had gone to work. She went into the bathroom to wash up and began thinking about how she was going to be forced to tell her parents. A feeling of overwhelming depression swamped her and she began to cry bitter tears. She raised her eyes to the mirror to look at her swollen body and tearstreaked face. As she confronted her image in the mirror, she suddenly realized why she was reluctant to tell her folks and what was so sad about the pregnancy. In the mirror her skin was white—she was white and the boy she had married in her

SOURCE: Williams, B. E. (1987) Looking for Linda: Identity in black and white. Child Welfare, 60(3), 207–216.

dream was black. The child she carried would not belong to either race (as she perceived it) and would have no home. She cried for her "bastard baby" (her words) and for herself with her white face. She knew then that she was "white" and that there was no home for her, either. In fact, at the point she even repudiated the love her black husband professed for her. Linda woke up sobbing, depressed, and alarmed. The dream was so vivid she examined her flat stomach and tried to figure out who and where her husband was. Dragging herself out of bed she went to the bathroom mirror (the same one in her dream) to examine herself. With disbelief and still groggy from sleep, she stared at the black face reflected.

## Background Case Material

Linda was a seventeen-year-old black girl who had been a resident of the Home for almost two years at the time of the dream. In school she was a senior, approaching graduation and facing termination of current living arrangements. The residents were welcome to stay in placement during the summer following high school graduation, working and saving money for a start in the "adult" world. They had to make plans to leave by mid-August. Linda was a ward of the court and the state juvenile justice system, which had agreed to continue monetary support for placement until that time. She had been in the care of various agencies since childhood, but with the advent of her seventeenth birthday, she was essentially free to go where she wanted.

There had been no contact with the family, in spite of repeated attempts on the director's part to encourage their participation. Linda reported that distance was the reason they would not come. As near as could be ascertained by the staff, they had written two letters during her stay. She was encouraged to call them at Christmas and again when she was approaching graduation. There was no response. The question arose as to how welcome she would be should she return to her hometown to work. She made the decision to remain in the vicinity.

Linda first came to the attention of the authorities on a dependent and neglect charge against the parents. The family lived in a border where Mexican Americans constituted the majority of the citizens. Black families were few and far between and black foster families practically nonexistent. So, although things were never really satisfactory, she was left in her own home for some years with a white caseworker keeping close tabs on the situation. Linda became very fond of her child welfare worker, who seemed to be the only bright spot in her existence. The worker dearly loved Linda and constantly took her on outings. The contrast with her neglectful and abusing mother was stark.

At school Linda did well with her white teachers. Because she was very bright and verbal, as well as frequently being the only black child in the classroom, she attracted the attention of well-meaning teachers who gave her a lot of time and attention. Many hours after school and on weekends were spent in various activities to which school personnel invited her. All of her role models were white, and it was obvious that she was not participating in what little black community there was. And no one wanted her to. She had become everyone's pet project, and they were accepting her as "one of us" and not perceiving her as a member of the black community. It was almost as though her daily brief periods at home were interludes in her real life in the white world.

When she grew to adolescence and went out of the neighborhood school into a central high school, she knew well how to navigate the white world. Although the opportunity for a choice of black friends broadened considerably, Linda chose not to associate with them, making friends among the "liberal" white teenagers. Her caseworker resigned, and another took her place. The new worker had heard such good things about Linda—what a rewarding case she was and what progress she was making under child welfare auspices—that she was immediately favorable. Linda never felt as close to her as the initial one, but apparently made the transition smoothly.

At fifteen Linda made her first "mistake." In solidly with the middle-class white teenagers who were trying their wings and their parents' patience, she began to experiment with drugs. Although she really didn't like drugs, she bought, sold, and used with the best of them. And they were caught. The other children were given probation and placed in the custody of their parents. Linda was sent to the detention center by shocked child welfare workers who had "done their best." Once at the receiving center, however, the workers could not forget what an exemplary child she had been and pleaded for treatment rather than a detention facility. The decision was "a child in need of supervision," rather than a psychiatric or juvenile delinquency case. Removing her from the home community seemed to offer the best solution, and she was sent across the state to a residential facility that had an excellent track record in the care of adolescents.

Linda was only the second black girl in the history of the Home. Welcomed with open arms by the staff, she immediately became a favorite. Likable, intelligent, friendly, and apparently happy to be there, her winning ways made the other girls appear surly. The staff was concerned that she might not be happy at the neighborhood high school, which had been integrated by means of crosstown busing. Fear of "contamination" by the discontented black students in that population prompted the decision to take her downtown every day to the central high school. A good socioeconomic mix, this was the only "naturally" integrated school in town. She was encouraged (as were all the children) to make friends and bring them home for supper or other activities at the Home. She did make friends—all white—and also soon had several white teachers whom she really liked. The staff was happy; Linda seemed to have settled in.

It should be noted that the staff of the facility was without exception white. A training site for the local state university graduate school of social work, even the social work interns were white. The board members, the physicians who furnished medical care, and the benefactors of the nonprofit institution were white, as was the surrounding neighborhood. How well Linda fit and what a credit she was to the Home always pleased the staff. Not so the two black boys in one of the boys' cottages. By comparison, they were always into some devilment and maintained close ties with their "irresponsible families." It seemed as if every time they went home for a visit, they came back obstreperous. Linda, however, always spent her holidays with a staff member and conducted herself with both liveliness and good manners.

## Discussion

Black psychiatrists Grier and Cobbs (1968) have denied the existence of positive self-esteem among blacks, while Foster and Perry (1982) point out that the prevailing view of blacks has been that they suffer from negative self-esteem manifested in feeling of self-hate and a lack of self-actualizing behavior. Oppressive social and economic conditions, racism, and discrimination, in combination with an attempt to identify with the values of the dominant white society, have contributed in a large measure to this negative self-image. Undeniably, color is a tag that is difficult to dispense with. Blacks become members of a highly visible victim group, thus lacking an inconspicuous avenue of escape from their disempowered status (Maguire, 1980). Pinderhughes (1976) emphasized that the most severely victimized adopt values of autonomy and isolation as a defense against the stresses that overwhelm them. Their autonomy is not based on growth and self-actualization, however, but on a feeling that they have been abandoned, are now alone and cannot expect help from anyone. One of the best-known defenses against powerlessness is that of identifying with the aggressor (Pinderhughes, 1979).

It does not take a complicated analysis of Linda's dream to recognize a psyche under stress. Stehno (1982) writes that the minority child's sense of well-being is developed in interaction with the inner, nurturing environment before he or she is directly confronted with the hostile wider society. This forms patterns of close involvement, including frequent interactions among and exchange of help with kin (McAdoo, 1982). Social workers must realize that individuals do not learn their coping behaviors or their mores, social drives, or values from the larger society. Children learn a particular culture and a particular moral system only from those people with whom they have close contact and who exhibit that culture in frequent relationships with them (Washington, 1982). Perceptual experiences, shared symbols, oral traditions, feelings and sentiments that make up ethnicity are learned and constitute the individual's nurturing environment (Davis, 1948).

What is the result when that nurturing environment is not that of the child's own family, or not even within the appropriate ethnic group? Linda, though remaining in her own home until age fifteen, was separated psychologically from her cultural heritage much earlier. A review of her childhood reveals only essentially negative relationships with a broader black community. Every helping or positive relationship was established with the white community. At no time in her seventeen years did Linda become involved with a warm, caring, or powerful black role model. All power and all goodness appeared to be vested in the majority-controlled systems with which she interacted—child welfare, juvenile justice, the Home.

Linda's family and ethnic group became merely shadow persons, existing in the background of the satisfying world that stroked her. Her lack of interest in and contact with them during her placement contrasted strikingly with the attachment and identification the other children, both black and white, had with their origins. And this was encouraged by those helping her. She was a satisfying case, quickly picking up the required behavior, excelling in the prescribed ways, warmly attached to her caseworkers and teachers, appreciative of and seemingly satisfied with the living arrangements at the Home. The houseparents particularly enjoyed having her because they did not have to compete with her family, who stayed out of their way, literally and psychologically. Each step away from a cultural identity earned her points. However, the color of her skin remained the same. Clark's assertion (1965) never was more true than in Linda's case: "It is still the white man's society that governs the Negro's image of himself."

Linda's dream brought to consciousness her dilemma. She was a creature of both worlds and citizen of neither. The "bastard child" within her was tragically not welcome in her family and her dual black-white identity would not serve her well in the wider world to which she was going. Her poignant cry to the case-worker, "Don't you understand? I looked in the mirror and I was white!" chilled her listener.

# Hilson Adolescent Profile

Hilson Research Inc.                                   HAP Narrative Report
## **HILSON ADOLESCENT PROFILE**

**Age 16**

**Agency 0555-2**          **Date 09/18/87**          **Case 72**     **Sex -M-**     **Race -0-**

## Introduction

This report is intended to be used as an aid in evaluating an adolescent's emotional adjustment, social skills, and behavioral patterns. These results are also designed to provide information to support classification, treatment, and case disposition decisions. While the HAP is not intended to be used as a sole source for making such decisions, it has been developed with the purpose of providing relevant data for further evaluation.

## Test Response Style—Validity Measure

This adolescent has not been entirely candid about his feeling and behaviors. He has favored socially acceptable responses, showing a tendency to deny minor faults or shortcomings to which his peers more readily admit. He has presented himself as a somewhat wary, guarded individual with an overriding need to be seen in a positive light. This test-taking strategy of attempting to portray himself as virtuous in all areas may have made the results of this test less valid, especially in areas where apparent emotional adjustment may be due to the denial of problems rather than to their nonexistence. Limited insight and strong concern for appearances are indicated for this adolescent.

## "Acting-Out" Behavior Measures: Specific "External" Behavior

He may be a habitual user of alcohol. He describes himself as a social drinker with a good alcohol tolerance. There may be a tendency for this person to use alcohol in an attempt to avoid painful feelings. A careful evaluation of his item endorsements and drinking habits is suggested.

This person may be a habitual user of drugs and has endorsed more drug-related items than have his peers. He is likely to use marijuana on a regular basis

449

and may also use other substances such as cocaine. A history of frequent drug usage and/or drug dependence is indicated. Similar adolescents find they are comfortable within a subculture that accepts the use of drugs as a routine part of life. The extent of this adolescent's drug involvement should be carefully evaluated.

Compared with others tested, this individual endorsed some items suggestive of antisocial attitudes and/or behavior. He may feel misunderstood by others and may participate in activities that deviate from social norms. Some conflicts with authority and difficulty accepting criticism may also be evident. If internalized conflicts are not reported on this test, insight regarding his behavior may be limited, making this individual a questionable candidate for success in traditional psychotherapy. A careful evaluation of items endorsed in this area is suggested to determine the extent of difficulty he experiences in adhering to society's rules and regulations.

## Attitudes and Temperament

This individual has endorsed items indicative of risk-taking or "thrill-seeking" behavior. He may seek a sustained level of excitement through a variety of experiences in a pattern similar to those of substance abusers. He may have some difficulty controlling behaviors requiring moderation (such as eating, drinking, gambling, or smoking). This adolescent may also have some detached, skeptical, or antisocial views about his position in society. He may feel that life is usually unfair and that self-serving motives are most appropriate.

## Interpersonal Adjustment Measures

A serious pattern of family conflicts is indicated. This adolescent shows evidence of an unhappy, perhaps disruptive, childhood, as well as alienation from family members and/or relatives. Although some alienation is recognized as a normal feature of adolescent growth, this individual displays significant homelife conflicts compared with peers. He may view his home situation as intolerable and a history of running away or other "acting out" behavior may be evident. A thorough evaluation of current relationships with family members is advised. If possible, the family should be involved in any treatment program developed for this individual. Family counseling/therapy may be considered as a useful treatment intervention.

At least one item was endorsed indicating he may have been physically abused. It is advised that this be verified in follow-up interviews with this individual and/or his family.

Endorsements suggested this individual may be experiencing some social/sexual adjustment difficulties. Although he may view himself as sexually knowledgeable and/or experienced, this adolescent may also have endorsed items suggesting difficulties with the opposite sex. There may be signs of social discomfort with peers, and item endorsements on this scale should be carefully evaluated for evidence of social/sexual problems.

## Internalized Conflict Measures

This adolescent has endorsed specific items indicating suicide has been considered and/or attempted. A thorough clinical evaluation is recommended to assess current suicide potential.

Item endorsements show similarities to the responses of individuals who suffer from psychoses or serious emotional disturbances. Unusual or bizarre thinking may be apparent at times. Because this adolescent has responded positively to items not usually endorsed by his peers, it is suggested that the item endorsements in this area be verified in a clinical interview.

This individual has endorsed items suggestive of auditory hallucinations and/or referential thinking. These should be examined more closely in follow-up interviews.

## Summary Statement

Overall, these test results suggest the presence of behavioral problems and/or serious emotional adjustment difficulties. Compared with his peers, this adolescent has significantly elevated scores falling outside the average range (see above report). Follow-up interviews and treatment interviews are recommended.

# HAP CRITICAL ITEMS FOR FOLLOW-UP EVALUATION

The following endorsed item(s) may provide useful leads for follow-up interviews and/or further investigations. Because individual items may have been endorsed in error, they should not be used alone as a basis for making decisions and should be verified by the tested individual and/or by outside sources.

## Alcohol and/or Drug Use

5. I like to drink a six-pack of beer, or have 4 or 5 mixed drinks. (T)
31. I have smoked marijuana without other people around. (T)
96. There have been times when I had trouble knowing what I was doing or what was going on around me. (T)
146. I go drinking with my friends at least once a week. (T)
157. I could easily drink a six-pack of beer, or four or five drinks. (T)
168. Sometimes I need a drink in order to relax. (T)
238. There have been times when I smoked marijuana three or four days a week. (T)
241. Some people, who do not know me really well, have said that I sometimes drink too much. (T)
244. I once sold a small quantity of drugs to a friend. (T)
248. I have tried cocaine more than once. (T)
264. I have used unprescribed pills to keep me going or to keep me calm. (T)
277. I have tried PCP (angel dust) or LSD to see what it was like. (T)
284. I have smoked marijuana more than two times in a week. (T)

## Family Conflicts

60. I have some enemies in my family. (T)
69. I have run away from home more than once. (T)
77. I have run away from home and stayed out overnight. (T)
235. I often have arguments with one or both of my parents. (T)
288. I have been physically abused in my life. (T)

## School Adjustment Difficulties

11. I have been suspended from school. (T)
58. In my last year at school, I failed more than one subject. (T)
121. I have had trouble being passed on to the next grade in school. (T)
257. I once had to repeat a grade in school. (T)
280. I have had to go to summer school to make up a failed course. (T)

## Trouble with the Law/Society

160. I have been involved in a stolen car incident. (T)
171. I was arrested over a minor incident. (T)
295. More than once I have taken small items from a store without paying. (T)
304. I have been out with friends when they wrote on walls or damaged some property. (T)

## Temperament

172. I used to have a really bad temper. (T)
252. When I become angry, I like to punch something.

## Depression/Suicide Potential

39. I have thought about killing myself. (T)
104. Someone in my family has tried to kill him/herself. (T)
126. I have tried to kill myself more than once. (T)
154. When I feel blue or depressed, I often stay in bed all day. (T)
204. I have seriously considered ending my own life. (T)
215. There have been times when I have thought a lot about ways to kill myself. (T)

## Health/Anxiety/Phobic Symptoms

108. I often have one of these: headaches, backaches, or neckaches. (T)
134. I usually get off a very crowded train or bus to wait for one less crowded. (T)
270. Sometimes, without warning, I have at least one of these: fast heartbeat, dizziness, feeling faint or fast breathing. (T)

## Counseling/Medication History

41. I have had counseling or therapy for a problem. (T)
84. I have attended a drug rehabilitation program. (T)

## Social/Sexual Adjustment

23. I have a close friend and we can talk about almost anything. (F)
247. I have had sexual experience with someone at least 5 years older than I am. (T)

## Unusual Suspicions/Thoughts

33. Someone has tried to poison me. (T)
132. I sometimes hear voices that others around me do not hear. (T)
213. I have sometimes heard voices that have tried to tell me what to do. (T)
236. I have special mental powers that few others know about. (T)

Critical Item total = 46

# Psychological Testing Instruments for Children & Adolescents

## Infant Development Scales

Brazelton Neonatal Behavioral Assessment Scales
1. Neurological intactness
2. Interactive behavior
   (a). Motor control (putting thumb in mouth)
   (b). Remaining calm and alert in response to stimuli (bell or light)
3. Responsiveness to the examiner and need for stimulation

Bayley Scales of Infant Development
1. Mental abilities (memory, learning, problem solving)
2. Motor skills
3. Social behaviors (social orientation, fearfulness, and cooperation)

Gesell Development Schedules
1. Fine and gross motor behavior
2. Language behavior
3. Adaptive behavior (eye-hand coordination, imitation, and object recovery)
4. Personal-social behavior (reaction to persons, initiative, independence, play responses)

Denver Developmental Screening Test
   (Can be administered by a person with limited training, screening test to indicate if more in-depth testing is needed.)
1. Developmental delays
2. Problems in personal/social, fine motor/adaptive, language, and gross motor skills

## Intelligence Tests for Preschool and School-Age Children

Stanford-Binet
   (Used with both preschool and school-age, usually administered to children between 2-8 years old. Disadvantage is that it gives only an overall score, doesn't address specific strengths and weaknesses. May not be good for bilingual/bicultural children.)

1. Vision
2. Eye-hand coordination
3. Hearing
4. Speech

Wechsler Scales consist of:
    Wechsler Preschool and Primary Scale of Intelligence (WPPSI) and Wechsler Intelligence Scale for Children-Revised (WISC-R). Most widely used to test cognitive functioning of school-age children. These scales include six verbal and six performance subtests.

System of Multicultural Pluralistic Assessment (SOMPA)
    This test is based on the WISC-R, and takes into account a child's handicapping condition and sociocultural background.

## Special Abilities Tests

Bender Visual Motor Gestalt Test
    1. Visual perceptual skills
    2. Eye-hand coordination

Peabody Picture Vocabulary Test
    (Originally designed to be used with persons who are nonverbal, mentally retarded, and/or have cerebral palsy.)

Detroit Test of Learning Aptitude
    1. Auditory and visual memory
    2. Concentration

## Testing for Mental Retardation

(An IQ score below 70 indicates that a client may be mentally retarded. However, a low IQ score by itself is not sufficient for diagnosis. The client's adaptive score must also be measured. The following three instruments measure adaptive behavior.)

Vineland Social Maturity Scale

American Association on Mental Deficiency's (AAMD) Adaptive Behavior Scales

Adaptive Behavior Inventory for Children

## Personality Tests

I. Objective tests, designed to determine predominant personality traits or behavior:

Minnesota Multiphasic Personality Inventory (MMPI)
    (can be used with adults and adolescents)

Personality Inventory for Children (PIC)

II. Projective tests give clients a stimulus, such as a picture to respond to—responses indicate problem areas.

Rorschach Test

Holtzman Inkblot Technique

Thematic Apperception Test (TAT)

Children's Apperception Test (CAT)

Michigan Picture Test

Task of Emotional Development Test

Blacky Pictures

Make-a-picture-story Test

SOURCE: Sheafor, B., Horejsi, C., & Horejsi, G. (1988). *Techniques and guidelines for social work practice*. Newton, MA: Allyn & Bacon.

# Multiaxial Assessment with the *DSM-IV-TR*

## Axis I: Clinical Disorders

- Disorders usually first diagnosed in infancy, childhood, or adolescence (excluding mental retardation, which is diagnosed on Axis II).
- Dementia, delirium, amnestic, and other cognitive disorders
- Mental disorders resulting from a general medical condition; for example, CNS infections
- Substance-related disorders
- Mood disorders
- Anxiety disorders: panic attack, agoraphobia, PTSD
- Somatoform disorders: somatoform disorder, conversion disorder
- Factitious disorders (intentional production of physical or psychological symptoms)
- Dissociative disorders: amnesia, dissociative fugue, MPD
- Sexual and gender identity disorders
- Eating disorders
- Sleep disorders
- Impulse control disorders not elsewhere classified
- Adjustment disorders (in response to an identifiable psychosocial stressor)
- Other conditions that may be a focus of clinical attention

## Axis II: Personality Disorders and Mental Retardation

- Paranoid personality disorder
- Schizoid personality disorder
- Schizotypal personality disorder
- Antisocial personality disorder
- Borderline personality disorder
- Narcissistic personality disorder
- Mental retardation
- Avoidant personality disorder
- Dependent personality disorder
- Obsessive-compulsive personality disorder
- Personality disorder not otherwise specified

## Axis III: General Medical Condition

Must be diagnosed by a physician

## Axis IV: Psychosocial and Environmental Problems

(Usually problems that have occurred during the past year)

- Problems with priority support system
- Problems related to the social environment
- Educational problems
- Occupational problems
- Housing problems
- Economic problems
- Problems with access to health care services
- Problems related to interaction with the legal system/crime
- Other psychosocial or environmental problems

## Axis V: Global Assessment of Functioning (GAF) Scale

Measurement of level of current functioning and measurement of highest level of functioning during past year. Anchored scale, 0-100

# Schizophrenia and Other Psychotic Disorders from the *DSM-IV-TR*

A. Essential features are a mixture of characteristic signs and symptoms (positive and negative) that have been present for a significant time during a one-month period (less if successfully treated), with some signs of a disorder persisting for at least six months
   1. Positive symptoms reflect an excess or distortion of normal functions (such as delusions, hallucinations, disorganized speech, grossly disorganized or catatonic behavior)
   2. Negative symptoms reflect a diminution or loss of normal functions (such as affective flattening in the fluency and productivity of thought and speech (alogia), in the initiation of goal-directed behavior)
B. Diagnostic Criteria
   1. Characteristic symptoms (two or more for most of one month)
      a. delusions
      b. hallucinations
      c. disorganized speech (such as, frequent derailment or incoherence)
      d. grossly disorganized or catatonic behavior
      e. negative symptoms (that is, flattened affect, alogia, or avolition)
   2. Social/occupational dysfunction
   3. Duration—signs of disturbance for at least six months
   4. Schizoaffective and mood disorder ruled out
   5. Not resulting from substance/general medical condition

## Schizophrenia subtypes

A. Paranoid type
   1. Preoccupation with one or more delusions or frequent auditory hallucinations
   2. None of the following is prominent: disorganized speech, disorganized or catatonic, or flat or inappropriate affect
B. Disorganized type (old Hebephrenic)
   1. All of the following are prominent
      a. Disorganized speech
      b. Disorganized behavior
      c. Flat or inappropriate affect

C. Catatonic type
   1. Marked by psychomotor disturbance; at least two of the following:
      a. Motoric inability as evidenced by catalepsy (waxy flexibility) or stupor
      b. Excessive purposeless motor activity
      c. Extreme negativism (motiveless resistance to all instructions) or mutism
      d. Peculiarities of voluntary movement as evidenced by posturing, stereo-typed movements, prominent mannerism, or prominent grimacing
      e. Echolalia (parroting) and echopraxia (parroting movements)
D. Undifferentiated type
E. Residual type
   Specifiers:
      Episodic with interepisode residual symptoms
      (with prominent negative symptoms)
      Episodic with no interepisode residual symptoms
      Continuous (with prominent negative symptoms)
      Single episode in partial remission (with prominent negative symptoms)
      Single episode in full remission
      Other or unspecified pattern

## Schizophreniform Disorder

A. Identical to schizophrenia, but of less than six months duration

## Schizoaffective disorder

A. An uninterrupted period of illness during which, at some time, there is either a major depressive episode, a manic episode, or a mixed episode concurrent with symptoms that meet criterion A for schizophrenia

## Delusional Disorder

A. Essential feature is the presence of one or more nonbizarre delusions that persist for at least one month
B. Diagnostic Criteria
   1. Nonbizarre delusions for at least one month duration
   2. Criterion A for schizophrenia has never been met
   3. Apart from the impact of the delusion(s), or its ramifications, functioning is not markedly impaired and behavior is not obviously odd or bizarre
   4. If mood episodes have occurred concurrently with delusions, their total duration has been brief relative to the duration of the delusional periods
   5. Not due to substance abuse effects
C. Subtypes
   1. Erotomania-delusions that another person, usually of a higher status, is in love with the individual
   2. Grandiose-delusions of inflated worth, power, knowledge, identity, or of a special relationship to a deity or famous person
   3. Jealous-delusions that individual's sexual partner is unfaithful

4. Persecutory-delusions that the person (or someone to whom the person is close) is being malevolently treated in some way
5. Somatic-delusions that the person has some physical or general mental condition
6. Mixed-characteristics of one or more of the above but none predominates
D. Unspecified
Bi-polar disorders from *DSM-IV-TR*

## Major Depressive Episode

A. Essential feature is a period of at least two weeks during which there is either depressed mood or loss of interest or pleasure in nearly all activities
B. Diagnostic criteria
  1. Five or more of the following for two weeks:
     a. Depressed mood most of the day, nearly every day
     b. Markedly diminished interest or pleasure in all, or almost all, activities most of the day, nearly every day
     c. Significant weight loss or gain (5% of body weight) or decrease or increase in appetite nearly every day
     d. Insomnia or hypersomnia nearly every day
     e. Psychomotor retardation or agitation nearly every day
     f. Feelings of worthlessness or excessive or inappropriate guilt
     g. Diminished ability to concentrate or think, or indecisiveness
     h. Recurrent thoughts of death, recurrent suicidal ideation with or without a plan
  2. Symptoms cause clinically significant distress or impairment in social, occupational, or other important areas of functioning
  3. Symptoms are not resulting from the direct physiological effects of a substance or a medical condition (for example, hypothyroidism)
  4. Is not bereavement

## Manic Episode

A. Essential feature is defined by a distinct period during which there is an abnormally elevated, expansive, or irritable mood, lasting at least one week
B. Diagnostic criteria
  1. Distinct period of abnormally and persistently elevated, expansive, or irritable mood of at least one week duration
  2. During the period of disturbance, three or more of the following, four if the mood is only irritable:
     a. Inflated self-esteem or grandiosity
     b. Decreased need for sleep
     c. More talkative than usual or pressure to keep talking
     d. Flight of ideas or subjective experience that thoughts are racing
     e. Distractibility
     f. Increase in goal-directed activity (socially, occupationally, sexually) or psychomotor agitation

g. Excessive involvement in pleasurable activities that have a high potential for painful consequences (spending, business ventures)
3. Does not meet criteria for a mixed episode
4. Mood disturbance is sufficiently severe to impair functioning or necessitate hospitalization
5. Symptoms not resulting from direct physiological effects of a substance or medical condition (for example, hyperthyroidism)

## Mixed Episode

A. Essential feature is characterized by a period of at least one week in which the criteria are met for both a manic and major depressive episode. Rapidly alternating moods (sadness, irritability, euphoria) accompanied by manic and major depressive symptoms
B. Diagnostic Criteria
1. Criteria met for both a manic episode and a major depressive episode (except for duration less than one week, in contrast to two weeks)
2. Mood disturbance is sufficiently severe to cause marked impairment in functioning
3. Symptoms not a result of direct physiological effects of a substance or a medical condition

## Hypomania Episode

A. Essential feature is a distinct period during which there is an abnormal and persistently elevated, expansive, or irritable mood that lasts at least four days
B. Diagnostic criteria
1. Distinct period (at least four days) in which there is persistently elevated, expansive, or irritable mood
2. During period of the mood disturbance, three of the following, or four if only irritable:
a. Inflated self-esteem or grandiosity
b. Decreased need for sleep
c. More talkative than usual or pressure to keep talking
d. Flight of ideas or subjective experience that thoughts are racing
e. Distractibility
f. Increase in goal-directed activity (socially, occupationally, sexually) or psychomotor agitation
g. Excessive involvement in pleasurable activities that have a high potential for painful consequences (spending, business ventures)
3. Episode is associated with an unequivocal change in functioning that is uncharacteristic of the person
4. Disturbance in mood is observable by others
5. Episode is not severe enough to cause marked impairment in social or occupational functioning or to require hospitalization, and there are no psychotic features
6. Symptoms do not result from the direct physiological effects of a substance or medical condition

## Serious Neurological and Cognitive Impairments from *DSM-IV-TR*

### Delirium

Disturbance in consciousness and changes in cognition that occurs over a short period of time. Rule out dementia, may change throughout the day. May come on over one to three days, or suddenly. More common in elderly, and children are very prone to development. Differential diagnosis—Dementia alone; Delirium superimposed on Dementia; or Delirium alone.

Grouped according to etiology.

General Medical Condition—(hypoglycemia, stroke, encephalitis etc.). Substanced-induced (e.g., cannabis, cocaine, hallucinogens, diazepam, alcohol withdrawl, etc.).
Multiple Etiologies—(such as viral encephalitis and alcohol withdrawl).
NOS

No single psychological variable can account for on-set of delirium but sleep and sensory deprivation have been implicated. The elderly and those recovering from surgeries (10-15%) and burn patients (30%) often experience.

Prodromal symptoms: restlessness, anxiety, irritability, and sleep disruption. Short onset after these symptoms appear.

**Mental Status Tests for Delirium:** Count backwards from 20. Draw the face of a clock (constructional tasks deficits); name objects (tests for dysnomia); write a sentence (tests for dysgraphia). Dysgraphia is one of the most sensitive indicators of delirium but can occur in other disorders too, such as dementia. Be aware of emotional responses to the confusion and delirium. EEG is either slowed or rapid.

**Questions to ask in looking for medical and substance-induced concerns:**

Is there a history of alcohol or drug usage?
Is the patient showing signs of sympathetic nervous system activity, such as rapid heart, increased blood pressure, sweating?
Does the person have high blood pressure?
Are there chest pains or other signs of cardiac distress?
Is there a history of insulin-dependent diabetes?
Is there a history of hypoglycemia?
Is there a history of pulmonary disease?

### Dementia

Multiple cognitive deficits that include impairment in memory. Experience aphasia—deterioration in language; apraxia—impaired abilities at motor activities. Agnosia—failure to recognize objects. Executive functioning—plan, sequence, monitor, and execute complex behaviors. Differential diagnosis—delirium, amnesia, mental retardation, schizophrenia, major depressive disorder. Can be understood as cortical and subcortical. Cortical involves cerebral cortex—amnesia, aphasia, apraxia and agnosia (that is, Alzheimer's disease). Subcortical involves grey and deep-white matter structures—basal ganglia, thalamus, brain stem nuclei, and frontal lobe projections of these structures. Subcortical disrupts arousal, attention, motivation, rate of information processing. Clinically observed as psychomotor retardation, defective recall, poor abstraction and strategy formation, and mood and personality alterations such as depression or apathy.

Grouped according to etiology.

Alzheimer's type
Vascular
General medical condition—(Parkinson's disease, syphilis, brain tumors, HIV infection; Huntington's disease; Picks disease; Cruetzfeldt-Jacobs diseases, head injury, etc.).
Substance Induced
Multiple Etiologies
NOS

### Differentiating Dementia syndrome of depression (pseudodementia) from primary dementia

Shorter referral times for depression
History of mood disorder
More depressed mood and delusions in depression
More behavioral deterioration in patients with primary dementia
Sleep disturbance is more severe and involves early morning awakenings.

*Anxiety Disorders*

*Panic attack* (term not codable—uses panic disorder)

A. Essential feature is a discrete period of intense fear or discomfort that is accompanied by at least four of thirteen somatic or cognitive symptoms. Attack has a sudden onset and builds to a peak rapidly (usually ten minutes or less) and is often accompanied by a sense of imminent danger or impending doom and an urge to escape.
B. Diagnostic Criteria (four or more of the following)
   1. Palpitations, pounding heart, or accelerated heart rate
   2. Sweating
   3. Trembling or shaking
   4. Sensations of shortness of breath or smothering
   5. Feeling of choking
   6. Chest pain or discomfort
   7. Nausea or abdominal distress
   8. Feeling dizzy, unsteady, lightheaded, or faint
   9. Derealization (feeling of unreality) or depersonalization (being detached from one's self)
   10. Fear of losing control or going crazy
   11. Fear of dying
   12. Paresthesias (numbness or tingling sensations)
   13. Chills or hot flashes

*Agoraphobia* (not codable—code specific disorder in which it occurs)

A. Essential feature is anxiety about being in places or situations from which escape might be difficult (or embarrassing) or in which help might not be available in the event of a panic attack or panic-like symptoms.
B. Diagnostic Criteria
    1. Anxiety about being in places or situations from which escape may be difficult if an attack occurs. Typically involves a cluster of symptoms that include being outside of the home alone, in a crowd or standing in line, being on a bridge, traveling in a bus, train, or automobile.
    2. The situations are avoided (such as, travel) or else endured with marked distress or anxiety about having an attack.
    3. Anxiety or avoidance is not better accounted for by another mental disorder; for example, social phobia.

*Panic Disorder without Agoraphobia*

A. Essential feature is the presence of recurrent, unexpected panic attacks followed by at least one month of persistent concern about having another panic attack, worry about the possible consequences of the attacks, or a significant behavioral change related to the attacks.
B. Diagnostic Criteria
    1. Both a and b
        a. Recurrent unexpected panic attacks
        b. At least one or more of the attacks has been followed by one month or more of the following
            i. Persistent concern about having additional attacks
            ii. Worry about implications or consequences (e.g., going crazy, having heart attack, losing control)
            iii. Significant change in behavior related to the attacks
    2. Absence of agoraphobia
    3. Not the result of physiological effects of a substance or a medical condition
    4. Other diagnoses ruled out

*Panic Disorder with Agoraphobia*

A. Essential feature is the presence of recurrent, unexpected panic attacks followed by at least one month of persistent concern about having another panic attack, worry about the possible consequences of the attacks, or a significant behavioral change related to the attacks.
B. Diagnostic Criteria
    1. Both a and b
        a. Recurrent unexpected panic attacks
        b. At least one or more of the attacks has been followed by one month or more of the following
            i. Persistent concern about having additional attacks
            ii. Worry about implications or consequences (e.g., going crazy, having heart attack, losing control)
            iii. Significant change in behavior related to the attacks

2. Presence of agoraphobia
3. Not the result of physiological effects of a substance or a medical condition
4. Other diagnoses ruled out

*Obsessive-Compulsive Disorder*

A. Essential features are recurrent obsessions or compulsions that are severe enough to be time-consuming (that is, that take more than an hour a day) or cause marked distress or significant impairment. Obsessions are persistent ideas, thoughts, impulses, or images. Compulsions are repetitive behaviors.
B. Diagnostic Criteria—either obsessions or compulsions.
   1. Obsessions
      a. Recurrent and persistent thoughts, impulses, or images that are experienced at some time during the disturbance, as intrusive and inappropriate and that cause marked anxiety or distress
      b. The thoughts, impulses, or images are not simply excessive worries about real-life problems
      c. The person attempts to ignore or suppress or neutralize with some other thought or action
      d. The person recognizes that the obsessions are products of his or her own mind (not thought insertion as in schizophrenia)
   2. Compulsions
      a. Repetitive behaviors (such as, hand washing) or mental acts (such as, praying, counting) that the person feels driven to perform in response to an obsession, or according to rules that must be rigidly applied.
      b. The behaviors or mental acts are aimed at preventing or reducing distress or preventing some dreaded event or situation
C. At some point during the course of the disorder, the person has recognized that the obsessions or compulsions are excessive or unreasonable.
D. They cause marked distress, are time-consuming, or significantly interfere with the person's normal routine, occupational functioning, or social relationships.

*Posttraumatic Stress Disorder*

A. Essential feature is the development of characteristic symptoms following exposure to an extreme traumatic stress or involving direct personal experience of an event that involves actual or threatened death or serious injury, or other threat to one's physical integrity. This includes witnessing an event that involves death, injury, or a threat to the physical integrity of another person; learning about unexpected or violent death, serious harm, or threat of death or injury experienced by a family member or other close associate.
B. Diagnostic Criteria
   1. Both of the following present:
      a. The person experienced, witnessed, or was confronted with an event or events that involved actual or threatened death or serious injury, or threat to the physical integrity of self or others
      b. The person's response involved intense fear, helplessness, or horror

2. The traumatic event is persistently re-experienced in one or more of the following ways:
   a. Recurrent and intrusive distressing recollections of the event, including images, thoughts, or perceptions
   b. Recurrent distressing dreams of the event
   c. Acting or feeling as if the traumatic event were reoccuring (flashbacks, illusions, hallucinations, etc.)
   d. Intense psychological distress at exposure to internal or external cues that symbolize or resemble an aspect of the event
   e. Physiological reactivity on exposure to internal or external cues that symbolize or resemble an aspect of the event
3. Persistent avoidance of stimuli associated with the trauma and numbing of general responsiveness (not present before the trauma), as indicated by three or more of the following:
   a. Efforts to avoid thoughts, feelings, or conversations associated with the trauma
   b. Efforts to avoid activities, places, or people that arouse recollections of the trauma
   c. Inability to recall an important aspect of the trauma
   d. Markedly diminished interest or participation in significant activities
   e. Feelings of detachment or estrangement from others
   f. Restricted range of affect (for example, unable to have love feelings)
   g. Sense of foreshortened future (for example, does not expect to have a career, marriage, normal life span)
4. Persistent symptoms of increased arousal (two or more of below)
   a. Difficulty falling or staying asleep
   b. Irritability or outbursts of anger
   c. Difficulty concentrating
   d. Hypervigilance
   e. Exaggerated startle response
5. At least one month duration of symptoms
6. Causes significant distress and functional impairment
   Specify if:
       Acute: Symptoms less than 3 months
       Chronic: Symptoms 3 months or longer
       With delayed Onset: Symptoms begin at least six months after the stressor

## Differential Diagnosis in Panic Disorders

Generalized anxiety
Depressive disorders
Schizophrenia
Depersonalization disorder
Somatoform disorder
Personality disorders
Hyper- and Hypothyrodism

Mitral valve prolapse (also acts as precursor to Panic Disorder)
Cardiac arrhythmias
Coronary insufficiency
Hypoglycemia
True vertigo
Drug and alcohol withdrawl

## Important Differential Diagnosis in Obsessive Compulsive Disorders

Schizophrenia
Other anxiety and depression

SOURCE: *DSM-IV-TR*

# The Scales of MMPI II Measure

**Scales**
**Validity and Clinical Scales**

VRIN–Variable Response Inconsistency

TRIN–True Response Inconsistency
F–Infrequency
FB–Back F
FP–Infrequency-Psychopathology
L–Lie
K–Correction
S–Superlative Self-Presentation
?–Cannot Say
1 Hs–Hypochondriasis
2 D–Depression
3 Hy–Conversion Hysteria
4 Pd–Psychopathic Deviate
5 Mf–Masculinity-Femininity
6 Pa–Paranoia
7 Pt–Psychasthenia
8 Sc–Schizophrenia
9 Ma–Hypomania
0 Si–Social Introversion

**Superlative Self-Presentation**
**Subscales**
(Forensic Report only)

S1–Beliefs in Human Goodness
S2–Serenity
S3–Contentment with Life
S4–Patience and Denial of Irritability and Anger
S5–Denial of Moral Flaws

**Supplementary Scales**
(Extended Score Report, Interpretive Reports, and Personnel Adjustment Rating)

A–Anxiety
R–Repression
Es–Ego Strength
Do–Dominance
Re–Social Responsibility
Mt–College Maladjustment
PK–PTSD/Keane
MDS–Marital Distress
Ho–Hostility
O-H–Overcontrolled Hostility
MAC-R–MacAndrew-Revised
AAS–Addiction Admission
APS–Addiction Potential
GM–Gender Role–Masculine
GF–Gender Role–Feminine

**PSY-5 Scales—part of the**
**Supplementary Scales**
(Extended Score Report only)

AGGR–Aggressiveness
PSYC–Psychoticism
DISC–Disconstraint
NEGE–Negative Emotionality/ Neuroticism
INTR–Introversion/Low Positive Emotionality

## Content Scales

(Extended Score Report, Interpretive Reports, Criminal Justice and Correctional Report, and Personnel Adjustment Rating)

ANX–Anxiety
FRS–Fears
OBS–Obsessiveness
DEP–Depression
HEA–Health Concerns
BIZ–Bizarre Mentation
ANG–Anger
CYN–Cynicism
ASP–Antisocial Practices
TPA–Type A
LSE–Low Self-Esteem
SOD–Social Discomfort
FAM–Family Problems
WRK–Work Interference
TRT–Negative Treatment Indicators

## Content Component Scales

(Extended Score Report, Interpretive Reports, and Personnel Adjustment Rating)

FRS1–Fears: Generalized Fearfulness
FRS2–Fears: Multiple Fears
DEP1–Depression: Lack of Drive
DEP2–Depression: Dysphoria
DEP3–Depression: Self-Depreciation
DEP4–Depression: Suicidal Ideation
HEA1–Health Concerns: Gastrointestinal Symptoms
HEA2–Health Concerns: Neurological Symptoms
HEA3–Health Concerns: General Health Concerns
BIZ1–Bizarre Mentation: Psychotic Symptomatology
BIZ2–Bizarre Mentation: Schizotypal Characteristics
ANG1–Anger: Explosive Behavior
ANG2–Anger: Irritability
CYN1–Cynicism: Misanthropic Beliefs

## Clinical Subscales—Harris-Lingoes and Social Introversion Subscales

(Extended Score Report, Interpretive Reports, and Personnel Adjustment Rating)

D1–Subjective Depression
D2–Psychomotor Retardation
D3–Physical Malfunction
D4–Mental Dullness
D5–Brooding
Hy1–Denial of Social Anxiety
Hy2–Need for Affection
Hy3–Lassitude-Malaise
Hy4–Somatic Complaints
Hy5–Inhibition of Aggression
Ma1–Amorality
Ma2–Psychomotor Acceleration
Ma3–Imperturbability
Ma4–Ego Inflation
Pa1–Persecutory Ideas
Pa2–Poignancy
Pa3–Naiveté
Pd1–Familial Discord

## Clinical Subscales—Harris-Lingoes and Social Introversion Subscales (Cont.)

Pd2–Authority Problems
Pd3–Social Imperturbability
Pd4–Social Alienation
Pd5–Self-Alienation
Sc1–Social Alienation
Sc2–Emotional Alienation
Sc3–Lack of Ego Mastery-Cognitive
Sc4–Lack of Ego Mastery-Conative
Sc5–Lack of Ego Mastery-Defective Inhibition
Sc6–Bizarre Sensory Experiences
Si1–Shyness/Self-Consciousness
Si2–Social Avoidance
Si3–Alienation–Self and Others

CYN2–Cynicism: Interpersonal
  Suspiciousness
ASP1–Antisocial Practices: Antiso-
  cial Attitudes
ASP2–Antisocial Practices: Antiso-
  cial Behavior
TPA1–Type A: Impatience
TPA2–Type A: Competitive Drive
LSE1–Low Self-Esteem: Self-Doubt
LSE2–Low Self-Esteem: Submissive-
  ness
SOD1–Social Discomfort: Introver-
  sion
SOD2–Social Discomfort: Shyness
FAM1–Family Problems: Family
  Discord
FAM2–Family Problems: Familial
  Alienation
TRT1–Negative Treatment Indica-
  tors: Low Motivation
TRT2–Negative Treatment Indica-
  tors: Inability to Disclose

# MAST (Revised):
# Michigan Alcohol Screening Test

The MAST is a simple test that helps assess if you have a drinking problem.

1. Do you feel you are a normal drinker? ("normal"—drink as much or less than most other people)
   Circle Answer: Yes No

2. Have you ever awakened the morning after some drinking the night before and found that you could not remember a part of the evening?
   Circle Answer: Yes No

3. Does any near relative or close friend ever worry or complain about your drinking?
   Circle Answer: Yes No

4. Can you stop drinking without difficulty after one or two drinks?
   Circle Answer: Yes No

5. Do you ever feel guilty about your drinking?
   Circle Answer: Yes No

6. Have you ever attended a meeting of Alcoholics Anonymous (AA)?
   Circle Answer: Yes No

7. Have you ever gotten into physical fights when drinking?
   Circle Answer: Yes No

8. Has drinking ever created problems between you and a near relative or close friend?
   Circle Answer: Yes No

9. Has any family member or close friend gone to anyone for help about your drinking?
   Circle Answer: Yes No

10. Have you ever lost friends because of your drinking?
    Circle Answer: Yes No

11. Have you ever gotten into trouble at work because of drinking?
    Circle Answer: Yes No

12. Have you ever lost a job because of drinking?
    Circle Answer: Yes No

13. Have you ever neglected your obligations, your family, or your work for two or more days in a row because you were drinking?
    Circle Answer: Yes No

14. Do you drink before noon fairly often?
    Circle Answer: Yes No

15. Have you ever been told you have liver trouble such as cirrhosis?
    Circle Answer: Yes No

16. After heavy drinking have you ever had delirium tremens (d.t.'s), severe shaking, visual or auditory (hearing) hallucinations?
    Circle Answer: Yes No

17. Have you ever gone to anyone for help about your drinking?
    Circle Answer: Yes No

18. Have you ever been hospitalized because of drinking?
    Circle Answer: Yes No

19. Has your drinking ever resulted in your being hospitalized in a psychiatric ward?
    Circle Answer: Yes No

20. Have you ever gone to any doctor, social worker, clergyman, or mental health clinic for help with any emotional problem in which drinking was part of the problem?
    Circle Answer: Yes No

21. Have you been arrested more than once for driving under the influence of alcohol?
    Circle Answer: Yes No

22. Have you ever been arrested, even for a few hours because of other behavior while drinking?
    Circle Answer: Yes No
    (If yes, how many times _____)

### Scoring for the MAST: Please score one point if you answered the following

1. No
2. Yes
3. Yes
4. No
5. Yes
6. Yes

7–22: Yes

Add up the scores and compare to the following:

        0–2: No apparent problem

        3–5: Early or middle problem drinker

        6 or more: problem drinker

# Examples of Circular Questions

I. Problem: Definition Questions: Whenever possible, ask for a description of the specific behaviors which are perceived to be problematic.

   A. *Present*
   - What is the problem in the family now?
   - What concerns bring you into therapy now? or: What concerns bring you here now?
   - What is the main concern of the family now?
   - What problems do the other children have?
   - For children: What changes would you like in your family?

   1. Difference
      - How is this different than before?
      - Has this always been true?

   2. Agreement/Disagreement
      - Who agrees with you that this is the problem?

   3. Explanation/Meaning
      - What is your explanation for that?
      - What does his behavior mean to you?

   B. *Past*
   - What was the problem in the family then?

   1. Difference
      - How is that different from now?

   2. Agreement/Disagreement
      - How is that different from now?
      - Who agrees with Dad that this was the major concern of the family then?

   3. Explanation/Meaning
      - What is your explanation for that?
      - What do you believe was the significance of that?

SOURCE: Fleuridas, C., Nelson, T. S., & Rosenthal, D. M. (1986). The evolution of circular questions: Training family therapists. *Journal of Marital and Family Therapy, 12*(2), 113–127.

C. *Future/Hypothetical*
  • What would be the problem in the family if things were to continue as they are?

  1. Difference
    • How would that be different than it is now?

  2. Agreement/Disagreement
    • Do you agree, Mom?

  3. Explanation/Meaning
    • If this were to happen, how would you explain it?
    • What purpose would that serve?

II. Sequence-of-Interaction Questions: Focus on interactional behaviors.

| *General Examples* | *Specific Examples* |
|---|---|
| A. Present<br>  • Who does what when?<br>  • Then what happens?<br>  • What next?<br>  • Where is she when this happens?<br>  • What does she do?<br>  • Then what do they do?<br>  • Who notices first?<br>  • What does he respond?<br>  • When he does not do that (problem definition), what happens? | • Ask Daughter: When Mom tries to get Sister to eat (to solve or prevent the presenting problem) and she refuses, what does Dad do? Then what does Mom do? What does Brother do? And what does Sister do? Then what happens?<br>• When Mom and Brother are fighting, what does Dad do?<br>• Does Dad get involved in that fight or stay out of it? Describe what happens.<br>• When Dad doesn't get involved in their fights, what happens? How does Mom react when Dad doesn't get involved and fight with Brother? |
| 1. Difference<br>  • Has it always been this way? | • Has Brother always behaved in this manner? |
| 2. Agreement/Disagreement<br>  • Who agrees with you that this is how it happens? | • Who agrees with you that Mom yells at Dad every time he stomps out of the house? |
| 3. Explanation/Meaning<br>  • What is your explanation for this?<br>  • What does this mean to you? | • How do you explain Dad's tendency to leave home often?<br>• What does Dad's behavior mean to you? |

| General Examples | Specific Examples |
|---|---|
| **B. Past** | |
| • Who did what then? | • What did Dad do on those days when Brother used to push Mom around? |
| • What solutions were tried? | • What did Dad do? |
| **1. Difference** | • How was Dad's behavior different? Describe what he used to do? |
| • How was it different? | |
| • When was it different | |
| • What else was different then? | • When did he do this? How often? |
| • How does that differ from how it is now? | • When did he change? |
| • Was it then more or less than it is now? | • How did Dad respond to the earlier situation? Then what happened? |
| | • How does that differ from how he responds now? |
| | • Was he gone more or less often then he is now? |
| **2. Agreement/Disagreement** | • Who agrees with Mom that Dad is more involved in the fights now? |
| • Who agrees with you? | |
| **3. Explanation/Meaning** | • How do you explain this recent involvement? |
| • How do you explain this change? | |
| • What does this change (or lack of change) mean to you? | • What does it mean to you that day after day, year after year, things between the two of you have not changed? |
| **C. Future/Hypothetical** | • What do you think Mom would do if Dad were to ignore Brother? |
| • What would she do differently if he did (not) do this? | |
| | • What will Dad do with brother when Mom begins to work nights? |
| **1. Difference** | • How would your parents' relationship be different if Mom were to return to school? |
| • How would it be different if he were to do this? | |
| **2. Agreement/Disagreement** | • Do you think Mom would agree that they would probably get a divorce if she were to return to school? |
| • Who would agree with you that this is probably what would happen? | |

| General Examples | Specific Examples |
| --- | --- |
| 3. Explanation/Meaning<br>• Tell me why you believe this would happen?<br>• How do you think your wife would explain it?<br>• What would this mean to you? | • Dad, why do you think your daughter and wife both agree that a divorce is likely should your wife return to work?<br>• What would a divorce between your parents mean to you? |

# Abusive Behavior Inventory
# Partner Form

Here is a list of behaviors that many women report have been used by their partners or former partners. We would like you to estimate how often these behaviors occurred during the six months prior to your beginning this program. Your answers are strictly confidential.

CIRCLE a number of each of the items listed below to show your closest estimate of how often it happened in your relationship with your partner or former partner during the *six months* before he started the program.

1 = Never
2 = Rarely
3 = Occasionally
4 = Frequently
5 = Very frequently

1. Called you names and/or criticized you.                                              1 2 3 4 5
2. Tried to keep you from doing something you wanted to do
   (example: going out with friends, going to meetings).                                 1 2 3 4 5
3. Gave you angry stares or looks.                                                       1 2 3 4 5
4. Prevented you from having money for your own use.                                     1 2 3 4 5
5. Ended a discussion with you and made the decision himself.   1 2 3 4 5
6. Threatened to hit or throw something at you.                                          1 2 3 4 5
7. Pushed, grabbed, or shoved you.                                                       1 2 3 4 5
8. Put down your family or friends.                                                      1 2 3 4 5
9. Accused you of paying too much attention to someone or
   something else.                                                                       1 2 3 4 5
10. Put you on an allowance.                                                             1 2 3 4 5
11. Used your children to threaten you (example: told you that
    you would lose custody, said he would leave town with
    the children).                                                                       1 2 3 4 5
12. Became very upset with you because dinner, housework,
    or laundry was not ready when he wanted it or done the
    way he thought it should be done.                                                    1 2 3 4 5

SOURCE: Shepard, C. E., & Campbell, J. A. (1991). *The Abusive Behavior Inventory*, Deluth, MN: University of Minnesota at Deluth, School of Social Work.

13. Said things to scare you (example: told you something "bad" would happen, threatened to commit suicide).          1  2  3  4  5
14. Slapped, hit, or punched you.          1  2  3  4  5
15. Made you do something humiliating or degrading (example: begging for forgiveness, having to ask his permission to use the car or do something).          1  2  3  4  5
16. Checked up on you (example: listened to your phone calls, checked the mileage on your car, called you repeatedly at work).          1  2  3  4  5
17. Drove recklessly when you were in the car.          1  2  3  4  5
18. Pressured you to have sex in a way that you didn't like or want.          1  2  3  4  5
19. Refused to do housework or child care.          1  2  3  4  5
20. Threatened you with a knife, gun, or other weapon.          1  2  3  4  5
21. Spanked you.          1  2  3  4  5
22. Told you that you were a bad parent.          1  2  3  4  5
23. Stopped you or tried to stop you from going to work or school.          1  2  3  4  5
24. Threw, hit, kicked, or smashed something.          1  2  3  4  5
25. Kicked you.          1  2  3  4  5
26. Physically forced you to have sex.          1  2  3  4  5
27. Threw you around.          1  2  3  4  5
28. Physically attacked the sexual parts of your body.          1  2  3  4  5
29. Choked or strangled you.          1  2  3  4  5
30. Used a knife, gun, or other weapon against you.          1  2  3  4  5

# Index

# ABOUT THE EDITORS

**Catheleen Jordan,** PhD, LCSW, is professor of social work at the University of Texas at Arlington, where she has taught since 1985. She is a licensed clinical social worker and currently co-chairs the Direct Practice sequence at the School of Social Work. Her areas of expertise are family assessment and treatment, and clinical research and program evaluation. She directed the School of Social Work's Community Service Clinic for five years. Jordan has served in various positions with the state and local National Association of Social Workers organization and served as state president (2007–2009). She is currently involved in clinical research with those who are homeless and dually diagnosed, as well as baby boomer populations. Jordan has numerous publications, including her chapter "Assessment" in the *Encyclopedia of Social Work* and *Family Social Work* with Canadian colleagues Don Collins and Heather Coleman from the University of Calgary.

**Cynthia Franklin,** PhD, LCSW, LMFT, is professor and holder of the Stiernberg/Spencer Family Professorship in Mental Health at the University of Texas at Austin, School of Social Work. Franklin is an internationally known researcher, scholar, and leader in school mental health practice, with more than one hundred publications in the professional literature on how to help at-risk youths. She is especially known for her innovative approaches to preventing high school dropout and graduating high-risk students. Franklin is one of the chief researchers to show how solution-focused, brief therapy works to help at-risk youths succeed in schools. She and colleague Mary Beth Harris also developed the solution-oriented "Taking Charge Group Intervention," which has been proved to help pregnant and parenting adolescent mothers stay in school and improve their attendance, academic achievement, and life goals. Before going into academia full-time, Franklin served in the ministry and conducted a clinical practice for ten years.